Praise for *The Ultimate History of Video Games*

"This book is extraordinary, with enough quotes, anecdotes, and [...]
more like a fast-moving novel than a literary tome."

—Pet[...]

"In the game industry, like in movies, an incredible amount happens behind the
scenes. This book tells it all."

—**Mark Cerny, creator of *Marble Madness* and cocreator of *Crash Bandicoot***

"From the advent of coin-op video games, through its transition to the consumer video
games industry, *The Ultimate History of Video Games* tells it as it is. An enjoyably
informative bird's-eye view of this entertainment medium."

—**Joel Hochberg, president of Rare, Inc.**

"*The Ultimate History of Video Games* is the definitive history of computer and video
games. Steven Kent takes readers from the arcade to the boardroom and introduces them
to the men and women who have transformed gaming from a garage hobby into the
current multibillion dollar industry of technology entertainment for the new millennium."

—**Arthur Pober, president of the Entertainment Software Rating Board**

"A great history of the video game industry! Steve Kent reports the inside story!"

—**Howard Lincoln, former chairman of Nintendo of America,
CEO of the Seattle Mariners**

"A must read for newcomers and veterans alike."

—**Michael Katz, former president of Sega, Atari, and Epyx**

"Steven Kent's passion for the video game industry illuminates every page. Despite all my
video game industry contacts over the years, I learned something new in every chapter."

—**Richard Doherty, director of the Envisioneering Group**

"Apart from the fact that Steve Kent is one of the big authorities on this thing we call
the video game, he can also make history fun."

—**Eddie Adlum, publisher of *RePlay Magazine***

"I certainly wasn't prepared for the engrossing, almost novel-like work that I discovered when I read *The Ultimate History of Video Games*. It was quite a pleasant surprise."

—**GameSpy**

"The book reads like a text version of one of those mammoth Ken Burns documentaries,
but without all the weird and pretentious poetry. The book leaves very few historical
stones unturned."

—**Happy Puppy**

"Highly recommended for any coin-op hobbyist's library."

—**Tim Ferrante,** *GameRoom Magazine*

"You'd be hard pressed to find a better book about the history of video games. In fact, you can't. It really is quite an engaging read. And you'll find yourself rereading sections for years to come."

—*Syzygy Magazine*

"Steve Kent has created a more compelling version of gaming history, one that relies heavily on anecdotes from the heavyweights of the gaming industry."

—**Game Informer**

"A thing of precious value. Kent's supremely exhaustive research ensures that nuggets of insight into what went on behind the scenes leap from nearly every page. Read this book now or forever be an unenlightened gamehead."

—*Edge Magazine*

"There have been a lot of books written about the video game business. None of them seem to get it. When people ask me about the video game business, I tell them to read *The Ultimate History of Video Games.*"

—**Ed Rotberg, creator of** *Battlezone*

"A fantastic account of the history of video games. Reads like a novel!"

—**Lenny Herman, author of** *Phoenix: The Fall and Rise of Video Games*

"Incredible insight into the creation of some of the biggest video games. Having been in this business for fourteen years, I was amazed by the amount of information and only wish the book could have been longer."

—**Ed Boon, creator of** *Mortal Kombat*

"I found this book fascinating to read. Besides reliving the stories about the people and the games, it goes into the inside stories and politics of the video games industry."

—**Ed Logg, creator of** *Asteroids, Centipede,* **and** *Gauntlet*

"A nostalgic, sweeping trip down memory brick road, *The Ultimate History of Video Games* is great for people who want to learn more about the early days of video games."

—**Tendo Box**

The Ultimate History of Video Games, Volume 1

From Pong to Pokémon and Beyond—
The Story Behind the Craze That Touched Our Lives
and Changed the World

Steven L. Kent

CROWN
NEW YORK

To Professor Alf Pratte, that rare individual
who understands the full responsibilities of journalism and teaching.

2021 Crown Trade Paperback Edition

Copyright © 2001 by Steven L. Kent

Published in the United States by Crown, an imprint of Random House, a division of Penguin Random House LLC, New York.

Crown and the Crown colophon are registered trademarks of Penguin Random House LLC.

Originally published by Prima Publishing, Roseville, California, in 2001 as *The First Quarter*. Subsequently published in trade paperback in the United States by Three Rivers Press, an imprint of Random House, a division of Penguin Random House LLC, New York, in 2001.

Library of Congress Cataloging-in-Publication Data
Kent, Steven L.
    The ultimate history of video games : from Pong to Pokemon—the story behind the craze that touched our lives and changed the world / Steven L. Kent.
        Includes bibliographical references and index.
        1. Video games—History. I. Title.
    GV1469.3 .K45   2001
    794.8'09—dc21   2001036497
    ISBN 0-7615-3643-4
    16

ISBN 978-0-7615-3643-7
Ebook ISBN 978-0-307-56087-2

Printed in the United States of America on acid-free paper

crownpublishing.com
21st Printing

Contents

Foreword

When Steven Kent asked me to write the foreword to this book, I was deeply honored and rather pleased. I then started to wonder what I would write! These feelings made me realize that what is so useful about this book is that is chronicles the beginnings of a new entertainment medium. Our industry's greatest problem has been one of identity—where, culturally, do video games fit? They don't fit into films, they don't fit into books, they don't fit into any existing pigeonhole. Twelve years ago, when I produced my first game, my greatest challenge was to try to get someone interested in it. After talking with Steven, I believe he has found a similar problem with placing this book. Thankfully, he persevered as I did.

However, now that we have this book, at last we have a faithful record on the cultural history of what I am sure will one day be one of the most important entertainment mediums in the world. It is shocking to me to open the first page and read through the first chapter and look back through the years of my life. Each chapter unveils a new episode in the history of computer games that coincides with my own history. What this highlights for me is that young people today think of computer games as a natural pastime, which was not always the case. They can't imagine a world without computer games, and what Steven's book does (and it is the first to do this) is set out the history of computer games that is both compelling and compulsive. I endorse and encourage you to read this excellent book.

—Peter Molyneux

Acknowledgments

In 1972, my physical education teacher took the class to a bowling alley in Kalihi, on the island of Oahu in Hawaii. As we walked past the familiar line of electromechanical games *(Night Bomber* was my favorite at the time), I noticed a game that seemed to be running on a television set or possibly a computer. My teacher sent the other kids off to bowl while he and I dropped a quarter into the machine and batted a square ball back and forth with rectangular paddles. Obviously, the game was *Pong.* One hour later, as the rest of the class finished bowling, I had a new addiction that has now lasted for nearly thirty years.

Four years later, I found myself playing Midway's *Gunfight* with a friend named Ed when two of the best-looking girls from my high school class came up to talk with us. (As anyone who knew me in high school will tell you, that was not a common occurrence.) I really wanted to talk to them. Ed really wanted me to talk to them, too; but every time I looked away from the game, he shot me. In the end, *Gunfight* won out, and I had proven my absolute nerddom.

Researching this book gave me the opportunity to interview Dave Nutting, the man who modified *Gunfight* for the U.S. market, and Al Alcorn, the engineer who built the first *Pong* machine. In fact, writing this book has given me the chance to meet most of the people who entertained me, addicted me, and caused me to spend an evening with Ed when I might have had more fun with Lisa. What I found out about these people was that the vast majority of them are kind, smart, and generous. With the exceptions of three people—Sam Tramiel, Ken Kutaragi, and Hiroshi Yamauchi—all of the people I asked for interviews granted them and put up with the endless hours of repetitive questions. In fact, such busy and important men as Ralph Baer, Nolan Bushnell, Al Alcorn, Masaya Nakamura, Minoru Arakawa, Howard Lincoln, Tom Zito, and several others granted me multiple interviews.

In the end, much of this book was cobbled together from information that I gathered from more than 500 interviews. While I would like to thank the people who generously donated their time for these interviews, many of which were several hours long, I feel it is equally important to thank the many people who helped me arrange everything. For every interview that went into this book, there was an average of two PR/communications people working to put everything together.

While writing this book, I found myself using a few published sources as well. One was KLOV, the Killer List of Videogames, which is located at *www.klov.com*. The people who created this amazing site do not receive advertising revenues and are not employed by the video game industry. They simply maintain this immense site out of love for the games.

I also relied heavily upon *Phoenix: The Fall and Rise of Videogames*, a brilliant book written by Leonard Herman. As I was finishing this book, a friend suggested that I call it "A Comprehensive History of Video Games." I could not do that. Lenny had already written the comprehensive book.

And while I am at it, on many occasions I also referred back to *Game Over*, by David Sheff. While both Nintendo of America and Nintendo Co., Ltd., in Japan, have been very generous with me, I have never interviewed Hiroshi Yamauchi. I learned about him by reading the works of Mr. Sheff.

I also wish to thank the many people who helped me get this manuscript knocked into shape. I am quite grateful to Lynelle Klein, who transcribed most of my interviews.

Also, I need to acknowledge the people who took time out of their busy schedules to help me check facts. Amazingly, Al Alcorn and Steve Bristow were kind enough to read the chapters about Atari for me; John Romero helped with the modern PC stuff; Richard Brudvik-Lindner helped with the Genesis years; and many others chipped in.

One thing I have learned while working on this project is that the gaming community is filled with people who know an awful lot about history and will do anything they can to preserve it. A number of people worked very hard to help me comb out errors that had crept into my text. When they first approached me to offer this help, I greeted them suspiciously. As we worked together, however, I realized that these folks did not want credit. They simply wanted to see history preserved correctly.

But they deserve credit. First and foremost, I wish to thank a gentleman at Colorado State who prefers to be known as "Zube." Meticulous and with far too much time on his hands, this fellow combed through my text and found pages of minutia and larger errors, all wanting correction. There were moments when I cursed Zube; but now I wish to thank him.

Then there was Tim Ferrante of *Gameroom Magazine*. One night, as I prepared to send my manuscript to Prima, Tim and I did a page-by-page search through the book. After three hours, I complained that I was tired, but he kept going. Only later did I realize that while I was in Seattle, where it was only 1:00 A.M., he was on the East Coast, and it was 4:00 A.M. for him.

I also owe debts of gratitude to Curt Vendel, Ken Gagne, and Lenny Herman, a true guardian of video game history. And all the way through this process, I frequently relied on help from my good friend, Jeremy Horwitz—once the world's best-connected video game player, now on his way to a fine career in law.

I also want to thank Eddie Adlum, Ingrid Milkes, Key Snodgress, and the rest of the staff of *RePlay Magazine*—the real experts on the coin-op industry—for taking the time to teach me about the workings of the arcade industry and for lending me valuable photographs to enhance my book.

Finally, I absolutely need to thank Steve Martin, David Richardson, and Andrew Vallas at Prima. These are the guys who shine up my work, and I am most grateful.

Timeline

1889

Fusajiro Yamauchi establishes the Marufuku Company to manufacture and distribute Hanafuda, Japanese playing cards.

1932

The Connecticut Leather Company is established by a Russian immigrant named Maurice Greenberg to distribute leather products to shoemakers.

1951

Yamauchi changes the name of Marufuku Co. Ltd. to Nintendo, a term meaning "leave luck to heaven."

United States passes new laws regulating slot machines. Marty Bromley, who manages game rooms at military bases in Hawaii, buys machines and opens Service Games (SEGA).

David Rosen, returning from service in the U.S. Air Force during the Korean War, opens portrait painting business in Japan.

1954

David Rosen starts Rosen Enterprises and begins shipping photo booths to Japan.

1956

Rosen imports $200,000 worth of coin-operated electromechanical games to Japan and starts the country's coin-op business.

1958

Physicist Willy Higinbotham of the Brookhaven National Laboratories in New York invents an interactive table-tennis–like game that is displayed on an oscilloscope.

1961

MIT student Steve Russell creates *Spacewar*, the first interactive computer game.

1962

Nolan Bushnell enters engineering school at the University of Utah.

1964

Rosen Enterprises, Japan's largest amusement company, merges with Service Games, which now has jukeboxes in over 6,000 locations, to form Sega Enterprises.

1965

Nolan Bushnell gets a summer job at a Salt Lake City carnival where he is in charge of the games midway.

1966

Ralph Baer begins researching interactive television games at Sanders Associates.

Sega releases *Periscope*, a game that becomes such a hit in Japan that U.S. and European companies begin importing it. This is Japan's first amusement game export. Because of the high cost of shipping, U.S. arcade owners charge players $0.25 per play, setting what will eventually become the standard price for playing arcade games.

1968

Ralph Baer patents his interactive television game.

1969

Gulf & Western purchases Sega.

Nolan Bushnell graduates from the University of Utah and accepts a job in California.

1970

Magnavox licenses Ralph Baer's television game from Sanders Associates.

1970

Bushnell begins work on an arcade version of *Spacewar* called *Computer Space.*

1971

Nutting Associates purchases *Computer Space* from Nolan Bushnell and hires him to help manufacture it.

Nutting begins shipping *Computer Space,* the first arcade video game machine.

1972

Magnavox begins demonstrating Odyssey in private showings. Bushnell attends a demonstration of the console on May 24, in Burlingame, California.

Bushnell Leaves Nutting and starts Syzygy with partner Ted Dabney. Finding that the name *Syzygy* is already taken, they rename their company Atari.

Atari engineer Al Alcorn creates *Pong.*

Magnavox releases Odyssey.

Magnavox sues Atari on grounds that *Pong* infringes on Ralph Baer's patents. Nolan Bushnell decides to settle out of court.

1973

Taito, Williams, and Midway enter the video game business.

1975

Atari creates prototypical *Home Pong* unit and sells idea to Sears Roebuck.

Namco begins making video games.

Strapped for cash, Nolan Bushnell approaches venture capitalist Don Valentine for funding.

Midway Games imports a Taito game called *Gunfight,* the first game to use a microprocessor.

1976

The Connecticut Leather Company, now known as Coleco, releases *Telstar,* a television tennis game.

Fairchild Camera & Instrument releases *Channel F,* the first programmable home game to use cartridges.

Exidy Games releases *Death Race*, a game in which players drive over stick figures. Protests about the game are featured on *60 Minutes*.

Bushnell sells Atari to Warner Communications for $28 million.

1977

Atari opens the first Pizza Time Theatre.

Atari releases the Video Computer System, also known as the 2600.

Mattel introduces a line of LED-based handheld video games.

Shigeru Miyamoto joins Nintendo.

Bally releases the Bally Professional Arcade home console.

Nintendo releases its first home video game in Japan.

1978

Bushnell is forced out of Atari and buys the rights to Pizza Time Theatre.

Ray Kassar becomes the CEO of Atari.

Nintendo releases *Othello*, its first arcade game.

Atari releases *Football* and Midway releases *Space Invaders*. Both games attract record business.

Magnavox releases the Odyssey2.

Cinematronics releases *Space Wars*, an arcade adaptation of the *Spacewars* game created at MIT.

1979

Capcom is founded in Japan.

Atari releases *Lunar Lander*, its first vector-graphics game. Later that year, Atari releases *Asteroids*, the company's all-time bestselling game.

Atari game designer Warren Robinett introduces concept of "Easter Eggs" to video games by hiding a room with his name in a 2600 game called *Adventure*.

Mattel Electronics introduces the Intellivision game console.

Milton Bradley releases Microvision, the first handheld programmable game system.

1980

Atari releases *Space Invaders* for the Video Computer System. The practice of selling home versions of arcade hits is started.

Renegade programmers fleeing from Atari create Activision, the first third-party game publisher.

Namco releases *Pac-Man*, the most popular arcade game of all time. Over 300,000 units are sold worldwide.

Minoru Arakawa opens Nintendo of America.

Williams releases *Defender*.

1981

Nintendo releases the arcade game *Donkey Kong*.

Atari releases *Pac-Man* for the Video Computer System.

Atari releases *Tempest*.

U.S. arcades revenues reach $5 billion as Americans spend more than 75,000 man-hours playing video games.

Arnie Katz, Bill Kunkel, and Joyce Worley begin publishing *Electronic Games,* the first magazine about video games.

1982

Coleco releases Colecovision.

Atari wins lawsuit accusing Magnavox of infringing on its *Pac-Man* license with K.C. Munchkin.

Atari releases *E.T.* for the Video Computer System.

Activision releases *Pitfall* for the Video Computer System.

Atari releases the 5200 game console.

General Consumer Electronics releases the Vectrex.

Midway releases *Ms. Pac-Man,* the biggest arcade game in American history.

When Warner Communications announces that Atari sales have not met predictions, Warner stock drops 32 percent.

1983

Nolan Bushnell opens an arcade company called Sente Games.

Yu Suzuki joins Sega.

Sega releases its first home console in Japan—SG-1000.

Cinematronics releases *Dragon's Lair,* the first arcade game to feature laser-disc technology.

Former Philip Morris executive James Morgan replaces Ray Kassar as head of Atari.

1984

Nintendo releases the Family Computer (Famicom) in Japan.

David Rosen and Isao Okawa purchase Sega Enterprises back from Gulf & Western for $38 million.

Coleco begins marketing the Adam Computer.

Hisao Oguchi and Yuji Naka join Sega.

Warner Communications sells Atari Corporation to Commodore Computers founder Jack Tramiel but retains the arcade division as Atari Games.

1985

Nintendo test-markets the Famicom in New York as the Nintendo Entertainment System (NES).

Russian mathematician Alex Pajitnov designs *Tetris.*

1986

Nintendo of America releases NES nationwide.

Sega releases its Sega Master System.

Atari releases the 7800 game console.

1987

Nintendo publishes *The Legend of Zelda.*

NEC releases the 16-bit/8-bit hybrid PC-Engine game console in Japan.

Sega unveils 16-bit Mega Drive game console.

1988

Square Soft publishes *Final Fantasy.*

Atari Games releases unlicensed games for the NES under its new Tengen label.

Tonka acquires the U.S. distribution rights to the Sega Master System.

Coleco files for bankruptcy.

1989

NEC brings PC Engine to the United States and releases it as TurboGrafx.

Sega releases Mega Drive in the United States as Genesis.

Nintendo releases Game Boy worldwide.

1990

Nintendo and Atari go to court over the rights to *Tetris*.

Nintendo releases *Super Mario Bros. 3*—the most successful non-bundled game cartridge of all time.

SNK brings 24-bit NeoGeo game console to the United States.

1991

Nintendo of America releases Super NES.

Sega recreates itself with a new mascot—Sonic The Hedgehog.

Galoob Toys releases the Game Genie.

Capcom releases the arcade game *Street Fighter II* giving arcades a needed boost.

1992

With Genesis outselling Super NES, Sega effectively takes control of the U.S. console market.

Sega ships Sega CD peripheral for Genesis game console.

1993

Panasonic begins marketing the 32-bit 3DO Multiplayer.

Atari launches the 64-bit Jaguar.

Broderbund publishes *Myst* for Macintosh Computers.

Id Software publishes *Doom* for PCs.

Virgin Interactive Entertainment publishes *The 7th Guest* on PC CD-ROM.

Senators Joseph Lieberman (D. of Connecticut) and Herb Kohl (D. of Wisconsin) launch Senate hearings on video game violence.

1994

The Interactive Digital Software Association is created in response to Senate hearings.

Nintendo releases *Donkey Kong Country* and retakes control of the U.S. console market.

Sega releases 32X, a peripheral that increases the power of the Genesis.

Sega releases Saturn in Japan.

Sony releases PlayStation in Japan.

1995

Sega releases Saturn in the United States.

Sony releases PlayStation in the United States.

Nintendo releases Virtual Boy in the United States.

Nintendo unveils the 64-bit Nintendo 64 game console in Japan.

1996

Nintendo sells its billionth cartridge worldwide.

Jack Tramiel sells Atari Corporation to disk drive manufacturer JTS.

Nintendo releases Nintendo 64 in the United States.

Nintendo discontinues Virtual Boy.

Sony unveils *Crash Bandicoot*.

1997

Sega discontinues Saturn.

Bandai releases Tamagotchi.

Tiger releases game.com handheld system.

Gumpei Yokoi, the creator of the Game Boy, dies in car accident.

DreamWorks, Universal, and Sega team up to form a new line of super arcades called GameWorks.

Nintendo releases *Goldeneye 007* for Nintendo 64.

Square Soft publishes *Final Fantasy VII* for PlayStation.

1998

Nintendo releases *The Legend of Zelda: Ocarina of Time* for Nintendo 64.

Pokemon, a line of Game Boy role-playing games that have ignited a craze in Japan, comes to American and starts a similar craze.

1999

JTS files for bankruptcy and sells Atari properties to Hasbro Interactive.

SNK Corporation brings the NeoGeo Pocket Color handheld game system to the United States.

Sega releases Dreamcast game console in the United States.

2000

Toshiba and Samsung announce plans to sell Nuon-equipped DVD players.

Sony releases PlayStation 2 in Japan.

Microsoft unveils plans for Xbox video game console at the Game Developers Conference.

Sega launches SegaNet Internet service for Dreamcast.

Sony launches PlayStation 2 in the United States.

SNK discontinues NeoGeo Pocket Color sales in the United States.

2001

Sega discontinues Dreamcast.

Sega chairman Isao Okawa dies.

Nintendo releases Game Boy Advance in Japan (March) and the United States (June).

Nintendo releases GameCube in the United States.

Microsoft releases Xbox worldwide.

The World Before Pong

You can't say that video games grew out of pinball, but you can assume that video games wouldn't have happened without it. It's like bicycles and automobiles. One industry leads to the other and then they exist side by side. But you had to have bicycles to one day have motor cars.

—Steven Baxter, former producer, *The CNN Computer Connection*

The Beginnings of Pinball

New technologies do not simply spring out of thin air. They need to be associated with familiar industries or ideas. People may have jokingly referred to the first automobiles as "horseless carriages," but the name also helped define them. The name changed them from nebulous, unexplainable machines to an extension of an already accepted mode of transportation.

Although video games are a relatively new phenomena, they benefited from a close relationship with the well-established amusement industry. The amusement industry, in turn, has long suffered from a lack of legitimacy. As it turned out, however, legitimacy would never be much of an issue for video games.

The beginnings of pinball can be traced back to Bagatelle, a form of billiards in which players used a cue to shoot balls up a sloped table. The goal of the game was to get the balls into one of nine cups placed along the face of the table. Abraham Lincoln was said to have played Bagatelle.*

No surviving records explain why the cue sticks in Bagatelle were replaced with a device called a "plunger," but for some reason the evolution took place and the game transformed into a new sport called "pinball" before the turn of the century.

If one event paved the way for today's computer and video game industry, it was David Gottlieb's *Baffle Ball*. The founder of D. Gottlieb and Company, David Gottlieb was a short, stocky man with a full head of brown hair and an ever-present cigar in his mouth. A showman and an inventor, he once made a living by taking carnival games to oil workers in remote Midwestern oil fields. He understood the balance of chance and skill that made games fun and had a talent for refining ideas to make them more fun. In 1931, Gottlieb created a game called *Baffle Ball*.

Baffle Ball used no electricity and bore little resemblance to modern pinball games. It was built in a countertop cabinet and had only one moving part— the plunger. Players used the plunger to launch balls onto a plane set at a 7-degree slope and studded with pins circling eight holes or "scoring pockets." Each scoring pocket had a certain point value attached to it. For a penny, players could launch seven balls.

---

* Whether or not Lincoln did in fact play the game, an old political cartoon shows him playing it during his presidency.

Baffle Ball did not have flippers, bumpers, or a scoring device. Players kept track of scores in their heads. Once they launched the ball, they could control its course only by nudging the entire *Baffle Ball* cabinet, a technique later known as "tilting." Sometimes they tilted so forcibly that the entire *Baffle Ball* cabinet could slide several inches during a single game.

At first *Baffle Ball* sales grew gradually, but within months, Gottlieb's game became a major success. By the time the game reached peak popularity, Gottlieb shipped as many as 400 cabinets a day.

Gottlieb, the first person to successfully mass produce pinball cabinets in a factory, became the "Henry Ford of pinball." His competitors worked out of their garages and couldn't compete.

> Imitators popped up immediately, more or less. I mean everybody got involved in the business, and, like I said, there were a lot of people building them in their garages.
>
> Gottlieb machines were a little more expensive. I think it was $16.50 for the machine, and that was $1.00 or $1.50 more than the competitors. But my grandfather used a better quality of walnut; I think the pins were a higher quality metal. He wanted it to be the Cadillac of pinball machines.
>
> **—Michael Gottlieb, grandson of David Gottlieb**

Once Gottlieb proved money was to be made, imitators followed. David Rockola created several successful pin games* before establishing his company as one of the most famous names in jukeboxes. Ray Moloney's first pinball machine, *Ballyhoo,* sold so well that he changed the name of his company from Lion Manufacturing to Bally.

Gottlieb's chief competitor was Stanford-educated Harry Williams. Having studied engineering, Williams brought a deeper understanding of mechanical workings to the industry. He entered the business as a West Coast distributor selling other companies' amusement machines but discovered he could purchase used pinball games and refurbish them with playfields of his own design for much less than it cost to buy new ones.

---

* Pin games is a slang term that members of the amusement industry often use to describe pinball machines.

In 1932, Williams decided to make pinball more challenging by limiting the amount of "body English" players could use. He designed a table with a device that contained a metal ball on a pedestal in its base. If players nudged the machine enough to knock the ball off the pedestal, the game ended. He originally called his device "Stool Pigeon," but when a customer complained that the machine had "tilted," Williams decided to call it a "tilt" mechanism. He tested this innovation in a game called *Advance.*

Williams later refined the "tilt" mechanism by replacing the ball and platform design with a pendulum device, which has been present in nearly every pinball game made since.

In 1933, Williams built *Contact*—the first "electric" pinball machine. The name *Contact* referred to its electrically powered scoring pockets (called "contact holes"), which knocked the ball back into the playfield to continue scoring points. Like the "tilt" mechanism, electric scoring pockets became a standard for pinball that is still used today.

> Previous to *Contact,* the skill for the player was to send the ball up on the playfield, have it roll around, and hope that his aim was such that the ball would somehow magically weave its way around through the pins that were nailed into the playfield.
>
> With the contact hole, you still needed to have some precision to get the ball into the cup, but getting the ball into the cup gave you something back. There was a sound, there was motion. Part of the fascination people have with pinball comes from those opportunities where the game takes over and does things.
>
> **—Roger C. Sharpe, author, *Pinball!****

Pay-Outs

Though he was well aware of Harry Williams's innovations, a different development frightened David Gottlieb more. Slot-machine manufacturers

---

* Readers interested in learning more about the history of pinball and seeing its color and pageantry should look for *Pinball!* by Roger C. Sharpe (E. P. Dutton, 1977).

began making pinball-like machines called "pay-outs," which combined pinball and gambling.

Gottlieb saw these machines as a threat to the entire industry. Pay-out machines first appeared in the crime-conscious 1930s, and Gottlieb suspected that politicians would outlaw the new machines and anything associated with them.

> Yes, there was a certain amount of skill involved, but basically the law looked at it as a gambling device. Pay-outs started out legally in many states and eventually ended up being operated mostly illegally in places where the police would look the other way, such as New Orleans. They were nickel games, by the way. They paid off in nickels. So it was a little gamble, but nevertheless it was gambling.
>
> **—Eddie Adlum, publisher, *RePlay Magazine***

Gottlieb's fears proved accurate. Politicians saw pinball as inextricably associated with gambling. When states passed laws prohibiting pay-out games, they usually outlawed all forms of pinball.

The most celebrated attack on pinball came from Fiorello LaGuardia, New York City's flamboyant mayor. As part of his ongoing crusade against organized crime, LaGuardia petitioned local courts for a ban against pinball. After six years of petitioning the courts, LaGuardia's request was granted. A Bronx court ruled pinball an extension of gambling and made it illegal.

LaGuardia celebrated by having the police confiscate pin games from around the city. He held a press conference in which he demolished several machines with a sledgehammer. The event was even shown on newsreels in theaters around the country.

> There was a gaming [gambling] connotation to the coin-operated amusement business. There was a photograph I remember very clearly—Fiorello LaGuardia, the mayor of New York City, by the waterside breaking up all these "games of chance" and throwing them into the sea to dispose of them. Today he'd have had an even greater problem with environmentalists.
>
> **—Joel Hochberg, president, Rare and Coin It**

Within three weeks of the Bronx court's ruling, the New York Police Department confiscated and destroyed more than 3,000 pinball machines. Mayor LaGuardia donated the metal scraps to the government to support the U.S. war effort against Nazi Germany. In all, he donated more than 7,000 pounds of metal scraps, including 3,000 pounds of steel balls. New York's ban on pinball remained in place for nearly 35 years.

Once New York City banned pinball, neighboring counties followed. The trend spread quickly.

The Battle for Legitimacy

Gottlieb believed that the only way to legitimize pinball was to prove that it involved more skill than luck. Years passed before he found proof.

In 1947, one of Gottlieb's engineers, a man named Harry Mabs, added an innovation to the game—six spring-powered levers that players used to propel the ball back into the playfield before it rolled out of play.

Gottlieb called them "flipper bumpers" and said that they proved that *Humpty Dumpty,* his latest pinball cabinet, was not just a game of chance because players scored most of their points by knocking the ball back into play with flippers rather than relying on luck and gravity.

> The flipper bat was quite a breakthrough because it gave the player a true means of exercising and developing skill. You could aim at targets now, rather than in the old days when you popped the ball up and just shook the shit out of the table and hoped that it went in the right hole or hit the right thing. The use of the flipper bat is probably the greatest breakthrough ever in pinball.
>
> **—Eddie Adlum**

> It [the introduction of the flipper] not only changed the basic landscape of the games themselves, but specific to the players, it really changed how they interacted with the games. It was a totally different entertainment form than it had been.
>
> More important, it was a remarkable change for the game designers and developers. What had been the prescribed way of doing game development

> for the previous decade had to be altered dramatically. No longer was it a situation of a person passively interacting with the game; now there was true influencing and greater control from the standpoint of the player.
>
> **—Roger C. Sharpe**

Gottlieb's "flipper games" became the salvation of pinball. Pushed on by a desperate need for respectability, other pinball manufacturers and distributors imitated *Humpty Dumpty's* flipper bats and called their cabinets "flipper games." In France, where pinball has a long and popular history, pinball machines are simply referred to as "le flipper."

After years of complaining about competitors stealing his ideas, Harry Williams found himself imitating rather than innovating, as he joined the growing number of pinball manufacturers adopting the Gottlieb flipper. Williams's first flipper game was called *Sunny.* By this time, Harry Williams owned his own Chicago amusement company, Williams Manufacturing Company, which he founded in 1942.

Though Harry Mabs created the first flippers, it was Steven Kordek, an engineer from a company called Genco, who discovered the best use for them. Kordek replaced *Humpty Dumpty's* six flippers—two at the top, two in the center, and two at the bottom—with two flippers along the bottom of the playing field. Kordek's innovation was introduced in a game called *Triple Action.*[*]

> I worked for a small company and I was always told to save money—and there was no way in the world that I was going to use six flippers.
>
> **—Steve Kordek, former pinball designer, Genco**

Most pinball machines created in 1947 had six flippers. When Kordek's two-flipper design was demonstrated in a trade show in January 1948, it caused an immediate stir. The industry has followed his basic design ever since.

Even as Gottlieb sought to legitimize pinball with flippers, Bally introduced *Bingo* machines—flipperless pinball machines with rows of pockets.

---

[*] Years later, Harry Williams hired Mabs as his chief designer. Mabs later recruited Kordek to work for Williams.

Bingo re-opened some of the wounds caused by pay-out games. Though pinball remained legal, most states outlawed *Bingo* machines permanently.

> People tried to operate *Bingo* machines legally and treat them as regular pinball machines, but because they were gambling devices, my grandfather didn't want to have anything to do with them.
>
> **—Michael Gottlieb**

Flippers were enough proof that pinball was a game of skill for some legislators. Satisfied by flippers and free-game rewards for high scores, some states relaxed their laws governing pinball. New York continued its ban into the 1970s.

A Growing Industry

> There were five game manufacturers in the beginning. It was Gottlieb making pinballs. It was Williams making pinballs and novelties. It was Bally's making pinballs, novelties, and slot machines, although the major industry didn't use those. It was Chicago Coin making pinballs and novelties. It was Midway making novelty games—target rifles and so on.
>
> There was a sixth, United Manufacturing. But just about the time I joined the industry in 1964, United was purchased by Williams, so that put it back down to five.
>
> **—Eddie Adlum**

The coin-operated amusement industry has two tiers of companies. The first tier includes companies like Gottlieb and Williams, which manufacture amusement equipment. The second is made up of local distributors and operators who place equipment in stores, bus stations, bars, restaurants, and bowling alleys and set up routes to maintain it.

Though flipper machines and other games have long represented a steady source of income, the jukebox defined the industry in the early going. During the 1940s and 1950s, jukeboxes were an integral part of the fabric of American society and the main source of income for amusement companies.

Known as music operators, these distributors placed jukeboxes and games in bus stations, restaurants, and ice cream shops. In exchange for permission to place their equipment in businesses, operators paid location owners a portion of jukebox and game receipts. They established routes and hired teams of technicians to maintain their equipment, empty the coin boxes, and place new records in jukeboxes. Keeping current with the latest music trends was essential to earning a good income and keeping location owners satisfied.

It was a competitive business. The music operator's entire livelihood depended on keeping customers happy. If a location owner thought he had received inferior equipment or old records, he could make arrangements with a new operator simply by picking up the telephone.

> In the mid-1960s, Gottlieb was the recognized leader [in pinball]. Bally was the recognized loser. In fact, I knew a salesman named Irv Kempner in New York City who worked for Runyon Sales Co. They were distributors of both Rowe jukeboxes and Bally pinballs, and one of the guys said the reason "Kempy" was the best salesman was because he had the worst pinball and the worst jukebox to sell.
>
> Today, Rowe is number one in jukeboxes, and Bally owned the pinball machine industry in the late 1970s and early 1980s.
>
> **—Eddie Adlum**

Novelty Games

> If you go to an old penny arcade, some of the equipment we consider antique today was quite popular in the days that I started [in the industry]. It makes me feel old.
>
> **—Joel Hochberg**

Historically, the oldest coin-operated amusement machines were known as novelty games. Before making *Baffle Ball,* David Gottlieb manufactured a novelty machine called the *Husky Grip* that tested a player's strength. By the 1940s, companies had already invented mechanical baseball games. Other games simulated horse racing, hunting, and Western gunfights. Over the years, the field has grown to include hockey, soccer (known by many as foosball), flying, and even building construction.

One of the most popular themes was the shooting arcade. Taverns began carrying mechanical pistol games in which players shot tiny ball bearings at targets on the other side of a small glass-enclosed cabinet. Larger shooting galleries with rifles became staples at arcades.

> We had some wonderful ideas like the *Seeburg Bear Gun,* a classic that old timers still remember. You took an actual rifle that had a cable attached to a console about 6, 8, 10 feet away, and the bear moved from left to right. He had light-sensitive targets in his stomach and on each side. As you shot, he would rear up and growl and turn in the other direction, and you just kept shooting until you ran out of bullets. It [*Bear Gun*] was a huge, big hit; a lot of people had it.
>
> We also had the *Six Gun* game where you had a great big mannequin dressed like a cowboy. He stood at one side and challenged you to a gun fight, and you stood on the other side and had a pair of guns mounted in a little stand-up frame. He would challenge you to draw, like a 1-2-3, and you would pull your gun, and he would lift his arm. If you got him, he would say, "You got me," and if he got you, he would say, "You lost. You're dead," that kind of thing.
>
> The *Six Gun* game was built like a Russian toilet so that it would last forever. And it did.
>
> By and large, you didn't go into an arcade in those days to play a specific game. You went into the arcade to go into the arcade. You went in there, got change for your dollar (of course, some games in those days were still on nickel play), and you just looked around to see what there was to play. You put a couple of nickels in here and put a couple of nickels in there until your dollar was used up.
>
> **—Eddie Adlum**

By the 1960s, novelty games had become quite sophisticated. Black lights were built into the cabinets to make objects glow against dark backgrounds. One game,

Chicago Coin *Speedway,* had a projection screen for a background. Players steered a race car in front of the screen, dodging the projected images of other cars. If the player came too close to a projected image, the machine made a banging sound to simulate a crash and the player went to the back of the pack.

These were the direct ancestors of modern video games.

Birth of a Visionary

If any one person has worked at every level of the amusement machine industry, it is Joel Hochberg. A jovial, quiet man with a self-effacing sense of humor, Hochberg entered the industry to remain near his ailing mother. He never imagined that years later he would help reestablish a multibillion dollar company and change the evolutionary path of the entire industry.

Born and raised in Brooklyn, New York, Hochberg earned an associate degree in electronics from the New York Institute of Technology. "I never wanted to find out how to make things tick; I wanted to know how to make them tick better." He got his degree in 1956 and began the selective interviewing process at Burroughs Corporation.

One Saturday, a neighbor who worked for Master Automatic Music asked Hochberg to help him repair a jukebox.

> He [Hochberg's neighbor] worked for one of the larger companies in the five boroughs area. He asked me one Saturday morning if I could help him. There was a very prominent location that was without music and would have been without music until Monday because the distributor was closed. It [having the jukebox shut off] would cost the company a lot of money, but I think more than the money was the lack of the entertainment required for the weekend in that location.
>
> **—Joel Hochberg**

It is nearly impossible to understand the impact that jukeboxes made on businesses in the 1950s. At that time, not having a jukebox meant that customers went elsewhere.

Though he had studied electronics, Hochberg knew nothing about jukeboxes. He opened the machine and found a problem with the amplifier. The jukebox worked within a few hours. Hochberg later found out that his neighbor had never really expected him to be able to fix the problem.

Harry Siskind, then president of Master Automatic Music, was impressed that Hochberg had fixed the jukebox and asked to meet him. Siskind didn't have a job to offer at the time but told Hochberg that he should consider working in the music operators business because he had the "ability to take things with a technical approach."

Accepting a job at Burroughs would have meant Hochberg moving to Pennsylvania, which, because of his mother's dire illness, he was unwilling to do. "My mother was deathly ill, and I really had no idea as to what the prognosis was. She was basically terminal, but I didn't know it. At least I didn't believe it."

Anxious to stay near his mother, Hochberg took a job at Tri-Borough Maintenance. "We did Brooklyn, the Bronx, Queens and Manhattan. We probably did all five boroughs, but it was called Tri-Borough because I think the individuals who formed the company came from three different boroughs." For a salary of $55 a week, Hochberg worked long hours six days a week and provided his own car. He began by repairing jukeboxes and pool tables.

At this time, New York distributors carried novelty games as well as jukeboxes—pinball was still banned. For the most part, novelty games represented only a small part of the business. The popular novelty themes of the times included shuffle alleys—indoor tabletop bowling lanes on which players used metal pucks to knock down miniature bowling pins. Other popular themes included racing, baseball, and shooting galleries. In New York, where pinball was still illegal, novelty games often turned a good profit.

> The biggest part of our business was shuffle alleys and ball bowlers. Remember, I came from the city [New York], and these were legal items. Every bar and grill, every tavern had a shuffle alley.
>
> Baseball was a very popular game. It used a bat and pitching mechanism. In some cases, lights on the playing field [were used to show bases with runners], and in other cases, men rotating on a motor carriage. You had some moving targets, some escalation ramps. You had home run areas that were predetermined, and of course, sometimes [home run] ramps came up and if you were able to hit them, your ball went out of the park.
>
> **—Joel Hochberg**

Wall boxes were another popular item in the industry. These were tabletop cabinets that linked booths and tables to a central jukebox. Each box had a song list, coin slot, and buttons for ordering songs. Restaurants, diners, and malt shops placed wall boxes on tables and in booths so that customers could select and order songs more conveniently.

> . . . and wall boxes were great for the industry because the machine would play a record once. It's conceivable if a record was popular, that four, five, or six people would select that record—but it would only play it once. The same situation holds true today. Jukeboxes don't dedicate songs to an individual; they just deliver the requirement to play.
>
> **—Joel Hochberg**

Always the innovator, Hochberg found a way to improve the system. He was the first engineer in his area to place volume switches behind bars and counters so that bartenders and restaurant managers could make the music louder upon request. Location managers welcomed the change. Before this, the only volume control was a knob hidden on the back of the jukebox so that customers couldn't get to it.

Though his mother died shortly after he started work at Tri-Borough, Hochberg continued working for New York amusement companies until 1961. This was during a period in which working within the amusement industry had its hazards.

> I've also had a situation where a gentleman who played the game after [I repaired it] lost a lot of money. So he was angry. He said, "If you didn't repair this game I wouldn't have lost." And he wanted to do a number on me.
>
> I've seen a man carrying a gun in his hat. I've had a shot fired at me. Let's change that. . . . Not fired at me directly but fired into the location while I was working on a *United Baseball* game.
>
> **—Joel Hochberg**

Once, when Hochberg showed up at a bar early one Sunday morning to service a machine, he was attacked and beaten. An investigation into the incident revealed that he'd been mistaken for the bartender.

> The next thing I knew, I was being brutalized by a couple of people who were very aggressive because they didn't know who to beat up. The indication was, he's in the bar on Sundays before the bar opens, so there were two people in the bar. They didn't ask what my name was or what the other gentleman's name was. They just came in there. It seems that there was some kind of local area issue, something that had something to do with a relative of one of the people. The bartender's wife was the sister of one of these fellows, and the bartender was mistreating the sister.
>
> **—Joel Hochberg**

Hochberg also remembers that many people liked him for what he did. Sometimes while working his route, he'd have to run outside to put money in a parking meter, only to discover that people had recognized his car and fed the meter for him.

In 1961 Hochberg took a job with New Plan Realty, which was opening the Cavalier, one of the world's first restaurant/arcades. Built in a new shopping center in Philadelphia, the Cavalier was an enormous endeavor with a 10,000-square-foot dining area and 2,500-square-foot arcade. Hochberg was hired to help build and manage the arcade.

The same year that Hochberg moved to Philadelphia, a group of socially awkward college kids began an experiment that would eventually change Hochberg's life.

CHAPTER 2

Forgotten Fathers

There's some question about how you define a computer game. Two interactive programs existed before *Spacewar,* in which you interacted with switches on the computer and you changed a display on the screen, depending on what you did with the switches. But they weren't particularly designed as games. And they weren't very popular because, as games, they weren't very good.

—Steve Russell, creator of *Spacewar*

The members of the Tech Model Railroad Club (TMRC) at the Massachusetts Institute of Technology (MIT) had their own language. They called broken equipment *munged.*[1] They called rolling chairs *bunkies.* They called garbage *cruft.* And they called practical jokes and impressive feats *hacks.*

Like most colleges, MIT had several campus organizations. The Tech Model Railroad Club appealed to students who liked to build systems and see how things worked. These were not typical college students. Many of them were short and most were unathletic. Some wore thick glasses. In the late 1950s and early 1960s, years before the invention of the pocket calculator, these were the kids who carried a slide ruler.

These strange college students, with their funny jargon and nerdy ways, did more to start the computer revolution than any Silicon Valley engineering team. Naturally curious, these MIT students had devoted their lives to intellectual tinkering. They believed in a cooperative society and imagined themselves living in a utopian world in which people shared information—sometimes without regard to property rights. Once they discovered computers, they became known as "hackers." Before that, they were simply nerds.

Some members of the TMRC explored MIT at night, looking for machines to examine. One night in 1959, Peter Samson opened a door in the Electronic Accounting Machinery building and found an IBM 407, a machine capable of creating and reading punch cards. To Samson, finding an unguarded computer was as exciting as discovering a new law of physics.

The IBM 407 was not a full-fledged computer. In order to make it work, Samson and his friends needed to "kludge" a plug board. They didn't mind the challenge—they'd joined the TMRC because they loved jury-rigging systems. Soon the IBM 407 became a major focal point in the lives of many TMRC members.

The Hulking Giant

Many computers of the 1960s were large enough to fill entire rooms. Their inner workings consisted of rows of expensive vacuum tubes; the standard building block for early electronics. Because vacuum tubes generated great amounts of heat, early computers needed cooling systems to prevent fires. Some even had water pipes running through them for cooling. Not only did vacuum tubes heat up, but they were also delicate. Certain computers, while in operation, required a dedicated technician to replace broken tubes.

Since 1960, silicon chips have replaced transistors, which replaced vacuum tubes, resulting in smaller, faster, and more powerful computers. Floppy disks and compact disks are used instead of much less efficient forms of data storage, such as punch cards and ticker tapes. A standard 3.5-inch floppy disk can hold as much data as a mountain of punch cards and offers faster access to the information.

For the gaming world, the biggest transformation is in the way computers display information. Early computers communicated via teletype. A few units had computer readout screens. Throughout the 1960s, the University of Utah, Stanford, and MIT were the only U.S. universities that had computers with monitors.

In 1961 MIT's two main computers were gigantic—an IBM 709, which the members of the TMRC called "the Hulking Giant," and the TX-O, one of the earliest computers to use transistors. Though it was considerably smaller than the Hulking Giant, the TX-O still required 15 tons of air-conditioning equipment for cooling. Unlike the 709, which used punch cards, the TX-O encoded data on long strips of paper tape.

Most students at MIT gravitated toward the IBM 709, causing the unregulated forces of the TMRC to develop disdain for it. They preferred the more efficient TX-O, which had been developed for military purposes. It was smaller, sleeker, and its military designers had given it a monitor. Working on the TX-O, several TMRC members quickly distinguished themselves as master programmers.

In the summer of 1961, Digital Equipment donated its latest computer to MIT, the PDP-1 (Programmable Data Processor-1). Compared to the Hulking Giant and even the TX-O, the PDP-1 was modest in size—about the size of a large automobile. It sold for a paltry $120,000, and like the TX-O, it had a readout terminal. The TMRC adopted it immediately.

In those days, when computers were as rare as nuclear reactors, hackers wrote programs for the good of the computer-loving community. TMRC members stored their PDP-1 programs on ticker tapes in a drawer near the computer, where anyone could try them out or even revise them. Creating a new program was considered an impressive hack. So was making a good revision.

Steve Russell, a fairly new Model Railroader who had just transferred from Dartmouth College, decided to make the ultimate hack: an interactive game.

Russell, a short, nervous kid, was fairly new to the club. He spoke quietly, wore glasses, and had curly hair. Though not a senior member of the club, Russell had earned the other club members' respect by helping a professor implement a computer language called "LISP."

Despite his nickname, "Slug," Russell was intensely smart and energetic. He was an avid reader of "B-grade" science fiction. He particularly loved Doc Savage, a Flash Gordon–like character. Reflecting that passion, Russell determined to set his interactive hack in outer space. He told the other club members about his plans and generated more than a little excitement.

There was one problem, however. Russell needed motivating. Over the next few months, fellow club members would ask about his progress and become frustrated. They complained that he was wasting time. In the end, Alan Kotok, a more senior member of the TMRC, had to push Russell into finishing his work. When Russell told Kotok that he needed a sine-cosine routine to get started, Kotok went directly to Digital Equipment, the PDP's manufacturer, to get it.

> Eventually, Allen Kotok came to me and said, "Alright, here are the sine-cosine routines. Now what's your excuse?" He'd gotten it out of the [Digital Equipment] users' library.
>
> Since I had run out of excuses, I sat down and wrote the program to run two spaceships on the CRT, which you controlled with switches. The prototype was completed in 1961 and the finished version in 1962.
>
> **—Steve Russell**

It took Russell nearly six months and 200 hours to complete the first version of the game: a simple duel between rocket ships. Using toggle switches built into the PDP-1, players controlled the speed and direction of both ships and fired torpedoes at each other. Russell called his game *Spacewar.**

---

* Some historians argue that Willy Higinbotham, a scientist at the Brookhaven National Laboratory, actually invented the first game. In 1958, Higinbotham programmed an oscilloscope to play an interactive tennis game. While this appears to be the first interactive game, it is an isolated instance. Apparently, neither Steven Russell nor Ralph Baer were aware of the existence of Higinbotham's game.

> It was a two-player game; there wasn't enough computing power available to do a decent opponent. I was the first person to not make money on a two-player computer game.
>
> They [the rockets] were rather crude cartoons. But one of them was curvy like a Buck Rogers 1930s spaceship. And the other one was very straight and long and thin like a Redstone rocket. They were commonly called the Needle and the Wedge.
>
> Except for the pacing, *Spacewar* was essentially like the game *Asteroids*. The spaceship controls were four switches. One let you rotate counterclockwise, another was for rotating clockwise, one fired your rocket for thrust, and the last one fired your torpedoes. The basic version used switches on the console, and your elbows got very tired.
>
> **—Steve Russell**

In typical hacker fashion, TMRC members revised *Spacewar.* Some of these additions improved the game so much that they became integral elements. By the time *Spacewar* was finished, Russell's simple game had an accurate map of the stars in the background and a sun with an accurate gravitational field in the foreground.

> I started out with a little prototype that just flew the spaceships around. Pete Sampson added a program called Expensive Planetarium that displayed stars as a background. Dan Edwards did some very clever stuff to get enough time so that we could compute the influence of gravity on the spaceships. The final version of that was done in the spring of 1962.
>
> **—Steve Russell**

Battles took place around Edwards's sun. The best players learned how to accelerate into the sun's gravitational field, loop around, and catch slower opponents off guard. Hovering too close or flying into the sun meant death. Another hacker added a hyperspace button. When trapped by an opponent, players could hit the button and disappear. The risk was that you never knew where your rocket would reappear. You could reappear safely across the screen, but you were just as likely to appear too close to the sun to save your rocket.

To add a touch of realism, Russell originally made his torpedoes unpredictable. Most flew straight, but some strayed. Judging players' reactions, he later recanted, replacing realism with dependability. His final version of the game had straight-flying torpedoes. Beyond these touches, Russell's primary vision of an outer-space torpedo duel remained intact.

Along with creating the first computer game, the members of the TMRC invented another first in electronic entertainment. Tired of sore elbows, Alan Kotok and Bob Sanders scrounged parts from the TMRC and assembled remote controllers that could be wired into the computer. These remotes were easier to use than the PDP-1's native controls since they had dedicated switches for every *Spacewar* function, including hyperspace buttons. This was the forerunner to the gamepad.

Though Russell's amazing hack created a sensation throughout MIT, he never made a penny from it. PDP computers were not a consumer commodity, particularly not arcade machines. "We thought about trying to make money off it for two or three days but concluded that there wasn't a way that it could be done," says Russell.

Eventually, Digital Equipment began using *Spacewar* as a diagnostic program for testing equipment. In effect, PDP buyers got the game free.

Steve Russell never graduated from college. He followed a professor to Stanford University and eventually moved into the private sector. In the 1970s, he met another legendary computer wizard.

> Steve Russell wound up years later in Seattle, working for a time-share computer company. They would bring in kids after school and have them pound on keyboards to see if they could make the computers crash.
>
> There was only one kid who could crash them no matter what they did. The kid was named Bill Gates. There's just this interesting little intersection of worlds that I just thought was a really fascinating thing.
>
> **—Tom Zito, president, Digital Pictures**

Spacewar was the first computer game. Steve Russell made no attempt to copyright his work or to collect royalties from it. He was a hacker and had created his game to show that it could be done.

The people behind the creation of the first video game did not share the Tech Model Railroad Club's utopian vision. Their capitalistic vision held up better in the courts of law.

The Father of Home Video Games

> I reported to the executive V.P. He knew what was going on. And he keeps asking me, "Baer, are you still screwing around with that stuff [video games]?" During the first couple of years and later on, I was subjected to his remarks like, "Stop wasting our money."
>
> When the millions started coming in, everybody remembered how supportive they had been of the project.
>
> **—Ralph Baer, former manager of Equipment Design Division,**
> **Sanders Associates**

The first video game was created by engineers at Sanders Associates, a New Hampshire–based defense contractor. Like many large contractors, Sanders had its share of sensitive and top-secret activities. But in 1967, some of the noises coming out of one Sanders research lab had many people wondering what was going on.

> For three months there were guitar sounds coming out of the little room on the fifth floor. It sparked all kinds of rumors.
>
> This is a military electronics company. Everything is classified. You don't walk in and out of any place without having either a key card or keys. And here's this room with guitar sounds coming out. All sorts of rumors started floating around about what we were doing in there.
>
> **—Ralph Baer**

The Equipment Design Division of Sanders was led by a stern and meticulous engineer named Ralph Baer; a man with a background in radio and television design who had been with the company for more than ten years.

Baer was born in Germany eleven years before Adolph Hitler took power in 1933, and he was largely self-educated. Being Jewish, he was kicked out of school at age fourteen. Two years later, his family moved to America, where he eventually took a correspondence course in radio and television servicing from the National Radio Institute.

Baer had a knack for realizing positive results from unlucky turns of fate. After joining the army in World War II, he studied algebra while stationed in England. One day, after a long study session "in the English mud," Baer was diagnosed with pneumonia. Three days after he entered the hospital, the rest of his platoon was sent to invade Normandy. He jokes that Algebra II saved his "collectives."

A year after he returned from the war, Baer enrolled at the American Television Institute of Technology in Chicago. It was his first formal education since being denied schooling in Germany.

After graduating with a bachelor's degree in television engineering, he took a job with a small defense contracting firm, turning down an offer from CBS because the salary from the defense contractor paid five dollars more per week. Baer quickly developed a solid reputation. When Sanders hired him in 1955, it was to manage a design department with a staff of 200. By 1960, the staff had expanded to 500.

Baer spent more than 30 years at Sanders. The first 15 years were dedicated to military projects. During this time, he weaned himself from vacuum tubes and began working on transistor technology and early microprocessors.

Among Ralph Baer's best attributes as an engineer was his methodical recording of every step of the inventing process. From the moment he began fleshing out new designs, Baer recorded the entire process, dated it, and filed it away. Because of his meticulous note-keeping, he knows exactly when and where he first got the idea to make games that could be played on a television.

> I'm sitting around the East Side Bus Terminal during a business trip to New York, thinking about what you can do with a TV set other than tuning in channels you don't want. And I came up with the concept of doing games, building something for $19.95. This was 1966, in August.
>
> Now you've got to remember, I'm a division manager. I have a $7 or $8 million direct labor payroll. I can put a couple of guys on the bench who can

> work on something. Nobody needs to know. Doesn't even ripple my over-
> head. And that's how I started.
>
> —**Ralph Baer**

The first man Baer allocated to game design was Bill Harrison. Once the concepts were roughed out, Harrison, well versed in transistor-circuit engineering, did most of the implementation. Baer describes Harrison as a young, talented technician who had educated himself on the workings of television sets by assembling a Heath Kit television set.

In his younger days, Baer was extremely austere or, as he later described himself, "uptight." Working with Harrison, he created early video games using a crude mechanism for transferring images onto the television screen. Their game designs, however, lacked entertainment value. The first toy they made was a lever that players pumped furiously to change the color of a box on a television screen from red to blue. Though Baer would later prove to be an excellent electronic toy and game designer, in the beginning his work was more about engineering than game design.

When he first presented his invention to the executive board, including the company founder Royden Sanders, most of the executives felt that Baer was wasting the company's time. Some suggested that Baer shelve the project. Others wanted to pull the plug on it entirely.

> My boss came up to play with our rifle; we had a plastic rifle by then. And he
> used to shoot at the target spot [on a television screen] from the hip. He was
> pretty good at it, and that kind of got his attention. We got more friendly.
> And it kept the project alive.
>
> —**Ralph Baer**

In 1967, Baer added another member to the team—Bill Rusch, who brought a needed understanding of fun and games.

> Bill Rusch was an engineer who worked for Herb Campman, the corporate
> IR&D director. I needed an engineer to work along with Harrison. I wanted

> two guys to work the problem, and Rusch came mostly because his boss
> didn't want him.
>
> My biggest problem that summer was motivating Rusch. He'd come in at
> 10 or 11 A.M. and spend an hour talking; he was lazy and frustrating as hell.
> Rusch was an extremely creative and extremely lazy, hard-to-motivate guy.
> Brilliant. Also, he played really hep guitar.
>
> But it's a good thing we had him, because he helped put us on the map.
>
> **—Ralph Baer**

To keep Rusch productive, Baer allowed him to continue working on a project that involved playing guitar chords through a box that dropped the sounds an octave, changing the notes to the pitch of a bass guitar. With Rusch on board, the games began to take shape. Rusch made a game in which one player chases another player through a maze.

The first ones were all two-person games. Baer's game machine was not powerful enough to control objects or run any form of artificial intelligence. In May or June of 1967, Rusch suggested a new game in which a hard-wired logic circuit projected a spot flying across the screen. Originally, the object of the game was for players to catch the spot with manually controlled dots. Over time, the players' dots evolved into paddles, and the game became ping-pong.

> So here we had a respectable ping-pong game going, and it wasn't long
> before we called it a hockey game. Remove the center bar, which we put up
> there to emulate the net, and now it's a hockey game. We put a blue overlay
> for blue ice on top of the screen so it looked more like hockey. We later added
> a chroma signal to electronically generate the blue background.
>
> We always had three controls—vertical control for moving the paddles up
> and down, a horizontal control for moving the paddles from left to right (so
> you could move close to the net if you wanted to), and what we called an
> "English control," which allowed us to put English on the ball while in flight.
>
> **—Ralph Baer**

Sanders Associates had a rough time in the late 1960s, downsizing from 11,000 to 4,000 employees. As a military contractor, Sanders couldn't suddenly go into the toy business, so Baer had to find a customer for his invention. He nearly licensed it to a cable company, but the depressed state of the cable industry prevented the deal from ever taking shape. As a last resort, Baer urged his bosses to notify television manufacturers about the project.

He had come up with the right audience. General Electric, the first TV manufacturer to evaluate Baer's toy, showed some interest. Then came Zenith and Sylvania. Both GE and Sylvania returned for second evaluations. RCA almost bought into the project—contracts were written but never signed.

In 1971, Magnavox hired a member of the RCA team that had nearly purchased the project. He then told other Magnavox executives about the television game he had seen at Sanders. Magnavox arranged for a demonstration of the television game and immediately saw merit in the idea. After months of the team working out details, negotiations were completed and the contract was signed by the end of the year. Production started in the fall, and early units were shown at Magnavox dealerships in 1972. Magnavox called the finished product Odyssey.

> Magnavox did a really lousy engineering job—[they] over-engineered the machine. Then they upped the price phenomenally so that the damn thing sold for $100. Here's this thing I wanted to sell for $19.95 coming out at $100. Then in their advertising they showed it hooked up to Magnavox TV sets and gave everyone the impression that this thing only worked on Magnavox TV sets.
>
> **—Ralph Baer**

While waiting for the Magnavox negotiations to finalize, Baer slipped into a deep depression. The military contracting industry was undergoing difficult times. Burdened both by Sanders Associates' troubled financial state and doubts about the value of his invention, Baer wondered if perhaps his bosses at Sanders were correct and he had wasted the company's time and resources.

After helping Magnavox set up an Odyssey engineering group, Baer returned to New Hampshire. He went back to working on military projects. This was after the layoffs, and few of Baer's friends remained with Sanders. During this period, he checked into a local hospital for an operation he had been putting off.

So I decided I was going to have my back operated on. I just wanted to get away from things. I went to the hospital. While I'm in the hospital, the first $100,000 comes in from the Magnavox license. And it was like somebody sticking the key in my motor and turning on the engine. My depression disappeared overnight.

—Ralph Baer

Ralph Baer and Steve Russell never met socially. They would, however, meet on opposite sides of some very important litigation. Russell, who never filed for a copyright or patent, would become the symbol for those trying to break into the business. Baer, whose employers jealously guarded all of his patents, would become the spokesman for people trying to protect their intellectual property rights.

Russell and Baer are the forgotten fathers of the industry. Because Steve Russell's game ran only on extremely expensive computers, it had no practical application. Outrageously priced and poorly advertised, Ralph Baer's game machine might also have gone unnoticed. But in 1972, the year Magnavox finally released Odyssey, another, rather similar, machine was about to change the way America played games.

Father of the Industry

Nolan at one point decided, as only Nolan can, that he wanted to run for the House of Representatives. And the way that Nolan's mind works, he decided that if he wanted to be a congressman, he'd better buy a house in Washington, D.C.

—Tom Zito, former reporter, the *Washington Post*

The son of a small-town cement contractor, he became a citizen of the world. A critic once called him "the smartest man who ever walked the earth," but a close friend describes him as having "the attention span of a golden retriever." He is Nolan Bushnell, an electrical engineer and inventor whose only true invention is a $16-billion industry.

Nolan Bushnell was born a Mormon in Clearfield, Utah, in 1943. Though he left both Mormonism and Utah behind early in life, he still speaks warmly of both. Bushnell has eight children. The rest of the country would call this a large family, but in the intensely Mormon town of Clearfield, Utah, the Bushnells would fit right in.

Bushnell's father died in the summer of 1958, leaving behind several unfinished construction jobs. Whether driven by youthful bravado or a sense of responsibility, 15-year-old Nolan, who already stood over six feet tall, fulfilled the contracts himself. "When you do something like that as a 15-year-old, you begin to believe you can do anything," says Bushnell.

Throughout his life, Bushnell demonstrated his love of ideas. In high school, he was a champion debater and studied philosophy as a hobby. He also demonstrated a deep-seated need for fun. As a teenager he strung electric lights along a kite and fooled neighbors into thinking it was a UFO. He stopped college roommates from using his toiletries by putting a deodorant label on a can of green spray paint. According to Bushnell, one rather unaware student painted both underarms before realizing he'd been duped.

In 1962, Bushnell enrolled in the University of Utah. As a freshman, he wrote a term paper stating his philosophy for an interesting existence: it expressed a constant need for change and a wanderlust that would punctuate his life.

> I said [in the term paper] that a bright person should be able to fundamentally master any discipline in three years—mastery meaning to hit the 90-percentile level. To become a truly immersed master, if you would, you could spend the rest of your life on the last 10 percent. But I felt that I wanted to be constantly on that 90 percent curve, which required me to keep changing venues.
>
> The way to have an interesting life is to stay on the steep part of the learning curve.
>
> **—Nolan Bushnell**

Bushnell describes himself as having received "two educations." After losing his tuition money in a poker game, he took a job running arcade games at Lagoon, an amusement park located north of Salt Lake City.

Bushnell worked full time during the summer. During the slower spring and fall seasons, he worked weekends. He began on the midway, talking people into trying to knock down milk bottles with a baseball at a quarter a shot. According to Bushnell, stacking bottles was the least important part of the job. The real trick was attracting players. The job taught him lessons he'd use the rest of his life.

> Remember I started out on the midway, selling balls to knock milk bottles over. So I'd say, "Come on over." If I got you to take one of my baseballs and give me a quarter, I was doing my job.
>
> I always said that I was doing the same thing with *Pong,* only I was putting myself in the box. The things I had learned about getting you to spend a quarter on me in one of my midway games, I put those sales pitches in my automated box.
>
> **—Nolan Bushnell**

Eventually, he moved from the midway to an in-park pinball and electromechanical game arcade. There he watched customers play games like Chicago Coin *Speedway.* He helped maintain the machinery and learned how it worked. Most important, he further honed his understanding of how the game business operates.

Though he majored in engineering, Bushnell divided his academic career among many interests, with special emphasis on philosophy. He eventually discovered the computer lab.

By this time, the University of Utah had emerged as one of the top schools for computer science. Led by Professor David Evans, who worked with ex-Harvard professor Ivan Sutherland to build a head-mounted virtual reality display in 1968, the Computer Science Department had some of the best equipment in the country.

> In the late 1960s, if you wanted to connect a computer up to a telephone or to a video screen, you only did it four places in the world or in the known uni-

> verse: the University of Utah, MIT, a college in Minnesota, or Stanford. And it
> was just serendipity that I went to school there.
>
> **—Nolan Bushnell**

As an undergraduate, Bushnell had only limited access to the computer lab. He was determined to explore, however, and eventually befriended some of the teaching assistants. In the end, Bushnell would become a regular, spending many late nights in the lab. He learned to program in FORTRAN and Gotran, two of the earliest computer languages.

Bushnell also learned about computer games. His favorite was *Spacewar,* Steve Russell's pioneering two-man combat game. Bushnell played it incessantly.

He also created some games of his own. Naturally charismatic, Bushnell talked senior students into helping him. He made computerized *Tic Tac Toe* and *3-D Tic Tac Toe.* But his best creation was a game called *Fox and Geese.*

> *Fox and Geese* was a very primitive game in which there were, it was either
> four or six Xs, which represented the geese, and one O, which was the fox.
> And if the geese completely surrounded the fox, they could kill it. But if the
> fox got any of the geese off by himself, he could kill the geese.
>
> So the idea was to have three geese touch the fox at the same time. And
> they were actually run by the computer. They had a very simple algorithm:
> They looked to see whether the fox was to the left of them or to the right, and
> they'd click one space toward that side in both the X and Y. So they'd constantly be converging on him.
>
> You were driving the fox around, trying to go after the goose and isolate it.
>
> **—Nolan Bushnell**

Though the students at the University of Utah teamed up to write seven computer games, *Spacewar* remained Bushnell's favorite. He continued his late-night *Spacewar* sessions all the way through school. By the time he graduated in 1968, he had committed the game and its many nuances to memory.

In 1969, a northern California engineering firm, Ampex Corporation, hired Bushnell as a research-design engineer for an annual salary of $10,000. He describes his first project as a "high-speed digital type recording system." He worked on the system for eighteen months before his wanderlust struck. For his life to be interesting again, he needed to slip back into "the steep part of the learning curve."

Bushnell saw himself as a stifled entrepreneur. He had ideas, talent, and ambition. Looking back on "both" of his educations, he decided to combine engineering and arcade games. In his typically strong entrepreneurial fashion, he turned his daughter's bedroom into a workshop. For the next few months, two-year-old Britta Bushnell slept in the living room while her father made a coin-operated version of Steve Russell's computer game, *Spacewar.*

Bushnell originally tried to build his game using a new and inexpensive Texas Instruments minicomputer but found that it was too costly and lacked the processing power to run a compelling game. The spaceships were shapeless and the game moved too slowly.

Undaunted, Bushnell found a way to improvise. Instead of building a general-purpose computer, he designed a specialized device capable of only one thing—playing his game. As an Ampex engineer, Bushnell was able to get most of the parts he needed free.

> Ampex had a policy that for hobbies, they'd give you the parts. Everybody called them "G-jobs." As long as it wasn't excessive. . . . they were just 15 or 20 cent items.
>
> And the ones Ampex didn't have, I got from Marshall Electronics. Every engineer ends up having friends who are salespeople—salespeople all have samples. So you just work your friend network and say, "Can you give me some of these? I'm working a new thing and I'll give you the order if it works."
>
> **—Nolan Bushnell**

It worked. Though it lacked the crisp graphics Russell had created on the $120,000 PDP-1, Bushnell's *Computer Space* retained all of the basic play value. It had the star and gravity field, the hyperspace jump, and the same outer-space physics. Even Steve Russell would have appreciated Bushnell's brilliant hack.

Once he created the circuit board, Bushnell found other ways to save money. He went to Goodwill and bought an old black and white television for a monitor. The coin-drop emptied quarters into an empty paint thinner can. Since the coin-operated video-game industry did not exist, and most of the electromechanical amusement industry was in faraway Chicago, Bushnell had to invent solutions constantly.

Having created a working prototype of his game, Bushnell now looked for a partner to help manufacture it. He found that partner in Bill Nutting, founder of Nutting Associates. Nutting, who had already begun dabbling in the coin-op business, hired Bushnell and licensed his game.

> We got *Computer Space* going and got a deal with Nutting. Nutting said they'd build it for us, but they had no expertise. They wanted me to join the company as chief engineer, and I agreed because Nutting had a couple of projects that they needed me to do. So I worked on their projects during the day and finished up *Computer Space* at night and on weekends.
>
> That's how I maintained my rights to things. And they actually later on tried to litigate and said they had a shop right and video game patents.
>
> **—Nolan Bushnell**

> Nutting Associates was owned by Bill Nutting, who had had a successful machine called *Computer Quiz*. It was one of the very first, if not the first, solid-state amusement machines ever developed. It came out probably around 1970. *Computer Quiz* was a trivia game, simple as that.
>
> But what's interesting is that Bill Nutting had a brother, Dave—they started out in the business together but had an argument that ended with them splitting up. Bill Nutting had Nutting Associates and Dave Nutting started Nutting Industries. Bill Nutting made *Computer Space* and Dave Nutting made *I.Q. Computer Quiz*.
>
> **—Eddie Adlum**

Always aware of the importance of presentation, Bushnell put special emphasis on creating an elaborate futuristic cabinet to hold his game. In his mind, the cabinet would be the huckster convincing people that they wanted to play—the same job he'd performed on the midway at the amusement park.

He ended up sculpting a cabinet with rounded corners out of modeling clay. Engineers at Nutting molded the final version out of fiberglass.

Because of its complex game play, *Computer Space* had pages of instructions explaining how to maneuver ships, steer clear of gravity, and jump into hyperspace. Nutting used the Dutch Goose, a bar just off the Stanford University campus, as a test site. No one in the bar had ever seen such a thing. Although *Computer Space* attracted some curious stares, it did not attract many players.

Whether he had succumbed to Bushnell's salesmanship or simply believed in the project, Bill Nutting went on to make 1,500 *Computer Space* machines. Bushnell personally demonstrated the game to coin-op distributors at the 1971 Music Operators Association* convention in Chicago.

> It was called *Computer Space,* and I saw it in 1971 at the MOA show in Chicago. As a reporter for *Cash Box* [a vending machine trade publication], I was strolling up and down the aisles where the machines were exhibited, with my camera and notepad. I ran into a great big, long, skinny hiker individual who appeared summarily to be known as Nolan Bushnell, who worked for a company named Nutting Associates.
>
> Nolan was hired on at Nutting Associates to fool around developing a game that had a television monitor in it. In those days the general public didn't call them monitors, they called them TV tubes.
>
> Nolan came up with a game called *Computer Space.* It was a wonderful try that went absolutely nowhere. It had a bizarre sculpted fiberglass cabinet, hourglass shape, lots of curves. I never played the game. All I can remember is that Nolan Bushnell was about the most excited person I've ever seen over the age of six when it came to describing a new game, describing it so much that I was backing up, trying to get away, while he was talking.
>
> **—Eddie Adlum**

The music operators at the convention saw little potential in *Computer Space,* and very few of them bought machines at the show. In the end, the game

---

* The Music Operators Association was later renamed the Amusement and Music Operators Association (AMOA), to reflect the importance of video games to the industry.

turned into a marginally expensive gamble for Nutting. The company didn't sell all of the original 1,500 machines and never built more.*

> *Computer Space* pulled in huge amounts of quarters at the Dutch Goose. But it would earn almost no money in a workingman's bar. The Dutch Goose is really a Stanford University hangout. . . .
>
> *Computer Space* obeys the first law—maintenance of momentum. [Bushnell is probably referring to Sir Isaac Newton's first law—objects maintain constant velocity unless acted upon by an external force.] And so that was really hard for people who didn't understand that.
>
> **—Nolan Bushnell**

Bushnell admits that the instructions were too complex: "Nobody wants to read an encyclopedia to play a game." He also blames Nutting for marketing the game badly.

> Nutting was literally about to go bankrupt. I mean, they really had some problems. And it [*Computer Space*] did okay, but it really didn't do nearly as well as it could have. Companies that are in trouble . . . when you get inside them, you figure out why they're in trouble.
>
> In some ways it was a blessing to have worked for Nutting. It didn't take very long to figure out I couldn't possibly screw things up more than these guys had. Seeing their mistakes gave me a lot of confidence in my ability to do better on my own.
>
> **—Nolan Bushnell**

After the failure of *Computer Space,* Bushnell decided to start his own company. He formed a three-way partnership with Ted Dabney, an Ampex engineer he'd brought to Nutting Associates, and Larry Bryan, also from Ampex. Each partner agreed to contribute $250. Bryan later dropped out of the partnership before contributing his money.

---

* Arcade historian Keith Feinstein located sales and shipping documents proving that Nutting Associates began shipping *Computer Space* in 1971.

The company's first step was to select a name. Looking through a dictionary, Bryan came up with *Syzygy,* a word describing the straight-line configuration of three celestial bodies—a solar eclipse is the syzygy of the earth, moon, and sun. When Bushnell applied for the name, the state of California responded that it was already in use. "A candle company already had it. They were sort of a hippie commune in Mendocino. We subsequently tried to find it out of curiosity. I think it had gone defunct by that time. I never did find it."

Because he could not use Syzygy, Bushnell turned to a word from the Japanese strategy game *Go.* He chose the rough equivalent of the chess term "check," naming his company Atari.

And Then There Was Pong

There were perhaps only five important game manufacturers and five pool table manufacturers and four jukebox manufacturers, and for all intents and purposes, that was the manufacturing side of the amusement machine business.

It stayed that way for quite some time—until 1972. In 1972, Nolan Bushnell, a rather clever electronics engineer from Northern California, adapted Ralph Baer's Magnavox toy for playing ping-pong on the television screen into a coin machine. As the world knows, he called it *Pong.*

—Eddie Adlum

My kid came home from school one day and said that Nolan Bushnell's daughter told the teacher that her father invented *Pong.* Well, I told him to go to Nolan's daughter and say, "If your daddy invented *Pong,* how come he had to ask my daddy to come fix his machine when it broke down?"

—Al Alcorn, former "sort of" vice president of engineering, Atari Corporation

In 1972, President Richard Nixon had all but locked up his re-election by visiting the People's Republic of China and the Soviet Union; the Supreme Court deemed the death penalty cruel and unusual punishment and ruled it unconstitutional; and an investigation by White House counsel John Dean found the Nixon administration innocent of any involvement in the attempted burglary of the Democratic Party headquarters in the Watergate apartment complex.

The Dow Jones Industrial Average hit 1000 points for the first time on November 14, 1972, and the economy looked brighter than it had in five years. Along with a healthy economy came thousands of start-up companies.

On June 27, 1972, Nolan Bushnell and Ted Dabney applied to have Atari incorporated. They founded their company with an initial investment of $250 each. Within ten years, Atari would grow into a $2-billion-a-year entertainment giant, making it the fastest-growing company in U.S. history.

Atari's first office was located in a Santa Clara industrial zone—a crude 1,000-square-foot space in an inexpensive concrete building, made to house start-up companies. These were lean times for the company. It existed on a few small contracts and the limited royalties Bushnell received from *Computer Space.*

Bally, now a very successful pinball and slot machine manufacturer, became one of Atari's first customers, signing a limited contract for Bushnell to develop new extra-wide pinball machines. Bushnell also continued working on a multiplayer version of *Computer Space,* which he hoped to sell to his old employers at Nutting Associates.

> We had a 2,000-square-foot facility. This was the original garage shop—you know, one of those places with a roll-up door, one office, and a bathroom. It had sort of a little reception area, and part of our requirement to the landlords was that they put in another office. That was Ted's lab.
>
> Incubator facilities like that are unique to California. They're cheap and they're made cheap because . . . what they really want you to do, and what Cole Properties, the ones that were running the building wanted, was to sign us for a long lease.
>
> Eighty percent of the companies [that sign up] don't grow or stay there for a long time until the lease is out. But some companies get really big

> quickly. And they'll say, oh, we'll let you out of the lease. You can just roll it
> into one of our other properties.
>
> **—Nolan Bushnell**

To create a steadier income base, Bushnell and Dabney started a pinball route that included a local bar, some coffee shops, and the Student Union building at Stanford University. Because they could buy the pinball machines cheaply and knew how to maintain them, the route became a profitable asset. It eventually became so lucrative, in fact, that when Dabney left the company, he accepted the route as part of his settlement.

The first full-time employee of Atari Corporation was Cynthia Villanueva, a 17-year-old who used to baby-sit Bushnell's children. She needed a summer job so Bushnell hired her as a receptionist. He instructed her to "put on the show," giving callers the impression that Atari was an established organization rather than a start-up company with more owners than employees.

> Nolan didn't want to answer the phone, he wanted to have somebody else
> answer it. So he hired a secretary, Cynthia. And when someone would call
> [she would make them wait and yell], "It's for you Nolan." We'd wait a cer-
> tain amount of time to make it sound like it was a bigger company, you
> know it would take longer to go get him.
>
> **—Al Alcorn**

Villanueva's responsibilities did not stop with answering telephones. Because of the company's limited budget, she was called upon to do everything from running errands to building electronic components and placing parts in cabinets. She stayed with Atari for more than a decade, remaining long after Bushnell and Dabney left.

Atari's second employee was a young engineer named Al Alcorn, whom Ted Dabney first met while working at Ampex. Alcorn had just completed a work-study program that allowed him to work summers at Ampex while finishing his engineering degree at Cal-Berkeley.

Short and sturdy, Alcorn was once a member of the same all-city high-school football team as O. J. Simpson. He was naturally gifted when it came to

electronics and had learned how to repair televisions by taking an RCA correspondence course in high school. When he got to college, Alcorn paid for his
education by working in a television repair shop.

When Alcorn finished his degree, he found the job market weakening and
was hired by Ampex. The company was going through rough times and had a
round of layoffs when Nolan Bushnell offered him a job working for Atari.
Alcorn agreed to move.

> Nolan hired me when Ampex was going through some setbacks. He offered
> me a job as the VP of engineering or sort of, VP of R & D or whatever title it
> was of this company called Syzygy.
>
> He offered me $1,000 a month and a chance to own stock in the company.
> The stock was worthless; most start-up companies fail anyway. I had actu-
> ally been making a little bit more than that, but I figured what the heck.
>
> Nolan had a company car. This was a concept I'd never thought of before
> or conceived of. It was an Oldsmobile station wagon, but like, wow, you can
> drive a car that isn't even yours and don't have to pay for it. What a concept!
>
> **—Al Alcorn**

Simply an Exercise

Shortly after hiring Alcorn, Bushnell gave him his first project. Bushnell revealed that he had just signed a contract with General Electric to design a
home electronic game based on ping-pong. The game should be very simple
to play—"one ball, two paddles, and a score. . . . Nothing else on the screen."

Bushnell had made up the entire story. He had not signed a contract or
even entered into any discussions with General Electric. In truth, Bushnell
wanted to get Alcorn familiar with the process of making games while he
designed a more substantial project. Bushnell had recently sold Bally executives on a concept for an outer-space game that combined the true-life physics
of *Computer Space* with a race track.

> I found out later this was simply an exercise that Nolan gave me because it
> was the simplest game that he could think of. He didn't think it had any play

> value. He believed that the next winning game was going to be something more complex than *Computer Space,* not something simpler.
>
> Nolan didn't want to tell me that because it wouldn't motivate me to try hard. He was just going to dispose of it anyway.
>
> **—Al Alcorn**

From his tenure at Ampex, Alcorn was already familiar with the transistor-to-transistor logic (TTL) involved in creating electronic games. He tried to work from the schematic diagrams that Bushnell had drawn while designing *Computer Space* but found them illegible. In the end, Alcorn had to create his own design, based on what he knew about Bushnell's inventions and his own understanding of TTL.

As he worked, Alcorn added enhancements that Bushnell had never envisioned. He replaced the expensive components with much less expensive parts. Bushnell's original vision included paddles that simply batted the ball in the direction it had come from. Feeling that this was inadequate, Alcorn devised a way to add English to the game and aim the ball with the paddles.

Instead of using solid lines to represent paddles, Alcorn broke the paddles into eight segments. If the ball hit the two center segments of the paddle, it flew straight back at a 180-degree angle. If the ball hit the next segments, it ricocheted off at a shallow angle. Hitting the ball with the outer edges of the paddle would send the ball back at a 45-degree angle.

Alcorn also added ball acceleration. The original game simply buzzed along at the same speed until someone finally missed the ball. Alcorn found the game dull and thought that speeding the ball during extended rallies might lend some excitement. He wrote the game so that after the ball had been hit a certain number of times, it would automatically fly faster.

A certain mythology has arisen about the creation of *Pong.* People have written about the meticulous effort that went into creating the resonant pong-sound that occurred whenever the ball struck a paddle. According to Alcorn, that sound was a lucky accident.

> Here I was developing this thing and feeling kind of frustrated because it already had too many parts in it to be a successful consumer product. So I

felt like I was failing, and Nolan didn't mention that the game had come off better than he'd expected.

Now the issue of sound . . . People have talked about the sound, and I've seen articles written about how intelligently the sound was done and how appropriate the sound was. The truth is, I was running out of parts on the board. Nolan wanted the roar of a crowd of thousands—the approving roar of cheering people when you made a point. Ted Dabney told me to make a boo and a hiss when you lost a point, because for every winner there's a loser.

I said, "Screw it, I don't know how to make any one of those sounds. I don't have enough parts anyhow." Since I had the wire wrapped on the scope, I poked around the sync generator to find an appropriate frequency or a tone. So those sounds were done in a half a day. They were the sounds that were already in the machine.

—Al Alcorn

Pong played more like squash than ping-pong. Thanks to Alcorn's segmented paddle, it had become a game of angles, in which banking shots against walls was an important strategy. Players controlled inch-long white lines that represented racquets, which they used to bat the small white square that represented the ball. The background was black.

The game was streamed through a $75 Hitachi black-and-white television that Alcorn picked up at a nearby Payless store. He set the television in a four-foot tall wooden cabinet that looked vaguely like a mailbox. Since the printed circuit boards hadn't been made, Alcorn had to hard-wire everything himself. The inside of the cabinet had hundreds of wires soldered into small boards and looked like the back of a telephone-operator's switchboard.

It took Alcorn nearly three months to build a working prototype. His finished project surprised Bushnell and Dabney. Instead of giving them an interesting exercise, Alcorn had created a fun game that became their flagship product. Bushnell named the game *Pong* and made a few changes, including adding a bread pan for collecting quarters and an instruction card that read simply, "Avoid missing ball for high score." To test the game's marketability, Bushnell and Alcorn installed it in a location along the Atari pinball route.

Our initial idea was to go into business as a contract design firm and sell our ideas to others for licensing. We had a contract with Bally to design a video game for them, and we saw it as being a big, pretty long project.

So I had Al do this *Pong* game, this ping-pong game. And, dammit, it was fun. We tweaked it a little and it was more fun, and we thought to ourselves, we'll get Bally to take this. We'll complete our contract way, way, way ahead of schedule and life will be happy in the Valley.

So I took *Pong* and offered it to Bally. I said, "Hey, you know we contracted to do a driving game but we got this game instead. Do you want this instead? Will this fill our contract for you?" They played it and said, "This is kind of fun, but it requires two players and if a guy's there all by himself he can't play it." And I said, "Well, we could probably put a one player version in." I sold them pretty hard.

—**Nolan Bushnell**

Andy Capp's Tavern

Andy Capp's was a peanut-shell-on-the-floor beer bar in Sunnyvale, California. It was nothing special, other than it had a game room in the back that was larger than any that you would see in a bar at that point in time.

—**Nolan Bushnell**

Once, when feeling particularly generous, Bushnell described Andy Capp's Tavern, the location where Atari first tested *Pong,* as a "rustic location." It was a shabby bar located in Sunnyvale, a much smaller town in the pre–high technology days of the early 1970s. Alcorn, who visited the bar while running the pinball route, remembers it as having four or five pinball machines, a jukebox, and a *Computer Space* machine. They installed the prototype in late September 1972.

We put it [the *Pong* prototype] on a barrel. He had old wine barrels to use as tables and we just put it on top of the table. It wasn't even a full size.

—**Nolan Bushnell**

Nolan and I sat there the first night and watched people play, and here's the scene. We're sitting there with a couple of beers, and a young man goes up and plays *Computer Space* while his friend plays *Pong*. While we're watching, the first guy goes over and tries *Pong* with his friend.

We went over to him afterward and asked, "Well, what did you think of that machine?" And the guy says, "Oh, it's a great machine. You know, I know the guys who designed it."

"Really! What are they like?"

So [he tells us] this whole bullshit story. I think he was practicing a line for picking up babes.

—Al Alcorn

One of the legends of video games is that two days after installing *Pong* in Andy Capp's Tavern, Alcorn got an angry late-night call from Bill Gattis, the tavern manager. According to the story, the machine had stopped working and Gattis wanted it hauled out of his bar.

In truth, Alcorn received the call from Gattis two weeks after installing the machine. It was a friendly call in which the bartender suggested that they fix the machine quickly, since it had developed quite a following. Alcorn frequently visited Andy Capp's while making maintenance runs on Atari's pinball route. He and Bushnell had selected the bar as a good test site because Gattis had always been cooperative.

He said to me, "Al, this is the weirdest thing. When I opened the bar this morning, there were two or three people at the door waiting to get in. They walked in and played that machine. They didn't buy anything. I've never seen anything like this before."

I went to fix the machine, not knowing what to expect. I opened the coin box to give myself a free game and low and behold, this money gushed out. I grabbed handfuls of it, put it in my pockets, gave the manager my business card, and said, "Next time this happens, you call me at home right away. I can always fix this one."

—Al Alcorn

Nolan Bushnell left for Chicago to visit a couple of pinball manufacturers a few days before Alcorn received the call from Andy Capp's Tavern. He had brought a portable *Pong* game to demonstrate to executives at Bally and Midway. Though Bushnell already had an inkling that *Pong* was doing good business at the test site, he had no idea how well it had done. When he returned, an excited Al Alcorn told him that the machine at Andy Capp's Tavern had stopped working because the quarters had overflowed. The news struck Bushnell like a revelation.

Surprised by *Pong*'s success, Bushnell decided that he should manufacture the game himself rather than sell it to an established game maker. The problem was, he had discussed the game with executives at Bally and Midway and stirred up some interest. Now he had to find a way to steer them away from *Pong* while keeping the door open for future projects. In the end, Bushnell played one side against the other.

> Nolan decided he didn't really want Bally to take *Pong* because he knew it was too good. So he met with Bally and Midway and decided to tell Bally that the Midway guys didn't want it. And so the Bally guys decided that they didn't want it.
>
> Then he told the Midway guys that the Bally guys didn't want it. He got them convinced that it was no good. [Once they heard Bally didn't want it] it . . . didn't take much convincing.
>
> **—Al Alcorn**

The Big Debate

There are unanswered questions in the history of video games. One question involves Ralph Baer, the designer of the Magnavox Odyssey, and Nolan Bushnell. It is a question of ownership.

In 1972, while Nutting Associates tried to market *Computer Space* as the beginning of a new generation of arcade games, Magnavox quietly circulated the Odyssey television game around the country in special demonstrations for dealers and distributors. Most demonstrations took place in private showings, but the new device was also displayed at a few trade shows.

The first show began on May 3, 1972, in Phoenix, Arizona. Three weeks later, Odyssey came to the San Francisco Bay area in a large trade show held in the town of Burlingame. According to Magnavox, a Nutting Associates employee named Nolan Bushnell attended the show on May 24. Depositions taken from Magnavox witnesses claimed that while at the show, Bushnell tested Odyssey.

Some time after Atari began marketing *Pong,* in 1972, Magnavox took the California start-up to court. *Pong,* Magnavox argued, violated several of Baer's patents. It infringed upon his patents for projecting electronic games on a television screen, and, more important, it infringed on his concept of electronic ping-pong.

> What they've always alleged was that there was a meeting or a distributor show somewhere in the valley, and I should have, would have, could have been there. So it's one of those pissing matches.
>
> **—Nolan Bushnell**

Atari was up against a stacked deck. First of all, the methodical Ralph Baer considered filing for patents an integral part of the invention process. During his life, Baer was awarded more than seventy patents and was once named "inventor of the year" by the state of New York. He documented everything.

By comparison, Bushnell, with his haphazard style, allowed the mundane details of invention and legal filing to escape him. Even when he created schematics, like the one he had made for *Computer Space,* they were often illegible.

More important, whether Bushnell attended the Magnavox show or missed it, there had been a show.* Magnavox could prove that it had demonstrated Odyssey in Burlingame prior to the creation of *Pong* and even prior to the incorporation of Atari. Magnavox also had Baer's patents and notes, all of which clearly predated *Pong* and *Computer Space.*

Bushnell considered his options. Magnavox had more lawyers and resources than Atari could ever hope to afford. His attorney urged him to take the matter to court, claiming they would win; but when Bushnell asked how much it might cost, the lawyer thought the expenses could be as much

---

* In later litigation, it was revealed that Bushnell not only attended the Burlingame show but also played the tennis game on Odyssey.

as $1.5 million—more money than Atari had to spend. Atari could not afford to fight, even if it won.

In order for his company to survive, Bushnell had to find another alternative. It came in the form of a settlement. Magnavox offered Bushnell a very inexpensive settlement proposal. Bushnell followed up by asking for special terms in the agreement.

> It was all settled outside and Nolan and Atari got extremely favorable terms. They paid very little. He got away with a very, very, very small licensing fee up front.
>
> Atari became a licensee under a prepaid arrangement. It paid some fixed sum, some ridiculous number like a few hundred grand. I don't remember the details. But he [Nolan] had an extremely advantageous, nonburdensome license from us. And as far as we were concerned, that was the end of our problems with Atari.
>
> If anybody had had any inkling of what was going to happen to this business at Atari, they would never have gotten those terms.
>
> **—Ralph Baer**

Bushnell played the legal action like a chess game. In exchange for settling, Atari became Magnavox's sole licensee. By this time other companies had begun making similar games. While Atari had already paid its licensing fees, future competitors would have to pay stiff royalties to Magnavox. In several later litigations, Magnavox zealously prosecuted all violators.

> Magnavox said, "For $700,000 we'll give you a paid-up license." And Nolan said, wisely, "You got it." So we had a paid license and everybody else had to pay royalties.
>
> That was negotiated in June of 1976, a very key date. It was a week before the consumer electronics show opened, and one of the caveats of that agreement was that Magnavox got the rights to any product we came up with in the next 365 days. Anything we released.
>
> So we said at one point, we're not going to release any consumer products for a year; we'll release them at the next CES [Consumer Electronics Show]. That was the only time we ever kept our mouths shut about a product, and it

was funny because when the Magnavox attorneys came by to analyze our stuff, we had Steve Bristow show them around. Bristow knew nothing about the consumer stuff—the stuff that Magnavox wanted.

—Al Alcorn

I helped negotiate that deal. We paid so little money, and yet we agreed that they would go after, as part of the settlement, all our other competitors. Well, we were the dominant people, and all of a sudden Magnavox said, "We'll help, we'll give you a sweetheart deal, and we'll beat up on everybody else."

—Nolan Bushnell

With the settlement signed, the case never went to court. Bushnell and Baer met in Chicago, on the steps of a courthouse, the day that settlement was sealed. Baer remembered being introduced to Bushnell and shaking hands. They exchanged pleasantries, then went in different directions.

Over the years, Bushnell became a national celebrity as the "father of video games." In the late 1970s, as he prepared to retire, Ralph Baer finally told his story to the press.

I finally got tired of being a shrinking lily and I started tooting my horn a little bit. But it didn't have any financial effect because it was all over by then.

I also didn't open up my mouth, didn't make any loud press for myself, because guys like Nolan were clients. He was a licensee. He put the business on the map. In fact, without him there would never have been any money in the till. If Nolan wants to say he was the great inventor, hooray Nolan. You're a nice guy, you made a lot of money for us, say anything you want to.

—Ralph Baer

Years later, Baer ran into Nolan Bushnell and Gene Lipkin, Atari director of marketing, on the floor of the Consumer Electronics Show. According to Baer, Bushnell introduced him as "the father of video games." Baer smiled and said, "I wish you would have said that to the press."

CHAPTER 5

The King and Court

We had vendor credit from Cramer Electronics. Banks wouldn't talk to us because we were obviously in the Mafia if we were in coin-op.

—Al Alcorn

Guilt by Association

More than thirty years had passed since Fiorello LaGuardia's crusade successfully shut down pinball in New York City, but the stigma of organized crime still plagued the coin-operated amusement business. Politicians and bankers remembered bingo and pay-out machines. When Joel Hochberg was assaulted by thugs while repairing a game in a Brooklyn bar, local authorities assumed it was a mob action and refused to believe that it was a case of mistaken identity. Conscious of their bad image, amusement operators tried to change the public's perception of the industry.

> *Jukebox* was considered within our industry to be a dirty word. It was a word associated with organized crime that would bring up images of racketeering, and we bent over backward to call it anything but a jukebox. My favorite was "coin-activated musical device." Of course, even people in the industry would call it a jukebox when no one was listening.
>
> **—Eddie Adlum**

As an all-cash business, the amusement industry naturally attracted suspicion and some members undoubtedly engaged in money-laundering activities. But most of the stories about the Mafia controlling the industry were exaggerations or myths. The truth was less interesting. "There isn't enough money in the business to attract that kind of people," according to Eddie Adlum, who began covering the coin-operated amusement industry in 1964.

> It's like a piece of ancient history that we'll grin and giggle about today. It was a sad thing when a little kid would go home and ask his daddy, "Daddy, are you a crook?" And the daddy had to say, "No, why?" And the kid would say, "Because my friend Joey says that all people who own jukeboxes are crooks."
>
> **—Eddie Adlum**

Even though Nolan Bushnell was quickly developing an understanding of the coin-operated machine market, had an attractive high-technology gadget that seemed like a sure hit, and had strong presentation skills—all necessary ingredients for financial backing—he found banks unwilling to lend him money. Lenders saw his machine as a new form of pinball. He might just as well have approached them about opening a casino or a racetrack.

Even if his ideas did not scare people, Bushnell's appearance did. He was tall and gangly, with unruly long hair. He looked more like a biker or a hippie than a gangster, but bankers were not impressed by bikers or hippies either.

In the end, only Wells Fargo was willing to take a chance on Atari, extending the company a $50,000 credit line. Though only a fraction of what Bushnell wanted, it was the best he could do.

For Atari to compete with such established coin-operated amusement companies as Bally and Midway, Bushnell needed to expand his facilities. By removing the concrete walls separating his space from an adjacent space in the building, Bushnell doubled Atari's size to 2,000 square feet. Bushnell leased another space and had the wall separating the two facilities torn down, doubling his space again to 4,000 square feet.

It wasn't enough. A few months later, Bushnell tried to get out of his lease with Cole Properties. Instead, he ended up moving operations to another Cole location, a defunct roller-rink a few blocks away. While Atari's administrative offices remained at the Scott Boulevard address, the new Martin Avenue facility served as the assembly plant.

The next step was hiring workers. Trusting the more technical issues of design and quality assurance to Al Alcorn, Bushnell and Ted Dabney decided to risk hiring untrained workers to assemble *Pong* machines. They went to a local unemployment office and hired nearly every prospect the office sent them.

> That's when we started bringing in these guys that we got at the unemployment office. There were members of motorcycle gangs and people who found that they could fence the televisions and buy heroin. We didn't think that any of that existed here. I mean, this was San Jose, California, really a very pristine community.
>
> **—Nolan Bushnell**

In the beginning, Atari offered a fun atmosphere but less than generous wages. New line workers made slightly above minimum wage—$1.75 per hour, plus benefits. One of the more popular benefits was "Friday night beer busts" on the loading dock. Employees also got to play free games.

As *Pong* orders mounted, however, it became impossible to keep up with demand. Bushnell hired nearly anyone who came in the door. Line personnel sometimes worked 16-hour shifts. Tensions mounted, and there was a failed attempt to unionize the company. A rift grew between management and the rank and file.

Atari also became a notorious Mecca of drug abuse. The Martin Avenue roller-rink facility smelled of marijuana. One ex-employee later quipped that "you could get stoned just breathing the air coming out of the building." Steve Bristow, who later became a vice president of the company, remembered the facility in a less extreme light. "Parts of the building smelled like pot, but I don't remember getting stoned just walking through."

Former Atari executives described the people manning the assembly line as long-haired bikers, junkies, and hippies. Even Bushnell admitted they made him nervous.

It didn't take long for some enterprising assembly-line workers to discover that they could supplement their low wages by stealing televisions and parts and selling them at local pawnshops.

> There was about a six-week period [when employee theft was rampant]. We figured out what was going on and then tightened things down, and that went away. The theft was incredible until we woke up and fixed it. We fired a lot of people, and there was still a lot of marijuana use.
>
> One of the kids set up a jar and took donations to help other employees with unwanted pregnancies. It was never an official Atari thing, but we didn't hide it [the jar] from vendors.
>
> **—Nolan Bushnell**

Other employees remembered the drug use as an ongoing problem. When the entire research and development team was asked to work on the line in a last-minute effort to meet deadlines for the 1977 holiday season, a newly hired designer named Roger Hector nervously took his place among the regulars. When he went to use the bathroom, he found empty syringes on the bathroom floor. "I was amazed with what went on," said Hector.

The Work Begins

> We were getting cash up front for *Pong* machines. I think we were selling them for $1,200—up-front cash—and it cost us about $300 or $400 to build them. So we had positive cash flow from the get go, and we were doing it without any venture capital or anything.
>
> **—Al Alcorn**

Though Atari's game production eventually evolved into a sophisticated assembly line, it began as a haphazard dash. Workers wheeled empty *Pong* cabinets to the center of the production facility, and employees took turns installing the various components until the machines were finished. The process was slow and undisciplined and resulted in the production of about ten machines a day, many of which did not pass quality testing.

> The first order was for ten units for Advance Automatic Sales in San Francisco. These were guys that I knew from my days at Nutting. Portale Automatic was down in Los Angeles, and that was my second order. They ordered ten.
>
> By that time, the word had gotten out. Advance Automatic had heard about what had gone on with Andy Capp's [Tavern].
>
> **—Nolan Bushnell**

Bushnell began using *Pong* at other locations on the Atari amusement route, as he drummed up business from other distributors. Word spread quickly. *Pong* had become one of the most profitable coin-operated games in history. Other machines collected $40 or $50 dollars a week. In those early days, *Pong* frequently brought in four times as much as other machines, often topping $200 a week.

As the route's profits expanded, Bushnell hired Steve Bristow, the engineering student at Cal-Berkeley who replaced Alcorn in the Ampex work-study program, to collect quarters along the route. Since Atari had just opened a game room in Berkeley, the route was a convenient way for Bristow to earn some income, and he received 1 percent of the receipts.

> We had the game route operation that was giving us cash flow. And he [Steve Bristow] was setting up the route in the summer, along with doing the other things, because we needed to do everything we could to build cash flow.
>
> We ran the first game room in Berkeley. It was Steve's job to maintain that game room and collect the money and bring it down to us. So while he was still in college at Berkeley that fall, this was his shtick.
>
> Steve usually took his wife on the route. When they'd go to collect, his wife would carry a hatchet. They were afraid because they were carrying hundreds of dollars' worth of quarters, and they couldn't carry a gun.
>
> **—Nolan Bushnell**

> We tried to get a permit to carry a gun, and they wouldn't let us have one, so we asked if there were any laws against carrying a hatchet. There weren't, so we took one along.
>
> **—Steve Bristow**

Word traveled quickly in the amusement industry. Though the first orders were small, they mounted. By the end of 1973, Atari had filled orders for 2,500 *Pong* machines. By the end of 1974, that number grew to more than 8,000. It became more popular than the best pinball machines of the day.

Interestingly, another company benefited from Atari's mounting success. Though the Magnavox Odyssey attracted very little attention when it was first released, the home entertainment system became increasingly more popular as *Pong* expanded into new markets. Atari's success spread quickly, and Odyssey rode in its solid-state wake, selling 100,000 units in its first year.

> . . . and I think if it hadn't been for Nolan showing up that summer with *Pong* and heightening the sensitivity to playing games on a television set, Magnavox's Odyssey wouldn't have sold as well as it did. There was definitely a complementary effect.
>
> **—Ralph Baer**

The King, the Queen, and the Five Princes

As Atari grew, Bushnell surrounded himself with people he knew and trusted. He suddenly foresaw greater success than he had ever imagined and no longer had time for people who did not share his vision.

Ted Dabney, Bushnell's longtime friend and co-founder of Atari, was the first casualty. According to Bushnell, Dabney still had a small-shop engineer's mentality. He wasn't ready to be part owner of an international company and slowed Atari's progress.

At first, Dabney refused to leave, and he and Bushnell traded accusations. In the end, however, Dabney took over operation of the profitable amusement route and received several shares in the company. Years later, Dabney sold his stock at a great profit. In exchange for his original investment of $250, Dabney became a millionaire.

> I bought him out two years into the business. What happened was that the business outgrew Ted, and he knew it. I mean, he was an engineer's engineer, and he liked being in the company, but all of a sudden it got too big for him.
>
> Ted ended up running the coin route. It was a very positive cash flow operation. When we sold off [Bushnell later sold Atari], he ended up with a large note for his shares and the operations, which he ran successfully for many years thereafter. I think, probably all totaled, it was worth about a million bucks.
>
> **—Nolan Bushnell**

In Dabney's place, Bushnell assembled a crew of Ampex expatriates and young gun executives. They became known around Atari as "the King, the Queen, and the Five Princes."

The group included Al Alcorn, who led Atari's research and development; Steve Bristow, who eventually became the vice president of engineering; Bill White, the chief financial officer; Gil Williams, head of manufacturing; Joe Keenan, one of Bushnell's next-door neighbors who would later be president of both Atari and Kee Games; and Gene Lipkin, vice president of sales. (Keenan, a married heterosexual, was referred to as the "queen" because he was second in command, not because of his sexual orientation.)

Of the members of Bushnell's team, Lipkin stands out as the only executive with a background in the coin-operated amusement industry. Before going to Atari, Lipkin worked at Allied Leisure Industries, a Florida game manufacturer.

Lipkin brought experience and savvy to the group. He rose quickly at Atari and proved to be a valuable asset.

> Allied Leisure was started by an old timer in our business named Dave Braun, basically to give his son Bobby something to do. Bobby was severely crippled.
>
> They had a factory in Hialeah, Florida, and they made a couple of pretty good motorcycle games. That's where Gene Lipkin got his start, working as the sales manager for Dave Braun and Bobby Braun.
>
> That motorcycle game was a good game, but it broke down a lot, and Gene ran around the country apologizing for the game as often as he was selling it.
>
> **—Eddie Adlum**

Bushnell still preferred working smart and fun to working hard and made sure that the men around him agreed with his philosophy. They held meetings in hot tubs, drank heavily, experimented with drugs, and named projects after sexy female employees. Sometimes Atari board meetings seemed more like fraternity parties than business meetings.

> It's an accurate part of the mythology that we played around with pot at our planning sessions and things like that. And it's actually, I think, a very interesting documentable piece of society that most of us played around. I mean this is the late 1960s, early 1970s.
>
> But then, very quickly, most of us said, "Hey, this isn't really effective. This isn't good." But by that time some of us had already destroyed our lives.
>
> **—Nolan Bushnell**

> I remember this board meeting . . . Nolan lived in Los Gatos in a very nice house on the hilltop with a hot tub out back. We had a board meeting in his tub. Nolan was saying how much money we were going to be worth, all these millions, and I thought to myself, "I'll believe this when I see it."

> Nolan needed some papers and documents so he called his office and said, "Have Miss so and so bring them up."
>
> We were in this tub [when she arrived], so he proceeded to try to get her in the tub during the board meeting. Nolan's attorney was miffed [because] we got his papers wet. He was not in the hot tub and he was not amused by any of this. That was the sort of fun we had.
>
> **—Al Alcorn**

In 1974, Bushnell added a final asset to Atari's arsenal. Steve Mayer and Larry Emmons, two of his former associates from Ampex, started a consulting company in Grass Valley, a small community near the California-Nevada border.

Bushnell respected Emmons's and Mayer's abilities and immediately began an exclusive relationship. Grass Valley became the Atari think-tank, the place Bushnell and his board went when they needed to plan a strategic move or devise some new and highly technical invention. Mayer and Emmons became the prime architects of many projects. "Grass Valley would build the technical stuff that people said couldn't be built," according to Bushnell.

> They [Mayer and Emmons] both worked with me at Ampex, and so I knew they were good.
>
> So we had this little group up in Grass Valley, California. We had kind of a reputation, you know, for smoking pot and things like that. And I think a lot of it came from the fact that we had a think tank in Grass Valley and people thought, "What is that? Grass Valley in California can only mean one thing."
>
> **—Nolan Bushnell**

Grass Valley was located deep in the Sierra Mountains near the Nevada border. It was a naturally scenic location, near towns that had once boomed during the silver rush. Atari executives adopted the Grass Valley facility as their company retreat. Bushnell and his board drove up for weekends and planning sessions. Trips to Grass Valley developed into an important part of Atari culture. In the end, the Grass Valley facility became so important that Bushnell bought it outright.

Unknown Territory

With Atari's growing success, Bushnell settled into the role of manager and lead promoter. He left the technical wizardry in the hands of Mayer and Emmons, while Alcorn and Bristow handled the practical matters of engineering.

Bushnell now focused his attention on the future. Though he dedicated some of his time to inventing new products, he spent most days trying to divine new paths for Atari's future. His steady inclination was toward unbridled growth. If there was an increase in orders, Bushnell wanted more workers. He implicitly believed that Atari would continue to grow as long as his research and development teams came up with new ideas.

One of Bushnell's first tasks was to apply for patents to protect Atari products. He remembered the lessons he had learned at the hands of Magnavox and wanted to avoid further problems. The solid-state technology behind *Pong* was completely original and Bushnell hoped to fend off imitators. Unfortunately, by the time the patent came through, it had no teeth. Countless competitors had already built and shipped imitations.

> Nolan filed for a patent on the motion circuit with a guy who was a patent attorney on the low end of the totem pole. We were a very small company.
>
> The guy was fundamentally incompetent. The patent was flawed because it was filed too late. We told him that, but he told us it didn't make any difference. It was patently wrong—pun intended.
>
> **—Al Alcorn**

By the middle of 1974, computerized ping-pong machines were in every bar and bowling alley across the United States, but Atari had made less than one-third of them. Bushnell called his competitors "the Jackals" because they had an unfair advantage.

CHAPTER 6

The Jackals

In those days it just took a long time to get patents through. That was a problem, so we tried to be fast and to out-innovate the competition.

—Nolan Bushnell

There were a handful of companies that came in to develop games like *Pong*. Nolan applied for a patent, but, of course, that patent wasn't awarded until many years later. I was there, by the way, when he got it. And at that time Nolan looked at the documents and said, "Well, great," but he decided not to do anything about it legally.

—Eddie Adlum

Success Has Its Problems

> The biggest accusation against Atari was that we caused radio interference at
> the exact frequency used by the Nevada Highway Patrol. It was absolutely true.
>
> It probably happened everywhere, but they figured it out in Nevada be-
> cause everything is so far apart. They'd get close to a bar and all of a sudden
> they couldn't communicate with headquarters. Then someone noticed that
> after 2:00 A.M., when the bars would shut down, it would be okay, so they
> knew it was something in the bars. They went around unplugging stuff and
> finally they unplugged a video game and the interference went away. So the
> Highway Patrol almost shut us down throughout Nevada.
>
> We had to create these big wire-mesh shields that shielded the computer
> and cut down the radio interference. We really tried to keep that puppy quiet
> because we didn't know if we were doing the same thing in New York, and
> the local authorities would never, ever be able to track it down there.
>
> **—Nolan Bushnell**

The Imitators

Now that Atari had established "television games" as an arcade phenomenon,
a number of factors conspired against the company's ability to preserve the
phenomena for itself. The first problem was that Nolan Bushnell couldn't
promote his machines without competitors trying to steal his ideas.

No sooner had *Pong* become the hottest innovation in amusement machines
than dozens of potential competitors began studying it. According to Al
Alcorn, engineers from rival game companies started visiting Andy Capp's
Tavern shortly after he installed the first *Pong* prototype.

More important, unlike Ralph Baer, Bushnell had no way to protect his
solid-state game technology. He filed for a patent, but the patent took so
long to arrive that other companies had already manufactured and sold
games using similar architecture. Bushnell had entered into an industry in
which success spawned imitation, and everybody considered *Pong* a success,
with *Pong* machines earning $200 per week.[1] There was no way to stop com-
panies from copying it.

Just as pinball manufacturers stole Williams's tilt mechanism and Gottlieb's flippers, they began making electronic ping-pong games. Within three months of *Pong*'s release, competitors with names like *Electronic Paddle Ball* started to surface. Ramtek, Meadows Games, and Nutting (the company that made *Computer Space*) were among the first companies to make their own versions of *Pong*. In the next few years, established manufacturers like Midway and National Semiconductor followed.

> Curiously, Atari did not build the number of *Pong* machines that the world would think. I don't know the actual number because the video-game industry generally begins with *Pong*, even though *Computer Space* pre-dated it as an actual video game.
>
> *Pong* was the beginning of the video era, a new idea in those days. People ripped it off. There were some companies that just came out of nowhere, saw what was happening with *Pong*, and said I want to get part of this action.
>
> **—Eddie Adlum**

Forgeries flooded arcades all over the world. As Atari expanded to overseas markets, its success attracted international attention. In 1975, an Italian manufacturer began imitating Atari's *Breakout*. Its forgeries were so well made that the only way to spot them was to check the address on the back of the machine. By this time, Atari had moved to San Jose. The Italians used the correct (current) address, while the Atari-made machines still had the company's old Santa Clara address.

Bushnell developed a grave dislike for his imitators. He called them "jackals" and believed that the only way to stay ahead of them was constantly to generate new games and ideas. He considered his imitators less creative and believed they would be unable to develop games on their own.

In an effort to stay ahead, Atari entered 1974 producing a new game every other month. Bushnell's new strategy allowed the competition to copy games, and Atari retaliated by coming out with new ones.

The problem was that, like everyone else, Atari was still basing its entire library on remakes of *Pong*. Other companies made paddle-ball games based on sports—*Handball* (*Pong* in a three-walled court) and *Hockey* (*Pong* with small goals and two paddles). Atari released *Pin Pong, Dr. Pong, Pong Doubles,* and *QuadraPong.*

> Early on in the history of Atari, I went to a meeting for distributors. Nolan and I and several other people sat around a lunch table. After we were done eating and shooting the breeze, Nolan came up with the unforgettable statement/question: "I wonder what else we can do with a video game than play tennis and hockey."
>
> He answered his own question with driving games like *Trak 10* and *Grantrak*. Very visionary guy.
>
> **—Eddie Adlum**

In the end, the Grass Valley think tank came up with the solution. In 1974, Mayer and Emmons began designing the first racing game. Later named *Trak 10*, the racing simulation was every bit as primitive as *Pong*. Players used a wobbly steering wheel to control a boxy-looking car as it sped around an oval track.

Although *Trak 10* had very basic graphics, it opened the gates for a flood of creative new ideas. One of Atari's next titles was *Gotcha*, a game in which a player with a box chased a player with an X through a maze. *Gotcha* received only a lukewarm reception from arcade owners, though. In later years, maze chases would become one of the most popular themes in video games.

Even though it proved unsuccessful in the arcades, Bushnell was always sentimental about *Gotcha*. His role in the company quickly shifted after that, as Bushnell became more involved in management than game design. More than a year passed before he came up with another design.

> Atari made the first sports game, *Pong*. They had the first maze game, *Gotcha*, and the first racing game, *Trak 10*. Imagine what would have happened if Bushnell had somehow managed to patent those ideas. You couldn't have had *Pac-Man* or *Pole Position*. The whole industry would have been different.
>
> **—Steve Baxter, former producer, *CNN Computer Connection***

While other companies remained bogged down with electronic ping-pong and tennis, Atari came out with its second game—*Space Race*, a game in which players dodged asteroids as they flew tiny spaceships across a screen. The game did poorly, and Bushnell decided to return to the safety of tennis games.

Within a few years, however, Atari experimented with new themes—*Steeple Chase,* a multiplayer game in which players jumped horses over gates on a treadmill race track; and *Stunt Cycle,* a game in which players jumped buses—capitalizing on real-life stunt man Evel Knievel's wave of popularity.

Atari established itself as the most diverse and prolific coin-operated video game company in history. The company developed an unwritten manifesto that did not allow designers to make games that had been done before. This legacy of innovation lasted more than a decade.

Though Atari was the first company to look beyond *Pong* for inspiration, other companies soon followed. In 1975, the movie *Jaws,* a story of a man-eating great white shark terrorizing a tourist town, set box-office earnings records and launched the nation into a frenzy. Beach resorts reported that tourists were afraid to go swimming, sometimes even in pools. The company Project Support Engineers (PSE) attempted to capitalize on shark mania with a game called *Maneater.*

Maneater was a shark-hunting game housed in a fiberglass cabinet shaped like the head of a shark. The distinctive cabinet made the game expensive to manufacture. Though the idea of hunting sharks initially attracted players, the game's unexciting play did not attract repeat customers.

In 1975, Midway, one of the companies that originally rejected *Pong,* emerged as Atari's closest competitor. Midway and Atari were very different organizations. While Atari had an established research and development department, Midway distributed games developed by other companies.

Gunfight, Midway's first major video game hit, was a shoot-out in which two players controlled cowboys who shot at each other from opposite sides of the screen. It was not an original concept; a Japanese firm had created the game, then licensed it to Midway for the U.S. market. When Midway's development team members first tested it, though, they found it less than entertaining. The graphics were blocky and the gunfighters' movements were quite limited. To try and salvage the game, Midway hired an outside designer, David Nutting, brother of Nutting Associates founder Bill Nutting. (Nutting and Associates went out of business shortly after the failure of *Computer Space,* and Bill Nutting spent the next few years flying missionaries and relief supplies into impoverished African nations.) Dave Nutting went on to create such classic games as *Sea Wolf, Gorf, Wizard of Wor,* and *Baby Pac-Man.*

While improving *Gunfight*, Nutting introduced new technology to the video-game market. The original game simply featured two cowboys shooting at each other. Nutting not only sharpened the graphics, he placed objects between the fighters. Sometimes cactus or stagecoaches appeared in the middle of the duel to add to the challenge. To power these changes, Nutting incorporated a microprocessor into the game's design, making *Gunfight* the first video game with a microprocessor.

Gunfight opened the way for Japan to enter the American video-game market. *Gunfight* was originally developed by a firm named Taito—the Japanese term for "Far East." Taito and Midway worked together until 1979. Their final project earned so much money that Taito abandoned Midway and opened its own U.S. operation.

The Visit

As Atari expanded its repertoire to include racing games, Nolan Bushnell and Gene Lipkin, vice president of sales, toured the country to find out what arcade owners and distributors thought about the future of video games. Lipkin, who had started in the business working for the Florida firm Allied Leisure, took Bushnell to have lunch with one of the most respected men in the amusement industry, Joel Hochberg, the New York City game technician who had moved to Philadelphia to manage an arcade-restaurant in 1961.

Hochberg moved to Florida to take a job working in a large amusement arcade owned by Mervin Sisken, the son of the man who brought him into the industry. They worked together for seven years, during which time Hochberg's knowledge of the industry earned him a national reputation.

When Hochberg and Sisken split under unpleasant circumstances, Hochberg opened an under-funded arcade of his own. Unable to afford help, he worked 14-hour days, 7 days a week. Despite the long hours, his debts mounted. Just as it looked like he might have to close, the owners of Allied Leisure contacted him, suggesting an attractive partnership. Hochberg moved from maintaining equipment to sales and design.

It was during this time that Atari released *Pong*. Hochberg tried the new medium and was impressed. Two years later, Gene Lipkin invited him to lunch to meet Bushnell.

> Nolan Bushnell came to visit me here in south Florida when we had the game room at Nathan's (a popular restaurant). Gene was working for Atari at that time.
>
> Nolan, pipe and all, made his way to south Florida to visit with me at our game center. His question was, "Do you think video games are here to stay?"
>
> The answer that I gave him was, "I don't think there's even a possibility of turning back. I think that the customer, the player, has gotten such a taste of technology utilized in a format that makes things appear to be so real, there's no chance of the industry turning back."
>
> I'm not quite sure why he asked that question since he was the pioneer.
>
> **—Joel Hochberg**

Though both Bushnell and Hochberg were in the same industry, they did not keep in touch with each other. Bushnell continued his tour, meeting with arcade owners and trying to satisfy his insecurity about the industry's future.

Hochberg continued with Allied Leisure for a while and eventually started his own business again. By this time he had established international relationships, which soon fostered unique advantages in the amusement industry.

In another decade, Bushnell and Hochberg would trade places. Bushnell would become the established authority, while Hochberg became a famous maker of games.

Only the Paranoid Survive

Atari's first years were filled with notable successes and important failures. When asked about the early years at Atari, Nolan Bushnell and those around him remembered the fun times, but they also recalled struggling to come up with new ideas. Bushnell's constant drive to expand the business depleted Atari's revenues, and growing competition cut into company profits.

Even in stressful situations, however, Atari's corporate philosophy of smart work and hard partying continued. Atari executives still had hot tub meetings and Grass Valley parties, though partying did not alleviate their concern for the future. Bushnell spoke publicly of long-term interest in computer games, but he privately questioned whether Atari's success had been the result of luck or skill. He knew he had outflanked the competition so far, but he wondered which company would pose the next serious threat. He needed a scheme to maintain his advantage.

Keeping that advantage was of dire importance because of a unique set of dynamics within the amusement industry. In the early 1970s, most cities had two or three dominant vending-machine companies competing to do business in every arcade and bowling alley. These companies inevitably controlled the bulk of the location-based amusement routes.

In the early 1970s, an unstated rule within the industry mandated that vending companies serving the same area should not buy equipment from the same manufacturer. If, for instance, the largest distributor bought Bally pinball machines and Rock-Ola jukeboxes, its competitors needed to carry products from other manufacturers. Bushnell's goal was to find some way to break that rule and sell equipment to competing distributors.

In 1974, Atari met that formidable competitor—a start-up company called Kee Games. Founded by Joe Keenan, Bushnell's next-door neighbor, Kee Games was supposed to have lured away two of Atari's "five princes": Gil Williams, of manufacturing, and Steve Bristow, of engineering.

A bitter rivalry began as soon as Keenan announced his new company. In public, Bushnell tried to appear magnanimous. But confidentially, he floated rumors that Keenan and crew were renegades not to be trusted.

> [We used to complain about Kee Games.] "Oh those bastards," you know, we'd bad-mouth them. They [the distributors] just loved it 'cause they thought we were all crooks anyway, and they loved the idea of being able to go around us. Sometimes we'd say Kee stole our engineer [Bristow]. We gave him to them.
>
> **—Al Alcorn**

At one point, the rivalry became so bitter that Atari executives made accusations about industrial espionage:

> One weekend I drove around to the back of the [Atari] building. While my wife talked with a security guard and kept him busy, I threw circuit boards and equipment through a window and loaded them into my car.
>
> **—Steve Bristow**

For years, Bushnell refused to believe that Bristow would take such a risk for what amounted to little more than an elaborate ruse. Kee Games, as it turned out, was created by Atari, and Bushnell and Alcorn sat on its board of directors. Rather than chance a real rivalry with an established amusement manufacturer, Bushnell had created a controlled competitor.

The stories of industrial espionage and bad feelings were an elaborate cover that had taken on a life of its own. When Bristow had his wife distract the security guard and slipped into his old office, he simply added more reality to the myths about the competition between Kee Games and Atari.

Bushnell's plan was to compete with himself, selling Atari products to the largest local distributors and Kee products to his competitors.

> Just like Andy Grove [former president of Intel] says, "Only the paranoid survive." I wanted to hijack the competition, so I created the number two guy.
>
> Joe Keenan was my next-door neighbor. I told him, "I'd like to hire you to set up a company and call it Kee Games. We'll make it look like it's Kee, for Keenan, and it will look like you've come in and started up a new coin-op machine manufacturer." We gave him our number two man in manufacturing and our number two man in engineering—Bristow and Williams.
>
> **—Nolan Bushnell**

> We made up a new company named after Joe Keenan—Kee Games. We made it sound like it was full of renegades. We gave him Steve Bristow to be the V.P. of engineering—gave him some designs to get started. Nolan and I were on their board. If any of the distributors wanted to check, they could see in the corporate records that we were part of the company.
>
> **—Al Alcorn**

The strategy solidified Atari's hold on the market. The only problem was that Kee Games became more dangerous than Bushnell anticipated. In 1974, while Atari's research and development team was still focusing on *Pong* and racing games, Steve Bristow designed an innovative combat game named *Tank*.

Tank had very primitive graphics. Players controlled either a black or a white tank that consisted of a square with a line sticking out of the front representing a gun turret. By December, the game had become a runaway hit.

While Kee Games scored well with *Tank,* Atari found itself falling behind. *Grantrak 10,* one of Atari's first driving games, had been very expensive to develop and even more expensive to distribute. The Grass Valley team designed the game, but after delivering it, Atari found that it was nearly unplayable. Alcorn fixed the game's control problems, but other complications followed.

It cost $1,095 for Atari to manufacture *Grantrak 10,* but because of an accounting error, the finished game was sold for $995. The company lost $100 on each unit sold, and *Grantrak 10* became Atari's bestselling game of 1974.[2]

> The only animosity was that Atari was dying and Joe Keenan was a great president who had skills that Nolan didn't have. They wanted to cut the cord and watch Atari die and they'd survive. And Nolan and I said, "No way."
>
> Ron Gordon, Bushnell's vice president of international sales and marketing, came back and said, "Okay, look here's what you do. Merge Kee Games back in with Atari and put Alcorn back in engineering. Let Joe be the president [of both companies]."
>
> That's exactly what happened, but there was a time when Nolan was just in tears. He saw his company dying.
>
> **—Al Alcorn**

Bushnell's scheme had worked, yet it began having negative effects. Through Kee Games, Bushnell had nearly doubled his distribution, but now he had to merge both companies to keep Atari alive. Atari's lackluster year, combined with the overhead costs of starting up and running a second company, had gouged deeply into Atari's profits.

Historically, several companies have created controlled competition in the past. Bushnell's coup was that he actually fooled the entire amusement industry into believing that Kee Games and Atari were bitter rivals. Even after the merger, when it became public knowledge that Bushnell had been a Kee board member all along, people had trouble believing it. Only one shrewd distributor had seen through the guise.

> The thing about it is that nobody in the coin-op business figured out what we'd done except for one guy, Joe Robbins. He was with Empire Distributing

> and later went to Bally. I remember him coming up to me at a trade show and saying, "Bushnell, you think you're pretty clever. I know your number, but I respect you. I knew what you were doing and you did it really well."
>
> **—Nolan Bushnell**

A 20-Year-Old Ho Chi Minh

> The personnel lady came in with a young candidate who had shown up on our doorstep. He was this real scuzzy kid. She said, "What shall we do?"
>
> I think I said, "We should either call the cops or we should talk to him." So I talked to him.
>
> The kid was a dropout and really grungy. He was 18 years old and he knew something. . . . He had a spark of brilliance. Don Lang, one of my engineers, was asking for a tech, so I said, "Great. I'll give you a job working for a real engineer."
>
> The next day Don came to me and said, "What did I do to deserve this?"
>
> I said, "What? You wanted a tech, you got a tech."
>
> He said, "This guy's filthy. He's just obnoxious. And he doesn't know electronics."
>
> The kid worked out in the end. His name was Steve Jobs.
>
> **—Al Alcorn**

Shortly after Atari re-absorbed Kee Games, Al Alcorn hired the man who would become the company's most distinguished alumnus—Steve Jobs. Though he went on to found such companies as Apple Computers and Pixar Animation Studios, at the time Jobs was little more than a skinny kid with long hair and a wispy beard. Several people described him as looking like a "20-year-old Ho Chi Minh." (Ho Chi Minh was the leader of North Vietnam during the Vietnam war.)

Like many luminaries in the computer industry, Jobs knew more about technology than social graces. He was dismissed as a hippie by most of his fellow engineers. According to Alcorn, Jobs once came to work with a jar of cranberry juice and told his supervisor he was fasting. "He said, 'If I pass out, just lay me on the workbench. Don't call the police, please. I'll be fine. I'm just a little weak right now.'"

Some co-workers complained that Jobs smelled bad. He offended others by openly treating them like idiots. In the end, Jobs's genius helped him emerge as a valuable employee, but by that time, he had managed to make enemies throughout the company.

> If he thought you were a dumb shit, he'd treat you like shit. That pissed certain people off. I liked him a lot. . . . Still do.
>
> **—Nolan Bushnell**

In 1975, Jobs decided to make a pilgrimage to India. At the time, several *Tank* machines had broken down in Germany. Alcorn offered Jobs a one-way ticket to Germany if he would fix the machines.

> He wanted to go to India to meet his guru. I said, "Fine, I've got a problem in Germany."
>
> The German distributors would take our boards and hook them up to 60-cycle monitors to make games, but they only had access to 50-cycle power and they had bad ground loops. I gave Steve a quick course in ground-loop power-supply repair and a one-way ticket to Germany. I figured it would be cheaper to get to India from Germany than it would be from here [California].
>
> I found out later that it would have been cheaper to leave from here.
>
> He fixed their problem, but they were freaked because Steve Jobs is the antithesis of the Germans. They're meat and potatoes and beer, and he's air and water and vegetables . . . maybe.
>
> **—Al Alcorn**

Jobs handled the problem without a hitch. When he returned from his pilgrimage several months later, Alcorn hired him back.

> Steve came back around the time that we were starting up the consumer stuff. Steve was wearing saffron robes and a shaved head. . . . gave me a

> Baba Ram Das book. Apparently, he had hepatitis or something and had to get out of India before he died.
>
> I put him to work again. That's when the famous story about *Breakout* took place. That's a big story that's often told wrong.
>
> **—Al Alcorn**

Breakout

Shortly after Jobs returned, work began on a game called *Breakout.* From the start, the game took on special significance. Nolan Bushnell created the concept himself.* (As things turned out, it was the last game Bushnell created at Atari. In fact, nearly twenty years passed before Bushnell designed another game.)

Breakout was a reiteration of *Pong,* in which players used the ball to knock bricks out of a wall at the top of the screen. Though Bushnell knew consumers would love *Breakout,* he worried about the cost of manufacturing the game.

In order to cut costs, Atari engineers tried to minimize the number of dedicated chips used in their games; tightly designed games had around 75.

In those days, Atari shipped approximately 10,000 copies of its most popular games. Because of repair costs and reduced circuit-board space, Atari saved approximately $100,000 for each chip removed before production. Bushnell wanted his engineers to reduce the number of chips in *Breakout* but got a less-than-enthusiastic response when he asked for volunteers.

> We had this bidding process. Nobody wanted to do *Breakout.* I remember that I figured that *Breakout* was going to be about a 75-chip game, so I'd give a bonus for every chip they took out.
>
> **—Nolan Bushnell**

Steve Jobs accepted the challenge. By this time, Jobs and his partner, Steve Wozniak, had begun developing the Apple II, generally regarded as the computer that launched the personal-computer industry. Wozniak worked for

---

* Years later, Steve Jobs claimed that he had developed the concept for *Breakout.* When asked about it, Nolan Bushnell simply responded, "Perhaps he did."

Hewlett Packard. He was a member of the Homebrew Computer Club, a group of early enthusiasts who built their own computers. Other Homebrew members considered Wozniak, or "Woz," to be the most brilliant member of the club. Jobs turned to Wozniak for help in minimizing *Breakout*'s circuitry.

> So meanwhile, Steve's friend, Wozniak, comes in the evenings. He would be out there during burn-in tests while these *Tank* games were on the production line, and he'd play *Tank* forever. I didn't think much of it; I didn't care. He was a cool guy.
>
> I found what really had happened is Jobs never designed a lick of anything in his life. He had Woz do it [redesign *Breakout*].
>
> Woz did it in like 72 hours nonstop and all in his head. He got it down to 20 or 30 ICs [integrated circuits]. It was remarkable. . . . a tour de force.
>
> It was so minimized, though, that nobody else could build it. Nobody could understand what Woz did but Woz. It was this brilliant piece of engineering, but it was just unproduceable. So the game sat around and languished in the lab.
>
> **—Al Alcorn**

Wozniak was able to remove more than 50 chips from *Breakout,* but his design was too tight. No one could figure out how he did it, and the manufacturing plant could not reproduce it. In the end, Alcorn had to assign another engineer to build a version of *Breakout* that was more easily replicated. The final game had about 100 chips.

Bushnell and Alcorn disagree on some of the details concerning Steve Jobs's bonus. Bushnell remembers offering Jobs $100 for each chip he removed. He claims Wozniak removed 50 chips and Jobs received a $5,000 bonus. Alcorn says that Jobs was told to reduce the design to a maximum of 50 chips and that he would receive $1,000 for every chip he removed beyond that mark. According to Alcorn, Jobs pocketed a $30,000 bonus.

Alcorn and Bushnell both agree, however, that Jobs misled Wozniak about the amount that he received. Jobs told Wozniak that the bonus was only one-tenth of what Bushnell actually paid.

I think we've got an order of magnitude problem here.

Jobs misled Wozniak, but Jobs got five grand and Woz got half of $500. I mean the macro-numbers are right, as it was told. I'm just saying that the denominator, the dollars per chip, is off.

—Nolan Bushnell

And Nolan says, "For every chip less than 50 I'll give you $1,000 cash bonus."

Now Jobs didn't use the money for his own personal gain. He put it into Apple. But still, the fact that Wozniak's best friend lied to him broke him up. That was the beginning of the end of the friendship between Woz and Jobs.

—Al Alcorn

According to Silicon Valley legend, Steve Wozniak discovered that he'd been misled many years later, while flying on a business trip and reading a biography about Jobs. Nolan Bushnell says that the legend is not true.

You want to know the real story? Woz was up here to a Sunday afternoon picnic at our house. We were talking and I asked, "What did you do with that $5,000?"

He says, "What?"

He was visibly upset. Wozniak's tender. I mean, he's really a good guy.

—Nolan Bushnell

Wozniak says that both stories are true. He first discovered Jobs's deception on the plane and he did later ask Bushnell for details at his house.

I got $375, and I've never really known how much Steve got. He told me he was giving me 50 percent, and I know he got more than $750. I knew he believed that it was fine to buy something for $60 and sell it for $6,000 if you could do it. I just didn't think he would do it to his best friend.

—Steve Wozniak

Dealing with Japan

Atari first began shipping *Pong* machines outside the United States as early as 1973. As its business expanded, Atari sought foreign partners to help with distribution and shipping laws. Namco became Atari's partner in Japan.

At the time, Namco was Japan's sixth- or seventh-largest arcade company, behind such sturdy giants as Taito and Sega. Unlike Taito and Sega, which were founded by a Russian and an American, respectively, Namco was founded by a Japanese entrepreneur named Masaya Nakamura.

A former naval engineer, Nakamura started his company with $3,000. He purchased two mechanical horse rides that he had to place on the roof of a department store because his competitors had exclusive arrangements with the best sites.

> I initially purchased two secondhand horse rides, and I talked a department store into allowing me to set them up in its roof garden. I operated the rides myself. I refurbished the machines myself. I would polish them and clean them every day, and I was there to welcome the mothers of the children as they arrived.
>
> **—Masaya Nakamura, founder and president, Namco**

Because of the size of the Japanese market and the country's enthusiasm for coin-operated entertainment, Atari created a Japanese branch to oversee importing and distributing games. Nakamura visited Atari's Japanese branch shortly after it was formed. He began purchasing games and met Bushnell.

In 1974, Bushnell decided to close the Japanese operation. He sold it to Nakamura, and Namco became Atari's chief Japanese distributor.

> Bushnell established Atari Japan and tried to expand his business. For various reasons, including poor maintenance and a selection of inappropriate locations, Atari Japan's business was not really doing well.
>
> **—Masaya Nakamura**

> We had real problems in Japan. Japan is a pretty closed market, difficult to get your product in . . . closed distribution. That's why we did the deal with

> Nakamura and Namco. He was willing to sort of break with tradition and start
> working with an American company. And he really made money on *Breakout*.
>
> **—Nolan Bushnell**

In 1976, Atari sent Nakamura *Breakout*. As soon as Nakamura saw the game, he recognized it as a sure hit. To his disappointment, however, Atari set special conditions for *Breakout*, allowing Namco to distribute the game but retaining exclusive manufacturing rights. In response, Nakamura asked for as many units as possible.

> This game *Breakout* was a wonderful game and I gave a very high evaluation
> to the game. Namco, through Atari Japan, had the sales rights on the prop-
> erty in Japan, and we were doing quite well. All of a sudden we encountered
> a great number of copies in the Japanese market.
>
> The game was called *Borokukuishi*. It's literally the Japanese translation of
> *Breakout*. And we saw more copies [units of *Borokukuishi*] than the original games
> that we were trying to distribute. It was to the detriment of our business.
>
> **—Masaya Nakamura**

The Yakuza

The Yakuza, most easily described as the Japanese Mafia, operates very differently than other criminal organizations. Unlike other gangsters, members of the Yakuza do not try to hide their identity. They often cover much of their bodies with tattoos. For years they were the only people in Japan who wore dark glasses. Many of them had missing fingers—cutting off fingers was a form of punishment within the organization.

In Japan's structured society, the Yakuza and the police coexist by setting limits on various illegal activities. Although the Yakuza frequently went beyond these limits, many of their activities involved nothing more spectacular than running the Japanese fish market and setting up concession stands at sporting events.

When it came to video games, a few Yakuza clans took a very aggressive stance. One clan tried to take over Konami, the company that made *Frogger* and *Contra*. When the owner of the company appealed to a friend in a rival clan for help, he touched off a war and had to go into hiding.

When Nakamura investigated the counterfeit *Breakout* machines, he discovered that a Yakuza clan had manufactured them. It was a dangerous situation.

> We knew exactly where the copies were being manufactured, and I instructed my staff to go to these factories for surveillance.
>
> They would watch from their car, then they would notice a car approaching them from behind and another car coming from the front, making their car immobile. They [the gangsters] would come out of their cars and make threats.
>
> **—Masaya Nakamura**

Nakamura met with the leader of the group that was manufacturing the counterfeit *Breakout* machines and asked him to stop. The man responded by offering to forge a partnership with Namco. According to Nakamura, the man offered to "suppress" Namco's competitors and make Namco the biggest company in the industry. Nakamura declined, fearing that the offer would lead to a takeover of his company and possibly the entire industry.

Rather than try to stand up to the Yakuza, Nakamura decided to work around them. He asked Atari to send more *Breakout* machines as quickly as possible, but shipments of *Breakout* continued at the same slow pace.

Nakamura and Bushnell disagree about what happened next. Nakamura says he flew to London to meet with Bushnell at an MOA (Music Operators Association, later renamed the Amusement and Music Operators Association) convention. He claims he explained the situation to Bushnell and asked for help but that Bushnell was in no condition to listen.

> My recollection is that Hide Nakajima and I traveled to London to attend a show, and Nolan Bushnell was there. Hide and I went to see him one morning to lodge a very strong claim against the copies in Japan and to ask for his assistance as the manufacturer who created the game, to counter the copies in Japan and do something about it.
>
> Unfortunately, when we met him, it was the morning after apparently a very long night of partying on the part of Nolan Bushnell and he very obviously had a

> hangover. He was in no physical condition to concentrate on our very serious claim. He took it very lightly.
>
> For that reason and for the sake of self-defense in terms of business, we decided to start manufacturing the game ourselves.
>
> **—Masaya Nakamura**

Since Bushnell and his associates had a reputation for partying, and liquor bars were prevalent at most MOA parties, Nakamura may have been naïve in his decision to discuss such an important topic at the show.

Unsatisfied after his meeting with Bushnell, Nakamura returned home and began manufacturing his own copies of *Breakout*. Before long, he flooded the Japanese market. The game was a huge success and Namco became one of the most dominant game manufacturers in Asia.

According to Bushnell, Atari knew nothing about Nakamura manufacturing the game. He assumed that Namco did not want more copies of *Breakout* because the game had not caught on. "It was doing so well in the rest of the world, we couldn't understand why they didn't like it in Japan."

The first time he heard about the counterfeits was when an Atari representative visited Japan and reported seeing far more machines than the company had shipped. Most of the machines had been built by Namco.

> The first sign that something was going wrong was *Breakout*. We shipped 15 *Breakouts* to Japan. All of a sudden, it turns out there were more *Breakouts* in Japan than there were in the rest of the world combined.
>
> **—Al Alcorn**

Breakout became the first issue in a growing rift that formed between Atari and Namco. The argument ended in a lawsuit that Atari won in the late 1970s.

CHAPTER 7

"Could You Repeat That Two More Times?"

Nolan sent this memo: "To: Engineering, From: Nolan, Subject: Products. You will have in one year a consumer *Pong* game, an eight-player *Tank* game, and a 12-person game for arcade midways."

The fact that we had no manufacturing capacity was not an issue to be brought up.

So I sent a memo back: "To: Nolan, From: Engineering, Subject: Your memo. One small issue, we have no money."

And Nolan wrote on my memo, "NO," in big letters, and sent it back to me.

—Al Alcorn

Gene Lipkin called me and said, "I need an advertising agency."

I said, "No, you don't. George Opperman [who worked for Atari] is doing very well."

He said, "No, not for the trade magazines. I need advertising for the general public."

I said, "For heaven's sakes, why?"

He said, "Because Nolan has come up with a device that you can plug into your home TV set that will play video games."

I said, "You're kidding."

He said, "No." They made a deal with Sears Roebuck, and home video was born.

—Eddie Adlum

A New Phase

In 1975, Atari released a consumer version of *Pong* and became the first company to make both arcade and consumer products.

Throughout Atari's early years, Nolan Bushnell constantly pushed his engineers to come up with a product that could expand his business. In 1974 an engineer named Harold Lee proposed a device that could do just that—a home version of *Pong* that could be attached to a television. Nolan Bushnell immediately recognized Lee's home unit as a logical next move for Atari.

Lee's timing could not have been better. The Magnavox Odyssey was now more than three years old and nearing the end of its retail life. Magnavox executives had committed two grave errors in marketing Odyssey: They allowed only Magnavox-exclusive dealers to sell the system, and their advertising suggested that Odyssey worked only on Magnavox televisions. Approximately 85,000 Odysseys were sold in the first year, and only 100,000 Odyssey systems were sold over the product's two-year life.

Alcorn and Lee, who worked together on *Home Pong*, decided to use the same basic digital technology used in Atari's coin-operated games. (Odyssey used much older analog architecture.)

> I hunkered down and worked with a guy named Harold Lee on the chip prototype. He designed the logic in the daytime, and he would give me a logic design that my wife would wire-wrap at home in the evenings and I would debug. I would give the corrected design to Harold and he would lay out the chip on the design computer at night to save money.
>
> **—Al Alcorn**

Once the design was approved, Alcorn, Lee, and an engineer named Bob Brown constructed a working prototype. Originally code-named Darlene, after an attractive employee, the finished product was called *Home Pong*.

With the price of digital circuits constantly dropping, Atari's digital home console ended up costing far less to manufacture than Odyssey. *Home Pong* had a sleeker cabinet and created sharper-looking images on television screens. Since it had Alcorn's segmented paddle design, it only required one knob per player. Odyssey used an extra knob for adding spin to the ball.

On the other hand, *Home Pong* played only one game—ping-pong. Despite its weaknesses, Odyssey could play twelve games.

The finished prototype was attached to a wooden pedestal that contained hundreds of wires. Alcorn and Lee had designed a chip that could replace the wires, but until the first prototype of the chip could be tested, the console could be built only with wire connections. Bushnell placed an order for chips, without even stopping to decide how to market *Home Pong*.

Breaking into Sears

In the fall of 1974, the first prototype of the *Home Pong* chip was delivered from the foundry. Alcorn and Lee carefully plugged it in and turned on the console. When they switched on the power, the game came to life. At that time, the chip in *Home Pong* was the highest performance-integrated circuit ever used in a consumer product. Alcorn ran to get Bushnell, and the design team celebrated.

The next day Bushnell and Gene Lipkin began approaching retailers about *Home Pong*. In later interviews Bushnell described being turned down by several toy stores. He says he got the same response from electronics stores. Electronics buyers, remembering that Magnavox had sold only 100,000 Odysseys, asserted that consumers weren't interested in television games. Toy-store buyers said that the asking price, $100, was too expensive. One buyer told Bushnell that his stores carried nothing that cost more than $29 unless it was a bicycle.

Lipkin didn't give up. He decided to approach department stores with *Home Pong*. Since Sears Roebuck was the biggest chain at the time, he started there. The buyers from the toy and electronics departments turned him down. As a last attempt, someone looked through the Sears catalog and noticed that the sporting goods department advertised Odyssey. Lipkin asked the operator to connect him to sporting goods.

> The guy [Tom Quinn] had done really well the year before on ping-pong tables. In the winter, Sporting Goods would sell some hockey equipment and a few basketballs and that was about it. To make his Christmas numbers, the Sears buyer was focusing on ping-pong tables and pool tables, and he thought consumer *Pong* might be just the thing for the family rec room.
>
> **—Nolan Bushnell**

> We talked to Tom Quinn and said, "Remember the Magnavox Odyssey? We
> got a better version. Would you be interested?"
>
> He said, "Sounds interesting. Next time I'm in California I'll stop in and
> see you."
>
> Three days later he was on our doorstep at 8:00 A.M. Now, none of us were
> there at eight o'clock, but he was. He was very excited about the prospect of
> this thing and proceeded to try to get an exclusive.
>
> We said, "No, we're too smart for that. We don't want an exclusive with
> Sears. It could be very dangerous."
>
> **—Al Alcorn**

Seeing Quinn's enthusiasm, Atari's executive team decided against signing an exclusive contract. Still convinced that the toy industry offered the best channel for selling *Home Pong,* Atari ran a booth at the January 1975 Toy Show in New York City.

Like most industries, the toy business had a unique protocol. Although hundreds of companies displayed toys at the show, the real business was conducted around town in private suites. During the show, toy companies set up meeting rooms so that they could close deals with buyers away from the floor. No one from Atari knew anything about setting up a private showing.

According to Alcorn, dozens of buyers stopped by Atari's booth, curious to see *Home Pong.* Although they said they liked it, no one placed orders because they had already finished buying products at private showings. Atari did not sell a single unit at the show.

Tom Quinn stopped by the Atari booth to say "hello" and ask how things were going. The staff at the booth lied, saying that the show was going well. A few days after the show, Lipkin called Quinn to ask for a meeting.

Before Quinn could purchase *Home Pong,* however, he needed permission from the head of the Sporting Goods department. At Quinn's suggestion, Alcorn and Lipkin flew to Chicago to demonstrate *Home Pong* at the Sears Tower.

Quinn set up a demonstration in a conference room on the 27th floor. A large group of executives in business suits flooded the room and watched as Alcorn hooked the prototype to a television set. When he turned the game on, nothing happened.

The Sears Tower has an antenna on the roof that broadcasts a signal on channel 3. The *Home Pong* prototype was set for channel 3, and the broadcast blocked out its signal. Quickly figuring out the problem, Alcorn removed a panel from the bottom of the prototype and made adjustments so that the prototype's signal could be picked up on channel 4.

I told Gene, "You cover for me."

I turned it [the prototype] upside down and opened the bottom up. I got it to work in about ten minutes. I was sweating now and ready to jump out the window. This was too much pressure for the kid.

So I finally played the game and it all worked and they were okay, but I could see that something was bothering them. They had seen something inside the prototype while I was adjusting it.

I said, "We'll replace the wires with a silicon chip that's the size of a fingernail."

Carl Lind, head of the department says, "Mr. Alcorn, you're telling me that you're going to reduce that rat's nest of wire to a little piece of silicon the size of your fingernail?"

"Yes, sir."

He looked at me, leaned over the table and said, "How you gonna solder the wires to it?"

—Al Alcorn

Once he received approval to carry *Home Pong,* Quinn asked Bushnell how many units he could manufacture by Christmas. Bushnell promised 75,000. Quinn responded that he needed 150,000. Bushnell agreed, fully aware that Atari did not have the manpower or facilities to fulfill such a large order. He would simply have to borrow the money. With the new business from Sears, Bushnell decided this was the time to expand.

The Wizard of the Valley

I read a story about Valentine. . . . In the story, a guy had gone into his office and Don intimidated him so badly that he passed out. Don denies it, of course.

—Trip Hawkins, founder, Electronic Arts and 3DO

Engineers and designers comprise only one side of the computer industry. The other side is made up of shrewd businessmen and investors who look at the latest technology in the same dispassionate way they view utility companies and pork bellies. Technological breakthroughs do not excite these people. A hefty return on investment does.

Known as venture capitalists, these businessmen do not part with money easily. They are willing to invest in promising companies, but they demand stock and control in exchange for their investment. Once, a venture capitalist fired the founder and chairman of a home computer company over a disagreement about the company's future.

Don Valentine, the founder of Sequoia Capital, was one of the computer industry's first and most successful high-tech venture capitalists. Extremely conservative and intense, Valentine had a reputation for intimidating prospective clients. Al Alcorn once bragged, "I have actually seen Don Valentine laugh."

As a venture capitalist, Valentine's work involved sifting through hundreds of proposals a year. He invested in a very small percentage of the companies that approached him.

According to Valentine, when Bushnell first came to Sequoia, he mostly talked about "coin-operated games for bars." Like the bankers Bushnell approached four years earlier, Valentine associated the coin-operated amusement business with organized crime. He was not interested. When Bushnell described *Home Pong,* however, he changed his mind.

> One of the things that I was concerned about and interested in was that there be a product or series of products that were designed for consumers. Only after we were persuaded that the company would be taken in the direction of a home product were we persuaded to invest.
>
> **—Don Valentine**

Valentine minimized the risk of investing in Atari by demanding an active role on the company's board of directors. He decided to raise the capital from a network of partners that included Time Inc., the Mayfield Fund, and Fidelity Venture Associates. Combined with Atari's annual earnings of $2.5 to $3.5 million, Valentine's capital opened a $10-million credit line at a bank.[1]

Valentine took longer than expected to close the deal. By the time he was ready, the new business Atari received through its merger with Kee Games had resulted in increased earnings. While Bushnell waited impatiently to open a new money line with Valentine's capital, his company amassed a balance sheet that was strong enough to get a loan. When Valentine finally decided to close the deal, Atari no longer needed him.

> What happens with venture capitalists [is that] time is in their favor usually. They love to delay and delay because the more they wait, the more they're squeezing your nuts and the more the deal gets better in their favor. In this case, we had pulled ourselves out of the fire. Things were going along pretty smoothly by the time Don was ready to cut the deal.
>
> I don't know the exact numbers, but two or three days before the deal was going to close, we had a board meeting and our corporate attorney told us, "You know, guys, the valuation on this deal is all wrong. You made the valuation back when you were in trouble. You're no longer in trouble. The deal is way out of whack."
>
> We had two choices. We could let the deal go as is or change the price— basically, double the price. If we pissed Don off, we knew we'd never get the deal. I think we still needed some money, and he was our only chance of getting financing because he was the top venture capitalist in the valley.
>
> We decided to roll the dice. We doubled the price Don had to pay us— double or nothing. If he didn't buy it and we went out of business, what the hell, we're all young.
>
> Don showed up that night with a station wagon full of champagne to celebrate closing the deal, and Joe Keenan told him, "Oh, by the way, we've doubled the price." Don blew up, but when he calmed down, he went ahead and did it at double the price.
>
> **—Al Alcorn**

Valentine took his role as a member of the Atari board seriously. He attended board meetings and participated in the decision-making process. Though he did not particularly enjoy video games, he took Atari games home and played them. Despite the culture clash, he visited the manufacturing facility to observe the progress.

According to Valentine, he had to hold his breath whenever he visited Atari. Straightlaced and conservative, Valentine did not smoke. He claimed that the manufacturing plant reeked of marijuana, and if he wasn't careful where he breathed, he sometimes accidentally inhaled it.

Valentine's association with Atari ended two years later. Though he profited from the investment, Atari was far from his most lucrative deal. A few years later, Steve Jobs and Steve Wozniak asked Valentine to help them start Apple Computers. In 1986, Valentine was approached by Cisco Systems, a company that pioneered the development of Internet equipment. He invested $2.5 million in the company in exchange for one-third of its stock. Over the next decade, Cisco's equipment became an integral part of the success of the Internet. By 1996, Valentine's one-third share of the company was valued at more than $10 billion.

The Wild Ones

Don Valentine was not the only partner who clashed with Atari's corporate culture. Sears Roebuck was a no-nonsense, button-down business as well.

By this time, Bushnell had used his new line of credit to purchase a manufacturing facility in Sunnyvale, California. One day, a number of Sears executives visited the new location for an inspection.

The plant was not yet in operation. Workers had recently installed a new conveyor line that Bushnell sometimes rode while in a box, as a diversion. The Sears executives arrived just in time to see Bushnell climbing into a box and "surfing" the line. They were shocked by his unorthodox behavior.

The difference in corporate cultures became even more apparent as the day went on. The Sears people had come in suits and ties. The Atari people wore T-shirts and blue jeans. By the end of the day, Bushnell was concerned that he had alienated his visitors.

Not wanting to leave a bad impression, Bushnell had one final chance to soften the situation. That night he and his board were scheduled to have dinner with the Sears team at a local Italian restaurant. In an effort to look more professional, Bushnell had his board attend the dinner dressed in suits and ties.

Unfortunately, the Sears executives, too, were worried about the impression they had made. Not wanting to appear too stuffy, they attended the dinner in T-shirts and blue jeans.

"Nolan Attacks"

> I thought of Nolan as the great visionary, someone who would be bored by day-to-day operations. Joe Keenan was the volunteer who took care of most of the day-to-day operation.
>
> **—Don Valentine**

For a brief period in 1975, Atari faced no emergencies. With the new factory in Sunnyvale, the company had enough manufacturing muscle to fulfill Sears Roebuck's order for 150,000 *Home Pong* consoles. Under Jim Tubb's direction, the manufacturing process moved along smoothly.

Through the merger with Kee Games, Joe Keenan became president of Atari. Because he was the least wild member of the original Atari board, Keenan made an excellent point man for working with Don Valentine and Sears.

During this time, Al Alcorn was vice president of research and development and Steve Bristow was vice president of engineering. Al's department focused largely on home game technology but also built a prototype of an extra-wide pinball machine and developed a high-speed modem. Bristow's team developed new arcade games. Of all the departments at Atari, Research and Development and Engineering were the departments that intrigued Bushnell the most.

Bushnell often visited. He looked over engineers' shoulders as they designed new games. Sometimes he saw ways to improvise and improve designs. On occasion he suggested changes.

Alcorn referred to Bushnell's visits as "Nolan Attacks" and said that they slowed the engineers' progress. According to Alcorn, Bushnell would approach engineers in the middle of the design process with solutions, and because he had not been involved with the projects from the start, his suggestions did not always work.

> Let me tell you what happens when you're Nolan Bushnell. You go into a lab and you sit down and you're talking with guys, and they're having a problem. And they'll say, "What about this?"
>
> Unless you're being very clear, sometimes junior guys think that you've told them what to do when in fact you're really asking, "Have you considered this solution?"
>
> Two or three times people thought they were following orders when in fact I was just trying to help them solve a problem they were having.
>
> **—Nolan Bushnell**

Hoping to keep Research and Development running smoothly, Alcorn made a new rule—engineers were not allowed to follow Bushnell's orders unless he repeated them three times. Bristow was even more straightforward: "Nolan could do and discuss anything he wanted, but my staff made no changes until I OK'd them." Since Bushnell rarely followed projects closely, he seldom checked to see if his suggestions were implemented.

Before long, Bushnell discovered Alcorn's strategy. He held a brainstorming meeting for the research and development staff in Grass Valley. During an opening speech, Bushnell said, "I understand there's a new rule that says you don't have to do what I tell you unless I say it three times. Well, I'm telling you now, when I tell you to do something, you do it."

An engineer sitting across the room shouted back, "Could you repeat that two more times?"

In an attempt to control Bushnell's visits, Alcorn set up a security system. Whenever Bushnell entered Research and Development, Alcorn distracted him by leading him from project to project. If Alcorn was out of the department when Bushnell arrived, his engineers could reach him with a special beeper.

> I couldn't keep him out; but when he went in, I'd just follow him around and tell the guys, "If you do what he tells you to do, you're fired. You're working for me, not him."
>
> **—Al Alcorn**

According to Alcorn, this strategy worked for a while, but Bushnell eventually concocted a method of monitoring Research and Development that even fooled Alcorn. He placed an ally in the department to tell him about each project. His informant had to be unimportant, someone so small and insignificant that Alcorn would never notice him. Bushnell's informant was Steve Jobs.

> Jobs was so low on the totem pole at Atari that I didn't care what happened to him. He was completely off the radar scope.
>
> **—Al Alcorn**

Reminders of a Risky Past

In 1976, two events reminded video-game manufacturers of their roots in the pinball industry. The first was the legalization of pinball in New York and Chicago.

The process began in early 1976 when Irving Holzman, the president of the New York Music and Amusement Association, applied to the New York City Council to have LaGuardia's 40-year ban on pinball removed. Gottlieb and Williams had been marketing special add-a-ball pinball machines in New York since 1972, and Holzman felt that the time had come to challenge the ban entirely.

The city council agreed to hold a hearing on the matter in April. One key testimony in the hearings came from Roger Sharpe, an editor at *Gentlemen's Quarterly*. Sharpe was an extremely gifted pinball player who, after completing a feature about pinball, had decided to write a book about the history of the pinball industry.

Sharpe testified about pinball and the skills needed to master it. He talked about the work that went into designing pinball machines and the popularity of pinball throughout the United States and in many countries around the world. After his testimony, Sharpe was asked to demonstrate his skill.

> Along with my testimony, I was supposed to give a demonstration to show that the game was based on skill, not chance.
>
> There's a funny aside to all this. There were two games set up. The second game was really a fall-back in case anything happened to the first. The cameras were all set up on the other game. We got to the end of my testimony

> and the head of the city council stood up and said, "I understand that you are now going to demonstrate pinball for us."
>
> I said, "Yes," and he said, "Not that game. Let's do that one over there."
>
> I guess he thought that the first game was fixed.
>
> **—Roger Sharpe**

Sharpe was directed to play a Gottlieb pinball game called *Bank Shot.* He began by describing the machine to the council, explaining its targets, rules, and objectives. After some explanation, Sharpe played two balls, acquainting himself with the machine and demonstrating the use of the flippers. On his third ball, he decided to prove that proper use of the plunger required skill.

> On the start of my third ball, I said, "Using the plunger takes skill as well."
>
> There were five lanes at the top of the playfield. I pointed to a lane and said, "If I pull this back just right, the ball is going to go right down this lane." It was kind of like Babe Ruth calling his shot.
>
> I pulled back the plunger. The ball went up, it went bounce, bounce, and right down the lane.
>
> "Alright, we've seen enough."
>
> I was supposed to play an entire game. The city council passed it [the petition to legalize pinball] six-to-nothing.
>
> August first of that year, which was my birthday, the mayor signed a law for pinball machines to be operated in the city.
>
> **—Roger Sharpe**

That year, 1976, was also the first year in which concerns were raised about violence in video games. Exidy Games, a company founded by former Ramtek executive Pete Kauffman, released a driving game titled *Death Race.*

Kauffman, a very quiet man, had originally planned to design games for other companies. *Destruction Derby,* his first project, was a game in which players steered cars around a screen trying to hit other cars. The computer-controlled drone cars were slightly faster than players' cars, but they traveled in zigzag paths. The only way to hit computer-controlled cars was to anticipate which way the drone would turn.

According to Kauffman, Chicago Coin bought *Destruction Derby* but refused to pay him his royalties. Kauffman responded by revising the game and re-releasing it himself.

The biggest change in the game was in the targets players hit with their cars. Kauffman renamed the game *Death Race,* and players ran over stick figures that were supposed to be skeletons escaping from a graveyard. When players ran over the skeletons, tiny crosses would appear in their places.

> *Death Race* was a spin-off from a game we did for Chicago Coin called *Destruction Derby,* in which you hit other cars. We licensed that to Chicago Coin, and they forced us into competing with ourselves by not paying royalties. We came out with *Death Race* to compete with our own game.
>
> **—Pete Kauffman, founder of Exidy Games**

> Pete came up with a game called *Death Race.* It's very tame by today's standards, but in those days it caused a big controversy.
>
> The player was asked to drive over running gremlins. They called them gremlins; the rest of the world thought they were stick people, real people, and the idea of the game, of course, was to kill them.
>
> Every time you made a hit, a little cross would appear on the monitor, signifying a grave. Nice game. Fun. Bottom line, the game really took off when TV stations started to get some complaints from irate parents that this was a terrible example to set for children.
>
> The industry got a lot of coast-to-coast coverage during news programs. The end result was that Exidy sales doubled or quadrupled.
>
> **—Eddie Adlum**

Though the *Death Race* machine did substantial business in arcades, many location owners refused to carry it. According to Kauffman, Exidy sold only 1,000 *Death Race* machines, just a fraction of the number of *Sea Wolf* and *Gun Fight* machines Midway placed that same year, but *Death Race* stirred up protests and was even discussed on CBS's *60 Minutes.*

When defending their game in public, Exidy spokespersons claimed that *Death Race* was about running over demons and had nothing to do with killing people.

In private, they agreed that the scandal had boosted their sales. When *Death Race II* arrived in 1977, it had the same basic theme—running over stick figures.

> Death Race did very well, but nobody wanted to be associated with it publicly because of the accusations from the press. It seemed like the more controversy . . . the more our sales increased.
>
> We did a sequel, but it was really just the same game. There wasn't anything new about it.
>
> **—Pete Kauffman**

Although no one could argue with Exidy's success, some competitors felt threatened by the public's reaction to Exidy's violent games. New York City had just legalized pinball, and *Death Race* threatened to cause the same kind of scandal that gambling machines brought to pinball.

> We were really unhappy with that game [*Death Race*]. We [Atari] had an internal rule that we wouldn't allow violence against people. You could blow up a tank or you could blow up a flying saucer, but you couldn't blow up people. We felt that that was not good form, and we adhered to that all during my tenure.
>
> **—Nolan Bushnell**

CHAPTER 8

Strange Bedfellows

I got the contracts out, I got the lawyers out, and I removed Nolan from office. Nolan was simply removed and he was put on the beach.

—Manny Gerard, former vice president, Warner Communications

Manny Gerard? Manny was a free spirit in a three-piece suit.

—Steve Bristow, former vice president of engineering, Atari Corporation

The New Champion

Sears executives calculated the success of the products in their catalog by comparing dollars to inches. They measured the amount of page space given to each product and matched it to the number of dollars grossed. In 1975, the reigning champion was an Adidas sneaker. By 1976, a new champion emerged.

> The previous record holder was Adidas tennis shoes. We blew that record away in total dollar volume. We also won the Sears Quality Excellence Award— something nobody knows or cares about, but they're pretty proud of it.
>
> **—Al Alcorn**

Magnavox sold 100,000 Odysseys. Atari sold 150,000 *Home Pong* machines in a single season. The first heyday of the home video-game console had begun.

New Competition

> Coleco was located in Connecticut, outside of Hartford. In their later years, they moved into what was once a high school. Before that they were on Asylum Street. That place was like an asylum.
>
> **—Ralph Baer**

With the success of *Home Pong,* an army of new competitors entered the home video-game market. Seventy-five companies promised to launch home television tennis games in 1976.[1] Obscure companies like First Dimension, of Nashville, Tennessee,[2] and established giants like RCA proposed game consoles that looked and worked like *Pong.*

Atari's most powerful competitors were Magnavox and National Semiconductor. Magnavox re-entered the market with Odyssey 100, a new console that, unlike its predecessor, only played tennis. Magnavox had more advertising muscle than other companies in the video-game business, but the poor sales of the original Odyssey did not impress retailers.

National Semiconductor, a company that once made chips for Atari's coin-operated games, posed a more significant threat. Atari and National

Semiconductor had stopped doing business with each other under unfriendly circumstances, back when Atari and Kee Games were separate companies.

Suspecting that Atari would not be able to pay its bills, National Semiconductor demanded that Atari pay cash up front for custom chips. Since Atari's income was generated by selling finished arcade machines, National Semiconductor's demand nearly paralyzed the company's cash flow. In the end, Steve Bristow, then working for Kee, developed discrete "piggyback" boards that were able to serve the same function as National Semiconductor's chips. Bristow's solution worked so well that Atari adopted it as well.

In 1976, National Semiconductor decided to compete with Atari in the consumer game business.

> They then proceeded to try to steal our consumer business. So they showed up at that same toy show with a bad version of our *Pong* game. It never sold.
>
> We then summarily handed them a copy of our patent, which we later found out was null and void. Fortunately, we didn't push it very far cause it could have backfired on us. You ever try to force a bad patent? You're in real trouble if you do.
>
> **—Al Alcorn**

Atari's most persistent competition came from a small company located across the continent—the Connecticut Leather Company, better known as Coleco.

> The company started with Indian crafts. From there, it became an outdoor products company, making above-ground swimming pools out of plastic.
>
> **—Mike Katz, former president, Coleco**

Coleco was a family business run by two brothers—Arnold and Leonard Greenberg. Arnold made most of the decisions. His associates described him as a short, anxious man with a quick temper and an aggressive desire to build his company into an empire. One person described him as a "buttoned-down lawyer who was very creative, very forceful, and willing to take great chances."

When Greenberg took over Coleco, the company produced kits for leather crafts. In 1956, Greenberg acquired equipment to manufacture plastics, and

Coleco became the leading manufacturer of above-ground swimming pools. Ten years later, Coleco took over Eagle Toys and entered the toy business, making tabletop hockey and football games.

In 1975, Greenberg decided that Coleco should expand its product line to include a home video game. His engineers designed a video tennis console called the *Telestar,* and Greenberg ordered the necessary chips from General Instrument, the microelectronics company that supplied chips to most video-game manufacturers.

In the beginning, Coleco's success seemed preordained. Of all the companies that ordered chips for console games from General Instrument, only Coleco received the quantities requested.

As it turned out, Coleco was the first company to place its order. Surprised by the number of orders received, General Instrument was unable to manufacture enough chips to satisfy its customers. As the first customer in line, only Coleco had its order filled and it looked as if the *Telestar* would have little competition if it reached the market by the proposed launch date of June 1976.

But Coleco ran into trouble when the prototypical *Telestar* console its engineers submitted for FCC approval did not pass interference tests. During the demonstration, FCC representatives discovered that the *Telestar* generated radio band interference. Greenberg was given a week to eliminate the problem and have his product approved or he would have to resubmit his product at a later date and go through the entire approval process over again. The process could have put them months off schedule as they waited for the FCC to reopen the case.

During this period, Coleco had been considering hiring Sanders Associates, the company that developed the original Odyssey, to develop future products. In desperation, both Greenberg and his chief engineer called Sanders for help. Ralph Baer, the man whose team designed Odyssey, agreed to find a way to block out *Telestar*'s interference if Greenberg signed the contracts he had pending with Sanders.

> The phone rings, and it's the chief engineer of Coleco. They had just been rejected by the FCC because they couldn't meet RFI [radio frequency interference] specs. They were told, and this was a Monday, that if they were not back by Friday, they would go to the end of the queue [for approval needed

> to sell their product]. At that moment, they had $30 million worth of game inventory, and that would have thrown them out of the Christmas business. . . . they were desperate.
>
> So here's this chief engineer on the phone with me, asking if we can help them overcome the problem. Meanwhile, Arnold Greenberg's on another line speaking to my boss.
>
> I said, "Sign the agreement, license the agreement, and we'll help you."
>
> They came the next morning, bright and early, from Hartford. They were there and signed the agreement. I took the machine up to the fifth floor of the building. We did radio frequency interference measurements up there. We made measurements and we found that they indeed were out of spec radiation was too high.
>
> **—Ralph Baer**

Baer tried several conventional methods of building a shield to block out the *Telestar*'s interference. Nothing worked. He went home frustrated at the end of the day. When he returned the next day, he stumbled across a possible solution.

> I came into the lab the next morning, scratching my head. Nobody was there yet; I was early. I walked around the lab, went outdoors to get the measurements started, and saw two pieces of equipment sitting on a bench connected by a piece of coaxial cable. The end of one of the cables was a ferrite toroid (ring).
>
> Later I asked somebody, "What's this for?" Miracle of miracles, the guy actually knew. They had been out in the field, they picked up external RF from some transmission, and they suppressed it by putting this toroid on it, which acts like a choke.
>
> **—Ralph Baer**

Baer made a new shield using the ferrite rings. When he tested it on the *Telestar,* the interference was within acceptable levels. He gave the shielded unit to Greenberg, who returned to Washington, D.C., and received approval to market his machine.

The *Telestar* came out in time for Father's Day, 1976. Coleco sold over $100 million worth of the consoles and rose to the top of the consumer game business. Its leadership, however, was short-lived. In August, Fairchild Camera and Instrument released a new game console that permanently changed the industry.

The Rise of Cartridges

Fairchild Camera and Instrument, one of the companies that pioneered the development of the transistor, released a new video-game console called the Channel F in August 1976. Several features made the Channel F different from other consoles. It had unique controllers with triangular handles at the end of long shafts. One person described the controllers as looking like the plunger on a device for detonating bombs.[3] More important, the Channel F played games stored on interchangeable cartridges.

The original Odyssey played twelve games hardwired into the console's circuitry. To change games, players inserted circuit boards into a slot in the front of the console. Inserting Odyssey circuit boards was, in effect, like changing dip switches inside the console. (Odyssey also came with plastic overlays to add color and backgrounds to its games. The Channel F had color games and did not require overlays.)

Like every other game system, the Channel F had tennis and hockey programmed into its circuits, but Fairchild released additional games stored in casings that looked like 8-track tapes. They called the game units "Videocarts." Each Videocart contained a microchip with a game programmed into it.

Though the Channel F never developed a large following, it changed the consumer market forever. Consumers no longer wanted single-game consoles at any price. RCA responded quickly by announcing that it had a new game console under development, Magnavox went back to the lab, and Atari's engineers stated that they had named a new computer chip after a bicycle.

Stella

By the middle of 1976, Atari was no longer the star of the Sears catalog. Coleco had stolen the home market, and the Fairchild Channel F had rendered *Home Pong* worthless. In fact, television games had become a bit of a joke.

Many consumers lost interest in playing video tennis shortly after purchasing their systems. Game consoles were being thrown in closets or unloaded at garage sales.

Atari executives had recognized the need for a new technology even before Channel F hit the market. Restless as ever, Nolan Bushnell no longer believed that Atari's previous consoles, which were designed with a single game hardwired into their chips, would continue to attract consumers. To compete with the Channel F, Atari would need a console that could read and process information like a full-blown computer. The new system would have to read and display information on a television screen. Nolan Bushnell turned to his Grass Valley team for help.

> Steve Mayer, brilliant man, basically solved the problem. All of the other companies were run by semiconductor companies that made them use a memory map as a frame buffer. We didn't want a frame buffer. Back in those days it was way too expensive.
>
> We wanted to find a way to make the system with minimum silicon. The other companies' video games were all done by semiconductor companies. We were the only one that did our own design.
>
> **—Al Alcorn**

Steve Mayer, one of the founders of the Grass Valley facility, looked for alternatives to the expensive Fairchild F8 microprocessor used in the Channel F. He found the MOS Technologies 6502, a general purpose microprocessor capable of creating images on a television screen in real time—nearly instantaneously. Building off the 6502, the Grass Valley team designed a custom chip they named "Stella," after an engineer's bicycle.

Though the Grass Valley engineers had the expertise to design the Stella chip, they could not manufacture it. Al Alcorn took the design back to Atari and consulted with his research and development team. In the end, they decided to bring in an expert to finish the project.

Harold Lee, who co-designed *Home Pong,* told Alcorn that the only person who could build a chip as complex as Stella was a man named Jay Miner—the chief microprocessor designer at Synertech, a company that created custom chips for Atari.

Following Lee's advice, Alcorn went to Synertech and asked the company to loan him Miner as a consultant.

> I went to Synertech and said, "I want Jay Miner to work on this project."
>
> They said, "No, he's our chief CPU chip designer."
>
> "But you don't understand. I really want him. I'll pay his salary plus I'll give you all the business you can handle to keep your factory full."
>
> They said, "You've got a deal."
>
> Miner ended up with two badges. He had a Synertech badge. He had an Atari badge. He was our chip guy.
>
> **—Al Alcorn**

After he had secured Miner to lead the Stella development team, Alcorn selected other members. The final team included Larry Wagner, a mathematician who was already programming games, and Joe Decuir, a skilled engineer.

Once the work started, Miner proved himself quickly. By most accounts, Miner was an austere and brilliant man. He often brought his small cockapoo, Mitchie, to work and usually remained at his desk late into the evening. When the team had problems, Miner invented ingenious solutions, and the team was able to finish Stella on schedule.

When a second member of the team approached Alcorn about bringing his dog to work, he received this response. "That mangy golden retriever?" Alcorn snapped. "You bring that animal here and I'll have the guards shoot it on sight. You start doing work like Miner and get yourself a decent dog and we'll talk about it."

Mayer's decision to use the 6507 microprocessor proved correct. Not only would Atari's new game system be less expensive to build than the RCA and Fairchild game consoles, it would process information more quickly. Officially named the "Video Computer System" (VCS), Atari's new console was more than a game machine; it was a computer with a eight-bit processor.

Bushnell worried that once he unveiled his new system, the "jackals" would start imitating it. The only way to stop them, he decided, was to saturate the market before his competitors came out with similar products. He would catch the market by surprise and take it by storm.

Before Bushnell could move ahead with his plans, however, he needed another infusion of cash. By this time revenues from *Home Pong* sales had practically disappeared, and the coin-operated business was drying up. Too many people had purchased *Home Pong* or a similar system and no longer wanted to spend quarters to play "television games."

Year of Transition

By 1976, video games had made a permanent impact on the arcade industry. In an interview with *RePlay Magazine,* Joe Robbins, a vice president of Empire Entertainment, declared electromechanical games extinct:

> Electro-mechanical games, with some exceptions, are becoming pretty rare offerings. The cost of making them has forced most manufacturers to cancel most production plans. This includes the once-popular gun types and baseball games, to name a few.
>
> The steady and abundant stream of TV games will slowly diminish. Right now, large runs are confined to only the best games. It is even becoming difficult to sell the TV game that is just good or marginal. And this trend is irreversible. The number of manufacturers will decrease—and so will the number of new games. But we will enter a new generation of TV or similar games. They will inevitably stimulate renewed interest, enthusiasm, and earnings.[4]

If Robbins was correct, Atari would certainly be one of the companies to benefit most, but Midway had also distinguished itself with games like *Sea Wolf,* the most popular game of 1976. While Atari mostly created tennis, driving, shooting, and tank games, Midway produced innovative games about gunfights and naval battles.

Sea Wolf represented a new high point in game presentation. Before *Sea Wolf,* most video-game cabinets looked similar. There were a couple of odd cabinets, such as *Computer Space* and *Space Race,* which were made out of fiberglass and had rounded corners, and *Maneater,* which had a cabinet shaped like a shark.

But for *Sea Wolf,* Midway attached a periscope in front of the screen for players to use for shooting torpedoes at ships and submarines. Hitting slow-moving ships earned few points. Hitting speedy PT boats earned more points.

The concept was not original. In 1966, Sega, the largest arcade company in Japan, created an electromechanical game called *Periscope* that used lights and plastic waves to simulate sinking ships from a submarine. *Periscope* was the first game to cost 25 cents per play. Prior to this, games cost a dime. Several arcade owners imported it to the United States, where it was imitated by many competitors—including Midway.

Sea Wolf, which was another creation of Dave Nutting, did solid business, selling more than 10,000 machines. (A later color version, *Sea Wolf II,* sold an additional 4,000 units.) With few exceptions, however, the coin-operated video game was declining, and most games sold under 5,000 units.

The public was losing interest. The novelty of playing games on a television had disappeared. Video games had been around for four years. People even had them in their homes. Unless someone could come up with a method for restoring the novelty, it looked like the industry would continue to stagnate.

The slow demise of video games did not necessarily hurt arcade owners. Pinball made a strong comeback in 1976. The first generation of solid-state pinball machines appeared in arcades. Though solid-state pinball machines played like older games, they had the advantage of scoring memory, allowing the game to recognize the playfield for the progress of each player from ball to ball.

Even Atari, the company that started video games, began manufacturing pinball games. Under Bushnell's direction, the company opened a special pinball division that created extra-wide pinball machines.

The Decision to Sell

Atari was one of the great rides. . . . It was one of the greatest business educations in the history of the universe.

—Manny Gerard

Around this time, Steve Jobs left Atari to dedicate himself to manufacturing and selling the computers he created with Steve Wozniak. Jobs asked Bushnell to invest in his company, but Bushnell declined. Jobs finally approached Don Valentine for capital. Valentine insisted on some special arrangements. Jobs agreed, and Apple Computer was born.

Instead of asking Valentine for more capital, Bushnell held a board meeting in which he discussed other options—going public or selling the company. Their first choice was to make a public offering of Atari stock, but after taking several steps toward the offering, the board decided that the slumping stock market would not support their move.

In the end, the board decided to put Atari up for sale. Over the next few weeks, Bushnell approached MCA, parent company of Universal Studios, and Disney. Neither company was interested.

> Everybody was losing interest in the digital watch and the pocket calculator, and most of the people we went to wondered why video games would be any different.[5]
>
> **—Nolan Bushnell**

One company that was interested in Atari was Warner Communications, a conglomerate with a strong presence in film, recording, and magazine publishing. Warner was owned by Steve Ross, a hardened entrepreneur who had risen from the streets of Brooklyn. By most accounts, Ross was a brusque man who expected results and had little patience for ineptitude.

Having worked his way out of poverty, Ross had grand intentions. He expected Warner to corner every facet of the entertainment industry. Toward that goal, he hired Manny Gerard, considered the best entertainment industry analyst on Wall Street, to acquire new companies for the Warner Communications fold. The first company Gerard selected was Atari.

The process began when Gerard received a telephone call from Gordon Crawford, an analyst at Capital Management. Crawford described Atari without saying its name and asked if Warner might be interested in acquiring the company. Gerard said yes.

The next step was for Gerard to fly to California and evaluate the operation. He met with Bushnell and Joe Keenan, observed the company's manufacturing facilities, and discussed Bushnell's future plans. By all appearances, Atari had a strong future.

> I was the guy who took the trip and looked at the company and got the lay of the land. I'm the lunatic who thought it was a good idea that we acquire it.

> I wrote an internal memo about it, in which I said I think we ought to acquire
> this company.
>
> —**Manny Gerard**

When Gerard returned to New York, he recommended the purchase to Steve Ross. Interestingly, he found Ross to be quite receptive.

> Steve Ross had just gone to Disneyland with his kids. They went into an ar-
> cade and all they played was *Indy 800,* and they were really fascinated with
> the game. One of the reasons this transaction occurred was because Ross
> understood the power of this game. He'd seen it at Disneyland.
>
> Actually, he really wanted an *Indy 800* game for his apartment, but it
> ended up that we couldn't get it in. It was too heavy.
>
> —**Manny Gerard**

At Gerard's suggestion, Steve Ross decided to buy the company. Ross's lawyers contacted Bushnell's lawyers, and representatives for both sides began outlining the details of the transaction. The negotiating process took four months.

Gerard wanted to keep Atari's management intact. He recognized Bushnell as one of the driving forces behind Atari's success. He also respected the company's team of engineers, whom he described as "loyal to Bushnell and very productive." According to Gerard, the entire industry was new to Warner; without Bushnell and his team, there was no reason to attempt entering the business. He did, however, express some concerns.

> I think we kind of understood Nolan, to some extent. Let me tell you what I
> felt about the whole management [team].
>
> The biggest problem with the company was that you had a bunch of
> babies—not literally, not as a character flaw. These were young guys. If
> they made too much money, I didn't know how we could motivate them.
> We couldn't give them too much money because they'd go live under a
> tree somewhere.

> Basically, they got a teeny bit of cash and the debentures of the subsid-
> iary, which were not secured by the parent. We took the outside investors
> out for cash, but the insiders had to take these debentures.
>
> **—Manny Gerard**

In the end, Warner Communications paid $28 million for Atari. It retained
Bushnell as chairman and Joe Keenan as president. The sales, marketing, engineering, and research and development departments also remained
unaffected. In theory, except for a seemingly endless supply of funding—
Warner invested $100 million in Atari—life at Atari would remain unchanged.

The entire deal almost fell apart, however, when Bushnell's ex-wife, Paula,
challenged it.

> If you want to know what appears to have triggered this, in the middle of all
> our negotiations, Nolan gets his picture in one of the San Francisco newspa-
> pers in a hot tub with his new girlfriend.
>
> This is not a great idea to start with. More than anything, I think his ex-
> wife was really unhappy about the pictures.
>
> Somehow it came up that she sued for recision of their divorce settlement.
> If she got recision, the deal would have been off. What the law says is, "If you
> buy 100 percent of the company and she gets recision, you've paid 100 per-
> cent of the price, you now get 75 percent of the company." In effect, she'd
> still own her half of his half of the company—that's 25 percent.
>
> We told Nolan, "We don't think this is a grand idea. This is not our first choice."
>
> **—Manny Gerard**

Warner responded by going directly to Paula Bushnell's lawyer and disclosing the entire deal so that she could no longer claim the transaction had
occurred without her knowledge. Nolan Bushnell then arranged a settlement,
in which she was paid to step out of the picture.

Once Paula Bushnell was satisfied, the deal could finally be closed. The signing
took place at a lawyer's office in San Francisco in October 1976. That night, executives from Atari and Warner celebrated the event with dinner at a French restaurant.

Years after selling Atari, Bushnell confessed that selling the company might have been a mistake. The roller-coaster ride of meeting each month's payroll had left him exhausted, and the idea of raising the capital needed to produce the *Video Computer System* overwhelmed him at the time. "I've often thought that if I had taken a two-week vacation and really rested and got away from the whole thing, I never would have sold the company."

According to Gerard, Bushnell seemed elated at the signing. "The day we signed the papers to close the deal, Nolan's comment was, 'I've been telling people I'm a millionaire for years, and at last I am.'"

Uneasy Partners

As was the case with Sears, the cultural clash between Atari and Warner became apparent even before the deal was signed. Gerard and Ross were very tough East Coast businessmen, unaccustomed to Bushnell's Californian style. Gerard once took his wife to Grass Valley. When she saw that many of the engineers had long beards, she commented that they looked like "the Smith Brothers [on the cough drops box]."

Once, to try to break the ice, Bushnell took several executives from Atari and Warner for a night cruise across the San Francisco Bay on his 42-foot sailboat, *Pong.* They left from Alameda and sailed to Tiburon. An accident on the way back to port left the Warner people less than impressed.

> There was this buoy, and we were up in the crest of the waves when the buoy was down and vice versa, and we never saw it. We were sailing along and suddenly we heard a loud KATHWANG as we hit the buoy—not side-swiped, but actually hit it with the point of the boat. It made a large sound, at which point the New York crowd looked a bit aghast.
>
> Someone went front to see if there was a crack on the outside. One of us went flying down below to see if there was any water coming in.
>
> **—Steve Bristow**

> Oh, was that a night! We sailed from Oakland across the bay to Tiburon. They managed to . . . oh, was that funny! They managed to bang the boat into a buoy. By the time we got back, it was like 11:00. We were freezing and wet and cold.

> That was hardly a win over. Yes, we took the boat. If that was perceived as a way to win us over, I can tell you . . . it wasn't too successful. I'm laughing because I remember that night. It was wonderful. It was a comic opera.
>
> **—Manny Gerard**

In January 1977, RCA released the Studio II: a game system with interchangeable cartridges. Though its only competition was the Channel F, the Studio II had a major design flaw that slowed its sales—its games were all black and white. Magnavox announced it would release a programmable game system called Odyssey 2 in September. Allied Leisure and Bally also announced new systems. It appeared as if the market might be too crowded by the time Atari released the VCS.

In October 1977, Atari released the Video Computer System, along with nine game cartridges. Atari engineers had worked hard to distinguish the VCS as the best system on the market. Like the Studio II and the Channel F, the VCS had controllers with dials for playing paddle games, but it also had a new device called a joystick, a pivoting lever in a pedestal, for controlling the tank and flying games on the *Combat* cartridge.* The VCS also had switches for selecting games, displaying games in color or black and white, and setting difficulty levels. None of these enhancements had ever been offered.

The profit margin on the VCS was low, but Atari executives planned to recoup their losses on software. It cost less than $10 to manufacture the game cartridges, which sold for $30. They set a precedent that would remain an axiom in the video-game industry: "Give away the razors so that you can sell the blades."

Unfortunately, very few consumers bought razors or blades that year.

One of the problems was shipping. According to Bushnell, Atari was unable to get the majority of its 400,000 game consoles on store shelves in time for the holiday rush. Other problems included lack of consumer interest in home video games, confusion over the glut of new products, and the success of a new line of handheld electronic sports games from Mattel and Coleco.

After Christmas 1977, the video-game market crashed. Manufacturers like Magnavox and Atari sold inventory at reduced rates. RCA pulled out entirely.

---

* Atari did not make the first joystick. German scientists developed the joystick during World War II for controlling guided missiles.

As it looked like the video-game market was dead, tensions increased between Bushnell and the new owners of Atari.

Adding to the tension was Bushnell's lack of enthusiasm about the business. Now that he no longer owned Atari, Bushnell seemed less interested in its day-to-day operation. He got involved in real estate, purchasing an enormous mansion in Woodside, California, from coffee-heir Peter Folger. Bushnell remarried. In a ceremony held in a courtyard on the grounds of his newly purchased mansion, Bushnell married Nancy Nino. Nearly 700 people were in attendance, including Steve Ross and Manny Gerard.

> [One thing] I think what I wasn't prepared for is that after we bought [Atari], basically Nolan and Joe [Keenan], having some money, went off and did their real-estate investments. They stopped paying attention to the business. That, I will tell you, I did not anticipate. They just refocused on something else.
>
> **—Manny Gerard**

> After I sold the company, I did take a couple of vacations and I think that was something that bothered Manny a little bit. It was just one of those things where I needed a certain amount of time.
>
> As it became clear that some of the things that were going on were things that I really disagreed with, it was harder and harder for me to really climb in and be as enthusiastic as before.
>
> **—Nolan Bushnell**

VCS sales continued at a steady-but-disappointing pace through 1978. Always wary of "the jackals" and convinced that the only way to stay ahead of the competition was to introduce new products, Bushnell wanted to discontinue the VCS and move on to the next-generation game console. Bushnell preferred moving to new technologies rather than spending time refining old ideas and letting his competitors catch up to him. He called his philosophy "eating your own babies" and said that if Atari didn't (eat its own babies), somebody else would.

> There was endless pushing and shoving. I'd go to meetings and Nolan, who
> kind of disappeared, would turn up and say, "This is what we're going to
> do." His own people were getting crazy with him.
>
> I used a phrase over and over with Nolan. "Nolan, you can't rule the com-
> pany by the divine right of king. You've got to be here, you have to pay
> attention. You can't just come in. . . . "
>
> —**Manny Gerard**

The Czar

In February 1978, Warner hired a consultant to help turn the company around.
Ray Kassar had extensive experience as a former vice president of Burlington
Industries, the largest textile manufacturer in the United States.

A Harvard graduate, Kassar claimed to know nothing about video games. He
had been with Burlington Industries for twenty-five years and distinguished
himself by becoming the youngest vice president in the company's history. This
experience, he felt, could be transferred to nearly any manufacturing situation.

> I came in as a consultant for Warner, but my title in the company at the time
> was general manager of the consumer division, which was, at that point,
> doing terribly.
>
> I mean, there was no infrastructure. They had no financial person. They
> had no marketing. They really had nothing. It was a disaster.
>
> —**Ray Kassar**

Most people who knew Kassar described him as autocratic but fashionable.
He wore tailored suits to work, insisted on being driven in a chauffeured lim-
ousine, and demanded very lavish treatment. He ate at only the finest
restaurants.

According to Kassar, his first assignment was to determine whether Warner
should liquidate Atari. After testing the VCS, Kassar was impressed and decided not to abandon it. He reported to Steve Ross that with some changes,
Atari could be a profitable company.

> My plan was to stay in California for as little time as possible. Warner really thought I was going to go out there and liquidate the company. That's what they wanted me to do. They were looking for me to give them a recommendation.
>
> Believe me, there's only one person who knows the full story and that is me. Even Manny Gerard doesn't know the full story 'cause he was sitting in New York. I was there. I was running the company.
>
> **—Ray Kassar**

Predictably, Nolan Bushnell and Ray Kassar found very little common ground. Kassar, who routinely arrived at work at 7:30 A.M., did not approve of Bushnell's "work smart, not hard" attitude. He was bothered by the stories of drug abuse among Atari's employees and felt that Bushnell's laid-back style did little to discourage it. He disagreed with Bushnell about the future of the VCS and wanted to use it as the lead product in Atari's Christmas lineup.

> The first or second week I was there, Nolan invited me to a management committee meeting. I arrived at his office at 3:00. Everybody was sitting around in jeans and T-shirts. In fact, when I first arrived at Atari, Nolan was walking around the company in a T-shirt that said, "I love to screw."
>
> Anyway, I arrived at this so-called management committee meeting and there were about six or seven of them drinking beer and smoking marijuana.
>
> They offered me a joint.
>
> I said, "No, I don't do drugs."
>
> And Nolan said, "Well, why don't you just relax? We're just kind of . . . "
>
> I said, "Look, are you having a meeting? If you're having a meeting, I'll stay. If you're not, I'm leaving."
>
> He said, "No, we're just going to drink some beer and wine." So I left.
>
> **—Ray Kassar**

The final battle came at a Warner Communications budget meeting held in New York City in November 1978. Atari had been mildly profitable, but Steve Ross was not satisfied. Bushnell's solution was to close down the pinball division and abandon the VCS.

In Bushnell's mind, the only way Atari pinball could succeed was to make specialty tables. Standard pinball playfields were 22 inches wide; Atari's first three tables were 29 inches wide. If Gerard insisted on making standard tables, Bushnell wanted to close down the division all together.

Gerard said that Bushnell also proposed discontinuing the VCS, but Bushnell said he only wanted to cut its price. Either way, his suggestions were in direct opposition to those of Gerard and Kassar. The battle lines were drawn.

> The ultimate parting with Nolan came at the budget meeting of Warner in 1978. Nolan came to the meeting, got up at the meeting, and everybody sat there in stunned amazement as Nolan said, "Sell off your remaining inventory of 2600s. [2600 was another name for VCS.] You've saturated the market. The market is saturated at the top. It's over."
>
> Remember, there were a lot of Warner people who didn't know nothing about nothing. And nobody in the room could figure what the hell Nolan was talking about.
>
> **—Manny Gerard**

> I said, "If, in fact, you guys are bound and determined to do regular pinball machines, I think we should close the division down because you aren't going to make any money."
>
> The battle was really over pricing the VCS. I felt that the strongest position would be to price the hardware lower and the software higher.
>
> **—Nolan Bushnell**

By this time, it was too late to make changes in the Christmas lineup. If Bushnell was right, Warner faced another holiday bloodbath.

The meeting erupted into a shouting match. Bushnell felt that Gerard and the entire Warner team had no feel for the electronics industry. Gerard claimed that Bushnell was no longer taking the business seriously. He said that Bushnell's decisions were erratic. Not only had Bushnell's recommendations caught the Warner people off guard, they even surprised Atari's executive team.

The day after the showdown, Gerard had a private meeting with Steve Ross, in which they discussed Atari's future. Ross wanted to know what Gerard thought would happen over the holidays. Gerard said that Atari had not saturated the market with the VCS and that he expected the system to sell well.

> The next day I got called into Ross's office, and he basically goes nuts, and I mean nuts. He says to me, "Oh my God, what do we do?"
>
> I said, "Look Steve, there are only two possible outcomes." It's now December 10th or thereabouts, and I said, "Steve, in my opinion, on December 26th there's going to be a game in every home in America, in which case we've got one of the biggest businesses you ever saw. If I'm wrong, we've got us a big problem. But what the hell, all we have to do is do nothing for two weeks, and we're going to know. Okay."
>
> He said, "I guess so."
>
> By December 26th we knew we had a monster business on our hands.
>
> **—Manny Gerard**

Shortly after the budget meeting, Gerard returned to California. While there, he heard that Bushnell was holding an Atari board meeting without Warner representation. This was the last straw. Gerard had an attorney draw up papers, and he dismissed Bushnell.

> There was this whole thing in which it came to my attention that Nolan was trying to call a board meeting with Joe [Keenan], and they said something about didn't I get my notice? I said to myself, this is untenable, then I got the contracts out, I got the lawyers out, and I removed Nolan from office.
>
> Nolan was simply removed and he was put on the beach. Okay?
>
> Then Joe asked to be put on the beach. That's a . . . word of ours, because by putting him on the beach, he was entitled to certain modest compensation in some bonus pool arrangements.
>
> I don't remember the numbers, but Nolan and Joe got 1 percent of this bonus pool, which, at that moment in time, he [Bushnell] believed was valueless. I believe what was going on was that they perceived they could make a fortune with Chuck E. Cheese, and who gave a shit about Atari anyway?
>
> **—Manny Gerard**

Bushnell's forced retirement knocked him out of the video-game industry. One of Warner's original stipulations for purchasing Atari was that Bushnell sign a seven-year noncompete clause. Once he left Atari, he was not allowed to work for any video-game company until 1983. On the other hand, he still received bonuses based on Atari's performance. If Gerard and Kassar ran Atari profitably, he stood to make some easy money.

Ray Kassar replaced Bushnell as the CEO of Atari. His autocratic style had angered a few Atari employees when he was just a consultant. Now that he was chief executive, he offended people in droves. Once Bushnell left, several of Atari's key figures followed within the next few years.

> A lot of us didn't know Ray when he was appointed to run the company, so he gathered the entire consumer engineering department in one of the cafeterias to talk about how he was going to run things.
>
> The question just came up, "What's your background?" He said it was from the textile industry, importing fabric and stuff like that.
>
> Somebody asked him, "Well, how are you going to interact with electronics designers?"
>
> He said, "Well, I've worked with designers all my life."
>
> I remember saying to myself, "What does he mean by that?"
>
> He went on to say, "The towel designers . . . "
>
> I was like, oh-oh, we're in for a lot of trouble. This is going to be a disaster. And it sure turned out to be a disaster.
>
> **—Alan Miller, former Atari game designer,**
> **cofounder of Activision and Accolade**

CHAPTER 9

The Return of Bushnell

Solid-state pinball was a really foolish market—they sold before they even finished building it. It was a wonderful market for Bally that only lasted about three years and went into the dumps. The reason it went into the dumps is because a video game called *Space Invaders* came out and captured the attention of everybody on the face of the earth.

—Eddie Adlum

Nolan started Chuck E. Cheese at about the same time that Warner bought Atari. You want to hear about Chuck E. Cheese?

—Al Alcorn

Arcades Reborn

In the spring of 1978, Taito approached Midway about distributing a new arcade game in the United States. The game had originally been invented as a hexadecimal test used for evaluating computer programmers. Someone decided to convert the test into a video game that Taito distributed in Japan, despite the unenthusiastic blessing of company executives. The game was called *Space Invaders.*

Space Invaders did very poorly for the first few months after being introduced to Japanese arcades. By the time the game was three months old, however, it started to show signs of life. More than a year passed between the time that *Space Invaders* was introduced in Japan and when it arrived in the United States. By that time, it had become an unprecedented phenomenon in Japanese arcades.

By the end of its arcade life, more than 100,000 units of *Space Invaders* blanketed Japan. So many people were playing the game that it caused a national coin shortage. The Japanese mint had to triple the production of the 100-yen piece because so many coins were glutted in the arcades.

> In 1978, Taito came out with *Space Invaders* in Japan. It was such an outrageous hit in Japan that many vegetable stores and other little stores would get rid of their vegetables and dedicate the whole store to *Space Invaders.* All told, worldwide, they say there were at least 300,000 *Space Invaders* games built, including counterfeit versions.
>
> **—Eddie Adlum**

Even after *Space Invaders'* triumph in Japan, Taito executives felt that the game's theme of defending space stations from an extraterrestrial attack was too different from other games to appeal to American audiences. Most of the top games of 1978 were based on popular themes such as driving, sports, and war. In *Space Invaders,* players moved a laser turret from side-to-side along the bottom of the screen, instead of controlling familiar objects.

The aliens in *Space Invaders* marched in a rectangular formation eight columns long and five rows deep. They marched horizontally, advancing toward the bottom of the screen. Players lost if the invading alien army reached the bottom or if players lost all their turrets.

To defend against the invaders, players had to shoot at the aliens with their laser turrets while avoiding descending enemy missiles. Four bases toward the bottom of the screen offered limited cover from missile barrages, but enemy fire could obliterate those bases quickly. Destroying an entire wave of aliens earned 990 points. Extra points could be earned by shooting flying saucers that flew across the top of the screen at 25-second intervals.

There was no way to beat *Space Invaders;* the alien waves kept coming until the player either gave up or was killed. The best you could hope for was to post the highest score of the day at the top of the screen.

After testing the game, Taito of America's vice president of product development Keith Egging predicted that *Space Invaders* would do well in the United States. He set up a prototype in a secret testing location in Colorado. The players' response convinced him that Taito had sold Midway a major hit.

> I was exceptionally confident that it would do good in this country. I had just started with the company [Taito of America], and they thought I was a nut. I said we could sell tens of thousands, and they said, "You can't sell that many."
>
> **—Keith Egging, former vice president of project development, Taito of America**

Midway introduced *Space Invaders* into the United States in October 1978, and American audiences adopted it almost immediately. Midway sold *Space Invaders* machines for approximately $1,700. The orders poured in so quickly that the company became backlogged. Arcade owners gladly paid the price; the game could pay for itself in a single month. In good locations, each machine earned between $300 and $400 per week.

Within a year, Midway manufactured and sold more than 60,000 *Space Invader* machines in the United States. Suddenly, video games were the most lucrative equipment a vendor could own.

> Not too long after I opened the game room, *Space Invaders* came out. What a great game. That was the first time I saw a cash box that represented a significant portion of the cost of [buying] the game in any one week. It was

> hard to believe that any game could capture the audience to the degree that
> it was capable of doing.
>
> I can remember only a few games that had that dynamic game-playing
> magnetism. You could probably count them on your fingers.
>
> **—Joel Hochberg**

In a 1982 interview, Taito import manager S. Ikawa tried to explain why so many people liked *Space Invaders*: "*Space Invaders* gives you a feeling of tension. A little neglect may breed great mischief."[1]

Though *Space Invaders* played the biggest role in revitalizing the coin-operated business, another game also had a major impact—Atari *Football*.

Contrary to a popular notion, *Football* was not the first game to use a trakball controller. According to Dave Stubben, who created the hardware for Atari *Football*, Taito beat Atari to market with a soccer game that used one. According to Steve Bristow, when his engineers saw the game, they brought a copy into their lab and imitated it.

Dave Stubben, a large and beefy man who often wore cowboy boots to work, cocreated *Football* with software designer Mike Albaugh. Stubben saw a partially completed football game called *X's and O's* that Bristow had begun around the time that he created *Tank*. Stubben improved Bristow's design by adding a smooth-scrolling playing field and trackball controllers.*

Few games absorbed more abuse than Atari *Football*, and few games have injured so many players. It was housed in a waist-high tabletop cabinet. Players stood beside the cabinet, pounding the trackball as hard as they could. On offense, players slapped the trackball to control their quarterback and make their receivers run. To build speed and to maneuver, players had to spin the trackball as quickly as possible. All over the country, people developed blisters on their hands.

Although the computer microprocessor that powered *Football* far exceeded dedicated circuits of games like *Pong*, it lacked the horsepower needed to display complex graphics. The teams in *Football* were represented by Xs and Os.

---

*The trackball was created by Jerry Liachek, the Atari mechanical engineer who created all of Atari's best coin-op controllers. Liachek worked on the handle for *Lunar Lander*, the joystick controller for *Star Wars*, and the dual joysticks for *Battlezone*.

Unlike *Space Invaders, Football* ran on a three-minute timer. Once the three minutes were up, players had to insert more quarters to continue. For the first three months of its release, *Football* was, quarter-for-quarter, as big a money maker as *Space Invaders*. The football season ended in January, and with it went most of Atari's *Football* business.

The Problem with Pizza

One of Nolan Bushnell's pet projects while working at Atari was finding new outlets for getting his games to the public. Video games had already found their way into bowling alleys, amusement parks, movie theaters, bars, pool halls, and arcades. In 1979, *Space Invaders* opened new doors as fast-food restaurants and even drugstores began experimenting with games.

The progress was slow, however, because much of the public still associated video games with pool halls, sleazy arcades, and vagrancy. Adding to the problem was a very effective war against video games launched by a woman named Ronnie Lamb, from Centereach, Long Island. She had seen a growing number of children playing the games and was appalled at the waste of time and money. She did not approve of the violence in many of the games and felt that arcades were not wholesome environments.

Ms. Lamb presented her concerns on *The Phil Donahue Show*. Her campaign resulted in a few small towns banning arcades and helped to sour the public's perception of video games and arcades. Despite arcades' growing popularity, few shopping mall owners would allow arcades to be built on their properties.

In order to reach a larger audience, Bushnell had to find a way to legitimize video games. He wanted to make them a family activity, and the only way to do that was to create locations in which parents were practically forced to let their children play them. The answer came in the form of a pizza parlor with a video game arcade and a built-in theater that showed a robot stage act.

Bushnell hoped that the restaurant would legitimize the arcade. The robotic show, he thought, could create a Disney-like atmosphere that would make children select his parlors over such other chains as Pizza Hut and Godfather's.

It didn't matter if the pizza was good or even mediocre; the arcade and robot show would attract kids. Once he lured customers, Bushnell hoped they would enter his arcade while their pizza was cooking. To help tempt them, he gave them a handful of free game tokens—enough to last five minutes. They would have to purchase more tokens if they wanted to spend additional time in the arcade while they waited.

> We were running out of locations, and opening a video game arcade in the 1970s was like opening a pool hall. Malls weren't interested in letting us open arcades. So Nolan figured, okay, I'll go into food service.
>
> What food are people used to waiting a long time to eat? Pizza. While they wait, we'll give them tokens to play games so they don't mind waiting a half hour for the pizza. We'll use these animatronic robots that Grass Valley engineered.
>
> It was a scheme where you could tell mall management, "I'm not putting in a video-game arcade, I'm putting in a pizza parlor with video games." But it was as big an arcade as you could possibly get in and still call it a pizza parlor.
>
> **—Al Alcorn**

Bushnell called his new venture Pizza Time Theaters. He named his restaurants Chuck E. Cheese after the robotic rat mascot.

Although Chuck E. Cheese restaurants were somewhat similar to the Cavalier restaurant/arcade that Joel Hochberg helped open in 1961, Bushnell's vision was unique. The Cavalier was designed to attract adults with games and food. Bushnell went after children, knowing that if they came, their parents would have to follow.

Bushnell began work on Chuck E. Cheese long before leaving Atari. He told a reporter that he had a rat costume on a mannequin in his office as early as 1974. Atari purchased an abandoned Dean Witter brokerage office in a San Jose outdoor mall and converted it into a Chuck E. Cheese restaurant in November of 1977.

The first Chuck E. Cheese was far smaller than later restaurants. Along with an arcade, the establishment had a food service area with three stages, from which a robotic animal band played family tunes. The eating area was laid out like a cafeteria, with tables in long rows.

Though Warner acquired the rights to Chuck E. Cheese when it purchased Atari, the project never interested Manny Gerard or Steve Ross. According to Bushnell, they eventually asked him to sell the entire franchise off.

> The project was started before Warner bought the company. They sort of
> said, "Okay, it's another one of Nolan's hare brains." They sort of tolerated
> it, but they figured it was going to be something that would go away. They
> didn't understand it.
>
> **—Nolan Bushnell**

When Bushnell left Atari, he asked to buy the rights to Chuck E. Cheese.
Ross sold him the entire project, including the rights to the robot technology, for $500,000. Bushnell paid the debt at the rate of $100,000 per year. Within
weeks of leaving the company, he began planning his second location.

Along with video games, Chuck E. Cheese had midway games that rewarded
players with tickets that could be redeemed for prizes. Bushnell had run similar games at the amusement park in Salt Lake City, Utah, while working his
way through school. He believed that the promise of winning prizes would
have enormous appeal to children.

> Skeeball was dying. The company [that made the games], Philadelphia Toboggan, was going out of business and all of a sudden Nolan recognized
> there was play value there. You've got to give him credit for this.
>
> The whole redemption idea was kind of a shady thing at the arcades, almost gambling, but Nolan realized that this was something the kiddies would
> love because they could spend time at the counter redeeming all those tickets.
>
> I don't know if he stole the idea from somebody else, but it was his drive
> and his vision.
>
> **—Al Alcorn**

Had the video-game industry remained in the doldrums, Chuck E. Cheese
might have quietly failed and disappeared. Instead, *Space Invaders* burst upon
the scene and the entire industry flourished. Since Chuck E. Cheese was one
of the places people were sure to find the games they were looking for, the
franchise rode the swell of excitement over hot titles like *Space Invaders*.

The second Chuck E. Cheese was far more ambitious than the first one.
Bushnell put it in a San Jose building that had once housed a Toys "R" Us
store. It was one of the largest Californian arcades of its time, with two floors

of video games and a spiral ramp running around a 20-foot tall revolving statue of Chuck E. Cheese.

By the end of 1979, Bushnell began selling Pizza Time Theater franchises. It cost approximately $1.5 million to construct a full-sized Pizza Time Theater. A properly run location could pay for itself in six months.

As it turned out, *Space Invaders* was only the tip of an iceberg that eventually turned Chuck E. Cheese and several other video game—associated ventures into billion-dollar success stories. The golden age of video games was about to dawn.

CHAPTER 10

The Golden Age
(Part 1: 1979–1980)

Nobody gets their first game published.

**—Theurer's Law (Atari doctrine named after Dave Theurer,
creator of *Missile Command* and *Tempest*)**

Games such as *Pac-Man* and *Space Invaders* were going into virtually every location in
the country, with the exception of maybe funeral parlors, and even a few funeral parlors
had video games in the basements. Absolutely true. I believe churches and synagogues
were about the only types of locations to escape video games.

—Eddie Adlum

The End of an Era

Once Nolan Bushnell left Atari, other notables soon followed. Within a few months of Bushnell's departure, Joe Keenan joined him. Gil Williams hung on for nearly two years; his last assignment was to set up a coin-op manufacturing plant in Ireland. Gene Lipkin remained a bit longer, then left the company under unpleasant circumstances.

As one of the company's original employees, Al Alcorn was caught in a tough position. He had been with the company since 1972 and helped develop its most successful products—*Pong, Home Pong,* and the Video Computer System. His name still carried weight at Atari, but he did not like the direction in which the company was headed.

As far as Alcorn was concerned, things had changed since Warner Communications took control. Under Bushnell, Atari was an engineering company. The leadership took risks and pioneered new technologies. When Ray Kassar replaced Bushnell as president, Atari became a marketing company. Instead of developing new technologies, Kassar preferred to push existing ideas to their fullest. Alcorn wanted to begin work on the next generation of home video-game hardware, but Kassar didn't even want to consider an alternative to the VCS.

Toward the end of 1978, Alcorn assembled a team of engineers and began designing a game console called Cosmos. Unlike the VCS, Cosmos did not plug into a television set. It had a light-emitting diode display. Both systems played games stored on cartridges, but Cosmos's tiny cartridges had no electronics, simply a four-by-five inch mylar transparency that cost so little to manufacture that the entire cartridges could retail for $10.

Alcorn's team included two new engineers. Harry Jenkins, who had just graduated from Stanford University, and Roger Hector, a project designer who had done some impressive work in the coin-op division. Both were assigned to work directly under Alcorn on the project.

> The perception was that Al was given a group of people to "play with." Harry Jenkins and Roger Hector were fresh hires. There was probably a bit of envy around the company because they did not have to actually deliver projects on time or budget but were more on a research and development–bent.
>
> **—Steve Bristow**

Borrowing a page from Odyssey, the Cosmos used overlays to improve the look of its games. Cosmos's overlays, however, were among the most impressive technologies ever created by Atari engineers.

Atari negotiated a deal with a bank for access to patents belonging to Holosonics, a bankrupt corporation that controlled most of the world's patents for holograms—a technology for creating three-dimensional images using lasers. Alcorn brought in two specialists, Steve McGrew and Ken Haynes, to develop a process for mass-producing holograms that could be used with his game.

McGrew developed a process for creating holograms on mylar. In later years, Haynes expanded the technology for other uses, such as placing 3D pictures on credit cards.

Alcorn used their mylar technology to create an impressive array of 3D holographic overlays for the Cosmos.

One of the first games developed for the system was similar to Steve Russell's *Spacewar*—an outer-space dogfight in which two small ships battled. The game took place in empty space with no obstructions, but the holographic overlay created an extremely elaborate backdrop with whirling 3D asteroids. The overlay did not affect the game. The ships could not interact with the backdrop, but the visual effects were spectacular.

Before beginning the project, Alcorn asked Ray Kassar for permission to create a new stand-alone game system. According to Alcorn, Kassar seemed uninterested but did not object. By the middle of 1980, Alcorn and his team had completed a working prototype. When they showed it to marketing, they were told that the department had no interest in selling anything other than the VCS.

> By this time, sales were up over a billion dollars. Everybody was fighting the idea of trying to get a new product out. You've got to realize that marketing had sold out [of the VCS] by April for the entire year. So the marketing department's only job was telling people, "I'm sorry, we're sold out."
>
> All of a sudden, here comes Alcorn with a challenge: "Let's get to work and let's sell a new product." Why would they want to do that?
>
> So here I am with this new product idea. Marketing didn't want to have anything to do with it. Manufacturing said they were too busy building VCSs to build a new product.

> I said, "Put that in writing." I then found a manufacturing place outside
> that could do a better job for less money.
>
> **—Al Alcorn**

Alcorn, Jenkins, and Hector had invested too much time in Cosmos to abandon it. Other engineers advised them to simply walk away from the project, but Alcorn decided to market the unit himself. He asked for space to show Cosmos at Atari's booth during the 1980 Winter Consumer Electronics Show in the Las Vegas Convention Center. Amazingly, the marketing department said yes.

By this time, Mattel and Bally had entered the market with newer, more powerful consoles, but no one seemed to care. The VCS had more games and a much larger installed base. A constant stream of buyers from toy stores and department stores flowed through the Atari booth. While they were there, several buyers stopped by the Cosmos table, where Alcorn, Hector, and Jenkins demonstrated the console themselves. The holographic overlays attracted a lot of attention.

A few months later, Alcorn, Hector, and Jenkins manned a similar display at the Toy Fair in New York City. Having learned from his failure to sell *Home Pong* on the floor of the show, Alcorn also set up a suite for private meetings. Among the visitors to the booth was Al Nilsen, the new toy buyer for JC Penney.

> The first time I saw Cosmos was at Toy Fair. I had heard the big deal about the
> hologram nature of it.
>
> From what I remember, I wanted to see more because they were only showing one very small demo game with it. That was the last that I ever heard about the product.
>
> **—Al Nilsen, former toy buyer, JC Penney**

> Harry, Roger, and I went to the winter CES in Vegas. We managed to get a
> part in the Atari booth, and we sold our product. We couldn't get any marketing guys to sell our product; we had to run the booth ourselves.
>
> We were at Toy Fair in New York a month later. This time we had the proper suite and the proper way to do it. And I think we had about a quarter million of them sold. Ray Kassar still wouldn't build them.

> I got it as far as I could. I had *Cosmos* tooled and sold, and there was nothing but Ray Kassar that could stop *Cosmos* from happening.
>
> Then he said, "No. We're not going to do it."
>
> **—Al Alcorn**

Although the response to *Cosmos* was not even remotely close to the response to the VCS, several buyers decided to gamble on the system. Alcorn returned to California from the Toy Fair with orders for 250,000 units. When he told Kassar that he wanted to begin manufacturing, Kassar derailed his plans. Despite the impressive number of orders, Kassar did not want to manufacture a game system that would compete with the VCS. Cosmos was never manufactured.

Alcorn and Hector long claimed that Kassar refused to manufacture the Cosmos because it represented competition for the VCS, but some of the people who tried the game console disagree. There were questions about the play value of its games.

> Cosmos was an attempt to do tomorrow's tech today. The holograms were only window dressing. The play action and the interest level proved to be very low. It was a cosmetic advance and a game-play setback.
>
> It was one of those things that looks like an advance, but it really isn't.
>
> **—Arnie Katz, the first full-time video-game journalist,**
> ***Electronic Games***

Kassar's decision to mothball Cosmos infuriated Alcorn, and he left the company. He hoped to receive the same retirement benefits that Bushnell, Williams, and Keenan were enjoying. According to Alcorn, being put "on the beach" by Manny Gerard meant receiving an expense account, a monthly check, and a company car.

> At that point I realized that if they were going to refuse this product, they weren't going to do any new products. And they never did. Atari developed several new products, but none of them ever appeared until after Ray left the company.

> So I said to myself, "All I do is develop new product that never comes out. Why would I want to be there?" I was getting huge bonuses, six-figure bonuses, but I just said, "Good-bye, I'm out of here."
>
> **—Al Alcorn**

Alcorn's plans, however, nearly did not come to pass. According to Warner Communications, Alcorn was not entitled to the same retirement package as Bushnell and Keenan. Warner attorneys claimed that Alcorn had negotiated his severance separate from the other board members and that he was not entitled to the same bonus-pool compensation.

By this time, Atari controlled 75 percent of the lucrative home video-game market and VCS sales were nearing $2 billion per year. The 1 percent of a bonus pool that Bushnell and Keenan received represented a substantial income. The case went to court.

> When we bought the company, everybody was represented by the same counsel except Al. He had separate counsel. I still remember those guys reading every page. The documentation doesn't have Al's name on it.
>
> Al's suit was that somehow the documents were wrong. Warner settled with him for other reasons, but I believe to the tips of my toes that he was wrong.
>
> The issue at hand was that the other guys kept 1 percent of the bonus pool. I think that's what it was about. Atari suddenly becomes this money gusher that got to be worth a goddamned shit load of money. I mean, that's the issue in a nutshell.
>
> Afterward, I said this to him, "Al, I know you believe you are right, and as surely as you believe you are right, I believe you are wrong." There was nothing personal in that. We had a fundamental disagreement about the facts, and we'll all go to hell without knowing any more about it.
>
> **—Manny Gerard, former executive, Warner Communications**

Warner settled and Alcorn, Atari's first full-time engineer, retired "to the beach."

Golden Age Begins

In 1978, Cinematronics released *Space Wars,* a coin-operated arcade version of Steve Russell's computer game that improved on the original by incorporating vector graphics.* Cinematronics was founded by Jim Pierce, Dennis Parte, and Gary Garrison in El Cajon, California, in 1975. Over the next few years, Parte and Garrison sold most of their shares in the business to Tom "Papa" Stroud.[1] Cinematronics and its games went fairly unnoticed until MIT graduate Larry Rosenthal joined the company. Rosenthal, who had done his master's thesis on *Spacewar,* the game created by MIT's Tech Model Railroad Club, had created a processor powerful and economical enough to run a full-scale version of the PDP Computer classic in an arcade machine. He convinced Stroud and Pierce to manufacture a game based on *Spacewar* using his processing technology. Appropriately enough, the game was called *Space Wars.*

Rosenthal's vector graphics technology gave him several advantages over designers using raster-scan screens. Images drawn with vector graphics can have sharp edges and crisp shapes. At the time, most raster-scan games had crude shapes—cars looked like rectangles, and people and animals looked like doodles. By contrast, vector graphics enabled designers to create fairly elaborate line art with stark contrast. Early vector-graphics hardware could not generate colors, so many companies placed colored plastic overlays on their games to create the illusion of color.

Feeling that he was not being paid enough for his innovations, Rosenthal left Cinematronics and tried to take his processing technology with him. Pierce and Stroud sued. The case was settled with Rosenthal selling his technology back to the company.

Vector graphics also enabled Cinematronics' game designers to animate more independent objects simultaneously than their competitors. Thanks to

---

*There are two kinds of monitors—vector and raster scan. Raster-scan technology, used in televisions, is based on an electronic beam painting images of the screen by constantly drawing and redrawing every row. Rather than going row by row, vector screens draw images by tracing lines from point to point, making them unsuitable for drawing pictures but excellent for displaying high-resolution outlines. Vector, or X-Y graphics, are displayed as lines. Rather than drawing an entire screen, a vector-graphics generator creates independent objects. The games *Asteroids, Battlezone,* and *Star Castle* were vector graphics games, as was *Space Wars.*

his vector-beam technology, the first game from Rosenthal's designer had forty independent objects at a time. Most raster-scan games had fewer than ten moving objects on a single screen.

After *Space Wars,* Cinematronics released a few more games that tapped into the science-fiction mania created by George Lucas's *Star Wars* movies. *Star Castle,* for instance, featured a Death Star–like space fortress with a giant cannon. Players flew tiny spaceships around the fortress, pecking away at its shields until they created a hole deep enough to destroy the fortress by shooting deep into its heart.

In 1981, Cinematronics released *Tail Gunner,* the first video game to feature three-dimensional animated objects.* In this game, players used a small chrome-plated joystick to target a gun in the rear of a large spaceship. The game was played from the first-person perspective—the player looked directly through the gunning station window, rather than over the shoulder of a character in the game. Because of the 3D effects, enemy fighters could turn and fly away rather than simply pass the ship.

Cinematronics emerged as one of the more successful companies in the wake of the *Space Invaders* phenomena. The company's biggest hit, however, would come with another innovative technology.

The Golden Days of Atari Coin-Op

In 1980, an Atari engineer named Howie Delman created a powerful vector-graphics generator for coin-op games. The first game that used his hardware was *Lunar Lander*—a game based on a common exercise in physics classes that was adapted for arcade use by Rich Moore. In this game, players had to dock a lunar lander on the moon, using limited fuel and dealing with a realistic simulation of the physics of lunar gravity. In order to succeed, players had to conserve fuel by using their thrusters as little as possible.

To dress up their game, Atari engineers created a massive two-handled lever for controlling the lander's booster engines. Springs on the lever made it snap back in place when it was released. Unfortunately, some younger players got their faces too close to the lever, resulting in complaints about children being hit in the face when the lever snapped back in place.

---

*Though *Night Driver,* a driving simulation published by Atari in 1977, featured 3D pylons along the side of the road, *Tail Gunner* is generally acknowledged as the first true 3D game.

Though *Lunar Lander* was never particularly successful, its vector-graphics generator was the impetus of Atari's most successful coin-operated game. Lyle Rains, vice president of the coin-operated games division, had an idea for a game in which players cleared an area of space by shooting asteroids flying around a small ship.

Rains described his idea to programmer Ed Logg and suggested that the asteroids should repeatedly get smaller when the ship shot them. Logg, who held a master's degree in math from Stanford University, thought he could expand the idea into a working game. He had recently completed the game *Super Breakout* and wanted to start his next project.

> Lyle Rains called me into his office and said, "I have this idea for a game in which you shoot asteroids." He said we needed something that keeps players from doing nothing, so I suggested throwing a saucer out to keep the player alert.
>
> I said, "Sure, I'll go do that." So I went up and started the project.
>
> I wanted high resolution. If you tried to put a little ship like the ship in *Asteroids* up on standard resolution, it would look like garbage; you couldn't tell what it was. Part of the deal I had with Lyle was that I'd go vector because, at the time, its high resolution was 1024 x 768, and at that resolution, the game would look nice.
>
> **—Ed Logg**

Within one week, Logg had a preliminary version of *Asteroids* running on his workstation. Within six weeks, the game was nearly complete. It featured the same basic control scheme as *Computer Space* and *Space Wars*. Players directed a small spaceship with five buttons—rotate left, rotate right, thruster rockets, fire, and hyperspace. When players jumped into hyperspace, they reappeared in a randomly selected spot on the screen or the ship blew up if they were hit by an asteroid or UFO while coming out of hyperspace.

The game began with a small spaceship in the center of the screen. Asteroids began floating toward the ship from every direction. Players had to rotate and move the ship to avoid getting bombarded, while shooting the advancing rocks into dust.

Asteroids had two classes of UFOs—large, slow-moving ones that fired a few wild shots while crossing the screen, and small, speedy ones shooting smart bullets that homed in on the player's ship. Around Atari, the saucers were known as Mr. Bill and Sluggo (after characters in a series of Clay Nation skits on the NBC comedy show *Saturday Night Live*), but when the nicknames were mentioned in an interview, a lawyer from NBC sent Atari a cease-and-desist order.

Players received 200 points for destroying large UFOs and 1,000 points for shooting small ones. Like *Space Invaders, Asteroids* rewarded players with extended lives at regular intervals.

The audience for coin-operated games had matured along with the industry in the seven years since Nolan Bushnell first created *Computer Space.* People were not intimidated by the controls in Cinematronics' remake of *Space Wars,* and they flocked to *Asteroids.*

In the beginning, most players lasted less than one minute per quarter. When players learned to maneuver and shoot, they could make their games last for hours. One teenager set the world's endurance record for *Asteroids* when he played a game for more than 36 hours. He earned so many free ships while playing that he was able to leave the game running and take breaks for meals.

Atari sold more than 70,000 *Asteroids* machines in the United States. The game did not do as well in Europe and Asia, however. Only about 30,000 units were sold overseas.

Logg's fellow designers later nicknamed him "Golden Boy" because of his long string of hits.

Inside Atari Coin-Op

The culture within Atari's coin-operated games division encouraged individuality. The quiet ones in the group were Ed Logg and Lyle Rains. Logg did not smoke, drink, or take drugs. He earned the respect of other department members by creating the most successful games. His string of hits included *Super Breakout, Asteroids, Centipede, Gauntlet,* and *Steel Talons.*

Like Logg, Lyle Rains was generally serious in nature but able to adjust to working with the wilder members of the division. According to some coin-op engineers, Rains never lost track of his executive status. Some programmers considered him guarded. One of the departmental jokes involved Rain's administrative assistant, an Asian woman from Hawaii who pronounced his name "Wyle Wains."

> She could say luau and Lanai, but for some reason she couldn't say Lyle.
>
> **—Lyle Rains**

After Bushnell left Atari, the people in the coin-operated games division began feeling alienated from other Atari personnel. Though they created many major hits—and Atari's bestselling cartridges were based on their arcade hits—the coin-operated game designers felt unappreciated by Ray Kassar, who focused most of his attention on home sales. Even worse, Kassar offered more praise to designers who adapted arcade games for the VCS than to the coin-op engineers who first created them.

> The kinds of things that went on were just wild. We were the company renegades. Atari, at that point in the early 1980s, was growing at an enormous clip, and coin-op really didn't grow too much. It stayed pretty small.
>
> Even though we were creating a lot of the titles that were the cornerstone for the consumer part of our business, we were kind of anonymous to a certain extent within the company because we were so small. But, by the same token, we didn't feel like we were going to take any crap from anybody either.
>
> **—Ed Rotberg, creator of *Battlezone***

> Ray always came off aloof to us. Outside of official tours, he only made one unannounced visit to the division, and that one day, nobody was in engineering. We all went out to see *Raiders of the Lost Ark*.
>
> I played poker with him once at a distributor meeting down in Pebble Beach. Nobody introduced me as the guy who did *Asteroids,* but I think he knew who I was.
>
> **—Ed Logg**

Coin-op's ironic sense of self often manifested itself in mischievous pranks. Kassar told *Fortune* magazine that Atari's game designers were a bunch of "highstrung prima donnas." The day after the interview was published, the entire division came to work wearing T-shirts that said, "I'm just another high-strung prima donna superstar."

An engineer made fun of Atari's slogan, "We take fun seriously," by circulating a memo that looked like an employment ad. "Looking for pilot. Must be able to fly at night without lights. Must have experience flying below radar range. Knowledge of Colombia-U.S. routes a plus. Must be comfortable handling large sums of cash. Atari. We take fun intravenously. Atari Recreation Pharms [short for Pharmaceuticals] Division."

The engineer was nearly fired.

A few months later, the entire division produced the "Outstanding in Our Field" video, a home movie–style spoof of life at Atari. The video took its name from a skit in which the narrator, Owen Rubin, describes the company's coin-operated engineers as outstanding in their field. As he speaks, the video shows the entire division standing in an empty field.

In one skit, two engineers heave an empty coin-operated cabinet from the top of their building. The narrator explains that "Not all of Atari's games are successful, but we know what to do with those," as the cabinet hits the pavement and shatters.

Two of the skits on the tape lampooned company commercials. One showed a young couple very absorbed in a game of Atari *Football.* The game is clearly a mismatch. The man, hardware engineer Howie Delman, is enjoying himself even though he is losing. As the camera backs away, it reveals that the woman is topless.

In the other parody, Ed Rotberg pretends he is a used-car salesman trying to sell an *Asteroids Deluxe** machine. "How much would you expect to pay?" Rotberg asks. "$3,900? $2,900?" He reveals the real price—$4,387. "Hell, no. We fuck you over completely!"

In another skit, the company's top designers visit "Club Atari," an Old Spaghetti Factory restaurant that they dressed up to look like a bordello. The programmers are greeted by women dressed in camisoles and clipped-up stockings as they straggle in. (Dona Bailey, probably the woman who had the greatest impact on arcade games as the cocreator of *Centipede,* appears in the video as one of the women of Club Atari.) Though they have two women each, the programmers congregate around an *Asteroids Deluxe* machine and forget about the club's other pleasures.

---

* A number of industry people, including coin-op game executives, acknowledged that *Asteroids Deluxe* was not one of Atari's better games.

Frank Ballouz, the coin-op division's marketing manager, also appears on the video. In his skit, he determines a game's future by throwing a dart. On the wall of his office is a dartboard with four cards taped around it. "Kill it." "Make 1,000." "Make 10,000." A fifth card, in the bull's-eye says, "Make 100,000."

Ballouz had a reputation for handling coin-op humor with stoicism. A group of engineers once smuggled a large ice sculpture of a swan into Ballouz's hotel room during a trade show in Chicago. When he returned to the room, he found the heavy sculpture in his bed. Ballouz dragged the sculpture to his bathtub and had to shower beside the unmelted portion of the statue the next morning.

Once Al Alcorn and Gene Lipkin dropped in on Ballouz while he was making an important telephone call. He ignored them. To get his attention, Lipkin leaned over Ballouz's desk and started a fire in his in-box. Ballouz responded by telling the person on the telephone, "A couple of VPs just lit the papers on my desk on fire. If it's all right with them, it's okay with me," and continued his conversation.

Coin-op even launched a little war with the building facilities department.

> Facilities decided to reserve some parking spots for themselves in front of our building so that no one else would have them. They would come out and paint lines on the spots, and every time they painted the lines, we would go out with a can of black spray paint and paint over their lines.
>
> Within 15 minutes there was no facilities parking
>
> No matter how many times they came out there, we would go out and paint the lines over again.
>
> **—Ed Rotberg**

Despite their minor rebellions, the engineers of Atari's coin-op division maintained incredibly tough standards. They seldom duplicated existing games. With only a few notable exceptions such as *Asteroids Deluxe* and *Space Duel,* programmers were not allowed to remake games already published. Other companies made new versions of *Space Invaders;* Atari looked for new ideas.

> Until about 1986, the attitude was that every game had to be completely new, completely different. It was much like saying if anybody ever did a

> fighting game, we shouldn't do a fighting game because that would be a derivative product.
>
> That kept the market very flexible. I think the players in the arcades in the 1980s were a lot more flexible because every time they went to the arcades and tried an Atari game, they were challenged to learn an entirely new control scheme, a new way of life.

—Mark Cerny, creator of *Marble Madness*

Another unwritten rule around the coin-operated division was that programmers never had their first game published. The rule was dubbed "Theurer's Law" after Dave Theurer, whose first game was *Four-Player Soccer*—a game that did not do particularly well.

Before manufacturing games, Atari tested prototype games in selected arcades to gauge player response. If a game had strong earnings, the company sent it to manufacturing. If a game did poorly, its design team could either find ways to improve it or abandon it altogether.

Atari coin-op had two unofficial in-house tests—the Stubben Test and the In-House Approval test. The Stubben Test, named for Atari *Football* designer Dave Stubben, was a measure of game durability. By most accounts, Stubben, who stood about six-feet-five and weighed 275 pounds, liked to break things. Once, while joking around with other Atari engineers at the lodge at Pebble Beach, Stubben kicked a door in. They tried to repair the damage using toothpaste as caulking.

When engineers wanted to test the durability of their designs, they took the games to Stubben. Few games ever survived. One man bragged that he had created an impregnable coin-drop door. Stubben smashed it in with one kick of his cowboy boot. He bent one joystick in half and ripped another controller right out of a cabinet.

While making the game *Paperboy,* Dave Ralston and John Salwitz decided to use handlebars instead of a joystick and had handlebars welded to the machine. When Salwitz told Mark Cerny, a skinny, brainy, 18-year-old who probably weighed less than 150 pounds, that the prototype was ready for the Stubben Test, Cerny pried the handlebars off himself. A dejected Salwitz took the handlebars back to the lab and looked for another way to attach them.

The other in-house test, and the programmers' first indication about how much players would like their game in the arcades, was the reaction the games got around Atari. While engineers built their prototypes, other coin-op employees often entered their labs and asked to play them. If a game was good, it usually developed a following. With *Asteroids* and *Tempest,* Ed Logg and Dave Theurer had to chase people away from their workstations.

The Rivalry

> In the late 1970s and early 1980s, our main competitor was Atari. I always looked at it as we had a hit, they had a hit, etc. It was great because we were creating a constant interest out there. Regardless of who had it, there was always something new, and people put their quarters in the slot and enjoyed what they were playing.
>
> **—David Marofske, former president, Midway Games**

Atari's biggest competitor was Midway games. Cash-rich Bally, a company renowned for slot machines and casinos, purchased Midway in the 1970s. By purchasing Midway, a major video-game distributor, Bally entered the electronics industry and acquired new technologies.

Since Taito executives decided to market their own games in the United States after their success with *Space Invaders,* Midway either needed to license games from a new partner or needed to begin developing games in-house. Midway found a partner in Namco, Atari's former distributor in Japan. In the beginning of 1980, Midway imported *Galaxian,* a game that improved upon the *Space Invaders* theme.

In *Galaxian,* players controlled a spaceship that moved laterally across the bottom of the screen and fired shots toward the top. Unlike *Space Invaders,* *Galaxian* had a color screen. The player's spaceship was white and red with yellow torpedoes, the alien ships had many colors, and the background in the game had a field of colorful twinkling stars.

Galaxian was more difficult than *Space Invaders.* Rather than marching in straight lines across the screen, the alien ships in *Galaxian* swooped down in changing formations. Though its profits were only a fraction of the money brought in by *Space Invaders, Galaxian* was one of the most successful games of its time.

> In those days, the [*Space Invader*] games became exceedingly popular in
> Japan, to the point that people were just going crazy over [them]. As their
> popularity began to wane, we introduced *Galaxian*. I must say that *Galaxian*
> was a far superior game.
>
> As you will recall, the *Invader* game was black and white, and it has ver-
> tical and horizontal movements only, whereas *Galaxian* was in color and the
> enemies attacked from various directions. So it was a significant improve-
> ment over the *Invader* game.
>
> **—Masaya Nakamura, founder, Namco**

Distributing games created by Namco and other foreign partners, Midway
challenged Atari's leadership in the arcade market.

Atari responded with *Missile Command*. Dave Theurer had just finished *Four-
Player Soccer* when a team leader named Steve Calfee suggested he make the game.

> *Missile Command* was based upon an old game called *Missile Radar* that
> Nolan had seen before he started Atari. In that game you tried to intercept
> missiles before they hit your base. We always brought this up at brainstorm-
> ing sessions.
>
> **—Steve Bristow**

> Calfee called me into his office and said, "Dave, we have something we want
> you to work on next. We want you to explore the idea of the U.S. being in-
> vaded by the USSR. We want your game to have this radar screen that shows
> missiles coming in."
>
> I walked out of his office and my spine was tingling because I just had this
> feeling that this was going to be fun and it was going to be hot. It was so
> relevant—that was in the middle of the Cold War.
>
> I just had this really, really good feeling about it.
>
> **—Dave Theurer**

Theurer, a relatively mild-mannered person who had to struggle to stay interested in *Soccer,* fell in love with the idea. Though he was known throughout
the division for constantly editing and re-editing his work, he managed to finish

Missile Command in approximately six months. Theurer had to make only minimal alterations to get the final version of the game ready for location tests.

> I just sat down and drew up a basic game idea, which is pretty much the way it turned out, except we got rid of the radar screen because that was too distracting. I hate radar screens because you can't see what's going on half of the time.
>
> **—Dave Theurer**

The finished game was fairly simple. Players launched missiles from three silos to protect six cities located at the bottom of the screen. The silos had limited numbers of missiles, so players could not waste them by shooting wildly. Once the missiles ran out, players had to sit and watch their cities explode.

Missile Command was controlled with a Magic 8-ball–sized trackball similar to the one used in *Football*. It was the perfect controller because it enabled players to move the aiming device quickly and accurately.

The game began with missiles appearing like streaks in the sky above the player's silos and cities. Players launched defensive strikes by firing their missiles in the path of the oncoming threat. As the game progressed, enemy jets and UFOs flew across the top of the screen and dropped clusters of warheads and an occasional bomb. If players were unable to hit enemy aircraft before they launched clusters, they'd have to waste shots mopping up.

> We added railroad tracks between the cities and missile bases. The cities were manufacturing the missiles and shipping them on the railroad tracks to the bases. If the incoming bombs blew up the railroad tracks, the missiles were stranded.
>
> It was all too complicated and we figured that it was going to confuse people, so we threw all the railroad track stuff away.
>
> We had submarines for a while, but we decided that it was confusing, so the submarines went.
>
> We were going to have a localities-option for the operator to set the machines to for the east coast or west coast or middle America. Then we'd label the cities according to where they were. But that got to be too complicated.
>
> **—Dave Theurer**

One day Theurer came up with an idea for creating an enormous explosion. When players lost their last city, he would make it look as if the entire screen had been destroyed by an atomic blast. When Calfee saw the explosion, he suggested putting the words *The End* in the middle of it.

> One lunchtime I had this urge to try something cool—I could make this huge explosion on the screen. So I just whipped it up one lunch hour. Steve Calfee walked through on his way back from lunch and said, "Why don't you put 'The End' in there?"
>
> So I stuck it in.
>
> Everybody liked it. The explosion made it into the movie *Terminator II*.
>
> **—Dave Theurer**

A Game About Eating

> *Space Invaders* was an outrageous hit, but it was nothing compared to the one that was to eventually become the icon of the video game business; and that was *Pac-Man*.
>
> **—Eddie Adlum**

Pac-Man was the invention of Toru Iwatani, a young pinball enthusiast who joined Namco shortly after graduating from college in 1977. Iwatani wanted to create pinball machines, but Namco was only manufacturing video games. As a compromise, he created *Gee Bee, Bomb Bee,* and *Cutie Q,* video pinball games that reached the United States in limited quantities.* Namco released *Bomb Bee* and *Cutie Q* in 1979, the same year *Galaxian* was released in Japan.

In April 1979, Iwatani decided to try something other than pinball. He wanted to make a nonviolent game, something female players might enjoy. He decided to build his game around the Japanese word *taberu,* which means "to eat."

---

* *Gee Bee* was the only game manufactured by Namco in 1978, and *Bomb Bee* was one of the only games manufactured by the company the following year.

> At that time, as you will recall, there were many games associated with kill-
> ing creatures from outer space.
>
> I was interested in developing a game for the female game enthusiast.
> Rather than developing the character first, I started out with the concept of
> eating and focused on the Japanese word *"taberu,"* which means "to eat."
>
> **—Toru Iwatani**

Iwatani was assigned a nine-man team to convert his concept into a game.
The first thing he produced was the character Pac-Man, which was a simple
yellow circle with a wedge cut away for a mouth.

> The actual figure of Pac-Man came about as I was having pizza for lunch. I
> took one wedge and there it was, the figure of Pac-Man.
>
> **—Toru Iwatani**

The next step was to create Pac-Man's enemies. Since the game was supposed to appeal to the female audience, Iwatani felt that the monsters had to
be cute. He settled on colorful "ghosts" that looked like mop heads with big
eyes. The maze, dots, and power pills came next. It took just over a year to
produce a working prototype of the game.

> The idea came up in April 1979, and the project team was put together in
> May. Location testing was a year later, in May of 1980. A private showing was
> done in June of 1980, and in July the game went on sale.
>
> **—Toru Iwatani**

The final game was exceptionally simple. Players used a joystick to guide
Pac-Man as he swallowed a line of 240 dots in the maze. Four ghosts swept
through the maze as well, trying to catch Pac-Man. The player lost if the ghosts
caught Pac-Man before he cleared all of the dots.

There were two ways to earn bonus points in *Pac-Man*. The first was to eat
fruit and objects. Cherries, strawberries, bells, keys, and other objects appeared
near the center of the maze at different intervals. Each time players cleared
the maze, the value of the fruit increased.

The other way of earning bonus points was to eat the ghosts. There were four large dots, or "power pills," located near the corners of the maze. When Pac-Man ate the power pills, the ghosts turned blue and Pac-Man could eat them for a brief time.

Around Namco, the reaction to Iwatani's game was not terribly enthusiastic. Namco produced four games in 1980. While *Pac-Man* was generally recognized as a promising game, most executives preferred *Rally-X,* a similar game in which players maneuvered a race car around a maze, collecting flags while avoiding other race cars. The other Namco games that came out in 1980 were *King and Balloon* and *Tank Battalion.*

> I did not imagine that *Pac-Man* would be an international hit of the magnitude that it was and is to date. People know *Pac-Man*. People who don't even know about video games know about *Pac-Man*. So, no, I didn't realize that it was going to be the hit that it is.
>
> **—Masaya Nakamura**

Before Namco showed *Pac-Man* to Midway, one change was made to the game. *Pac-Man* was originally named *Puck-Man*, a reference to the puck-like shape of the main character. Nakamura worried about American vandals changing the "P" to an "F." To prevent any such occurrence, he changed the name of the game.

When Midway president David Marofske saw Namco's four new games, he thought *Rally-X* was the hottest prospect.

> There were actually four pieces that Namco was showing at that time. Of the two best games, one being *Pac-Man* and the other one being *Rally-X,* I sort of thought that *Rally-X* was the favorite.
>
> **—David Marofske, former president, Midway**

Buyer and analyst response at the October AMOA show further confirmed that *Rally-X* was the best game in the group. Of all the video games at that show, *Rally-X* received the most favorable comments.

Once they hit the street, however, *Pac-Man* quickly overshadowed *Rally-X.* More than 100,000 *Pac-Man* machines sold in the United States. Several companies published *Pac-Man* strategy guides. *Pac-Man* appeared on the cover of *Time* magazine, inspired a hit song, and translated into a popular Saturday morning cartoon show. Some arcades purchased entire rows of *Pac-Man* machines.

The video-game industry changed in the wake of *Pac-Man's* success. Before *Pac-Man,* the most popular theme for games had been shooting aliens. After *Pac-Man,* most games involved mazes. Arnie Katz, editor and founder of *Electronic Games,* the first magazine about the industry, called these games "maze chases." Soon there were maze chases involving mice *(Mappy),* eyeballs *(Eyes),* penguins *(Pengo),* fish *(Piranha),* even a personified fire hydrant that slurped up water and spat it at bipedal flames. Like Pac-Man, the heroes of some of these games were relatively helpless. Other games, such as *Targ* and *Eyes,* were tank battles set in mazes.

The video-game business quickly became a wildly lucrative enterprise, and arcades grew to be as common as convenience stores. Hotels replaced gift shops with arcades. Grocery stores placed video games near their entrances. Some doctors even placed games in their waiting rooms.

To reflect the growth in the video-game side of the business, the Music Operators Association changed its name to the Amusement and Music Operators Association.

Despite the success of his game, Iwatani never received much attention. Rumors emerged that the unknown creator of *Pac-Man* had left the industry when he received only a $3,500 bonus for creating the highest-grossing video game of all time. They were untrue.

> I don't recall receiving anything special, although I am told that I received some recognition in my semi-annual bonus.
>
> **—Toru Iwatani**

According to Namco president Masaya Nakamura, Iwatani received a very small bonus—less than $3,500.

> Maybe he received some bonus but nothing really to write home about. He did not leave the company. He now performs a very important function within our R & D group. He's the general manager.
>
> —**Masaya Nakamura**

In Japanese business, summer and winter bonuses are considered an important part of the overall employment package. Japanese employers seldom award bonuses to employees for performing the work they were hired to do. Iwatani's next game, *Libble Rabble,* did not create much of a stir in Japan and was never exported to the United States. Shortly after the release of *Libble Rabble,* Nakamura promoted Iwatani to manager of research and development as a token of respect.

A New Competitor

Pac-Man was not the only overlooked game at the AMOA show that year. Few people noticed when Williams Electronics, the leading pinball manufacturer, unveiled its first video game since *Paddle Ball,* a rip-off of *Pong.* The game was called *Defender.*

Eugene Jarvis, creator of *Defender,* had broken into the amusement industry designing wide-body pinball machines at Atari. He realized the pinball division would be closed shortly after Bushnell left the company, so he quit and spent a few months vacationing in Costa Rica. When he returned, another Atari pinball veteran named Steve Ritchie asked him to come to Chicago to help produce pinball games for Williams. They teamed up to build three groundbreaking pinball games— *Lazerball, Firepower,* and *Gorgar.**

In February 1980, Williams executives decided to enter the arena of video games. They asked Jarvis to design their first title. He had to start by designing a hardware platform for running his game.

> The first step was getting a hardware system going. We debated the merits of color versus black and white. We kind of said, "Okay, we've got to go with the future, we've got to be hip dudes, so we're going to go color."

---

* *Gorgar* was the first electronic game to feature synthesized speech.

> The next question was deciding how many colors.
>
> For *Defender*, we decided we'd go all out and make every pixel on the screen capable of sixteen colors. It was like, "Wow! This was more colors than you'll ever need."
>
> I don't even know if the game had a name at that point.
>
> **—Eugene Jarvis**

Jarvis, who described himself as a fan of violence and action, wanted to give his game a title that would justify the game's violence.

> I had to have this whole justification for why you were there and what you were doing. A lot of games fall short. They just put you there, and all of a sudden you're beating people up and you start to wonder, "Why am I beating these people up?"
>
> There was actually an old TV show called *The Defenders* about attorneys back in the 1960s, and I kind of liked that show. You know, if you're defending something, you're being attacked, and you can do whatever you want.
>
> **—Eugene Jarvis**

According to Jarvis, space battles provided the most popular theme for games at the time. Placing *Defender* in space appealed to Jarvis because it covered up the inadequacies of his hardware.

> At the time, space was just the happening thing. It was very easy to do space because space is very abstract.
>
> We had limited graphic ability—just making a person look like a person was very difficult. It was almost as if you wanted to go to more abstract outer-world themes because that way people couldn't say, "You know, that thing looks like shit."
>
> **—Eugene Jarvis**

Jarvis's first inclination was to create a game similar to *Space Invaders.* After several aborted attempts, he began trying to design something closer to *Asteroids.* He liked the controls in *Asteroids,* which let players go anywhere on the screen.

When his programmer began creating the game, Jarvis changed his mind because he didn't like the way the game anchored him into a single screen.

In his next attempt, Jarvis created a world that was far larger than the screen.

> I came up with scrolling the screen, making the field larger than the actual screen. The *Defender* world turned out to be three and one-half screens or seven screens or something. Having a universe that was larger than the screen, that was just a huge, huge breakthrough.
>
> My original idea was to go one direction. I tended to want to go left to right. My friend told me that was bogus, that you needed to be able to go backward. Changing the program to make it go backward was a pain in the ass, but he finally talked me into it.
>
> **—Eugene Jarvis**

By July, Jarvis found himself far behind schedule. He had his spaceship, his scrolling world, and his controls, but he still needed to create allies to defend and enemies to attack. He needed to finish the game before the upcoming trade show, which took place in mid-September.

Jarvis decided to defend astronauts—humans in space. He spent weeks creating tiny men who actually walked on the surface of the planet while players shot enemy aliens out of the sky. The process took too long. Jarvis's boss began pushing him to finish the game, even if it meant taking the astronauts out.

> Somewhere during that time, I just wanted to put all my stuff in a box and quit. I don't know why I didn't actually quit. Everyone was hassling me on spending so much time on these little astronaut guys.
>
> Around this time, a really talented guy joined the team. His name was Sam Dicker. He was about nineteen years old.
>
> He did some really incredible effects for the game. All of a sudden, we were blowing up things, we had some sound going, and it was starting to get fun.
>
> **—Eugene Jarvis**

Jarvis did not finish the game on time. He ended up spending several hours completing *Defender* on the floor of the show.

Defender was Williams Electronics' biggest seller. More than 55,000 units were placed worldwide.

In making *Defender,* Jarvis had created one of the toughest games in arcade history. Players controlled a fighter craft as it defended the inhabitants of a small planet, ten astronauts in stasis, from alien abduction.

In the beginning, the alien invaders slowly dropped from the sky in an effort to snare an astronaut and fly back into space. When aliens escaped with an astronaut, they turned into fast-moving mutants. If the aliens managed to capture every astronaut, the planet exploded and the player found himself flying through hyperspace being chased by a seemingly endless supply of aliens.

Defender had an elaborate control panel with a joystick for controlling altitude and five buttons for firing weapons, dropping smart bombs, accelerating, changing directions, and jumping into hyperspace.

Beginning players seldom lasted more than a few seconds on *Defender,* and mastering the game became a badge of honor. Some players let the aliens capture their astronauts, then shot them as they tried to escape. They would catch the astronauts as they fell back toward the planet and carry them on the front of their fighter. Other players preferred to let the aliens take the humans because so many aliens attacked them in hyperspace that they easily built up their scores. Different players came up with their own solutions for conquering *Defender's* very intense play.

> I came into an arcade on a Friday night and there was a crowd of people four deep around this game, putting in their quarters and lasting maybe 35, 40 seconds. *Defender* was a very ferocious game—very difficult controls.
>
> They were seeing the special effects in the game and they just, they wanted to do it. And one after the other, they were throwing quarters in. *Defender* made $700 its first week. I have never seen a quarter-a-play video game make money like that—not before or after *Defender*. It was the most phenomenal collection anyone had ever seen.
>
> It was a hell of a game. . . .
>
> **—Larry DeMar, video-game and pinball designer, Williams Electronics**

Battlezone

In November 1980, Atari released a game with an updated version of a familiar Atari theme—tank warfare. The game was titled *Battlezone*.

Though Ed Rotberg is credited with creating *Battlezone*, the game was a group effort from the beginning. Rotberg used Howie Delman's vector-graphics generator because it offered enough power to create a three-dimensional environment. He also asked other designers for help.

> The idea that we should do a first-person tank game came out of a company brainstorming session. Morgan Hoff was the project leader, Jed Margolin was the electrical engineer, and I did the programming.
>
> Roger Hector did the models [for the enemy tanks]. I went to Roger and said I needed something that looked like a tank but used as few lines as possible because we had only so much processing power back then.
>
> We needed a missile and we needed this and that, so Roger did all the artwork. He did the background as a line drawing that we had converted into a series of vectors, and there was a volcano in it.
>
> We worked in labs and I was in a lab with Owen Rubin, who would always come in and say, "When are you going to make the volcano active?"
>
> I was trying to make a game, and every day Rubin came in with, "When are you going to make the volcano active? When are you going to make the volcano active?"
>
> Finally, I said, "Look, I'm trying to make this game here. If you want the volcano active, write the damn code yourself."
>
> I came into work the next day and there, sitting on my desk, was a bunch of code. That's how we got the active volcano in *Battlezone*. It was really the only code in the game that was not written by me.
>
> **—Ed Rotberg**

Like *Sea Wolf, Battlezone* had a distinctive periscope-like viewer. Players pressed their faces against it to see the screen. The viewer in *Sea Wolf,* however, pivoted and was used to aim torpedoes. The one in *Battlezone* was a stationary plastic structure that enhanced the feeling of being inside a tank. It could not be used for aiming, however, since the player's tank only fired straight ahead.

To this day I don't like it [the viewer]. I was concerned with coin drop. It isolated players and gave them a feeling of immersion, but it blocked other people's view of the game.

—Ed Rotberg

In *Battlezone,* players used two large joysticks to maneuver their tanks as they hunted enemy vehicles. A radar scope in the top of the screen showed the position of enemy vehicles. The key to the game was using the scope to evade enemy attacks.

Battlezone featured several kinds of enemies—slow-moving standard tanks, super tanks, and anti-tank missiles. Sometimes flying saucers appeared as well.

Rotberg created a three-dimensional plain for his battlefields. In this silent world, Roger Hector's volcano could be seen spewing boulders along the horizon. Blocks and pyramids scattered throughout the plain added depth and provided players with cover from enemy attacks. Though all of the objects were shown as line art, *Battlezone's* realistic depiction of tank warfare attracted attention that Rotberg later came to resent.

CHAPTER 11

The Golden Age
(Part 2: 1981–1983)

We only mentioned *Space Invaders* and *Pac-Man,* but there were a few others that made it into that boom period, which lasted until June of 1982. It was only a short-lived thing, but it got everybody's attention, including the national media.

—Eddie Adlum

Ron's accountant called me up and said, "We've got to incorporate Ron." I started laughing and said, "Ron is nearly bankrupt. Why would we incorporate him?"

He said, "Don't you know? Nintendo is just going wild selling this *Donkey Kong* coin-op game."

—Howard Lincoln, chairman, Nintendo of America

Arcade's Biggest Year

In 1981, 15-year-old Steve Juraszek of Arlington Heights, Illinois, scored 15,963,100 points in a 16-hour game of *Defender*. He set a new world's record, became an instant celebrity, and got his picture in *Time* magazine. Local school officials were not impressed. The game began during school hours. Juraszek was banned from leaving school grounds for playing hooky.[1]

Arlington Heights was not the only town that saw a connection between video games and truancy. The Pittsburgh City Council enacted an ordinance that prohibited minors from playing video games during school hours and threatened to revoke the license of any arcade that ignored that ordinance.

Several small towns, including Babylon, New York, pushed for laws to monitor the operation of video-game arcades. In Oakland, California, the city council voted to ban minors from visiting arcades during school hours, after 10 P.M. on weeknights, and after midnight on weekends. A dispute over zoning laws between Aladdin's Castle, a large chain of arcades, and the city of Mesquite, Texas, ended up before the Supreme Court (*City of Mesquite v. Aladdin's Castle, Inc.*, 455 U.S. 283 [1982]).

Other countries also struggled with the growth of video games. In November 1981, Philippine president Ferdinand Marcos banned video games and gave arcade owners two weeks to destroy them.[2]

A *Time* magazine cover story reported that Americans dropped 20 billion quarters into video games in 1981 and that "video game addicts" spent 75,000 man-years playing the machines. The article went on to explain that the video-game industry earned twice as much money as all Nevada casinos combined, nearly twice as much money as the movie industry, and three times as much money as major league baseball, basketball, and football.[3]

America was covered with arcades. According to a *Play Meter Magazine* study, there were approximately 24,000 full arcades and 400,000 street locations. In all, according to the 1982 study, more than 1.5 million arcade machines were in operation in the United States.

Nameless Stars

Despite the popularity of their games, Atari's designers were forbidden to take credit for their work. Whether Atari president Ray Kassar thought competitors would try to buy his designers away or simply felt that they didn't deserve the publicity, he seldom allowed his designers to meet reporters and never let them put their names on their machines. When Steve Bloom interviewed Atari coin-op engineers in a book called *Video Invader*, he had to change their names. He referred to Dona Bailey and Ed Logg, creators of *Centipede*, as Dona Taylor and Ed Lodge.*

Tension continued to mount between game designers and management at Atari. By this time, such software companies as On-Line Systems** and Broderbund were making consumer versions of popular coin-op games for Apple, Atari, and Commodore home computers. Ken Williams, founder of On-Line, treated his designers like rock stars, lavishing them with publicity and bonus checks.

At Atari, only managers and executives received public accolades. Some coin-op engineers began referring to Lyle Rains as "Hollywood Lyle" because he appeared before the media so often. A number of publications mistakenly credited him with the creation of *Asteroids*.

Military Battlezone

Shortly after *Battlezone* was released, a group of retired Army generals contacted Atari. The officers wanted to license a more realistic version of the game to be used for training soldiers. The new version of the game would require several technical features and had to be built within a few months, in time to be demonstrated at an important trade show. Despite his vigorous protests, Ed Rotberg was asked to take the project.

> I didn't think it was a business that we should be getting into. You've got to remember what things were like in the late 1970s, and where those of us who were in the business came from—our cultural background. There were any number of jobs to be had by professional programmers in military industries or in military-related industries. Those of us who found our way to video

---

* Craig Kubey released *The Winner's Book of Video Games* the same year. Kubey's book was published by Warner Books, part of the Warner Communications empire that owned Atari. It listed Logg, Bailey, and several other Atari designers by their correct names.

** Later renamed Sierra On-Line.

> games . . . it was sort of a counter-culture thing. We didn't want anything to
> do with the military. I was doing games; I didn't want to train people to kill.
>
> Since *Battlezone* was my baby, and it was *Battlezone* that they wanted to
> convert, and there was a deadline to get it done, I agreed to do the proto-
> type if they [his bosses] would promise that I would have nothing to do with
> any future plans to do anything with the military. They gave that assurance
> to me, and I lost three months of my life working day and night and hardly
> ever seeing my wife.
>
> **—Ed Rotberg**

Military Battlezone was much more complex than the original game. In the
arcade game, players could only shoot straight ahead, and their projectiles
flew in a straight trajectory unaffected by gravity. The military version was
considerably more realistic.

> The changes were extensive. First of all, we were not modeling some fantasy
> tank, we were modeling an infantry fighting vehicle that had a turret that
> could rotate independently of the tank. It had a choice of guns to use. In-
> stead of a gravity-free cannon, you had ballistics to configure.
>
> You had to have identifiable targets because they wanted to train gun-
> ners to recognize the difference between friendly and enemy vehicles. So,
> there were a whole slew of different types of enemy vehicles and friendly
> vehicles that had to be drawn and modeled. Then we had to model the phys-
> ics of the different kinds of weapons.
>
> **—Ed Rotberg**

Rotberg deeply resented being forced to work on the military version of
Battlezone. His next project was a game called *Dragon Riders* that was based on the
novels of fantasy writer Ann MaCaffrey. Had it been completed, *Dragon Riders*
would have been the first game based on a novel. Atari never licensed
MaCaffrey's books and the game never made it out of production.

Rotberg's final project at Atari was a game called *Warp Speed.* This was a high-
speed outer-space flight simulation in which players attacked a well-armed
space fortress. Rotberg left Atari before the project was finished.

The people who completed *Warp Speed* decided to use the joystick from *Military Battlezone* on their game. Around this time, Atari struck a licensing deal with another Bay-area legend—film maker George Lucas. With its ships and activities altered to replicate the battle over the Death Star, and voices from the movie added to the game, the game was released as *Star Wars*.

Donkey Kong

> Our coin-op engineers were really tough, arrogant guys. They didn't believe anybody made a coin-op game as well as they did.
>
> One day they came in and they wanted to take the rights to manufacture a game called *Donkey Kong* for coin-op in the United States. What that told me, knowing our coin-op people, was that it must have been a hell of a game.
>
> **—Manny Gerard**

During the golden age of arcades, a few Japanese companies earned huge profits through U.S. operations. Namco prospered through its partnership with Midway. Taito had made so much money from *Space Invaders* that it opened its own U.S. operation—Taito America.

A few Japanese companies, nevertheless, seemed unable to crack the American market. One of these was Nintendo, a nearly 100-year-old playing-card manufacturer that had recently expanded into making toys and electronic games.

By 1980, Hiroshi Yamauchi, president of Nintendo Company Limited, decided that his company needed a U.S. office if it was going to break into the American arcade market. He hired his son-in-law, Minoru Arakawa, to establish an American operation.

Yamauchi did not hire Arakawa out of family loyalty. Arakawa had just spent three years overseeing the building of a Canadian condominium project for a Japanese construction firm. He had a proven track record as a manager. More important, he had experience running the North American office of a Japanese firm.

In April 1980, Arakawa set up an office in Manhattan and a warehouse in New Jersey. His first distributors were a couple of entrepreneurs named Ron Judy and Al Stone, who owned a Seattle-based trucking company but moonlighted as game resellers. They had been purchasing Nintendo arcade games through a firm in Hawaii and marketing them in the continental United States.

Arakawa offered to cover their expenses and pay them a large commission if they would become consultant-representatives of Nintendo of America.

> Ron and Al had a small trucking company, Chase Express, and I was their lawyer. They came in one day and said that they had discovered coin-operated video games. This was actually before they had been involved with Nintendo.
>
> They started importing Nintendo video games through Hawaii. These were games that Nintendo Company Ltd. produced and exported to the United States. Not a lot of games but a few.
>
> At some point they hooked up at a trade show with Mr. Arakawa, who by now had set up Nintendo of America. Mr. Arakawa engaged Ron and Al Stone on a consulting basis. The term of the deal was that they would be paid on a commission basis.
>
> Their responsibility was to go around and set up the distribution throughout the United States and Canada for Nintendo of America coin-op games.
>
> **—Howard Lincoln, chairman, Nintendo of America**

Their first game, *Radarscope,* did not sell well, even though it had done fairly well in Japan. Yamauchi told Arakawa that *Radarscope* would be a hit. Nintendo shipped 3,000 copies of the game to the United States.

Around this time, Arakawa discovered that locating his operation on the East Coast added two weeks to the time it took to ship games from Japan. He decided to relocate his headquarters to the West Coast and settled in Redmond, Washington.

Radarscope did not appeal to American audiences, and Judy and Stone were unable to sell all 3,000 units. Since Nintendo of America covered their expenses, they did not incur debts, but they also received very little income since they were being paid a straight commission.

> The fact that it was one of the most expensive games in the industry and we were not an established line with the American distributors . . . we had some difficulty selling the entire amount of the shipment from Japan.
>
> **—Al Stone**

> *Radarscope* and *Heavy Fire* and mediocre games were available. *Radarscope*
> was the number two game after *Pac-Man* [in Japan], so it was pretty popular
> . . . very popular at the September show, in Japan. And we had Ron Judy and
> Al Stone very excited [about bringing the game to America].
>
> It's a shooting game, like *Galaxian* from Namco but more sophisticated.
> We brought it to the United States . . . I think too many games, about
> 3,000 *Radarscopes*. We saw them pile up. We sold 1,000, and had 2,000 left.

—Minoru Arakawa, president, Nintendo of America

As president of Nintendo Co. Ltd., Hiroshi Yamauchi ran his company in a notoriously imperialistic style. Before taking over the family business, Yamauchi had his dying grandfather fire relatives working for Nintendo so that he could consolidate his power base. As Nintendo expanded operations from Hanafuda playing cards to toys, Yamauchi acted as sole judge of new products. If a concept appealed to him, it went to market. Since Yamauchi's instincts were almost always correct, Nintendo generally thrived.

Breaking into the American market, however, proved baffling to Yamauchi. Arakawa reported failure after failure. *Space Fever* did not attract business. Arcade owners did not like *Sheriff*. Judy and Stone were able to sell a scant 1,000 units of *Radarscope*, the game Yamauchi hoped would take America by storm. Two thousand *Radarscope* machines sat stacked in the New Jersey warehouse. If Yamauchi was going to establish Nintendo in the United States, he would need something that Americans had never seen before.

Fortunately, there was a project that looked very promising. In 1977, Yamauchi had hired a creative young college graduate with a degree in industrial design named Shigeru Miyamoto.

Miyamoto was somewhat of an anomaly in Kyoto, Japan. He played the banjo, loved bluegrass music, and collected Beatles albums. Above all else, Miyamoto loved designing toys. Years later, after establishing himself as the greatest designer in the video-game industry, Miyamoto told a reporter that he still wanted to design toys, not video games.

Ironically, one of Miyamoto's first jobs at Nintendo was to create the art for the outside panels of *Radarscope* and *Sheriff* cabinets. In 1979, Yamauchi called Miyamoto to his office and asked him if he could design an arcade game. Miyamoto excitedly said yes.

> What I wanted to do was to make fun toys, interesting toys. They [Yamauchi] knew that I had been doing kids' toys, but nobody expected me to get involved in the video-game business.
>
> When I was first hired, I did artwork for game cabinets. I was actually making some game characters before I started *Donkey Kong,* so when I knew that I was going to be given a chance to make a game, I was very excited.
>
> **—Shigeru Miyamoto, creator of *Donkey Kong***

Miyamoto did not have to worry about the technical aspects of game creation. The cabinets already existed—Yamauchi planned to build Miyamoto's game by converting unsold *Radarscope* machines. To make sure the project proceeded smoothly, Yamauchi assigned Gumpei Yokoi, the dean of Nintendo's engineering team, to oversee the implementation of Miyamoto's ideas.

Like Eugene Jarvis, Miyamoto began by inventing an elaborate story to explain his game. The story involved a gorilla escaping from its master, a carpenter, and kidnapping his girlfriend. First the gorilla climbed to the top of a seven-story construction site. When his master followed, the ape rolled barrels at him. Players helped the carpenter leap over the barrels as he followed the gorilla.

Once the carpenter reached the top of the foundation, the chase moved to a five-story structure made of steel girders. This time the carpenter had to avoid marching flames while pulling the pins that held the girders together.[*] Once the structure collapsed, the carpenter and his girlfriend were reunited.

Because of his desire to penetrate the American market, Yamauchi wanted the game to have an English name. Since Miyamoto spoke only a little English, he used a Japanese-English dictionary to find the correct words for the title. He wanted to name the game after the ape—"Stubborn Gorilla." Looking through the dictionary, Miyamoto selected the word *donkey* as a synonym for "stubborn" and the word *Kong* for "gorilla."

Masaya Nakamura may not have foreseen the success of *Pac-Man* and Michael Kogan may not have predicted the impact of *Space Invaders,* but Hiroshi

---

[*] The original version of the game also included a level where the carpenter chased the gorilla through a cement factory. The level involved jumping vats of cement on a conveyor belt. This level was not included in the Nintendo Entertainment System version of the game.

Yamauchi immediately recognized the potential of *Donkey Kong*. He called his son-in-law and told him that a new game was coming that would make Nintendo one of the hottest game companies in American arcades.

The news could not have come at a better time. Ron Judy and Al Stone had nearly bankrupted themselves, and Arakawa was having trouble covering the costs of his floundering operation. Around this time, Mario Segale, the landlord of Nintendo's warehouse, visited Arakawa to complain that the rent was late. After threats and angry words, Segale accepted Arakawa's promise that the money would arrive shortly. Arakawa later immortalized Segale by renaming Jumpman, the carpenter in *Donkey Kong*, Mario.

Arakawa wanted to file a trademark patent on the new game, so he asked Ron Judy to recommend a good lawyer. Judy and Stone took Arakawa to meet their lawyer, Howard Lincoln, the day they learned that Nintendo's new super game would be called *Donkey Kong*.

By this time they were deeply in debt and anxious to abandon Nintendo. The only reason they had stayed was Arakawa's solemn promise that the next game out of Japan would be a major hit. The name *Donkey Kong* did not inspire their confidence.

I remember that day. The fellow who was setting up the distribution for Nintendo Coin-Op was a client of mine named Ron Judy. Ron was compensated with a commission based on game sales. The games that had come in that year had not been strong, so Ron was really strung out.

Poor Ron. I can still see him sitting there when Mr. Arakawa said, "We have this new game and we need to get it trademarked. The name of the game is *Donkey Kong*."

And I said, "Pardon me. What was that? *Donkey Kong?* How do you spell that?"

I remember Ron saying, "Yeah. Can you believe that? *Donkey Kong!*" It was at a point in time when Ron was thinking, "What have I gotten myself into? None of these games have been great. I didn't earn any money, and now the final blow is a game called *Donkey Kong*, which even my lawyer can't understand."

—Howard Lincoln

Just as Al Alcorn had learned about *Pong*'s appeal by placing it in Andy Capp's Tavern, Arakawa discovered he had a hit by placing *Donkey Kong* in two Seattle bars—the Spot Tavern in South Seattle and Goldies, a bar near the University of Washington. Stone and Judy persuaded the managers of the bars to let them use their locations as test sites. When both test locations cleared more than $30 per day for an entire week, the managers asked for more machines.

It didn't take long for *Donkey Kong* to develop a following. Because of a lack of funds, Arakawa, Judy, and Stone converted the 2,000 *Radarscope* machines stockpiled in the warehouse into *Donkey Kong* machines themselves. Soon the entire inventory had been sold, and orders kept rolling in. Arakawa decided to manufacture more machines in the Nintendo of America warehouse in Redmond because it took too long to ship them from Japan.

> At any rate, the game went out to a few distributors who managed to get some operator to put it out before the playing public, and the thing broke out of the box. Smash hit!
>
> I caught the buzz early on, just from talking to distributors, and I flagged it in *RePlay* and said this was something to keep your eye on. It went crazy. I think they ended up selling 67,000 *Donkey Kongs*.
>
> **—Eddie Adlum**

The straight-commission pay schedule that had nearly bankrupted Ron Judy and Al Stone suddenly turned them into millionaires. Toward the end of 1981, Lincoln received a telephone call from their accountant. He had been expecting the accountant to call about filing their bankruptcy notice. Instead, the accountant asked Lincoln to incorporate them to protect their immense earnings.

Bug Shooter

After *Asteroids,* Ed Logg teamed up with Dona Bailey and created one of the few games that appealed to female players as well as male—*Centipede.*

Before going to Atari, Bailey spent three years at General Motors, where she helped design the microprocessor-based cruise control in the Cadillac Seville. In 1980, she applied for a job at Atari because she enjoyed playing video games. Once she got the job, she found herself in an odd position—the only female programmer in the coin-op division.

> I was doing this *New Yorker* profile on Nolan [Bushnell] and Dona was work-ing for him at Sente Games. What I really remember about her is that she was charming. Dona was one of my heroes because *Centipede* had always been one of my favorite, favorite, favorite games.
>
> I remember going out to dinner with Dona. She was just so anxious to talk to me because her dream in life was to be able to write for the *New Yorker,* and here I'm just this guy writing this profile on Nolan and talking about it.
>
> I said, "So it must be really cool making video games." And she said, "What I'd really like to do is be a writer."
>
> She gave me a story that she had written. It was tremendous. She was a terrific writer.
>
> **—Tom Zito**

Ed Logg got the idea for *Centipede* from a book of game ideas, in which it was listed as "Bug Shooter." Bailey asked if she could work on the project, so Logg fleshed out the game and turned it over to her.

> I did all the self-tests. I did the graphics, too. It came from an idea called *Bug Shooter.* I asked her [Bailey] to go ahead and put mushrooms up and use a trackball. That stuff was my idea, and I did about half the code.
>
> At the time, the mushrooms were not shootable. If I remember right, it was basically a spider-like creature, a centipede, and the shooter, and that was really it. The mushrooms were static—you shot the centipede and noth-ing was left behind.
>
> Dan Van Elderen reviewed the game and said, "It would be nice if . . . " Dan wanted to shoot the mushrooms and I agreed that something needed to be done.
>
> I thought about it a while and said, "Well, I need to add something that creates mushrooms and other things to destroy them," and so on. So that's where other ideas like the fleas that brought more mushrooms came from.
>
> **—Ed Logg**

In *Centipede,* players used a trackball to move a cursor shaped like a snake's head along the bottom of the screen. The goal of the game was to shoot quick-moving centipedes as they appeared at the top of the screen and snaked their way down. The centipedes were composed of eleven sections with legs. Each time a section was hit, it turned into a mushroom, and the rest of the centipede continued its nimble march.

The playing field in *Centipede* was covered with mushrooms that could be shot away. Whenever the centipede collided with a mushroom, the centipede changed directions. Some players developed strategies in which they set traps by creating mushroom formations that forced the centipede to drop down the side of the screen.

Along with the centipedes, players shot bouncing spiders, scorpions, and fleas that dropped from the top and left mushrooms in their wake.

One of Dona Bailey's chief contributions to the game was its unusual color scheme. While other game designers used bright colors, she chose pastels. The first stage of the game had a lime-green centipede scurrying through a patch of green mushrooms with orange edges. The next centipede was pink and traveled through a patch of pink mushrooms with white edges. Nobody knows precisely why *Centipede* appealed to women, but several people believe that Bailey's pastel colors were part of the attraction.

On October 28, 1981, Tournament Games held a three-day national video-game championship in the Chicago Exposition Center. Tournament Games, a company that had extensive experience promoting tournaments for such bar games as billiards and darts, heralded the event as a major new sporting contest in which 10,000 to 15,000 of the world's best video-game players would go head-to-head on a single game—*Centipede.*

Tournament Game's experience with billiards and darts tournaments did not translate to video games. The company invited the winners of local video-game tournaments to compete, but contestants had to pay for their own transportation and lodging. Walk-on contestants had to pay a $60 registration fee. These expenses were too high for the teenage crowd that frequented the arcades, and less than 150 people signed up for the competition.

Competitors were invited to practice before the event, but the 250 *Centipede* machines that Tournament Games installed were not set on free play. The contestants not only had to pay to practice, but the machines had internal timers that stopped their games after three minutes.

The "Open Singles" winner of the tournament was Eric Ginner, who received a check for $12,000. Ok-Soo Han, one of less than a dozen women who entered, won $4,000 as the top female competitor. Both checks bounced. In the end, Atari covered the checks to avoid bad publicity.

> Atari and another company [that] had done tournaments like foosball and billiards and games of that sort organized the tournament. There was supposed to be a $50,000 fund, but it turned out that these guys didn't have enough funds to pay it off. So I guess everybody turned and sued Atari.
>
> **—Ed Logg**

First-Person Space Invaders

Despite a growing list of competitors and mounting internal problems, Atari remained one of the strongest companies in the industry. By this time, so many new companies were manufacturing arcade equipment that no one company could hope to control more than half the market as Atari had in the past.

In 1981, Taito America had its first American-made hit—*Qix*, a highly innovative game that one reviewer described as a cross between an *Etch-a Sketch* and *Star Wars;* Sega distributed *Frogger*, a game in which players helped a frog cross a busy highway and an alligator-filled stream; Stern attracted crowds with *Berzerk;* and Midway imported several strong titles from Namco and released domestic hits created by Dave Nutting and other American designers. Smaller companies like Nichibutsu, maker of *Crazy Climber*, and Konami also made their mark.

Toward the end of the year, Atari released a new game by Dave Theurer, designer of *Missile Command*. The game was called *Tempest*.

Tempest did not start out as an original idea. Shortly after finishing *Missile Command*, Theurer went hunting for his next game in the book of game themes that had been compiled at company brainstorming sessions. The idea that caught his eye was called "First-Person Space Invaders."

Since his game would be played from the first-person perspective, Theurer needed the efficiency of a vector-graphic generator. As it turned out, a new X-Y generator that created color lines was under development. *Tempest, Star Wars, The Empire Strikes Back, Gravitar, Black Widow, Space Duel, Quantum,* and *Major Havoc* were the only games Atari ever released that used the color X-Y generator.

It took Theurer six weeks to create a preliminary version of *First Person Space Invaders.* The project was almost derailed when he demonstrated it at a coin-op meeting.

> I got *First-Person Space Invaders* up pretty quickly. Gene Lipkin, the head of coin-op, and Frank Ballouz played it at a meeting and said, "This game is not that fun. It's basically *Space Invaders* from a different perspective."
>
> They said I should kill the game if I couldn't do something special with it.
>
> I told them about this nightmare I had about monsters coming out of a hole in the ground and you had to kill them before they got out of the hole or they would kill you. "I can take *First-Person Space Invaders,* put it on a surface, wrap that surface around a circle to make a cylinder, and rotate the cylinder to make a different game out of it."
>
> They said go ahead and try it, so that's what I did.
>
> **—Dave Theurer**

In Theurer's new game, players shot at creatures as they climbed to the top of geometrically shaped holes. The game was controlled with a heavy knob that players spun like a dial. The knob originally controlled the hole's rotation. When players began feeling nauseous, Theurer adjusted the controls so that the player's gun rotated instead of the hole. The game attracted a lot of attention around the coin-op division.

> *Tempest* took a year and had about 21K [of code].* When I started the game, the cylinder actually rotated and your player stayed still. People said it made them sick to their stomach, so I switched it so that the player moved around. That solved the problem.

---

* K refers to 1,024 units of memory.

> I wanted to do something special when you got a high score, and I love fireworks and explosions, so I made fireworks at the end if you got on the high score table.
>
> People loved it [*Tempest*]. They came into the labs to play it. That's how you knew you had something hot—if you had trouble developing your game because people played it while you were trying to debug it.
>
> **—Dave Theurer**

Theurer switched from a black and white vector-graphics generator to the color X-Y generator during the project, but the technology proved somewhat unstable. Though it created beautiful colors and had the same high-resolution images created by older vector-graphics hardware, the new color generator tended to overheat.

> I was working on the game, trying to figure stuff out, and all of a sudden the monitor stopped working. I couldn't figure out why it wasn't working anymore. I was just sitting there and all of a sudden it stopped.
>
> I looked up on the bench where the monitor was sitting, and five or six of the resistors and components had melted themselves out of the PC board. They had gotten so hot that they had melted the solder.
>
> Those color X-Y monitors were flaky. They were a big problem throughout the testing period and they continued to be a big problem in the field. They just don't last very long. It's not good for sales if things are continually breaking.
>
> **—Dave Theurer**

More than any game before it, *Tempest* seemed to move at the speed of light. Players used a spinning knob to control a fast-moving C-shaped polygon that moved around the top of geometric cylinders with a spider-like crawl and shot at flippers (large red Xs), fuseballs (multi-colored balls), pulsars (yellow lines that gave deadly shocks) and other enemies as they tried to climb out of the tube.

Tempest was an immediate hit, but some arcade owners complained about it. It had maintenance problems and broke down frequently. Before long, Theurer heard rumors about kids playing the game for hours on a single quarter. One story was that they had found a code that gave them forty free games.

In a business that depended on the average player lasting less than two minutes per game, machines that dolled out free credits were a big liability.

When Theurer first heard about the problem, he assumed it was caused by the "flaky" hardware. Upon further examination, he discovered that he had created the flaw.

To protect against piracy, a growing problem in the arcade business, Theurer had imbedded a security code in the game. The code checked the placement of different objects on the screen and caused the game to shut down if images were not in the correct space.

Before shipping, Theurer, who had a reputation for repeatedly fussing over details, discovered that an Atari logo was not perfectly centered. He moved it slightly. It seemed like an inconsequential change, but if players hit a certain score, it caused the security code to malfunction and the player received forty credits.

> If players got something like 179,480 points, the game would crank a 40 into the coin counter. It would do other weird things, too, like double the vector generator multipliers so everything would be twice as big, but nobody wanted that. They just wanted to get the 40 free credits, so the kids figured out how to do it.
>
> **—Dave Theurer**

Around the time that Theurer finished *Tempest,* Atari announced a new bonus plan to reward designers for creating hit games. The plan took effect shortly after *Tempest* was released.

> Atari pissed me off. After *Missile Command,* they came up with a new bonus plan that paid about ten times as much, but they weren't quite sure when they were going to put it into effect. I was working on *Tempest,* and they waited to see how well *Tempest* was going to do. Then they said the first game after *Tempest* would be the first game on the new bonus plan.
>
> Talk about making me mad. It cost me perhaps a million dollars.
>
> I don't know who made the decision. I mean, Ray Kassar was president of the company at the time. They were owned by Warner Brothers, so there was plenty of money to go around.
>
> **—Dave Theurer**

The Peak

The growth of the industry continued into 1982, and video games appeared in unlikely places. The Hilton Hotel in Rye Town, New York, opened Bagatelle Place. Named after the forerunner of pinball, Bagatelle Place was a formal arcade with thirty-three video games, a cappuccino bar, and a strictly enforced dress code.[4]

In Nevada, casinos cleared out gambling equipment and set up small arcades. In Hawaii, an enormous arcade took up nearly half of a floor in the Rainbow Bazaar, a large tourist center in Waikiki. In the early 1980s, Hawaii experienced record tourist business and Waikiki real estate was among the most expensive in the world.

The company that earned the most profits was not, however, Atari or Nintendo—it was Midway. Midway was about to release a product that would become the most successful game in the history of the American arcade industry—*Ms. Pac-Man.*

MIT Strikes Again

Toru Iwatani, the Namco employee who designed *Pac-Man,* was not involved with the creation of *Ms. Pac-Man.* It was created, instead, by nine college students, led by two MIT students, Doug Macrae and Kevin Curran.

As a junior, Macrae created a small coin-op route on the MIT campus with a Gottlieb Pioneer pinball machine that he received from his brother and three *Missile Command* machines that he bought on his own. The route was very lucrative in the beginning, but *Missile Command* soon began losing popularity. One problem faced by small-route operators was the cost of keeping current. People lost interest in older games as new ones arrived, and before long, the only people playing them could milk an hour of play out of a single quarter.

Other small-time operators would have had to abandon their machines or sell them cheaply, but Macrae was studying engineering. He and another student named Kevin Curran decided to update the *Missile Command* machines and give them a new life.

> The spring of our senior year, Kevin and I got interested in designing games rather than just operating them. I had a computer graphics background,

> and Kevin had an electrical engineering background, and the two of us kind of said to ourselves, "Well, how do we get into the design of video games?"
>
> The process was a little bit daunting, in that we looked at mainly the arcade games and didn't really know how you'd go about building cabinets or getting involved in the hardware. . . . so we came up with the idea that we'd do enhancement kits.

—Doug Macrae, cofounder, General Computer

Rather than creating new games, Curran and Macrae decided to build "PAL" boards that would fit onto the circuit boards of existing games and modify game play. Their first project was to revitalize Macrae's *Missile Command* machines.

Curran and Macrae moved off campus and set up shop in a rental house. The business at this point was a five-man operation. They borrowed money from Macrae's mother and from their coin-op route and purchased equipment. Then they took apart one of the *Missile Command* machines and studied its design.

> We started disassembling the code to *Missile Command* on this emulator, figuring out exactly what all the code did. Then we designed a board that would mount on top of the *Missile Command* game and would cleverly overlay code that we wrote onto the original Atari code. The way we did it actually was we had a board that was watching the addresses and was deciding when to overlay our code on top of the original Atari code.
>
> We were very concerned about copyright infringement because if we just modified their code and sold new ROMs, we thought we would be infringing on the Atari copyrights and end up sued within minutes.

—Doug Macrae

The new game, which they called *Super Missile Attack,* was basically an accelerated version of *Missile Command* with a few new enemies. Along with the usual missile-packing jets and UFOs, the new version also featured a laser-shooting UFO and a new color scheme.

The *Super Missile Attack* modifications brought players around MIT back to *Missile Command,* and Curran and Macrae wagered that it would have the same impact around the country. *Missile Command* was a fairly expensive game, so Curran and Macrae decided to try and sell their "enhancement kit" on the market.

> And we started selling these boards or these kits out of the back of *Play Meter Magazine* and *RePlay Magazine* for $295 dollars. We were taking phone calls in the bedrooms, we were producing them in the basement, we were designing in the living room and shipping out of the dining room of this house in Brooklyn.
>
> **—Doug Macrae**

It cost Curran and Macrae approximately $30 to make a board, which they then sold for $295. They called their company General Computer and sold more than 1,000 enhancement boards over the summer.

Somewhat pleased with themselves and their new business, they decided to modify an even more popular game for their next project. They settled upon the most popular game in the world, *Pac-Man.*

Modifying *Pac-Man* was more difficult than working with *Missile Command.* Dave Theurer, the designer of *Missile Command,* had created a very logical and minimalistic code for his game. It was easy to understand and to work with. The programmers who worked with Toru Iwatani on the creation of *Pac-Man* had not been as efficient, and their code was twice as long.

By August 1981, while Curran and Macrae had disassembled the code and begun to build an enhancement, a new development threatened to shut them down. Atari charged them with copyright infringement and took them to court.

> We disassembled the code, documented it all and how it worked, etc., and then looked at how to make modifications to make it a little more difficult and a little more interesting. And we were developing this enhancement kit as a separate board and kit again. We were ready to take it to market in August of 1981, and, at that point, we ended up sparring in court with Atari in front of Justice Keating, who was the original Boston bussing judge. It lasted almost two months.
>
> **—Doug Macrae**

Though the case was ostensibly about copyright infringement, Atari was not worried about people altering the code in its games. The bigger issue with Atari was the concept of enhancement boards. Its arcade business would be crippled if operators could simply update old equipment instead of purchasing new machines. From Steve Ross to Ray Kassar, the Atari executive board wanted General Computer stopped at all costs.

> We believed we had very moral high ground, in that we had not copied their code. We had the game operator pull the ROMs out of the Atari game and put them into our board, plug our board into the Atari board, and then we overlaid our code on top of it, so, we viewed that we were actually relatively free of copying their code.
>
> As it came out in court, there were some very difficult issues about trademark dilution and misrepresentation of origin that were going to get sorted out in court under Justice Keating, which had never really been decided before. Up to this point, video-game enhancers had just blatantly copied code, did all kinds of things wrong, and they were pretty clear cut cases for Atari and also Bally to go attack and pretty much put out of business. Ours was a much greater case about whether we had the right to enhance a video game.
>
> We went a couple of rounds with temporary restraining orders and injunctions and, eventually, the general counsel of Atari, Skip Paul, came to us and said, "What are you guys really after here?"
>
> **—Doug Macrae**

Skip Paul, Atari's general counsel and later the president of Atari Coin-Operated Games, decided to look for an amicable solution. He asked Curran and Macrae what they hoped to accomplish. When they told him that they simply wanted to make video games, he made a deal with them. Atari would drop the case with prejudice—meaning that Atari would admit it was a wrongful suit—and pay them $50,000 per month for the next two years to develop games if they would stop making enhancement kits.

Curran and Macrae agreed.

> The one thing that got carved out of the agreement was that we actually had an enhancement kit to *Pac-Man* in development at the time, and we did not want to

> throw it in the trash. The agreement that was written up stated that we would
> never produce an enhancement kit again without permission from the original
> copyright holder of the game . . . or the original manufacturer of the game.
>
> Atari assumed that no one would ever give us permission.
>
> **—Doug Macrae**

In an attempt to salvage their work on *Pac-Man*, Curran and Macrae flew to
Chicago and met with David Marofske and other executives at Bally-Midway.
Their plan was to bluff Bally into accepting a deal.

They went to the meeting armed with court papers that showed that Atari
had dropped its lawsuit with prejudice. "We just beat Atari in court," Macrae
told the Bally executives, "and we're going to launch this enhancement kit.
We just want your blessing."

> We thought we were being very clever, convincing them that we were going
> to launch this enhancement kit, and I think we probably could have gotten
> their blessing.
>
> One thing we did not take into account was that Bally had just success-
> fully made *Pac-Man* the biggest-selling video game of all time. Their
> production lines had just shut off and they had nothing to put into produc-
> tion after that. They did not have the next game.
>
> I believe Dave [Marofske] was the one who came up with the idea of say-
> ing, "Well, guys, how about we talk sequel rather than you selling it as an
> enhancement kit?"
>
> **—Doug Macrae**

The enhancement kit designed by General Computer turned *Pac-Man* into
a new game called *Crazy Otto*, in which *Pac-Man* had legs. In the whirlwind
negotiations that followed, Curran and Macrae were told that the new game
had to be faithful to the *Pac-Man* image and that the legs were not acceptable.
They decided to create a female character.

> As we kicked it around and what the sequel should be, we came up with the
> idea of, well, it should be the female *Pac-Man*. We originally burnt the

> ROMs for production under the name *Pac-Woman*, but as we were getting
> ready to go into production, several females inside of Midway objected,
> saying, "That's kind of an inappropriate name" and that we should put a
> surname in front of it.
>
> I never understood why.
>
> We chose *Miss Pac-Man* and got very close to going into production. Then
> someone pointed out to us that in the third animation (the cartoons between
> levels of the games) *Pac-Man* and the female *Pac-Man* get together and have
> a baby. We would have had all kinds of people talking about the fact that
> they had a baby out of wedlock, which would have been very bad.
>
> We scrambled and came up with Mrs., then changed it to a fifth name,
> Ms., because we were trying to make everyone in life happy and all of
> this happened in the final 72 hours before the production line was sup-
> posed to start up.
>
> **—Doug Macrae**

Midway never built an actual *Ms. Pac-Man* board. It simply built *Pac-Man*
boards, then added General Computer's enhancement kit.

By this time, maze chasing had become the most popular theme in the
arcades. Some manufacturers updated the theme by making the characters
move fast or by adding shooting to the game, but most maze chase games still
looked a lot like *Pac-Man*.

> We had thought that the *Ms. Pac-Man* image gave the game its own identity.
> We changed the artwork and changed the speed and presented it to Mr.
> Nakamura [president of Namco]. After going back and forth for a while, we
> introduced it to the marketplace.
>
> **—David Marofske**

Like *Pac-Man* and *Centipede, Ms. Pac-Man* appealed to female players. It had
the same basic game play as *Pac-Man*. The game still involved clearing a maze
while avoiding four mop-like ghosts named Inky, Pinky, Blinky, and Sue—
the latter of which Macrae named after his sister. (The fourth ghost in *Pac-Man*
had been named Clyde.)

The biggest difference between *Pac-Man* and *Ms. Pac-Man* was that *Ms. Pac-Man* featured four mazes instead of the single maze in the original game. *Ms. Pac-Man* was also faster. The ghosts in *Pac-Man* followed preset paths. By running in certain patterns, players were able to confuse them and play nearly indefinitely. There were no known patterns to fool the ghosts in *Ms. Pac-Man.*

General Computer also created several cosmetic changes. The fruits and bonus objects in *Pac-Man* appeared just below the center of the maze. In *Ms. Pac-Man* they marched around the maze. The main character, Ms. Pac-Man, was still a yellow ball with a mouth but had comic touches—a red bow and lipstick. Like *Centipede,* the pinks and blues in *Ms. Pac-Man's* color scheme added a feminine touch.

Midway sold 100,000 *Pac-Man* machines and more than 115,000 *Ms. Pac-Man* machines in the United States. Other than *Pac-Man* and *Ms. Pac-Man,* no arcade game has ever sold more than 100,000 units in the United States.

General Computer later built *Junior Pac-Man* for Bally Midway. Later, Bally/Midway contracted with Dave Nutting to build *Baby Pac-Man,* a maze-chase game with a pinball machine attached. At certain points in the game, the action went from the chase on the video monitor to the pinball machine.

Curran and Macrae sued Midway, claiming that they had come up with the concept of a Pac-Man family and that they should receive royalties from all Pac-Children games. They won the suit.

Though *Baby Pac-Man* was never a popular game and its royalties amounted to little, the litigation resulted in huge royalties on merchandise with images of Pac-Man and his family.

Digital Me

In 1980, Ralph Baer, inventor of the Magnavox Odyssey, birthed an invention to personalize video games—a camera that could shoot pictures of players' faces, digitize them, and load the images into games. He thought that arcade manufacturers could place the camera in the marquee of their cabinets and paste players' faces on characters in their games. The camera could also snap a photograph of a high-scoring player and post it next to his score.

> The idea was to put a small, inexpensive black and white video camera into the arcade game and point it down toward the face of the player. The player would

> see his own face digitized on the screen, smile until he liked the way he looked, and push a button, and the digitized picture would be stored in RAM and available for use, either during the game to become the head of a player or used in the credits to appear next to the scores and the initials of the player.
>
> I figured every confirmed video-game player in the city of Chicago and New York would be running around from arcade to arcade to get his mug up. It seemed like a surefire hit to me, so I built the preliminary piece of equipment and took it to Chicago to Marvin Glass and Associates.
>
> We had John Pasierb, the chief engineer of Bally/Midway, come over and look at it. And he got very interested immediately.
>
> **—Ralph Baer**

Executives at Midway expressed great interest in Baer's camera and commissioned him to install the prototype into one of their machines. Baer installed his camera in an arcade machine and rigged it to take pictures of players who got high scores. Midway set up the game in a Chicago test site.

According to Baer, the game did well the first day. The second day ended in disaster, and a Midway executive told Baer that Midway was no longer interested in his invention.

> To make a long story short, they put it on display in an arcade in Chicago and it did very well the first day. The second day some guy gets up on a chair, drops his pants in front of the camera, and that's the end of the product.
>
> **—Ralph Baer**

During this time, the rock group Journey was one of the most popular musical acts in the United States. Some Midway designers wanted to make a game based on the group.

In *Journey,* the game, players helped drummer Steve Smith jump through space, using drums as trampolines. They helped keyboard player Jonathan Cain run through a minor obstacle course, guitarist Neal Schon float through a low-gravity cave, bass guitarist Ross Vallory jump over several exploding platforms, and lead singer Steve Perry slip through a maze of deadly gates.

Journey was the first game to incorporate digitized graphics. Black and white photographic images of the musicians' faces appear throughout the game. The images were captured using Ralph Baer's camera.

> There's a postmortem. We salvaged all that money we put into that game by digitizing the heads of some rock group that was popular at the time and using the heads as characters in a game. That was the outcome, but the concept of a camera in a machine just went by the board because of that one instance.
>
> **—Ralph Baer**

The game play in *Journey* was not particularly innovative, but Midway executives believed that the digitized likenesses of the band would attract an audience. In past years they might have been right. By the time *Journey* came out, the arcade business was beginning to fade and pictures of rock stars were not enough of a draw to save a bad game.

> *Journey* was, between you and me, a disappointment. I thought it was a better game than it got credit for, but the market had started to soften.
>
> Like I say, I was a little disappointed. I thought that from a market standpoint, it was a nice piece.
>
> **—David Marofske**

The Changing Tides

> There's a joke that on June 21, 1982, at approximately 4:30 P.M., the video game business fell over a cliff. People stopped playing them, and operators stopped buying them. And that pall lasted for many, many years and nobody's been able to figure out why.
>
> To this day, even though it happened well over a decade ago, you still hear people talking about the bust. Not the boom, but the bust.
>
> **—Eddie Adlum**

The video game industry began its decline in mid-1982. The industry didn't crash; it simply stopped growing.

The first people to feel the effects were entrepreneurs who placed games in restaurants, grocery stores, and fancy hotels. Games in low-traffic locations no longer earned enough money to pay for their operation. Many of these entrepreneurs defaulted on the loans they had made to purchase their games.

At the time, several companies had recently built new super arcades on the belief that the business would continue to expand. Arcades like Castle Park, a multimillion-dollar 17,000-square-foot operation in Riverside, California, needed thousands of customers per week to survive. As interest waned, these large new arcades attracted too few customers to meet expenses. They were the first casualties of the shake up.

> So the fallout from the video bust in mid/late 1982 was a sad one for this business. People lost money putting games in places where they shouldn't have gone. Lobbies of Chinese restaurants, for example. You're just not going to make money on a machine in the lobby of a Chinese restaurant, you're just not.
>
> When the bloom came off the rose, those machines came out of those locations.
>
> Unfortunately, a lot of distributors had extended too much credit to new-comer-operators and ended up with a lot of debt. A million dollars in unpaid bills was not unusual from a single distributorship.
>
> The people who devoted much of their money to video games ended up with a lot of unnecessary cabinetry, hardware, monitors, and games that had absolutely no resale value whatsoever. They started visiting the city dump and pushing them over the hill.
>
> **—Eddie Adlum**

As the big arcades disappeared, smaller ones received enough business to survive. For a short time, the business seemed to correct itself. Many arcade owners purchased new equipment and tried to hang on until business picked up again. It never did. The coin-operated video-game business continued a fairly steady decline for the next fifteen years.

No one knew why the business had slumped. Some of the most memorable games in video-game history arrived after the arcade business began to fade. Gottlieb released *Q*bert*, Nintendo released *Donkey Kong Junior*, Sega released *Pengo*, and Williams released *Joust* and *Robotron 2084*, but the business continued to wane.

> We could just say it's a fickle public. We do know that movies got better. We do know that CD records made their appearances. And we also know that the stuff that we sell is generally called "novelty," and novelty is not forever, you have to constantly freshen it.
>
> We tried to freshen it, but apparently not to the point where the public would play it with the reckless abandon that they were playing before.
>
> **—Eddie Adlum**

Jungle Who? Jungle What?

Toward the end of 1982, Taito America came out with an adventure game called *Jungle King.* In this game, players helped a Tarzan-like hero rescue a woman from savages. The game involved swinging across a jungle on vines, swimming through alligator-infested waters, dodging falling boulders, and jumping over cannibals.

Edgar Rice Burroughs, Inc., the entity that held the rights to Tarzan, claimed that *Jungle King* infringed on its property and demanded that Taito change the title of the game and its content. Rather than face an expensive legal battle, Taito agreed.

Jungle King became *Jungle Hunt.* Although Taito did not change the game itself, the Tarzan character was replaced with an explorer in a Patagonian jungle suit. The original hero had made a Tarzan yell as he swung from vine-to-vine, but the new hero made no sound at all.

In the beginning, most lawsuits over video games involved two game manufacturers suing each other over patents. After the golden age of arcades, much of the litigation involved ideas, titles, and names. The most bizarre suit involved Universal Studios. The judge handling the trial called it "a tale of two gorillas."

CHAPTER 12

The Battle for the Home

Oh, I mean . . . there are lots of anecdotes from those days. One of them was about this day I'll never forget, when I walked across the street to the engineering building on Borregas, and went into coin-op engineering, downstairs—consumer engineering was upstairs. This is probably in 1979. . . .

Anyway, they had this *Space Invaders* machine in coin-op engineering. I looked at it and went back to Kassar's office and said, "Ray, take this goddamned *Space Invaders* and move it up to consumer. Make a consumer cartridge and license the goddamned name."

He just looked at me, and the only thing he said was, "Of course. Why didn't I think of that?"

I said, "'Cause you're very busy running the whole company."

—Manny Gerard

Those of us who stayed at Atari called ourselves the Dumb Shits Club. They made $50 million and we made $20,000.

—Warren Robinett, former programmer, Atari

Atari Consumer Division

A core group of four programmers was hired in early 1977 to design games for the Video Computer System (VCS), Atari's programmable video game console. Within a year, Atari hired four more programmers, and after a few more months the team grew to twelve. Larry Wagner managed the division.

Nolan Bushnell was already having problems with Warner Communications as he prepared to launch the VCS, but he remained at the head of Atari through the October 1977 launch of the system and into 1978. With Bushnell in control, programmers frequently came to work late, stayed late, and enjoyed the relaxed atmosphere. Bushnell encouraged their laid-back attitude and had no problem with them partying after, and sometimes during, work hours. The programmers in the fledgling VCS project genuinely liked Bushnell, but there were occasional inconveniences.

> Nolan would come through the game developers area every couple of weeks and make comments on the games that made a lot of sense. Then he would come two or three weeks later and tell you to reverse what he had told you the last time.
>
> We started taking Nolan's comments with a grain of salt and asking, "Do his comments really make sense?" A lot of times we ignored him because he would frequently spin you around in circles every two to three weeks.
>
> **—Alan Miller, former programmer, Atari**

The VCS Team

Atari recruited talent for its VCS team in a haphazard way. Instead of visiting engineering schools and placing employment advertisements around the country, it simply placed ads in local newspapers. Amazingly, many of the people Atari selected proved to be masters at pulling a lot of power out of the Stella chip's overtaxed hardware. During the VCS's six-year life span, they found ways to expand its native capabilities and make it perform tasks that went far beyond anything that Al Alcorn and Jay Miner had ever envisioned. Alcorn may have called the VCS an "empty box," but the people who made games for it turned it into a full-fledged computer.

One of the first programmers Atari hired was Alan Miller, a graduate of Cal-Berkeley who had become addicted to such early coin-op games as *Space Race* and *Tank* during his final year of college. He responded to an Atari employment ad in 1977.

> My first interview was with Larry Wagner, the guy who headed up the software group, and one of their hardware engineers, Joe Decuir.
>
> The boss of the Micro Electronics Group, Bob Brown, was away at the time I was interviewing, so I didn't have a chance to meet him. Bob was one of the technology leaders who I really respect. He understood technology and how to motivate technical people. I was very happy to work for him.
>
> **—Alan Miller**

Unlike the engineers in the coin-op division who enjoyed socializing as a group, the people programming games for the Video Computer System formed cliques and never integrated. Owen Rubin, a coin-op engineer who helped design computer development systems for the consumer division, described the environment as "cutthroat." Coin-op engineers generally stayed at Atari for years, but VCS people seldom lasted more than a year or two.

> I was just there for a year and a half.
>
> There really were kind of two rival cliques when I was there. There was one group: Al Miller, Bob Whitehead, Dave Crane, and Larry Kaplan, who, for some reason, kind of formed their own little clique.
>
> Me and my two friends, Tom Reuterdahl and Jim Huether, were sort of another clique.
>
> **—Warren Robinett, early VCS programmer**

Life in the consumer division was not as wild as it was in coin-op. The programmers did not engage in petty battles with the maintenance department or go to movies. They did not pull pranks on their managers. Coin-op engineers worked in teams, consumer programmers worked alone. Most important, through its first year and a half, the consumer division was a financial black hole. Coin-op earned millions of dollars, much of which was used to cover losses accrued by the consumer division.

Unlike coin-op engineers, who wrote their code and then gave it to data entry people to input, consumer programmers entered their own code. Wagner generally assigned them their first game, but they were usually allowed to come up with their own concepts after that.

> It typically took about 3 or 4 months to make a game, so the process was very fast paced.
>
> Most of the first games were based on existing coin-op games. I came on board and they assigned me to do a game called *Surround* that was similar to a number of arcade games. At least I didn't have to come up with a concept. That helped speed things along.
>
> **—Alan Miller**

In the beginning, programmers were responsible for creating every element of their games. The same person who created the concept was also responsible for the programming, art, and even the sound effects. The look of VCS games improved, however, when an artist named Marilyn Churchill was brought in from the marketing department to help. A lot of the first games for the VCS were based on popular arcade and board games of the time.

As they started their second generation of games, Atari's VCS programmers came up with their own concepts, developed new skills, and accelerated up the learning curve. To make their deadlines, programmers worked long hours, for which they felt inadequately compensated.

> After my first game, I was given free rein there to come up with all my own concepts and implement them myself. We did all the implementation in those days, including the music and the graphics.
>
> We did the music, what little there was. I can't say I'm a great musician, but I like music a lot.
>
> I thought making games was a pretty creative, unique act that warranted compensation. I think I was making $27,000 or $30,000 a year at that time. It was not aggressive engineering compensation, frankly, even for that era.
>
> **—Alan Miller**

The first games for the VCS were fairly plain. After designing *Surround*, Alan Miller went on to create cartridges based on *Hangman* and *Concentration*. Warren Robinett's first game was *Slot Racers*. Other early games included *Pong* and *Breakout*.

Within a year, however, the games became more intricate. David Crane created a football game and Miller created *Basketball*, a home video game shown from a 3D perspective.

> Of the games I did at Atari, the one I like the best was the *Basketball* game. It was one-on-one or one against the computer. VCS hardware was designed explicitly to do the *Tank* kind of game, and the basketball game took sports to a new level of realism on the VCS. It had a really good playability.
>
> I was on the basketball team in high school and loved the sport. Wish I was better at it.
>
> —**Alan Miller**

Change Comes to Atari

The team had four games ready by the time Atari unveiled the VCS at the Consumer Electronics Show in June 1977. By the time the system was released in October, there were nine game cartridges: *Combat, Street Racer, Air-Sea Battle, Surround, Blackjack, Basic Math, Indy 500, Video Olympics* (variations of *Pong*), and *Starship*.

The Video Computer System retailed for $199 and came with a cartridge called *Combat*. Designed by Larry Kaplan and Larry Wagner, *Combat* supposedly contained twenty-seven unique games. Most of the games, however, were variations of the arcade game *Tank*. In fact, the menu of games on the outside of the *Combat* cartridge contained the following list:

    1–5 TANK®
    6–9 TANK-PONG™
    10–14 INVISIBLE-TANK™
    15–20 BIPLANE
    21–27 JET-FIGHTER™

Most of the variations in the games involved trading out bullets for missiles and empty battlefields for mazes.

Despite shipping problems and slow sales through Christmas, the VCS outsold the Fairchild Channel F. This was not enough for Warner chairman

Steve Ross. He was disappointed with Atari's sales and wondered if purchasing the company had been a mistake. Bushnell's answer, abandoning the VCS and developing a more powerful home console, infuriated him.

Bushnell's struggles were well known throughout Atari. When he was forced out of the company in 1978, many people believed the company had lost its soul. They expected Warner to impose a stricter culture. When Ray Kassar introduced himself as Bushnell's replacement at a company-wide meeting, nobody trusted him.

> Ray came on to run the company about a year after I was there. I don't have positive feelings about him at all. He had no understanding or appreciation of the industry, no understanding or appreciation of fundamental technology. He was destined to run that company into the ground.
>
> **—Alan Miller**

> Naturally, when I came, they were all very suspicious. People get nervous when any new guy comes in. They were afraid, I don't deny that, but I really had great respect for the programmers because I knew that's where the products came from. I did everything to encourage them.
>
> **—Ray Kassar**

Kassar's East Coast "high society" mannerisms offended many Atari employees. The programmers and engineers at Atari did not care about Kassar's Harvard credentials or his tailored suits. They viewed these traits as peculiarities and made fun of them in a rash of Kassar-jokes.

In Kassar's mind, his job was to raise corporate revenues. As he surveyed Atari's situation, he recognized that the company needed a focused marketing plan for its consumer products. He needed to build a quality-assurance program. Sears was complaining about defective VCS units, and no one knew how to respond. In fact, according to Kassar, the company's relationship with its retail partners was beginning to disintegrate.

Kassar was ready to fix Atari's problems, but he demanded rewards for his work. He filled his office with expensive furniture and converted the executive dining room into a place of fine dining. Chefs from many of San Francisco's most expensive restaurants were brought in to prepare daily meals.

> Ray came on board to run the company and, frankly, nobody liked him. He was just a totally different kind of guy. The tech guys used to wear shorts to work. Ray was a really high society type and people just couldn't identify with him. Didn't like him. I don't think it was because of anything that he did overtly, it's just that he was different.
>
> He always wore very heavy cologne and you could literally smell if he had been through the area. People used to joke about that all the time.
>
> **—Alan Miller**

Like Kassar or hate him, one fact that no one could dispute was that Atari grew exponentially under his supervision. In 1977, the year before Kassar became CEO, Atari had $75 million in sales. Under Kassar, Atari became the fastest-growing company in the history of the United States,* as the company's sales exceeded $2 billion within three years.

> We went from $75 million to $2.2 billion and made a lot of money. They don't talk about all the money we made for the company. One year we made $400 million after taxes. It was the most profitable company in the world.
>
> **—Ray Kassar**

The First Easter Egg

> They decided that security was really important, so they installed one of those magnetic keypad systems. It was universally hated by all the tech types, who were sort of anarchists anyway. You had to have your little electronic key to get through the doors, and there was no way to get around it.

---

* Since that time, several high-tech companies have surpassed Atari's record.

> One night Warren Robinett went down to the cafeteria to get some food. It was late, and he had forgotten his wallet upstairs. His key, the little mag card he needed to get back in the office, was in his wallet [so he was stuck]. He started looking around the building for some way to get back in and he found that the tool room for the coin-op people was open, so he took some tools out and literally broke down the door to consumer engineering. The alarms did not go off.
>
> It turned out that the security system recorded the comings and goings of legitimate employees. You could break down the door and it would not register a thing.
>
> **—Alan Miller**

Atari's coin-op engineers felt that Ray Kassar did not appreciate their accomplishments and accused him of paying attention only to the game designers in the consumer division. What they did not know was that the consumer division designers also disliked him.

By all appearances, Kassar did not trust his employees. Shortly after taking over, he had an extensive security system installed. Employees had to carry magnetic identification cards to enter buildings and secured areas. Though electronic-security systems were fairly standard in the computer industry, many Atari employees counted Kassar's increasing security as one more step toward destroying the company's relaxed culture.

Kassar's policy about programmers not receiving publicity infuriated all of the company's designers, but one consumer programmer, Warren Robinett, found a way around it. He had just finished his first game, *Slot Racers,* and decided to make his next project a graphic version of *Adventure,* the pioneering all-text computer game created by Will Crowther and Don Woods.

Like the computer game, Robinett's *Adventure* would take place in a medieval world with dragons and caverns. The original game, however, took place in an enormous universe. In order to beat the game, players had to create maps. Because Robinett's game was for the VCS, it was restricted in size to 4K of code. The VCS, with its memory limitations and joystick controller, was not suited for text-based games. Robinett had to draw his dungeon and dragons.

> I played *Adventure* at the Stanford Artificial Intelligence lab. One of my room-mates was a grad student. He took me over there and we played it and I thought that it was a really cool, great, amazing thing. I had just finished *Slot Racers* and I was trying to figure out what game to do next. I decided to do a video-game version of *Adventure*.
>
> It presented several problems because it was all text. You'd get a text description of the room you were in and what was around you, and you'd make commands like, "pick up wand," "take bird," "go north," "go south," "wave wand," and things like that. It was all noun-verb descriptions for movements or actions, and it took up quite a bit of memory to give these text descriptions.
>
> I decided I'd do the "go north/southeast" thing with the joystick and I'd show one room at a time graphically on the screen. The rooms were all interconnected. If you drove your cursor off the edge of the screen, you popped into the next room.
>
> **—Warren Robinett**

In the original *Adventure,* players found weapons and other inventory, much of which they carried with them throughout the game. Because Robinett had to show graphic representations of each item, he limited players to carrying one inventory item at a time. Making the proper selection for each situation was crucial, since a certain sword might defeat one enemy but be useless against another. Throughout the game, pesky bats tried to fly away with whatever objects players carried.

> I made the decision to allow you to carry just one object at a time, and that turned out to be a good thing because it meant you had to make strategic choices. If you had a treasure and a weapon and you wanted to go somewhere, you had to pick which one you were going to take.
>
> It was also a good choice because the graphics on the 2600 were so limited and it kept things from getting too cluttered on the screen.
>
> **—Warren Robinett**

Robinett began *Adventure* in the days when programmers were expected to create their own artwork. He describes his dragons as looking like ducks and admits that the entire game looked a bit primitive. When he was about half-way through, he got bogged down and started another project. He did not return to finish *Adventure* for nearly six months.

When he returned, Robinett decided to create a hidden room. The room would have a special surprise for anyone who found it, and the keys to open the room would be readily available, but Robinett made the keys and location of the room so obscure that he doubted that anyone would ever discover them.*

To access Robinett's secret room, you had to find "the dot," a single gray pixel in the center of a wall of the exact same color. If your cursor touched the single interactive dot on that noninteractive wall, it would indicate that you could pick it up.

> I called it "the dot" and it was just one pixel. It was the smallest, most insignificant little object you could possibly have, and it was gray. It was the same color as the background. That made it even more insignificant because [even if you found it], you could lose it and maybe not find it again.
>
> It was hidden in part of one of the mazes in which you couldn't see very far. The area was even inaccessible—you had to use the bridge to cross the wall to get into it. You had to make a map of the whole maze and then you would discover that there was one little tiny chamber that you couldn't get to unless you used the bridge to cross the wall. And then if you went in there, you'd run into the dot and you could pick it up.
>
> If you picked up this little dot, the one pixel dot that was hidden inside the inaccessible part of a large maze, and you brought it back and you messed around with it long enough, you found that it could get you through this wall and into the secret room in which I filled the screen with the words, "Created by Robinett." It [the message] was in every color in the rainbow because I made the graphics go through the entire color palette. I wanted my name in colored lights.
>
> **—Warren Robinett**

---

* He got the idea from the Beatles' *White Album,* which allegedly had a message that could only be found if people played the album backward. According to Robinette, the game became an experiment to see if anyone could ever find his hidden secret.

No one knew about Robinett's secret room. He did not tell his friends at work about his little prank. If word got out, he would have been fired. It cost approximately $10,000 to manufacture games at that time. Robinett's secret room took up 5 percent of the storage on the *Adventure* cartridge, and he was afraid that if Atari executives discovered it, they would insist on deleting it and remastering the game.

> I was the only person creating the game, and nobody went through our programs with a fine-toothed comb to see what might be in there. The hard part was keeping it a secret for a year until the game came out. I didn't even tell my two buddies, Jim Huether and Tom Reuterdahl. I felt that if I couldn't keep the secret myself, how could I expect them to keep a juicy secret like that?
>
> **—Warren Robinett**

Atari manufactured nearly 300,000 copies of *Adventure*. In 1980, after Robinett had left Atari, a 12-year-old boy from Salt Lake City sent a letter to Atari to inform the company about a strange thing he had discovered in the game *Adventure*. He had found the dot and opened Robinett's secret room.

Robinett's prank created a sensation. Arnie Katz, Joyce Worley, and Bill Kunkel, the publishers of a magazine called *Electronic Games,* reported the story. They referred to the room as an "Easter egg." The popularity of Robinett's hidden room was also noticed at Atari. In the future, entire games would be built around hidden surprises.

The Great Migration

The 1978 introduction of *Space Invaders* ignited interest in consumer video games, as well as arcade games. Atari's *Video Computer System* did not sell particularly well through the 1977 Christmas season, but its sales were better than expected throughout the rest of the year. As Christmas 1978 approached, however, a new competitor emerged.

Magnavox returned to the video-game industry with Odyssey 2: a game console that the electronics manufacturer hoped to pass off as something more by adding a built-in keyboard. The keyboard did not fool consumers into believing that Odyssey 2 was a computer. Consumers did not see Odyssey 2 as somehow being on a par with Apple. It was a video game system, and despite having launched the first home game system, Magnavox could not hope to compete with Atari. By the end of 1978, Atari had sold its entire inventory of over 400,000 warehoused VCSs and had to step up the production of new units.

> I had built the company and I had developed the marketing plan. They never advertised their products before, so we spent five million dollars in advertising and that's when it started taking off.
>
> **—Ray Kassar**

Early in 1979, Manny Gerard made a suggestion that further increased Atari's leadership in the video-game industry. Like everyone in the industry, Gerard knew about *Space Invaders.* One day it occurred to him to license *Space Invaders* and convert it into a cartridge for the *Video Computer System.* Kassar loved the idea.

Taito agreed to license *Space Invaders* to Atari. It was the first time that an arcade game had ever been licensed for home use. Kassar, whose marketing sense proved nearly uncanny, predicted that a home version of *Space Invaders* would be such a major hit that people would buy VCSs just to play the game. He focused most of his advertising budget into promoting the game. The result was the bestselling game of 1980.

> When they came out with the *Space Invaders* cartridge, all hell broke loose. There were contests. It was a big deal. That was the beginning of licensing coin-op games as consumer products.
>
> **—Manny Gerard**

With the success of the VCS, Atari expanded its consumer division as quickly as possible, but many of its employees were unhappy. Under Kassar, the executive team knew nothing about technology and corporate policy. Executives discouraged programmers from taking ownership of their games. Kassar would not even allow them to see sales figures.

> Under the Kassar regime, management became sort of brain dead about technology. They didn't know the limitations of technology.
>
> The straw that broke the camel's back was that we lost respect for Atari. They were not committed to doing great stuff anymore. That was a huge change from when we all started there. When we started, we were very idealistic, hardworking, and committed to creating great stuff.
>
> **—Alan Miller**

Atari's first and most significant defection began in 1979 when Alan Miller, one of the first VCS programmers, left the company. He wanted more money and more ownership of his products. He considered game designing an art and wanted to be treated like other popular artists. When he complained about this to a few friends within the company, they agreed. With the support of Crane, Kaplan, and Whitehead, Miller tried to renegotiate his job.

By this time, more than twenty programmers were in the consumer division. The VCS had already surpassed all sales projections, and Kassar and his staff felt extremely comfortable with the system's future prospects.

> I put together a closed contract based on contracts I had read about for [popular] writers and musicians. I presented it to management and told them I wanted to negotiate for more compensation, and we kicked that around for quite a while.
>
> At some point, Larry [Kaplan], Dave [Crane], and Bob [Whitehead], who were my best friends at Atari, became aware of what I was doing and they wanted to try to negotiate on that basis, too. The four of us became a group.
>
> We moved up through the ranks, talking with our boss, George Simcock, then John Ellis, who was first in command of consumer engineering, and then Ray [Kassar] directly. At one point they told George Simcock that they would come to some kind of agreement, but ultimately they just put their feet down and said no.
>
> I remember one guy told us, "For the kind of money you're wanting I can go out and hire six guys."
>
> My reaction was, "You can hire them, but I don't think they can do the kind of job that we're doing." I don't think I actually said that to him.
>
> **—Alan Miller**

Joe Decuir, one of the hardware engineers who developed the VCS, left Atari to open his own engineering firm shortly before Miller submitted his demands to Kassar. When Kassar rejected his proposal, Miller went to Decuir and asked him which law firm he used to start his company. Decuir suggested Wilson, Sonsini, Goodrich & Rosati, a firm with a good reputation for handling start-up companies.

Miller and his friends visited the law firm and told an attorney about their plan to open an independent company that made games for the VCS. The attorney listened to the plan and carefully considered the patent infringement ramifications of making software for Atari's hardware.

The group members clearly had enough technological know-how to make good products, but their lack of business acumen showed. They had the creative talent but needed an administrator.

> We went to Decuir's law firm and talked to some of the attorneys there. They started looking for venture capital funding for us. They started the process of getting us incorporated and started pulling us together as a company.
>
> They said that we had an interesting technological opportunity, but they thought we really needed a management type to handle the administrative and marketing side of things.
>
> **—Alan Miller**

Wilson, Sonsini, Goodrich & Rosati eventually recommended Jim Levy, a businessman with experience in the music industry, as the right person to handle the business side of the new game company. When they met, Miller and his friends agreed and asked Levy to join them. They decided to call their company Activision.

In the meantime, Wilson, Sonsini, Goodrich & Rosati also contacted Sutter Hill, a Palo Alto venture capital firm. Sutter Hill agreed to invest in Activision and placed one of its executives, Bill Draper, on its board of directors.

> Bill was on our board of directors—really influential and smart guy. He ultimately became George Bush's cochairman when Bush ran for president against

Ronald Reagan. When Bush became vice president, Bill left our board of directors to go to Washington and perform in many high-level functions. I think he also worked at the United Nations for a while.

—Alan Miller

Activision opened its doors in April 1980, with David Crane, Alan Miller, and Bob Whitehead as its original programmers. Larry Kaplan joined the company a few months later. By the summer Consumer Electronics Show, in June of 1980, they were ready to show their first products.

I saw Jim Levy at the January CES show in Las Vegas, when he announced that Activision had been formed with Alan Miller and Bob Whitehead. I thought he was nuts.

There were so many cartridges available to Atari players from Atari, that we couldn't imagine that any consumer needed more cartridges. Nobody thought that they [consumers] would perceive any kind of difference in the graphics between the Activision cartridges and the Atari cartridges, and we couldn't conceive of anyone paying $3 to $5 more at retail for cartridges from a company that no one had ever heard of.

Because of that and the fact that Jim didn't have any money because he was in the start up, we bought him dinner on the first night of the show.

—Michael Katz, former marketing director, Mattel Toys

As Activision prepared to release its first games that fall, Atari took the company to court. It was a simple case. Atari's lawyers claimed that their company had engineered the VCS and held claim to its technology. Activision, they said, had no right to create games for its hardware.

This was not the first time in history that an independent company had created software for another company's computer system; but it was the first time anyone had sued over it. Atari had no choice. Its entire business model was built around selling console hardware as cheaply as possible and making profits from software. Suddenly, Activision was gouging into its profit base.

They sued us repeatedly. We were the first independent video-game publisher. Before us, games were published by hardware manufacturers. I'm very proud of the fact that we created this independent video-game publishing industry.

We had the best games in the industry, as far as I was concerned. Dave Crane and Bob Whitehead were fantastically talented. Larry Kaplan joined us a few months after we started, so we had four designers who were clearly among the top designers in the world.

The first game I did was *Checkers,* which was not a big seller. Dave, I think, did *Dragster;* Bob Whitehead did *Boxing;* Larry did a *Bridge* game. And those were all good solid games. But the second round [of games was] much stronger. I did a *Tennis* game; Dave did *Laser Blast;* Larry did *Kaboom!*

—Alan Miller

Atari sued us every six months for the span of a year and a half, and I attended all the depositions, acting as technical interpreter for our attorneys. This was all technical stuff.

I met one of the court reporters who was taking depositions at that time, and we started dating and ultimately got married, and we've been together now for fifteen years. That was a positive benefit of the lawsuit. About the only positive benefit I can think of.

—Alan Miller

If Kassar ever regretted not negotiating with Miller while he was still at Atari, he never admitted it. They never met again, and Kassar publicly scorned Activision as a parasite in the video-game industry. Kassar always believed that he had treated his programmers with respect.

I always realized that one of the key groups really [was] the programmers, because without cartridges, without games, we had nothing. I spent a lot of time catering to those programmers. I think eventually they respected me. I really favored the programmers. . . . spent a lot of time with them.

—Ray Kassar

> After every quality designer in the company left, Atari went, "Gee, we're
> gonna lose all our designers." Talk about closing the barn door after the
> horses have left, Atari didn't just close the barn doors, they wallpapered
> them in velvet. Atari started paying royalties to the bums they had left.
>
> **—Bill Kunkel, former executive editor, *Electronic Games***

A Real Contender

Atari's early history was spent creating successful products and fighting off
imitators. With the growing success of the VCS, new companies began entering the market. Coleco returned to the market with a bizarre triangular
console, the Telstar Arcade, which had a steering wheel for driving games on
one panel, a pistol for shooting games on another, and knobs for games like
Pong on the third. The games were stored on triangular cartridges that plugged
into the top of the console. The system never caught on.

Mattel, the world's largest toy manufacturer, also released a video-game
console in 1980, the Intellivision. Mattel had already enjoyed phenomenal
success with a line of unsophisticated handheld video games in which players
controlled light-emitting diodes that represented football players and sports
cars. Mattel executives believed that their marketing position and name would
help them create a niche in video games, so they formed a special division
that specialized in video games called Mattel Electronics.

Intellivision had a newer and more powerful CPU than VCS, slightly more
memory, and played better-looking games. Intellivision games tended to have
more detailed graphics.

> Two things made Intellivision good. The graphics [on the Intellivision] were
> superior, less stick figure—oriented, with more bright and vibrant colors.
>
> The second thing was the lineup of sports games. Baseball, football,
> hockey, soccer, backgammon, bowling. Mattel wanted to have every single
> sport under the sun, all licensed from the right organizations, from the Ameri-
> can Backgammon Players Association to the U.S. Chess Federation, to Major
> League Baseball. Sports really brought new players to video games.
>
> **—Al Nilsen, former electronics buyer, JC Penney**

Along with more detailed graphics, the Intellivision also played more intricate games. The controllers on the VCS were paddles and a joystick. The controllers on the Intellivision included a 12-key button pad. It also had a disk that worked like a joystick. Players pressed on the disk to make characters move. Unlike Atari's joystick, which could only move characters in eight directions, the disk on the Intellivision controller could move objects in sixteen directions, adding more precision to games.

> We sold about 100,000 units in 1980. By our third year, we did well over a million units. We progressed upward after that into 1983, which was the peak year. As I recall, we did something like 3.5 million units on a worldwide basis that year.
>
> **—Paul Rioux, former senior vice president of operations,**
> **Mattel Electronics**

Back at Atari

> I remember one top programmer who was on drugs. You know, these were guys who would come in at 2 A.M. and work till midnight the next night, then disappear for two days. That's how programmers operate, and I had to accept that. I mean, I didn't say, "You have to be here at eight o'clock and leave [at a certain hour]." I understood that this was a very talented breed of people.
>
> I remember one guy came in. He was stoned out of his mind. He just wanted to read poetry to me, and I sat with him for four hours because he was one of our top programmers, just to let him feel that I understood him and I cared about him.
>
> At the end he said, "You know, I really appreciate what you've done for me." I mean, that's what I had to put up with.
>
> **—Ray Kassar**

VCS sales continued to grow, despite unrest in the consumer division. By mid-1979, Robinett, Reuterdahl, and Huether had become the old men of the division. It was no badge of honor. The programmers who left had formed their own companies; those who stayed were still making less than $30,000 per year. In June, Reuterdahl decided to leave Atari and Robinette felt even more isolated.

> Every time somebody left, we'd go out to lunch and end up drinking beer. We stayed at the bar until pretty late sometimes.
>
> The Friday that my friend Reuterdahl was quitting, we all went out drinking. At four o'clock, after I had been drinking for four hours and was pretty smashed, I started thinking about some of the things that were going on at Atari and got kind of pissed off, so I went over to a telephone and called up corporate headquarters and asked to speak to Ray Kassar.
>
> I thought it would be a little bit harder to get through to the president than it was. I got him on the phone and told him I was pissed off at management, and the next thing I knew, I had driven over to the building, and there I was, drunk, talking to the president of the company.
>
> **—Warren Robinett**

Robinett turned in his resignation the following month and took an extended trip to Europe.* While he was gone, Activision released its first products and became an overnight success. During that same period, Bill Grubb, who had been Atari's vice president of marketing, formed Imagic, another independent game company. He took several top programmers with him. Like Activision, Imagic became an overnight success.

> Ray Kassar was pissed at Grubb for taking all these people, particularly Mark Bradley. (Bradley had been the national accounts manager at Atari.) He offered Mark the world to stay there, but Mark and Bill worked together at Black and Decker for many years before then and they were very close personal friends.
>
> Ray told Mark . . . he said, "I promise you, I will do everything in my power to destroy your company." He was furious that Mark was leaving and that Imagic had taken all these key programmers from him. It was a real personal vendetta with Ray. That manifested itself not much later.
>
> **—Jim Whims, former executive, Imagic**

---

* The secret room in *Adventure* was discovered while Robinett was in Europe.

Defections from the consumer division had become a common event by this time, and Jim Huether was the last of the original programmers who remained. When Robinett returned from Europe, he applied for a job at Imagic but did not like the way Grubb treated him. Grubb offered him a job but only after insulting him. Regarding the pay as too low, Robinett declined the job.

> One night I was out with Huether and Reuterdahl, drinking beer. After about six pitchers, we decided we must be dumb shits to not be millionaires like the other guys . . . the eight filthy rich guys who were our coworkers when we started at Atari. We decided to form the Dumb Shits Club to celebrate our stupidity and bad choices. The requirement for membership: you had to have designed games for Atari and never made any money from it.
>
> We later elected Jim Huether the president of the Dumb Shit's Club because he was the only one of the original group of twelve that stayed at Atari after three or four years had elapsed.
>
> **—Warren Robinett**

In the end, Robinett was one of four people who received a grant from the National Science Foundation to create educational software for teaching children math. When the grant money expired, the four formed their own software publishing firm called the Learning Company. In 1995, SoftKey International purchased the Learning Company for $600 million.

A Case of Two Gorillas

I remember sitting in the Coleco booth (at the Toy Fair trade show in 1981) even before it was announced. They brought out an 8 x 10 photograph of the new system and said, "We're coming out with this. It's got a TI (Texas Instrument) chip in it. Stay tuned."

—**Al Nilsen, former electronics buyer, JC Penney**

This is a dispute over two gorillas.

—**Judge Robert W. Sweet, U.S. District Court, S.D. New York**

The Beginning of Handheld Games

> Our big success was something that I conceptualized—the first handheld game. I asked the design group to see if they could come up with a game that was electronic that was the same size as a calculator.

> **—Michael Katz, former marketing director, Mattel Toys**

In 1976, Mattel began work on a line of calculator-sized sports games that became the world's first handheld electronic games. The project began when Michael Katz, Mattel's new product category marketing director, told the engineers in the electronics group to design a game the size of a calculator, using LED (light-emitting diodes) technology.

The engineers returned with a strip of red plastic that housed several rows of LEDs, which could be moved and controlled like shapes on the screen of a video game. Players could control lights as they moved across the strip, making them go forward, backward, up, or down, using four directional buttons.

The unit had built-in collision detection. If the player's light made contact with other lights on the strip, the toy registered it.

Simple as this unit was, it became the basis for the first generation of portable electronic games. With the right packaging, Katz decided that the toy could be marketed as either a racing game or a football game. He decided to go with racing.

> We developed a prototype of an obstacle avoidance game in which you had to guide your one LED, avoiding two or three other rows of LEDs that were coming down. It wasn't themed; it was just game play that we tested that turned out to be fun. Then we had to theme it.

> We could have themed it as football. We could have pretended the LED was a running back, but we knew we had a better game coming along from the developers at Mattel that was going to make for a better football game, so we chose auto racing.

> We tested themes with kids by showing them drawings of what the actual game would look like and having them play the prototype. Racing came in second [to football], so we themed our first game as an auto race.

> **—Michael Katz**

Katz's team made no effort to make the LEDs look like race cars. They were simply lights on a vertical plastic strip with three lanes painted on top. The object of the game was to guide a light from the bottom of the strip to the top four times without colliding with other LEDs. Each trip represented a lap around the race course. The game was called *Auto Race.*

After *Auto Race,* Mattel released *Football.* In this game, players controlled an LED on a horizontal strip with ten lines representing yard lines. The LED represented a quarterback who could either pass the ball or scramble across the strip ten times for a touchdown.

Selling for $25 to $35, Mattel's handheld sports games were a great success, generating more than $400 million in sales. Mattel formed an electronics division that followed *Football* and *Auto Race* with *Basketball, Hockey, Baseball,* and eventually the Intellivision game console.

Simon

In 1975, Magnavox filed a suit against Atari, claiming that Nolan Bushnell attended a demonstration of the Odyssey game console in Burlingame, California, and stole Ralph Baer's concept of electronic table tennis. In an ironic twist, Baer attended a 1976 trade show and stole an idea for a portable game from Bushnell.

> Howard Morrison, who was a principal at Marvin Glass [a firm that designed toys], and I went to an MOA [Music Operators Association] show and saw a thing called *Touch Me,* made by Nolan [Bushnell]. It had four buttons and made some horrible noises.
>
> We said, "This has all the earmarks of a great game." And we sat down and came up with the concept for *Simon.*
>
> **—Ralph Baer, designer of Magnavox Odyssey**

Bushnell's toy had a row of lights that flashed patterns and made sounds that players had to memorize and repeat. Baer, working closely with Marvin Glass Associates, improved the game by replacing the sounds with distinct musical notes. His toy had four bright-colored buttons that lit up and played musical notes when pressed.

> I went through *Compton's Encyclopedia for Kids* to find an instrument that
> had four notes that could be played in any sequence without sounding dis-
> sonant. It turned out to be the bugle, C-G-E and B, I think. That's how I
> determined the four notes that are played in *Simon;* notes that sound har-
> monious no matter what sequence you play them in.
>
> **—Ralph Baer**

Baer's prototype had a square case and square buttons. After applying for
a patent for the toy, engineers at Marvin Glass Associates replaced Baer's
square case with a round one, with four buttons forming a ring. They called
the game *Simon.*

Simon played three memorization games. All of the games involved repeating patterns. In the first game, *Simon* played musical patterns. Players competed
with the machine by watching the buttons light up and listening to the musical notes, then repeating the pattern by pressing the buttons in the correct
order. The game lasted until the player made a mistake.

Game two was exactly the same, except that players added one note to the
pattern after every turn. The pattern simply became longer until the player
made a mistake. In game three, players competed against each other instead
of the machine.

Marvin Glass Associates sold *Simon* to Milton Bradley Electronics, a toy company already in the electronic games industry with *Comp IV,* the electronic version
of the board game *Mastermind. Simon* was a major hit during the 1977 Christmas
season.* Despite *Simon's* success, however, Atari did not file suit against Marvin
Glass Associates, Milton Bradley, or Ralph Baer for copying the idea.

> First of all, I don't think he [Bushnell] had a patent. Second, I think the scheme
> he had implemented was an old scheme—following a sequential light. *Simon's*
> claim to fame was the association of discrete sounds with each light. A whole
> lot of people played *Simon* by ear.
>
> **—Ralph Baer**

---

* As of this writing, Milton Bradley is still manufacturing *Simon.*

Handheld electronics were extremely popular in the late 1970s and early 1980s. Most of the earliest games were either sports simulations or memory games, though Mattel experimented with electronic handheld versions of popular game themes such as *Sub Chase.* In 1980, several companies saw the success of Atari's Video Computer System (VCS) version of *Space Invaders* and realized that a big demand existed for home versions of arcade games. Soon afterward, handheld versions of arcade games began appearing in stores.

Nintendo and Mego Electronics created lines of credit card–sized toys with liquid crystal screens that played games and displayed the time. The Mego Time Out series featured original games such as the *Exterminator, Fireman,* and *Flag Man.* Nintendo manufactured the Game and Watch series, which included original games and simplified versions of *Donkey Kong* and other popular Nintendo arcade hits.

Not all portable games were the size of paperback books or credit cards. Joyce Worley, a founder of *Electronic Games* magazine, dubbed the larger gadgets "tabletop games." In 1981, three companies introduced new lines of tabletop games that looked like miniature arcade machines. These games would have simplified versions of such top arcade hits as *Pac-Man* and *Galaxian,* housed in eight-inch cases that were scale models of arcade cabinets.

Nintendo and Tiger Electronics made some very good tabletop games, but the company that earned the reputation for making the best tabletop games was Coleco—the leather company that nearly cornered the market for *Pong*-style television games.

Coleco Comes Back

After nearly going bankrupt in 1976 with the collapse of the *Home Pong* generation of games, Coleco barely survived to the end of the 1970s. Arnold Greenberg, CEO of Coleco, however, had not lost his entrepreneurial ambitions, and he was impressed with the handheld game industry's potential for growth. Shortly after Mattel released *Football,* Coleco entered the market with a similar game titled *Electronic Quarterback* that had a lower price tag and more features.

Whether he was following a set plan or making decisions as he went along, Greenberg seemed to have discovered a way to ride the market. He hired Michael Katz, the Mattel executive who had overseen the launch of *Auto Race* and *Football,* to establish Coleco's marketing department. Greenberg became very aggressive about developing new products.

> Arnold knew that I had been responsible for Mattel's handhelds and he asked me if I wanted to come to Coleco and be part of what he thought would be a wonderful turnaround and establish the first marketing department that Coleco really ever had. He offered to make me vice president of marketing and to give me stock options that I didn't have at Mattel.
>
> The timing was good because we got into all kinds of other handheld games, including the Head-to-Head series, which were two player games that sold very well. We got licenses and designed tabletop games that looked exactly like miniature arcade games, like *Pac-Man* and *Donkey Kong.* They sold extremely well.
>
> **—Michael Katz**

By 1980, the handheld game market began fading, but it didn't matter to Greenberg. He no longer cared about handheld games; he wanted to create a video-game console that could play arcade-quality games. Coleco had made enough money during the heyday of handheld games to begin the research and development phase of building the new console, and Greenberg was ready to try to steal some of Atari's enormous share of the market.

Greenberg had a tough reputation as an employer. He was known to have a temper and to browbeat his executives. According to Michael Katz, Greenberg's driven nature often caused him to live up to his rough reputation, but Katz described him as "tough, smart, eloquent, and fair."

> People give me credit for working for both Arnold Greenberg and [Jack Tramiel, the volatile founder of Commodore Computers] in one lifetime and surviving. They ask, "How could you work for Jack Tramiel?" and I say, "I worked for Arnold Greenberg for three and one half years."
>
> Arnold was incredibly bright and articulate, just a wonderful, spontaneous speaker. I think [he was] a very good leader. . . . dynamic and very tough and demanding.
>
> **—Michael Katz**

In 1981, Coleco began manufacturing tabletop versions of arcade hits. It wasn't just the game play in these tabletop toys that resembled the arcade originals; the cabinets were scale models of arcade machines, right down to the artwork on the outside panels. In order to do this, Greenberg arranged licensing agreements with eight arcade companies, including Sega, Bally/Midway, Exidy, Centuri, Universal, and Nintendo. These arrangements became very important to Coleco with later projects.

Greenberg used his relations with arcade companies to expand his business in another direction. Activision had already launched its first titles by this time, and third-party publishers had become part of the business. Just as Greenberg had seen an opportunity in manufacturing handheld games, he suddenly saw a gold mine in becoming a third-party publisher. Instead of creating new games, however, Greenberg wanted to convert arcade hits into VCS and Intellivision cartridges.

> Atari, of course, was out there with its 2600 and Mattel was coming out with Intellivision, so we decided that we would basically become a third-party supplier of programming. We decided to program for Atari and Intellivision at the same time that we were developing ColecoVision.
>
> There were basically two strategies at work. We would take these licenses and use them not only in the major systems, but also put them into the handheld category. That was very appealing to Nintendo at the time. That's why we got *Donkey Kong* from Nintendo, because they saw that we could maximize their potential revenue stream by putting this product across a number of formats that existed at that point in time.
>
> **—Al Kahn, former executive vice president, Coleco**

> When I found out that we did not take the consumer license to *Donkey Kong,* and that Coleco got it, I asked how could that happen. They said, "Well, it was two dollars a cartridge, and you don't understand. It would have fucked up our cost structure."
>
> I remember I looked at them and I said, "Guys, you got an 88 percent gross margin on cartridges. Don't you understand that a year from now you will walk on shards of broken glass to get a two-dollar cartridge deal?" Now

> that decision basically put Coleco in the business because without *Donkey Kong*, they couldn't have gotten anywhere.
>
> **—Manny Gerard, former vice president, Warner Communications**

ColecoVision

> Arnold, to his credit, felt that the world was ready for a new game system. Atari had been out with the 2600, and that was replaced basically by Intellivision, and Arnold thought that Coleco could come out with a game system that would be better and everyone would trade up.
>
> **—Michael Katz**

It took nearly two years for Greenberg's team to develop ColecoVision, its new super game console. Greenberg began telling retailers about the system toward the end of 1981, unveiled it at the January Consumer Electronics Show in 1982, and began shipping it in July.

Though ColecoVision had only the standard eight-bit processor, 8K of RAM (random access memory) with an additional 16K of video RAM found in other game consoles, it had several other features. Five years had passed since Atari began developing the VCS. The price of technology had come down so much that Coleco could afford a chip with the memory mapping and frame buffers that Atari left out of Stella, the processing chip in the Video Computer Systems. These added features gave the ColecoVision smoother animation and more arcade-like graphics than the Intellivision and the VCS.

Coleco powered the ColecoVision with a chip set from Zilog that was so advanced, it could even handle video images. When Hasbro engineers began experimenting with interactive video in 1985, they used a modified ColecoVision game console.

> The reason we chose ColecoVision to do this kind of down-and-dirty prototype was that it had been designed initially to be able to pass video through it. You could do what I call the wallpaper game, that is, a game in which you

> have moving video in the background with computer graphics imposed on top of the video.

> **—Tom Zito, former president and CEO, Digital Pictures**

Even with its technological superiority, Coleco faced a tough challenge because its fledgling system had very few games. Atari had more than 100 games for the VCS by 1982, and Atari executives offered huge sums of money for exclusive licensing agreements with arcade companies. Far fewer games were on the market for the Intellivision, but Mattel had already carved out a niche with its realistic sports simulations.

Coleco did not have enough money to compete with Atari for big licenses, but Coleco's marketers had a knack for selecting small games with strong followings. Coleco secured licenses for *Mr. Do, Lady Bug, Cosmic Avenger,* and *Venture.* And ColecoVision's powerful processor generated games that looked like they belonged in an arcade. Coleco's good relations with Sega resulted in a *Zaxxon* cartridge that sported excellent 3D effects.

> ColecoVision was a real step forward. It was indisputably the best machine counting hardware and software . . . the best platform of those early consoles. Michael Katz, no relation, was a genius at finding little known coin-op games that translated beautifully to the home market.

> **—Arnie Katz, former editor in chief, *Electronic Games***

Katz's marketing team even invented a way to compete with Atari's enormous software library, by creating an adapter that enabled the ColecoVision to play VCS games.

In some ways, using the adapter defeated the purpose of purchasing ColecoVision,* as VCS games looked just as primitive on the ColecoVision as they did on the VCS.

---

* ColecoVision generally sold for $195. By this time, Atari had cut the price of the VCS to $135, in preparation for releasing a new game console called the 5200.

Coleco's crowning achievement, however, was a six-month exclusive license with Nintendo for *Donkey Kong,* a game whose worldwide popularity was surpassed only by *Pac-Man.**

Nintendo was still a small company in 1981, and Minoru Arakawa, president of Nintendo of America, decided that an outside company with established contacts would do a better job marketing *Donkey Kong* than he would be able to do. He decided to work with Coleco because Greenberg offered to do both game cartridges and a tabletop console.

> A couple of things popped up [around Christmas of 1981]. One was the ColecoVision agreement, in which Nintendo was going to license Coleco to do the home video game. . . . give them the home video-game rights to *Donkey Kong.* The *Donkey Kong* success had been so great that they needed help with merchandise licensing of their properties.
>
> **—Howard Lincoln, former outside legal counsel, Nintendo of America**

Once they had made contact with Nintendo, Coleco's representatives moved slowly. They preferred to work with executives at Nintendo's Japanese headquarters. What they did not know was that Howard Lincoln, the outside legal council of Nintendo of America, wrote the contract.

This was all new territory to Lincoln. In creating the contract, he discovered that companies traditionally accepted all liabilities on their games—

---

* In 1978, an Atari executive named Joe Robbins made a foresighted agreement that gave Atari exclusive rights to *Pac-Man.*

> Skip Paul and Ray Kassar told Joe [Robbins], "You go over to Japan and talk to Namco, but don't sign anything with them." We [Atari] felt that they owed us money.
>
> A week later Joe comes back. He's had his picture in the paper, signing this deal with the Japanese and playing with [Masaya] Nakamura on a golf course. He agreed to give them $1 million, and they got to renew their contract, but we got the rights to their coin-op games. At that point they had no hits at all.
>
> It was like Jack and the Beanstalk, and Joe came back with these worthless beans.
>
> Well, one of those beans was a little game called *Pac-Man.* In retrospect, it was the best buy of the decade, but at the time, I think it pretty much cost him his job.
>
> **—Al Alcorn**

that is, Nintendo would accept responsibility for any legal action against Coleco involving *Donkey Kong*. Since he could see no reason why Nintendo should accept such liabilities, Lincoln decided to write a clause that made Coleco responsible for the content of the cartridge.

> I came up with a clause in our agreement that cleared Nintendo of all liability from Coleco's product. I hadn't drafted many of those things [manufacturing agreements], so I was looking in a form book and, typically, you would have the licenser indemnify the licensee or at least make a representation that you own the mark. I asked myself, "Why would we want to do that?"
>
> We drafted the agreement and sent it to Yamauchi. Yamauchi confronted Eric Bromley from Coleco and said, "Sign the license agreement."
>
> He said, "Well, our attorneys haven't seen it."
>
> I think Yamauchi basically said, "Sign the damn thing. You guys are getting ready to ship the product. If you want a license, sign now."
>
> So they signed it.
>
> **—Howard Lincoln**

On February 1, 1982, Coleco and Nintendo signed an agreement in which Coleco paid Nintendo an undisclosed amount of money and promised royalties of $1.40 for every *Donkey Kong* cartridge and $1 for every tabletop machine sold.

Coleco created an excellent version of *Donkey Kong* that came closer to matching arcade gameplay and graphics than any earlier game cartridge, selling it exclusively as a pack-in with ColecoVision as an incentive to purchase the system, which went on sale in July 1982. After six months Coleco began selling VCS and Intellivision versions of *Donkey Kong*.

> We knew that we had to have a hot piece of software to launch the product because software sells hardware. We got it from a little company called Nintendo—*Donkey Kong. Donkey Kong* was exclusive to ColecoVision for the first six months, and we packed it in with the system. If you owned an Atari or Intellivision, you couldn't get *Donkey Kong* for the first six months.

> It was a pretty good marketing strategy. Six months later, when enough
> people had bought ColecoVision, we wanted the profit from the Atari and
> Intellivision owners, so we sold *Donkey Kong* as third-party software.
>
> **—Michael Katz**

Fortune magazine later wrote:

The uncontested smash hit of the year was Coleco, which celebrated its
50th anniversary last year (1982) by more than doubling sales to over
$500 million and quintupling earnings to about $40 million. The Hart-
ford-based toy manufacturer is headed by two brothers: Arnold C.
Greenberg, 49, president and chief executive officer, and Leonard, 55,
chairman. It has long specialized in plastic swimming pools, tricycles,
and hand-held electronic games, but in 1982 it introduced three successful video products: tabletop games, cartridges that fit Atari and
Intellivision equipment, and its own ColecoVision.[1]

Battle of the Kongs[2]

O. R. Rissman, the president of an American handheld game manufacturer
named Tiger Electronic Toys, first saw *Donkey Kong* while visiting Tokyo in the
summer of 1981. He liked what he saw. When he returned to the United States,
he sent a letter to Universal Studios, requesting a license to make video games
and handheld games based on King Kong.

Loretta Sifuentes, a Universal/MCA vice president involved in licensing
properties such as King Kong, received Rissman's request. Before entering such
agreements, Universal's licensing department typically conducted trademark
searches to monitor retail activity.

At the time, Universal's only active King Kong license was with Ben Cooper, Inc., a company that manufactured King Kong masks and costumes.
Sifuentes ran a trademark search on September 25 and discovered several minor uses of King Kong.

This report revealed numerous third-party trademark registrations of
the King Kong name often in conjunction with a picture of a gorilla.

Universal's merchandising and law departments decided not to take any action against those listed in the report because there was very little activity in licensing King Kong at Universal.[3]

Unaware of *Donkey Kong* and satisfied that everything was in order, Universal Studios granted Tiger the license in September 1981.

Nintendo of America began selling *Donkey Kong* in July 1981. By October, the game was selling at the rate of 4,000 arcade units per month.

Sifuentes ran another trademark search in January 1982, which revealed a pending agreement between Nintendo and Coleco for the cartridge and table-top license of *Donkey Kong*. She took the information to Steven Adler, another Universal vice president in charge of licensing, and the two executives decided to go to an arcade and evaluate the game.

After analyzing the game play, Sifuentes and Adler concluded that no one was really interested in licensing King Kong and that Tiger probably planned to use its King Kong license merely to copy *Donkey Kong*. They discussed whether they should continue offering licenses for King Kong. No action was discussed or taken to challenge the *Donkey Kong* application.[4]

In April 1982, Sid Sheinberg, president of MCA and Universal, heard about *Donkey Kong* and asked Robert Hadl, a lawyer with copyright experience working as the Universal vice president in charge of legislative matters, about the game in a memo. At Sheinberg's request, Hadl took his children to an arcade and played *Donkey Kong*. Unlike Sifuentes, Hadl decided that *Donkey Kong*'s story of a giant gorilla breaking loose and carrying a woman to the top of a building came too close to the story of King Kong.

Around that time, Sheinberg arranged a meeting with Arnold Greenberg to discuss Universal Studios investing in Coleco. Greenberg had no reason to suspect that the meeting was about anything else. Video games were in their heyday. Warner Communications had made a great deal of money through its ownership of Atari, Gulf/Western had recently purchased Sega, and several other large companies had expressed interest in breaking into the video-game industry.

The meeting was held on April 27, 1982. It began with a splashy Hollywood luncheon and ended with Sheinberg threatening Arnold Greenberg.

> Universal called me and Arnold out to California. We thought we were going out there to meet with Universal people to talk about how we could work together, you know, maybe even form some kind of venture together or something of that nature. We met with Sid Sheinberg and Lou Wasserman, and I remember they had Steven Spielberg there.
>
> And then Sid pulled Arnold on the side and said, "You know something, we're going to sue you if you don't give us some kind of a royalty on *Donkey Kong* because you're in violation of our copyrights as it relates to King Kong."
>
> Arnold came back and was very concerned because here we were going to ship ColecoVision, which included *Donkey Kong* inside the package. He was concerned that Universal might try to get a temporary restraining order or something.
>
> **—Al Kahn**

On April 28, Universal sent telexes to Nintendo and Coleco, claiming "sole and exclusive ownership of all rights (except book publishing rights) in and to the name, title, character, and story 'King Kong' and 'Kong' . . . including, without limitation, the right to exploit, license and sell games, toys, video displays and other forms of merchandising based upon or using the 'King Kong' name, title and character."[5] Sheinberg demanded that Nintendo and Coleco stop marketing *Donkey Kong,* destroy all *Donkey Kong* inventory, and submit a complete account of profits made through the game. He also threatened to take the case to court if both companies did not settle within 48 hours.

After considering his options, Greenberg decided to back down. Universal Studios was so big and its legal resources were so vast, he could see no way to stand up to it in court. By May 5, Greenberg agreed in principle, obligating Coleco to pay royalties to Universal. The formal agreement was signed one week later.

> Arnold was very concerned, so he signed a deal with Universal, which was really a strange deal. It was a covenant not to sue. It wasn't really a license agreement for Universal. Arnold started paying royalties on any shipments of *Donkey Kong* to Universal in exchange for Universal's pledge not to sue Coleco.
>
> **—Al Kahn**

Hiroshi Yamauchi, president of Nintendo Co. Ltd. in Japan, was baffled and angered. First Nintendo could not penetrate the U.S. market. Now that it had, an enormous and powerful company was threatening to sue him.

Nintendo and Coleco were not the only companies that received threatening messages from Universal. When Robert Hadl discovered the licensing agreement with Tiger Electronics, he angrily called a meeting with Loretta Sifuentes.

> He was upset upon learning that Universal had licensed Tiger, and "wanted to know on what basis [Universal] had made a license," noting the Tiger agreement to be a lousy license because it offered only a small return to Universal and because its exclusivity provision could prevent Universal from concluding its agreement with Coleco.[6]

On May 4, Sheinberg sent a mailgram to Tiger Electronics, threatening to terminate its licensing agreement unless Tiger submitted its game for approval. Tiger sent materials explaining the game the following day.

Minoru Arakawa and Howard Lincoln flew down to represent Nintendo in a meeting with Coleco and Universal Studios on May 6. Robert Hadl restated the claim that *Donkey Kong* infringed upon Universal's trademark for King Kong. Lincoln responded that Nintendo had run a trademark search and found numerous unlicensed uses of "King Kong," and that he had discovered that Universal had only applied for the name within the last decade.

Greenberg did not inform Arakawa and Lincoln about his arrangement with Universal. Instead, he urged Arakawa to sign an agreement with Universal.

> I didn't realize that Coleco had already cut a deal with them behind our back, prior to the time we had the first meeting. We were puzzled by how Coleco kept pushing for an agreement. We knew that we had drafted the agreement with Coleco such that we didn't have any liability vis-à-vis Coleco, but we suspected that Universal didn't know that.
>
> **—Howard Lincoln**

The day after their meeting with Nintendo, executives from Universal discussed purchasing $30 million of Coleco debentures in a separate meeting with Coleco executives.

Sheinberg canceled Universal's marketing agreement with Tiger Electronics on May 8, stating that the proposed King Kong game was substantially similar to *Donkey Kong*. Rissman not only refused to let Universal terminate the agreement but also in a later letter began questioning Universal's ownership of the name.

During the May 6 meeting, Robert Hadl said he would have a document—a chain of title—sent to Nintendo. The chain of title was important because it would establish Universal's claim on King Kong. The document did not arrive.

Howard Lincoln called Hadl the following week, asking for the chain of title. Hadl restated his demand that Nintendo pay Universal royalties on *Donkey Kong* but did not send a chain of title.

Minoru Arakawa had great faith in Howard Lincoln. Based on Lincoln's recommendation, he chose to fight Universal rather than settle out of court. The decision could have cost Arakawa his job. Even when his father-in-law, Hiroshi Yamauchi, questioned this decision, Arakawa continued to support Lincoln.

The next time that Arakawa and Lincoln met with Universal was a luncheon at Universal Studios. Lincoln and Arakawa called Hadl and said that they wanted to set up a meeting. Hadl arranged a small luncheon with the Nintendo executives and Sid Sheinberg on May 21, believing that Nintendo was ready to concede Universal's ownership of King Kong and settle the dispute. He was wrong.

> Mr. Arakawa and I decided that we would go down and simply tell him that we've come to tell you to your face that we would pay you if we thought we were liable, but we had done our homework and we were not prepared to pay anything because we hadn't done anything wrong. We just wanted to essentially look him in the face and tell him that. It seemed to be the honorable thing to do.
>
> As it turned out, maybe Hadl had led him [Sheinberg] to believe that we had come down to reach some type of a monetary settlement with him. And it was really funny because it was not what he was expecting and his reaction was shock.
>
> —Howard Lincoln

Lincoln and Arakawa had decided not to give in to Universal's demands, even if it meant that they would have to present their case in court. Lincoln had researched Universal's claim and come to the conclusion that the claim on King Kong was weak at best. If he was right, Universal Studios' lawyers would not be able to win in court, despite their unlimited legal resources.

Arakawa, Lincoln, Hadl, and Sheinberg had a quiet meal at Universal Studios. As the lunch finished, Sheinberg, possibly hoping to win over Arakawa the same way he had enticed Greenberg, mentioned that Nintendo might have future business dealings with Universal after settling the *Donkey Kong* affair.

Lincoln responded with a calculated and unflinching statement, telling Sheinberg that after a full investigation, he did not accept Universal's claim to King Kong and that Nintendo would not pay the studio royalties on *Donkey Kong.* Sheinberg exploded. "You'd better start saving money to pay your attorney's fees," he shouted, then added that Universal was very litigious and that the "litigation department even turned a profit."[7]

Realizing that the case would end up in court, Hadl reopened discussions with Tiger Electronics, stating that Universal would consider issuing a nonexclusive license to Tiger if it altered its *King Kong* game by: (1) putting a fire hat on the hero character; (2) replacing the barrels the ape was throwing with bombs; and (3) making the floors of the building the hero was climbing horizontal instead of slanted. These changes were supposed to differentiate Tiger's *King Kong* game from *Donkey Kong.* O. R. Rissman demonstrated the new game to Hadl at a Sears store in early June, and the changes were approved.

On June 29, 1982, Universal filed suit against Nintendo, claiming that Universal Studios owned all rights to King Kong by virtue of agreements with RKO Pictures, Inc., the studio that made the original *King Kong* movie, and the heirs of Merian C. Cooper, the man who wrote *King Kong.* That same day Universal also announced its licensing agreement with Coleco.

Sheinberg's attack did not stop with the lawsuit. By this time, Nintendo had grossed more than $180 million from sales of approximately 60,000 *Donkey Kong* arcade machines. Nintendo had also licensed the *Donkey Kong* name and character to more than 50 companies, for everything from cereal boxes and board games to Saturday morning cartoons.

Determined to make an example out of Nintendo, Universal obtained a list of all of Nintendo's licensees, contacted them, and threatened them with litigation if they did not abandon their relationships with Nintendo. The only licensee that stayed with Nintendo was Milton Bradley, whom Universal never took to court.

As they prepared for their day in court, Howard Lincoln and John Kirby, the lawyer that would represent Nintendo in court, flew to Nintendo's Japanese headquarters to take depositions. At this time, Lincoln first met Hiroshi Yamauchi. He also took statements from Shigeru Miyamoto, the man who had designed *Donkey Kong*.

> I met Mr. Miyamoto in connection with the *Donkey Kong* litigation on my first trip to Kyoto. I was such a poor international traveler. . . . My car stalled on the way to the airport and I almost missed my plane. Then I checked my bags to Tokyo, even though we were going to Osaka.
>
> I got to Kyoto and met Mr. Yamauchi for the first time. And it was in connection with the litigation that I first met Mr. Miyamoto. He was a young guy, really young. I remember that he came into Yamauchi's office where there's a big and very formal conference room. Yamauchi and Arakawa and other people were there.
>
> The door opened and there was a disheveled—I wouldn't call it disheveled—but he was a little bit disheveled and his hair went in ten different directions. And it was this guy, Miyamoto. At that time, I don't think I really knew what it was that he had accomplished in creating *Donkey Kong*.
>
> He had showed us the drawings and the way in which he had come up with the game, but he was working for Mr. Yokoi [the head of engineering] at the time. As I recall, he was new to Nintendo and pretty much a junior guy.
>
> **—Howard Lincoln**

As they prepared to meet Universal in court, Arakawa offered Lincoln a job at Nintendo. Lincoln accepted. By the time the case went to court, Lincoln was the senior vice president of Nintendo of America, rather than its outside counsel.

The case was heard before Judge Robert W. Sweet of the United States District Court for the Southern District of New York and lasted for seven days, during which time Kirby had a Nintendo employee demonstrate *Donkey Kong* in the court, then compared the game with clips from the movie *King Kong*.

As it turned out, Universal Studios did not own King Kong. In fact, Universal's profit-earning litigation department had recently proved that no one owned the character. In 1975, Universal had taken RKO to court, claiming that the original King Kong was more than forty years old and was now public domain.*

Judge Sweet ruled that Universal's claims were not valid. Sid Sheinberg's words about profiting through litigation were repeated somewhat ominously in the Judge's summary of the case.**

Throughout this litigation, Universal knew, as a result of the RKO litigation, that it had no rights to any visual image of King Kong from the classic movie or its remake.[8]

Nonetheless, Universal, when it seemed beneficial, made sweeping assertions of rights, attempting to extract license agreements from companies incapable of or unwilling to confront Universal's "profit center."[9]

Once Nintendo demonstrated that King Kong was public domain, Universal's lawyers were unable to demonstrate that remaking *King Kong* gave Universal Studios ownership of it. In the end, no chain of claim was ever delivered, in or out of court. Universal's lawyers were also unable to prove "the likelihood of confusion between *Donkey Kong* and King Kong,"[10] and Universal's efforts to scare the companies that licensed *Donkey Kong* gave Nintendo grounds to seek extensive damages for lost revenues.

Tiger Electronics did not fare much better than Universal. Judge Sweet ruled that Tiger's *King Kong* game infringed upon *Donkey Kong* and let Nintendo choose to collect either statutory damages or Universal's profits from licensing the game. Nintendo chose to collect Universal's licensing fee, which totaled $56,689.41.

. . . *Donkey Kong*'s particular expression of a gorilla villain and a carpenter hero (with or without a fire hat) who must dodge various obstacles

---

* This action was taken to clear the way for Dino DiLaurentis to remake the movie.

** Nintendo's lawyer, John Kirby, reminded the court of Sheinberg's angry claim while cross-examining him.

(whether bombs or fireballs) while climbing up ladders (whether complete or broken) and picking up prizes (umbrellas and purses) to rescue a fair-haired (whether knotted or pigtailed) hostage from the gorilla is protractible against Universal and its licensees.[11]

Judge Sweet's decision cleared Nintendo and placed Universal in the unfortunate position of having to answer to the companies it had threatened. Coleco wanted its royalty money refunded. Atari had agreed to pay royalties on the VCS version of *Donkey Kong*, which came out a few months before the case went to court. After Nintendo won, Atari also demanded its money back. Even Ruby-Spears, the company that did the *Donkey Kong* cartoon show, lodged a claim against Universal Studios.

Tiger Electronics released its *King Kong* game on a cartridge for the Atari VCS and also as a handheld electronic game.

> Suffice it to say that when Nintendo won [its] suit from Universal, Coleco went back at Universal and said, "Hey, what about us?" And Universal then bought some Coleco stock and basically as a payback for the moneys that Coleco had paid to Universal on the royalties side.
>
> **—Al Kahn**

Nintendo's counterclaims did not go to court until May 20, 1985. On July 29, 1985, Judge Sweet ordered Universal to pay Nintendo $1.8 million for legal fees, photocopying expenses, costs incurred creating graphs and charts, and lost revenues.

By the time the case was concluded, the video-game industry had nearly vanished and Coleco had entered the doll business.

CHAPTER 14

The Fall

They reached a pinnacle in interactive game design with *Robotron*. If I was on a desert island and I had AC, I'd have *Robotron*. There's no question.

—David Thiel, former sound engineer, Gottlieb

But Atari's biggest coup this season will probably be extraterrestrial: this week Atari will launch its first *E.T.* video game in time to hit toy shelves in November.

—William D. Marbach with Peter McAlevey, "A New Galaxy of Video Games,"
Newsweek, **October 25, 1982**

Spielberg wanted to make *E.T.* into a *Pac-Man* game, but I wanted to do something original. In retrospect . . . Maybe it wasn't such a bad idea.

—Howard Scott Warshaw, former game designer, Atari Corporation

In the Arcades

No one realized that the arcade business had begun to collapse in 1982. Arcade owners, still believing that all it would take to set the business right was a few good games, watched for hits and tried to rebuild their businesses. And some of the best games of all time came out between the end of 1982 and the middle of 1983.

Robotron 2084

> I was thinking about the novel *1984*. There was a lot of excitement about the whole Orwell thing and [the year] 1984 was upon us, and I was noticing that things were not at all like they were in the book.
>
> I'm kind of a science-fiction guy, and I was thinking about it and . . . well, decided that probably not too much is going to happen in the next couple of years. It was really going to be 2084 when the ship runs out and it's not going to be humans subjugating humans, it's going to be robots doing the subjugating.
>
> **—Eugene Jarvis, creator of *Robotron 2084***

Eugene Jarvis and Larry DeMar left Williams shortly after completing *Defender*, the first game Jarvis created as an independent consultant. They started a consulting firm called Vid Kidz that designed games for Williams. Then, in 1981, Jarvis crashed his MGB and broke his right hand.

Jarvis's arm was still in a cast when he and DeMar began their next project. As they had with *Defender*, Jarvis and DeMar started by fleshing out a story about the game. They decided the game would be about an Orwellian world. Since 1984 was only three years away, it was obvious that the world was not in sync with Orwell's timetable, so they set their game in 2084 to give mankind an extra century to create a viable Big Brother.

Mankind had created a race of robots to use as servants in Jarvis and DeMar's story, but the robots had evolved to the point when they no longer needed humans, so they took over the world.

> The idea is that right now we have all these machines that are serving us. They're getting more and more intelligent, and at some point we'll see computer rights activists because these things will be so smart and you'll be

> talking to them and they'll be your buddy and they'll be your information
> agent on the Internet, and then some guy comes along and unplugs your
> computer and screws up your hard disk or something and it's like, wait a
> minute, that was murder! It's like killing your dog or something.
>
> So, computers are running around, trying to help our lives and scooping up
> our shit and everything, and finally they realize, "What do we need these guys
> for? I mean, they're nasty people, they build nuclear bombs, they kill each other.
> We're having all these problems with them. What's the equation here?"
>
> **—Eugene Jarvis**

When *Robotron 2084* begins, robots have conquered the world. Players cannot hope to restore mankind. The game has no end; it simply repeats until the player runs out of lives.

Players control a tiny hero with a large head and thick glasses, whom Jarvis thought looked like Elton John. The hero and his family are the last humans, and the robots, according to Jarvis, want to catch them and put them in a zoo.

As usual, Jarvis wanted a game in which players were surrounded by enemies. He prided himself on creating games with nearly unwinnable circumstances. In this case, every scene in the game began with the hero and his family completely surrounded by robots. In order to survive, players had to help the hero dodge and shoot the robots and save family members, while avoiding mines and projectiles. The game moved at a frantic pace.

> In almost every game like *Space Invaders* or *Galaxian,* everything comes down at
> you. Our idea was that being in the center of something would cause incredible
> panic. Things are coming from all sides and you are just like, "Oh, my gosh!"
>
> **—Eugene Jarvis**

Jarvis's car accident played an important role in the designing of *Robotron 2084.* With his hand in a cast, Jarvis was laid up in bed for a few days. While trapped in bed, he thought about a popular game from Stern Electronics, in which players helped a man run through a maze while shooting slow-moving robots. Jarvis loved the game but hated its joystick-button configuration because the same joystick was used for moving the character and aiming his shots.

When Jarvis returned to work, his cast made him unable to handle the standard joystick and button configuration used with most games, so he and DeMar rigged a two-joystick controller by attaching two Atari 2600 controllers to a panel. In this configuration, one joystick controlled the hero and the other aimed his gun.

> It was the first game to introduce the twin joystick, which let you fire in one direction and move in the other. It's a very challenging control, most people cannot . . . probably 80 percent of the population cannot pat their head and rub their stomach at the same time. You actually have to be fairly coordinated with both hands, and you have to be able to deal with running away from something and shooting in another direction.
>
> —Eugene Jarvis

Williams sold less than 20,000 *Robotron 2084* machines and considered it a success. In later years, *Robotron 2084* would become one of the most highly esteemed trophies among video-game collectors.

Q*BERT

D. Gottlieb & Company, the group that helped found the coin-operated amusement industry with *Baffle Ball,* entered the video-game industry late. Columbia Pictures owned Gottlieb & Company by the time Gottlieb produced *Reactor.* Coca-Cola owned Columbia Pictures, so some Gottlieb employees joked that Coca-Cola was their boss.

Gottlieb had only one hit video game—a quirky little title named *Q*Bert*. The project began when an artist named Jeff Lee drew a stack of cubes on his computer screen in a tribute to M. C. Escher.

> Being a fan of the great Dutch artist M. C. Escher, the master of optical illusions, I constructed a stack of triad-based cubes. Admiring my derivative handiwork, it struck me, there's a game in here somewhere![1]

Lee created an Escher-like pyramid of blocks and a two-legged character with no arms who hopped along the blocks and shot enemies with projectiles that he fired from his hose-like nose. He called the game "Snots and Boogers."

Gottlieb had recently hired a programmer from Bell Laboratories named Warren Davis. Though he was assigned to a game called *Protector,* Davis sometimes roamed around the office, hoping to try his hand at other projects as well. One night Jeff Lee's 3D blocks caught his eye.

> *Q*Bert* was kind of a Skunk Works project. Warren Davis was a good programmer who had no track record whatsoever doing games; he just thought it would be a fun thing to do.
>
> Warren saw this stuff that Jeff Lee was working on, these shaded cubes that filled his screen, and asked if he could have a copy of the art. He started playing with it and said, "You know, the problem with this is that it shouldn't cover the screen like this." So he made a pyramid out of it.
>
> **—David Thiel**

Davis's biggest contribution to the game was changing its theme from shooting to strategy. Davis eliminated the nose-gun and changed the goal of the game to saving the main character rather than killing enemies.

One night a Gottlieb employee named Ron Waxman saw the game and told Davis that the blocks should change color whenever the armless character jumped on them. With that suggestion, the game finally had a clear goal: changing all of the blocks to a particular color while avoiding enemies.*

During a meeting, another Gottlieb employee named Richard Tracy suggested that the game and its main character be named Q*Bert, a name that he derived from the words "Cube" and "Hubert."[2]

The game began taking shape. Q*Bert's enemies became more ludicrous than menacing. They were comic animals that included a bouncing snake named "Coily," a mop-headed gremlin named "Ugg," and a tiny hood in shades named "Wrongway." Lee suggested creating two rather harmless imps named "Slick" and "Sam," who made extra work for Q*Bert by changing the blocks he had touched back to their original colors.

Lee and a sound engineer named Dave Thiel came up with a humorous device for giving Q*Bert a distinctive personality. They set the game up so

---

* Rick Tighe, a techie, suggested sticking the pinball knocker in the cabinet. It went off when Coily fell off the cubes, making a loud "thwack."

that when Coily, Ugg, or Wrongway caught him, or when players ran Q*Bert over the edge of the blocks, he gives a trailing-away scream followed by a sickening thud. At other times he muttered angry gibberish words and a word balloon appeared above his head with messages like "@!#@!"

> Now, in parallel with this, completely independently and having nothing to do with what Warren and Jeff were up to, I had been tasked with using this speech chip that was on a pinball sound board. It was a really unpleasant task because the technology was crummy. You had to manually put together these units of speech, these little sounds, and try to make it say things. It's not the same as joining letters together on paper and ending up with words.
>
> We wanted the game to say, "You have gotten 10,000 bonus points," and the closest I came to it after an entire day would be "bogus points."
>
> Being very frustrated with this, I said, "Well, screw it. What if I just stick random numbers in the chip instead of all of this highly authored stuff, what happens?" It sounded alien. It sounded like somebody should be able to understand it, but, of course, you couldn't understand it because it was gibberish.
>
> By that time, Warren had Q*Bert bouncing around on the cubes, and I said, "Have I got something for you."
>
> **—David Thiel**

*Q*Bert* was released in 1983. The game's popularity resulted in licensing deals for lunchboxes, board games, and a Saturday morning cartoon. Gottlieb sold approximately 25,000 *Q*Bert* arcade machines.

Dragon's Lair

In 1983, Cinematronics, the pioneering arcade company that led the move toward vector-graphics games in the late 1970s, released *Dragon's Lair.*

The game, which combined computer engineering and a Pioneer laser disc machine, had animated cartoon graphics that looked like something out of a Walt Disney cartoon. Understandably, it resembled a Disney cartoon, because it was created by Don Bluth, a former Disney animator who had worked on films such as *Robin Hood, The Rescuers,* and *Pete's Dragon.*

> Don Bluth had been in Disney's inner circle, one of the chosen heirs of the company, and he decided to leave Disney and go off on his own. No one had ever left Disney's inner circle before, and Disney did everything it could to have him blacklisted.
>
> **—Rick Dyer, founder, RDI Technologies**

In *Dragon's Lair*, players helped a knight named Dirk as he rescued Princess Daphne from an evil castle. The game play was like a cross between an old-fashioned Saturday morning serial and a series of multiple-choice questions. The screen would show an animated sequence in which Dirk faced some new danger and players had to respond by moving Dirk with a joystick or pressing a button to make him draw his sword.

In one sequence, for instance, Dirk walked into a room in which a boiling beaker of liquid sat on a table under a sign reading "Drink me." Left to his own devices, Dirk would drink the liquid and die, but players could save him by pulling the joystick to the right, causing him to leave the room.

If he drank the potion, players saw an animation of Dirk gasping. After three mistakes, the screen showed a picture of a partially skeletal Dirk scowling at the player.

Cinematronics had been in Chapter 11 for a year when it released *Dragon's Lair*. To complete the project, Cinematronics established a partnership with RDI Technologies, a company that later tried to market a home laser-disc game system.*

Due largely to public fascination with the new technology, *Dragon's Lair* was an immediate and profitable hit. Cinematronics sold more than 16,000 *Dragon's Lair* machines in 1983, for an average price of $4,300.[3] Coleco purchased the home rights to the game, giving Cinematronics an additional $2 million. *Dragon's Lair* was so successful that Cinematronics released a follow-up game called *Space Ace* within a few months.

> Steven Spielberg loved *Dragon's Lair*. After seeing the game, he contacted Bluth and they worked together on some films.
>
> **—Rick Dyer**

---

* Because Coleco owned the rights to *Dragon's Lair*, RDI was unable to offer the games as one of the titles for its new system.

A battle formed between Cinematronics, Don Bluth, and RDI Technologies. Though Bluth began work on *Dragon's Lair II* shortly after finishing *Space Ace,* the game did not come out until 1991. By the time it did, both Cinematronics and RDI Technologies had gone out of business. Leland, a Texas-based company, released *Dragon's Lair II: Time Warp* into the arcades.

Mylstar (formerly Gottlieb), Atari, and Williams all joined Cinematronics in releasing laser-disc games, but *Dragon's Lair* was the only game of its kind to become a hit.

Society Gone Games

By the middle of 1982, even as the arcade industry began its lengthy fall, video games crept into other areas of American popular culture. Video jockeys talked about video games on MTV. Walt Disney Pictures made a movie, *Tron,* in which actor Jeff Bridges saved the world by entering a super computer and defeating an evil program in a series of video game—like battles. The first movie to feature computer-drawn special effects, it inspired two arcade games from Bally/Midway—*Tron* and *Discs of Tron*—as well as several home game cartridges from Mattel. Arcade games were also used in the backgrounds of dozens of movies.

Consumers no longer had to go to the store to buy games; they could purchase them from home. Columbia House, the parent company of the Columbia Record Club, opened the Columbia Cartridge Club. Other companies, such as Tele Soft, Inc., and VideoLivery, set up toll-free lines to let shoppers call in orders for the latest games. Some companies even began experimenting with delivering games over modems and cable television.

Software manufacturers also experimented with new topics for games. In October 1982, Caballero Control Corporation released three X-rated games for the Atari VCS. The games—*Custer's Revenge, Bachelor Party,* and *Beat 'Em & Eat 'Em*—were more crude than sexual. They retailed for $49.95.

Of the three games, *Custer's Revenge* received the most attention. The game involved helping Custer escape from battle by dodging arrows. Once safely away from the battlefield, he would find and rape an Indian woman tied to a stake.

Actually, there were several attempts to do adult games in 1982 and 1983. Caballero, a company that did Swedish erotica, put out three cartridges for the VCS under the name Mystique. One was *Custer's Revenge,* a game in which you ran along, left to right, dodging Indian arrows. If you did that successfully, you got to rape an Indian girl who was tied to a pole.

As you might imagine, Native American groups loved this game. There were protests all over the country. Women Against Pornography did a lot of picketing against it.

I remember talking to a representative of that organization and telling her that in my opinion, the best way to keep the game from selling was to ignore it. These were games that most people wouldn't touch with a ten-foot pole.

They trained all their energy on *Custer's Revenge* and they succeeded in helping it sell twice as many copies as the other adult games. Mystique sold approximately 80,000 copies of *Custer's Revenge* at a time when games were starting to sell half a million or more.

—Arnie Katz, former editor in chief, *Electronic Games*

Another sign of the video-game industry's growing strength was its continuing expansion. In 1982, Activision replaced Atari as the fastest-growing company in the history of the United States. Riding high with such hits as *Pitfall* and *River Raid,* Activision had $150 million in sales in 1982.

Activision was extremely successful. At one time, before Compaq came along, it was considered the fastest-growing American company in history. We grew from zero to $160 million in annual sales in three years.

—Alan Miller, cofounder, Activision

In April 1982, Atari released one of the most anticipated video-game cartridges of all time—the VCS version of *Pac-Man.* Demand for the game was so immense that Atari executives believed that many consumers would purchase VCSs just to play *Pac-Man.* Atari manufactured 12 million *Pac-Man* cartridges.

In 1982 we shipped 12 million *Pac-Man* cartridges. It was a record. I mean, to ship 12 million of one product at a retail price of $25.75 was extraordinary.

—Ray Kassar, former president and CEO, Atari

> We were the first retailer ever to go and do national network television advertising behind a software title. That was April 6, 1982, the launch of that little guy called *Pac-Man*. We sold over a million *Pac-Man* cartridges.

> **—Al Nilsen, former toy buyer, JC Penney**

The video-game industry became frenzied with excitement with the release of *Pac-Man*. Drugstores opened video-game counters, toy stores fought for the latest cartridges, and Kmart and JC Penney challenged Sears's claim as the largest video-game vendor. In the end, JC Penney, led by a savvy toy buyer named Al Nilsen, narrowly inched out Sears to become Atari's number-one retail partner.

General Computer and Atari

> Kevin [Curran] and I, as we found out later, were naïve students. We kind of misunderstood what they meant and thought they really were paying us money to develop video games since that's what the contract stated.
>
> Later, years later over beers, we were all laughing at the fact that the intent was to pay us $50,000 a month for two years to go away.

> **—Doug Macrae, cofounder, General Computer**

In August of 1981, Atari took General Computer to court to stop it from making enhancement boards. The case was settled out of court. General Computer agreed to make video games for Atari and stop making enhancement boards, and Atari dropped the suit and paid General Computer $50,000 per month for the next two years in exchange for first refusal rights on all games they might make.

Doug Macrae and Kevin Curran, founders of General Computer, immediately set up a larger shop and hired programmers to help design and build new games. What they did not understand was that Atari did not expect to receive games; the $50,000 per month was Atari's way of buying them out of the industry.

Within 90 days, they called Atari, asking how they could submit their first game—an arcade game called *Food Fight*.

> Atari did not hear from us for about 90 days, and we called them up and said, "We've got our first video game we'd like you to take a look at." They

sounded kind of shocked, saying, "We did not really expect it. . . . sure."
And we brought out to them the game *Food Fight.*

—**Doug Macrae**

Food Fight was a fast-paced chase game, in which Charley Chuck, a blonde-haired boy, picked up pies, bananas, and other foods and threw them at chefs as they tried to corner him. It was a simple game in which the goal was to eat the ice cream cone on the other side of the board. The boy throwing the food was designed to look like Jonathan Hurd, the lead programmer on the project. Atari bought the game and published it.

Though *Food Fight* was not a particularly successful game, the speed with which General Computer created the game impressed Atari executives. Asked if they could also make games for the VCS, Curran and Macrae said they could and began making what turned out to be some of the most popular cartridges Atari ever offered.

Between 1982 and 1984, General Computer hired a pool of seventy engineers, making it much larger than Atari's internal VCS research and development team. Curran and Macrae produced seventy-two games during that time, including the VCS versions of *Ms. Pac-Man, Centipede,* and *Pole Position.*

The Atari 5200

Toward the end of 1982, Atari finally made the hardware upgrade that Nolan Bushnell had suggested in 1978: a new and improved game console called the Atari 5200. Shaped like a large, rectangular wedge, the 5200 had the same processor as the Atari 400 home computer and retailed for $250.

Atari's engineering team was particularly unhappy with the 5200. In the months before its launch, team members passed a petition around the research and development department to try and get the system dropped unless new controllers were added. When they gave the petition to Ray Kassar, however, he decided to ignore it and pushed the system through manufacturing.

At its launch, Atari released translations of *Super Breakout, Pac-Man, Centipede, Space Invaders, Defender, Missile Command,* and *Galaxian* to support the new system. (More than half of the games for the 5200 were developed by General Computer.) In all, twelve cartridges were ready at the time of the launch.

Most reviewers and analysts were impressed. *Newsweek* called the 5200 "a quantum improvement over the standard 2600 (with the release of the 5200, Atari began referring to the VCS as the 2600)."[4] *Video Games* magazine called the 5200 "a classy act" and complimented the unit for its special effects, its high-resolution color graphics, its ability to handle several moving objects at one time, and its sophisticated sound synthesizer.[5]

Despite its strengths, the 5200 had a few strikes against it. It cost more than ColecoVision, yet its graphics were not as attractive. It had a fairly small library of games, and Atari's programming team could not devote its full attention to the 5200 because it was still making games for the huge 2600 user base. According to Arnie Katz, editor in chief of *Electronic Games,* the 5200 was "a buggy, unpleasant system with basically the same old games turned up a notch in terms of audiovisual quality."

The 5200's biggest problem, according to *Electronic Games* executive editor Bill Kunkel, was its controller. The joysticks on the 5200 did not center themselves, making it harder to control the action. Other joysticks had self-centering springs, but the joysticks on the 5200 simply fell over.

> The 2600 was fading. ColecoVision had already passed it, so they moved to their next-generation system, which was the 5200.
>
> The 5200 had several strong titles. They ported over all the best 400/800 computer games on to 5200 cartridges.
>
> But the 5200 was a doomed system because of one simple thing: it had the worst controllers in the history of the business—this non-centering joystick. Dead fish floppo joysticks. Just try playing *Dig Dug* or *Pac-Man* with a floppo joystick.
>
> **—Bill Kunkel, former executive editor, *Electronic Games***

Vectrex

In 1982, General Consumer Electronics (GCE) released a product that bridged the gap between tabletop electronics and video game consoles—the Vectrex. Standing approximately 14 inches tall, the Vectrex had a 9-inch black-and-white vector-graphics monitor built into its cabinet, a slot for game cartridges, and an extremely bulky built-in game pad.

Rumor had it that GCE president Ed Krakauer was traveling in the Orient when he was approached by an Asian businessman. The businessman had a warehouse full of monitors that had been built for use in cardiogram machines. According to the rumor, the businessman offered to sell Krakauer the monitors for less than it cost to build them (the company that originally ordered having refused delivery). Krakauer bought the monitors and had an engineering team design a game console around them. The system name: Vectrex.

Retailing for $199, the Vectrex was a great success, and GCE sold its entire inventory. Unfortunately, once Krakauer's supply of monitors ran out, so did his business. When Krakauer returned to Asia, hoping to secure a good price on another shipment of monitors, he discovered that ordering vector monitors from a manufacturer was far more expensive than purchasing them from a distressed supplier, so he pulled the plug on his business.

According to Hope Neiman, one of the first GCE employees, this legend about the warehouse of unwanted monitors is completely inaccurate.

> The story about the monitors was not true. In fact, it was a real problem for us to get 9-inch monitors made because nobody really was doing them anymore. Everything was going bigger and bigger in those days.
>
> We made the monitors in Hong Kong.
>
> **—Hope Neiman, former marketing director,**
> **General Consumer Electronics**

Ed Krakauer, Lee Chaden, and Shelly Morrick, the founders of GCE, envisioned making a game console with a built-in screen from the day they started their company. There was no chance encounter in Hong Kong and no warehouse filled with cut-rate monitors.

Developing the console required capital. Like Coleco, GCE used revenues from the lucrative handheld-games market of the late 1970s to develop a videogame console.

> Development was very costly. In order to create some additional cash flow, we created these three game watches—*GameTime, ArcadeTime,* and *SportsTime.* The latter two both featured little joysticks on the watch, in addition to a single button.

> Each of them had a feature that allowed you to turn the sound off. This totally endeared us to parents. You could play them in school without your teacher knowing that you were really playing. I think they sold for $39.95.
>
> **—Hope Neiman**

Like many small companies, GCE had a small staff and a small budget. Many of the company's games were developed by outside programmers since only three people were on GCE's research and development team. When Toys "R" Us refused to carry *GameTime* on the grounds that GCE was too small to advertise, GCE created demand for its products by sending thousands of free samples to subscribers of *Boy's Life,* along with notes that instructed the kids to request *GameTime* at local toy stores. So many kids went into Toys "R" Us stores asking for the product that the company began carrying GCE products.

Before GCE could market the Vectrex, the company ran into funding problems. Looking for a partner, Hope Neiman flew to Massachusetts and presented the system to executives of Milton Bradley, a company that had raked in huge profits from such early portable games as *Simon.*

> We were going to have to get the cost of the unit down and probably lose money, which is what happens today, in order to get the hardware into people's hands. That was going to take a major investor. The industry was hot and the public markets were bad.
>
> In the mid-1980s, you couldn't go public and expect to achieve anything as far as a reasonable return on your investment. The industry was very hot and Ed was very well connected, so we got a lot of interest. I presented before every major studio. I presented to all the major toy companies, venture capitalists, you name it. We probably did fifty presentations in the span of a month.
>
> [The executives at] Milton Bradley felt they had really missed the boat on the business; after all, Mattel had become a major player with Intellivision. Their management was somewhat stodgy and they sort of knew that this would be sort of a cool thing to do, but they weren't sure that they really wanted to do it.

> They decided to buy the company. They initially bought the company, saying they were going to leave us alone because we had shown them that we were a success.

—Hope Neiman

The Vectrex's vector-graphics screen proved to be both a bane and a blessing. Hardcore video-game enthusiasts liked its high-resolution images. Vector-based games like *Tempest* and *Star Trek* were still big in the arcades at the time, so many arcade fans knew about the advantages of vector graphics. Many parents also liked having a game system with its own monitor because that made it possible for them to watch television while their children played games.[*] A *Newsweek* author praised the Vectrex's graphics in a holiday article about the video-game phenomenon.

The general public, however, considered vector graphics boring when compared to the colorful arcade translations available for the Video Computer System (VCS), the Intellivision, and particularly the ColecoVision.

In an effort to add color to its games, GCE borrowed a page from the Magnavox Odyssey and created plastic overlays for players to place over their screens. This scheme might have come across as completely ridiculous had Cinematronics not used a similar scheme to add color to the arcade version of *Star Castle* a few years earlier.[**]

Milton Bradley demonstrated the Vectrex at the Winter Consumer Electronics Show in 1982 and began shipping it in October of that year. The system retailed for $199 and had an *Asteroids*-like game called *Mine Storm* burned into its circuits. Additional game cartridges sold for $30 to $40. The entire shipment sold out, grossing approximately $80 million.

The Field

Atari, Coleco, and Milton Bradley weren't the only companies hoping to cash in on the video-game craze in 1982. Mattel released a voice module that en-

---

[*] According to Neiman, one reason Vectrex remained active in European markets after disappearing in the United States was that most European homes had only one television.

[**] One of the most popular Vectrex games was an excellent translation of *Star Castle.*

abled certain Intellivision games to speak. Magnavox, still trying to reenter the market with Odyssey 2, also released a voice module. In May 1982, Astrovision released the Astrocade, a system originally launched as the Bally Astrocade by Bally in 1978.

The most improbable product of 1982, however, came from Zircon International, which relaunched the Fairchild Channel F, with some enhancements, as the Channel F II.

In a *Newsweek* article on October 24, 1982, reporters William D. Marbach and Peter McAlevey summarized the industry and its best prospects for Christmas.

> Here they come. *Zaxxon, Smurf, E.T., Donkey Kong* and more; a new generation of video games—and game machines—is gobbling its way onto toy-store shelves like so many Pac-Men. By and large, the entries are a startling leap forward. Manufacturers have taken maximum advantage of recent advances in semiconductor technology to create state-of-the-art fun. For the first time, the graphics and play action of home games are beginning to approach the quality of video-arcade games. In some cases, home-video makers have even vaulted ahead with games that "talk."
>
> The new products will all be out just in time for Christmas. Manufacturers are gunning for each other like starship pilots facing an onslaught of alien ships. The stakes are huge: the booming video-game industry has become almost as big as the movie business and a single top-selling home video-game cartridge may soon be able to outsell all but Hollywood's biggest blockbusters.[6]

The Big Surprise

On December 7, 1982, Atari announced that it expected a 10 to 15 percent increase in sales in the fourth quarter. Until that announcement, Atari executives had been talking about an increase of 50 percent. Analysts were shocked. Atari had never given any indication that sales were not on target. The news set off a panic.

By the time the New York Stock Exchange closed on December 8, Warner stock had fallen 16¾ points to 35⅛ and the video-game industry had begun to collapse.

Warner Communications was further embarrassed a few days later when it was discovered that Atari president and CEO Ray Kassar had sold 5,000 shares of Warner stock 23 minutes before announcing the company's sales figures. He said that the announcement had nothing to do with his transaction and eventually returned the money, but the damage was done.

> I sold 5,000 shares of Warner Communications, which represented 1 percent of my total holdings.
>
> The timing was unfortunate, but the reason I sold those shares was that I had been working with my investment counselor on a new investment opportunity that developed and they needed that amount of money. I think it was about $82,000. So I sold the stock, and I reported the sale to the company.
>
> There was an SEC investigation. It was resolved, and there was no action. If I was really bailing out, I would have sold hundreds of thousands of shares of Warner Communication, not 5,000 shares.
>
> **—Ray Kassar**

Atari had deeply rooted problems that eventually infected the entire video-game industry. During its heyday, Atari became top-heavy with marketers and other executives. As several ex-Atari people later described the situation, the company had entirely abandoned its carefree youth and become a home for MBAs.

With the continuing growth of video games, some executives began to believe that they could sell anything as long as it came packaged as a video game. Purina created a game titled *Chase the Chuck Wagon,* a video-game version of a television commercial for Chuck Wagon dog food. Atari even released a video-game version of the Rubik's Cube.

> We had 24- and 26-year-old MBAs running around making multimillion-dollar decisions. I remember shortly after I first joined Atari, I guess I had been there for less then a month, and they had just signed up to do a video rendition of Rubik's Cube.
>
> There was a woman who was running the marketing for the North American side of the business, and she came up to me and asked me if International [the International division of Atari] would be interested in marketing it internationally. And I said, "No. Absolutely not."

> She was quite surprised that I could make a decision that quickly, and she said, "Well, why wouldn't you be interested in it?"
>
> I said, "Well, you're going to have to help me understand why a $40 electronic rendition of this product is better than the $3.98 [original] rendition that is more portable and that I can take anywhere I want. When you can convince me of that, I'll be happy to consider this for International."
>
> *Rubik's Cube* went on to be an incredibly bad disaster.
>
> **—Steven Race, former vice president, Marketing and Communications,**
> **International Division, Atari**

The first indication of trouble came in May 1982, but no one seemed to notice. Atari manufactured 12 million copies of *Pac-Man,* even though the company's research showed that less than 10 million people actually owned and used its 2600s. Atari manufactured over two million extra copies on the theory that millions of people would buy the hardware just to play *Pac-Man.*

In an effort to get the game manufactured quickly, Atari contracted with a programmer named Todd Frye, promising him a royalty on every *Pac-Man* cartridge the company manufactured. With a deal like that, Frye made money even if the game was bad. According to industry rumors, he made over $1 million.

Whether it was bad programming or a weakness in the hardware, Frye's version of *Pac-Man* had slow, jerky animation and the ghosts flickered so badly that they kept disappearing from the screen. Atari sold seven million copies of *Pac-Man;* many people were so disappointed with the game that they asked for a refund.

> The first real chink in the armor, though, was Atari's edition of `Pac-Man`, which was a terrible job. It was amazing that they produced such a flickery, unresponsive game. And although they sold many copies, paradoxically the more copies they sold, the more people they turned off.
>
> **—Arnie Katz**

A few retailers canceled their orders over the summer, but no one at Atari saw any cause for alarm. The big vendors, JC Penney, Sears, and Kmart, all stayed on track. Ray Kassar may have discussed these problems with Manny Gerard, the Warner executive watching over Atari, but both men remained completely confident. Atari still garnered 70 percent of Warner's operating profits.[7]

Atari's problems continued with the production of *E.T.,* a game based on Steven Spielberg's blockbuster movie. Many analysts later blamed Kassar for the disaster, but it actually began with Steven Ross, the head of Warner Communications.

> Steve Ross called me. He was very anxious to have Spielberg make movies for Warner, and he said he just made a deal with Spielberg to produce *E.T.* as a cartridge.
>
> He asked me what I thought. I said, "I think it's a very dumb idea. We've never really made an action game out of a movie."
>
> And he said, "Well I've also guaranteed Spielberg a $25 million royalty regardless of what we did."
>
> **—Ray Kassar**

Atari was poised for another great year when Ross approached Spielberg about licensing *E.T.* The *Pac-Man* cartridge had been a disappointment, but Kassar and Gerard still claimed that Atari's sales would be up by 50 percent for the fourth quarter. Ross might not have known the full extent of the *Pac-Man* debacle and had felt confident that a game based on *E.T.* could be a huge bestseller.

Ross told Spielberg that the game should be out in time for Christmas. Since they made the deal in late July, that left very little time to design and manufacture it.

> I asked Steve, "When do we have to produce this?"
>
> He said for Christmas of 1982.
>
> This was in July when he called me, the end of July.
>
> I said, "Steve, the lead time to produce a game is at least 6 months between semiconductor deliveries and programming and all that. It's impossible."
>
> He said, "Well, you have to do it because I promised Spielberg we'd have it on retail shelves for Christmas."
>
> We had literally six weeks to produce a brand new game, manufacture it, package it, and market it. It was a disaster. I mean, the programmers hated it. Nobody liked the game.

> Then he [Ross] ordered us to produce almost five million of these games.
> I told him, "Steve, that's crazy. We never make five million of a product until
> we have some market testing."
>
> He said, "Well, it's going to be a big hit because of Spielberg and *E.T.*" So
> we made five million and practically all of them came back.
>
> **—Ray Kassar**

None of the VCS programmers wanted anything to do with *E.T.* because it came with an unrealistic deadline and high expectations. In the end, Kassar turned to Howard Scott Warshaw, a young programmer whose other games, *Yar's Revenge* and *Raiders of the Lost Ark,* were both million-sellers.* Kassar was so anxious about this project that he forgot his normally aristocratic pretensions and called Warshaw himself.

> It was late July when they first called me up to do it, after my boss, other
> programmers, and everybody else told them to forget it. Ray called me up
> personally. Because of some other interactions I had had with Ray before, I
> think he just had a feeling that I would do it.
>
> So he called me up from Monterey and said, "Howard, we need *E.T.*" This
> was like July 23, and he said "We need *E.T.* by September 1. Can you do it?"
>
> I said, "Yeah, provided we reach the right agreement."
>
> **—Howard Scott Warshaw, former VCS programmer,**
> **creator of Atari's *E.T.***

E.T. became infamous throughout the video-game industry for its dull play and disappointing story. The game involved leading Spielberg's cute

---

* Warshaw's first game, *Yar's Revenge,* was the bestselling original game Atari released for the VCS. It was about Yar of the Rassak Solar System. The joke was that Yar was Ray spelled backward and Rassak was Kassar. The game was Ray's revenge on Activision.

Warshaw told a friend in the marketing department that the name was a secret joke between him and Kassar and that Kassar loved it, even though Kassar had never heard about it. He asked his friend not to tell anyone, because he didn't want anything to influence getting the name approved. The friend immediately made sure the name stuck. Warshaw's next game was *Raiders of the Lost Ark.*

extraterrestrial away from various dangers as he tried to assemble an intergalactic device to phone home. The game's graphics were primitive, even by Atari 2600 standards, and E.T. spent most of the game falling into holes.

Riding on the heels of the *Pac-Man* disaster, *E.T.* was too much. Atari had managed to sell millions of *Pac-Man* cartridges, but the majority of *E.T.* cartridges remained in dead inventory. Atari tried to buy its way out of the hole by licensing top arcade games, often spending millions of dollars for exclusive rights.

> Basically, we'd zap them. They had last right of refusal, so we'd just come up with a bid that was wild; then, of course, Atari would be forced to beat it.
>
> Atari was getting it from two sides. Atari was getting it from not only the glut of the market, but also they were paying unbelievable amounts of money for these software titles. You know, the bidding on these software titles was just mind blowing.
>
> **—Al Kahn, former executive vice president, Coleco**

Not even home versions of the latest arcade hits helped. Consumers had already begun losing interest in video arcades, and in 1983, they stopped purchasing video games. The industry that had shown such miraculous growth through most of 1982 suddenly became a black hole.

Warner Communication's Atari, which pioneered home video games with such classics as *Space Invaders* and *Asteroids,* has lost $356 million so far this year, dropped 3,000 employees from its payroll of 10,000 and finished moving all of its manufacturing facilities to Hong Kong and Taiwan. Plagued partly by sluggish sales of Intellivision games, the electronics division of Mattel has run a $201 million deficit in 1983, while laying off 37 percent of its 1,800-member work force. Activision estimated that it lost $3 million to $5 million in the past three months, despite scoring hits with its new *Enduro* and *Robot Tank* games. At Bally, the leading manufacturer of arcade video machines, profits are off 85 percent.[8]

> I think I'm responsible for some of the problem. I think Ray is responsible for a lot of the problem. Neither one of us is responsible for the fact that a market just went away in an eye blink.

> Steve Ross blamed me to some extent. He blamed Kassar. The truth of the matter is, you can't blame me for the market imploding, but you can certainly pin some of the blame for the Atari problems on me and I in turn will tell you that you have to blame Kassar for some good chunk. He was running the show. It was on his watch and tangentially on my watch.
>
> **—Manny Gerard, former vice president, Warner Communications**

Atari was stuck with enormous inventories of worthless game cartridges. With no hope of selling them, Atari dumped millions of cartridges in a landfill in the New Mexico desert. When reports came out that people had discovered the landfill, Atari sent steamrollers to crush the cartridges, then poured cement over the rubble.*

By the end of 1983, Atari had racked up $536 million in losses. Warner Communications sold the company the following year.

---

* This was not the first time Atari destroyed unwanted cartridges. The practice had gone on for years. According to several sources, the concrete slab under Atari's Borregas Street warehouse is filled with crushed cartridges.

CHAPTER 15

The Aftermath

I went to visit Nolan at this small toy company he owned called Axlon. I walked in and asked to see him and was told, "Mr. Bushnell's in a meeting."

About three minutes later a door bursts open and Nolan comes through with a big smile on his face. He says, "Manny Gerard, the man who fired me from Atari."

I said, "Right, Nolan. And the guy who made you a millionaire."

Nolan stopped in his tracks and said, "I guess you're right."

—Manny Gerard, former vice president, Warner Communications

"My name is Nolan Bushnell, but I'm not God," he told them. "I need to build factories."

If not God, then Prometheus—about to be unbound. At midnight on September 30, 1983, a seven-year noncompete agreement, which Bushnell had signed when he sold his pioneering Atari Inc. video game company to Warner Communications Inc. in 1976, was due to expire, and a grand party had been organized to celebrate his release.

—Steve Coll, "When the Magic Goes," *Inc. Magazine*

The Rich and Famous

With the unlikely and unqualified successes of Atari and Chuck E. Cheese, Nolan Bushnell became a Silicon Valley legend and a world-renowned high roller. He purchased two personal jets, bought mansions, took up yachting, and developed a taste for the finer things in life. When he decided that Northern California needed a truly fine restaurant, he had one built—the Lion and Compass.

Bushnell mingled with the biggest names of his time, entertaining actors and politicians and doing frequent interviews with financial publications. He even considered making a bid for a seat in the United States House of Representatives.

> I met Nolan in the late 1970s. I was a reporter at the *Washington Post.* My recollection is that I met Nolan at a party at Bob Woodward's house. Bob was his next-door neighbor in Washington.
>
> Nolan used to own a Learjet and he loaned it to George Bush when Bush was Ronald Reagan's vice presidential running mate, and he sort of got interested in politics that way. And he got put on some Presidential commission as a result of what he did.
>
> **—Tom Zito, former reporter, the *Washington Post***

In 1981, Bushnell founded Catalyst Technologies, an incubator firm that housed and funded several high-tech start-up companies. In exchange for building space, access to office equipment, and funding, Bushnell received a piece of each company.

The companies he selected reflected his tastes. Through Catalyst, Bushnell became involved with companies working on high-resolution television monitors, cable television, and robotic toys. For him, the Catalyst building was a kind of dream factory that was funded by the ever-growing success of Chuck E. Cheese and Pizza Time Theaters.

In the three years since Bushnell had started Pizza Time Theaters, the company had opened 204 restaurants, and he expected that number to grow to 277 by the end of 1983. Behind the scenes, however, Bushnell's empire faced a previously unforeseen danger in the form of a new restaurant chain that would challenge Chuck E. Cheese. The chain, ShowBiz Pizza, was nearly identical to Chuck E. Cheese.

Like Chuck E. Cheese, ShowBiz restaurants served pizza in a cafeteria-like theater, in which customers watched musical reviews performed by robotic animals. Chuck E. Cheese had a streetwise rat, ShowBiz had a bear named Billy Bob leading a band called the Rock-a-Fire Explosion. Both chains featured large arcades in which patrons played video games and children rode coin-operated rides while waiting for their orders.

The similarity was no accident. ShowBiz Pizza was founded by Robert Brock of the Brock Hotel Group—the largest Holiday Inn franchise in America at the time.[1] Brock first became aware of Pizza Time Theaters in 1978, shortly after Bushnell opened his second location in San Jose. He contacted Bushnell the following year and inquired about opening a chain of 200 Chuck E. Cheese restaurants in the Midwest.

Brock decided against licensing Chuck E. Cheese, however, when he met Aaron Fletcher, an inventor manufacturing robotic characters similar to the ones in Chuck E. Cheese that looked better and cost less. Instead of buying Bushnell's franchise, he decided to compete against it.

> Two weeks after returning to [his corporate headquarters in] Topeka, Brock no longer wanted to be a franchisee; he wanted to be a franchiser. Brock demanded that Nolan tear up the contract. Nolan refused. Brock went ahead anyway and negotiated a contract with Fletcher. Nolan sued Brock for breach of contract, and Brock countersued Nolan for misrepresentation.[2]

Bushnell successfully demonstrated that Chuck E. Cheese had been a unique idea and that ShowBiz was an imitation, and the courts ruled in his favor. Although he was not successful at shutting Brock's chain down, Bushnell received a percentage of the annual revenues from the first 160 ShowBiz restaurants.[3]

ShowBiz wasn't the only problem. More concerned about robots and video games than food, Pizza Time executives had their restaurants serving cheap pizza at premium prices. With poor quality food and the popularity of video games evaporating, people had no reason to go to Chuck E. Cheese, and the company's revenues began falling by the end of 1982.

Pizza Time Theaters was operating in the red by the middle of 1983. The company's repeat business fell off,[4] and one-time business was not enough to cover the costs of running the restaurants. Amazingly, Bushnell claims that he was unaware of the problems. A professional management team ran the company while he developed Catalyst industries and traveled.

> I was aware that some store sales were dropping in certain parts of the country where we had built too many operations. The professional managers were the problem, not the solution.
>
> The rap that really pisses me off is being characterized as an inept manager. I believe that the real story of Atari was one of real sound financial management because I don't believe that there are 100 people, certainly not any of the people who are so critical of me. Not one of them could have built that company with no cash.
>
> **—Nolan Bushnell**

Adrift at Sea

> Nolan bought a yacht. He built a special yacht and he entered that big race, but he wasn't a great sailor. No matter what you say about Nolan, he is one colorful dude.
>
> **—Manny Gerard**

As far as Nolan Bushnell was concerned, Chuck E. Cheese was doing well, his Catalyst companies were going to pay off, and the end of the noncompete agreement Warner Communications had him sign before purchasing Atari was at hand.

Behind the scenes, Bushnell had already reentered the video game industry. In January, eight months before he could officially enter the business, he closed a deal to purchase Videa Inc. for $2.2 million. Videa was a game company founded by three of Atari's brightest alumni—Roger Hector, Howie Delman, and Ed Rotberg.

Hector, who had worked with Al Alcorn on Cosmos, was a natural leader and had experience working with holographic images. Delman, a brilliant engineer, built *Lunar Lander,* Atari's first vector-graphics game. (Atari's later vector-graphics games were also built around Delman's hardware.) Rotberg, widely considered one of Atari's best game programmers, was the man who designed *Battlezone.*

> Nolan purchased Videa about 18 months after Rotberg, Dilman, and I started it, then changed the name to Sente. We had actually put together a really good group of people and were working on laser discs.
>
> **—Roger Hector**

The name Sente held a special significance for Bushnell—like the name Atari, Sente came from a Japanese strategy game called Go. In chess terms, *Atari* meant "check," *Sente* meant "checkmate." In Bushnell's mind, naming his new company Sente was a way of telling the world that he was going in direct competition with Atari.

Bushnell purchased Sente as a subsidiary of Pizza Time Theaters. He hoped to distribute the games he made throughout the restaurants, possibly releasing them to Chuck E. Cheese restaurants first, as a way to draw new customers.

As he waited for the moment in which he could begin working with Sente in the open, Bushnell took up yachting and entered the Transpac Yacht Race. By this time, he had amassed a fortune estimated to be over $200 million dollars; he could afford a hobby like yachting. Bushnell invested a lot of money into hiring a top crew and constructing a special yacht, which he christened *Charlie.*

The Transpac is a race between California and Hawaii that takes place in July. With an excellent crew and a well-designed boat, Bushnell won the nine-day race his first time out.

According to a popular electronics industry legend, Bushnell received a telegram upon docking. The message began, "BAD NEWS IN THE SECOND QUARTER, STOP."

According to the story, Bushnell didn't even wait to receive his trophy. Upon reading the message, he went straight to the airport and flew home on the next available flight.

> The stories are absolutely true. I found out about the problems right after the race. I didn't know about it until I called from Hawaii.
>
> We had hired a guy to run the restaurants named George Hellick, who really screwed things up. He changed many of my operating ratios, and when

> I got back from the Transpac was when I had the fights with the board to go back to the same ratios that had generated the profits.
>
> **—Nolan Bushnell**

In March 1984, Pizza Time Theaters filed for Chapter 11 bankruptcy protection. Bushnell retired from the company later that year.

In a strange twist, ShowBiz Pizza absorbed Pizza Time Theaters and maintained both chains for several years. In 1990, Show Biz adopted Chuck E. Cheese over Billy Bob Bear as its mascot.

Ironically, the keel broke loose from Nolan's yacht as his crew sailed it back to California. Without its keel, *Charlie* drifted listlessly and had to be rescued. The same thing was about to happen to Nolan Bushnell's career.

Big Changes at Atari

> We wound up selling games to Atari. I think Ray's [Kassar] final act at Atari was buying our games.
>
> I went to his office and we struck a deal. We had created three VCS game cartridges and I brought them to him. I said, "Here, check it out. They're done. We're making them available to you."
>
> He said, "I'll buy them," and the deal was done. He said, "Come in next week. We'll have a check for you."
>
> I came in next week and they had a check, but he was gone.
>
> **—Roger Hector, Videa Inc.**

Ray Kassar resigned as CEO of Atari in July 1983. His last months with the company were tainted by the revelations that he had sold 5,000 shares of Warner Communications stock right before making the announcement that Atari's profits were lower than expected. Steven Ross, the chairman of Warner Communications, never stopped blaming Kassar for Atari's problems.

Ross's problems did not stop at Atari's doorstep. The financial roller coaster Atari put Warner through shook many investors' confidence in Ross, and Rupert Murdoch, the Australian publisher baron, was poised to attempt a hostile takeover of Warner Communications.

Ross turned to Herbert Siegel, chairman of Chris-Craft Industries, for help in fighting off Murdoch's takeover; but that placed 29 percent of Warner voting stock in Siegel's hands. Ross needed to make Atari profitable or cut his losses. Against this backdrop, Ross hired James Morgan to replace Kassar.

Morgan was only forty-two years old, but he had already developed a big name in business circles. Before going to Atari, he worked in the tobacco-marketing division of cigarette giant Philip Morris, where he managed such brands as Virginia Slims and Merit. Morgan was a chain-smoker who openly criticized Atari's past management team.

According to *Time* magazine, Morgan was promised $8.5 million over a seven-year period to move to Atari, along with performance bonuses that could raise his pay to over $25 million.[5]

Like Kassar, Morgan had no background in technology and knew nothing about computers. He had no idea why the average American would want a home computer and was appalled to discover that few people at Atari had any answers either. One of Morgan's heroes was Lee Iacocca, the maverick businessman who had turned Chrysler Corporation around and made it profitable a few years earlier. Perhaps one reason Morgan accepted the job at Atari was to see if he could follow Iacocca's example.

> If Atari's offer seemed baffling, Morgan's acceptance was even more un-expected. By all accounts, he was on a very short list for the presidency of Philip Morris. Yet Morgan, who had previously never even listened to outside offers, resigned 48 hours after having lunch with Warner chair-man Steven Ross.[6]

Morgan's first order of business was to cut back Atari's excess expenses. In his opening months as CEO of Atari, he cut Atari's domestic workforce from 9,800 employees to 3,500 and made preparations to move manufacturing from California to Hong Kong and Taiwan.

It would take more than austerity to save Atari.

Commodore and the Tramiels

One major force changing the market was a new line of inexpensive home computers. Cheap and only marginally more powerful than the game consoles of the time, these stripped-down processors did word processing, played games, and cost twice as much money as an Atari 5200 or a ColecoVision.

Atari had been selling inexpensive computers for years, and IBM introduced the $699 PCjr in 1983, but it was another company—Commodore International—that broke the market wide open.

Jack Tramiel

Commodore International was founded by Jack Tramiel—possibly the most complex person ever to enter the computer industry. He was a Polish Jew, a survivor of the Nazi concentration camps who came to America and worked his way from poverty to fortune.

As a teenager, Tramiel was sent to Auschwitz, a particularly savage Nazi concentration camp. While the people around him died, Tramiel discovered a way to survive. The Germans were building the Autobahn and asked for volunteers to help with the roadwork. It was unpleasant work, overseen by guards who sometimes took pleasure in beating their workers. Even as a teenager, however, Tramiel understood that the Germans had to feed their volunteers to keep them working, so he volunteered and survived six years in Auschwitz.

After being liberated at the end of World War II, Tramiel moved to the United States and became a Horatio Alger story. He joined the U.S. Army and was sent to Fort Dix, in New Jersey, where he learned how to repair typewriters. He saved his money and in 1954 started a typewriter repair store in the Bronx.

In 1955, Tramiel moved to Toronto, where he founded Commodore International and won a contract to assemble typewriters for a foreign firm. In a few years, Commodore began manufacturing its own adding machines. Commodore ran into trouble several years later and Tramiel had to close his manufacturing plant. Rather than go out of business, he worked with Ricoh to get his products made.

As his business grew, Tramiel developed an eye for catching trends. Realizing that calculators would replace electromechanical adding machines, he set up a partnership with Casio in the 1960s. By 1969, Commodore owned its own calculator manufacturing plant.

In 1976, Tramiel purchased a small chip manufacturer named MOS Technologies for $800,000. This was Tramiel's biggest break. MOS made the 6502 microprocessor, the chip that would become the heart of the Apple II and Atari 400 and 800 computers.[7]

Jack Tramiel, and later his sons, entered Silicon Valley with cutthroat East Coast business techniques that earned them enemies throughout the computer industry. Tramiel was well known for hardball business practices and notorious for purposely paying company debts late. Around Commodore, he referred to his business philosophy as "the religion." Executives who were unprepared to practice Tramiel's religion quickly found themselves unemployed.

This arrangement may seem a little like loan-sharking, but Commodore always knew how to make good use of other people's money. The company's accountants routinely crunched cash, cut costs to the bone, stretched out payables to vendors, and made dealers pay up fast.

A good example came in 1981 when the prime rate topped 18 percent. To take advantage of the high interest, Commodore practically stopped paying bills so it could deposit as much money as possible in interest-bearing accounts. That year, Commodore earned substantial interest income.[8]

Commodore struggled to stay solvent but lost $4 million on $56 million in sales in 1976. Jack refused to pay vendors. Why should he? He was losing his shirt. Lawsuits flew in all directions.[9]

> Commodore did its usual Jack Tramiel stunt—not paying the bill.
>
> If your guys are dumb enough to keep shipping him product, he lets them keep shipping. Pretty soon Commodore owes them so much money that they run out of cash flow and they find themselves out of business. At that point, Commodore comes in and buys the company for a song, then forgives its own debt.
>
> **—Al Alcorn, former vice president, Atari**

Tramiel had an explosive temper. He was known for pounding desks as he spoke, yelling at employees, and doing mass firings. *California* magazine once listed Tramiel third on its list of "Bosses from Hell."

The darkest accusation about Jack Tramiel, however, dates back to his early days in Canada. During that time, Commodore became associated with the Atlantic Acceptance Corporation and one of the biggest financial scandals in Canadian history.

In 1965, a financial firm named Atlantic Acceptance collapsed, leaving behind millions of dollars in unpaid loans. A four-year investigation into the collapse revealed fraud on the part of C. Powell Morgan, the president and controlling stockholder of Atlantic Acceptance, who was also the chairman of Commodore.[10] The investigation also showed that Atlantic Acceptance had made large loans to Commodore.

> What was wrong with that? The Canadian report said there had been heavy insider trading of Commodore stock for the apparent purpose of bolstering share prices. It also stated that Commodore issued misleading financial statements and letters to shareholders. The report said Tramiel and his partner had created two companies "with nominal capital and no assets," borrowed from Atlantic and re-lent to Commodore at a higher interest rate, pocketing the difference. The report went on to say that Powell Morgan had paid a "notoriously fraudulent stock promoter with established links in the world of organized crime" to tout Commodore stock in Europe through a financial newsletter, with Tramiel's knowledge and consent.[11]

Tramiel was never indicted, and C. Powell Morgan died before the commission investigating the Atlantic Acceptance collapse concluded its work. He later moved his headquarters back to the United States.

Tramiel made up sayings that were bandied about his company. One of his sayings was, "We need to build computers for the masses, not the classes."* Making computers for the masses meant finding a way to sell a low-cost, fully functional computer. To do this, Tramiel bullied his engineers to find cheaper ways to manufacture components and stripped costly luxuries from products.

He also saved money through vertical marketing. Owning MOS Technologies provided him with an inexpensive source for computer chips. Years later,

---

* Another Tramielism was "Business is like sex—you have to be involved."

when he wanted to sell dot matrix printers with his computers, Tramiel purchased a printer manufacturer and was able to market printers at stripped-down prices. When Commodore unveiled the Pet Computer in 1977, it was the first home computer to retail for under $1,000.

In 1980, Jack Tramiel survived a mid-flight airplane fire while entertaining two important software developers on his corporate jet, which was jokingly referred to as the Commodore "Petjet." During the flight, the wiring on a coffeemaker caught on fire while the jet was headed from Chicago to Commodore's California headquarters.

> They didn't smell the smoke until it was too late. They grabbed the fire extinguishers, but they didn't work. Within minutes, the entire right side of the jet was engulfed in flames. The jet shot through the sky like a Roman candle. Only the thin air and altitude kept the whole thing from exploding in mid-air. Smoke began to fill the cabin.
>
> Most horrifying of all, no airports in the area could handle their landing.[12]

By skill or by luck, the two men flying the jet managed to keep it together until they reached an airport in Des Moines, Iowa. With the electrical system destroyed, the pilot had to stop manually. The jet skidded past the end of the runway, but all of the passengers were able to walk away from the scene.

Tramiel later told an employee that the near-fatal incident was God telling him "not to fly so high."[13]

In 1981, Commodore released a home computer called the VIC-20 that sold for under $300. The VIC-20, which came with 5K of RAM and 16-color graphics, was a pricing coup for its time. Backed by commercials with William Shatner* as its spokesperson and sold through regular retail outlets instead of computer stores, the low-end machine was a major success. While Atari began faltering in 1982, Commodore sold over 800,000 VIC-20s worldwide.**

In August 1982, Commodore launched the Commodore 64 (C64), a personal computer that company executives claimed rivaled the $1,000 Apple II

---

* Atari hired Alan Alda as a spokesman for its computers and Mattel hired George Plimpton.

** Commodore had a particularly strong following in Europe.

in power but sold for $600. By the following January, Commodore was shipping 25,000 C64 computers per month.[14] The Commodore 64 went on to become a turning point in the history of home electronics, propelling Commodore into practically unheard of financial success.

> People lucky enough to have purchased 100 shares of the [Commodore International] stock in 1977 for under $2 a share would hold over $70,000 worth of stock [as of 1983].[15]

The public's interest in video games seemed to have been replaced by a fascination with home computers. Atari, Mattel, and Coleco now scrambled to find ways to compete.

The Demise of Coleco

Though 1982 was a banner year for Coleco, the crash of the video-game market made Coleco CEO Arnold Greenberg nervous. Going into the future, he wanted something more than ColecoVision. Greenberg's drive took his company in two directions.

Greenberg's pet project was the Adam Computer, and he abandoned the ColecoVision to manufacture it. Adam was a complete computing solution. It came with a master console that contained an audio cassette–like high speed data recorder and a slot for playing cartridge games, a letter-quality printer, and a 75-key keyboard, all in one box. The complete Adam setup sold for $600, but Coleco also built a partial Adam kit that could be plugged into a ColecoVision, which retailed for $400.

Coleco unveiled the Adam computer in 1982, promising to ship 500,000 units in 1983. Production took longer than expected, however, and less than 100,000 Adams reached store shelves that year.

> No one had a word-processing package at that time. This was the first one that was bundled. . . . You had the printer, the computer, and the CPU and everything, including the software at about $600, so it was an unheard of price for that kind of equipment.
>
> Basically, there was no one out there really competitive in terms of price, and we had done a terrific marketing job and everybody wanted one.

> Arnold was convinced that Adam was going to be a billion-dollar business, so he decided to make two companies out of Coleco. He was going to make a toy company on one side and an electronics and computer company on the other side.

—Al Kahn, former executive vice president, Coleco

Coleco also ventured into the toy business.

In 1982, Greenberg heard about a small toy company near Cleveland, Georgia, called Appalachian Artworks. Xavier Roberts, the 28-year-old owner of the company, was a dropout from nearby Truett-McConnell College, where he'd studied sculpting. Before dropping out, Roberts had created a line of pudgy baby dolls that he called "Little People."

Roberts's Little People were so popular that he left school and set up a business selling Little People out of an old clinic that he called Babyland General Hospital. Roberts's dolls were not manufactured at Babyland General, they were "delivered." Employees dressed like doctors and nurses (i.e., assembly workers) brought them into viewing rooms in beds of cabbage.

Instead of selling his dolls, Roberts put them up for "adoption." Adoption rates ranged from $125 to $2,000, depending on the doll. The more expensive adoptees came with furs or diamonds. One thing Roberts stressed was that each doll was unique and had its own name and identity. They even came with adoption papers and birth certificates. More than 250,000 people had adopted Roberts's handmade dolls by the end of 1983.

Greenberg heard about the dolls and decided to introduce Babyland General Hospital to the world of mass production. Coleco licensed Roberts's concept and renamed the dolls "Cabbage Patch Kids." Under the direction of Al Kahn, senior vice president of marketing, Coleco manufactured 2.5 million Cabbage Patch dolls in 1983. Kahn and Greenberg had grossly underestimated the appeal of their pudgy little dolls.

Cabbage Patch Kids sold out as quickly as Coleco could ship them. Stores ran out of stock as Christmas rolled around, and shoppers sometimes broke into near-riot frenzies as they tried to grab the dolls wherever they could find them. Even stores that jacked up the price of the dolls from $25 to $50 sold out, and many enterprising scalpers found that they could resell the dolls for over $100. According to Kahn, Coleco hoped to do $1 billion in Cabbage Patch sales in 1984.

The news was not as positive on the electronics side of Coleco's operations. Committed to meeting his 1983 shipping date, Greenberg pushed the Adam into production before it was ready. More than half of the computers Coleco shipped in 1983 were returned as defective.

> Dave Rosen [the founder of Sega] tells me that he went to see the Adam at the CES show. When Eric Bromley explained what was inside the Adam, Dave said it became clear to him that Eric didn't have a clue what he was talking about, and he knew it was time to sell his Coleco stock because it was about to drop 20 points.
>
> **—Michael Katz, former executive, Coleco**

> He [Arnold] didn't really think the toy company was going to mean much because he was really banking on Adam being the big slam dunk.
>
> It certainly was marketed beautifully. Everybody wanted Adam, but it wasn't ready to ship. It had glitches in the programming, etc., which certainly should have been fixed before the machine was released.
>
> The program wasn't totally debugged, and the printer still had some issues that had to be worked out. Arnold was fully committed to bringing Adam to market for Christmas, and he was not going to let anything stop him.
>
> **—Al Kahn**

Wall Street was not impressed. Over the next year, Coleco's stock dropped from 22 points per share to 13. Greenberg claimed that his company had fixed the problems when he released his next shipment of Adam computers, but the public wasn't interested. "It's almost impossible to resurrect a lemon like that," one analyst told *Financial World*.[16]

By this time, Coleco's electronics sales were nearly nonexistent. When Atari dropped the price of the 5200 in 1984, Coleco responded by dropping the price of the ColecoVision and giving a Cabbage Patch doll to people who purchased both a console and a game cartridge.

Adam sales were equally dismal. Unable to re-ignite public interest in its computer, Coleco discontinued the Adam in January 1985. Cabbage Patch Kids were still popular at that time, but their popularity peaked that year.

Still hoping to save his company, Greenberg acquired the company that published *Trivial Pursuit* in 1986. He was too late to catch the *Trivial Pursuit* fad. In 1988, Coleco filed for bankruptcy.

Mattel Drops Out of the Race[17]

> The hardware price spiral really impacted the hardware manufacturers, who were breaking even before that on the hardware system. As things started to spiral down, they spiraled down very, very quickly. . . . The hardware came down $50 or $60 or $70 in an 18-month period. If you're selling 2 million units or 3 million units and you're losing $70 a unit, you're talking about significant losses.
>
> **—Paul Rioux, former senior vice president of operations,**
> **Mattel Electronics**

It is impossible to piece together the conflicting stories surrounding the collapse of Mattel Electronics. According to former Mattel Electronics vice president Paul Rioux and other former employees, 1983 was a banner year for the Intellivision.* That October, however, *Time* reported that Mattel had a $201 million deficit and a layoff of over 600 employees.[18] Asked about rumors that they planned to close the electronics division in 1984, Mattel executives told *Fortune* that they would not.[19]

By the end of the year, Mattel canceled all new hardware projects. The following March, Mattel closed the division down and sold it to Terrence Valeski, Mattel Electronics senior vice president of marketing and sales, for $20 million. Valeski believed that the 3 million people who owned Intellivisions still constituted a viable market. He and his partners renamed their company Intellivision Inc. and later changed it again to INTV, but after 1983, Intellivision was never a major force in the video game industry again.

---

* According to Leonard Herman *(Phoenix: The Fall & Rise of Video Games)*, video game sales were actually up in 1983. He reports that Atari, Mattel, Coleco, and other competitors sold a combined 7 million consoles and 75 million game cartridges in 1983, 15 million more cartridges than they sold in 1982. Herman also claims that only 27 percent of those games were purchased from clearance bins.

"Freedom Day"

> Yeah, Bushnell is quite a showman. He had this huge party to which he brought safari animals from a game park. There were animals all over. The food was great, but the place stunk of elephant shit.
>
> **—Eddie Adlum, publisher, *RePlay Magazine***

With the end of his noncompete agreement in sight, Bushnell dropped too many hints about his planned reentry into video games, and Warner Communications filed a lawsuit against him for breach of contract. Warner executives didn't mind his involvement with the video game industry through Pizza Time Theaters because it was an arcade and a big customer, but Sente Technologies was a direct competitor.

Bushnell held a party to celebrate the end of his noncompete agreement on September 30, 1984. At 12:00 midnight, the moment that the agreement expired, he officially announced his involvement with Sente Technologies. (He even referred to this event as his "Freedom Day party.") He might also have unveiled his new line of games at that time, but the suit knocked him off schedule. His next "magic" hour, he announced in several trade papers, would be on December 9, 1984.

> Nolan sort of came back into the games business with great hoopla. There was a huge warehouse over in Fremont that was rented, and we had jungle animals from the local wild animal theme park that were brought in. The whole warehouse was dressed with palm trees and volcanoes and rivers and tons of dirt brought in and these animals and their trainers were walking around. And this was all part of, sort of the showbiz presentation of the whole Sente system.
>
> **—Roger Hector**

Bushnell held a larger party to mark the unveiling of the Sente line. He rented game animals from Marine World's Africa U.S.A. and had them walk around the floor to create atmosphere. At 10:00 A.M., the guests gathered around a stage.

There was a large box on stage with an alarm clock on it. When the clock struck 10:08, Bushnell burst out of the box to celebrate his freedom. He then introduced his customers to his new Sente concept—arcade machines that played games stored on cartridges.

> Bushnell came along with an idea that was in his head right practically from the early 1970s, and that was to make a universal cabinet and just change the software with a cartridge.
>
> He wasn't the first to come up with such a "system"; that was Nintendo. Nintendo had some wonderful games like *Hogan's Alley* and so on, where you just changed the cartridge. Made a lot of money.
>
> Nolan came out with the Sente system. As he said, instead of two grunts on a truck moving video games around, one girl in a Pinto with an attaché case could change the game. What was wrong with Sente system was that while everything made sense, the games weren't any fun to play.
>
> **—Eddie Adlum**

Bushnell needed money to build his games, so he tried a new tactic—he strong-armed the distributors who came to his show. Instead of simply showing his games and asking for orders, he told the distributors that no companies could buy into his system unless they ordered hardware ahead of time. Because he was Nolan Bushnell, the father of video games, founder of Atari, and genius behind Chuck E. Cheese, several companies gave in to Bushnell's strong-arm tactics.

> And so there was this big hoopla presentation and Nolan stood up at the right moment and pitched the deal. And the industry, the buyers, the distributors out there were just lathered up. And they wrote checks on the spot for all of this stuff. We had a tremendously successful launch.
>
> **—Roger Hector**

Unfortunately, Sente Technologies was doomed to fail before it ever got started. Bushnell purchased it through Pizza Time Theaters before the financial problems became apparent, so Sente was a subsidiary company. When Pizza Time Theaters declared bankruptcy in March, 1984, Sente was tainted.

Bally purchased Sente Technologies from Pizza Time Theaters, but Sente's hardware was expensive and all but one of its games got bad reviews. Shortly after purchasing Sente, the president of Bally shut it down.

CHAPTER 16

Album Covers

I thought to myself, "Yeah, boy, if you are going to be able to get computers from retail stores, this is going to become a mass market. Let's see now, I want to start a company to make entertainment software. When can I do that?"

That afternoon I did some analysis and I decided that by 1982 the technology would have made enough progress that I could start an entertainment software company. By that time there would be enough of these devices in homes to support a software company.

—Trip Hawkins, founder, Electronic Arts

I wound up writing a *New Yorker* profile on Nolan. We sort of remained friendly, then lo and behold, in November of 1984, Nolan called me up and said, "Hey, I'm starting a toy company and I'd like you to come be vice president of marketing."

I had covered the toy business a bit as a reporter and I said "No way. I don't know anything about marketing."

He said, "Sure, nobody does. Just come on out and do it."

—Tom Zito, former vice president of marketing, Axlon Inc.

New Faces

The success of the Commodore 64 was previously unheard of among home computer manufacturers. In 1983, Commodore surpassed Apple in overall sales and became the first computer company to report a $1-billion sales year.[1] At the January 1984 Consumer Electronics Show, Commodore posted an enormous back-lit sign boasting sales of more than two million VIC-20s and one million Commodore 64s.

Unlike Atari and Coleco, companies that barely broke even on their hardware and recouped their investment by selling software, Commodore sold hardware profitably and did nothing to discourage outside software development. As Tramiel saw it, every time a developer created a good program, he created a new reason for people to buy a Commodore computer.

> But the key factor was our manufacturing cost, which in the end determined whether we would make money or not.
>
> The cost of making a VIC was estimated by the press at under $60, while the Commodore 64 was thought to be slightly more expensive. One reporter estimated that Commodore could sell the Commodore 64—introduced at $595—for as low as $99 and still make a profit.[2]

The Commodore 64 had a slot for game cartridges, and the manufacturer also sold a separate floppy disk drive. Since floppy disks cost less to make and held more information than cartridges, both entertainment and serious software makers preferred publishing their products on disks, even though the overall install base of users with disk drives was smaller.

Commodore's success attracted a new breed of game companies.

The Birth of Electronic Arts

The biggest and most successful game company that emerged during the Commodore 64's reign was Electronic Arts, a company with a central tenet that ran counter to the entire fabric of the computer and video game industries—promoting game designers.

Electronic Arts was founded by Trip Hawkins, a visionary man who could generally be described as half salesman and half technophile. In many ways, Hawkins was the antithesis of the computer industry executives who preceded him. Other executives had engineering and business backgrounds; Hawkins was a marketer—Harvard educated and outwardly cultured. He was the kind of man who fits in better with Wall Street analysts than engineers. It wasn't just education that set him apart, it was his handsome facial features, his taste in suits, and his polished public demeanor. In 1995, *People* magazine included Hawkins in its annual list of the fifty most attractive people.

Hawkins's sense of style, learned or natural, had an air of sophistication. Other industry executives threw huge parties for the press and buyers at trade shows; Hawkins held small dinners at trendy restaurants.

Hawkins first got the idea to enter the computer industry in 1975, during his time at Harvard. While at school, Hawkins struck up a friendship with a home computer enthusiast. One day the friend told him about a home computer he had seen for sale. Whereas the friend was excited by the technology that home computers represented, Hawkins was intrigued with computers becoming a consumer item.

> I thought about how many of these computers there were [in people's homes], and what they cost, and market penetration rates, and how people would purchase them, and how big an audience you might need to support if you opened a software company, and how big of a fraction of them [computer owners] would be interested in the kind of things that I wanted to do.
>
> I don't remember a single number from the analysis, but I remember deciding that 1982 was the year it could all be done. I never forgot that, and from then on, I was always thinking in the back of my mind, 1982, 1982, 1982.
>
> **—Trip Hawkins**

After graduating from Harvard, Hawkins enrolled at Stanford, where he earned an M.B.A. Both opportunistic and persuasive, Hawkins used his status at Stanford to establish himself around Silicon Valley. As part of his graduate studies, he researched projects on the future of personal computing and used these projects as excuses to introduce himself to top executives.

> I did a study on personal computing. I used it as a calling card, so I had an excuse to call up every company in the business. I got to know all the pioneers in the business at that time, guys like Chuck Peddle, the guy who

> designed the 6502 microprocessor and . . . the Commodore Pet. You know,
> guys like Steve Jobs.
>
> Apple actually called me to ask me about the study, and I said, "Well I'm
> looking for a job. Why don't I come in and we can talk about the study?"
>
> That's how I got in for my job interview at Apple. Of course, they thought
> that they were basically acquiring an instant market-research department.
>
> **—Trip Hawkins**

Hawkins, Apple Computer's 68th employee, was involved in many of the company's biggest projects. He helped to formulate the strategy Apple used to establish the Apple II as a business machine. Hawkins was with Steve Jobs when Jobs made the fateful visit to Xerox and saw a prototypical workstation with pop-up windows for menus and a mouse controller.

Once at Apple, Hawkins worked his way into the company's inner circle. When the company went public, the 26-year-old Hawkins became a multi-millionaire. He also made valuable contacts, including Don Valentine, the venture capitalist who helped Nolan Bushnell expand Atari and Jobs and Wozniak start Apple. When 1982 rolled around and Hawkins prepared to start his company, he went to Valentine for funding.

> I heard about Don Valentine and thought, this is the guy who I want on my
> board, so I went to see him. I said, "Well, you know, here's what I'm doing at
> Apple, and I'm thinking about leaving to start this company and do this
> other stuff."
>
> I was nervous that he would be critical of me because I was leaving a big
> company like Apple, you know, "Who the hell am I to think I'm ready to start
> a company?" And "Gee, you're leaving Apple in the middle of your project?
> Aren't you a follow-through kind of guy?"
>
> Instead, he said, "Quit dragging your feet. Get the hell out of Apple. When
> you're ready, I'll provide an office for you."
>
> **—Trip Hawkins**

> We knew Trip Hawkins a little bit at Apple as one of the marketing guys. He
> went to Harvard. He looked like he went to Harvard.

> We invited him to come live in our office while he was organizing his company, writing his [business] plan, and hiring people. The first territorial people at Electronic Arts all began working in our office, and the company was started in our office.
>
> Sequoia (Valentine's venture capital firm) was not an especially large company at that time. At one point they had twice as many people as we did.
>
> **—Don Valentine**

With Valentine's backing, Hawkins began to assemble his company. He hand-picked people he thought were dynamic and smart, invited them to meetings at his home, and persuaded them to join his team. Hawkins also actively proselytized game designers.

The best way to find game developers at the time was to attend computer trade shows. Hawkins walked the floors of these shows, looking for the designers he wanted and then talking to them about his plans. He found Bill Budge, David Maynard, and Dan Bunten, the programmers who became the heart of his design team.

Hawkins and crew decided to name their new company "Electronic Arts" during one of the evening meetings at Hawkins's house. They chose this name to emphasize the artists and artistry of the games he would publish.

In the meantime, Hawkins continued meeting with Budge and other designers he hoped to attract. He told them that game designers should be treated like stars. In an industry that was still rife with the stories of Atari's abusive attitude toward designers, Hawkins's message sounded very attractive.

Promoting designers was only one of several innovations Hawkins had planned. In the early 1980s, computer game makers still sold their games in plastic bags with labels. Hawkins found the situation laughable and proceeded to apply his marketing wizardry to revolutionize the way computer games were packaged.

Hawkins referred to his packaging as "album covers." Album covers were custom-made boxes with professional art and the designers' names placed prominently on the label. In Hawkins's mind, having the best games in the store meant nothing if the packaging didn't attract buyers. With better packaging and a stable of established designers, he would create a following to make Electronic Arts the industry leader.

Of all of Hawkins's progressive proposals, the one involving the most risk was his decision to challenge the distribution system. At the time, companies that distributed software to retailers kept most of the revenues from software sales. Hawkins didn't like the distributors' stranglehold on the market and wanted to pay them a smaller commission. When he proposed the idea at a board meeting, Don Valentine objected.

> Everyone was selling [their games] to distributors at a 55 percent discount. I said, "We're going to go to some of these distributors, and we're going to offer them 52 percent."
>
> Valentine said, "Who the hell are you people to think that you can just rewrite any of the rules of the industry? What makes you think you can get away with that?"
>
> I said, "We really don't have any choice. Either we're going to pull this off or we're not going make it."
>
> Pushing a lower discount worked. Don pounded his fist on the table at our next board meeting and said, "You people have to continue to challenge convention."
>
> **—Trip Hawkins**

Electronic Arts shipped its first products on May 21, 1983. Of the six products launched, three quickly became bestsellers.

> In terms of commercial success, *Hard Hat Mack* was a bestseller, *Archon* was a classic bestseller, and *Pinball Construction Set* was a classic bestseller. It was a really remarkable debut set of products.
>
> We just started cranking out products. The next month we released more, and within six months we had 25 or 30 different products. By that time we were supporting Apple II, Commodore 64, and Atari 800.
>
> **—Trip Hawkins**

By 1984, the video game industry had collapsed and Commodore 64 sales plateaued. Toward the middle of the year, Commodore started reporting Atari-sized losses, and Apple, for all of its market strength, was not proliferating the way Commodore or Atari had. Shortly after Electronic Arts made its splashy debut, the computer-game industry looked as soft as the video game industry.

> It was a really brutal period for the industry. I wouldn't de-emphasize that. You'd put out a product on the Apple II and be pleased if you sold 15,000 units.
>
> When I started EA, I made a list of all the companies I had ever heard of that made video games or floppy disk games, and there were something like 130 or 131 other companies. Today I would say that maybe 6 of those guys are still in the business.
>
> **—Trip Hawkins**

During this period, Hawkins abandoned his strategy of promoting game designers. He still treated them with respect and gave them credit for the work they did, but the emphasis at Electronic Arts clearly shifted from popularizing designers to promoting games.

In 1984, that new emphasis led Electronic Arts to place new names on its labels, the names of famous sports figures. Hawkins had a friend who had a friend who knew the agent handling the Philadelphia '76ers basketball star Julius Irving—better known as "Dr. J." Using this connection, Hawkins asked Irving's agent if his client would be willing to let Electronic Arts use his name and likeness in a computer basketball game.

It was the first time a computer game company had licensed an athlete's name. Though earlier games had been made based on movies such as *Tron, Krull,* and *Star Wars,* and Mattel had acquired licenses from the NFL and the NBA, no one had ever approached an individual sports star. Electronic Arts paid Irving a $25,000 fee for his name and image.

> Of course, you'd be lucky to do anything today for even ten times that amount.
>
> Anyway, he agreed to do it, making it possible for us to have his agent ask Larry Bird's agent, why don't you do it and why don't you do it on the same terms that we're doing it?
>
> **—Trip Hawkins**

The game was called *Dr. J and Larry Bird Go One-on-One.* Though the game had cutting-edge graphics for the time, the limited processing power of the Commodore 64 and Apple II could only support characters that looked like bad doodles and moved like cardboard cutouts. The people designing the game, however, got several pointers from Irving (Bird was less involved and less interested), which helped them add some finer points to the game.

Dr. J and Larry Bird Go One-on-One was a huge bestseller for its time, leading Electronic Arts to begin work on a game based on another sports legend—John Madden. Though no one knew it at the time, *John Madden Football* would become the most enduring sports series in computer and video game history. It would also play a decisive role in determining the leaders of two future generations of video game consoles.

A Change at Commodore

The 1965 collapse of Atlantic Acceptance left Commodore with substantial financial problems. Short on capital and tainted by scandal, Tramiel turned to Canadian investor Irving Gould for help. Gould purchased a controlling share of Commodore stock for $500,000.[3] Though he later sold 8 percent of his stock back to Tramiel, Gould remained the power behind the scene at Commodore.

According to a few reports, Gould scrutinized Tramiel's every move. Tramiel could not borrow money without Gould's signature, and Gould kept Commodore on a strict leash. The relationship was rumored to be turbulent. *Fortune* magazine once reported that the volatile Tramiel often threatened to quit the company.[4]

At a Commodore board meeting on January 10, 1984, Tramiel made the threat one final time.

The board had met to discuss the company's future. Tramiel went to the meeting planning to unveil his dream of bringing his sons together to run Commodore. He wanted to name his oldest son, Sam, as president. He wanted his next oldest, Gary, to run the company's finances, and his youngest son, Leonard, who had just earned his Ph.D. from Columbia, to work in Commodore's software division.[5]

Gould had other ideas. He wanted Marshall Smith, a 54-year-old finance specialist from the steel industry, to take over the company. According to one report, Tramiel threatened to quit the company, and Gould said, "Fine."

On Friday, January 13, 1984, Jack Tramiel officially resigned as the CEO of Commodore International. On February 21, Marshall Smith moved into Tramiel's office.

Changing Times at Atari

When James Morgan took over Atari in September, 1983, he found a company in complete disarray. Atari was now composed of dozens of departments that seldom communicated with one another, housed in nearly fifty buildings spread throughout Silicon Valley. The departments' animosity and political infighting were crippling the company. Alan Kay, the head of Atari's research center, described the venomous brinkmanship to a *Time* reporter in terms that made the company's executives sound like spoiled children playing on a small boat. "For a while the company was playing 'Ha, ha, your end of the boat is sinking.'"[6] In the article, the reporter concluded with the statement that "it turned out that everybody was on the same boat."

Morgan's first move was to cut the domestic payroll down from 9,800 employees to 3,500. Next he turned to foreign labor for manufacturing, sending 3,000 jobs to Hong Kong and Taiwan. He also sold off Atari's excess buildings, condensing the company's sprawling operations down from forty-nine buildings to four.

A few months into his new job, however, Morgan discovered that he could not turn to Warner Communications for help. When he submitted his 1984 budget in March, Warner executives vetoed it. According to Ross, Atari would have to find its own funding.

Morgan revised his budget, trimming his operating expenses from $600 million to a mere $150 million. He cut an additional 550 jobs, and dumped 20 million old cartridges into the marketplace at $2 each to clear out old inventory.

Realizing that simply cutting expenses would not save Atari, Morgan pushed for new products. On May 21, Atari announced the development of a powerful new game console, the 7800 ProSystem, and a deal to create games with LucasFilm, the company that made the *Star Wars* and *Indiana Jones* movies.

> The 7800 just sort of showed up at our door one morning. It was developed by an outside firm, and I think it was originally called the 3600 or something like that.
>
> **—Jerry Jessop, former engineer, Atari**

The 7800 had actually been developed by General Computer, the same Boston company that had designed *Ms. Pac-Man* and made nearly half of the cartridges for the 5200.

In the summer of 1984, Atari announced plans to release a new game controller called the Mindlink. Mindlink was a bizarre product—a game controller that supposedly directed game play by reading electrical impulses in players' heads. It would come packaged with a *Breakout*-style title, *Bionic Breakthrough.*

Companies frequently incur losses while downsizing and cutting inventory, but Warner Communications was completely unprepared for the $425 million second-quarter losses Atari reported in 1984. When Morgan returned to New York, claiming he needed more money to run the company, Ross decided to rid himself of Atari once and for all.

In June, rumors started floating around Atari that Warner planned to sell or close the company. Morgan held a meeting in which he promised his employees that Ross still had confidence in Atari and that he had no plans to sell out. Morgan was wrong.

The Deal

In early July 1984, Warner Communications announced an agreement to sell Atari Corporation to a new owner—Jack Tramiel.

Tramiel did not acquire all of Atari. Warner retained the coin-operated games division and renamed it Atari Games.*

The final agreement was extremely convoluted. On the surface, Tramiel paid $240 million dollars for the home computer division of the failing video game giant. This, however, was only part of the story.

Tramiel and his company, Tramiel Technologies Limited, paid Warner Communications $240 million in promissory notes, based on Atari's future performance. In effect, Warner had loaned him the money to buy the company.

The deal also involved exchanging stocks. Tramiel Technologies, Jack Tramiel's company, received warrants for Warner stock and a promise from Warner to cover certain debts and expenses. (That promise proved to be significant. Tramiel contacted Warner on at least one occasion and received a multimillion dollar

---

* Warner retained Atari Games (the coin-op division), which later sold technological assets to Mitsubishi and BSR.

cash infusion.) In exchange for Atari and warrants for stock, Warner received warrants for 14.3 million shares of Tramiel Technologies' stock.

Although Warner certainly offered Tramiel good terms for purchasing Atari, the interesting question was why did Tramiel want the company? Atari had good facilities and tremendous name recognition, but within the industry, the company's name carried negative connotations.

Several analysts believe that Tramiel wanted to use Atari as a vehicle for wreaking revenge on Commodore. While later developments showed that he had no qualms about using Atari to jab at his former company, some of Tramiel's friends believed that he reentered the computer business for the sake of his sons.

In his book *The Home Computer Wars,* former Commodore employee and Tramiel confidant Michael Tomczyk suggests that Tramiel purchased Atari to bring his sons and his Commodore family together. Bernie Stolar, another friend of the Tramiels, believed he made the move to ensure his family's financial security.

Imperial Storm Troopers

> Everybody was expecting something draconian to happen. When they first walked in the building, someone got on the PA system and did the line from *The Empire Strikes Back.* I think it went, "Attention, Imperial storm troops have entered the base."
>
> **—Kelly Turner, former employee, Atari**

In the beginning, Atari Corporation and Atari Games were headquartered in adjoining buildings, and the people working in the newly independent coin-op company silently watched as their former associates were demolished.

The Tramiels cared little about soothing nervous employees' feelings. Jack and Sam Tramiel set up offices, interviewed workers, and decided how to realign the company. The people who witnessed their takeover described them as tireless, energetic, and merciless. Within a short time, the number of employees on Atari's worldwide payroll was reduced to 1,500.

Everywhere he looked, Tramiel saw excesses. He had inherited a 300-person marketing division. In contrast, during its heyday Commodore had 25 employees in marketing. Tramiel wanted to reduce the number of secretaries, engineers, and administrators.

> I sat there and watched Atari go from 5,000 people in 25 buildings back down to like 200 in coin-op, 200 in consumer in three or four buildings. It was the Tramiel fire sale of Atari.
>
> It was an interesting split. He [Tramiel] had control of his side for probably a day or two before he realized that we were two different companies. Our buildings had connecting doors and they decided to seal them up.
>
> It became a very "us and them" kind of atmosphere, which was too bad. I hated watching the consumer people have to go through interviews because it was a bloodbath.
>
> I was happy to be at coin op.
>
> **—Kelly Turner**

In typical fashion, Tramiel did not care whom he offended. According to one story, he once stopped a demonstration of existing Atari products by shoving them onto the floor. When a programmer Tramiel supposedly wanted to keep mentioned that his wife had a job, Tramiel told him that his wife should stay home. Offended by Tramiel's chauvinistic attitude, the programmer began looking for another job later that evening.

> We made several successful games for the 2600 and most of the big games for the 5200. When the Tramiels came in, we quickly realized that we were not going to be able to forge a profitable relationship with them, so we started making programs for the Mac.
>
> **—Doug Macrae, cofounder of General Computer,**
> **codesigner of *Ms. Pac-Man***

> The "Tramiel Fire Sale" was not restricted to the wholesale reduction of jobs. Atari's new management sent crews to evaluate the company's assets. Carts filled with computer and office equipment soon lined the walls. Equipment deemed unnecessary was either sold off or stolen. According to one ex-employee, equipment theft reached epic levels.

> It's funny, I was actually in Greece the day that Atari sort of went "tapi-oca" and was sold to the Tramiels, so I missed it. The way I had it described to me, it sounded like the last days of Vietnam, in which people were push-ing helicopters off aircraft carriers so they could get the fighters down, because the fighters were worth more than helicopters. Well, it sounded like the same thing at Atari.
>
> I heard stuff was just flying out the doors and out the windows. If it wasn't nailed down in the last couple of days there, people were walking out the door and stuffing it in their cars.

—Steve Race, former vice president, Atari Europe Division

On September 13, Jack Tramiel described his plans for resurrecting Atari at a closed-door meeting for venture capitalists in a luxurious San Francisco hotel. During that meeting, Tramiel reportedly told his audience that he planned to build Atari's sales from $500 million to somewhere between $1.2 and $1.5 billion within one year.[7]

As the meeting progressed, Tramiel was reportedly asked if he seriously believed that he could keep Atari afloat even through Christmas. He responded that he could and that he planned to release a new line of high-quality, low-cost home computers the following year. Amazingly, Tramiel seemed to believe that he could turn Atari around. Even more amazingly, he convinced several venture capitalists attending the meeting that he could as well.

Axlon, A. G. Bear, and Nemo

> I grew up in the New York area. I think I was six or seven when I started going to the movies every Saturday. In high school I was just fanatically interested in movies. In fact, when I got out of high school I decided that I wanted to go to film school and enrolled in NYU. Of my fellow students, the guy who's become the best known, is Brian DePalma. Marty Scorsese was my cinema-tography professor.

—Tom Zito, former vice president of Marketing, Axlon Inc.

The *Washington Post* gave Tom Zito one of the most enviable jobs in America, just a few days after he graduated third in his class from Georgetown University.

> The first four years I was at the *Washington Post,* I was the rock critic. I went to 250 rock and roll shows a year and got every record ever made for free. It was like every kid's dream! It was great.
>
> After about four years, I went to my editor and said, "You know, I'm out of adjectives. I can't do this anymore." I'm partly deaf now as a result of all that rock and roll, but I still love music.
>
> I did that for four years, then there was other stuff that I wanted to do besides write about rock and roll, so I became a general assignment reporter. I covered the first couple of space shuttle shots. I covered Gary Gilmore's execution.
>
> **—Tom Zito**

While working at the *Post,* Zito began writing articles for the *New Yorker* and *Rolling Stone* on the side. As video games came into vogue, Zito often found himself writing about the industry.

In 1984, the *New Yorker* assigned Zito to profile Nolan Bushnell and the video game phenomenon. Bushnell was focusing most of his attention on Sente Technologies at the time. Always gracious to reporters, he showed Zito around, and they struck up a friendship. A few months later, Bushnell called Zito and asked him to move to California and work at one of Bushnell's pet companies—Axlon Inc.

Axlon was a manufacturer of high-tech toys. The company's products included a line of hand puppets called Party Animals that had sensors in their mouths. When you opened their mouths, the sensors activated a little sound chip that produced howls or barks, depending on the animal.

Zito's first project was A. G. Bear, a mechanical teddy bear whose sound sensor enabled it to mumble in response to noise. The idea was that if children talked to A. G. Bear, it mumbled back to them. Unfortunately, Axlon's intelligent teddy bear was no match for Teddy Ruxpin, a more articulate talking bear released by Worlds of Wonder that same year.

> Interestingly enough, Teddy Ruxpin killed us. When you stripped everything away from Teddy Ruxpin, it was basically a television set for little kids. Kids would put a tape in Teddy and put it on its chair and sit down in front of the chair to watch Teddy tell a story.

> We had all kinds of child psychologists telling us how good A. G. Bear was and what a wonderful product it was for kids; but if you put kids in a room with Teddy Ruxpin and A. G. Bear, they'd run in and grab Teddy Ruxpin. I learned this in horror in focus groups. . . .
>
> Fortunately, our first year at Christmas, Teddy was very much in short supply. I think a lot of people bought A. G. Bear because they couldn't get Teddy Ruxpin.

—Tom Zito

Zito, a bachelor whose family and friends lived on the East Coast, developed a close relationship with the Bushnell family. He visited their home often and thought of their children as nieces and nephews. It was a relationship he valued.

In 1985, Zito's fascination with movies and video games merged into the idea of creating interactive games using video footage instead of animated characters. He believed that controlling real people instead of cartoons would give games impact.

Zito asked Bushnell for permission to explore "interactive television." Bushnell liked the idea and told him to assemble a small team. Zito's team included Steven Russell, the man who made *Spacewars* while studying at MIT; Rob Fulop, the Atari programmer who designed the VCS versions of *Missile Command* and *Night Driver;* David Crane, the charter member of Activision who created *Pitfall;* and other industry pioneers.

As they explored ways of interlacing video images and computer graphics, the team discovered that the ColecoVision's graphics chip had been designed to allow it to place video game images over a clear background. They learned later that Coleco engineer Eric Bromley had hoped to do games with video images in the background, but the company abandoned the idea because of costs.

Zito and his team hoped to take advantage of Bromley's design. They wanted to stream video images transmitted through a cable signal into a ColecoVision, then add interactive images. The team was able to build a prototype for testing its ideas with a limited budget but needed more money to take the idea any further.

> We basically finished the design of the ColecoVision machine and added syncable video. When I put together a budget, it looked like it would cost

> about seven million dollars to get a machine, along with a couple pieces of software, ready so that we could introduce this thing. Initially, it was a game machine, but the vision all along was that it would basically be a cable box, and you'd be able to get video games or any kind of interactive programming over cable.
>
> Nolan said to me, "Well, if you want to do this, you're going to need to raise the seven million bucks, 'cause we don't have it."
>
> **—Tom Zito**

If Zito was going to complete his project, he needed to take on a partner who could fund it. That partner turned out to be a toy company—Hasbro. Hasbro agreed to spend the $7 million to fund the project in exchange for the video game rights to the technology. Zito named the venture Nemo.

Within six months, however, the partnership was strained. Hasbro wanted the Nemo project to move at a faster pace, but delays in engineering prevented it. After some discussion, Hasbro told Zito that he could either continue the project on his own or Hasbro would take it over, but the company would no longer finance Nemo while under the Axlon umbrella. Forced to choose between Bushnell and Nemo, Zito went with his project, costing him an important friendship.

Upon leaving Axlon, Zito formed a company of his own called Isix. Because of the amount of space required to store digitized video footage, Isix's games could not be stored on computer diskettes or in a game cartridge. Isix's engineers developed two solutions for the problem—broadcasting the footage as a cable signal or storing it on video cassettes. Either way, the video footage had to be looped from an outside source and through a console that added the interactive programming before it could be played.

By the middle of 1986, Zito's team had produced three short trial games. They made a four-minute interactive mystery called *Scene of the Crime*, a baseball game called *Bottom of the Ninth Inning*, and an interactive music video using the song "You Might Think I'm Crazy" by the Cars.

Zito's next step was to make an interactive movie. He hired a director and had members of his team write the script. His original plan was to do an interactive movie based on the *Nightmare on Elm Street* movies—a series of popular horror films featuring a maniac named Freddie who shredded people to death in their dreams. Negotiations with the studio fell apart, however, so Zito decided to create a script with original characters. He hired Terry McDonell, a future editor of *Esquire* and *Men's Journal,* to write the script.

The final version, titled *Night Trap,* was about fledgling vampires attacking a group of teenage girls during a slumber party. As apprentice vampires, the villains did not have fangs; in fact, they wore black stockings over their heads. They simply sneaked around the girls' house, trying to trap them, then sucking their blood with a device that used a power drill. The game was more silly than violent.

Night Trap was not a typical video game. The point of playing was to protect the girls by catching the vampires with booby traps. One of the girls was the late Dana Plato, the actress who played the older sister on the NBC sitcom *Different Strokes.*

Players would scan the rooms of the house, looking for vampires and trying to spring traps at the right moment to catch them. If players' timing was right, the game would show a video clip of a vampire being trapped. If they missed, the game would show a clip of the vampire leaving the room and possibly even catching a victim.

In 1987, Zito made a second full-sized game called *Sewer Shark.* In this game, players guided a futuristic fighter craft through tunnels. The game showed clips of the fighter streaking toward junctions, at which point players had to direct it toward openings. If they guided it in the right direction, the game showed a video clip of the fighter going through the opening. If the player made the wrong choice, the game showed video clips of spectacular collisions. Zito hired a special-effects wizard who had worked on the movie *2001* to help produce the game.

Hasbro stopped funding the Nemo project shortly after the filming of *Sewer Shark.* Zito toyed with the idea of marketing the games as arcade laser-disc games, but the laser disc fad had ended. With no funding and nowhere to sell his ideas, Zito packed *Night Trap* and *Sewer Shark* in a warehouse. Several years passed before video game technology caught up with Tom Zito's dream.

In the meantime, a new force was emerging in the electronic entertainment industry.

Prior to working on Nemo, I went back to New York for Christmas [in 1985], and I needed film so I went to a camera shop. All these boys were crammed around this counter, playing with a new toy. I went to see what they were playing, and they had this new video game system by Nintendo. It looked better than anything out before it, and I thought, this could be big.

—Tom Zito

CHAPTER 17

We Tried to Keep from Laughing

All the headlines said, "Video games are dead," and here was this little upstart company that no one had ever heard of called Nintendo that said they were going to bring video games back again. Everybody seemed to think that it was a joke. "Oh yeah, they say they can bring video games back again."

—Herb Weisbaum, consumer affairs correspondent, *CBS News*

Here it is 1985, Christmas of 1985, and Nintendo has just introduced the NES in the New York market, as well as in FAO Schwartz stores nationally. It's a home run . . . a hit! It's a sell-out.

So I'm saying, "Who's gonna be interested in this?" And I said, "Well, I'll bet the toy companies are gonna be very interested in something like this because . . . Nintendo is gonna clean your clock next year. I mean, Nintendo is going to launch nationally and they're gonna be represented by Worlds of Wonder.

—Tom Zito, founder, Digital Pictures

The Rising Sun

The American video game market may have crashed in 1983, but the international market continued almost unimpeded. Atari marched on in Europe and Japan. Even the Canadian market remained fairly active throughout most of 1984. Atari, Mattel, even Vectrex sales continued in foreign markets.

Nintendo, the arcade giant that created the games *Donkey Kong* and *Popeye,* introduced a new game console to the Japanese market in May 1983.* Christened the Famicom (for Family Computer), the new console was a testament to innovation and economic engineering.

Nintendo built the Famicom around the 6502 processing chip, a close cousin of the 6507 that Atari used in the original Video Computer System (VCS). Technology had evolved, however, and Nintendo's engineers were able to reap more power from the chip. Along with added memory, the Famicom had a number of components (including a second processor for generating graphics) that had been either unavailable or too expensive in 1976, when Miner and Alcorn designed the VCS. This upgraded architecture allowed the Famicom to produce more colors and more detailed graphics than the VCS or any system before it.

> It was amazing because it was basically a re-warmed VCS, even going so far as having the same processor in the box as the VCS. [The Famicom had] a better graphics display chip, but the basic processor was the same. And the reason that they could have a better look was that addition of slightly more RAM in the thing so you could address more pixels; that's all.
>
> **—Tom Zito**

Of the Famicom's many innovations, the most important was its controller. The VCS was initially designed to play sophisticated versions of *Pong* and *Tank* and came with both paddles and joysticks, but most of its games used a joystick. That turned out to be a weakness. VCS joysticks were versatile for their time but were uncomfortable to hold. To use them, most players had to

---

* For a full account of the design and launch of Famicon, read *Game Over* by David Sheff. Mr. Sheff's book is a 400-page account of the history of Nintendo from 1889 to 1994 and offers a thorough account of the Nintendo story.

grip the square base with one hand and move the stick with the other. People often complained that their hands cramped or their fingers locked around the base after long stretches of game playing. Also, the stick, not designed to withstand the kind of stress players often placed on it, often broke.

Mattel had added a measure of ergonomics, durability, and sophistication to game controllers with its Intellivision game pad, which featured a flat disk that players pressed with their thumbs. Though it took players a while to get used to the disk, most felt that the Intellivision controller added precision to gaming.

For the Famicom, Nintendo designed a new kind of controller that was derived from the +-shaped direction pad that its lead engineer, Gumpei Yokoi, developed in the late 1970s for the Game & Watch LCD games. Somewhat similar in concept to the disk on the Intellivision controller, the Famicom controller allowed players to maneuver characters by pressing on the + pad with their left thumb.

The design of the Famicom's controller was both elegant and functional. The joystick, once the symbol of video gaming, was about to be replaced by a newer and more universally applicable device. Most people found the Famicom controller easier to use and more comfortable to hold.*

The Famicom controller was easier to use than the Intellivision controller. Nintendo's + pad was more intuitive than Mattel's disk. Intellivision's controller also included a twelve-button membrane keypad that was cumbersome to use. The Famicom controller had a simple two-button design.

The Japanese launch of the Famicom was not without problems. A bad chip set in the original design caused the system to crash during certain gaming conditions. Hiroshi Yamauchi, president of Nintendo, decided to recall the entire first shipment of Famicoms and replace the chips. Though it cost Nintendo a small fortune and alerted retailers to problems with the new console, Yamauchi decided that protecting the Nintendo name was more important than preserving the initial momentum of his sales.

After that initial setback, the Famicom became a spectacular success. Nintendo sold more than 500,000 Famicoms within two months of introduc-

---

* Two medical conditions were later attributed to prolonged use of the Nintendo controller. Thousands of people developed calluses on the tips of their thumbs. The second and more serious condition was sore wrists, a condition later dubbed "Nintendonitus."

ing the system into stores. Encouraged by his success with Japanese consumers, Yamauchi set his sights on exporting his game console to the United States. The only problem was that no one in America seemed particularly interested in video games any longer. As far as retailers and software makers were concerned, the U.S. video game industry was dead.

> It seemed like all the print media wanted to keep writing about was the death of video games. I mean, they just loved to write that story. "Video game sales are dead, video games are gone, video games are history."
>
> Then I'd go to CES [the Consumer Electronics Show] and see all this stuff, and think, "Where are these people coming from? It isn't dead." It was very interesting.
>
> **—Herb Weisbaum**

> Retailers took a tremendous financial beating because of the way the Atari business had fallen apart. I mean, with the demise of the old 2600 business, you wouldn't even try bringing up the words *video game* with some of these buyers. It was like they were going to pull you out to the parking lot and shoot you if you said the words *video game*.
>
> **—Jim Whims, former vice president, Worlds of Wonder**

Left at the Altar

> Mr. Yamauchi said, "Why don't you contact the Atari people?"
> So I called Ray [Kassar], and the next thing we knew, we were going down in a corporate jet to Warner.
>
> **—Howard Lincoln, chairman, Nintendo of America**

One lesson Hiroshi Yamauchi learned from his attempts to break into the U.S. arcade market was that popularity in Japan did not automatically translate into success in America. Ron Judy and Al Stone, the men who represented Nintendo's products to arcade distributors, struggled to get people to take their products seriously. Even *Radarscope,* one of the top arcade games in Japan, had gone unnoticed in the United States. Had it not been for the runaway success of *Donkey Kong,* Nintendo might have never carved a niche in the U.S. market.

Yamauchi had heard the stories that the U.S. video game industry was collapsing. Atari had already announced its low earnings by this time, and Warner Communications stock had already dropped. The worst was yet to come, but Yamauchi certainly knew that the 1982 Christmas season had not lived up to expectations. Even so, he believed that the Famicom was different, that it was the best video game console ever made. What he needed, however, was a powerful network to market the system on a worldwide basis. Even with its strong presence in the arcade business, the name Nintendo meant very little to retailers outside of Japan.

With no presence in the retail channel and no way of making inroads, Yamauchi decided that Nintendo needed a partner to represent the Famicom in America. He decided that the best partner would be Atari. At Yamauchi's suggestion, Nintendo of America vice president Howard Lincoln contacted Atari early in 1983.

Ray Kassar was still running the company when Lincoln called, but his tenure was coming to an end. The call came four months after Kassar's announcement about not reaching sales goals, and Warner stock was still in decline, due to investor doubts about Atari's future. Investors also had doubts about Kassar himself. The allegations of insider trading were public by this time, and Kassar, Atari's once lofty CEO, was fighting for his corporate existence.

Lincoln called Kassar to suggest a partnership. He had been authorized to offer Atari a license to sell the Famicom internationally in every market except Japan. Lincoln's offer was fairly straightforward. In exchange for allowing Atari to sell the system under its own label, Nintendo would receive royalties on every unit sold and have unlimited access to sell software for the system.

The offer placed Atari in a no-lose situation. Licensing the Famicom did not necessarily equate to making a good faith effort to market it. What Lincoln and Yamauchi did not know was that General Computer, the Massachusetts game developer that had produced most of the games for the 5200, had begun work on a new game system for Atari—the 7800.

If the new system proved to be more powerful than the Famicom, the license would have enabled Atari to smother the Famicom globally. If, on the other hand, the 7800 did not sell well, a partnership with Nintendo could provide Atari with an escape hatch. Kassar asked for a meeting.

Lincoln and Minoru Arakawa, president of Nintendo of America, flew from Seattle to Atari headquarters in Sunnyvale, California, to explain the details of the partnership.

A meeting was set up, and Kassar told Arakawa he would send the Warner Communications corporate jet, a Gulf Stream, to collect him and Howard Lincoln. En route to the airport, Arakawa asked Lincoln if he expected lunch to be served on the plane. Lincoln said there would probably be no food on the short hop between Seattle and Sunnyvale. Arakawa was starved, so the two headed to a restaurant before meeting the jet at a private airport.

The jet, fitted with leather couches and gold-plated ashtrays, was empty except for Arakawa, Lincoln, and the crew. Once it was airborne, the pretty attendant set up dining tables with linen tablecloths and asked if the two were ready for lunch. Arakawa threw Lincoln a dirty look when she served paté, fresh poached salmon, and Dom Perignon.[1]

Lincoln and Arakawa received royal treatment during their visit at Atari. Not only did they meet with Manny Gerard and Ray Kassar, but Steve Ross, president of Warner Communications, stepped into the meeting to shake their hands. When they finally sat down to discuss the partnership, several of Atari's top executives crammed into the conference room to listen. As far as Lincoln and Arakawa could tell, things were going better than expected.

> We got down there and, god, what a cast of thousands: Ray Kassar, Manny Gerard, Steve Ross, Skip Paul. . . . And we were just getting hammered with one question after another.
>
> **—Howard Lincoln**

> Everybody said, "Oh, that's a good idea. We'll buy it."
> The negotiations started, but the price . . . they didn't buy it. After we started negotiations, we created games to show them . . . *Defender, Centipede,* those [kinds of] games.
>
> **—Minoru Arakawa**

The next step in the negotiation process was for Nintendo to demonstrate the Famicom. Yamauchi sent several Famicom consoles to Atari's research and development labs and invited members of Atari's executive staff to watch a demonstration of the system at his corporate headquarters in Kyoto, Japan. Kassar did not attend that showing but sent a delegation led by Skip Paul, Atari's legal counsel.

After the initial demonstration of the Famicom console, negotiations evolved into a three-day struggle over prices and royalties. Paul claimed that Kassar and Gerrard were interested in making a deal but wanted to make some changes in the contract. Lincoln had to make sure that Nintendo's best interests were not compromised. Both Kassar and Yamauchi, the only men with the authority to approve a final deal, appeared anxious to iron out the details.

On the third day of negotiations, Lincoln warned Paul that Yamauchi was getting annoyed with all of the haggling and delays. Paul excused himself to call Kassar. When he came back, he said he had received final approval and that a contract should be drawn up.

> I mean, it was a done deal. We spent a week putting this thing together, this elaborate agreement in Kyoto. Skip Paul was over there. . . . we had the whole thing put together. It was a deal.
>
> **—Howard Lincoln**

The deal never went through.

The collapse began at the 1983 Summer Consumer Electronics Show in Chicago. While all appeared to be moving smoothly, Coleco debuted the Adam Computer. It was playing *Donkey Kong,* a game Nintendo had licensed to Coleco.*

Yamauchi, Arakawa, and Lincoln went to the show expecting to finalize their marketing arrangement with Atari. Instead, they received an angry message from Kassar, claiming that Coleco's use of *Donkey Kong* on the Adam breached the licensing agreement Atari had made with Nintendo for the home-computer rights to the game.

---

* Nintendo sold the video game console rights to Coleco. Atari purchased the home computer rights for the game.

> You have to understand that *Donkey Kong* was the main reason anyone would
> be interested in working with Nintendo. *Mario Bros.* and our other games
> were good B-titles, *Super Mario Brothers* had not come out yet, and the only
> game that did better than *Donkey Kong* was *Pac-Man*.
>
> If Coleco had *Donkey Kong,* Atari had no reason to work with us.
>
> **—Howard Phillips, early employee, Nintendo of America**

> And then at the June 1983 CES, Coleco introduced Adam. And they had *Don-*
> *key Kong* running on Adam. They only had the home video game rights. And
> the next thing we knew, they [Kassar] were screaming and yelling at us and,
> oh . . . they claimed that they couldn't go through with the Family Computer
> deal until we straightened out the mess with *Donkey Kong*.
>
> **—Howard Lincoln**

In an effort to pacify Atari, Lincoln called for a meeting that evening with
Arnold Greenberg, president of Coleco. Perhaps Arakawa and Lincoln remem-
bered how quickly Greenberg had backed down when threatened by Universal
Studios, or they may simply have been enraged that Coleco had made a new
version of *Donkey Kong* without clearing it, but they sat back and watched as
Hiroshi Yamauchi put on a show for Greenberg.

Yamauchi entered the room abruptly and, without addressing anyone, stood
at the end of a table. He became, as one of those present put it, "unglued."

He began with a breathy, high-pitched tirade in a Marlon Brando
monotone and quickly became loud and abusive. With a piercing cry, he
swung his arm in an arc in front of him, shooting his outstretched index
finger toward Greenberg.

Yamauchi's diatribe, all in Japanese, completely stunned everyone
in the room, with the possible exception of the Arakawas.[2]

Yamauchi demanded that Coleco refrain from showing or selling *Donkey*
Kong on the Adam Computer, and Greenberg backed off, though he had legal
grounds to challenge that demand. Atari had purchased only the floppy disk
license; the Adam version of *Donkey Kong* was cartridge-based.

Even with Coleco out of the way, the deal between Atari and Nintendo never took place. Kassar was fired the following month, and no deal was ever signed.

First Impressions

We kind of all looked at it and chuckled as we walked through the show because we all knew that video games were dead. This was the age of the floppy disk, the Commodore 64, the Apple IIc, the IBM PC, and the little one, what did they call it? . . . it was PC Junior.

Everybody was talking about the Amiga and the Atari ST. That was where everybody thought the business was, really. Nobody thought that Nintendo had much of a chance, and they kind of all laughed at what [Nintendo was] doing.

—Greg Fischbach, founder, Acclaim Entertainment

Nintendo was a company ruled by strong personalities. Back at Nintendo Co. Ltd. (NCL), the Japanese parent, Hiroshi Yamauchi controlled his company with an imperial hand, seldom complimenting workers' successes and often criticizing them harshly for mistakes. One person he openly criticized was Minoru Arakawa, who was both his son-in-law and the president of Nintendo of America.

When Nintendo could not break into America's burgeoning arcade business, Yamauchi blamed the failures on his son-in-law. Though he never accused Arakawa of ruining the deal with Atari, he did not hesitate to voice his opinion that a more competent person would have no trouble marketing the Famicom in the United States.

Minoru Arakawa was quiet-natured, sometimes jovial, and very determined. He surrounded himself with friends in whom he had complete confidence. During his tenure as president of Nintendo of America, Arakawa sometimes sided with his employees even when it put him in direct opposition with Yamauchi himself.

The Famicom continued to sell extremely well in Japan through 1984. Nintendo managed to sell more than three million game consoles in the eighteen months since its release. As 1985 rolled around, Yamauchi decided to make another attempt at breaking into the American market. There would be no more discussions of partners. However, he now believed that the best course would be to market the system through his American offices.

In the 1980s, the ideal place to unveil new consumer electronics products was at the Consumer Electronics Show. CES was held twice a year—January, in Las Vegas, and June, in Chicago. Both shows were held in enormous convention centers, with sprawling show floors large enough to hold row after row of spacious one- and two-story booths.

CES served the entire electronics industry, not just the video games branch of it.* During the CES's peak years, video and computer game companies reserved nearly half the floor space for the show; the other half sported televisions, stereos, video cassette recorders, refrigerators, car alarms, and the like.

CES had the atmosphere of a carnival. Large companies such as Sony, Panasonic, and RCA generally set up huge, flashy booths with walls of televisions displaying their latest achievements. Stereo and record companies blared music in their booths, and auto alarm companies brought in cars to broadcast their goods. Many companies hired attractive models in sexy outfits to work their booths. Some even brought in actors or actresses.** One section of the floor was sectioned off for adult film and software makers. It was not unusual for exhibitors in this section to bring in actors and actresses from pornographic movies to work in their booths.

Companies often spent as much as $5 million on a single show. They could spend up to $1 million alone on floor space and another $500,000 to host a spectacular party one night of the show. CES gave electronics companies an opportunity to impress retailers and journalists, and no expense was spared in that attempt.

Arakawa decided to officially unveil the Famicom at the January 1985 show in Las Vegas. Instead of calling the system the Famicom, a name that both Arakawa and Lincoln agreed might not appeal to American consumers, they decided on Advanced Video System (AVS).

---

* In fact, for many years, people organizing the CES treated video game makers like the industry's ugly stepchildren. Computer game and video game companies eventually formed their own trade show, the Electronic Entertainment Expo (E3).

** One year a company called 3DO hired the San Diego Charger's cheerleaders to appear in its booth. A few reporters described this as gratuitous, because 3DO did not publish a football game that year.

At the time, Arakawa had serious doubts about Nintendo's ability to re-start the video game market. He did not know if retailers would bother looking at a new system, and he had no idea what kind of competition he might face at the show.

Nintendo rented a small booth in a corner of the Las Vegas Convention Center and set up a simple display that included a basic Famicom (with an AVS label), a computer keyboard, a music keyboard, and twenty-five games.

> We didn't even know if we really wanted to get into the home video game business in the United States. We got a mixed reception at the show.
>
> The reaction, as I recall, was that anybody who would get into the video game business was nuts. They liked the hardware, though, and the games.
>
> **—Howard Lincoln**

> In January 1985 we introduced the Advance Video System with the music keyboard and keyboard and computer exercise, and it wasn't popular at all. Everybody really thought we were crazy or dumb.
>
> **—Minoru Arakawa**

Arakawa manned the booth himself. One person who saw him there described him as a small Japanese man who looked completely lost. Although a few retailers stopped by the booth and several people commented on the quality of the games, no one placed orders.

After returning to Seattle, Arakawa and Lincoln decided to reposition the Famicom. The people who played Nintendo's games liked them, but buyers for big department stores and toy stores were not interested in reentering the video game business. If the Famicom was going to break into the U. S. retail circuit, it would have to be marketed as something other than a video game system.

The solution came in the form of a light pistol and a little robot.

Nintendo's arcade division had two successful arcade shooting games called *Hogan's Alley* and *Duck Hunt*. (*Hogan's Alley* was popular enough to have been used in Steven Spielberg's film *Back to the Future*. The hero of the movie, played by Michael J. Fox, was supposed to be completely addicted to the game.) By adding a light gun, which was called "the Zapper," to the Famicom, Nintendo turned the system into a virtual shooting arcade—allowing Lincoln and Arakawa to position it as a gun game instead of a video game.

The robot, called Robot Operating Buddy (ROB), was developed by Gumpei Yokoi and the engineers of Nintendo's Research and Development Team number 1, the same team that developed the Game & Watch handheld games and the arcade hardware for *Donkey Kong*. ROB was a small plastic robot that worked in conjunction with two Famicom games—*Gyromite* and *Stack-Up*. Technologically speaking, ROB was a pretty simple toy that offered very little play value. It was mostly a decoy designed to prove that the Famicom was not just a video game.

> When we first got the robot, it did not look like anything that you could associate with the fun and excitement of our arcade games. When you put the batteries in, he made this horrible grinding sound and his arms slowly closed and slowly opened. It was scary.
>
> At the same time, he did this really cool thing. He did this technology thing where he would look at the screen. It was new technology; he could somehow read what was going on on the screen.
>
> That allowed the consumer retailers to think about it as a new toy.
>
> **—Howard Phillips**

As they prepared for Summer CES in June, Lincoln and Arakawa came up with a new name for the Famicom. Instead of calling it the Advanced Video System, they changed the name to the Nintendo Entertainment System (NES).

> In the spring of 1985, we added this robot. At the June 1985 show, we had a booth, and we launched the product as the Nintendo Entertainment System.
>
> We changed our position. We were selling a robot game, not a video game. It also let you play *Duck Hunt*, *Wild Gunman*, and *Hogan's Alley*.
>
> **—Howard Lincoln**

As he had done in January, Arakawa chose to run a small, quiet booth at the 1985 show. Although this booth, about 600 square feet, was larger than the one he had rented in Las Vegas, it was tiny compared to most booths on the floor. Arakawa purposely positioned ROB as his center attraction.

Though the NES was far from the hit of the show, several buyers expressed interest in it. As Lincoln and Arakawa had predicted, retail buyers were more receptive to gun and robot games than they were to video games. They inspected the NES carefully, and many commented that they liked the games. At the end of the show, however, there were again no orders.

Though he was disappointed by the lukewarm response, Arakawa did not give up. In an attempt to test whether the retailers' hesitance reflected consumer opinion, he hired a marketing firm to test the NES on focus groups. The response was disappointing.

Arakawa observed sessions as they took place. From behind a one-way mirror, he watched a random sampling of young boys play the NES and heard them say how much they hated it. Typical was the comment of an eight-year-old who said, "This is shit!"[3]

Arakawa faced several low points during his career with Nintendo of America. He faced hardship when he tried to establish Nintendo's arcade games. He faced another low point when Ron Judy and Al Stone, the men distributing Nintendo arcade games, wanted to leave him. He'd also braved the threats of Sidney Sheinberg, president of Universal Studios, but his latest challenge was the toughest. This was the first time Arakawa ever actually talked about backing away.

After the focus tests, Arakawa called his father-in-law and suggested giving up. He began to believe that the American video game market had shut down for good.

The Beginning of Rare

There was a certain situation that took place right around 1983. I happened to go to Japan and see the Nintendo Entertainment System. . . . the Family Computer. As soon as I saw the Famicom, I said, "That's it. This is the system that we've been waiting for." So I purchased a system and sent it to the UK, and that was the start of that latest and greatest group called Rare.

—Joel Hochberg, former Allied Leisure executive,
former coin-op repairman, cofounder of Rare Ltd.

By 1983, Joel Hochberg had been in the arcade and coin-operated game business for twenty-seven years. He had started as a repairman in 1956 and worked his way into the executive team of Allied Leisure in the 1970s.

While at Allied, Hochberg traveled to Europe and Japan to attend amusement industry trade shows and seek out international partners. One relationship he created was a partnership with Zilec, a small British company that made arcade conversions.

During one of his frequent trips to England, Hochberg attended a trade show and met Chris and Tim Stamper. Chris Stamper was a 19-year-old game designer for Zilec. Tim, his 16-year-old brother, was still in school.

The Stampers were a unique team. Chris was an electronics genius who, as a boy, had built an oscilloscope. Chris often took Tim to work with him. Both brothers—Tim in particular—had an air of confidence. They felt that they knew what made some games good and others bad.

> There's a dispute about this. Tim doesn't agree with me. But I'm almost positive, unless that was his charming personality I'm thinking of, there was an ATE show—Amusements Trade Exhibition Show. Chris attended it as a member of Zilec. I attended it as an independent, and Tim was there as an interested individual without any direct association. Very young guy. And I was very taken aback because here was a young man, very bright, very set in respect to what he thought a very good, successful product should look like, what it should represent on screen.
>
> **—Joel Hochberg**

Hochberg met the Stampers during the end of the *Space Invaders* era. A lot of changes were taking place within the industry. Centuri had bought Allied Leisure, and Hochberg decided to start his own business. Although the game business had fallen off in the United States, the worldwide market was still fairly strong. The Stampers wanted to leave Zilec and start their own company.

During one of Hochberg's visits, Chris Stamper revealed that he wanted to leave Zilec. He wanted to start a company with Tim, now nineteen, for more creative freedom and larger rewards. Hochberg's first reaction was to try and convince him to stay at Zilec, but Chris was determined. When that failed, Hochberg decided to set up a partnership with the Stampers.

Chris and Tim Stamper set up a game company called Ashby Computer Graphics (ACG) and began publishing games for the Sinclair Spectrum, a tiny computer that sold very well in Europe but never caught on in the United States.

> I visited with Tim and Chris and we discussed certain possibilities. Chris was absolutely set on the fact that he wanted to do games for Sinclair Spectrum (a small personal computer that Timex unsuccessfully tried to market in the United States). They did a host of games for the Sinclair Spectrum in 1983 and 1984.
>
> **—Joel Hochberg**

One of Tim Stamper's first games, *JetPac,* was a major success by Sinclair standards. Nearly one million people owned Sinclair Spectrum computers in 1983, and ACG sold more than 300,000 copies of *JetPac.*

> It was incredible penetration for a single product.
>   We had an advantage—we'd been working on an arcade product. We just took that expertise and transferred it directly to the Sinclair Spectrum.
>
> **—Chris Stamper**

Toward the end of 1983, Hochberg visited Tokyo. While there, he saw a Famicom and instantly recognized it as the future of video games. He purchased a console and sent it to the Stampers to get their reaction.

The Stampers were not immediately impressed. Nintendo had not begun exporting Famicom from Japan at the time, and the Stampers were not convinced that they wanted to deal with the Japanese market. They preferred to work on computer games. At the time, it seemed as if computers were the only viable market for electronic games. With a little prodding from Hochberg, the Stampers agreed that they would design games for the Famicom system if Nintendo started shipping to the United States and Europe.

In order to make games for the new system, however, they needed to obtain system specifications, schematics, and a license to make games from Nintendo. As an arcade owner, Hochberg was familiar with Nintendo of America. He made an appointment with Minoru Arakawa and flew out to Redmond, Washington, to propose a partnership.

I contacted Nintendo and found out that they were not completely interested in sharing the technical specs with us. My question to Mr. Arakawa was, "Why?"

He said, "You have to prove that you have the technical expertise," which was not a bad answer.

Chris spent a good deal of time, practically six months, reverse engineering the hardware and then proceeded to do for me an audiovisual display, very simple but utilizing graphic and other capabilities of the hardware that would show what we could do. We really weren't interested in giving Nintendo a product; we were interested in giving Nintendo a view of what could be done.

When I sent that off to Nintendo, Mr. Arakawa said, "I like what I see. Now please do a game."

But he still did not give us the technical specs at that point.

—Joel Hochberg

Joel came to me and I said, "If you are so good, why don't you make a game without tools?" It was a good test.

—Minoru Arakawa

I reverse engineered the NES. I had an understanding of the coin-op hardware that was out there, so I had a very good idea what the Nintendo actually contained.

We got about 99 percent correct. There were just a few things we didn't know about. But the interesting thing was the stuff that we discovered in the machine that was not documented. That instantly gave us an advantage that other developers didn't have.

—Chris Stamper

The Test

We decided to test the American market in New York. Everybody thought that we were going to die, that it was suicide.

—Minoru Arakawa

By the summer of 1985, Nintendo of America president Minoru Arakawa had become convinced that Americans no longer had any interest in video games. When he called Hiroshi Yamauchi to recommend pulling out, however, Yamauchi refused to consider the idea. He didn't care about CES shows or focus groups. The Famicom was flying off shelves in Japan, and as far as he was concerned, the NES would sell just as well in America.

To prove this, he suggested testing the NES in the toughest market in America. That market, everyone agreed, was New York City.

> I don't know who came up with the idea of starting out in New York. It was clear that New York would be the toughest market; New York was the entertainment capital. Mr. Yamauchi made the comment, "Well, then, it would be a really fair test because if you could do a good job in New York, you could pretty much do anything anywhere."
>
> **—Howard Lincoln**

CHAPTER 18

The Seeds of Competition

We visited Activision at that time. Greg Fischbach was the head of their international department, so he attended the meeting. After the meetings we tried to sell Greg Fischbach on why he wanted to become a licensee.

Later we found that Fischbach reported to the president or chairman of the company that Activision should not get involved with video games.

—Minoru Arakawa, president, Nintendo of America

This also wraps back to another story that they [Howard Lincoln and Minoru Arakawa] love to tell about a memo that I wrote when I was at Activision. After having met with them sometime in 1986, I sent a memo to Jim Levy (president of Activision) saying the business, in essence, doesn't work because there's no margin in it.

They never knew about the existence of this memo until several years later when it came out in a court case.

—Greg Fischbach, former vice president of the International Group, Activision

Hitting It Big in the Big Apple

The last vestiges of the Atari VCS era had crumbled by the beginning of 1985. Jack Tramiel, the man who purchased Atari from Warner Communications one year earlier, had already announced his intention to concentrate on home computers instead of video games. By the end of 1985, Coleco had abandoned the Adam Computer and squandered its Cabbage Patch Doll earnings just to stay afloat.

Against this tumultuous backdrop, Nintendo sent a small team of executives and seasoned employees to spearhead the American launch of the Nintendo Entertainment System (NES) in New York City.* Everything about Nintendo's New York test marketing efforts seemed small, except the $5 million advertising budget.

The effort began with Nintendo of America president Minoru Arakawa personally leading a group of thirty employees to the small New Jersey warehouse he had leased through the end of the year. The group included Ron Judy, one of the two entrepreneurs who had been with Nintendo of America from the beginning; Don James, who had been with Nintendo of America since its early New York days; and Gail Tilden, who was in charge of advertising.

> We sent a number of our employees back to Hackensack. We rented houses for them or we rented apartments. And we also had an apartment in New York City, but the warehouse was in Hackensack.
>
> **—Howard Lincoln, chairman, Nintendo of America**

> We sent thirty or forty people from Redmond [Washington] to New York. Most of them were married persons, and they left wives or husbands behind. They were there for three or four months.
>
> **—Minoru Arakawa, president, Nintendo of America**

The first shipment of NES systems arrived in a neat stack that barely took up half of the trailer on which it was transported. The boxes were stored in the warehouse, and the team began the arduous task of trying to get retailers

---

* For a more complete account of the New York launch, see *Game Over*.

to accept Nintendo's products. Most store owners did not want to look at video games, let alone waste floor space selling them. In fact, team members were cautioned not to use the term *video game*. The NES was to be sold as an "entertainment system."

At this point, the biggest selling points for the Nintendo Entertainment System were the Zapper gun and the games *Duck Hunt* and *Hogan's Alley*. Some retailers also liked the Robot Operating Buddy and some of the early arcade translations, like *Donkey Kong*, *Baseball*, and *Tennis*. When Nintendo went to New York, *Super Mario Brothers*, which would become the linchpin during the national launch of the NES, had not been introduced.

As often was the case with Arakawa, he surrounded himself with exceptional people. Whether visiting the headquarters of major chains or stopping by the manager's office of a local shopping mall, Judy and the rest of the team were tireless. The advertisements Tilden arranged with a local advertising agency were so effective that they set the tone for Nintendo ads well into the next decade.

Even so, most of the 500 retailers who sold the NES that Christmas might not have taken the merchandise if it were not for a risky offer made by Arakawa himself—a money-back guarantee. Going against the wishes of Nintendo Co. Ltd. president Hiroshi Yamauchi, Arakawa authorized his sales force to say that Nintendo would buy back any merchandise that retailers wished to return. The only thing retailers provided was floor space. Nintendo lugged in the merchandise, set up the displays, and bought back any unsold product.

> We rented a truck so that we could deliver orders, and we let people order the systems risk-free. We did the merchandising. We trained their people. We did everything. Then we really spent a lot of money on TV.
>
> **—Minoru Arakawa**

> They shipped it in the New York area in the Christmas of 1985. And it worked. I mean, they sold through. And they sold through with the little robot thing that they had attached, much to everybody's surprise.
>
> I think one of the gutsiest things Arakawa ever did was to take the inventory risk with respect to the launch of that product.
>
> **—Greg Fischbach, president, Acclaim Entertainment**

The Nintendo team's hours were exhausting. Team members approached retailers and demonstrated the system to customers by day, then delivered products and set up displays by night. One night, two team members went to deliver a merchandising display at a Macy's store in an area that Howard Philips described as a scary part of town. While Philips went into the store to arrange for the delivery, his partner remained outside to guard 19-inch televisions that would be used in the display. While he waited, a knot of aggressive young men gathered around. When Philips returned, he found his partner nearly frantic but still guarding the televisions.

After three months of exhaustive work, the Nintendo Entertainment System could be found in hundreds of stores throughout the New York area, including FAO Schwartz and Toys "R" Us.

> I went home to New York to spend Christmas with my parents that year. I went to Willoughby's, a camera shop on 32nd Street, to buy some film for my father, and there were all of these kids, these boys huddled around this counter at the shop. I went over to see what they were looking at, and it was a new video game system from Nintendo.
>
> **—Tom Zito, founder, Digital Pictures**

The NES was not a smash hit, but Nintendo did manage to sell 50,000 units, about half of the systems that had been shipped from Japan. It was enough to prove Yamauchi's point that video games were not dead. Amazingly, a large percentage of the retailers that carried the NES decided to continue carrying it after the holidays.

In February, Arakawa expanded his test to Los Angeles. But this test had none of the urgency of the one in New York. Nintendo continued its policy of offering to buy back merchandise and provided displays for stores, and reports of the company's success in New York made Los Angeles retailers more receptive than their New York counterparts had been.

The success of the Los Angeles test is best gauged in terms of the number of stores that accepted Nintendo's offer. Spring and summer are typically slow times for toy retailers, many of whom expect to incur small losses throughout the year, then cover their losses with highly profitable holiday sales. A large number of local department stores, electronics stores, and several toy stores began carrying the NES at that time. Though the system only sold moderately well, Arakawa interpreted retailers' willingness to stock his product as a sign of future success and expanded his test to include Chicago and San Francisco.

The Return of Jumpman

Shigeru Miyamoto, the man who designed *Donkey Kong,* built the game around two main characters. One was the eponymous villain, a giant ape that stole a woman and hurled barrels at the man trying to save her. The other was Jumpman, the chubby, mustachioed carpenter who leaped barrels, climbed ladders, and saved the day. Over time, Jumpman underwent an interesting evolution.

The first step in Jumpman's evolution was a name change—he became Mario in his next outing, a game called *Donkey Kong Junior.* Next, Miyamoto gave Mario a brother named Luigi and converted him from a carpenter into a plumber in the 1983 game *Mario Bros.* Up to this point, Mario always appeared in small games in which you could place the entire field of play on a single screen. That changed in 1985, with the release of *Super Mario Bros.*

Super Mario Bros. took Mario out of his single-screen setting and placed him in a huge, vivid world. Instead of simply climbing ladders and moving around on platforms, players now controlled him as he ran through a seemingly endless, brightly colored countryside filled with caverns, castles, and giant mushrooms. The landscape was much too expansive to fit on a screen. In this new game, the camera followed Mario as he ran forward through his two-dimensional world. Arnie Katz, editor of *Electronic Games,* dubbed it a "side-scrolling" game.*

The goal of the game was to help Mario rescue a princess from a dragon named Bowser. To do this, players had to fight or slip past walking turtles, flying turtles, and little mushroom-shaped men called Goombas.

Super Mario Bros. contained several elements that attracted attention. It had bright cartoon-like graphics, fast action, and a sense of humor. It also took

---

* *Super Mario Bros.* was not the first side-scrolling game. *Scramble, Defender, Super Cobra,* and several others predated it by several years.

Warren Robinett's concept of hidden "Easter eggs" to a new level with entire hidden worlds.* Most people continued playing *Super Mario Bros.* to find all of Miyamoto's Easter eggs long after they finished the game. If players knew where to look, they could find free men and coins hidden in mid-air, not to mention beanstalks that took Mario into the clouds, mushrooms that made him big, flowers that enabled him to spit fireballs, and stars that made him invulnerable. *Super Mario Bros.* did very well in Japanese arcades and attracted some attention to the failing U.S. arcade industry.

By the end of the year, Nintendo engineers succeeded in creating a home version of *Super Mario Bros.* for the Famicom. This product defined the difference between games for the old Atari systems and games that could be played on Nintendo cartridges. Although the home version of *Super Mario Bros.* was not identical to the arcade game, it was an extremely close approximation.

By the end of 1985, Nintendo began packaging *Super Mario Bros.* with the Famicom. This marketing move was so successful in Japan that Yamauchi and Arakawa decided to do it in the United States. It took a few months to create an American version of the game, and the cartridge was available by the time Nintendo of America went national—the end of 1986.

A Partner

Although 1985 was not a great year for video game sales, it was an excellent year for the five ex-Atari executives who had started a toy company called Worlds of Wonder. The head of the company was a man named Don Kingsborough, a former Atari vice president, who decided to start his own business when he ran across an invention that he believed would be a surefire hit as a toy.

> There were a lot of former Atari guys putting together this company called Worlds of Wonder. I didn't really know Don all that well. . . . . He was really on the domestic side of the business, and we had very little interaction.
>
> I joined Worlds of Wonder as the executive vice president of marketing and then eventually the managing director of international. You know, we started the company up literally around Don's swimming pool.

---

* At one point in the game, players could even walk through a brick wall to enter a seemingly endless underwater world.

> There were some guys from Disney who did the talking presidents. They
> wanted to do this talking teddy bear. Well, he was not nearly the incarnation
> that we finally brought out. When I first saw him, I called him Biafra bear
> because he was like this little skinny bear that looked like he needed fatten-
> ing up. He looked like he was a refugee from Biafra or someplace.
>
> **—Steven Race, former director of international marketing,**
> **Worlds of Wonder**

Building off the original animatronic technology, Kingsborough and company designed a plush teddy bear with a tape recorder built into its back.
Children could place tapes in the recorder, and the bear's mouth would move
as it appeared to tell stories and talk. The bear was named Teddy Ruxpin.

Once they had their product, the founders of Worlds of Wonder next set
out to build a sales force. They could have tried to hire salespeople from within
the toy industry but instead decided to go with people they knew who would
be aggressive. They hired ex-Atari sales representatives.

> We hired most of the old Atari reps to represent us because we knew that if we
> hired the toy reps, we'd have to go through channels. These guys ran Atari.
>
> When it came to selling Teddy Ruxpin, they went right over everyone's
> head and got right in to see the senior people. All the key retailers we showed
> Teddy Ruxpin to, to the man with one exception, all just melted and said,
> "Holy shit, this is it! This is it. This is the product this year."
>
> **—Jim Whims, former executive vice president, Worlds of Wonder**

Teddy Ruxpin was the toy sensation of the 1985 holiday season. Stores could
not keep it in stock; public demand was too great. The following year, Worlds of
Wonder came out with another major hit, Laser Tag. With these two products,
the company became a major player in the toy industry and an attractive partner to Minoru Arakawa, who wanted a marketing partner to distribute the NES.

> They approached us in 1986. They approached us. Kingsborough and Arakawa
> got together with Howard [Lincoln] and the senior management team and
> [they] said, "Listen, Whims and Bradley come from the video game business.

> You obviously have a strong relationship with the retailers, both with Teddy Ruxpin and Laser Tag."
>
> The rumor was that Toys "R" Us gave us a $100,000,000 order at Toy Fair that year. . . . Actually, they did; it wasn't a rumor. With that type of clout, we were able to work closely with the buying community to ensure that Nintendo didn't get put on the back burner and that, in fact, it was a priority for the buying community.
>
> **—Jim Whims**

The offer Arakawa made to Kingsborough bore no resemblance to the one he had made to Atari. The Atari offer involved licensing—Nintendo would allow Atari to manufacture the NES and sell it as an Atari product. Arakawa wanted Worlds of Wonder as distributor. He simply wanted Worlds of Wonder representatives to market the NES, along with Teddy Ruxpin and Laser Tag. He hoped that being associated with the two hottest toys on the market would open doors to stores such as Sears, and he was willing to pay a fee for the help.

As former Atari employees, Kingsborough and many of his executives were very familiar with the NES. They had seen it launched as the Famicom in Japan, and most of them agreed that it was much more powerful than prior console systems. With this in mind, Kingsborough accepted the offer.

> I will always remember the first sales meeting we had where we introduced the Nintendo 8-bit to the sales force. Arakawa came down, and we had the Nintendo people presenting the product, and we said, "This is a product we're going to be supporting on a nationwide basis."
>
> Everyone was sitting in the bar after dinner that night, and these guys who had been Atari's three biggest reps grabbed me and said, "Can we talk to you?"
>
> They pulled me aside and said, "We want to let you know that we think you're making an enormous strategic mistake by getting involved in the video game business again." Now these are three Atari reps who made millions of dollars in the video game business already. They said, "Listen. WOW is the hottest company in the world right now. You've got the hottest toy company in the world right now. The video game business is a black smear and it's just gonna drag you down into the abyss."

> And I'll always remember that discussion.
>
> The obvious answer was, "Well, listen, I'm glad you feel that way, but I have to tell you, if you want to sell Teddy Ruxpin and you want to sell Laser Tag, you're gonna sell Nintendo as well. And if you feel that strongly about it, then you ought to just resign the line now."

—Jim Whims

As Arakawa expected, the association brought new clout to Nintendo. Worlds of Wonder representatives had access to all of the top buyers. Suddenly, demonstrations of Teddy Ruxpin and Laser Tag expanded to include the NES as well. By that time, however, a new competitor had arrived on the scene.

An Old Competitor

> Yes, the Master System was a better piece of hardware than the NES. Remember, they had two extra years to develop it.

—Peter Main, vice president of marketing, Nintendo of America

The NES was not the only Japanese game console introduced in the United States at that time. In October 1986, Sega introduced a console called the Master System that featured the Zilog Z-80 processing chip and 128K ("K" in this case stands for kilobits which are one-eighth the size of the kilobytes normally referred to as "K".) nearly twice the memory of the NES. The Master System's additional memory and microprocessor made it more powerful than the NES.

Though it was a more powerful unit, Sega's Master System, marketed as the Mark III in Japan, had not fared well in that country, where Nintendo controlled more than 90 percent of the market.

> Unfortunately, it was probably launched about a year and a half to two and a half years, maybe two years after Nintendo. By that time, it was a Nintendo culture in Japan, and it was very, very difficult to launch a similar technology in Japan.

—David Rosen, chairman, Sega Enterprises, Ltd.

The controllers that came with the Master System appeared to be patterned after NES controllers—rectangular, with a directional pad rather than a joystick. In what appears to have been a small concession to the previous generation of game systems, Sega also manufactured tiny joysticks that could be screwed into the center of the directional pads.

Sega planned to market two forms of game media for the Master System. The first was standard cartridges. The other was a plastic card that looked like a credit card with little metal connections on one end. The cards could not store as much data as cartridges, but they sold for less. In the end, however, Sega published very few games on cards.

Like Nintendo, Sega was a company with a strong arcade presence. Sega's long line of hits included early favorites such as *Astro Blaster, Monster Bash,* and *Turbo,* as well as classics such as *Pengo.* Sega distributed *Frogger* in the United States, though the game was created by Konami. One difference between the two companies is that while Nintendo slowly pulled away from its coin-operated games business, Sega remained very committed to making arcade games. Within the next few years, Nintendo focused all of its development efforts into making cartridges for the NES. Sega, on the other hand, had never launched a consumer product in the United States. Instead, it had licensed games to companies such as Coleco, while continuing to create games for arcades that could then be translated into home games.

To attract consumers, Sega packed a home version of *Hang On,* the number-one game in arcades, with the Master System. *Hang On* was a motorcycle racing game that did not translate well to the constraints of a home system. The arcade game had handlebars for controllers. A deluxe version even had a model of a motorcycle upon which people sat as they played. The home version seemed slow and plain in comparison.

The Battle

> Now you are playing with power!
>
> **—Nintendo's advertising slogan**

> Now there are no limits!
>
> **—Sega's advertising slogan**

The marketing arm behind Sega's American release was considerably smaller than Nintendo's. Formed in April 1986, Sega's consumer products division consisted of two men, Bruce Lowry and Bob Harris, working with a couple of administrators out of a small room in the back of the company's coin-operated games offices.

Lowry and Harris arranged for advertising and set up demonstrations for retailers. Harris, who had come from the J. Walter Thompson advertising agency, helped create the packaging for the Master System. Within two months of joining Sega, Harris and Lowry had to set up and man an 1,800-square-foot booth at the Summer CES in Chicago. Some show attendees had never heard of Sega, and a few mistook the company for Saga Foods, commenting that it was strange that a food distributor would enter the video game business.

Although the Master System was not as widely distributed as the NES, it could be found in most major cities across the country in time for the holidays. Many electronics stores displayed the NES, the Master System, and the recently re-launched Atari 7800 side by side. Of the three game consoles, the Atari 7800 was the least expensive. Since it played both 2600 and 7800 games, it also had the largest library. The problem was that all of the games for the 7800 looked obsolete when compared to the top games for the two newer systems, and the 7800 eventually disappeared from store shelves.

The Master System was the most expensive of the trio, selling for about $10 more than a similarly equipped NES. The NES Control Deck, which included the console, two controllers, and a *Super Mario Bros.* cartridge, sold for $129.95; the basic Master System package sold for $139. The Nintendo Action Set, which included everything in the Control Deck packaging plus the "Zapper" light gun and the game *Duck Hunt,* sold for $149, as did the Master System and gun set, which included the "Light Phaser" and the game *Safari Hunt.*

Nintendo had several advantages right from the start. The marketing clout Nintendo received from its association with Worlds of Wonder opened doors to retailers, which remained closed to Sega. Anyone who wanted to sell Teddy Ruxpin and Laser Tag, including Sears and Toys "R" Us, was going to hear about the Nintendo Entertainment System.

Nintendo also had a stronger identity. In 1981, the biggest year of arcades, *Donkey Kong* was second only to *Pac-Man* in popularity. A *Donkey Kong* cartoon show had aired on television, and Nintendo made succeeding games that featured Donkey

Kong and Mario as heroes. Also, Nintendo arcade games all looked very similar. They had similar cabinet designs, the same style of art, and often the same themes. When Nintendo broke from its traditional Mario-style game with *Punch Out* in 1983, *Donkey Kong* could still be seen sitting in the audience. By doing this, Nintendo established an identity and created mascots that would remain valuable through the next decade. Though Sega broke into the U.S. arcade market before Nintendo did and had more games in its library, no theme ran throughout these games. They included everything from race cars to jet fighters.

Nintendo's biggest advantage was its library of games, and the advantage was apparent right from the start. *Super Mario Bros.* was more popular in arcades than *Hang On,* and Nintendo did a much better job of capturing its game in the home version. People went to stores asking for the "new video game system that plays that Mario game." Very few people ever seemed aware of the *Hang On* cartridge.

> There were seventeen games—all Nintendo games or games that Nintendo had licensed—that we were marketing as Nintendo games. The hardware had some software, along with the robot, packed in. But there were seventeen cartridges created, including *Super Mario Brothers, Baseball, Tennis,* and *Golf.* There was a karate game, *Kung Fu,* and *Donkey Kong Math.* It was our educational series.
>
> **—Howard Lincoln**

Nintendo's software advantage ran deeper than just the packed-in game. With *Donkey Kong, Donkey Kong Junior, Golf,* and *Popeye,* Nintendo had a substantial list of its own arcade games. Internally developed products, later referred to as "first-party" games, would eventually become a defining component in the operation of a video game company.

Hiroshi Yamauchi recognized the importance of setting up strong relationships with successful game publishers and arranged exclusive partnerships with Bandai, Capcom, Hudson, Konami, Namco, and Taito. (Although Bandai [a leading Japanese toy manufacturer], Taito [publisher of *Space Invaders*], and Namco [publisher of *Pac-Man*] were the most respected names at the start, Capcom and Konami eventually emerged as Nintendo's most influential partners during the 1980s.)

Shortly after the NES's national launch, Capcom released home versions of such arcade games as *Trojan, Ghosts 'N Goblins,* and *1942.* The text in many of these games was hastily translated and often contained grammatical errors.

The Hunt for American Software

> I think there may have been three or four licensees in the marketplace at that point, but no more than that. We were the seventh licensee that Nintendo had in the U.S. and the first U.S. company that Nintendo did business with.
>
> **—Greg Fischbach**

Although several top Japanese game companies signed licensing agreements with Nintendo, the American companies showed little interest. Game publishers such as Sierra On-Line, Broderbund, and Electronic Arts were more interested in making games for computers than for consoles, and toy companies like Milton Bradley and Mattel had left the industry entirely.

> And the entertainment companies like 20th Century, Paramount, and some of the other companies that had been involved in the video game business in 1982, 1983, and 1984 had been burned badly and therefore weren't too interested in coming back into the business again. So they wanted to shy away from it.
>
> **—Greg Fischbach**

> We spent a lot of time in the spring of 1986 trying to convince American software publishers, Electronic Arts, Broderbund, and Activision as an example, [to make games for the NES]. We were trying to say, "Hey, we got this great licensing program, and we want you to be part of it. This is the deal." And none of them took it.
>
> We ended up with four companies, all of whom were actually subsidiaries of Japanese companies. They were all coin-op companies—Data East, Konami, Capcom, and Bandai—and all of them were licensees of Nintendo Company Ltd. in Japan.
>
> **—Howard Lincoln**

One interesting twist from the early days of Nintendo occurred when Lincoln and Arakawa visited Activision. They demonstrated the NES and discussed their business model and how they planned to avoid the traps that destroyed Atari. One of the executives at the meeting was Greg Fischbach, vice president of Activision's international group. Fischbach approached Arakawa after the meeting, and the two men discussed Nintendo's licensing deal. Not long after the meeting, Arakawa received a call letting him know that Activision was not interested in making games for the NES.

> Greg Fischbach was president of the international department, and he attended the meeting. Then after the meeting we tried to sell Fischbach on why we wanted them to become a licensee. Later we found out that Greg Fischbach reported to the president of the company or chairman that he shouldn't do it.
>
> **—Minoru Arakawa**

One reason companies would not sign licensing agreements with Nintendo was that the terms of the agreement seemed entirely one-sided. Yamauchi had analyzed Atari's downfall and decided that Atari had allowed it to happen by letting the market flood with mediocre games. To prevent this from happening to Nintendo, Yamauchi implemented strict controls. Atari was caught off guard when companies like Activision and Imagic began making games for the 2600. To prevent this from happening to his system, Yamauchi protected it with a security chip that locked out unauthorized cartridges. This meant that the only way to make games for the NES was to allow Nintendo to manufacture them, and Nintendo maintained final authority in deciding which games would be manufactured and in what quantities.

> Most U.S. businesses weren't too interested in Nintendo's trading charges, which required that you purchase all of your inventory requirements from Nintendo, that you purchase them in Japan, and that you purchase them for a fixed price. In essence, Nintendo really controlled how much inventory was put into the marketplace. [The company] also made you open up a letter of credit guaranteeing payment for the goods at the time that you made the order.

> If you came out of the toy business, like Hasbro and Mattel, that really
> wasn't the way you did business . . . especially if you were the size of Hasbro
> or Mattel.
>
> **—Greg Fischbach**

At the same time that he courted established companies, Arakawa was not entirely cooperative with the lesser-known companies that approached him When approached by small design houses, he sometimes authorized companies to make games for the NES without giving them the design specifications they needed to understand the system.

The first American company to sign a licensing agreement with Nintendo was Acclaim Entertainment. The agreement was signed in 1988. Amazingly, Acclaim got the agreement before it ever published a game.

Three ex-Activision executives—Jim Scoroposki, Rob Holmes, and Greg Fischbach—founded Acclaim. Fischbach, the vice president who wrote the memo cautioning against involvement with Nintendo, left the company in 1986 and moved to New York to take a job with RCA Records as president of RCA International. When the company was bought out seven months later, Fischbach lost his job.

During his tenure with RCA, Fischbach kept in touch with Holmes and Scoroposki and met with Scoroposki socially. One day over lunch, Scoroposki mentioned Nintendo. He had visited the Nintendo booth while attending the Winter CES in Las Vegas, and had come to the conclusion that the company really might restart the video game business. He believed that Nintendo might sell two or three million NES decks and that retailers would be clamoring for software. They could meet that need by starting a company that would import popular titles from Japan.

> I got on the phone that next week and called Arakawa. He wasn't available.
> Then Howard [Lincoln] called me back, and I told him what I wanted to do. I
> said that we didn't have a name for this company, but I was interested in
> setting up a company and we were interested in becoming a licensee.
>
> **—Greg Fischbach**

Arakawa had not taken Fischbach's telephone calls because he was attending the annual Toy Fair trade show in New York. Lincoln arranged a meeting with Fischbach in Arakawa's hotel room. After a long discussion, Arakawa agreed to extend a license to Fischbach's still-unnamed company, and Lincoln faxed the agreement the following day. Once he obtained the license, Fischbach flew to Japan to find some games.

As president of Activision's international group, Fischbach had visited Japan several times and had several contacts in Tokyo. He began his search in Akihabara, Tokyo's electronics district.

> The Akihabara is like 42nd Street in Manhattan—big, wide boulevards, about six lanes across and with buildings on either side that are anywhere between eight and fourteen stories high that are just chock full of any kind of electronic gizmo or gadget that you could ever think of, from capacitors all the way up to television sets and washing machines and refrigerators. It's kind of like this hub of electronic hardware and software, and it's about three or four blocks long with big, wide sidewalks and streets that are just littered with people.
>
> **—Greg Fischbach**

Fischbach went to Japan in March 1987 and returned with three games. In June, even before the games were ready for market, Fischbach, Scoroposki, and Holmes decided to make a big splash as they announced their new company at the Summer CES. They rented a huge booth at the show that they decorated with an enormous sign bearing their company's new name—ACCLAIM. They wanted to convince passing retailers that Acclaim would be a major force in the video game industry. The image Fischbach tried to create proved prophetic.

Scoroposki's belief that licensing with Nintendo would be a lucrative move also proved true. Acclaim Entertainment released its first game in August 1987—a space combat game called *Star Voyager* that Fischbach jokingly referred to as "the game that never ends." Nintendo required licensees to make a minimum order of 1,000 cartridges; Acclaim ended up selling more than 100,000 copies of *Star Voyager.* Acclaim exceeded 200,000 in sales of its next game, *3D World Runner,* and more than one million copies of *Tiger Heli*—a game that Taito released in Japan but decided against releasing in the United States.

Over the years, Acclaim became one of Nintendo's most influential partners, and Fischbach never told Arakawa or Lincoln about the memo he had written after their visit to Activision. In 1989, however, the memo surfaced during a court battle between Atari Games (the coin-operated games division that Warner Communications did not sell to the Tramiels) and Nintendo.

> In one of those litigation deals with Atari games, our attorneys discovered this document. It was a memorandum from Greg to the president of Activision, basically saying, "I've met with Arakawa and Lincoln and I don't think that it makes any sense to get into this business."
>
> We had a lot of fun reminding Greg about that.
>
> **—Howard Lincoln**

Partnership Lost

> And eventually, the tail ended up wagging the dog, as Nintendo grew and that business flourished. And our toy business, you know, went away.
>
> **—Jim Whims**

Despite their hesitation to represent Nintendo, Worlds of Wonder salespeople soon discovered that the NES was their hottest product. The demand for Teddy Ruxpin in 1986 was at an all-time high; but by 1987, neither Teddy Ruxpin nor Laser Tag did very well. Nintendo, on the other hand, continued gaining momentum. Americans purchased 3 million NES consoles in 1986. Sales more than doubled the following year. This translated into huge commissions for toy representatives from Worlds of Wonder, but it also caused Nintendo to reconsider the relationship.

> Several reps wound up making over a million dollars a year in commissions. They [Nintendo] finally capped people like Mike Needleman and, . . . oh, who was the guy in Boston? Richard Tuckley. They capped them to a million dollars apiece.
>
> It was an easy deal. You just said, "Here's your lucky day. I've got an extra 50,000 pieces of NES." Easy sell.
>
> **—Steve Race**

Disaster struck Worlds of Wonder as the 1987 Christmas season approached. Mistakenly confident in the continued popularity of Teddy Ruxpin, Worlds of Wonder management grossly overestimated its inventory needs. The company ended up with so many extra copies of the expensive robotic bear that it faced bankruptcy.

In October, Minoru Arakawa contacted Worlds of Wonder to break off the partnership. Nintendo now had so much clout that it no longer needed a distribution partner. By coincidence, Arakawa contacted Don Kingsborough about discontinuing the Worlds of Wonder relationship around the time that Kingsborough was preparing to lay off his sales force. Arakawa decided to hire them instead. Ironically, Worlds of Wonder connected Nintendo with the exact sales force it had once tried to enlist through Atari.

Pac-Man, the most successful arcade
character of all time, at E3.

Donkey Kong—the 300-pound gorilla that put Nintendo on
the map.

After selling Atari to Warner Communications, Nolan Bushnell bought back the rights to Chuck E. Cheese Pizza Time Theaters. Atari made Bushnell famous, but it was "the rat" that made him rich.

David Rosen, the man who brought photomats, bowling alleys, and arcade machines to Japan, then led Sega to the United States.

Bushnell hired his neighbor, Joseph P. Keenan, to work for Atari. Keenan went on to become the president of Kee Games, and later, Data East USA.

Roger Hector and Nolan Bushnell at the launch of Sente.

▓ Workers assemble *Centipede* machines.

▐ Atari's Don Osborne demonstrates the *Star Wars* coin-op "cockpit"
to George Lucas.

Possibly the greatest coin-op designer of all time, Dave Theurer created *Missile Command, Tempest,* and *I*Robot.*

COURTESY OF DAVE THEURER

COURTESY OF *REPLAY MAGAZINE*

Former Disney animator Don Bluth provided the artwork for *Dragon's Lair,* the first laser disc–based arcade game. Some pundits thought *Dragon's Lair* would be the game to restore the arcade business, but with an average price tag of $4,300 and requiring special maintenance, laser disc games were a short-lived fad in arcades.

COURTESY OF ED LOGG

Nicknamed "Golden Boy" by his coworkers, Atari's coin-op engineer Ed Logg has a history of hits that includes *Asteroids, Centipede, Gauntlet,* and the Tengen version of *Tetris* for the NES.

COURTESY OF *RePlay Magazine*

Pete Kauffman, chairman of Exidy, was the bad boy of arcades. His pedestrian demolition game, *Death Race,* inspired a feature on the television news magazine *60 Minutes,* and he later created a game called *Chiller* that was so amazingly morbid that most American arcades refused to carry it.

COURTESY OF ED ROTBERG

Ed Rotberg, creator of *Battlezone,* left Atari shortly after working on the military version of the game.

COURTESY OF *RePlay Magazine*

Parent-activist Ronnie Lamm appeared on the television talk show *Donahue* to warn about the evils of video games.

In 1981, Tournament Games held the world video-game champion- ships in Chicago. The attendance was low, and the checks given to the winners bounced.

In 1981, video arcades were as common as convenience stores, and arcade games could be found just about anywhere.

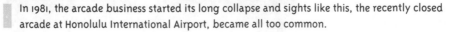

In 1981, the arcade business started its long collapse and sights like this, the recently closed arcade at Honolulu International Airport, became all too common.

Toru Iwatani (pictured here between Yasuhiko Asada, Namco president, and Kazuo Ito, Namco general manager) only made one famous game before being bumped up to management. However, that sole game was *Pac-Man*, the most popular arcade game in the world.

The arcade business's brightest star, Namco's *Pac-Man* appeared on Saturday morning cartoons, breakfast cereal boxes, and the cover of *Time*.

Though it did not do particularly well in the international market, *Ms. Pac-Man* was the most successful game ever released in American arcades.

Minoru Arakawa, president of Nintendo of America, had to battle to break into the U.S. market, then struggled again to revive the home game market.

Seattle attorney Howard Lincoln convinced Arakawa not to surrender when sued by Universal Studios over *Donkey Kong.* Arakawa was so impressed that he made Lincoln vice president of Nintendo of America.

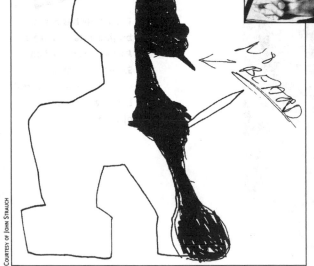

This doodle, created by attorney John Strauch, played a large role in a court decision that cost Nintendo $250 million in the Alpex case. The decision was later overturned. (See pages 394–395.)

Having created Donkey Kong, Mario, Zelda, Yoshi, and Star Fox, Shigeru Miyamoto (pictured here with awards from the Academy of Interactive Arts and Sciences) is generally regarded as the most successful game designer in history.

Donkey Kong was the game that enabled Nintendo to break into the U.S. arcade business.

COURTESY OF S. KENT

COURTESY OF NINTENDO OF AMERICA

The Nintendo Entertainment System (NES) and the Super NES, the systems that solidified Nintendo's place in video game history.

Russian mathematician Alexey Pajitnov (seen here visiting his old apartment in Moscow) created *Tetris,* the best-selling video game of all time.

COURTESY OF NINTENDO OF AMERICA

COURTESY OF NINTENDO OF AMERICA

The late Gumpei Yokoi, dean of Nintendo's engineers, devised the toys that helped Nintendo expand from manufacturing playing cards, created the hardware for Nintendo's first arcade games, and led the team that made Game Boy.

Game Boy. . . . Atari engineers laughed when they saw its crude, monochrome screen. Twelve years, 115 million units, and more than 450 million cartridges later, Game Boy reigns unrivalled as the most popular game system of all time.

By the time former Mattel president Tom Kalinske was appointed president and CEO of Sega of America, Nintendo already controlled more than 90 percent of the video game industry. Kalinske chose to take Nintendo head-on.

Brilliant, temperamental, and an extreme perfectionist, Sega's Yuji Naka created *Sonic The Hedgehog*, *NiGHTS*, *Burning Rangers*, and *Samba de Amigo*.

The creation of *Sonic The Hedgehog* signaled a new direction and attitude for Sega. It also meant the end of Nintendo's unchallenged dominance of the home game industry.

Sega's top arcade hit-maker, Yu Suzuki, is known for his sophisticated taste in wine, cars, and technology.

Capcom's Shinji Mikami, creator of the exceptionally gory *Resident Evil* games.

Crazy Taxi creator, Hisao Oguchi.

Hironobu Sakaguchi of Square Soft thought *Final Fantasy* would be his swan song as a game designer.

Created by Andrew Gavin and Jason Rubin of Naughty Dog, produced by Universal Interactive, and published by Sony Computer Entertainment, *Crash Bandicoot* games became Sony's unofficial answer to Mario and Sonic. (Pictured here is concept art from the latest *Crash Bandicoot* game, which is being developed and published by Universal.)

In 1994, Nintendo allowed Tim Stamper and a team at Rare, Ltd. to use their new rendering technology to revive Donkey Kong. The result was *Donkey Kong Country*.

Moviephile and *Metal Gear* creator, Hideo Kojima.

Sort of a cross between Clint Eastwood and Toshiro Mafune, Solid Snake is the mercenary hero of Konami's *Metal Gear Solid*.

John Romero, cocreator of *Doom* and *Quake*.

During the 1993 joint hearings, Senator Joseph Lieberman displays a light pistol used in video games.

Nintendo's Donkey Kong enters the ring in a PR event for *Super Smash Bros.*

Because of the lasting popularity of the Pokemon craze in Japan, Nintendo opened a "Pokemon Center" store a few blocks from the main subway station in Tokyo.

COURTESY OF MICROSOFT

In 2001, Microsoft plans to enter the video game industry with its new Xbox game console.

COURTESY OF S. KENT

COURTESY OF S. KENT

Seamus Blackley, whose past resume includes such impressive feats as working on the super collider and such low points as *Tresspasser*—a terrible *Jurassic Park*–based first-person shooter on PC—is the main designer of Xbox.

Having helped his company launch a very successful line of PC peripherals, Microsoft "chief Xbox officer" Robert Bach is now assigned to break into the video game hardware market.

Nintendo teamed up with IBM to design a custom-built 64-bit chip for GameCube. Because Nintendo was so quiet about the system, many skeptics doubted its ability to compete with Sony's PlayStation 2 and Microsoft's Xbox. Big mistake. GameCube may look like a toy, but going into the 2001 Christmas season, it could compete with anything on the market.

With the launch of PlayStation 2, Sony officially launched the most recent generation of video game hardware.

Twenty years and 100 million Game Boys later, Nintendo of America president Minoru Arakawa and Mario still have reason to smile.

First appearing in the 1981 game *Donkey Kong* as a carpenter named "Jumpman," Nintendo's Mario is the elder statesman of the gaming industry.

CHAPTER 19

The Birth of Sega

When I was a youngster, I went to Coney Island. Like everybody else in New York City, I played the games in the penny arcades. That was really my total knowledge of the business.

—**David Rosen, cofounder, Sega Enterprises**

David Rosen and Michael Kogan . . . just a couple of guys living it up in Tokyo.

—**Bernard Stolar, chief operating officer, Sega of America**

The Meaning of Sega

Sega is not a Japanese word; it is an abbreviated form of Service Games. Though the company is headquartered in Japan and has a Japanese corporate culture, it was founded by Americans.

The history of Sega can be divided into two distinct stories. One is the story of Sega; the second is the story of David Rosen.

The Beginnings of Sega

> My Dad was in Hawaii when the Japanese bombed Pearl Harbor. He ran the slot machines on the bases. When they bombed Pearl Harbor, there was a note on one of the slot machines that said, "In case of another attack, jump under this machine. It's never been hit yet."
>
> **—Lauran Bromley, president, Bromley Incorporated**
> **(daughter of Marty Bromley)**

Service Games began in May 1952, shortly after laws were passed restricting the use of slot machines in the United States. Prior to those laws, a man named Marty Bromley managed game rooms with slot machines, pinball tables, and other coin-operated amusement devices on several military bases in the U.S. Territory of Hawaii. In 1951, after the laws changed and the government confiscated the slot machines, Bromley and his father purchased them from the government, then shipped them to Japan, where they set up game rooms for servicemen stationed there.

By most accounts, Japan of the early 1950s was practically a Third World nation. The country's industries were greatly depleted during the war years, many of its factories had been destroyed, and a large portion of the workforce had died. Though the United States was a generous victor, Japan's recovery was slow.

Bromley set up a lucrative trade. He branched out into jukeboxes and opened a manufacturing plant called Nippon Kikai Seizo. By 1960, Service Games, also known as Nippon Koraku Bussan, was one of the three largest coin-operated entertainment companies in Japan, along with Taito and Rosen

Enterprises Ltd. By this time, Bromley had two partners, Dick Stewart and Ray LaMaire, who stayed in Japan and managed the business.

In 1964, they took on a new partner, a man named David Rosen.

> There are two people who played a very important role in the opening and establishing of the coin machine industry in Japan. Dick Stewart and Ray Lemaire had come to Japan in 1952 and, sharing an office as a bedroom, had from scratch built a major operation on the U.S. military bases. They called their company Service Games. From this start they expanded into the Japanese marketplace, establishing a jukebox operation that reached a total of over 5,000 locations. To service this route they had established branch offices in every major city in Japan. By this time they had two companies, Nippon Goraku Bussan and Nippon Kikai Seizo, which they merged into one. The company had an extraordinarily well-developed corporate infrastructure and, like my company, had taken the best from both business cultures: Japan and the United States. It was with this company, named Sega, that I merged Rosen Enterprises Ltd., and Sega Enterprises Ltd. came into being.
>
> **—David Rosen**

> Twelve years after Service Games was formed, Mr. Rosen came in. He was already established, and he already had his own company.
>
> **—Lauran Bromley**

A Tough Guy from New York

> You know, game machines, like a theater seat or a plane seat, depend on occupancy and depend on the time that they are used. If you charge $1 per play, but it's only used ten times a day, you only make $10. Really, all you're selling is time. Our machines were constantly going. I mean, [they were] going from morning to night.
>
> **—David Rosen**

David Rosen was tall and thickly built, with dark hair and a strange calm intensity that suggested the ability to carefully consider issues under any circumstances. He could be friendly and quietly intimidating at the same time. He had served in the U.S. Air Force during the Korean War. In 1951, as Marty Bromley started his slot machine business, Rosen was stationed in the Far East. He traveled to locations such as Shanghai and Okinawa but spent most of his time in Japan.

While serving in Japan, Rosen came to believe that the Japanese people were too industrious to remain in their present circumstances. Seeing an opportunity, he started up a business even before he was discharged. After finishing his commitment with the Air Force, he returned to the United States, hoping to further his college education and establish his business.

> My first business was actually involved in art, strangely enough, which is about as far from the current business as you could be. In those years Japan was still in an economic postwar strata and, consequently, there was still a lot of unemployment at the time. A lot of the artists were doing portrait painting based on photos. I established a company in the United States that sent photos back to Japan to be made into portraits.
>
> **—David Rosen, founder, Rosen Enterprises, Ltd.**

When his portrait business failed, Rosen decided to return to Japan and start a new business that he would run while living in Japan. He studied the people and their needs and found an intriguing possibility.

> At that point in time, the people in Japan had a great need for ID photos. You virtually needed an ID photo for school applications, for rice ration cards, for railway cards, and for employment, obviously.
>
> We're talking about 1953, 1954, and the photo studios generally charged what was then 250 yen, and it took two or three days to have the photos done. My thought was that we had, in the United States, photo mat studios that charged 25 cents, and you could get four photos. They were called Photomats—little booths that were completely automated.
>
> **—David Rosen**

American Photomat booths were not an ideal solution, however. Upon returning home, Rosen discovered that Photomat pictures faded after one or two years. If he wanted to bring Photomats to Japan, where the pictures would be used on official IDs, he needed to find a way to produce pictures that could last for four or five years.

After some research, Rosen discovered that the problem was easily solved. Photomat pictures were made without negatives—an automated camera snapped the shot, then flashed the image on positive paper. If this process were carried out adhering to certain temperature specifications, the pictures would not fade for several years. The booths, however, lacked temperature controls. The people who ran the companies that made the booths believed that their customers viewed the pictures as having only novelty value.

Adding temperature controls would have been too expensive, so Rosen came up with a more practical solution. He left the automated camera device in the booths and placed workers behind the booths to develop the pictures by hand while monitoring the temperature. With the economy as weak as it was, Rosen had no problem hiring workers.

> I took some older machines that were in the United States, redesigned them, and brought them into Japan. This was the beginning of 1954. We put out the first couple of booths, and it turned out to be wildly successful. We charged . . . I believe it was 150 to 200 yen, which was less than the 250 yen [charged by photographers], and obviously we were able to develop it in about two or three minutes. The Japanese for this business was *Nifun Shashin,* which means "two-minute photo," and Photorama was the name of the brand.
>
> This became so successful that it enabled me, over a short period of time, to open up well over a hundred such locations throughout Japan. There were different times when people would go through school applications and what-not, and it was not unusual at those times of the year for the lines to get into the booth to be an hour, hour and a half.
>
> **—David Rosen**

If anything, Rosen's Photoramas proved too successful. Although his prices were only slightly cheaper than those offered by photographers, the convenience of picking up pictures within a few minutes attracted customers in droves. As his business grew, photographers started to complain and eventually protested to the U.S. consulate. When the consulate asked Rosen for help, he offered to license Photorama franchises. According to Rosen, this may have been the first franchising business in Japan.

Franchising led to some immediate profits but ultimately killed the business. Although Rosen was able to double his locations by licensing nearly one hundred operations, franchising invited competition. There was no patent on Photorama technology, so other companies were able to move in and imitate the booths. In the early 1960s, Rosen finally closed his Photorama business. By this time, however, he had managed to open several new ventures and move in a different direction.

> To import any product into Japan in the early 1950s and mid-1950s, and even pretty much going into the late 1950s, you had to apply for a license through the Ministry of International Trade and Industry (MITI). It didn't matter if you were a Japanese company or any other nationality, you could not import anything without a license.
>
> The licenses generally went into three categories. Category one was absolute necessities. Category two items were non-necessities but something desirable. And category three was luxury. Well, luxury was nearly impossible; I mean, there were no dollars there. And absolute necessities were such things as oil, certain foodstuffs, etc. So those problems existed, as I say, simply because of a lack of dollars, not because they were trying to block imports coming into Japan.
>
> **—David Rosen**

Japan received a tremendous financial boost from the presence of the American military during the Korean War. The United States used Tokyo as a base throughout the war, and American procurement of goods and workers brought a rich infusion of dollars into the Japanese economy. As a result of that new prosperity, Rosen decided to import a limited number of "luxury" items in 1956. After considering his options, he decided to bring in some coin-operated electro-mechanical games.

> It took me over one year with a lot of effort and certainly a lot of introductions
> to convince the MITI that these games were something that would be good for
> leisure. They finally granted a license to me for $100,000, which meant that I
> could purchase $100,000 worth of merchandise [in the United States].
>
> **—David Rosen**

According to Rosen, the U.S. amusements market was fairly stagnant when he arrived. The arcades that carried the games attracted a fairly rough clientele, and all of the games came from a few Chicago-based companies. With the exception of pinball, the amusement industry had gone flat, creating a buyers' market in which many distributors were glad to sell used machines to Rosen at bargain rates. He paid approximately $200 per game, then had to pay nearly twice that price to the Japanese authorities in order to import them.

Most of the games Rosen imported, such as *Bear Gun* from Seeburg, involved shooting. These were big, heavy machines that required a lot of space. With *Bear Gun,* for example, the player stood nearly fifteen feet from the target. These games were also very solidly constructed and seldom broke down.

Due to the success of his Photorama operation, Rosen had more than one hundred locations in which he could place his machines. He charged 20 yen per game. At the time, the trade rate was 360 yen to the dollar, so Rosen was letting people play for less than the ten cents per game that was standard in the United States. Like his photomats, Rosen's coin-operated games were a huge success. With shipping and duties, Rosen paid less than $1,000 to import each game. Even at 20 yen per game, it took less than two months for the games to earn back that investment. Within a year, the Ministry of International Trade and Industry approved Rosen's request to return to the United States and purchase $200,000 worth of games.

> At this point in time I became known as a very live customer because most
> distributors in the United States had warehouses filled with used equipment
> that they really had no marketplace for.
>
> In those years, trade-ins were a very big part of any distributor's busi-
> ness. Operators buy games and two years later they trade them in. At that

> time, the distributor's price to the operator for new games was maybe $695,
> $795, and he would take a trade-in and give $50 or $100 for an older game.
> The trade-ins just piled up in warehouses.
>
> **—David Rosen**

Through the Photorama business, Rosen had developed strong relationships with the owners of the Toho and Shochiku movie theater chains and was able to place arcades in their lobbies or in adjoining spaces. While Namco founder Masaya Nakamura was still operating horse rides on the rooftops of Tokyo department stores, Rosen had at least one arcade in every city in Japan. His closest rivals were Service Games, which by this time had cornered the jukebox market with "Sega" jukeboxes, and Taito, the amusement company founded by Michael Kogan. Though they were all fiercely competitive, Rosen, Kogan, and the principles of Sega formed strong personal ties.

After the success of his arcades, Rosen searched for new ways to expand his business. He bought the rights to an indoor golf game, in which a computer read the speed and direction of a ball that players hit into a net, and set up a golf course franchise. The Japanese, however, considered golf an outdoor activity, and Rosen's business did not flourish. Next, he tried building a business around slot cars. This idea touched off a brief fad. Then he was approached by AMF to help establish a bowling alley.

> At that time there were bowling installations in military bases and there was
> one bowling installation in Tokyo, but it was sort of quasi-American mili-
> tary. It really wasn't in the civilian marketplace. I decided that I would open
> up the first bowling center.
>
> It had to be put into a very high traffic, high entertainment area. I picked
> an area of Tokyo that was full of restaurants and theaters called Shinjuku.
> Well, getting space in Shinjuku was very, very difficult; next to impossible. I
> decided to open up fourteen lanes, but the only way I could find that much
> space was to build on top of one of the existing [movie] theaters.
>
> This was a real challenge because the president of that particular theater chain
> was a friend of mine. We had to do this without affecting the theater. . . .

> no vibrations, no noise in the theater. It was really an engineering feat. Until
> we rolled the first ball down, we really couldn't be sure it would work.
>
> **—David Rosen**

Rosen's bowling alley was an unqualified success.

> This particular bowling center went on to establish records in the bowling
> industry. The way they measure the success of an alley is by lines bowled in
> a day. At that point in time, a typical bowling center in the United States
> would do 40 to 45 lines per day. The centers that held records were situated
> in Hawaii. They were doing about 60 per day. We did 110 per day.
>
> We only closed four hours a day, between 2:00 and 6:00 in the morn-
> ing. We were originally opened 24 hours, but the police said, "Please close
> for a few hours."
>
> **—David Rosen**

Ironically, it was the only bowling alley Rosen ever opened. Once again, his success paved the way for competitors. Before long, Brunswick opened several bowling alleys around Japan, with Sega or Taito arcades in their lobbies. Thanks to its theater arcades, Rosen Enterprises, Ltd., remained the biggest amusement game company in the business, but its closest rivals gained ground.

A New Arrangement

Smaller competitors started popping up around Tokyo toward the end of 1964, and Rosen began discussing a three-way merger with Michael Kogan of Taito and the three men who controlled Service Games—Marty Bromley, Dick Stewart, and Ray LaMaire. Kogan eventually decided against joining with the other companies; but Sega and Rosen Enterprises did join forces to form Sega Enterprises, Ltd.

Though Rosen Enterprises had a stronger hold on the amusement games market at the time of the merger, Service Games was a much larger company. Its assets included a thriving jukebox trade that at one point reached approximately 6,000 locations, a considerable manufacturing facility, several bowling alley arcades, and more than thirty branch offices. Under the new agreement, Rosen became president and CEO of Sega. Within a year of his becoming president of the company, Rosen used Sega's manufacturing plant to build its own games.

Nearly ten years had passed since Rosen imported his first *Bear Gun* and *Coon Hunt* games, and he felt that game quality had not changed much over that time. Due to increased competition, he switched from purchasing used games to buying new ones, driving the money he spent per game from $200 to as much as $695. The switch yielded little value to the consumer. The coin-operated amusement industry was so stagnant that the new games were almost identical to the used ones Rosen had imported earlier.

In 1966, Sega began manufacturing its first game, *Periscope,* which put a new spin on the shooting games Rosen had imported since 1956. The game was an attack submarine simulation. Players scanned a stretch of ocean through a periscope, then fired torpedoes at ships as they crossed the horizon. The ocean was a wide bed of plastic that looked like a windy, wave-tossed sea, and the torpedoes were really only strings of lights, but *Periscope* had great sound effects and the overall effect was very impressive for its time. The game was expensive to make and cost 30 yen to play—twice the price of earlier games.

Periscope was so successful in Japan that distributors from the United States and Europe flew in to see it. The game had been designed for use in Sega arcades and was not built well for export; but when international orders came in, Sega engineers redesigned it so that it could be shipped elsewhere. Rosen gave the game a $1,295 price tag, making it far more expensive than games manufactured in the United States. When U.S. operators complained that Sega wanted too much money and that a $1,200 game would never pay for itself, Rosen responded that they should set *Periscope* at 25 cents per play instead of the usual 10 cents. *Periscope* became the first game to be set at that price.

> Sega made its mark in this country when it brought over a gigantic target rifle called *Periscope*. What was interesting about *Periscope* was not only that it was the biggest machine ever built—I think the thing ran 10 feet deep by 6 feet wide by 6 feet high—it introduced quarter-play. It was so successful in the arcades that it brought people off the street. People came into

these arcades just to play that game. I would say that in my time, *Periscope* is one of the great successful novelty machines.

—Eddie Adlum

With the success of *Periscope,* Sega suddenly became an exporter rather than an importer of games. Sega engineers began designing as many as ten new games each year—all of which were available for export. Within three years of the merger, Sega had become so successful that Rosen, Bromley, and the other principals began discussing a public offering on the Japanese market. That idea turned out to be too ambitious. Had they succeeded, Sega would have been the first foreign-owned company to enter the exchange since the end of World War II.

Rather than selling shares of their company, Rosen, Bromley, Stewart, and LaMaire ended up selling their company altogether. Approached by Kidder Peabody with the suggestion that several large American conglomerates would be interested in purchasing the company, they spoke with a few companies and finally sold to Gulf & Western in 1967.

All four of those boys (Bromley, Stewart, LaMaire, and Rosen) were involved with Sega until they sold it in 1968. From what I gather, Ray, Dick, and Dave had more money than they had ever seen, and they were going to retire. My father would have been in his fifties at that point. They got an offer from Gulf & Western and decided to retire, and that lasted all of six months; then three of the boys (Bromley, Stewart, and LaMaire) started Segasa of Spain.

—Lauran Bromley

Though the sale of Sega included a stipulation that required Rosen to remain as CEO and chairman through 1972, it allowed him to move his headquarters to the city of his choosing. After trying Hawaii for a few months, he established headquarters in Hong Kong and stayed there until 1976. It was during this time that he established a strong relationship with Charlie Bluhdorn and Jim Judelson, the chairman and president, respectively, of Gulf and Western. Bluhdorn offered Rosen the opportunity to go into partnership with G & W in establishing a Far East conglomerate similar to G & W. The company was formed with Sega as a subsidiary. However at that time the market conditions in the Far East did not allow for an acquisition program of the type required to emulate G & W's success in the United States. In 1974 Bluhdorn, recognizing Rosen's restlessness and entrepreneurial spirit, offered to spin out Sega into a U.S. listed company, which Rosen as chairman, CEO, and second largest shareholder could use as a vehicle to grow Sega.

During this time, Sega acquired an established American arcade company called Gremlin as its manufacturing arm. Teamed up with Gremlin, Sega ended the 1970s as a major supplier of video games in the United States and Europe.

> While profits kept rising in the 1980–1982 periods, I became very concerned regarding the economics of the industry. I felt that sound fiscal principles were being ignored and that the wild expansion would lead to a very serious bust. In a major industry distributor meeting hosted by Sega, I gave a speech in which I forecasted that the industry was just around the corner from a major disaster, if there was not a change in the way business was being conducted.
>
> **—David Rosen**

Rosen advocated that manufacturers and distributors start manufacturing and selling kits to the operator, allowing them to convert older games without having to purchase completed cabinets. According to Rosen, the idea stunned the audience and some people booed him. "My speech was considered blasphemy," he later wrote of the event.

In the late 1970s Bluhdorn asked Rosen to join the Paramount Group, and his headquarters were moved to the Paramount studio lot. Barry Diller, the chairman of Paramount, and Michael Eisner, the president of Paramount, joined the Sega board, and Rosen joined the Paramount board.

In late 1981 Rosen proposed that Gulf & Western buy out the minority shareholders, including himself. The decision was to buy out the minority shareholders. Rosen agreed to stay on as corporate advisor, and was there to see the collapse of the coin-op and consumer markets a few months after the buy-out in 1982. In 1983, however, about one year after the crash of the arcade industry, the oil giant started looking for ways to get out of the video game industry. Gulf & Western sold Sega's U.S. assets to Bally/Midway, then contacted Rosen and offered him the opportunity to buy back the Japanese operation for $38 million. Rosen put together a team of backers and assumed control of the company in March 1984. After the buy-back, Hayao Nakayama, one of Rosen's backers, became CEO.

Having witnessed the crash of the arcade industry, Nakayama decided to diversify Sega's activities to include home products. Nintendo had already launched the Famicom, so Nakayama turned his attention toward America.

CHAPTER 20

The New Empire

I just love playing Mario on my Atari.

—Yasmine Bleethe, actress on *Baywatch*

Every dog has its day, and this one is having a big day.'

—Trip Hawkins, founder, Electronic Arts

It can carry a glass of water to you, or a glass of milk, or whatever, so It's really hot.

—Ernie Anastos, former anchorman, *WABC-TV Eyewitness News*

The Last Vestiges of Anonymity

Nintendo began marketing the Nintendo Entertainment System (NES) in 1985 with a single sales territory—New York City—and 100,000 game consoles. By the following Christmas, the NES could be found in stores coast to coast and in 1.9 million homes. With a new sense of confidence, Nintendo president Minoru Arakawa sponsored a survey called the North Pole Poll as he prepared for the 1986 holiday season. In the survey, children were shown the toys that retailers considered to be their top prospects and asked to choose a favorite. Some of the candidates included Rambo action figures, Teddy Ruxpin, Barbie, and baseball gear. The number one pick was the NES.

To publicize the results, Nintendo's PR firm produced a video news release about the survey and sent it to television stations across the country. Scores of news shows ran the story, including WABC TV in New York City. The problem was that while an ever-growing body of children knew about Nintendo, the message had not yet reached most adults. When *WABC Eyewitness News* anchors Ernie Anastos and Roz Abrams discussed the story on the air, they clearly had no idea what the NES was or even how to pronounce the name Nintendo.

The segment began with Nintendo's prepackaged video release about the North Pole Poll. Once the clip ended, Anastos tried to sound knowledgeable as he said: *"Nine-tendo,* that is the high-tech video entertainment system."

"I think that is part of *Nine-tendo,* there," agreed Roz Abrams, pointing at a Robot Operating Buddy (ROB), which came bundled in the deluxe NES package.

"Let's see if we can push this button here," said Anastos. He flipped the power switch on the back of the robot and it began rotating its arms to the right in a slow and grinding motion.

Assuming an air of expertise, Roz leaned forward and pushed the robot's arms down. "It's part video game, part computer, part everything, and it goes up and down and all around, and if you have all of the pieces. . . . "

"It can carry a glass of water to you, or a glass of milk, or whatever, so it's really hot," added Anastos.

The Pitfalls of Success

NES sales increased exponentially as Nintendo began its national sales campaign. According to Nintendo's internal records, the company sold 1.8 million game consoles in the 1986 fiscal year, 5.4 million in 1987, and 9.3 million in 1988. In 1989, Nintendo changed its fiscal year from September–August to March–February, leaving the company with a seven-month fiscal year in 1989. During that seven-month period, Nintendo sold 5.3 million game consoles, and another 7.6 million in 1990.

Nintendo's earnings soared as well. In 1987, Nintendo sold more than $750 million worth of games and hardware in the United States. That figure more than doubled in 1988 to $1.7 billion. By 1990, Nintendo had sold more than 350,000 cartridges worldwide. Nintendo sales alone accounted for one-tenth of the Japanese-American trade deficit.

Aware of the complexities that their company's success might bring, Arakawa and Howard Lincoln hired two outside firms—McCann-Erickson and Foote, Cone & Belding—to handle advertising. Arakawa hired a public relations firm, too—Hill and Knowlton. The largest PR firm in the world at the time, Hill and Knowlton represented the nation of Kuwait just before and during the Gulf War.

As the NES gained prominence, Nintendo became a lightning rod for protests from several groups. One challenge Hill and Knowlton's account executives faced was trying to help Nintendo create a positive image at a time when Americans were becoming increasingly upset about the Japanese–American trade imbalance.

> That was a time when Japanese influence in American business was really picking up, and there was a certain animosity toward Japanese companies. You'd call reporters in certain quarters and they'd basically say, "Three strikes and you're out." Strike one was that the video game industry was supposed to be dead; two was that they'd never heard of a company called Nintendo before; and three came when they said, "Oh, so they're Japanese!"
>
> **—Richard Brudvik-Lindner, former group supervisor and head of Nintendo of America Account Team, Hill and Knowlton**

Protests came from all directions. Educators and parents complained that Nintendo was distracting children from their studies, a 1989 study stated that Nintendo was partially to blame for a 10 percent decrease in the cardiovascular fitness of American schoolchildren,[2] and Jewish groups protested that the outline of the third dungeon in a game called *The Legend of Zelda* was an inverted swastika. When a Seattle-based group called Families for Peace protested outside Nintendo headquarters during the 1987 holidays, Hill and Knowlton executives had to scramble to preserve their client's reputation.

> Families for Peace decided they were going to protest against the war toys that Nintendo was creating and shipping. Nintendo had their little Zapper light gun and, of course, a lot of the games involved shooting or things of that nature.
>
> That was a big test for Nintendo because they were a Japanese company and Arakawa hadn't faced protest before. . . . Mr. Arakawa didn't have a cultural reference for how to deal with this. Howard Lincoln had a legalistic way of dealing with it, but it wasn't going to do much for them in terms of their public persona, especially at that critical juncture. He took a very lawyerly, legalistic approach. We convinced them that what they needed to do was really soften Nintendo's image at the time, so we went out and bought a whole bunch of Christmas trees and lights and decorations. We bought some white plastic sheeting that we put over the Nintendo sign at the entrance, and we put these Christmas trees up and covered up the name.
>
> We had to cover the name because we assumed there would be news cameras. Here was this crowd of families marching up and down in front of Nintendo. . . . Families for Peace. There were moms pushing strollers with babies, holding signs that said, "No guns," and "Nintendo breeds war."
>
> **—Richard Brudvik-Linder**

In an effort to create a softer image, Arakawa turned to Howard Phillips, one of Nintendo's first employees. Phillips, the company's product analysis manager, was Nintendo's most skilled video game player. He was energetic, enthusiastic, and a natural evangelist for video games. Though he was originally sent to the New York launch to work in the warehouse, he proved more valuable as a salesman and product demonstrator.

Phillips made the perfect spokesman for Nintendo not only because of his skill as a gamer and his enthusiasm, but also because of his appearance. With short red hair and a youthful demeanor, Phillips had the bright smile and the wholesome countenance that Nintendo needed to counteract bad publicity.

Dressed in bow tie and jacket, Phillips went on publicity tours, judged contests, became the president of the Nintendo Fan Club, wrote columns for the *Nintendo Fun Club News*—the forerunner to *Nintendo Power Magazine*—and eventually starred in a *Nintendo Power* comic strip called "Howard and Nester."

Phillips played along as Nintendo and its PR firm portrayed him in a slightly nerdy fashion. His relaxed mannerisms made him instantly likable, and he knew how to build on his own affability by making himself open and approachable. In 1986, Nintendo began promoting him as "the man who plays games for a living." The campaign lasted until he left the company in 1991. During that time, he became somewhat of a luminary. "I wasn't as big as a movie star, but I was as recognized as the actors in network television shows. I was probably as recognized as the guy from *McGyver*." Near the end of Phillips's time at Nintendo, one survey found that 59 percent of boys between the ages of nine and eleven could identify him.

Here to Stay

> We were not convinced that video games had a long life. We knew that if the market was flooded with poor quality video games, it'd blow up overnight.
>
> **—Howard Lincoln, chairman, Nintendo of America**

Although they conceded that Nintendo had done better than expected during its national launch, many journalists and toy industry analysts believed that the resurgence of video games would be little more than a brief fad. This put Nintendo in a dangerous position. Parents would not spend $80 purchasing an NES for their children if they believed the video game craze was ending, and buyers for the big retail chains might refuse to carry Nintendo products if the industry was shaky. In a pamphlet called *The Facts on Home Video Games,* Howard Phillips listed four insufficiencies of older game systems that might have led to their demise:

1. Limited in graphics and depth of play
2. Played at their best only in arcades
3. Restricted to few colors
4. Constrained by poor audio qualities, with a limited variety of sound effects

Nintendo spokespeople often attempted to distance their company from Atari when dealing with the media, a difficult task considering that its sales force was comprised of Atari salespeople. They began spreading the message that Nintendo had analyzed Atari's mistakes. In a 1986 interview on the Financial News Network, Nintendo of America director of sales Bruce Donaldson stressed inventory management and system security as the reasons Nintendo would last longer than Atari had.

> Very important to the Nintendo System, at this point in time, [is that] it cannot be what we refer to as "reverse engineered." Nobody can buy a unit, from an engineering standpoint, take it into [his] factory, and figure out how to make software. There are security codes built into our entire system.
>
> **—Bruce Donaldson, former director of sales, Nintendo of America**

Donaldson was mistaken. A British software development house called Rare Ltd. reverse engineered a Famicom in 1984. And in 1988, engineers at Salt Lake City–based Sculptured Software reverse engineered the NES to create their own game authoring equipment, then created a thriving trade selling NES development kits to other software developers. Other companies such as Tengen, the home game division of Atari Games, invented technologies to disable the security chip that Nintendo embedded in the NES to lock out unlicensed games.

> We were very concerned about the quality of the games. If we didn't come up with good quality from our associates, we thought that we might go like Atari. So we really had to be strict with our quality screening system.
>
> **—Minoru Arakawa**

Nintendo's most important message was game quality. According to Lincoln and Arakawa, the game companies of the Atari age had gotten sloppy and released too many identical games. To prevent this, Lincoln created very strict terms that gave Nintendo unflinching authority over the licensing agreement that publishers had to sign to make games for the NES. American companies such as Activision and Electronic Arts, which did not have to deal with these restrictions when they made games for personal computers, took a wait-and-see approach with the NES.

When Nintendo of America first began marketing the console, the only licensees making games for the system were Japanese companies. These companies reaped tremendous benefits during the first year that the NES was out. The first three games that Capcom released for the system—*1942, Ghosts 'N Goblins,* and *Commando*—all sold over one million copies. By 1987, several U.S. firms recognized the value of doing business with Nintendo and signed licensing agreements.

> There were a lot of myths that were built up over the years about how Nintendo was arrogant and Nintendo had a really restrictive licensing program and all of that. But from our point of view, these guys were all making a ton of money.
>
> Atari Games got all upset because they felt that they weren't getting enough games, so they illegally reversed engineered the NES and copied our security chip. We got in a lot of litigation with them, so all of this stuff was kind of cumulative.
>
> When we set up this third-party licensing program in 1986, we came up with a program by which we identified ways that we could control the quality of software that was going to reach the market. We said two things. We said, "If you want to be a third-party licensee, you have to agree that you will only publish five games a year on our system, and you have to agree that the games will be exclusive to the Nintendo Entertainment System for a period of two years." From our point of view, those clauses worked as a quality control mechanism.
>
> **—Howard Lincoln**

Over the next decade, Lincoln learned that controlling third-party games was not as important as having a healthy library of original games. When a company named 3DO launched a highly sophisticated game console in 1994, Lincoln commented that he was not worried about 3DO as a competitor because it did not publish its own games. When a reporter later asked why he'd been so confident, Lincoln responded, "The first-party games are the products that differentiate your hardware."

The Home Game Company

With more than 60,000 units sold in the United States, *Donkey Kong* was Nintendo's biggest arcade hit. The arcade industry began its long collapse the year after *Donkey Kong* was released, and Nintendo's arcade fortunes eroded quickly. Nintendo released *Donkey Kong Junior* in 1982 and sold only 30,000 machines, 20,000 *Popeye* machines (also 1982), and a mere 5,000 copies of *Donkey Kong 3* (1983).*

In 1982, Universal Sales made arcade history with a game called *Mr. Do!* Instead of selling dedicated *Mr. Do!* machines, Universal sold the game as a kit. The kit came with a customized control panel, a computer board with *Mr. Do!* read-only memory (ROM) chips, stickers that could be placed on the side of stand-up arcade machines for art, and a plastic marquee. It was the first game ever sold as a conversion only. According to former Universal Sales western regional sales manager Joe Morici, the company sold approximately 30,000 copies of the game in the United States alone.

In 1983, Nintendo released the VS System, a line of arcade games with double-screens on which two players could face off against each other or play alone. In 1987, Nintendo replaced the VS System with Play Choice 10, a line of arcade machines that worked like a jukebox with ten interchangeable boards. All of the games for Play Choice 10 were modified versions of NES cartridges.

Despite the strategic move away from creating original arcade games, Lincoln and Arakawa did not take the arcade business lightly. Play Choice 10 had great marketing potential. They could prerelease highly anticipated games on Play Choice 10 to build public awareness with negligible development costs. Wealthy from home game sales, Nintendo remained the largest advertiser in *RePlay,* a magazine that tracked the arcade business, for years after the company stopped developing arcade content.

With its software development focused on home games, Nintendo began churning out the most detailed and diverse game lineup ever seen in the consumer market. In 1987, Nintendo released three extremely significant games.

---

* In fairness, *Donkey Kong 3* was not as impressive a game as the original *Donkey Kong* or *Donkey Kong Junior.* The earlier games featured unique challenges; *Donkey Kong 3* was little more than a clever adaptation of *Space Invaders.* Lack of innovation may have hurt the game's sales.

The Legend of Zelda

Nintendo's biggest game in 1987, *The Legend of Zelda*, was created by Shigeru Miyamoto, the same man who created *Donkey Kong* and *Super Mario Brothers*. By this time, Hiroshi Yamauchi, the president of Nintendo Co. Ltd. in Japan, recognized Miyamoto as a rare talent upon whom his company's future would depend.

The Legend of Zelda was a role-playing game in which players helped a young elf boy named Link explore a huge territory as he fought monsters, collected treasures, and explored dungeons. The ultimate goals of the game were to defeat an evil monster named Ganon and rescue Zelda, the princess of Hyrule. Before you could do that, however, you had to locate pieces of a magical tablet called the Triforce that were scattered across a vast playfield. In many ways, *The Legend of Zelda* was Miyamoto's most brilliant game. It combined a well-thought-out fairy tale with perfectly crafted game mechanics. It was also Miyamoto's first free-roaming game. Unlike *Super Mario Bros.*, a side-scrolling game in which players could move only forward or backward, *The Legend of Zelda* was played from the top-down perspective, allowing players to move the hero in any compass direction.

When the first prototypes of *The Legend of Zelda* arrived in the United States, Minoru Arakawa was not sure how people would respond to a complex game with text windows in it. He worried that perhaps the game was too complicated for American audiences. To test this out, he had several employees try the game. In order to give the game a fair chance, Arakawa arranged for Japanese-speaking workers to sit with American employees and translate any Kanji that appeared in the text boxes.

> It was all in Japanese, which made it really hard to play, but it was just so compelling that we kept playing it and playing it. The way the game mechanics worked, the fact that it did this great thing with that sword . . . It had great mechanics. Typical of Miyamoto, it had puzzles. You would come across things that would be on the island or behind a door or whatever, and you could see them, but you couldn't have them.
>
> **—Howard Phillips**

As he tested *The Legend of Zelda* on his employees, Arakawa noticed a disturbing trend. Most American workers who played the game did not warm up to it instantly. They all ended up giving the game high marks, but Arakawa noticed that some people needed as much as ten hours before they understood the game and enjoyed it.

> *The Legend of Zelda* was a different kind of game and, also, it took a long time until people really liked the game. I hoped people would be patient enough and understand that it was a different game and enjoy it, and I was worried at the time.
>
> **—Minoru Arakawa**

Housed in a shiny gold cartridge, the American version of *The Legend of Zelda* required more megabits of storage space than any other game released for the NES up to that point, and it came with an internal ten-year battery, enabling it to store three players' progress so that they would not have to start again after every game. *The Legend of Zelda* was the first game to include an internal battery. It also came with more documentation than earlier games, including a thick instruction booklet that identified most of the monsters and weapons in the game and a large fold-out map of the fantasy land of Hyrule. As a final precaution, Arakawa added a toll-free telephone number that players could call if they needed help with the game.

> The game was so different that we were afraid that people couldn't figure out how to play and [would] give up, so we put the 800 telephone number in the game [booklet] so that they could call us for free and we could answer any questions about the games.
>
> We released the *Legend of Zelda* on June 27, 1987. All of a sudden, the telephone started ringing. We hired four people to answer questions over the telephone, and those four people were busy all the time, so we increased from four to five, 10, 20, 40, 50, and we ended up with 200.
>
> **—Minoru Arakawa**

Customers called nonstop and asked questions about more than *The Legend of Zelda*—they wanted to know about every game. To cover the calls, Arakawa expanded his telephone bank to ten full-time operators, but it wasn't enough.

He continued expanding the telephone operation, running ads in the help-wanted sections of the *Seattle Times* and the *Seattle Post Intelligencer* for people who "want to play games for a living." By 1990, more than 200 people were working on the help lines, and the toll-free number became too expensive to maintain. Expecting to reduce the number of calls, Arakawa approved the suggestion to keep the help center as a free service but eliminate the toll-free number. Throughout the 1990s, the help center continued to maintain a staff of 200 operators, fielding an average of 100,000 telephone calls, 3,500 e-mail messages, and 1,900 letters per week. During the holidays, the staffing grew to 500 operators fielding as many as 250,000 calls.*

Mike Tyson's Punch-Out

The second major game of 1987 was *Mike Tyson's Punch-Out,* a home adaptation of an arcade game that Nintendo had released in 1983. Both the arcade game and the NES cartridge were designed by Genyo Takeda and Nintendo Co. Ltd.'s Research and Development Team 3, a team of engineers that generally focused on hardware.

The original arcade game, which was simply called *Punch-Out,* was a boxing game in which players took on five fictitious fighters as they fought for a shot at a championship belt. An early first-person game, players saw the game from within the head of an "up-and-coming boxer." The fighter the player controlled was depicted as a wire mesh character. Although *Punch-Out* was ostensibly about boxing, it was really a puzzle game. In order to win, players had to learn the patterns used by the computer-controlled boxers. A fighter named "Bald Bull," for instance, would charge at the player. If he landed a punch at the end of his charge, he would score an instant knockdown. The player could either dodge Bald Bull's charge and respond with a properly timed counterattack, or hit him at a precise moment in his charge to knock him to the canvas.

The home version of *Punch-Out* featured more than twice as many opponents as the arcade game. While the home version did include three of the original fighters—Glass Joe, Bald Bull, and Mr. Sandman (who was the world champion in the arcade game)—it also had five all-new opponents, including Mike Tyson, who had recently been crowned heavyweight champion of the world.

---

* In 1998, the help center held a small party to celebrate call number 64 million.

Arakawa thought up the idea of licensing Mike Tyson himself. He attended one of Tyson's early fights during a trade show and was impressed by the young boxer's power and skills. Arakawa decided that adding the super-powerful heavyweight's name to the upcoming boxing game would make it more attractive. Nintendo's legal team approached Tyson with an offer that was rumored to be $50,000* for a three-year period, and the fighter agreed. (It should be noted that Nintendo took a chance licensing Tyson, since the agreement was signed prior to his winning the WBC title from Trevor Berbick on November 22, 1986.) When Arakawa told Takeda the idea, Takeda agreed and began adding Tyson's image to one of the fighters in the game.

> I watched Tyson fight during CES. This was before he became champion. He was so powerful and strong and we all fell in love with him, so we decided to license him. Japan liked the idea, too. Fortunately, the *Punch-Out* game was under development for the home [console], so I contacted Mr. Takeda and asked him to convert it to *Mike Tyson's Punch-Out.*
>
> He changed the master board to include Tyson, and Tyson [the boxer] was quite successful. He won every fight before he became champion, so we were very pleased.
>
> **—Minoru Arakawa**

Unlike the arcade game, the home game was played from the third-person perspective. Players controlled a tiny boxer in a black tank top named Little Mac, who was so short that his head barely reached his opponent's belt lines. As he prepared to release the game, Arakawa confided to Howard Phillips that the Little Mac character was designed to look like him.

> When he first got *Punch-Out,* Arakawa said, "Little Mac, that's you."
>
> I said, "What are you talking about?" and he said, "It looks just like you."
>
> I told him, "He looks nothing like me," but Arakawa kept saying that repeatedly. I don't know if he was just pulling my leg.
>
> **—Howard Phillips**

---

* Nintendo refuses to specify the amount.

If Takeda's team members wanted Little Mac to look like Howard Phillips, they failed. Little Mac had black hair; Phillips's hair was red. Their faces were also unalike.*

Nintendo, a company that worked hard to maintain a clean image, came to regret its association with Tyson. After winning and unifying the heavyweight crown in 1987, Tyson became involved in a well-publicized divorce from actress Robyn Givens. During the proceedings, Tyson was accused of beating Givens. When Nintendo's three-year agreement with Tyson ended, the company quietly removed his name and image from the game and re-released it as *Punch-Out!* with a new champion named "Mr. Dream."

Both *Mike Tyson's Punch-Out* and *The Legend of Zelda* became million-sellers.

Metroid

Metroid, the third major game to be released by Nintendo in 1987, was a futuristic adventure in which players controlled a space explorer named Samus. Created by Nintendo's Research and Development Team 1—the team led by Gumpei Yokoi, the man who created the hardware for *Donkey Kong*—*Metroid* was a difficult game to beat. It involved a lot of precision jumping, one of the tougher skills in video games. It featured several large side-scrolling and vertically scrolling maps and stands out for having some of the most innovative and challenging levels of any NES game. It was also one of the first games to feature a female hero. Samus wore a large space helmet throughout the game. She could have been a man, a child, or a robot. Once she destroyed the final enemy character, a creature called "Mother Brain," she removed her helmet. Only then did players find out that Samus was a woman.

Metroid became a symbol of Nintendo's ability to make adult-oriented games. In later years, Nintendo tried to attract older consumers to Game Boy and Super NES by releasing *Metroid* versions for those systems.

The Library of Licensees

Nintendo's third-party licensees also provided impressive games in 1987. Konami, a company that would distinguish itself as one of Nintendo's four

---

* Glass Joe, the first opponent in the game, looked a bit more like Phillips and has the same hair color and length. It is possible that Arakawa was mistaken.

most influential licensees, made good use of its five-game allotment in 1987. A successful arcade company with such past hits as *Frogger* and *Time Pilot*, Konami's first offerings included *Gradius*, a side-scrolling space shooter; *Track & Field* and *Rush 'N Attack*, two decent translations of arcade games; *Castlevania*, a side-scrolling adventure in which players controlled a whip-toting vampire hunter; and *Double Dribble*, a basketball simulation.

Konami sold more than 1 million copies of *Gradius*, its first NES title, in Japan before shipping it to the United States. The game contained a secret code that would enable players to equip their spaceship with an array of weapons. To get the weapons, players had to hit the directional pad on their controllers up twice, down twice, left, right, left, right, "B," "A," and then "Start" buttons. Konami used the same secret code in many of its later games.

Data East, another licensee with a strong arcade pedigree, used its game allotment to convert popular arcade games into home cartridges. Data East's first offerings included *Tag Team Wrestling*, *Karate Champ* (the first side-view martial-arts tournament game), *Burgertime* (which had been released for ColecoVision, Intellivision, and several Atari systems in the early 1980s), and *Karnov*.

Taito, which along with Konami was one of the original four licensees, released home versions of three arcade games in 1987—*Elevator Action*, *Legend of Kage*, and *Arkanoid*. In later years, *Arkanoid* became somewhat of a collectors' item because it had an adapter featuring a knob that enabled NES controllers to move paddles across the bottom of the screen. *Arkanoid* was basically an updated version of the Atari game *Breakout*.

Some companies rushed to publish NES translations of arcade games that they licensed from other companies. SNK Corporation licensed the NES rights to the arcade hits *Ikari Warriors* and *Ikari Warriors II: Victory Road* from a company called Irem. Sun Soft Corporation licensed a 1983 driving simulation called *Spy Hunter* from Bally/Midway.

Of all of Nintendo's early licensees, however, the one with the most staying power in the industry was Capcom. With an unmistakably strong arcade presence and a particularly aggressive marketer at the helm of its U.S. affiliate, Capcom released a mixture of arcade translations and original games that attracted a strong following.

> Capcom is another coin-op company, a very good coin-op company. They
> were especially good at creating the games and doing the smart marketing.
> Sometime, from inventory-risk point of view, they made mistakes by being
> too aggressive, and they ended up in trouble back in those days.
>
> **—Minoru Arakawa**

Fighting for Survival

Nintendo and Sega were neighbors during the 1987 Winter Consumer Electronics Show. Sega's big product at the show was a pair of 3D glasses for the Master System. The glasses were designed by Mark Cerny, the young game designer who created *Marble Madness* for Atari Coin-op. Now working for Sega, Cerny moved to Japan shortly after leaving Atari.

Sega's 3D glasses reflected their creator's gift for sensible design. They were molded out of durable plastic, lightweight, and large enough to fit over prescription eyewear. The glasses were not meant to replace the television but rather to enhance it. Players watched the game through the glasses, and transparent liquid crystal displays within the eyepieces focused the picture on the screen and added 3D effects.[*] Cerny's glasses were one of the big hits of the trade show.

> We were showing off what we felt was the next step in this technology, these
> 3D glasses that used a shuttering effect. Next to us . . . right next to us be-
> cause we were side by side, Nintendo was showing their knitting machine.
> They actually had a big to-do for knitting potholders and stuff like that.
>
> I remember seeing Howard Lincoln and Arakawa in the hallway between
> our booths, and I started laughing and said that I felt that I was taking two
> steps forward in technology and I didn't know where they were going with
> the pot holders.
>
> **—Bruce Lowry, former president, Sega Consumer Products**

---

[*] Ten years after Sega released its 3D Glasses, a number of smaller companies released products that utilized the identical technology to enhance PC games.

Sega had a number of small victories during this period. Macy's and FAO Schwartz carried the Master System right alongside the NES, and Target stores promoted the console quite heavily. Film critics Siskel and Ebert compared the NES and Master System on a special holiday program, concluding that they preferred Sega's hardware. Ebert, who wore corrective eyeglasses, even commented that he could wear his glasses under the 3D Glasses.

These were fleeting victories at best, however. Nintendo controlled somewhere between 86 to 93 percent of the market by the end of 1987. By the time Sega had sold 100,000 Master Systems, Nintendo had already sold more than 2 million NES units and the gap was widening. Nintendo had better market awareness and more money for advertising. Sensing that an established marketing partner with inroads into the American toy industry might have more luck competing with Nintendo, Sega Enterprises CEO Hayao Nakayama pulled the plug on the in-house consumer division in the beginning of 1988 and signed a two-year licensing agreement with Tonka Toys. Neither Bruce Lowry nor Bob Harris, who was vice president of sales and marketing, wanted to move to Tonka's Minnesota headquarters; and both ended up leaving Sega.

> While we had gotten into all the retailers they [Nintendo] did, we simply did not have the resources to compete against Nintendo's huge marketing budget, and the decision was made to look for a partner. We hooked up with Tonka, and they took over the distribution and put a tremendous amount of money into marketing dollars. They put over $30 million into marketing.
>
> **—Bruce Lowry**

Another Big Year

Toy sales generally drop sharply after the holidays, but Nintendo sales remained strong in January and February of 1988. With more than seven million users, the demand for new games remained steady all year long. So did the requests for game hints and information about upcoming titles. Nintendo tried to satisfy consumer curiosity with a free quarterly newsletter called *Nintendo Fun Club News,* but the newsletter wasn't enough. It began as a 12-page, two-color publication in the spring of 1987, but by winter it had expanded to 32 full-color pages. After releasing the spring 1988, issue of *Nintendo Fun Club News,* Arakawa decided it was time for Nintendo to publish a full magazine. The magazine was named *Nintendo Power.*

> There were quite a few publishers making video game magazines in Japan, and no one was doing one in the United States, so we decided to do it ourselves. I felt Gail Tilden was the perfect person to do the editing on the magazine. She had just had a baby and wasn't in the office, so I called her up and asked her to start our publishing department. She accepted, and she came with the baby in her arms two weeks after she got out of the hospital.
>
> **—Minoru Arakawa**

Nintendo Power, which was released bi-monthly, was larger and far more sophisticated than *Nintendo Fun Club News.* Each issue was approximately 100 pages long and featured game maps, tips from game counselors, and descriptions of upcoming games. *Nintendo Power* ran no advertisements, though it glibly plugged products made by Nintendo. By 1989, more than one million people subscribed to *Nintendo Power.*

One of *Nintendo Power*'s most popular features was "NES Achievers," a two-page spread that listed the names of people who either completed or got exceptionally high scores on popular NES and Game Boy games. The competition to get on this list was fierce and not always restricted to kids.

> I had my name in *Nintendo Power Magazine* several times for top score on *Game Boy Tetris.* It got to the point that they wouldn't print my name again, so I had to use a fake name. . . . my first name backwards and my last name backwards. Evets Kainzow.
>
> I saw the fake name in there one day, and I thought it was somebody else and said, "Oh, my God, his score is better than mine!" I was trying to figure it out, then I noticed that Evets Kainzow lived in Saratoga, and I remembered sending it in.
>
> **—Steven Wozniak, cofounder, Apple Computers**

Inventing the Ultimate Video Game

As Nintendo's popularity grew, so did complaints about video games interfering with school studies. Rather than taking a defensive approach, the public relations team from Hill and Knowlton recommended that Nintendo take a proactive stance and proposed an event that would cast the company in a pro-education light.

> There was a fair amount of backlash starting to develop about this time, and people felt that video games were an insidious stealer of children's energies and creativity. There were a lot of things we did to try to put a more human face on Nintendo, including sponsoring a contest that promoted the process of inventing and creativity among kids.
>
> **—Richard Brudvik-Lindner**

The contest was called the "Invent the Ultimate Video Game" competition. Kids of all ages were invited to submit original ideas for video games to be judged by Nintendo. They did not have to make an actual game; they simply needed to send documentation explaining their ideas. Of the more than 10,000 entries received, 10 finalists were selected and flown to Washington, D.C., in February 1989, to exhibit their ideas at an event that would be held in the rotunda of the Senate office building. Many of the games that were selected had a decidedly educational theme. A female finalist, for instance, came up with a game that simulated a presidential election. The winner of the competition was fifteen-year-old Jeffrey Scott Campbell of Aurora, Colorado, who received the grand prize: a $3,000 scholarship.

> I presented the trophies at the competition and talked with a lot of reporters. This one TV reporter came up to me, and we spoke for quite a while. We had a friendly conversation, then he said, "Are you ready to do the interview?"
>
> I said yes, and he put his microphone in my face and said, "Why is it that video games are so bad for kids?"
>
> I thought for a few seconds, then I said, "They're not."
>
> He said, "Let's try this again," and asked the same question. Then I thought for a few seconds and said, "They're not." He wanted to get me arguing, and

> I thought this was the best way to make sure that he did not get any useable
> tape from me.
>
> **—Howard Phillips**

Not a Political Statement

In 1988, Konami released an NES side scrolling shooter game called *Contra*. The game started out like a fairly typical war game with soldiers running through a jungle, shooting at enemies. Before long, however, the action moved out of the jungle and into a futuristic-looking fortress filled with alien creatures and lasers. (Despite the picture of an alien standing between two soldiers on the box, some people saw the title and thought the game referred to the guerrillas Ronald Reagan had sent aid to in Nicaragua.) Toys "R" Us refused to carry the game, stating that it was too violent. When Minoru Arakawa called Toys "R" Us headquarters and told the buyers that the violence in the game was within acceptable limits, the retailers picked up the game. It sold exceptionally well.

Nintendo's product analysts scrutinized and screened games before approving them for publication on the NES, but some things slipped through. When Jaleco, a company best-known for the million copy–selling baseball simulation *Bases Loaded*, submitted *Maniac Mansion* as a possible NES title, Nintendo made the company change some of the background art. Originally created by LucasArts for the Commodore Amiga, *Maniac Mansion* featured naked Greek statues. Once the statues and a few mildly suggestive lines of dialog were changed, the game was approved. Unfortunately, Nintendo's screeners had not discovered an Easter egg that was well hidden deep within the game.

> You had to sneak into a character named Weird Ed's room and steal his hamster. You would then run down to the kitchen undetected and put the hamster in the microwave oven, at which point the hamster would explode into a little charred mess complete with sound effects. Then you could hand the charred hamster back to Weird Ed.
>
> That actually was one of the only ways you could die in *Maniac Mansion*. If you pulled off that trick, you would end up as a little tombstone, and then you could move around the game as an invisible ghost-like character.

> It was just one of those nice little tricks that was buried in the game, and it was buried so well that they never found it until the first 250,000 copies had sold. When we did the second run, they made us change it.

> **—Mike Meyers, former product manager, Jaleco**

A Holiday for Sequels

As the holiday season approached, Nintendo could not ship in enough inventory to satisfy demands. Orders had been placed for 8.4 million NES consoles. Nintendo was only able to deliver 7 million. Because of the cost of making cartridges, Nintendo executives generally preferred multiple small manufacturing runs and making customers wait for games rather than risking overstocking inventories. This policy made shortages of top products a Nintendo holiday tradition.

Blockbuster releases also generally resulted in holiday shortages. In 1988, Nintendo released two blockbuster games in time for the holidays—the sequels to *Super Mario Bros.* and *The Legend of Zelda.* Excitement over the games grew so feverish that some Nintendo outlets took pre-orders. Both games had fundamental changes in their game play that made them unlike their predecessors. Although both games were good, neither lived up to expectations.

Like *The Legend of Zelda, Zelda II: The Adventure of Link* was an adventure game in which players led a young elf through a sprawling kingdom, exploring dungeons and fighting monsters. The game had many of the same monsters and supposedly took place in the same fantasy world as *The Legend of Zelda,* but the earlier game was exploration-based while *The Adventure of Link* focused more on combat.

The second sequel of the 1988 holiday season, *Super Mario Bros. 2,* was even more dissimilar to its predecessor. The only thing it shared with the original *Super Mario Bros.* were the lead characters, a few clever puzzles, and the same cute, innocuous sense of humor. The play mechanics of *Super Mario Bros. 2* were entirely new. *Super Mario Bros.* was a fast-moving game of exploration and precision jumping, in which players always raced against the clock. Much of the action occurred in acrophobic environments, where players sped across tall mushrooms or dangling steel girders. There was always a sense of vertigo, as one misstep could cost Mario a life. *Super Mario Bros. 2,* on the other hand, took place at a slower and more plodding pace. Players located puzzles in the original *Super Mario Bros.* by jumping and bumping walls and blocks as they ran. Many puzzles in the sequel were hidden under clumps of grass. To find them, players had to pull every plant they passed.

Part of the reason the *Super Mario Bros. 2* bore so little resemblance to the original *Super Mario Bros.* was because it was not a true sequel. The game that was released in the United States as *Super Mario Bros. 2* was originally released in Japan as *Doki Doki Panic.*

> *Mario 2* was a gap filler. In Japan it was called *Doki Doki Panic* and it had some little Arabian guy. They just took the Arabian guy out and replaced him with Mario, and I think there were some changes to the girl to make her more like a Mario-ish heroine; but they only made very limited changes.
>
> **—Howard Phillips**

Shigeru Miyamoto, the man who created *Super Mario Bros.,* had little to do with the making of *Doki Doki Panic.* He did create a sequel that was released in Japan. Though Miyamoto's sequel was similar to the original *Super Mario Bros.,* it was determined that the game had elements that might irritate American consumers.

> There were two things in the Japanese *Super Mario 2* that made it not so palatable. At the time, I didn't really know if Miyamoto had driven these changes or not, and it made me question whether he just lucked out to begin with.
>
> In the Japanese *Super Mario 2,* the very first thing that happens is that this mushroom pops out of a block and you think, "Oh, great, go grab it." It's a poison mushroom. In the first Mario game, all the things that popped out were good. They added this new jeopardy that when you were looking for something surprising and good, it might be surprisingly bad.
>
> The other thing he did was add in this driving rain. It came at a 45-degree angle so that Mario would be cruising along, and this wind would pick up and it varied with time. Sometimes it would blow slow and you'd move pretty quickly, and then sometimes it'd blow hard. You had to time your jumps to

> the wind, but again, the winds were unpredictable and you had to guess. Those two things were classically un-Miyamoto, in that [they were] random and out of the player's control.
>
> Maybe Miyamoto was depressed at the time he made *Mario 2,* or maybe he delegated somebody else to do some level design, and that person added a couple of developments.
>
> **—Howard Phillips**

Though it was quite different from the original *Super Mario Bros., Super Mario Bros. 2* was a major hit. Nintendo sold 6.76 million copies of the game worldwide.

CHAPTER 21

The Legal Game

A "computer program" is a set of statements or instructions to be used directly or indirectly in a computer in order to bring about a certain result.

—**United States Congress**[1]

All computer software exists as electrical pulses, yet Congress explicitly extended copyright protection to computer software as a literary work.[2]

—**Judge Fern M. Smith, District Court, North District of California**

If you stack the notes from my appearances in court and measure them end-to-end, that stack would probably be about two feet long. If you take all of the paperwork from all of Magnavox's cases, it would be at least 200 feet, enough to fill two storage rooms in a private storage facility in Chicago.

—**Ralph Baer, former manager, Equipment Design Division, Sanders Associates**

Lasting Decisions

Video game companies began taking each other to court before the term *video game* was even coined. Magnavox, the first console manufacturer, sued Atari, the first commercially successful arcade company, as early as 1973, coming the year after the introduction of *Pong*. At the time, people did not know whether to call *Pong* a "computer game" or a "television game."

There have been hundreds of legal actions throughout the history of video games. Many of these actions, such as Magnavox's protection of its technology patents, have resulted in insignificant trials or out-of-court settlements. Other cases have had important ramifications for future copyright protection and antitrust actions.

Data East v. Epyx

In 1984, Data East released a game titled *Karate Champ*. Though it was not the first two-player fighting game,* it was the first two-player martial arts tournament game and the progenitor of a genre that in the early 1990s would become extremely popular. In *Karate Champ*, players controlled a martial artist as he battled computer-controlled fighters in tournament-style combat. (*Karate Champ* had two-player simultaneous action as well.) It featured several realistic blocks, kicks, and punches and had large, relatively human-looking characters. The game was a modest hit in the arcades.

In October 1985, Data East released a home version of *Karate Champ* for the Commodore 64 computer. One month later, the British company System III released a similar game titled *International Karate*. When California-based Epyx, Inc., licensed the game and released it as *World Karate Championship* for the Commodore 64 in April 1986, Data East took Epyx to court, claiming that the "overall appearance, compilation, and sequence of the audio visual display of the video game *World Karate Championship* infringed upon *Karate Champ*." Data East also claimed that *World Karate Championship* infringed upon its trademark and trade dress. The case went before Judge William A. Ingram of the United States District Court for the Northern District of California.

Upon looking at both games, Ingram found several areas of similarity to support Data East's claim:

---

* The first two-player fighting game was *Warrior*, released by Cinematronics in 1979.

A. Each game has fourteen moves.

B. Each game has a two-player option.

C. Each game has a one-player option.

D. Each game has forward and backward somersault moves and about-face moves.

E. Each game has a squatting reverse punch wherein the heel is not on the ground.

F. Each game has an upper-lunge punch

G. Each game has a back-foot sweep.

H. Each game has a jumping sidekick.

I. Each game has a low kick.

J. Each game has a walk backwards position.

K. Each game has changing background scenes.

L. Each game has 30-second countdown rounds.

M. Each game uses one referee.

N. In each game the referee says, "begin," "stop," "white," "red," which is depicted by a cartoon-style speech balloon.

O. Each game has a provision for 100 bonus points per remaining second.[3]

World Karate Championship borrowed other elements from *Karate Champ*. Both games featured fighters in either red or white karate *gis*, and both featured bonus rounds in which players earned extra points by breaking bricks or dodging dangers. The court recognized that as both games depicted karate tournaments, some duplication was inevitable. Karate in general, and karate tournaments in particular, included standard features such as karate *gis*, certain moves, and referees. Matches at karate tournaments involve two fighters earning points by performing combat maneuvers. The fights are scored by referees who award certain points for various moves. In his decision, Judge Ingram also noted that both games were made for the Commodore computer and that various constraints were inherent in the use of that computer. Even granting these constraints, the judge found too many similarities to ignore.

The district court found that except for the graphic quality of Epyx's expressions, part of the scoreboard, the referee's physical appearance, and minor particulars in the "bonus phases," Data East's and Epyx's games are qualitatively identical.[4]

Based on these findings, Judge Ingram ordered Epyx to recall *World Karate Championship* and *International Karate*. His decision was overturned, however, by Judge Stephen S. Trott of the United States Court of Appeals, Ninth Circuit.

> To establish copyright infringement, Data East must prove ownership of a valid copyright and "copying" by Epyx of the copyrighted work. It is undisputed that Data East is the registered copyright owner of the audio-visual work for each version of "Karate Champ." Thus we need only determine whether Epyx copied "Karate Champ." This sounds simple and straightforward. It is not.[5]

According to Trott, there was no direct evidence that System III, the original creator of *International Karate,* had access to the Commodore computer version of *Karate Champ.* He listed Judge Ingram's 15 similarities and identified them as inherent to the sport of karate. According to Trott, "karate is not susceptible of [sic] a wholly fanciful presentation."[*] In his decision, the judge stated that the only parts of the game that could be protected by a copyright were the areas in which Data East made creative contributions—namely the scoreboard and the background scenes. These, however, were the areas in which *Karate Champ* and *World Karate Championship* were most different.

> Based upon these two features, a discerning 17.5-year-old boy could not regard the works as substantially similar. Accordingly, Data East's copyright was not infringed on this basis either.[6]

Trott found in favor of Epyx and reversed Ingram's decision. Epyx was allowed to market *World Karate Championship.* This decision would have a decisive impact on several future decisions, including another case with Data East. In 1993, Capcom released the game *Street Fighter II,* which became an international arcade sensation. Shortly after the game was released for home systems, Data East released the fighting game *Fighter's History,* which had similar combatants

---

[*] In later years, *Mortal Kombat, Street Fighter II,* and other "completely fanciful" martial arts games that built off the *Karate Champ* formula would dominate both the home market and the arcade industry.

and moves. Capcom took Data East to court, claiming infringement, but the courts ruled in Data East's favor.

Atari Games Corporation v. Nintendo of America

In 1985, Steven Ross, president of Warner Communications, divided Atari into two companies and sold off shares of each. He sold 75 percent of Atari Corporation, formerly known as the consumer division, to Jack Tramiel. He kept 40 percent of Atari Games Corporation, the arcade division, and sold the rest to Masaya Nakamura, founder of Namco. Nakamura had hoped to develop synergy between the two companies. Instead, he found the arrangement unsatisfactory and decided to sell his stake in Atari. Backed by a group of employees and Time Warner, Hideyuki Nakajima, the man Nakamura sent to manage Namco's American operations, bought Atari Games in 1987.

Nakajima is generally remembered as a smart and extremely likable man with a long history in the video game industry.[*] When Nolan Bushnell first opened Atari Japan, in 1973, he hired Nakajima to manage it. One year later, Bushnell sold the operation to Namco and Nakamura hired Nakajima to continue running the company.

> He was very "American" for a Japanese man. Culturally, they are different people, but he was almost like an American with a Japanese accent. Just a really neat man. I remember I was at an Atari convention down in Hilton Head, and I asked him some sort of a philosophical question about the industry and he looked at me and said something like, "That is a strange question for the preacher to be asking."
>
> I really got a kick out of that. Here was this big deal from Namco and Atari calling me "the preacher."
>
> **—Eddie Adlum, publisher, *RePlay***

Shortly after taking over Atari, Nakajima decided to leverage some of Atari's arcade games as consumer products. He could not publish the games under the Atari banner because the consumer rights to the Atari name belonged to

---

[*] Nakajima died of lung cancer on July 11, 1994.

Atari Corporation. Instead, Nakajima created a wholly owned subsidiary of Atari Games called Tengen.*

At the time, the only viable outlet for video games was the hugely lucrative Nintendo Entertainment System (NES) market. Sega was not licensing games for the Master System, and the Atari 7800 had barely made a dent in the market. To break into the market, Nakajima knew he would need to become a licensee of Nintendo, so he met with Nintendo president Minoru Arakawa and senior vice president Howard Lincoln in 1987 to discuss the terms of their licensing agreement.

Nakajima wanted special privileges that had not been granted to other licensees.** As the only company with access to the Atari library, he felt Tengen had more to contribute, but Arakawa insisted that all licensees receive the same terms. Nakajima ultimately agreed to Nintendo's terms and signed on as a licensee in December 1987. What Arakawa and Lincoln did not realize was that they were entering into a trap.

It is not known if Nakajima ever planned to honor the licensing agreement, but Atari engineers began trying to discover ways around the security devices in the Nintendo Entertainment System a full year before he signed the agreement. (The NES had a custom-designed security chip containing a protocol called "10NES programming" that detected unlicensed cartridges and prevented them from working on the console.)

> Atari first attempted to analyze and replicate the NES security system in 1986. Atari could not break the 10NES program by monitoring the communication between the master and slave chips themselves. Atari analysts chemically peeled layers from the NES chips to allow microscopic examination of the object code.*** Nonetheless, Atari still could not decipher the code sufficiently to replicate the NES security system.[7]
>
> **—Judge Fern M. Smith**

---

* Keeping with Atari tradition, Nakajima named the company after a term from the game *Go. Tengen* refers to the center of a *Go* board.

** Nintendo licensees could publish only five games per year. Once a game was published on the NES, it could not be released for other platforms for two years. Nakajima requested that both stipulations be waived.

*** This is a figurative statement.

Nintendo Co, Ltd., did not have this security system when the Famicom was released in Japan. The system was designed for the NES, and it was built around a special chip that was placed in all consoles and cartridges. The chips worked like a lock and key, communicating signals in an initialization process. The NES simply ignored cartridges that lacked the security chip, and Atari's engineers were unable to duplicate it.

In 1988, as Nakajima agreed to release licensed versions of *Pac-Man, RBI Baseball,* and *Gauntlet,* his lawyers found another method of analyzing the security chip. They illegally obtained a reproduction of the 10NES program through the Copyright Office by signing a false affidavit stating that they needed it for use in a copyright infringement suit Nintendo had filed against them. The suit was entirely fictional.

> After deciphering the 10NES program, Atari developed its own program—the Rabbit program—to unlock the NES. The Rabbit program generates signals indistinguishable from the 10NES program. . . . The Rabbit gave Atari access to NES owners without Nintendo's strict license conditions.[8]
>
> **—Judge Fern M. Smith**

Submitting the false affidavit was a mistake that would haunt Atari in future court actions. According to several accounts, a team of Atari engineers running a "Clean Room" operation was close to breaking the 10NES code. By illegally obtaining a reproduction of the code from the Copyright Office, Atari tainted the operation.

> Some paralegal went to the copyright office, got the information and showed it to somebody at Atari. The fact that he had access to it basically means that somebody had the information and showed somebody at Atari, [which] basically means that we had knowledge of it. So, some paralegal fucked up!
>
> **—Ed Logg, game designer, Atari Games Corporation**

On December 12, 1988, with three NES-licensed games on the market and a complete understanding of NES marketing and security, Atari filed suit against Nintendo, alleging that Nintendo was "improperly using its patent and greater market share to monopolize the home video game market." Atari asked for $100 million in damages. All of the pieces were in place. Through the original licensing agreement, Atari had obtained access to retailers. Through the Copyright Office, it had obtained a complete understanding of NES technology. Atari could now manufacture its own cartridges, and the court action would work as a preemptive strike against any injunctions Nintendo might file.

One unanswered question about this case is why Hideyuki Nakajima chose such an aggressive tact for dealing with Nintendo. Some people quietly speculate that it dated back to licensing disagreements between Hiroshi Yamauchi, president of Nintendo, and Namco president Masaya Nakamura. Nakamura received some preferential treatment when he originally signed Namco as a Nintendo licensee, but when the contract expired, Yamauchi refused to renew those preferential terms. The change in terms led to an angry rift between Nintendo and Namco.

> Mr. Yamauchi tried to take away all of the special provisions of the contract that Namco enjoyed as a first licensee, and because of that, the relationship suffered. I became very upset about the whole situation at that time, but looking back, that was just his business management philosophy. I shouldn't have become upset about it, although I must admit that I was pretty upset at that time. But I have no ill sentiments now.
>
> When you consider the technical expertise and the depth of the technical know-how of Namco, which Namco currently possesses as reflected by the success of Namco games, Nintendo may have lost a lot more than Namco by taking that approach.
>
> **—Masaya Nakamura, founder, Namco**

One event that may have added to Hideyuki Nakajima's resentment of Nintendo, and Minoru Arakawa in particular, was a small dinner gathering at Arakawa's house in August 1988, at which Nakajima was a guest. According to several accounts, Arakawa, Howard Lincoln, and Nakajima had just finished dinner and gone out on a deck to talk. While they were outside, Arakawa, known for taking short naps whenever the urge struck, fell asleep for a few minutes. According to Lincoln, Nakajima seemed offended when he left the party later that evening. (Nakajima may have taken offense to Arakawa's falling asleep, but it should be noted that Atari had already used the false affidavit to obtain the reproduction of the 10NES by that time.)

> I've heard that story many times, and I don't know that that influenced or impacted the licensing decision. I do know that there was a fairly consistent falling out between Nintendo and Atari Games. What the ultimate rationale behind that was, I don't know that we'll ever fully know, but as far as Mr. Arakawa's dozing off with Hide, I somehow doubt that was the cause. I think Hide was bigger than that.
>
> **—Ted Hoff, former senior vice president of Sales and Marketing,**
> **Atari Games Corporation**

Nakajima took an unusually aggressive stance toward Nintendo, and Arakawa responded by taking an uncharacteristically patient approach toward Atari Games. Ever since the Universal Pictures suit over *Donkey Kong*, Nintendo had a reputation for using the legal system to its advantage. In this case, however, Nintendo waited eleven months before responding to Atari's charges by lodging a suit of its own. In November 1989 Nintendo launched a countersuit, accusing Atari of patent infringement, breach of contract, unfair competition, and tortious interference with contract. Before filing the suit, Nintendo took other measures, sending letters to retailers warning them not to carry Tengen products. Stores caught selling the games, the letters warned, would be subject to legal action.

This strategy caught Atari off guard and proved effective. Nintendo was the most lucrative product in the toy industry at the time, and many retailers would simply collapse if Nintendo cut off their supplies. Nintendo cartridges were one of the few toy products that sold steadily all year long. Though a few retailers such as Toys "R" Us considered ignoring Nintendo's demands, every major chain eventually removed Tengen cartridges from its shelves and refused future shipments. Caught with expensive inventory and no sales outlets, Atari asked the courts to stop Nintendo from threatening customers. Judge Fern Smith responded by enjoining both Atari and Nintendo from interfering with each other's customers. Both companies appealed the decision, and the injunction was lifted on both sides, opening the way for Nintendo to continue threatening retailers who stocked Tengen products.

The court battle went much the same way, with Atari's lawyers making small gains, then finding themselves in a bad position. They attempted to make the point that the data stream created by the security chips during the authentication process was not protected by copyright law. On this issue they were correct. The copyright laws that protect computer software clearly stated that while programs could be covered by a copyright, the data they produced could not. Under that interpretation, Atari had the right to copy the data stream created by 10NES.

Atari also argued that Nintendo's lock-out security gave the company an unfair advantage in the marketplace and that duplicating the code was the only way to break into the market. Atari then took the case one step further, asking for information that would ensure compatibility with future Nintendo consoles. The judge declined that motion.

> By requiring independent game developers to carefully study a particular security system and discern which program instructions are truly necessary for present compatibility, console manufacturers will have a limited period of time in which to control the market for compatible games. In this time period, some third party game developers are likely to enter license agreements with Nintendo, particularly if they have limited resources. After a relatively short period of time, however, other developers will enter the game market with independently produced, but still compatible games. In addition, if third party developers who entered license agreements later find the license agreements to be onerous, there still exists the option of reverse engineering the security system after the expiration of their license agreement. Thus, a fair use defense which allows copying for present compatibility balances the incentives for both the game developers and console manufacturers.
>
> The extension sought by Atari would destroy this balance by eliminating the console manufacturers' lead time.[9]
>
> **—Judge Fern M. Smith**

The case came down to a few simple points. Since Atari did not dispute Nintendo's ownership of 10NES, the trial revolved around two specific questions: Was Rabbit a direct copy of 10NES? And would companies need to copy the program to compete in the market? The question of copying was solved when Nintendo showed that Atari had duplicated nonfunctional parts of the 10NES code.

> In particular, the Court finds that the existence of program elements in the Rabbit program which serve no function other than authenticating the console firmly establish illicit copying.[10]
>
> —Judge Fern M. Smith

Nintendo's lawyers were also able to prove that there was more than one way around the NES security system and that Atari did not need the illegally obtained reproductions from the Copyright Office to access the NES.* The judge found in favor of Nintendo, but the battle with Atari was only beginning.

Tetris

The most notable casualty of the war between Nintendo and Atari Games was the Tengen version of the game *Tetris,* a game that was created by Soviet mathematician Alexey Pajitnov while working at the Computer Center of the Moscow Academy of Science. Pajitnov came up with a computer game in which players organized two-dimensional geometric shapes. The blocks would fall from the top of the screen, and players had to rotate and place them before they landed. If the player organized the blocks into complete and unbroken lines as they landed, the blocks would disappear. If the line was broken, it would remain on the screen and blocks would pile on top of it. The game ended when the blocks reached the top of the screen.

Pajitnov developed the game on an Electronica 60, an antiquated computer that was the Russian clone of the PDP (Programmable Data Processor) computers made for the Department of Defense by Digital Equipment.** Because his computer could display only alphanumeric characters, Pajitnov teamed up with Vadim Gerasimov, a gifted young hacker with access to a PC, to create a better-looking interface for the game.

---

* This point would become pivotal in later cases.

** Steven Russel developed *Spacewar* on a PDP-1. Pajitnov's Electronica 60 was considerably more powerful, the equivalent of a PDP-11.

In 1986, a friend of Pajitnov's sent a copy of *Tetris* to the Institute of Computer Science, in Budapest, Hungary. It was there that Robert Stein, president of the London-based software company Andromeda, happened to see the game.

> Sometime in 1986, Robert Stein was in Hungary and saw *Tetris*. . . . just one of the pirate copies. I didn't call them pirated back then, I gave it out myself everywhere. So, he feels that this is a really good game and approached the Computer Center and wanted to make a license and publish it. He had no idea what it means to deal with the Russians, with the Russian bureaucracy.
>
> **—Alexey Pajitnov, creator, *Tetris***

Stein contacted the Moscow Academy of Science and began negotiating with Pajitnov for the rights to *Tetris*. Thinking Pajitnov had the authority to make a deal, Stein next began calling executives at large software publishers with an offer to license the game. He sold the European computer rights to *Tetris* to Mirrorsoft and the American rights to Spectrum Holobyte, both backed by British publishing magnate Robert Maxwell. Stein had not counted on the difficulties of dealing with the Soviets, however, and granted these rights before securing them for himself. Mirrorsoft and Spectrum Holobyte released versions of *Tetris* in January 1988. The Soviets did not sign Stein's contract until the following month. Stein's contract specifically gave him control of the personal computer versions of *Tetris* created for Western markets.

> He finally came to us and said, "Well, I want this right, I want those rights, I want those rights." So, basically, because we promised him the PC rights, they were given to him, and we legalized our relationship at this point. But the game was on the shelf already and I do believe that he sold his video rights as well without having an agreement. He approached us immediately, asking for all the rights, but we didn't know who the hell he was.
>
> **—Alexey Pajitnov**

Then the confusion began. Spectrum Holobyte sold the Japanese computer and coin-op rights of *Tetris* to an entrepreneur named Henk Rogers, who had strong ties to Nintendo. At the same time, Mirrorsoft sold the exact same rights to Atari Games. Mirrorsoft wielded more power in the Maxwell organization, so the rights went to Atari. Atari, in turn, sold the Japanese coin-operated game rights to Sega Enterprises and the Japanese console and PC rights to Rogers. What nobody realized was that Stein had never received the rights to make any of these deals.

After looking over the various arrangements, Rogers realized that no one owned the handheld rights to *Tetris,* so he flew to Moscow and met with the Soviets. He had hoped to secure the rights as an agent for Nintendo. Nintendo was preparing to unveil the Game Boy, and Arakawa thought *Tetris* would be the perfect lead title for the new handheld game system. While Rogers was there, the Soviets surprised him by offering the worldwide video game rights as well. He had been under the impression that Atari and Mirrorsoft controlled those rights, and fearing a legal battle with those companies, Rogers brought Nintendo into the negotiations. On March 22, 1988, Howard Lincoln and Minoru Arakawa signed a contract with representatives of Electronorgtechnica (ELORG), the Soviet agency handling the transaction, sealing the worldwide home video game rights to *Tetris.*

Atari Games had already begun work on the Tengen version of *Tetris* for the NES by that time.

> I was there when they locked up *Tetris.* The *Tetris* story was kind of an interesting one, and to this day the people at Tengen believe that the Russians double dipped. The product was in negotiation for licensing, and at virtually the same time, the product was licensed to two companies. We had manufactured *Tetris* and put it on the market, and, in fact, it became the number one seller on the Nintendo platform.
>
> **—Ted Hoff**

On March 31, nine days after signing the contract in Moscow, Lincoln and Arakawa sent a fax to Hideyuki Nakajima, informing him that Nintendo had secured video game rights to *Tetris.* Two weeks later, Atari Games quietly filed for a copyright for the game.

Atari released its Tengen version of *Tetris* in May, 1989; Nintendo released its version one month later. The Tengen version, which was created by veteran arcade designer Ed Logg,* had both single-player and two-player modes and looked almost exactly like the arcade game. Nintendo's version was a single-player game. Most reviewers agreed that Tengen had done a better job with the game.

Judge Smith, who handled the case concerning Atari's duplication of the 10NES, presided over the *Tetris* case as well. The trial hinged on determining who had legal ownership of the game. Nintendo's pedigree was obviously stronger. Nintendo had signed statements from Soviet officials confirming the sale and a note signed by Stein, defining computers as PC computers with, among other things, a keyboard and a monitor. Recognizing that Nintendo would almost certainly prevail when the case went to trial, Judge Smith granted Nintendo's motion to force Atari to recall its cartridge. The case ended without a trial, however. On November 13, 1989, Smith canceled the trial and ruled that Nintendo owned the rights to the game.

> I think to this day, anyone you talk to will certainly say that the best *Tetris* was the two-player *Tetris* that came out on Nintendo and was published by Tengen. Without a doubt, it was the best *Tetris*. At one point, you could look in the back of any of the gaming magazines and find people who would be willing to pay you $300 for a Tengen *Tetris* cartridge.
>
> There were 268,000 of them locked up, bolted, padlocked in Milpitas on Sycamore [Street]. If people knew that they were $300 each and knew that there were that many of them, they probably would have picked the lock. But that was a well kept secret in a dark room. And those cartridges were never shipped. When I left the company two years ago, the cartridges were still under lock and key. My understanding is that they were subsequently destroyed.
>
> **—Ted Hoff**

Nintendo sold more than 3 million copies of its NES *Tetris* cartridge and more than 40 million copies of *Tetris* cartridges for Game Boy. (The game

---

* Logg, best known for creating the arcade games *Centipede, Asteroids,* and *Gauntlet,* deserves some credit for Atari's coin-operated version of *Tetris.* He converted the code he made for the Tengen NES cartridge to work in the coin-operated game, then Atari engineers Greg Rivera and Norm Avellar finished the game. The Tengen *Tetris* cartridge was finished nearly four months before it was released. Atari sat on it while the arcade game was hot.

came packed in with the system.) Pajitnov, the creator of the game, did not make any royalties from any of these sales, but his association with the game enabled him to emigrate to the United States. In 1996, all of the rights that ELORG had sold expired and reverted to Pajitnov. Hoping to help Pajitnov finally profit from the game, Henk Rogers helped him establish the Tetris Company, Llc., which would then control all rights to the game. From that time on, companies that made games based on *Tetris* had to purchase the rights from Pajitnov.

Sega Enterprises, Ltd. v. Accolade, Inc.

> Ordinarily in a trademark case, a trademark holder contends that another party is misusing the holder's mark or is attempting to pass off goods or services as those of the trademark holder. The other party usually protests that the mark is not being misused, that there is no actual confusion, or that for some other reason no violation has occurred. This case is different. Here both parties agree that there is misuse of a trademark, both agree that there is an unlawful mislabeling, and both agree that confusion may result. The issue here is—which party is primarily responsible?"
>
> **—Judge Stephen Reinhardt**

In 1984, Bob Whitehead and Alan Miller, two of the original VCS programmers who left Atari and started Activision, founded a software company called Accolade. Accolade started out as a computer game company, but when Sega released the Genesis in 1989, Whitehead and Miller decided to convert some of their PC titles to work on the new console.

> They had licensed approximately thirty other companies, and the licensing deal, it turns out, is a very expensive deal. One pays them between $10 and $15 per cartridge on top of the real hardware manufacturing costs, so it about doubles the cost of goods to the independent publisher. It winds up with the consumer generally paying a lot more for the cartridge, but that's the licensing deal, and they have a right to establish whatever they consider to be a fair deal.

> We chose to not accept the licensing deal and instead to independently study the system, figure out how to do games for it, and then publish several games for the system.
>
> **—Alan Miller, cofounder, Accolade**

Mike Lorenzen led a team of Accolade engineers that purchased a Genesis console and three game cartridges, then wired the console so that they could make printouts of the executable code of the games. They compared each game's code to locate identical chains, believing that all of the games would use the same programming instructions to disable any security locks Sega placed in the Genesis. They used this information to create a "development manual" for making Genesis games.

> According to Accolade, at this stage it did not copy Sega's programs but relied only on the information concerning interface specifications for the Genesis that was contained in its development manual. Accolade maintains that with the exception of the interface specifications, none of the code in its games is derived in any way from its examination of Sega's code.[12]
>
> **—Judge Stephen Reinhardt**

Accolade released *Ishido,* its first Genesis game, in 1990. Previously released as a Macintosh and PC computer game, *Ishido* was a strategy board game in the same vein as *Go.*

Like Nintendo, Sega created security systems in its consoles to guard against software pirates and unlicensed publishers. In 1990, the company unveiled Genesis III, a slightly modified version of the Genesis console that included an externally developed security system called the Trademark Security System (TMSS).

> The most recent version of the Genesis, the "Genesis III," incorporates the licensed TMSS. When a game cartridge is inserted, the microprocessor contained in the Genesis III searches the program for four bytes of data consisting of the letters "S-E-G-A" (the "TMSS initialization code"). If Genesis III finds the TMSS

> initialization code in the right location, the game is rendered compatible and will operate on the console. In such case, the TMSS initialization code then prompts a visual display for approximately three seconds which reads "PRODUCED BY OR UNDER LICENSE FROM SEGA ENTERPRISES LTD" (the "Sega Message").[13]

> —Judge Stephen Reinhardt

With Genesis III, Sega created a double security gate. To make unlicensed cartridges, software publishers had to discover how to unlock the security system, then face charges of misrepresentation since the TMSS authentication process triggered the licensing message. Though all officially licensed games were Genesis III compatible, *Ishido* would not operate on the new console. Accolade did not learn about this development, however, until the Winter Consumer Electronics Show in January 1991, when Sega did a demonstration in which the new version of the Genesis screened the *Ishido* cartridge. By this time, the company was preparing five games for release.

Caught in a vulnerable situation, Accolade engineers scrambled to discover what piece of code the licensed cartridges used to satisfy TMSS. They found their answer in a tiny segment in the "power-up" sequence of the game code that had no identifiable function. Lorenzen noticed it during his first round of reverse engineering and even sent a memo to Miller, stating that "it is possible that some future Sega peripheral device might require it for proper initialization."[14] That code sequence was added to the games *Star Control, Hardball, Turrican,* and *Mike Ditka Power Football* before Accolade put them on the market. Accolade released a fifth game, *Onslaught,* as well, but the game code did not have the TMSS file in the correct location and would not run on Genesis III consoles.

On October 31, 1991, Sega Enterprises filed suit against Accolade, accusing the company of trademark infringement and unfair competition. One month later, Sega added copyright infringement to its charges. Accolade lodged a counterclaim, accusing Sega of false designation of origin and unfair competition. Among other things, the counterclaim stated that Sega injured Accolade's reputation by falsely attributing itself as the source of the unlicensed games.

The case was supposed to be heard by Judge Robert F. Peckham, a judge who had tried similar cases and whose views were thought to be sympathetic toward entrepreneurs.

> The case was originally assigned to a federal judge here in San Francisco named Peckham, with whom we had some familiarity. We had been the plaintiff in a copyright infringement case and knew his thoughts on the copyright process and intellectual property laws in general associated with computer technology. We felt very comfortable with having him as the judge.
>
> Unfortunately, he had a heart attack early on in the case and the case had to be reassigned. We were reassigned to a brand new federal judge named Barbara Caulfield, and she was a disaster.
>
> **—Alan Miller**

When the two sides met in court, Sega asked Judge Caulfield to bar Accolade from manufacturing Genesis-compatible games and for Accolade to abandon future attempts to reverse engineer Genesis technology. For its part, Accolade asked the court to stop Sega from manufacturing or selling Genesis III consoles.

Sega began the case by establishing that Accolade's games contained illegal reproductions and adaptations of Sega Enterprises, Ltd.'s copyrighted material. Accolade defended its position by appealing to the Fair Use Doctrine.

> The criteria to be considered in determining whether a particular use is fair use include:
>   1. The purpose and character of the use, including whether such use is of a commercial nature or is for nonprofit educational purposes;
>   2. The nature of the copyrighted work;
>   3. The amount and substantiality of the portion used in relation to the copyrighted work as a whole; and
>   4. The effect of the use upon the potential market for or value of the copyrighted work.[15]
>
> **—Judge Barbara A. Caulfield**

In Judge Caulfield's decision, she stated that the Fair Use Doctrine offered Accolade no protection. Since Accolade was a game manufacturer, the Genesis-compatible games were clearly made for financial gain. They would compete with Sega-licensed games in the marketplace, and she felt that they might indeed diminish the value of Sega's copyrighted work.

> Accolade's game cartridges compete directly with those of SEL [Judge
> Caulfield's notation for Sega Enterprises Ltd.], which has likely lost sales as a
> result of Accolade's copying. In addition, since SEL's disassembled code is
> an "unpublished work," it is subject to a narrower scope of fair use.[16]

> **—Judge Barbara Caulfield**

As to the charges of trademark infringement, Judge Caulfield sided with Sega.
In her decision, she pointed out that Accolade copied the S-E-G-A code that
triggered the Sega logo and licensing message. Accolade's lawyers explained that
there was no way of knowing that the TMSS code would bring up the trademark and licensing messages when the code was added to the games. Accolade
engineers had simply recognized that this small file could be found in games
that worked on the new console and was not present on games that were
screened out. In her decision, Judge Caulfield dismissed this argument.

> Accolade boldly inserted SEL's code into its games before SEL released the
> Genesis III into the marketplace, and thus without fully realizing the conse-
> quences. Accolade took that risk, and cannot now shift the responsibility to
> SEL and SOA (Sega of America).[17]

> **—Judge Barbara Caulfield**

Accolade's lawyers argued that Genesis III would not read a game unless it
contained the TMSS code, and by definition the code would trigger the trademark messages. This argument, however, was severely weakened when a Sega
engineer named Takeshi Nagashima was called to testify. Nagashima claimed
that competitors could create games that would work on Genesis III without
the TMSS code. He then produced two cartridges that did not have the code.
When he demonstrated them before the court, they ran without displaying
S-E-G-A or the licensing message. Sega offered the cartridges for inspection
by Accolade's defense team but refused to allow Accolade engineers to inspect the cartridge or to reveal how the code had been modified.

On April 3, 1992, Judge Caulfield ruled in favor of Sega and enjoined Accolade from "disassembling, translating, converting, or adapting" the codes in
Sega's games. She also ordered Accolade to stop manufacturing, distributing,

and developing Genesis-compatible products. The decision meant that Accolade, a relatively small company, was stuck with thousands of worthless cartridges. Six days later, at Sega's request, Judge Caulfield added an order that Accolade recall all Genesis-compatible games within ten business days. Though the recall was quickly repealed, the rest of Caulfield's injunction remained in effect for several months.

> She imposed an injunction against Accolade from doing any work at all with Sega cartridges. We could not sell the cartridges we had developed. We had to immediately stop development on all of our Sega-related products. This was just terrible. Just to fight the injunction, we had to pay at least a half million dollars in legal fees, and the commercial damage associated with this injunction ultimately proved to be somewhere around $15 to $25 million to our company.
>
> She bought Sega's argument that it was impermissible to study computer systems and figure out how they worked, and in addition, to bring out competitive software. This was a fundamental step backward from the way that product development had always been done in the Valley and in general throughout the world.
>
> **—Alan Miller**

Accolade appealed the decision, and the case went before Judge Stephen Reinhardt of the Ninth Circuit Court of Appeals on July 20, 1992. Judge Reinhardt interpreted the Fair Use Doctrine differently than Judge Caulfield. He understood the doctrine to suggest that when there is no other means of understanding how a system works, and when a legitimate reason exists for needing to gain that understanding, reverse engineering was indeed a fair use of copyrighted technology. He applied a similar approach toward the false trademark message.

> The question is whether the computer manufacturer may enjoin competing cartridge manufacturers from gaining access to its computers through the use of the code on the grounds that such use will result in the display of a false trademark. Again, our holding is based on the public policies underlying the statute. We hold that when there is no other method of access to the

> computer that is known or readily available to rival cartridge manufacturers, the use of the initialization code does not violate the Act even though that use triggers a misleading trademark display.[18]

> —Judge Stephen Reinhardt

Judge Reinhardt noted that the TMSS file, which contained somewhere between 20 and 25 bytes of data, was minuscule when compared to the 500,000 to 1,500,000 bytes of data contained in the entire game. The data in the games, according to Reinhardt were overwhelmingly original and deserved to compete in a free market. This, he felt, was to the benefit of the public.

> There is no basis for assuming that Accolade's *Ishido* has significantly affected the market for Sega's *Altered Beast,* since a consumer might easily purchase both; nor does it seem unlikely that a consumer particularly interested in sports might purchase both Accolade's *Mike Ditka Power Football* and Sega's *Joe Montana Football,* particularly if the games are, as Accolade contends, not substantially similar.[19]

> —Judge Stephen Reinhardt

Sega's attorneys defended the original decision by pointing out that their client had invested time and capital designing and manufacturing the Genesis. Even after Genesis shipped, Sega continued spending millions of dollars marketing it. They characterized Accolade as a "free rider," benefiting from time and investment. Reinhardt dismissed this argument, however, as the "'sweat of the brow' rationale for copyright protection."

He was also unimpressed with Nagashima's demonstration of a game cartridge that initialized in Genesis III without activating the trademark signals. Reinhardt stated that "At most, the Nagashima affidavit establishes that an individual familiar with the operation of TMSS can discover a way to engineer around it." Just as Judge Caulfield had said that Accolade took a risk in adding the TMSS code and could not be excused by claiming it did not know that using the code would result in a trademark abuse, Judge Reinhardt now held Sega responsible for attaching its trademark to an unlicensed game.

> Sega knowingly risked two significant consequences: the false labeling of some competitors' products and the discouraging of other competitors from manufacturing Genesis-compatible games. Under the Latham Act, the former conduct, at least, is clearly unlawful.[20]
>
> **—Judge Stephen Reinhardt**

Though he did not completely absolve Accolade of all wrongdoing, Judge Reinhardt struck down the injunctions handed down by Judge Caulfield. The immediate ramifications of Judge Reinhardt's rulings were short lived. Within a year of the trial, Accolade released a basketball game titled [Charles] *Barkley Shut Up and Jam!* as an official Sega licensee. The long-term ramifications of the case were significant, however. *Sega Enterprises v. Accolade* has been cited in nearly every video game trial involving reverse engineering and unlicensed products since 1993.

States of NY and MD v. Nintendo of America

In 1988, Nintendo announced that there was a worldwide shortage of the ROM chips used in Famicom and NES game cartridges. All publishers, Nintendo included, would be given chip allotments that averaged approximately 25 percent of their original orders. This development had a two-edged effect. Many company executives complained that they were not able to sell as many games as they hoped. On the other hand, the shortage ensured that nearly every cartridge that was manufactured that year got sold. Consumers seemed to purchase anything they could find as long as it carried the label "Nintendo."

> Overall, our licensees enjoyed the shortage because everything they produced got sold, but everybody wanted to have a little more than allocated.
>
> **—Minoru Arakawa, president, Nintendo of America**

Some licensees simply accepted the shortage, while others accused Nintendo of purposely inventing the shortage in an effort to further control the market. Hide Nakajima and Atari Games accused Nintendo of America of unfair competitive practices. Other nonrelated complaints were leveled against

Nintendo as well. In a 1989 case, the Tramiels accused Nintendo of shutting Atari Corporation out of the marketplace and filed a $500 million suit. In another suit, filed in 1991, Nintendo found itself in court against the attorneys general of all fifty states and the District of Columbia.

The attorneys general accused Nintendo of a variety of offenses that seemed to borrow from all of the suits that had been filed against Nintendo. They accused the company of price fixing, shutting out competitors, overregulating licensees, and bullying retailers. New York Attorney General Robert Abrams, who led the investigation and ensuing case, said that Nintendo threatened to slow down or cut off supplies to retailers who lowered the price of the games by as little as six cents. When the case finally went before Judge Sweet, the same New York judge who presided over *Universal Studios/MCA v. Nintendo,* it focused mostly on allegations of price fixing and ended in a settlement.

The results of the case are almost humorous. On October 17, 1991, Judge Sweet approved a rather absurd settlement in which Nintendo agreed to mail coupons giving consumers who had purchased NES systems between June 1, 1988, and December 31, 1990, a $5 discount on the purchase of their next game cartridge. To make sure that the people who might have purchased the consoles got the message, Nintendo agreed to run advertisements in *TV Guide, USA Today,* four video game magazines, and 800 newspapers. According to the terms of the agreement, Nintendo would have to make up the difference if the coupon sales added up to less than $5 million in discounts. Nintendo also agreed to pay the states and the District of Columbia $1.75 million for their administrative costs and $3 million for other uses.

> Nintendo will pay $3 million to the Attorney Generals for use at the States' option for one of the following purposes: antitrust enforcement, deposit into a state antitrust revolving fund, defraying the costs of experts used in multistate antitrust investigations, benefiting those unidentified consumers for whose benefit the settlement was entered, or payment into a state's treasury.[21]
>
> **—Judge Robert Sweet**

In an article titled "Please, Br'er Fox! Don't Throw Me in the Briar Patch!" *Forbes* described the settlement as less than punishing for Nintendo.

The deal Nintendo cut to settle antitrust complaints by the Federal Trade Commission and some states turns out to be another shrewd move by the Japanese videogame manufacturer. Nintendo agreed to mail 5 million $5 coupons good on Nintendo cartridges, plus pat-myself-on-the-back letters from some local attorney generals. That's some punishment. Nintendo has just put a new 16-bit machine on the market, but the coupons are only good for the old eight-bit cartridges. So the deal helps clear old inventory as well as bring in lookers for the more powerful new sets.

Please, Br'er Attorney General . . . ![22]

The FTC investigation may not have resulted in a large punitive settlement, but it served notice to Nintendo of America and its parent company in Japan that more investigations could follow if complaints continued. Though there is no proof that company executives made this decision because of the lawsuit, in October 1990 Nintendo announced that its licensees were free to manufacture their own cartridges and to publish games on competitors' consoles.

> In about, I think it was 1989 or 1990, we made a business decision that we did not need the exclusivity clause. Now, it's true we were in litigation with Atari Corp. We were in litigation with Tengen and the FTC was moseying around; but we made a decision that we would no longer require the exclusivity clause. We would no longer enforce it and we would not put it into any new agreements.
>
> Those clauses, from our point of view and from our lawyers' point of view, were perfectly legal under the antitrust laws. It was determined to be that way by a jury and by multiple courts, including a court of appeals, in the various litigations that we had.
>
> **—Howard Lincoln**

Lewis Galoob Toys v. Nintendo of America

In 1990, Lewis Galoob Toys obtained the U.S. manufacturing rights for a device called GameMage that enabled players to access hidden codes that designers placed in games as Easter eggs. Releasing the product in the United States as Game Genie, Galoob packaged the "game enhancer" with a "programming manual" containing codes for hundreds of games. Through Game

Genie, players could enter up to three codes at one time, codes that made games easier or gave players extra lives. The game *Contra,* for instance, allowed players to give their soldiers powerful weapons or set the game up so that the enemy soldiers did not shoot their weapons. The codes for *The Legend of Zelda* could give players endless supplies of bombs, let them purchase items in the game for free, and make Link, the hero of the game, invincible. Spokespeople for Galoob said that Game Genie added new life to old games, but Nintendo saw it as a threat and notified the toy manufacturer that the device infringed on copyrighted material. Galoob took Nintendo to court to ask for a declaration that Game Genie did not infringe upon protected material; it also tried to pacify Nintendo by offering to license the product through the company. The offer was declined.

In June 1990, Nintendo applied for an injunction to bar the toy manufacturer from distributing Game Genie. In a preliminary hearing, Judge Robert W. Schnacke granted Nintendo's request on the likelihood that Nintendo could win the case. In April 1991, the case went to court before Fern Smith, the same judge who had presided over *Atari Games Corporation v. Nintendo of America.*

Judge Smith's interpretation of the Fair Use Doctrine would prove central to both Nintendo's and Galoob's case. Nintendo claimed that Game Genie was a derivative work. It did not play original games; rather, it altered the copyrighted work of other companies. Nintendo's lawyers compared it to the unauthorized "speed-up kits" that were used to enhance arcade games. They referenced the case of *Midway Manufacturing v. Arctic International,* in which a judge barred a company called Arctic from selling chips that accelerated the arcade version *Galaxian.** Judge Smith, however, disagreed with Nintendo's argument, citing that Game Genie did not physically incorporate portions of any copyrighted works and that it in no way diminished the game market.

One interesting question that emerged in this case was whether Galoob was in fact infringing on Nintendo's copyrights or whether the real perpetrators would be consumers using the device. The argument suggested that Game Genie was simply an adapter onto which consumers attached a game car-

---

* In the Arctic case, arcade owners replaced the original chips with new ones that incorporated Namco's original programming along with new code. A more accurate comparison would have been *Atari Games v. General Computer,* since the chips General Computer created to accelerate *Missile Command* were used to enhance Atari's chips and modified, rather than borrowed, the original code.

tridge. The decisive factor in the case, however, was that Nintendo's lawyers could not demonstrate to Judge Smith's satisfaction how Game Genie impacted their client's business.

> Nintendo has failed to show any harm to the present market for its copyrighted games and has failed to establish the reasonable likelihood of a potential market for slightly altered versions of games at suit.[23]
>
> **—Judge Fern Smith**

While Judge Smith was unable to certify that Game Genie users would not infringe on Nintendo's copyrights, she did conclude that Galoob had not violated the Copyright Act and ruled in favor of the toy manufacturer, ordering Nintendo to pay the company $15 million for lost sales. When the case came up for appeal before Judge Jerome Farris in 1992, he affirmed Judge Smith's opinions. Nintendo did not concede defeat, however, until the U.S. Supreme Court declined to hear arguments on the case on March 22, 1993, sealing the decision.

Alpex Computer Corporation v. Nintendo of America

With the exception of the original Magnavox Odyssey, which had several games hardwired into its circuitry, all of the home television game consoles that retailed in the early 1970s were single-game (or dedicated) systems. In 1974, Alpex Computer Corporation created and patented a technology that enabled consoles to play multiple games stored on ROM chips stored in game cartridges. The first company to license Alpex's technology was Fairchild Camera and Instrument, which used it in the Channel F game console released in 1976.* Two years later, Alpex applied for patent protection on that technology and received patent number 4,026,555, also known as the "555 patent."

After receiving its patent, Alpex embarked on a campaign to enforce it, selling nonexclusive licenses to companies that infringed. Magnavox, Atari, Mattel, Bally, and Coleco were just a few of the companies that Alpex contacted. Though the other settlement sums are not public, it is known that Atari paid $380,000 to settle the affair.

---

* The Fairchild Channel F was the first game console to use interchangeable game cartridges.

Alpex declared Chapter 11 bankruptcy and ceased operation in 1983. As the company dissolved, creditors found that its only valuable asset was the "555 patent."

> In 1983, after the settlement with Atari and another with Magnavox, counsel for Alpex sent infringement letters to approximately seventy companies. These letters announced that Alpex had recently granted licenses under the patent to Atari and Magnavox and stated that Alpex had "recently obtained information indicating that your company manufactures and/or sells video game cartridges and/or consoles which may infringe the subject patent."[24]
>
> **—Judge Kimba Wood**

Of the seventy companies that received the letter, six companies expressed interest in settling without litigation. By 1985, Alpex had won licensing agreements in suits against ten companies.* Most companies preferred to pay Alpex rather than risk a court battle. This was especially true of Japanese companies, which were supposedly scared that U.S. jury awards might reflect anti-Japanese sentiments.[25] Sega Enterprises, for instance, elected to purchase a license from Alpex in 1993. Nintendo, however, refused to settle, so Alpex sued for willful infringement of the "555 patent."**

The case, which was tried before Judge Kimba Wood*** of the South New York District in Manhattan, hinged on a question of technology. Nintendo claimed that while the NES did use interchangeable cartridges, the bit mapping technology developed by Alpex was not powerful enough to handle the sophisticated images in NES games.

> The television raster comprises numerous discrete dots or bars, approximately 32,000, which the cathode ray beam illuminates on a standard cycle, which in turn creates the image on the television screen. The patented invention

---

* Alpex had an ongoing suit with Parker Brothers, the result of which was stayed pending the results of the case against Nintendo.

** At one point Nintendo offered a $3.9 million settlement.

*** Bill Clinton nominated Kimba Wood for the post of Attorney General after the nomination of Zoe Baird was withdrawn. The process ended with Janet Reno getting the position.

> requires sufficient RAM to accommodate each of the approximately 32,000 memory positions needed to represent the raster image. The RAM holds at least one "bit" of data for each position in the memory "map" of the raster. Accordingly, this video display system is called "bit-mapping."[26]

> —Judge Glen Archer

According to Nintendo's defense, Alpex's RAM-based technology was simply too slow. Nintendo's lawyers claimed that the NES featured a patented "picture processing unit" (PPU) that received pre-formed "slices" of data.

> The PPU receives preformed, horizontal slices of data and places each slice in one of eight shift registers, each of which can store a maximum of 8 pixels. These slices of data are then processed directly to the screen. The PPU repeats this process to assemble the initial image on the screen. Thereafter, it repeats the process as necessary to form changes in images throughout the progression of the game. Nintendo refers to the PPU as an "on-the-fly" system.[27]

> —Judge Glen Archer

The case turned into a debate about whether "on-the-fly" graphics did indeed differ from the technology in the Alpex patent. Nintendo maintained that while Alpex's bit-mapping was fast enough for games with "linear player images," it lacked the speed for games with "animated cartoon characters," such as *Mario*. The highlight of the case was when John Strauch, lead attorney on the Alpex team, cross-examined Nintendo expert witness Stephen Ward. Strauch questioned Ward about the differences between linear player images and animated cartoons. Strauch tried to corner Ward into explaining the precise differences between the two kinds of graphics. Ward, either unwilling or unable to specify, refused to be pinned down, although he maintained that he could detect concrete differences, having viewed hundreds of games.

To clarify, Strauch drew a stick figure that he identified as a drawing of a hockey player. Ward agreed that the character would definitely be classified as a linear image. Next, Strauch colored the figure red and asked if it was still a linear image. When Ward said that it was, Strauch drew a bulge on the player that he identified as a hip and asked if it was still linear. Ward answered that they had "entered into a region" in which he had no answer. Strauch next added two little arms and asked if they were still in the gray area in which Ward could not distinguish between linear images and cartoons. Ward said, "I believe that one could arbitrarily decide to draw the line either way in that case."

"Now using your terminology and understanding, we are using your terminology the way you want to define this, if I add a nose, are we still in a situation where we can put this one on either side of the line?"

Ward responded, "I think that at some point when you add features that make it look like a human form, for example, then it is no longer a linear player image, and if you keep adding noses and arms, then you do cross that line."

Strauch: Let me add a tiny tail here. Let's say this is an animal combination human-animal cartoon. Just adding a tiny tail. Have we yet reached the point where you are willing to say that it is not a linear image player?
Ward: We are getting close to that point, yes.
Strauch: Okay. Why don't we put a beard on it. Where are we now?
Ward: Okay. I am willing to say that it is not a linear image player.
Strauch: Okay, so now I know how you are drawing the line. If we have a nose, two little arms, a tail, more hip, and the configuration I have drawn, except for the beard, you don't know whether it is a linear image player or not; but if we add the beard, it is not.[28]

According to Alpex attorneys John Strauch and Thomas Young, members of the jury tried to duck behind the rail of the jury box so that the rest of court would not see them laughing during this exchange. The jury agreed with Alpex, finding that Nintendo willfully infringed Alpex's patent and that 118 of the games that had been introduced for the NES before the patent expired on July 31 infringed on the "555 patent." Alpex was awarded $208 million for damages. Stating that she saw "scant" evidence of willful infringement, Judge Wood did not add further punitive damages to the award, but she allowed interest and legal fees to be tacked on, bringing it to $252 million—one of the largest patent awards in history.

Judge Glen Archer of the Federal Circuit did not see substantial evidence of infringement when the case went to Federal Appeals Court on November 25, 1996. After a thorough investigation of the bit-map and "on-the-fly" technologies, he ruled that there was insubstantial evidence that the devices operated in the same way. Based on his findings, Judge Archer reversed the original decision.

CHAPTER 22

The Year of Hardware

Nobody, including me, thought that Game Boy would take off like it did. Game Boy is the most perfect example in the industry that you can't be sure about anything, and anytime that somebody shows me something that I have doubts about, I remind myself that I had doubts about Game Boy, too.

—Don Thomas, former director of customer service and marketing,
Atari Corporation

Nintendo was extremely dismissive about Sega. I think there was some concern about Genesis, but they were generally very dismissive. The feeling at Nintendo always was that Sega was kind of a second-class outfit.

—Richard Brudvik-Lindner, former group supervisor, Nintendo of America Account,
Hill and Knowlton Public Relations

A Part of Society

By 1989, Nintendo had become a regular fixture in the news. The media reported on the company's phenomenal record sales and press events and sometimes covered curious anecdotes associated with the company. The "Hands-Free" Controller, developed by Nintendo engineers to enable quadriplegics to play games, earned the company print and broadcast attention. To use this special controller, players rested their chins on a lever that worked like a steering device. A tube running from the controller to their mouths replaced the "A" and "B" buttons. "A" button functions were accessed by blowing into the straw, and "B" button functions were accessed by sipping.

The press also covered humorous human-interest stories such as an incident involving a burglar who noticed a Nintendo Entertainment System (NES) and couldn't resist trying it. Somebody noticed the criminal and reported him to the police. On arrival, the police found the burglar in front of the television, playing a game.* In another story, a bomb squad blew up an NES on the runway of Los Angeles International Airport. Airport security officers X-rayed the NES inside a suitcase and, unable to identify it, called the bomb squad. Fearing the unfamiliar object to be a bomb, the police detonated it.

> I was quoted in *USA Today* on the front page that day, or . . . the next day and . . . something to the effect of "Well, we know we have a great product, but people don't usually get quite such a bang out of it."
>
> **—Richard Brudvik-Lindner**

Unauthorized and Never Sued

Nintendo guarded against unlicensed companies making unauthorized NES, Game Boy, and Super NES cartridges, but an Arizona-based company, Wisdom Tree, slipped through its net unchallenged.

Wisdom Tree was the offshoot of Color Dreams, a company founded by U.S. engineers who reverse engineered the NES and found a way around the lock-out chip. Using this technology, Color Dreams published games such as

---

* This story has been confirmed by people who worked for Nintendo at the time, though the details may be exaggerated.

King Neptune's Adventure, Pesterminator, and *Metal Fighter.* One of the company's titles, *Menace Beach,* featured material considered highly risqué by NES standards. The goal of the game was to help a hero rescue his kidnapped girlfriend. Pictures of the chained-up woman were flashed throughout the game, and she had on less clothing in every shot. In the beginning, she wore a blouse and skirt; by the end of the game she was in a bikini.*

In 1989, Color Dreams spun off Wisdom Tree, a company that made NES games with Christian themes. For the most part, Wisdom Tree games were fairly indistinguishable from other video games and had the same basic side-scrolling, object-finding, enemy-shooting play. Some of the games had biblical trivia quizzes between rounds, and the themes of the games were adapted to convey biblical ideas. Wisdom Tree's first game, *Bible Adventures,* was released in December 1990. After a slow start, the company sold approximately 350,000 copies.

> Basically, what we were doing was taking the garbage out and putting Bible content in. That's the whole reason for the company to begin with. We marketed almost 100 percent into the Christian bookstore market, not through secular channels. It took a while to get in. We got picked up by Focus on the Family, which gave us pretty much of an industry okay.
>
> **—Brenda Huff, co-owner, Wisdom Tree**

Wisdom Tree eventually published seven NES games, along with four games for Game Boy,** three for Sega Genesis, and one for the Super NES. The company's library included several original games published by outside contractors and a couple of cosmetically altered Color Dreams games. *Sunday Funday,* for instance, was a thinly disguised version of *Menace Beach.* While the owners of Wisdom Tree were openly Christian, their game designers did not necessarily share their beliefs. People who later worked with the man who programmed *Bible Adventures* say that after working day and night on the project, he went to Las Vegas and blew his earnings in less than a week.

---

* *Menace Beach* was far tamer than *Peek a Boo Poker, Bubble Bath Babes,* and *Hot Slots,* three unlicensed games published by the Taiwanese software company Paneision, which featured *anime*-style drawings of naked women.

** Two of Wisdom Tree's Game Boy cartridges were not really games. The company published cartridges containing the text of the King James and New International versions of the Bible.

Wisdom Tree presented Nintendo with a prickly situation. The general public did not seem to pay close attention to the court battle with Atari Games, and industry analysts were impressed with Nintendo's legal acumen; but going after a tiny company that published innocuous religious games was another story. In 1994, Wisdom Tree tested Nintendo's ability to turn the other cheek by licensing the mazes and code to a game called *Castle Wolfenstein 3D* and converting them into an unlicensed Super NES game called *Super 3D Noah's Ark.* This was this one of the few unlicensed games to appear on the Super NES. In *Castle Wolfenstein 3D,* players ran through dungeons killing Nazi soldiers and guard dogs as they hunted for Hitler. In *Super 3D Noah's Ark,* which featured the exact same mazes, players shot food at little goats that had escaped from their pens.*

Ignoring Wisdom Tree was the only logical course of action. *Super 3D Noah's Ark* was released toward the end of the 16-bit generation, as growing numbers of people began using computers to play games. Though Wisdom Tree was one of the last companies to manufacture and sell NES and Super NES games, the company's focus eventually turned to publishing games for PCs.

The Return of Sega

One of my first jobs here was to take the Master System back from Tonka and bring it over to Sega. Then we closed down a lot of the development. We did not have the money to do anything big; our main focus of 1989 and 1990 was obviously Genesis.

—Paul Rioux, former executive vice president of finance,
Sega of America

Sega's alliance with Tonka did not prove completely satisfactory for either company. Despite its strong toy distribution network and a very generous advertising campaign, the Minnesota toy truck company sold considerably less than one million Master System game consoles in two years. When the con-

---

* This game was built into a special adapter that attached to any licensed Super NES cartridge. The chip in the licensed cartridge would disable the security chip, allowing the Super Nintendo to read the game.

tract expired, Sega quietly took back the system and inherited large inventories of unsold game consoles and cartridges. Clearing out Master System inventory, however, was not a major priority at the time. Sega had spent the last two years developing a powerful new game console that had twice the processing power of the NES/Famicom, and the product was finally ready for release in Japan.

Sega's new system, called the Mega-Drive, featured an impressive array of hardware. It was built around the 16-bit Motorola 68000 processing chip, the same chip that Apple used to power the Macintosh computer. This chip could process twice as much data per cycle as the 8-bit MOS Technologies 6502 chip Nintendo used in the Famicom. The Mega-Drive had a 512-color palette and could display as many as 64 colors on screen at any one time, compared to the NES's 52-color palette. The Mega-Drive even had a separate 8-bit processor for sound. All of that power translated into games with larger and more detailed characters, more complex graphics, faster action, and a game console that could compete with coin-operated game machines in the arcades.

With its headquarters in Tokyo, Sega Enterprises had the infrastructure needed to market the Mega-Drive in Japan. Bringing the system to the United States was another story. Hayao Nakayama, CEO of Sega Enterprises, and David Rosen, the chairman, had already experienced the problems of launching a game console through a small start-up operation. Nintendo, a company that had only recently entered the home video game market in the United States, had completely smothered the Master System out of the market by 1988. Attaching itself to Tonka, a strong company that knew little about the game business, also failed. In an interesting twist, Rosen decided to enlist the same company that Nintendo had tried to enlist before launching the NES—Atari Corporation.

> Dave Rosen came to Atari and asked if we'd be interested in taking over the manufacturing, marketing, and distribution of Genesis. We came very close to making a hefty licensing deal so that Atari could jump into the 16-bit fray before Nintendo. The negotiations went pretty far down the stream, and as I recall, they fell apart when Jack [Tramiel] and Dave Rosen couldn't agree to the terms. Then Sega decided to do it themselves.
>
> **—Michael Katz, president, Video Game Division, Atari Corporation**

Everybody's Expert

Video game companies have a certain incestuous relationship, and it is not uncommon for top employees to take jobs with their competitors. Bruce Lowry, for instance, resigned his job as Nintendo vice president of sales to become the president of Sega of America. When he left Sega, he moved to Europe to help Ron Judy run Nintendo of Europe. But of the many job shifters in the industry, few have had as illustrious a career as Michael Katz.

In the late 1970s, Katz, as marketing director at Mattel, oversaw the creation of the first handheld video games. From there, he moved to Connecticut to become vice president of marketing at Coleco. After five years at Coleco, he received an intriguing telephone call.

> I was contacted by headhunters representing some venture capitalists and told about a company named Epyx, which they described as a $1.5 million computer game company losing $400,000 a year in Sunnyvale. I was anxious to get back to California, where my two kids lived. I hadn't lived in San Francisco for about seven or eight years, and my goal was to get back there.
>
> I didn't know anything about Epyx and I had never heard of a venture capitalist. I liked the fact that I was being offered a CEO slot and some stock in a start-up, but I wasn't quite sure whether I wanted to do something risky like that. I had to make the decision on a January night in Connecticut. I was trying to get a fire started in my fireplace and it wouldn't start. As I was leafing through a computer gaming magazine, I came upon an Epyx ad. Just as I turned the page and discovered it, this flame burst in the fireplace. It was a complete coincidence. The fire that I'd been trying to start burst into a flame, so I considered that a divine message that Epyx was where I should go.
>
> **—Michael Katz, former president, Epyx**

Katz became the president of Epyx in February 1983 and changed the company's entire focus. The company had severe financial problems and only had enough cash to maintain operations for approximately six months. Under Katz's direction, the company created three new product lines and hired Chiat Day, the same advertising agency that handled Apple Computer. Another of Epyx's new directions was the acquisition of outside software developer StarPath, which was led by Bob Brown, one of the engineers involved in the creation of the Atari 2600. StarPath had abandoned a project based on the Olympic games. With the real Olympics only a year away, Katz had the company finish the project, which was released for the Commodore 64. *Summer Games* was released in 1984 and was followed up in 1985 with a sequel, *Winter Games.* Over the following years, these thematic "Games" titles became Epyx's signature series and included a tremendously popular product called *California Games.*

Katz's biggest interest, however, was in marketing hardware, not software. When two inventors named RJ Mical and Dave Needle approached Epyx in 1986 with a design for a color handheld video game system, Katz urged the board to adopt the project (which later became the Atari Lynx). Epyx eventually did work with Mical and Needle, but by that time Jack and Sam Tramiel had already lured Katz to accept a position at Atari Corporation.

> I had lunch with Jack and Sam Tramiel one day, and they said, "What do you want to do?"
>
> I said, "I want to form an Entertainment/Electronics division at Atari. I want to bring back video games, and that can help fund the new division. It can also fund the ST computer," which was what Jack and Sam were all excited about.
>
> So they said, "You can become president of the entertainment electronics division if you also become president of the video game division and become head of sales and marketing for the computer division." I said that sounded fair. So in one lunch, which is what Jack and Sam are like, we made a deal. I got a new job and became head of the video game division, which, in Jack's mind, had the main objective of getting a lot of profits so that the company could develop the ST computer.
>
> **—Michael Katz**

Katz moved to Atari in 1986 and oversaw the rerelease of the Atari 7800 game console. Unlike the Master System, the 7800 was not meant to compete with the Nintendo Entertainment System head-on. Atari introduced it as a low-end alternative system that sold for $30 less than its competitors. The 7800 barely dented Nintendo's billion-dollar market, but it contributed to Atari's best year since the fall of 1982. In 1988, Atari reached $452 million in revenues.

> We brought back Atari video games as the low price spread for three or four years and made a hell of a lot of profit. As I recall, we made about $80 million of profit over that period. We brought back the 7800. We needed software for it, but, of course, this was the period when Nintendo created the market again in the U.S. and Nintendo had a lock on all the hot arcade titles. Nobody else, whether it be Atari or Sega or anyone, could get the hot arcade titles because Nintendo had exclusives.
>
> It occurred to me that the standard for the last few years had not been arcade games. There was a core group of computer gamers who knew all the hot computer games, so I went to those companies who were just doing computer format. I went to Doug Carlstom at Broderbund, to Ken Williams at Sierra, to Gilman Louie at Spectrum Holobyte, and to Alan Miller at Accolade, and asked if we could license games like *Hardball* and *Lode Runner*.
>
> **—Michael Katz**

By the beginning of 1989, Katz needed a break from work. He had not taken a two-week vacation since graduating from college in 1967, and the Tramiels were notorious for placing high expectations on their executives. Tired and needing time to decide what he wanted to do with the rest of his life, Katz left Atari Corporation and spent the next three months traveling around the world. While he was gone, Sega released the American version of the Mega-Drive. It was called Genesis.

Genesis

Sega of America launched Genesis in two markets, Los Angeles and New York, on August 14, 1989. The console sold for $189 and came with a single controller and the game *Altered Beast*. There were five additional games available at launch: *Thunder Force, Tommy Lasorda Baseball, Super Thunder Blade, Space Harrier II,* and *Last Battle*. A second wave of games arrived one month later.

As the game that came with the console, *Altered Beast* played an important role in convincing consumers about the power of Genesis's 16-bit processor. NES games generally had small characters occupying only a limited area on any game screen. The shape-shifting hero of *Altered Beast* was nearly half as tall as the screen and had recognizable facial features. The snakes, wolves, enemy sorcerers, and other creatures that attacked him were also large and clearly drawn. In size, game play, and graphics, the Genesis version of *Altered Beast* was amazingly similar to the arcade game on which it was based.

In October, as the Genesis market expanded from New York and Los Angeles to a nationwide campaign, Sega of America announced the hiring of a new president and CEO, Michael Katz.

> Dave Rosen asked me if I wanted to come to Sega and become president, so I joined Sega in October of 1989 and spent a year. And every day, the chant that I was supposed to be saying and our troops were supposed to be saying was "Hyakumandai," which means a million units in Japanese because Nakayama felt we should be selling a million units.
>
> We had to differentiate ourselves from Nintendo, and once again we couldn't get hot properties from the arcades other than Sega's own arcade titles. Just like it was at Atari, it became a matter of figuring out a way to position ourselves strongly when we couldn't get the hottest arcade titles. So we decided to get the hottest personalities instead.
>
> **—Michael Katz**

As the head of Sega, Katz's first goal was to establish an identity for Genesis. The marketing team came up with a two-part approach. On one hand, team members needed to demonstrate the superiority of Genesis over the NES. They needed to show that Genesis games had better graphics and sound and looked more like arcade games. Realizing that most consumers were more interested in games than technology, Katz's team members did not want to focus too heavily on the 16-bit processor. Instead of reciting technological achievements, they developed an advertising campaign that challenged Nintendo head-on. Sega's new marketing mantra was, "Genesis does what Nintendon't."

> Sega came out slamming us in their commercials. They were naming us by name, and that was really a big deal. It's like somebody calling your team "crap." We took it good-naturedly and competed the best we could.
>
> **—Don James, vice president of design, Nintendo of America**

The second part of Katz's marketing rollout was to circumvent the lack of arcade properties by creating a library of instantly recognizable titles. Nintendo could dominate the arcade translation business; Sega, meanwhile, would contract athletes and celebrities and create games with their names and images. Under Katz's direction, Sega created *Pat Riley's Basketball, Arnold Palmer Golf, Buster Douglas Boxing,* and *Joe Montana Football.*

> Joe Montana became the ultimate example. We paid $1.7 million up front. I fought to convince Nakayama and the Japanese that we needed Montana, and I gave Joe Montana the check. We also had Michael Jackson, we had Pat Riley, and we had Tommy Lasorda. Buster Douglas was my selection, too. He got knocked down in his first challenge after he won the championship, but that was okay because the royalty was on a sliding scale and that meant we didn't have to pay as much. He gave up the title right after he had gotten it.
>
> **—Michael Katz**

Shortly after starting at Sega, Katz convinced Nakayama to sign a five-year agreement with 49er quarterback Joe Montana. The deal enabled Sega to use Montana's name and image in a football game. Once the licensing deal was signed, the next problem was finding the game itself. Sega did not have a large U.S. game production facility at that time, and Sega of Japan had not designed a football game. By coincidence, a small software company, Mediagenic,* had a game under development. According to the team that had worked on the project, the game was approximately 30 percent finished, but Mediagenic executives said that it could be finished by October, or November at the very latest, so Katz decided to purchase the game.

> We didn't know about all the internal turmoil that was going on at Mediagenic. Basically, they deceived us over a period of four or five months that the game was proceeding on schedule. We—Sega—were naive and irresponsible. We should have known.
>
> The game wasn't very far along at all, but we didn't discover that till about September or October. By the time we found out, the only way we

---

* The company was formerly known as Activision.

> were gonna get a game out near Christmas would be to find another game
> that was either mostly finished or completely finished, and convert it.
>
> —**Michael Katz**

In desperation, Sega turned to Electronic Arts, one of its first American licensees. Well known for its sports games, Electronic Arts had been publishing the *John Madden Football* series for four years. The first *Madden Football*, released for the Apple II computer in 1986, was so successful that Electronic Arts began updating its team rosters and playbook and rereleasing it on an annual basis. Electronic Arts president Trip Hawkins agreed to help, and his designers put together a game that Sega could name *Joe Montana Football* and publish under its first-party label. The game was released in January 1990. Electronic Arts released a Genesis-compatible version of *John Madden Football* later that year.

The finished versions of *Joe Montana Football* and *John Madden Football* were so completely different that few people would have guessed that the same company had made them. *John Madden Football* featured a playbook partially designed by Madden himself. As an NFL broadcaster and former Raiders coach, Madden helped Electronic Arts' designers create a game realistic enough to appeal to football purists.

Joe Montana Football, on the other hand, was an arcade-style game that emphasized fast action over realism. Unlike *John Madden Football*, which had all 28 NFL teams, *Joe Montana Football* had a 16-team roster and a simplified playbook built around a passing-intensive offense that discouraged running plays.

Although the *Joe Montana* series did not last as long as the *Madden* games, it helped establish Sega's reputation among sports fans and Genesis as the leading video game platform for sports simulation. Electronic Arts developed only the first *Joe Montana* football game. Blue Sky, an independent development company, created Sega's later football games. Founded by George Kiss, who worked with Michael Katz at Coleco, Blue Sky went on to make several important Genesis hits, including *World Series Baseball* and *Vectorman*.

> I think Joe Montana earned something like a $2.5 million or a $3.5 million
> royalty over the course of the five years of our agreement. The Japanese were
> originally concerned that he wouldn't even earn the money that we paid him
> [in advance], so I was gratified to hear that.
>
> —**Michael Katz**

Of all the games that Sega released in 1989, *Michael Jackson's Moonwalker* made the biggest impression on the media. Not only did the game contain synthesized versions of such hits as "Smooth Criminal," "Bad," "Billie Jean," "Beat It," and "Thriller," it also had Jackson and chorus lines of villains dancing to choreographed moves that looked like they belonged on MTV. Loosely based on Jackson's *Moonwalker* video, the game followed Jackson as he explored pool halls, graveyards, and other secret hideouts in search of kidnapped children. Just like the video, the game ended with Jackson turning into a robotic alter ego as he battled a nefarious criminal named Mr. Big.*

Sega's marketing team was led by Al Nilsen,** who constantly reminded the press that Jackson had added his own creative suggestions during the development of the game. Jackson even released a statement saying that Genesis was the first game console that had enough power to handle his music. In this, however, the pop star was wrong. The first system powerful enough to handle his music was the Master System. Sega published an eight-bit version of *Michael Jackson's Moonwalker* as well.

Sega of America may have slowed down its Master System marketing effort with the launch of Genesis, but it did not abandon the retailers in the video game channel. Sega released Master System versions of such Genesis hits as *Michael Jackson's Moonwalker, Ghouls 'N Ghosts, Golden Axe, Columns,* and even *Sonic The Hedgehog.* It also released the Power Base Converter, a pricey adapter that allowed consumers to play Master System cartridges on their Genesis consoles.

Electronic Arts Does

> When we announced the Nintendo deal, the stock went up. When we announced the Sega deal, the stock went down because the market was so ignorant about what was going to happen. Of course, by the end of that year, everybody realized that the wheels were falling off the 8-bit market, and we were getting punished for that. They still didn't appreciate the 16-bit

---

* Actor Joe Pesci played Mr. Big in the music video. The character in the video game was an excellent likeness.

** Nilsen was the JC Penney buyer who handled video game orders during the late 1970s and early 1980s.

> [systems]. A lot of people in the period from 1989 to 1990 just assumed that Sega was not going to do anything.
>
> **—Trip Hawkins**

Electronic Arts' relationship with Sega produced significant rewards for both companies. Genesis quickly became a lucrative new outlet for Electronic Arts, and Sega benefited from having a line of sophisticated games that appealed to an older audience more than most games on the NES.

Nintendo approached Electronic Arts about making games for the NES in the mid-1980s, long before Sega announced Genesis. But Hawkins did not want to make games for the eight bit console. He and many other Electronic Arts board members felt that the NES was not powerful enough to run their computer games and they did not want to downgrade their games to run on it. Like many people at the time, Hawkins was openly disdainful of console games and critical of Nintendo's chances of success. The difference was that Hawkins waited too long to change his mind. By the time he realized that Nintendo was going to succeed, Electronic Arts' stock was tumbling and the eight-bit market showed signs of aging.

> We decided that Genesis would do really well and that we had very appropriate content for it. We did not want to be in this business the way it was currently being run, the way Nintendo did it with that one-sided licensing agreement, and Sega was trying to clone almost everything about Nintendo. I thought, look at what Atari is doing. They have reverse engineered the machine and are selling their own games. If Atari wins that lawsuit, that will open up the market and you won't need to have one of those oppressive licensing agreements.
>
> **—Trip Hawkins**

In 1989, Electronic Arts' technicians successfully reverse engineered both the NES and Genesis. Though the NES market was considerably larger and his company eventually released a few games for it, Hawkins felt that Genesis was a better fit for his company's goals. Electronic Arts' programmers were familiar with its 16-bit 68000 processor, having worked with it while making games for the Atari ST, Commodore Amiga, and Apple Macintosh computers. Converting games to work on Genesis also required less work since the most popular computers had 16-bit processors at that time. Only one obstacle remained: waiting to make sure that Sega did not change the architecture of its game console before releasing it in the United States. (Hawkins was aware of the security chip Nintendo added to the Famicom before shipping it to the United States as the NES.) When Genesis proved nearly identical to Mega-Drive, he decided to move ahead with his plans.

> We decided to go ahead and publish our own stuff on Genesis. Then, before we did that, we went to Sega and said, "Look, before we embark on this path, maybe there's a way for us to work out a more reasonable arrangement."
>
> So in June of 1990, we signed a very unusual and much more enlightened license agreement with Sega. Among other things, we had the right to make as many titles as we wanted. We could approve our own titles; there was not this sort of oppressive restriction on our rights of expression, and, of course, the royalty rates were a lot more reasonable. We also had more direct control over manufacturing.
>
> **—Trip Hawkins**

Electronic Arts' first two Genesis games, *Populous* and *Budokan: The Martial Spirit,* were released in June 1990. In August, Electronic Arts released a miniature golf simulation called *Zany Golf* and that fall released the first Genesis version of *John Madden Football.*

> At that time, we would be pretty happy if we released a computer game that sold 50,000 units. That was considered to be a significant milestone of success. We thought, Well, what would it take for us to sell 50,000 on the Sega Genesis? We decided that if they had an installed base of 500,000 units, we would be able to sell 50,000.
>
> After *Madden* came out, they probably reached 500,000 machines in North America, and by that time we had probably sold well over 100,000 units. That was pretty healthy penetration, and it just got better and better after that.
>
> **—Trip Hawkins**

TurboGrafx

> I started at NEC in 1987, and within about two months I got this call, and they said, "Hey, NEC's doing this new project in Japan that's a video game system. We want you to check it out and think about whether you could introduce it in the U.S." It was ironic because I didn't go there having any thought of NEC doing anything in the video game space, and yet almost right away they started doing video games.
>
> **—Ken Wirt, former vice president and general manager,**
> **NEC Technologies**

Sega was not the only company to release a new video game console in the United States in 1989. NEC, one of Japan's leading computer manufacturers, and Hudson Soft, a leading video game publisher, teamed up to enter the market with a system called TurboGrafx-16 (TurboGrafx).

> Hudson and NEC designed PC Engine, but a lot of it was Hudson's game experience because they were one of the top developers for the Nintendo Famicom. Hudson was a very colorful company. It was started by two brothers named the Kudo Brothers. They were eccentric software entrepreneurs, and they grew up kind of next to the railroad tracks on the island of Hokkaido, which is the northern island of Japan.
>
> **—Ken Wirt**

In the very beginning, TurboGrafx had a few small advantages over Genesis. NEC had a good reputation as a computer company and strong name recognition among PC owners. TurboGrafx was also older than Genesis. NEC released it in Japan as the PC Engine a full year before announcing plans to ship it to the United States, and the launch was tremendously successful. More Japanese consumers purchased PC Engines in 1988 than Famicoms, and a small core group of U.S. video game enthusiasts had bought imported PC Engines for prices averaging approximately $500. American game magazines such as *Electronic Gaming Monthly* and *Video Games and Computer Entertainment* mentioned the console. In May 1989, NEC announced plans to release the system in the United States.

NEC had some distinct disadvantages, too. Sega was an established arcade company, and American consumers knew the Sega name from the Master System and arcade games. Some people even remembered the tabletop games and ColecoVision cartridges from the early 1980s. Sega also had a stronger following among game enthusiasts. By the time Mega-Drive was released in Japan, it was much bigger news in the U.S. press than PC Engine.

NEC did not have to search very far to find an executive to handle the introduction of its new game console. Ken Wirt, who joined NEC's computer division a few months before the launch of PC Engine, had spent more than a year as a vice president in Atari's consumer computer division. Recognizing the value of his past experience, executives at NEC headquarters in Japan sent Wirt their new console and some games and asked him to evaluate the system. His initial reaction was positive.

> They sent over some PC Engines and I checked it out. The quality was great. At the time, we were comparing it to the Nintendo Famicom and the Sega Master System, and it did an awful lot better than either of those did. It played faster and the graphics were better and it had some interesting styling. And the game cartridges were those little IC cards. I mean, it had a lot of interesting things going for it.
>
> **—Ken Wirt**

Technologically, TurboGrafx was a curious hybrid of 8- and 16-bit technology. NEC's marketing department fiercely maintained that it had both a 16-bit custom graphics processing chip and a 16-bit central processor, but critics charged that both systems were built around 8-bit chips. TurboGrafx clearly lagged behind Genesis in overall power, though it could display far more colors on the screen.*

> As I recall, TurboGrafx was a hybrid design of 8- and 16-bit technology. From a marketing standpoint, driving the idea that it was a 16-bit system was pretty important. From a marketing standpoint, that was a complicated story to tell.

---

* TurboGrafx could display 241 colors at a time. Technically, Genesis could display only 61 colors at one time, though a method for displaying 128 colors was developed in later years.

> Of course, the competition wanted to tell the 8-bit part of the story, and NEC wanted to drive the 16-bit component of the story. In hindsight, maybe it wasn't a good idea to let that battle line be drawn because neither side was 100 percent right. Perhaps telling a more sophisticated story would have been of more value.

> **—Stephen Boogar, former vice president of sales, NEC Home Electronics**

Instead of storing games in cartridges, NEC published its games on plastic cards that looked a lot like the cards used on the Master System. But NEC's held a lot more data. The game that came packed with the system was a slow-paced, side-scrolling adventure called *Keith Courage in Alpha Zones* that highlighted TurboGrafx's ability to display several colors. In the future, however, TurboGrafx games would have the potential to be much larger than Sega games. NEC announced that it would release a CD-ROM add-on device called the TurboGrafx-CD within a few months after the fall release of the main console. (CD-ROM disks could store nearly 260 times more data than TurboGrafx cards.) The console launched in New York and Los Angeles in late August, just two weeks after the launch of the Sega Genesis, and retailed for $199.

> The video game business was hot at the time that we launched, and we had tons of orders from all the big retailers. Kmart, Wal-Mart, Babbages, everybody had these giant orders. We had a big introduction ceremony in New York in the original customs building. There must have been 200 press people at this thing, and it was covered on CNN, and there was a big media splash about the introduction.

> **—Ken Wirt**

Unaffected and Overconfident

> I thought Nintendo screwed up three different times. One was being so late bringing its 16-bit in to counteract Genesis. Number two was not making Game Boy a color system a lot quicker to counteract not only our Game Gear but also the Lynx. Number three was not taking care of mom and dad

> by making a downwardly compatible component that accepted 8-bit soft-
> ware on the Super NES. It didn't have to enhance the software, just to accept
> it so mom and dad didn't complain about tossing $500 out the door on
> little Johnny's NES.

> **—Bob Harris, former director of creative services and advertising,**
> **Sega of America**

The executive team at Nintendo greeted the news about Sega's Genesis and
NEC's TurboGrafx with indifference. Looking back years later, several
Nintendo employees have offered various explanations about why they did
not take Genesis seriously. Some people said that the first Genesis games
did not leave an overwhelming impression. Others said that Japanese Mega-
Drive sales figures were so low that Genesis didn't seem like much of a threat.
Several people admitted that since Nintendo had a U.S. install base of over
20 million, Sega seemed like an upstart, an upstart that Nintendo had easily
beaten a few years earlier.

> The other failing was this blind faith that since they were Nintendo and
> they were successful, no one could ever defeat them. That they worked so
> hard and had done so many things right and were given such positive
> acclaim from people and had made so many people in the industry wealthy
> that you just couldn't imagine them looking anywhere else because we'd
> made them so happy.

> **—Howard Phillips, former game master, Nintendo of America**

At the same time, Nintendo had just passed new milestones, and the business continued to expand. Nintendo's sales for the year topped $2.3 billion,
and the company's licensing program grew as well. Knowing that under the
terms of their agreement, they could not publish more than five games per
year, two licensees—Konami and Acclaim—asked for second licenses. This
allowed Acclaim to publish five additional games as LJN, and Konami to publish its additional games as Ultra. Two of the first games that Konami published
under the Ultra label were exceptionally successful—*Teenage Mutant Ninja Turtles,*

a game based on comic-book heroes that became a cartoon show and a motion picture, and *Metal Gear,* a game about a soldier in a special forces operation.

The big news around Nintendo in 1989 was the pending release of a new handheld game system, the first handheld video game to use interchangeable cartridges since Milton Bradley released Microvision in 1979. Named Game Boy, the new unit was designed by Gumpei Yokoi and Nintendo's Research and Development Team 1, the team that created Game & Watch and designed the hardware for *Donkey Kong.*

Typical of Yokoi's engineering, Game Boy was inexpensive, lightweight, and efficient. It was the same size as a calculator, had stereo sound, a black-and-white liquid crystal display (LCD) screen, and could run for ten hours on four AA batteries. Though Game Boy was designed around an eight-bit processor, it was not compatible with the Nintendo Entertainment System, and its cartridges were only slightly bigger than a book of matches.

Yokoi was not alone in his interest in handheld games. Unaware that Yokoi was creating Game Boy in Japan, Rare Ltd. cofounder Chris Stamper built a handheld game system that played NES cartridges. When he completed the project, Stamper and Joel Hochberg, Rare's American partner, demonstrated the unit to Nintendo of America.

> We had no idea that Nintendo was working on a portable system when I arranged a meeting with Mr. Arakawa and Howard Lincoln, to show them a portable system that we had developed that used NES carts. There were a number of problems, of course, such as battery life. It was cumbersome in comparison to what Game Boy in its final form actually looked like because it accepted a larger cartridge.
>
> At my meeting with Howard and Mr. Arakawa, they took me into their confidence and told me about this Game Boy project and suggested that we forego any development of this project that we were working on.
>
> **—Joel Hochberg, cofounder, Rare and Coin-It**

In a shrewd maneuver, Nintendo of America president Minoru Arakawa decided to use *Tetris* as the cartridge that came packed in with Game Boy. It was a perfect match. The puzzle game's simple graphics lent themselves well to Game Boy's LCD screen, and its style was ideal for travel and quick breaks. The *Tetris* cartridge also fit into advertising campaigns that Nintendo ran in later years, after discovering that Game Boy had a stronger appeal to adults than the NES did.

Nintendo originally released three cartridges—*Baseball, Breakout,* and *Golf*—that retailed for $20 at the time that Game Boy was launched. A few weeks later, Nintendo released the Game Boy cartridge *Super Mario Land* with a barrage of advertisements based on the science-fiction movies of the 1950s. Though it had the look and feel of other Mario games, *Super Mario Land* took the plumber in new directions. In this game he flew a spaceship and rode in a submarine. Shigeru Miyamoto had not overseen the creation of this game; Yokoi produced it himself specifically to support his Game Boy system.

Unlike the other hardware systems that came out in 1989, Game Boy was an immediate success. According to an article in *Time* magazine, the one million Game Boys sent to the United States in 1989 met only half the demand for the product.[1] That allotment sold out in a matter of weeks. Game Boy was a juggernaut. Its sales did not slow down, even when it was confronted with a technologically superior product.

Atari Lynx

Jay Miner, the man most associated with the design of the Atari 2600, founded Amiga in 1982. In 1983, he hired a young programmer named RJ Mical* who had a fanatical passion for creating operating systems. Tall, athletically built, and openly goofy, Mical was the antithesis of the standard programmer. Working under Miner, Mical learned a new appreciation for the relationship between hardware and software.

> Everything I learned at college and everything I learned until going to Amiga suggested that hardware was hardware and software was software, and the way things are done is that you invent a bunch of hardware and give it to the software guys. There's a much better way of thinking that I learned at Amiga. For the first time, the hardware and the software were created together. There

* Mical's biggest claim to fame at Williams was helping design the arcade game *Sinistar.*

> was a great flow of communication, a mutual design coming into existence
> at the same time.
>
> **—RJ Mical, operating system designer, Amiga**

While working at Amiga, Mical struck up a friendship with a hardware guru named Dave Needle. Both men shared the same "Yin and Yang" philosophy about the interrelationship of hardware and software. They both left Amiga in 1985. Needle took a job with Apple Computer and Mical became an independent contractor. A few years later, however, while eating at a Mexican restaurant, they began discussing projects they could build together. The conversation turned to video game systems. Needle grabbed a napkin, and they sketched the basic plan for a handheld video game system with stereo sound and color graphics.

Mical and Needle originally planned to design their system around a 16-bit processing chip but decided it was not a practical idea. The chips they looked at would have had heat problems, and when they evaluated the components needed to support the 16-bit processor, they decided the system would be bulky and heavy. They switched to an 8-bit 6502 chip from the same family of chips used in the NES and Atari 2600.

Mical and Needle did not have the money needed to build and market a game system, so they began searching for a company that would buy their idea. They contacted Epyx and demonstrated their idea toward the end of Michael Katz's tenure as president of the company. They did not know that Katz had urged the company's board of directors to accept the project. Over the next few months, they entered a lengthy and friendly negotiating process that ended with them accepting stock in Epyx and taking positions with the company. They called the project "Handy Game."

Though Katz had managed to keep Epyx running, he was never able to completely solve its financial problems. The company, needing financial backing in order to bring out a new game system, invited several potential partners to view Handy Game while it was under development. In 1988, Nintendo sent Don James to have a look at it.

> Someone from Epyx contacted us and said, "Hey, we've got this thing and
> do you guys want to look at it?" I don't think they actually offered it to us,
> but we found out about it and I flew down and had a look.

> I went down and they showed me what they were doing. It was really just a screen at that point. It was difficult to see the screen because it faded in and out if you moved it around. You had to have it just the right angle to see the screen really well. My personal thought was that, because of that and because it just chewed through batteries like crazy, it wouldn't ever really catch on that well.
>
> **—Don James**

> Nintendo sent somebody to look at what we were doing, but he didn't seem interested. It was like he came to see us even though he had already made up his mind that he wasn't interested.
>
> **—RJ Mical**

Needle and Mical learned a new phrase while working on Handy Game—"emag tresni." For them, the phrase became a sort of Murphy's Law. It meant that no matter how carefully you worked, and no matter how meticulously you checked every detail, something was bound to go wrong. In this particular case, the mistake occurred as Needle designed Handy Game's screen with engineers from Sharp Electronics. Needle and a Japanese engineer discussed every point in the design, but at some juncture, they slipped up on one digit slot in the binary coding, and instead of listing a "1," the engineer placed a "0."

> If you didn't have a game in the slot when you turned it on, the screen would display the message, "Insert Game." Because of the error, the message came out inverted. It said, "EMAG TRESNI."
>
> **—RJ Mical**

Epyx's financial problems increased throughout 1988, and the company ended up selling Handy Game to Atari Corporation. Many of the employees at Epyx resented the idea of working with Atari. Mical and Needle disliked the idea of working with Atari so much that they left Epyx. A few months later, Epyx collapsed.

Atari changed the name of the system from Handy Game to Lynx to highlight the fact that up to eight Lynx consoles could be daisy-chained together using link cables. The system was launched in October 1989 to rave reviews. Lynx was designed to accommodate both left- and right-handed play, and it had one of the finest LCD screens of its time. The screens on Game Boy and later handheld systems tended to blur when showing fast movements. Lynx's screen handled speed without blurring, though it scratched very easily. Color graphics and a crisper screen were not enough, however. While Toys "R" Us and most of the dedicated video game stores carried Lynx, Atari could not give it the marketing and retail support that Nintendo gave Game Boy. Atari's poor reputation with retailers, and fear of Nintendo, caused many retailers to avoid the system. Originally retailing for $199, it cost twice as much as Game Boy and was never widely advertised. Many stores pulled Lynx from their shelves within a year. It was available mostly through mail order thereafter.

Run for the Money

It was embarrassing to talk to retailers when I first joined the company. They hated us because we never did what we said we were going to do. Fortunately, they did not like Nintendo either. In those days, Nintendo was so arrogant.

—Tom Kalinske, former president and CEO, Sega of America

Indeed, when Apple president Michael Spindler was asked in March 1991, which computer company Apple feared most, he quickly answered, "Nintendo."[1]

[Laughs] They should have feared Apple more.[2]

—Bill Gates, chief operating officer, Microsoft

The NES Hits Its Apex

Nintendo's best year . . . The best year for the NES, the most lucrative year for the NES, was 1990, which was also the first full year that Sega Genesis was on the market.

—Peter Main, executive vice president, Nintendo of America

With the 1989 releases of Genesis and TurboGrafx, Nintendo found itself lagging in technology behind the competition; but amazingly, technology did not seem to matter. Nintendo sold more than 17 million copies of *Super Mario Bros. 3* worldwide, setting a lasting sales record for a game cartridge that was not packed in with console hardware.* There were other hits, too. Sun Soft scored a major hit with *Batman,* a game that built off the popularity and storyline of the Tim Burton movie. Konami scored a major hit that year as well with *Teenage Mutant Ninja Turtles,* the first game to be published under the new Ultra label.

In 1987, Nintendo of America president Minoru Arakawa met with executives of Konami—one of Nintendo's three most successful third-party partners—to discuss a problem they saw in their licensing agreement. According to the agreement, third-party licensees were allowed to publish only five games per year. Konami had published a long line of bestselling games, including *Castlevania, Blades of Steel, Double Dribble,* and *Life Force,* and the five-games-per-year clause was holding the company back from realizing additional profits. Based on the games' quality and torrid sales, they argued, Konami should not be limited to five games per year.

Another third-party publisher had the same complaint. Acclaim, Greg Fischbach's Long Island–based game company, also asked for permission to publish more games. Having created such games as *Double Dragon II, Iron Sword,* and several games based on WWF wrestling, Acclaim was another one of Nintendo's top licensees.

After considering their arguments, Arakawa found a way around the rule. He gave Konami and Acclaim second licenses so that they could publish an additional five games under different names. Acclaim adopted the name

---

* By comparison, Nintendo sold in excess of 30 million copies of the original *Super Mario Bros.* and Game Boy *Tetris* cartridges, both of which were packed with hardware systems.

LJN for its second license and Konami published additional games under the name Ultra.

> I think Konami and Acclaim were doing so well that we thought we had a good reason to give them another license. The other licensees did not like it.
>
> Konami had a really good manager [Emil Highcamp] in the States. He was not only doing marketing and sales, he was also a good product manager. He sometimes went to Japan and asked the R&D people at Konami [headquarters] to come up with this type of game or that type of game. Once he was watching TV and saw *Teenage Mutant Ninja Turtles* and got an idea, so he licensed it and asked Japan to make it into a game.
>
> **—Minoru Arakawa, president, Nintendo of America**

Under the Ultra label, Konami sold approximately 4 million copies of *Teenage Mutant Ninja Turtles,* giving Ultra a heady send-off. One of Ultra's next titles, *Metal Gear,* also helped establish the product line. But Ultra's days were numbered. The Ultra license was only for the Nintendo Entertainment System (NES), and that system was coming to an end.

Even with earnings of $3.34 billion and 48 million Nintendo Entertainment Systems sold worldwide, Nintendo executives knew that they could not control the market with obsolete hardware. Work had already begun on the new 16-bit game console that they hoped would help them shut competitors out of the market.

A Change at Sega

> I think Mike Katz was the guy who did a lot of the things that ultimately led to Sega's success with Genesis.
>
> **—Howard Lincoln**

Breaking Nintendo's hold on the international video game market proved to be more than a matter of technology for Sega. Nintendo controlled more than 90 percent of the international market. But whether Sega's 16-bit game console was sold as the Mega-Drive in Japan or the Genesis in the United States, the unit was simply not catching on. With memories of the failed Master System still vivid in his memory, Sega Enterprises CEO Hayao Nakayama decided to shake up Sega of America, in the hope that new ideas might lead to new success.

In mid-1990, Nakayama bumped into an old acquaintance named Tom Kalinske who was visiting Tokyo on business. As they spoke, Nakayama told Kalinske that he now worked at a company called Sega that had a new game console that he hoped could steal the market away from Nintendo. Kalinske, who was working for a struggling toy car manufacturer called Matchbox, almost laughed. "You're competing with Nintendo! They're huge!" he said.

According to a 1995 article, Nakayama offered Kalinske the position of CEO of Sega of America on the spot.[3]

Tom Kalinske

> And so Nakayama-san was not happy that we hadn't sold a million units. In January, about fourteen months after I started there, I was replaced by Tom Kalinske who, of course, I'd known from Mattel, where we had worked together.
>
> **—Mike Katz, former CEO, Sega of America**

Thomas J. Kalinske was a natural choice for president and CEO of Sega of America. An affable man with clean-cut all-American good looks, he graduated from the University of Wisconsin with a degree in marketing and spent years in advertising before joining Mattel as a product manager in the early 1970s. While at Mattel, Kalinske's bold style caught the eye of top executives, and he moved up quickly.

Mattel, the largest toy company in the world, had plenty of room for a tomcat like Kalinske to grow. He began with preschool toys, then was asked to oversee the Barbie line. At the time, Mattel marketed Barbie as a single line of dolls with accessories. Kalinske's team changed the strategy, breaking the line into several segments such as Malibu Barbie. "When I started on the Barbie business, worldwide, it was $42 million; when I left the company, it was $550 million; today, it's $1 billion."[4] As Kalinske rose through the ranks of Mattel, his responsibilities expanded and he oversaw several research and development teams. One of those teams formed the nucleus of Mattel Electronics.

> I was a VP of marketing at the time, and one of my product development groups developed the first portable games. We introduced them on Father's Day. Nobody thought it was going to be successful, and, of course, the products were phenomenally successful. Within that same group, they developed the Intellivision technology. But what happened was that because it was clear the electronics business was going to become such a major part of the company, we decided to create a totally separate company. Once we made that decision and staffed it with some new hires and with some e-toy people, I never had anything to do with it again.
>
> **—Tom Kalinske**

A rising star at Mattel, Kalinske tracked the new electronics division's meteoric ascent and fall.

> I eventually ended up on the board of directors of Mattel Inc., and during that time period the Intellivision company would report its results back in. So I had some involvement at a board level with them and how they were doing. All of a sudden one day the guys from Mattel Electronics said, "Oh my god, the bottom has fallen out. Atari just lost all its money, and we're losing all this money, and it looks like we're gonna lose $350 million."
>
> **—Tom Kalinske**

Twelve years after he started at Mattel, Kalinske began a three-year stint as president of the company. During this time, he went toe-to-toe with television network executives over advertising sales. "We were spending millions of dollars, and the networks treated us like dirt," says Kalinske. "They had McDonalds and other big companies, and they acted as if they were doing us a favor by giving us advertising time."

Mattel came up with an alternative medium for reaching children—a cartoon series and a line of toys called *HeMan and the Masters of the Universe.* The idea was to create a hit cartoon series for non-network television where advertising was more affordable. The idea worked. "*Masters of the Universe* ended up getting a 7.5 rating at a time when the networks' shows weren't getting a 7.5 rating. From that point on, the networks were much easier to work with."

After sixteen years with Mattel, Kalinske went to Matchbox for a short period, then replaced Michael Katz, who had spent the last year trying to find a foothold in the market. In truth, Katz has seldom been given enough credit for his role in Sega's success. Much attention has been given to the rise in profits under Kalinske, jumping from approximately $100 million in sales in 1990 to over $1 billion by 1993. Much of this success, however, grew out of programs started by Katz.

> We started the aggressive advertising campaign "Genesis does what Nintendon't." We concentrated on games that Americans would play. . . . sports games, specifically, and some other products. And we attempted to develop a mascot character like Mario.
>
> **—Michael Katz**

Several people who worked under Kalinske when he first joined Sega say that he did not know much about video games but that he was a fast learner. In the early days, marketing executives and engineers had to brief him before meetings with reporters, and some Sega of America employees wondered if he was right for the job. Playing off his Mattel background, some reporters dubbed Kalinske Sega's "Ken doll" spokesperson, suggesting that he was a good-looking figurehead with little else going for him. The label was grossly inaccurate. According to those who worked with him, Kalinske studied hard and quickly developed an understanding of the industry. He demonstrated the ability to make tough decisions and the willingness to defend his decisions when challenged by the Japanese board of directors of Sega Enterprises. He also surrounded himself with industry-savvy advisers such as Steve Race, an Atari veteran and one of the founders of Worlds of Wonder; Bob Harris, who had helped launch both Master System and Genesis; Paul Rioux, who had worked on Intellivision; and Al Nilsen, who had been JC Penney's merchandise buyer during the Atari's heyday.

> Tom focused on retail and how to represent the company and third-party relationships. I mean, that was Tom. He made sure that the best people outside of us wanted to work on Genesis.

Shinobu Toyoda was the vice president of licensing, and he was the man behind building the Sonic franchises and licensing in and out. He wanted to go to Hollywood. To this day he works in Los Angeles at our Sega PC offices. He's the one who wanted to do the Paula Abdul game. He's the one who would go down to Hollywood and go onto all the sets to get licenses like Batman. He was the one who made sure Sonic was on every bath towel and all of that stuff, and he worked very closely with the Sonic cartoon.

The guy who was most underrated and the guy who doesn't get a lot of positive press was Paul Riuox. I can tell you from firsthand experience . . . I got to sit and watch all these guys, and Paul Rioux was the guy who pushed hard to improve the quality when the quality wasn't there. He was the guy who saw the value of making money in peripherals. He was the "make it happen" guy, the sort of nuts and bolts guy who would be involved in all aspects. He didn't have the most romantic job, but I assure you, he was a really key part of the success.

You know, it was a real triad, though. If all three of them [hadn't been] there, I really feel like we wouldn't have been successful. The chemistry between the three was essential.

—Michael Latham, former director of Omega Group, Sega of America

A student of classic marketing, Kalinske believed in the Gillette school of "giving away the razors to sell the blades." Above all else, he felt that Sega had to get as many Genesis consoles into consumers' hands as possible and as quickly as possible. Working with his executive team, Kalinske developed a four-point strategy that he believed could weaken Nintendo's hold on the market. His plan included dropping the price of Genesis from $189 to $149, with the eventual goal of getting it down to $100; replacing *Altered Beast,* the first bundled game, with a game called *Sonic The Hedgehog* that was under development at the time; assembling a U.S.-based team to create games more suited to American tastes; and adopting strident advertising campaigns that challenged Nintendo head on.* Kalinske prepared a presentation with these

---

* While Tom Kalinske often takes credit for creating advertising campaigns that challenged Nintendo "head on," it should be noted that the "Sega does what Nintend-don't" campaign began under Michael Katz. It should also be noted that Nintendo later responded to this campaign with "Nintendo is what Genes-isn't."

suggestions and flew to Japan to present them to Nakayama and the board of Sega Enterprises. The board nearly rejected his ideas.

> It was like I'd hit them with a bucket of cold water. They asked, "Are you out of your mind? You want to lower the price until we don't have any profit at all? You want to take out our regular software and put in our best software? You want to take on this company that has 92 percent of the market in an advertising campaign?"
>
> That's essentially what they told me. I thought, "Well, this is the shortest career anybody ever had. I guess I'd better start looking for something else to do."
>
> As the other guys got up to leave, Nakayama turned and said, "On the other hand, he was hired to make decisions for the U.S. market, and if that is what he thinks needs to be done, he should go ahead and do it."
>
> **—Tom Kalinske**

Kalinske returned to Sega of America with Hayao Nakayama's approval on all four suggestions. The next step was putting his plan to work.

Sega's Secret Weapon

A large portion of Kalinske's recovery plans would fall on the shoulders of *Sonic The Hedgehog,** a speedy blue rodent in red tennis shoes.

Sonic was the creation of Yuji Naka, a young game designer whose credentials included *Phantasy Star,* a role-playing title generally remembered as the best game ever released for Sega Master System, and *Ghouls 'N Ghosts* for Genesis, a flawless translation of a popular Capcom coin-op game. Of the games released around the launch of Genesis, *Ghouls 'N Ghosts* stands out among the finest.

An exacting and relentless micromanager, Naka was well known for expecting nothing short of perfection from those who worked on his team. Like the programmers who created the games for the Atari 2600, Naka generally preferred to do everything from game layout to the music and even writing the code himself.

---

* The "T" in *Sonic The Hedgehog* is capitalized. Sega marketing wizard Al Nilsen had the "The" registered as Sonic's middle name.

> Not just programming, everything . . . the graphics, the pictures. I'm really careful about everything. It's not exactly the building of the program itself that concerns me, it's the overall flow of the program. In my mind, working as a producer or director means handling all aspects of a game, including the music, graphics, pictures, and everything.
>
> **—Yuji Naka, creator of *Sonic The Hedgehog***

Naka's demanding managerial style sometimes gave way to outbursts. Unlike other creative teams, Naka's team suffered from heavy turnover as burned-out programmers, designers, and artists looked for less demanding work elsewhere. Mild-mannered in public, Naka was said to be given to emotional flare-ups when under stress. He had already established himself as one of Sega's most respected console game creators in 1989, when the company-wide call went out to create a new mascot that could compete with Nintendo's Mario.

> Mr. Nakayama expressed the idea to the company that it would be a good thing for Sega to develop a mascot character—one that could be sort of, that could do for Sega what Mickey Mouse does for Disney. As a result of that, numerous artists and designers from the company submitted design ideas and suggestions and sketches for what this character would be. A lot of ideas were considered, like kangaroos and rabbits, and we were kind of thinking along the lines of a jumping, hopping kind of character.
>
> Mr. Oshima [Masato Oshima] was the artist whose character design sketch was accepted. He's the one who essentially drew the hedgehog. It's a very stylized hedgehog.
>
> **—Roger Hector, former head, Sega Technical Institute**

Naka wanted to make a game that was similar to the *Super Mario Bros.* games, only simpler. *Mario* games used two buttons, so *Sonic* should use one. Mario collected coins, so Sonic collected rings. The way Naka's people differentiated Sonic from Mario was by making the hedgehog faster and giving him "attitude." Mario games were slow and friendly, Sonic games would be fast and the eponymous groundhog would glare at the camera and tap his foot impatiently if the player did not move quickly enough.*

> The Japanese, unbeknownst to us, created a character with *Sonic The Hedgehog*. We, in America, thought Sonic was ridiculous because the hedgehog was a little known animal and it was in blue. We thought it was silly, but to the credit of the game, which was so good, the character became established.
>
> I think it was because the game was a good game on its own anyhow. The character could have been anything, but it was a hedgehog that would have died a dismal death had it not been for a very good game.
>
> **—Michael Katz**

Moreover, Sonic traveled through a surreal world designed to show speed. His two-dimensional side-scrolling environment included loops, steep cliffs, and pinball-esqe bumpers from which he could launch at high speeds. Compared to *Sonic The Hedgehog,* even the fastest racing games of the time seemed slow. Players had to make decisions in advance and react quickly to survive each level of the game. When Sega at last unveiled *Sonic The Hedgehog,* the response was one of astonishment. Magazines praised it as one of the greatest games ever made and proof that Genesis could do more than the *Golden Axe* and *Moonwalker* side-scrollers for which it had become known.

People at Nintendo, however, remained unimpressed.

> It was pretty much a typical Nintendo reaction at first. [People said] "Look, they're trying to copy us with *Super Mario Bros.* and it's the same kind of a game. They can't really do anything as good as we do it." Over time, there was this kind of dawning realization that this was . . . not such a bad product. It was the same thing with Genesis, in general.
>
> **—Richard Brudvik-Lindner, former group supervisor and head of Nintendo of America Account Team, Hill and Knowlton**

---

* Sonic's foot tapping was not original. It first appeared in *Major Havoc,* an Atari vector-graphics coin-op game created by Owen Rubin.

Sonic The Hedgehog was released in the United States in 1991. As part of Kalinske's proposed plan, it replaced *Altered Beast* as the game that came bundled with the system. People who had purchased the old package with *Altered Beast* within a few-months grace period were allowed to mail in for a free copy of *Sonic,* in effect giving them an extra game at no charge. The *Sonic* cartridge was also sold separately for those who already owned Genesis.

Sonic was an immediate hit, and many consumers who had been loyally waiting for Super NES to arrive now decided to purchase Genesis. After struggling for more than a year, Sega was suddenly seeing success. The fiercest competition in the history of video games was about to begin.

The Super Family Computer

Japan remained loyal to Nintendo, ignoring both Sega's Mega-Drive and NEC's PC Engine (the Japanese name for TurboGrafx). When Nintendo Co. Ltd. announced that its 16-bit Super Family Computer (Super Famicom) would go on sale in Japan in November 1990, nearly 1.5 million people pre-ordered the console.

The November 21, 1990, Japanese launch of Nintendo's 16-bit Super Famicom was an international media event. Tens of thousands of people lined up in front of department and electronics stores the night before, hoping to pick up the coveted new console. According to some reports, many parents called in sick to work so that they could join the lines of waiting shoppers. All of Tokyo was slowed down by the crowds, and a frenzy began when news spread that Nintendo had shipped only 300,000 consoles. The pushing and shoving were so chaotic that the Japanese government later asked Nintendo and other video game companies to restrict future hardware releases to weekends.

In terms of technology, the Super Famicom, which would be released in the United States as the Super NES, was an improvement over both Genesis and TurboGrafx. Like Genesis, Super NES had a true 16-bit processor rather than the 8-bit/16-bit hybrid in TurboGrafx. Nintendo's Research and Development Team 2, led by Masayuki Uemura, designed the console around visual and audio performance rather than processing speed. It displayed more colors. Genesis had a 512-color palette; Super NES could display 32,000 colors. Along with its central processor, the Motorola 65816 chip, it included a Sony stereo chip and two customized graphics chips that were nicknamed PPU-1

(Picture Processing Unit) and PPU-2. Powered by PPU-1 and PPU-2, Super NES's architecture included seven special modes for handling graphics, the best-known being "Mode 7 Graphics," which enabled designers to set parameters for effects such as scaling and rotating backgrounds. What the Super NES lacked, and what would ultimately become its technological Achilles' heel, was the sheer processing power of Genesis.

Nintendo's strongest selling point, however, was the game that came packed in with the Super NES console—*Super Mario World.* Shigeru Miyamoto, who by now was seen as video gaming's greatest star, created an enormous and sprawling game that expanded the Mario universe. By this time, Miyamoto had started working with teams of designers. He may have created the original *Donkey Kong* with only two people to write code, one person for hardware, and another for music, but the 16-bit *Super Mario World,* also known as *Super Mario Bros. 4,* was a much bigger effort created by what Miyamoto would later remember as a fifteen-person team.

Super Mario World built on earlier *Super Mario Bros.* games. It marked the return of the bright colors that had been a trademark of the original *Super Mario Bros.* (although they were replaced with washed-out colors in the series' second and third installments). This was also the game in which Nintendo introduced Yoshi, a friendly dinosaur who carried Mario on his back. "Too much of a good thing," complained one video game magazine. Others extolled it as the greatest game ever made.

Nintendo set aside $25 million for marketing and prepared to release Super NES in the United States at a retail price of $199 on September 1, 1991.* With Sega having recently dropped the price of Genesis, the $200 cost of Super NES seemed high. As one magazine put it, "Hold on to your wallets, Nintendo fans. *Super Mario Bros. 4* is on the way. But it could be a mixed blessing for all those addicted to the *Mario Bros.* series of home video games—and a cash-register bonanza for the Japanese company that sells them."[5]

As the time grew closer, however, it became clear that the market was shifting. The launch of *Sonic* had revitalized Genesis sales. The ABC sitcom *Roseanne,* starring comedienne Roseanne Barr, ran an episode in which Barr and her working-class husband splurged to purchase a Super NES for their son while

---

* That date was eventually changed to September 9, which would later become the launch date of Sony's PlayStation and Sega's Dreamcast as well.

telling him that they would not be able to afford to buy him such an expensive gift. When he heard this, the boy was nonplussed and exclaimed that he would simply visit a friend who owned a Genesis. There was a real market analogy to the one in the sitcom. Tired of waiting for Super NES to arrive and unhappy about the $200 price tag, many consumers decided to take a chance on Genesis. Unlike the Japanese launch in which Super Famicom had outsold both competitors combined in presales alone, Super NES would debut against an established product.

> By the time Nintendo produced Super NES this fall, Sega already had 150 different 16-bit cartridge games on the market vs. 12 for Nintendo, and its player was retailing for $150, or 25 percent less than Nintendo's. While no one knows who will ultimately win this spirited battle for Christmas sales, the feisty underhog has sold a million Genesis systems this year, vs. 700,000 for Super NES.[6]

In the meantime, NEC, already shut out by Sega, now faced desperate times as it tried to market TurboGrafx against a second competitor. Having already failed at increasing its sales by introducing new technologies—the TurboGrafx-CD and a handheld console called TurboExpress that played games designed for the TurboGrafx game console, as opposed to the scaled-down games played on Game Boy and Lynx, NEC lowered the price of its base system to $99.

> The basic issue was that Genesis had much better-known games. They got Electronic Arts' support and they had *Madden Football* and all that stuff. And they had a lot more marketing dollars. And, you know, marketing dollars count.
>
> **—Ken Wirt, former vice president and general manager,**
> **NEC Technologies**

In a move designed to increase market share, NEC Technologies has lowered the suggested retail price of its TurboGrafx-16 system to $99.99. In addition, the company will offer the new TurboGrafx-16 system SKU, called the "Bonk SuperSet," at a suggested retail price of $149.99 and will lower the suggested retail price of its TurboGrafx-CD player from $399 to $299. NEC's 16-bit TurboExpress portable remains priced at $299.[7]

The Battle Begins

A conventional wisdom in the video game industry is that consumers purchase new hardware when the economy is strong and stick to software when the economy is tight. In 1991, the United States economy was in recession. It didn't matter. Nintendo easily sold its entire first shipment of 1 million Super NES consoles when they went on sale on September 9. Estimates of the exact number of Super NES units sold in the United States over the next three months range from Sega estimates of just over 1 million to an internal Nintendo figure of 2.2 million.[8] According to the NPD Group, a company that tracks sales figures, Sega outsold Nintendo in 1991. According to NPD figures, Sega finished the year with 55 percent of the market, while Nintendo's share was 45 percent. (This figure did not include TurboGrafx, NES, or Master System sales.) And the competition was just heating up.

The All-American Game

> Mr. Yamauchi was subjected to a great deal of scrutiny. . . . a great deal of discrimination. He was really dragged through the mud. And it took him six months to put that deal together.
>
> **—Howard Lincoln**

Toward the end of 1991, U.S. Senator Slade Gorton (Republican, Washington) requested a meeting with Minoru Arakawa and Howard Lincoln. The three met at Nintendo of America headquarters in Redmond, Washington. During the meeting, Gorton asked Lincoln and Arakawa if they were baseball fans. Neither one was. Next he asked them if they knew that the Seattle Mariners, the local pro baseball team, was up for sale.

> I think we'd [only] been to one Mariner game, but that was it. Trip Hawkins (founder of Electronic Arts) had come up and taken us, and we actually had gone to the owner's suite where we met Jeff Smulyan (owner of the Mariners).
> We didn't have any interest in baseball. We probably had some kind of a vague idea that the Mariners had been put in play, that Jeff Smulyan had put

> the team up for sale, and that if they could find a local buyer, they could
> keep it. But there were no local buyers coming.
>
> **—Howard Lincoln**

Gorton finally came to the point, asking them if Nintendo could help keep the Mariners in Seattle by buying the team. If Nintendo did not purchase the franchise, the Mariners would very likely move to Florida, where a group of investors was prepared to buy it. Lincoln's response was less than favorable.

> And I think I said it immediately, "Bull." I mean, would Major League base-
> ball go along with a Japanese investor, a Japanese element?
>   His comment was, "That's going to be a problem, but that can be over-
> come by having minority local ownership."
>
> **—Howard Lincoln**

Lincoln and Arakawa were noncommittal. Lincoln worried about the back-lash among major-league owners. He also worried about how Nintendo Co. Ltd. chairman Hiroshi Yamauchi would react to the bad publicity and protests that might erupt from the news that a Japanese company was purchasing an American baseball team. Arakawa, on the other hand, had lived in Seattle for the last fourteen years and wanted to give back to the city.

> About two weeks later he [Arakawa] came in my office and said, "Oh, re-
> member that meeting we had with Senator Gorton about baseball?" I said,
> "Yes." And he said, "Well, Mr. Yamauchi has decided to buy the team."
>
> **—Howard Lincoln**

Lincoln and Arakawa decided to work through Senator Gorton, who was visiting Russia when Yamauchi decided to purchase the baseball team. By the time he returned, Lincoln and Arakawa were on the Big Island of Hawaii, staying at a large vacation property that Nintendo had purchased. On Christmas day, they called Gorton at home and told him the news. In an effort to stave off trouble, Yamauchi did not purchase the Mariners alone.

He formed a consortium called the "Baseball Club of Seattle" with John Ellis, chairman of Puget Sound Power & Light; John McCaw of McCaw Cellular Communications; Frank Shrontz, CEO of Boeing; and Chris Larson of Microsoft. The consortium met Smulyan's asking price of $100 million for the Mariners, with Yamauchi personally contributing 60 percent and taking the controlling voice.[9] As Lincoln predicted, baseball fans and club owners did not welcome Yamauchi's decision.

> In *Super Mario Land,* one of Nintendo's most popular games, Mario the plumber must travel through four kingdoms, dodging arrow-dropping bees (Bunbuns), defeating bomb-carrying turtles (Nokobons) and jumping over man-eating plants (Pakkuns) so he can rescue Princess Daisy from the evil Tatanga.
>
> In Nintendo's newest game, Hiroshi the billionaire must negotiate his way through a hostile country, avoiding the venomous Jingos and skiing past the antagonistic Moguls so that he can rescue Ken Griffey, Jr., from the clutches of the Tampa Bay Baseball Task Force and save the day for the beleaguered Rain People.[10]

Nintendo's purchase of the Mariners was ill timed. The nation was in the midst of an economic recession that many economists and politicians blamed on Japan. Those opposed to the sale pointed out that Japan did not allow foreign investment in its baseball league, as proof that Yamauchi should not be allowed to buy his way into the major leagues. Baseball commissioner Fay Vincent stated that he doubted the sale would go through, and a national poll showed that 61 percent of Americans preferred to keep Japanese investment out of major league baseball.[11]

Lincoln had anticipated the American backlash to the offer. What he did not expect was a Japanese backlash as well. In Japan, where the economy was strong and the people enjoyed a favorable trade imbalance with the United States, Hiroshi Yamauchi was accused of arrogance and criticized for bringing negative attention to the current prosperity.

> He made the decision, he did it, and then all sorts of flack broke out. There was a backlash in both the United States and Japan. . . . a negative reaction. We

had, I think, anticipated the negative reaction in the United States. I was a little bit surprised that there was a negative reaction to some extent in Japan. That really was because there was a negative reaction in the United States.

—Howard Lincoln

The final sale was approved when three-fourths of team owners in the American League and a simple majority of owners from the National League voted to support it. Since the purchase, Yamauchi has proved to be one of the least vigorous and involved team owners in baseball. In 1999, he would appoint Howard Lincoln chairman of the team, but other than that, he has always left Mariner affairs in the hands of Lincoln and the team's front office.

He [Yamauchi] has never seen a single Mariner game. He's never met John Ellis, our CEO. He's never met any of the other Mariner owners. He's never attended a game. He was going to come if we made it to the World Series, but he's never had to. He's never met a Mariner player. He's never met Ken Griffey, Jr.

—Howard Lincoln

In 1994, Yamauchi did become involved with the Mariners for one brief moment. Early that year, Hiroshi Yamauchi called Arakawa and Lincoln to tell them about a great opportunity for the team—a Japanese pitcher whom he thought might do well in the major leagues.

The crowning blow came one year late when Mr. Yamauchi called and said, "There is this great Japanese pitcher, Nomo. I want the Mariners to get this guy, and I've made arrangements so that the agent will come first to the Mariners with Nomo. I'm not worried about the budget, anything like that. I want the Mariners to sign this guy."

—Howard Lincoln

Arakawa and Lincoln agreed to have Hideo Nomo try out for the team. He flew out to Seattle, but during a physical, the Mariners' team doctor said he had a "bad arm." Lincoln called Yamauchi and told him that they had decided to turn Nomo down. A short time later, the Los Angeles Dodgers signed him, and he finished the season as Rookie of the Year.

> He was a starter in the All-Star game. Both the Mariners and the Dodgers made the playoffs and this is the real tough one. During the playoffs, you've got this team with a Japanese owner. They did not broadcast the Mariners' games in Japan. The Los Angeles Dodgers' games were being broadcast all over Japan. So Mr. Yamauchi was a little bit torqued.
>
> **—Howard Lincoln**

CHAPTER 24

The War

I was tricked into this job!

—Yoshiki Okamoto, producer of research and development, Capcom

Sega of America had this whole Game Institute. Our whole strategy was to hold on and wait for the next game from [Shigeru] Miyamoto.

—Howard Phillips, former "man who plays games for a living" spokesman,
Nintendo of America

Acclaim Breaks Ranks

In 1990, Sega Enterprises CEO Hayao Nakayama called Greg Fischbach, CEO of Acclaim Entertainment, about licensing some of his company's games for use on Genesis. Fully aware that making such an agreement would infringe upon the exclusivity clause in Acclaim's licensing agreement with Nintendo, Fischbach agreed. Acclaim had already risen to the top tier of Nintendo's third-party partners and published several bestselling games. Fischbach welcomed the opportunity to market his products to a new audience and felt it was time to revisit the terms of the licensing agreement. After careful consideration, Fischbach and cochairman Jim Scoroposki attempted to contact Nintendo of America president Minoru Arakawa to discuss their decision. When they were informed that the Nintendo executives were in Germany on business, Fischbach and Scoroposki called him and asked for a meeting. Arakawa suggested that they get together for dinner on Sunday evening, so Fischbach made travel arrangements and had his German office make arrangements at a restaurant about 25 minutes outside of Frankfurt.

Fischbach and Scoroposki arrived in Frankfurt early Sunday afternoon. They went to Arakawa's hotel, where they met him, his wife, and Howard Lincoln. The five of them could not fit into one cab, so Fischbach and Scoroposki went in one cab while the Arakawas and Lincoln followed in a second.

Have you been to Germany? Narrow two-lane roads and fast . . . Everybody drives fast in Germany. And they use Mercedes 300 series sedans as taxicabs—little bright ones, kind of cream color.

We were going to make a left-hand turn into the road that leads to the restaurant, and for whatever the reason, our taxi driver [didn't] see an oncoming car. We got broadsided and ended up in a ditch on the side of the road. Howard, Mr. Arakawa, and his wife watched this happen, and it looked like we were dead. It wasn't a good precursor to the dinner or to the conversation.

Nothing really happened, we got scratched up a little bit. The car was totaled, but we walked away. We got into their car and still went to dinner because we were men on a mission. We had a really enjoyable meal. Mr. Arakawa was really quite nice about it and understood what we were doing and why we were doing it.

—Greg Fischbach

When asked about that meeting, Howard Lincoln later remembered it a little differently. Their stories were fairly similar up until the accident; but after the accident, Lincoln remembered a few additional details.

> We grabbed Jimmy and we grabbed Greg and put them in our cab and took them to this restaurant. Jimmy had glass in his head and these guys were in a state of absolute shock, and the only thing they wanted to do was to have a couple of scotches. They forgot what it was that they had come to tell us: that they were going to do third-party publishing on Sega. They completely forgot what they had come for.
>
> Both Arakawa and I knew what they were getting ready to tell us, but we didn't say anything. The entire night we just sat there and we just got these smiles on our faces, waiting for them, and then we let them go that night. The next day they called and said, "Oh, we remember now why we had come to see you."
>
> **—Howard Lincoln, former Executive Vice President, Nintendo of America**

Rare Becomes Scarce

Acclaim was not the only company to break ranks. Within the next few years, Konami, Tecmo, Taito, and nearly every other one of Nintendo's third-party partners would begin publishing games on Genesis. The two most notable holdouts were Capcom, which licensed a few games to Sega for Genesis rather than publishing them, and Square Soft, which maintained exclusivity with Nintendo throughout the 8- and 16-bit eras.

In 1992, one of Nintendo's most influential development partners—Rare Ltd., the British-based development company founded by Joel Hochberg and the Stamper brothers—completely vanished from the game publishing world. Rare had become a fixture in the Nintendo camp, creating more than fifty NES games that were published by such companies as Acclaim *(Iron Sword)*, Milton Bradley *(Marble Madness)*, and Nintendo itself *(Slalom* and *R.C. ProAm)*.

With the outset of the Super NES, Rare created two games for Tradewest— *Battletoads in Battlemaniacs* and *Battletoads & Double Dragon: The Ultimate Team.* Then, after having kept up a pace of designing ten games per year, Rare went silent.

> We [Joel Hochberg, Tim Stamper, and Chris Stamper] went to a developers' conference at Nintendo of America, and we didn't like what we saw. Too many companies were making 8-bit games for a 16-bit machine.
>
> We had just visited Nintendo, and we went to the Bellevue Red Lion Hotel, and we were talking about company posture and direction. We were busy and we had a lot of opportunity, but there was a situation taking place that I was not comfortable with and I'm sure that they were uncomfortable, and I said, "Let's do something original. Let's pay close attention to what our company's requirements happen to be for moving forward." Those requirements were not taking somebody else's products and porting them over from the NES to the Super NES.
>
> **—Joel Hochberg, cofounder, Rare Ltd.**

> As creative people, we didn't want to be a sort-of conversion house for major third-party developers.
>
> **—Chris Stamper, cofounder, Rare Ltd.**

The last few years had been particularly lucrative ones for Rare, and the company had enough money to experiment. As an artist, Tim Stamper was not satisfied with the idea of making games that looked like everybody else's. Chris, his brother, always the technical wizard, suggested that they could develop a new technology that would change the look of games. Chris Stamper was the engineer who discovered the NES's ability to run split-screen games. If he believed that he could create some new graphics technology for Super NES, there was every reason to believe him. The decision was made, and Rare Ltd. withdrew from actively designing games.

A Street Fighter from Japan

In 1982, Konami hired Yoshiki Okamoto, a young college student studying graphic arts in Osaka, to create posters and character art. The standard Japanese practice was to hire students in March or April, shortly after graduation; but Okamoto was given a part-time job in December with the understanding that he would work full time upon graduating that spring.

Looking back on his time at Konami, Okamoto, who did not particularly enjoy video games before joining Konami, would later decide that his employers never intended to hire a graphic artist and that he was tricked into becoming a game designer. A few months after he started with the company, Okamoto's boss asked him to try his hand at designing a game. It was supposed to be a driving game in which players earned a license by driving through streets filled with hazards and bad drivers. Okamoto did not like the idea. Since joining Konami, he had become fascinated with a Namco game called *Bosconian*, in which players controlled a spaceship as it flew through minefields, battled enemies, and attacked space stations.

Okamoto, a freewheeling individualist with a penchant for speaking his mind and a notoriously short attention span when bored, decided that creating a space game would be more fun than creating a game about earning a driver's license. Without telling his boss, Okamoto began work on a game that built upon *Bosconian* rather than the one his boss had asked him to do. This was a dangerous decision. Okamoto's boss knew him well enough to be suspicious, and the design team had to simultaneously create code for a driving game that they could show whenever executives came to check in on them, at the same time that they made the space combat game.

> Then my boss asked if the driving simulation game was finished and came to check up on me. What I showed him was a totally different game concept, and he really got angry. The driving game was supposed to be a real simulation, but when he came, I showed him *Time Pilot*.
>
> I said, "Why don't we do a location test?" He did the location test and [the game] got really good reviews, so he forgave me. At that point my boss said, "I told you so."
>
> **—Yoshiki Okamoto**

Okamoto designed only two games during his time at Konami, but both games were considered classics. The first, *Time Pilot,* was a space combat game in which players flew a futuristic fighter craft through squadrons from different time periods. It began with waves of World War I-era bi-planes, then went to World War II, and eventually progressed to a futuristic battle against UFOs.

Gyruss, Okamoto's second game, was a *Tempest*-like space combat game in which players control a fighter that circles around the outside of the screen, shooting at enemies as they emerge from the middle. Amazingly, having just created two of Konami's most successful games of the time, Okamoto was fired.

> I asked for a raise and they said they would give me a really small raise. But I wanted a little more, so I threatened to quit. So the next day, when I came to work, they fired me.
>
> So I went to Capcom because it was the only company that would take me. At that time, Capcom was a really small company. I was the second person they hired for R & D.
>
> **—Yoshiki Okamoto**

In 1984, Capcom, which was located in Osaka, was a fledgling company with only two game designers—Yoshiki Okamoto and Tokuro Fujiwara. Both men had seemingly endless talent and energy. A competition formed between them and that competition created enough synergy to make Capcom a leading force in video games.

Okamoto created a couple of little known games after arriving at Capcom, then designed *1942,* a top-scrolling flight game in which players controlled an American fighter flying a World War II mission over the Pacific theater. He then followed up with a similar game called *1943.*

Okamoto's next few games did not do well. As Okamoto struggled to come up with new ideas, Fujiwara created such Capcom classics as *Commando* and *Ghosts 'N Goblins.* Okamoto became worried about his job. He created a "soft porn" version of Mahjongg, a tile game that is popular in Asia, but in the meantime, he needed a special project—something big. The answer came from another Osaka-based game company—Taito. While looking at competitors' games, Okamoto ran across *Double Dragon II: The Revenge* and realized that with some of Capcom's newer technology, he would be able to improve upon this style of the game.

Double Dragon II was a two-dimensional side-scrolling gang-fighting game in which players walked along streets, fighting off muggers of all types. It featured simplistic three-button combat controls, with one button for attacking enemies to the left, one for attacking to the right, and one for jumping. One problem with the game was its antiquated graphics. The combatants looked short and childishly scrawled. Capcom's research and development engineers had recently come up with new and more powerful hardware that could make much more realistic-looking characters and backgrounds. The end product was a game called *Final Fight*.*

With its simpler controls and much more sophisticated graphics, *Final Fight* improved upon the *Double Dragon* formula. Instead of having three buttons and a joystick, Okamoto's game had only "attack" and "jump" buttons. Players could execute several moves as they fought off attackers, but they did not have to master these moves to have fun with the game. The art was the biggest improvement. The characters in *Final Fight* looked cartoonish and moved stiffly, but they had human proportions and detailed faces. One of the enemies was a giant who looked and fought like Andre the Giant, a real-life professional wrestler. Released in 1989, *Final Fight* was one of Capcom's most successful games to date, but it was Okamoto's next game that made him famous.

Okamoto's next project was a sequel to a 1987 game called *Street Fighter*. The original *Street Fighter* was a one-on-one martial-arts fighting game. As Okamoto's team members created their version of what a *Street Fighter* game should be, they decided to include three elements from that game: secret moves that allowed players to throw fireballs, a character named Ken, and a character name Ryu.

> The sales division said that we needed to make another *Street Fighter;* they had been asking for it for a long time. At one of the trade shows, *Final Fight* was shown with the title of *Street Fighter II,* but all the operators said, *"Hey, that's not Street Fighter."*
>
> Originally, I wanted to change all the characters, but some of the players still liked Ryu and Ken.
>
> **—Yoshiki Okamoto**

---

* Okamoto did not design *Final Fight*. By the time he began work on the project, he had already been promoted to producer.

It took ten months to complete *Street Fighter II: The World Warrior.* The game was a major undertaking and several artists worked on each of the fighters. The team created multiple hidden moves for each of the eight main characters in the game. Okamoto personally believed that this game would be just as successful as *Final Fight,* but once the concepts and art were complete and the fate of the game was in the hands of the programmers, he became nervous. Restless by nature, he found it impossible to sit around the office waiting to see the final results, so he often went off to play baseball to distract himself. These were nervous times for Okamoto. He had committed a great deal of time and resources to *Street Fighter II.*

Like *Final Fight* before it, *Street Fighter II* brought marked improvement to an already existing genre. Not only did it have the same kind of clean, ornately detailed, yet somewhat cartoony look that distinguished *Final Fight,* it also had a colorful cast of international brawlers. Along with returning martial artists Ryu and Ken, it featured ten other fighters, including a fire-spitting Hindu mystic, a lumbering Sumo wrestler, and a one-eyed kick boxer. Each character had unique abilities and special moves. Okamoto was well aware of the arcade prestige given to players who master hidden moves and difficult games, and he wanted to use that prestige to his game's advantage.

The game was a major international success. Its combination of brutal action, hidden moves, humorous characters, and bright graphics appealed to players all over the world. Released in 1991, *Street Fighter II* brought much-needed business to the dwindling American arcade industry. This was the first game since the mid-1980s that actually attracted players to arcades. More important, arcade owners bought multiple *Street Fighter II* machines and set them up in rows, the way they used to set up *Pac-Man* machines a decade earlier. Capcom will not release the final numbers, but some outsiders have estimated that more than 60,000 *Street Fighter II* arcade machines were sold worldwide. According to a former Capcom spokesperson, the arcade version of *Street Fighter II* earned more money than the movie *Jurassic Park* made in box office receipts.

Street Fighter II was even more successful as a game cartridge for Super NES. Capcom released it exclusively for the 16-bit Nintendo console and went on to sell more than 2 million copies of the game, making it the first third-party hit for the Super NES. In 1992, as Genesis started to pull away in sales, having the only home version of *Street Fighter II* gave Nintendo a needed edge.

Battle of the 16-Bitters

> Was Genesis ever as advanced a machine as Super NES? Technically, no. I thought we were able to do better software then they were. They both are good machines, but I think the big advantage we had was we initially were able to do better software and it took them a long time to get up to speed on doing as good a [job on their] software.

> **—Tom Kalinske, former president and CEO, Sega of America**

Nintendo sold 3.4 million Super NES consoles in 1991, a long-lasting record for first-year sales of new game hardware. This gave Nintendo a good share of the market. But with a one-year lead and more sales overall in 1991, Genesis continued to have the larger 16-bit install-base in the United States.*

> They [Nintendo] always claim that there was a time after the launch when they pulled ahead of us, but our research said that there wasn't. They had a phenomenal initial launch. If you mean in terms of a month, I'm sure there was a month when they outsold us. You know, I'm sure they outsold us for a few months.

> **—Tom Kalinske**

> The fact is that the home video game market is made up of three categories, and having a good year in one category does not give you the right to claim overall superiority.[1]

> **—Peter Main, vice president of marketing, Nintendo of America**

Going into 1992, Sega had several advantages over Nintendo, including a much lower sales price and a larger library of games. Nintendo was slow in

---

* Genesis never amassed a significant install-base in Japan. Sega Enterprises CEO Hayao Nakayama may have allowed Tom Kalinske to drop the price and change the game that came with the console, but he had no intention of following Kalinske's example. Though Mega-Drive sales would increase briefly with major events such as the release of the new *Sonic The Hedgehog* game, Sega remained a distant third behind NEC and Nintendo throughout the 16-bit generation.

getting games to market, and some of the early Super NES games such as *U.N. Squadron* and *Bill Laimbeer's Combat Basketball* were not particularly fun. There were too many golf games early on, and the anticipated third-party titles, such as Konami's *Contra 3: The Alien Wars,* were slow in coming. Sega had ten games for every game on Super NES, and Sega's internally produced titles were getting better and better. Sega had a long line of arcade hits to draw from and several licensed contracts with Disney, as well as with such sports stars as Joe Montana and David Robinson. Capcom may have released only a Super NES version of *Final Fight,* but one of Sega's internal development teams created *Streets of Rage,* a similar side-scrolling gang-fighting game with bigger levels, tougher enemies, and amazing original music.

Not only were there more games for Genesis, but Sega also continued to produce titles at a faster pace. The market seemed to stop and take note every time Shigeru Miyamoto released a new *Mario* or *Zelda* game, but those games generally arrived at the rate of one per year. Sega released several anticipated games like *Streets of Rage* and *ToeJam & Earl* throughout the year. These games may not have been as widely anticipated as a *Mario* game, but they often had an edgy irreverence about them that helped shape the way people perceived Sega. More important, they gave Genesis owners something to look forward to buying in the near future, while Super NES owners had to wait for the Christmas season.

> Every week we would have an executive review of the games we had in progress. And the meeting would involve anybody who wanted to join. . . . marketing, manufacturing executives would be there, producers, etc. We would review the games in a conference room that was called the Loony Bin. It was kind of funny.
>
> When you watch the television commercials, they're very irreverent, very cutting edge, and this kind of . . . this attitude pervades throughout the entire company. When we had these meetings with Tom Kalinske and all the executive VPs in the room, you could say anything you wanted to. It was very interesting because people were swearing in the meetings and making off-color remarks. But it was all accepted. It was just part of the company culture, people could say anything about the game. They'd say things like, "That thing really sucked." Or, "That character really blows," and the executives were right there, taking it all in and very serious about it.
>
> **—Terry Huang, former public relations manager, Sega of America**

Sega's advertising continued to evolve as well. While Nintendo's advertising seemed stuck in a Mario-esque world of cute images appealing to preteen kids, Sega turned to a noisy underground image. Sega commercials always ended with the "Sega Scream": some character screamed "Sega" into the camera. This new marketing approach, combined with an emphasis on sports games, *Sonic The Hedgehog,* and new lines of edgy games, changed some basic market demographics. Sega was becoming cool to high-school students, and the cooler Sega became, the less people were ready to admit that they liked Nintendo. When a Sony marketing team ran focus groups, they found that teenage boys who owned a Super NES console would not admit it.

> I saw that our primary audience was over eighteen years of age. Nintendo tended to focus on younger kids. We attempted to focus on an older crowd. Forty percent of our business is over eighteen years old. Teenage and college-age kids have adopted the Sega Scream. I was backstage at a rap concert, and I watched rappers who did not know who I was meet each other with the Sega Scream.
>
> **—Tom Kalinske**

As the year progressed, Nintendo sought to eliminate one of Sega's advantages by lowering the price of the Super NES console from $179 to $149. Nintendo of America vice president of marketing, Peter Main, would later comment that he wished they had gone with a $149 price tag from the start. "I could have sold an extra million," said Main. Sega responded to the Nintendo price drop by reducing the price of Genesis to $129.

According to the TRST data, sales information recorded by the industry-tracking NPD Group, Nintendo sold 5.6 million Super NES consoles in 1992, edging out Sega by 10 percent. Sega still had a larger install base and sold more software, but the momentum seemed to be moving in Nintendo's direction.

As Nintendo and Sega squared off for top honors in the 16-bit arena, NEC officially pulled out of the market, turning the sales of TurboGrafx over to a newly created company called Turbo Technologies Inc. that it formed with Hudson Soft. The writing was on the wall for TurboGrafx and had been since before the release of Super NES. The system had developed a cult following but it would never have a genuine hit game in the United States. Even *Bonk,* its mascot game, was almost unknown to the general consumer. (By comparison, a 1993 study showed that more American kids recognized Mario and Sonic than Mickey Mouse.) Turbo Technologies continued marketing various versions of the TurboGrafx into 1994, then closed shop as Atari and 3DO entered the market.*

The ROM Race

In what may have been the oddest race in video game history, Sega and Nintendo began developing devices for a new storage format called CD-ROM and raced to deliver CD-ROM peripherals to retail. In truth, CD-ROM was anything but new. Computer companies had been using them as a method of mass storage for years prior to Nintendo and Sega making their discoveries, and NEC beat them by two years with TurboGrafx-CD. Sega announced plans for the Mega-CD, the Japanese version of the CD-ROM, drive in early 1991. The plan was to release the unit in Japan by late 1991, then in United States the following year.

Around Sega of America, the general reaction to the Mega-CD announcement was euphoric. The drive was seen as a way of turning the technological tables in Sega's favor and driving yet another nail into Nintendo's coffin. Sega of Japan and its partner on the project, Sony, handled all of the design work, shutting out Sega of America executives until the project was completed. As late as mid-1991, Japanese executives continued to keep the unit hidden from Sega of America, finally sending a crippled "dummy" drive to the U.S. that summer to show them what it looked like.

> When you work at a multinational company, there are things that go well and there are things that don't. They didn't want to send us working Sega CD units.** They wanted to send us dummies and not send us the working CD units until the last minute because they were concerned about what we would do with it and if it would leak out. It was very frustrating.

---

* It should be noted that NEC was not the only straggler in the market at that time. SNK, a leading arcade company, released a 24-bit console called NeoGeo in 1990. NeoGeo was a name familiar to arcade goers, as SNK's coin-operated NeoGeo was popular with arcade owners.

NeoGeo was expensive. The base unit, which came with only a controller, sold for $399—$200 more than the Super NES. The full set, which included a game and two controllers, sold for $599, and additional cartridges (which had the exact same code as the arcade game) routinely sold for $200.

** Sega CD was the name of the American version of Mega-CD.

> Somehow they had sent some ROMs, or we had procured ROMs somehow, and we had a dummy unit that was missing its ROM. I always liked to work late at night, and so did Shinobu Toyoda,* so it was like one in the morning and he came to me with this chip and with the Sega CD and the ROMs and said, "Can you actually make this work?"
>
> I thought, "Yeah, I probably could." So, I put the chip in. There were a couple of other things that were unhooked, but we fixed it and plugged it in. So Shinobu and I were the first people in the U.S. to see the Sega CD boot up. Our take on it was one of wonder from the product development side, but as soon as we started to program for it, I think . . . I think the wonder went away quickly.
>
> It was literally a mass storage extension of the Genesis. It wasn't a new system, and that was always the confusion internally. The internal people believed it to be a completely new system with new abilities. It did have small expansion abilities, but they were not significant.
>
> **—Michael Latham, former executive producer, Sega of America**

Although Mega-CD, which would arrive in the United States in 1992 as Sega CD, had a more powerful processor and handled more colors than the Genesis processor, the single-spin CD-ROM drive was meant only to expand the size of games. Genesis and Super NES cartridges generally ranged in size from 8 to 16 megabits, but a single CD-ROM could hold 640 megabytes—320 times more data. With over 600 megabytes of storage, Sega CD could play games with digitized video. Before the company could launch the new medium, however, Sega would need games to support it. As luck would have it, several suitable games already existed.

The Nintendo Play Station

Nintendo also announced plans to manufacture a CD-ROM drive. Like Sega, Nintendo turned to Sony Corporation as a partner. At the Winter Consumer Electronics Show in January 1992, Nintendo claimed that it could manufacture and distribute the drive within the year. The problem was that Sony was proving to be a very dangerous partner. Sony executives had already

---

* Shinobu Toyoda was the vice president of licensing at Sega of America and the executive who worked most closely with Japan.

revealed plans to release their own CD-based video game system called the Play Station, and Nintendo executives wondered about the wisdom in giving them access to Nintendo's system by having Sony make a Super NES–compatible CD drive.

After reconsidering the situation, Nintendo executives allowed Sony to announce plans for the drive at the Consumer Electronics Show, then appeared the next day to say that they had struck up a deal with Philips N.V., the Dutch conglomerate, instead. Sony executives were shut out and humiliated. Ken Kutaragi, the young engineer whom Sony had placed at the head of the Nintendo project, went to Sony CEO Norio Ohga to plead for permission to keep the Play Station project alive, stating that the system could be built into a stand-alone unit. He proposed looking ahead to the next generation of game hardware and creating something that would immediately render Super NES obsolete.

Having just been humiliated by Nintendo, Ohga accepted Kutaragi's suggestion and brought it to the company board. The general reaction was unfavorable. Nintendo clearly had too much control over the market, and attempting to break in would be too risky. An internal battle ensued, with Ohga almost alone in his support of the venture. In the end, he decided to gamble on Kutaragi and approved the project.

As Kutaragi quietly started work on his project, Nintendo executives began looking for suitable games. One of the first projects to catch their eye was *The 7th Guest,* a breakthrough puzzle game that was being developed by a Medford, Oregon, company called Trilobyte.

> We got a call one day from a guy working with Don James's group at Nintendo. They were trying to find games that would be appropriate for their CD-ROM drive that was eventually going to happen, and he gave me a call and said, "Do you have any CD-ROM titles that you're working on that we should have a look at?"
>
> I said, "Oh, wow, I've got something that you've got to see. It's called *The 7th Guest.*" So he flew down probably about a week and a half later and was given the tour of the company and shown the product. He said that he was very excited. Within a couple of days later, his boss Don James came down and took a look, and from there, they started negotiating a deal to purchase

the rights to *The 7th Guest* for the Nintendo CD-ROM player. A deal was eventually struck, and Nintendo got all CD-ROM game console rights to the product and Virgin (the game's publisher) was paid, I believe, $1 million up front.

**—Seth Mendelsohn, former senior game designer,
Virgin Interactive Entertainment**

Nintendo never released its CD-ROM drive. Nintendo first announced delays and then claimed that the unit would be ready by August 1993. Behind the scenes, Nintendo was slowly closing down the project. By 1995, Nintendo would be the only major video game company that did not have a CD-based game system.

The Birth of Digital Pictures

With the collapse of the Nemo project, which he had begun in conjunction with Hasbro, Tom Zito had placed his live-action video games, along with office equipment and other supplies, in a Rhode Island warehouse and largely forgotten about them. What he did not know was that Sega and Nintendo had a new medium with enough storage space to handle his games and that a desperate search for games with digital video was underway.

Ken Melville was working at this company and happened to have a prototype copy of *Sewer Shark* in its original version on videotape. So he calls me up and says, "The weirdest thing happened today. Mickey Schulhof and Peter Guber were in here the other day. They saw *Sewer Shark*; they were blown away by it. I think they're trying to buy this company because they believe that this company owns *Sewer Shark* and has technology to do products like *Sewer Shark*."

Now Guber was the head of Columbia Pictures, which was owned by Sony, and Schulhof was the chairman of Sony U.S.A. It just so happened that my younger brother, Bob Zito, was Mickey Schulhof's PR guy.

I called my brother on the phone and told him the story and he said, "That doesn't sound at all possible."

"I really can't believe that's true." He said, "I'm gonna be with Mickey two weeks from now. If the opportunity comes up, I'll ask him. I'll get back to you."

About two hours later, my phone rang and it was my brother. He said, "Is this thing set in sewers?" I said, "Yeah," and he said, "You shoot at rats and bats?"

> I said, "Yes."
>
> He said, "And you own rights to this?"
>
> I said, "Yeah."
>
> He said, "I think you better take a red-eye to New York."

—Tom Zito, founder, Digital Pictures

As Nemo collapsed, Zito had purchased the rights to the video-based games that he had helped create for it, thinking they might some day be useable. With clear rights of ownership in hand, he met with Schulhof, who signed him up to create games for the Nintendo Play Station. Zito then formed a company called Digital Pictures. He spent the next year reworking two of the games that had been created for Nemo—*Night Trap* and *Sewer Shark*—so that they would run on the ill-fated Play Station. When the Sony/Nintendo partnership failed, Zito turned to Sega.

> So then, in the meantime, Sony had gone off and started off with a Play Station of its own. And we started doing all this stuff for Sega CD; and the rest, as they say, is history. And meanwhile, I met Shinobu Toyoda at Sega and was aware that Sega was coming out with a CD system. When Sony went away, we sort of changed the focus of our development afterwards and started doing stuff for Sega CD rather than for Sony.
>
> The incredible irony of it was that the video we plugged into the Super Nintendo was just terrific because Super NES could display 256 colors at once. Sega CD could only put up 32 colors at a time, so you had this horrible grainy look to the images.

—Tom Zito

Sega CD was released in the United States on October 15, 1992; it retailed for $299 and Zito's game, *Sewer Shark,* came packed in the box. Digital Pictures became one of Sega's most important partners, creating several original games for Sega CD.

Tom Zito, CEO of tiny Digital Pictures, is one of the first to take advantage of the technology. Zito, who used to write for the *New Yorker* and *Rolling Stone,* spends some $2 million filming real actors for his CD-based interactive games. Corey Haim *(The Lost Boys)* and Debbie Harry (*Hairspray*) are among the performers who have starred in his miniproductions. His most interesting title this Christmas is *Prize Fighter,* directed by Ron Stein, who choreographed some boxing sequences in the 1980 Martin Scorsese classic *Raging Bull.* Besides trying to knock out a series of actors portraying boxers, you, the game player, become part of a story. In this case, a crippled boy on the sidelines cheers for you.[2]

PCs Get Game

Sega and Nintendo found themselves facing a new and increasingly more dangerous opponent in the early 1990s—PC computers. Just as the Commodore computer had caught up to Atari and Coleco a decade earlier, personal computers threatened to eclipse the new generation of video game manufacturers as the era of multimedia began.

The evolution to multimedia began as sound became more common on computers. Companies such as Roland and Turtle Beach had long offered sound cards that could handle audio files, and even most of the early PCs came with cheap speakers built in. But few people owned early sound cards and the sound that streamed through PC speakers was tinny at best.

In 1989, a company called Creative Labs, founded by a Singaporean entrepreneur named Sim Wong Hoo, introduced a reasonably priced PC sound card called Sound Blaster. The card, which featured an 11-voice FM synthesizer, input/output jacks, and a MIDI/joystick port, became the top-selling add-on card in the PC market. Sound Blaster was not the first sound card; it was not even Creative Labs' first sound card, but it was the first sound card to see this kind of success, and Sound Blaster compatibility became a standard throughout the industry.* Soon companies such as MediaVision and Gravis released their own Sound Blaster–compatible cards.

---

* In truth, Macintosh computers were much more suited for gaming than PCs. Macintosh monitors had slightly higher resolution than standard PC monitors and Apple computers did not have all of the compatibility problems that still haunt PCs.

Unfortunately, former Apple president Michael Spindler did not want people to see Macintosh as a gaming computer and did nothing to encourage companies to make games for them.

With the advent of Sound Blaster, PC game companies became very aggressive about adding audio to their games. Origin Systems, a company with a well-earned reputation for making technically superior games that would only run on the latest and most powerful personal computers, published a game called *Wing Commander* that began with a virtual conductor directing a symphony.

The next big move toward multimedia came in the form of CD-ROM drives. Soon companies such as Viacom New Media, Hyperbole Studios, and ICOM were flooding the market with "interactive movies" that featured bad scripts, amateurish acting, and minimal interactivity. Sanctuary Woods, a software publisher that would eventually produce a few impressive products before going bankrupt, released a series of interactive comics called *Victor Vector and Yondo.* CD-ROMs had provided the entertainment industry with a new frontier, and a wave of entrepreneurs rushed to take advantage of it.

Of the droves of games that flooded the market during the first years of multimedia, three stood out as the kind of "killer applications" needed to launch new technologies. The first was *Myst,* a game that was funded by a Japanese video game publisher called Sunsoft.

Myst was the creation of Rand and Robyn Miller; brothers who had moved to Spokane, Washington, to start up a game development company called Cyan Studios. They had sold a handful of games prior to coming up with an idea for a surrealistic adventure with elaborate puzzles. They needed funding, however. One of the first companies they approached was Activision; but they were turned down. Then they ran into Sunsoft.

> We hooked up with Sun, which is a Japanese company, in 1991. They said, "We want a big epic CD-ROM product," and we said, "We're ready. We'll tell you what we need."
>
> They funded it well. It ended up that they funded half of the project. It cost more than what we thought; but at the time, we had a relationship with Broderbund as well. When we showed *Myst* to Broderbund, they just fell in love with it.
>
> **—Rand Miller, cofounder, Cyan Studios**

As a video game company, Sun Soft cared little about PC rights. The way the final contract was laid out, Sun Soft gave the Millers $350,000 in exchange for the console rights and went on to release *Myst* on 3DO, Jaguar CD, PlayStation, and Saturn. None of those versions sold particularly well, but Sun Soft's investment still paid for itself in less than one month. Working with Broderbund, the Millers released their game for Macintosh and it became a runaway hit. In 1994, Broderbund released a PC version. It became a hit, too. *Myst* went on to become the first CD-ROM game to sell over one million units. It remained on the computer game's bestsellers list for three years. Broderbund eventually sold four million copies of the game.

While *Myst* started out on Macintosh, then migrated to PC, the next multimedia blockbuster went in the opposite direction. *The 7th Guest,* the Virgin game that was licensed by Nintendo, brought a similar mixture of puzzle-solving and exploration to PCs. As a showcase for technology, *The 7th Guest* was a masterpiece. It featured a photo-realistically rendered virtual haunted house with live-action video of actors portraying ghosts. With far less puzzles than *Myst* and not nearly as visually appealing, *The 7th Guest* did not enjoy the same long-lasting success, and critics would later pan it. "A lot of people bought it, and a lot of people bought hardware just so they could play it," game designer Graeme Devine would later say in defense of his game.

The third game, and the one that has had the most long-lasting impact on the gaming world, was *Doom,* a first-person perspective game in which players stepped into the head of a marine who shoots everything he sees, as he works his way toward a confrontation in the depths of Hell.

Doom was a true team effort, created by a group of young computer enthusiasts who had started a company called id Software. Formed on February 1, 1991, id consisted of John Romero, the well-known creator of dozens of computer games and a legend among hardcore gamers; John Carmack, a somewhat otherworldly but brilliant programmer with a nearly unequaled ability to create incredibly complex graphics engines; Adrian Carmack, a talented artist with a gift for bringing gore and horror to life; and Tom Hall, the main designer of *Commander Keen,* id's first product and a game that helped establish the company's reputation.

Romero first came across the idea of 3D games when he called an old friend at Looking Glass, a company that was designing a game called *Ultima Underworld.* Intrigued by the concept, he brought it up with John Carmack to see if it would be possible for them to create a similar game.

> John talked with some of the Looking Glass people and they were saying
> that they were doing a texture-mapped game. I said I could do that, and
> the next month—we were doing games every month—I did *Catacombs 3D*,
> which was our first 3D game. It was about running around in dungeons
> with trolls and stuff.
>
> **—John Carmack, cofounder, id Software**

In 1992, id released its first hit game, *Wolfenstein 3D.* The game took its
name from an Apple II game created by a man named Silas Warner. Players viewed *Wolfenstein 3D* through the eyes of a commando shooting his
way through a labyrinth filled with Nazi soldiers, SS men, vicious dogs,
and eventually, Adolf Hitler. Although it was an exciting game with great
graphics, part of *Wolfenstein*'s popularity sprang from its shock value. In
previous games, when players shot enemies, the injured targets fell and
disappeared. In *Wolfenstein 3D,* enemies fell and bled on the floor.

> With *Wolfenstein,* the shock was only half of the attraction. The main draw
> was the super-fast 3D rendering engine and movement. Most of the raves
> came from the pure adrenaline rush of speeding at 70 frames per second
> through corridors and mowing down Nazis.
>
> **—John Romero, cofounder, id Software**

id games were distributed via a unique method called "shareware." The
idea was that consumers could download the first section of the game for free
from the Internet or order it by mail. If they liked the game, they could purchase the rest of it by contacting the publisher. Shareware offered small
companies the chance to market their games and computer tools without
having to compete with larger, more powerful companies for retail shelf-space.
In the case of *Wolfenstein 3D,* the game was broken into three separate missions,
the first of which was available as shareware. id and Apogee, the firm that
marketed id's early games, maximized profits by creating several *Wolfenstein*
games at once—the basic three missions, *The Nocturnal Missions,* and the *Spear of
Destiny* missions, which were sold as a retail product.

> *Wolfenstein 3D* was a trilogy; it had three episodes. That's sort of a shareware thing. Then we did *Spear of Destiny,* which is a retail version of *Wolfenstein.* It was a completely new adventure but with the *Wolfenstein* engine.
>
> **—John Romero**

id's next hit, and the first game published under the id label, was *Doom.* It took John Carmack six months to create the graphics engine, with Tom Hall leading the game and map designs. Partway through the project, however, Hall left and John Romero took over, programming *DoomEd*—the game's map editor, while at the same time doing programming and map design. When the project was complete, everyone in the company knew they had a sure-fire hit. Not only did *Doom* have more gore than *Wolfenstein 3D,* it was decorated with Satanic symbols and populated with demons, images that thrilled gamers but infuriated critics of the gaming industry. Since it was originally released as shareware, however, the critics did not notice it until a few months after its release. In the meantime, *Doom* created a phenomenon unlike any PC game before or after it.

> We put out a press release in January of 1993 saying what our next game (*Doom*) was going to have in it. From January to December, all of 1993, the entire Internet thing was really growing and we had newsgroups about *Doom* already. . . . before the game was out.
>
> So we'd leak out a little bit more information. There would be an alpha that would leak or a beta that would leak, and people just started going nuts. So when the game was released, it crashed the University of Wisconsin's computers two times because there were so many people hitting it for *Doom.* . . . We just knew that when the game came out [in stores], that this was it. This thing was great.
>
> **—John Romero**

Doom set a precedent for computer games. It established the 3D first-person shooter genre, a popular style of gaming that would top the bestseller lists for years. Though it was not the first first-person shooter, it set the standard by which such games as *Duke Nukem 3D, Jedi Knight, Unreal,* and *Descent* would be judged. *Doom* also brought attention to shareware, validating it as a viable means of software delivery and establishing the idea of free demonstration copies as a marketing method.

Doom also demonstrated the entertainment power of multiplayer games. One of the game's better options was "death match," a mode in which players could hunt each other in teams instead of going after demons and monsters. *Doom* would become a lightning rod in later years. It would become a focal point for those who wanted to regulate or end the perceived stranglehold that the largest companies held over the entire interactive entertainment industry. Even as id completed its game, powerful forces were gathering in Washington, D.C. The gaming industry was about to come under an attack that would be felt from Redwood City, California, to Redmond, Washington.

CHAPTER 25

Moral Kombat

I have been a parent for 16 years, a wife for 20, a teacher in Royal Oak, Michigan, for 23, and a woman since the day I was born. Let me tell you, in all of my labels and all of the hats I wear, I find that so extremely offensive, and the only words you can say to the manufacturers and shareholders of the company is, "shame on you."[1]

—Marilyn Droz, Congressional testimony, expert witness, 1993 Joint Hearings

Roses are red, Violets are blue, So you had a bad day, Boo hoo hoo.

**—Public letter to Tom Kalinske, Howard Lincoln, former chairman,
Nintendo of America**

A Van Damme Big Game

Ed Boon worked on six pinball games at Williams before moving into coin-operated video games. The first two video games he worked on were arcade-style football simulations—*High Impact* and *Super High Impact.* John Tobias began his time at Williams working with Mark Turmell, creator of *Smash TV, NBA Jam, Wrestlemania: The Arcade Game,* and *NFL Blitz* and almost unquestionably America's last significant arcade game designer. Tobias worked on Turmell's team as he created *Smash TV* and *Total Carnage*—games that revived the same basic double-joystick gameplay that Eugene Jarvis originally created for *Robotron 2084.* Having just finished recent projects, both men were available in 1990 when the call went around Williams for a fighting game to compete with *Street Fighter II.* Boon and Tobias teamed up to do it.

To make their game stand out from the flood of *Street Fighter II* imitators, Boon and Tobias decided that they would use digitized graphics rather than traditional animation. Having already manufactured *Narc* and *Terminator 2,* Williams had the technology to create the game, and Atari had already proved that such a game could be made, with *Pit Fighter.* In designing their game, Boon and Tobias wanted to make their combatants as large as possible, while still being small enough to move around the screen freely. They also wanted to attach their game to a known personality, someone who fit the image of the kind of fighting they would show in their game. Martial-arts movies were enjoying a resurgence of popularity at the time, and Boon and Tobias believed that attaching their game to either Aikido master Steven Segal or European star Jean Claude Van Damme would attract players. This, however, proved unlikely. Segal, who had made quite a stir with *Above the Law* and *Hard to Kill,* had already agreed to appear in another game. When they contacted Van Damme's agent, he told them that his client, the self-professed "Fred Astaire of Karate" who had recently starred in such movies as *Kickboxer* and *Bloodsport,* was in discussion with Sega.

Rather than look for an older or lesser-known martial artist, Boon and Tobias decided to create an entire universe of their own. They created an elaborate mythology with complex characters fighting each other for the chance to represent Earth in a battle against an evil monster in a cosmic tournament that would decide the fate of humanity. The entrants in this tournament were as colorful as the tournament itself. There was Liu Kang, the strong and silent

Bruce Lee–type; Raiden, the god of thunder; two mystic ninjas—Scorpion and Sub-Zero; a female special forces agent named Sonya Blade; a gangster with a metal plate covering part of his face, named Kano; and a movie star named Johnny Cage.

> Johnny Cage was just kind of a play on the whole Van Damme thing. I mean, when Van Damme didn't pan out, we kind of still had this role that was slowly being created, and we just thought, well . . .
>
> **—Ed Boon, game designer, Williams/Bally/Midway**

If one lesson from *Street Fighter II* was not lost on Boon and Tobias, it was the importance of hidden moves. In the ten short months it took to create the game, they fashioned layer upon layer of special moves and hidden secrets. By the time their game appeared in arcades, it contained special characters, moves, and ways of ending the fights.

> Reptile was a last minute idea. Someone came up with the idea of doing a green [ninja] as opposed to the red (Scorpion) and blue (Sub-Zero), and having him be this hidden feature that is seen very rarely. We knew that the rumors were running kind of rampant about the game and as a last ditch effort we just threw Reptile in, saying, "Let's make this come out very rarely so only a few people will see it." We hoped that the people who saw it would talk about it with a lot of conviction; but since no one else would have seen it, everybody would kind of call them liars. You wouldn't know if somebody was telling the truth or not if you said, "There's a guy, a green ninja, and you fight him at the bottom of the pit."
>
> The things that had to happen to make Reptile come out were so rare. . . . You had to have flawless victories as you defeated opponents, do a fatality, and something had to fly in front of the moon. It was a very rare occurrence that all three things happened, but they happened.
>
> **—Ed Boon**

Boone and Tobias named their game *Mortal Kombat*. The name probably referred to the background story about mortals entering a fighting tournament against beings from another dimension; but critics would later say that it came from the game's "fatality" moves. Each match in *Mortal Kombat* was for the best of three falls. When a combatant was defeated the second time, he or she would stand in a swaying stupor for a few seconds, allowing the victor to finish the match with special signature moves called "fatalities."

> Other fighting games had this thing where you would get dizzy, and the other guy would get a free hit on you, and you had to accept the fact that you were going to get hit. We hated the idea of being the guy who's dizzy, but it was great to be the guy who was walking up to go beat the crap out of him, so we moved that to the end of the fight where damage was already done. We had this dizzy animation, and then at one point somebody suggested, "Let's make it gruesome." And everything just kind of built on that. It became a huge part of the game. We didn't know that was going to be such a big attraction. It just happened.
>
> **—Ed Boon**

Fatalities ranged from Kano wrenching his opponents' hearts out of their chests to Scorpion pulling out their spines and skulls. These were not the kind of graphic cinematic sequences you might see in a movie—they were fast with a splash of animated blood and no kinds of incisions. Knowing how to perform *Mortal Kombat*'s fatalities became a sign of prestige around arcades because they were not easily executed. Once you won the fight, you had to get within range of your opponent and then know special combinations of joystick moves and buttons to punch. When the game first came out, some arcade goers would stand around watching other people, in the hope of catching a glimpse of one of the fatalities.

> At the time, we thought these button and joystick combinations were going to be so hard to do that nobody would ever figure them out. I think the first time we put *Mortal Kombat* out at a test location, in that first weekend somebody found it.
>
> **—John Tobias, former game designer, Williams/Bally/Midway**

The fighting game craze had already revived the arcade business when Williams began shipping *Mortal Kombat.* The game was an instant hit, easily eclipsing *Street Fighter II* in overall popularity with American audiences.

At the time that *Mortal Kombat* was released, Acclaim Entertainment had a contract for the exclusive rights to the home-console versions of Williams arcade games. The partnership would prove very profitable for both companies. Under cofounder Greg Fischbach's leadership, Acclaim had set up the biggest and best sales networks of any of Nintendo's third parties.

Acclaim put great quantities of effort and money into the *Mortal Kombat* license, creating a $10 million marketing campaign and stocking nearly $40 million worth of inventory. Acclaim's designers created authentic versions of *Mortal Kombat,* complete with all of the special moves, for both Genesis and Super NES.[*] Super NES, with its multiple processors, was particularly well suited for *Mortal Kombat,* and the game looked and moved very much like the arcade game. It was not, however, tailor-made for Nintendo's entertainment standards.

> I guess it was June 1993 that Nintendo of America was confronted with *Mortal Kombat* as a home video game that Acclaim was doing. We had game standards that we were enforcing all along. We made a list of what you can and can't do: "No excessive blood and violence and what not." "No sex." Applying those standards to *Mortal Kombat,* we told Acclaim [designers] that they would have to tone down their version of *Mortal Kombat,* which, I believe, was going to come out in September of 1993.
>
> We spent a whole summer screwing around, trying to decide how to handle that issue. Ultimately, we decided that the death moves or finishing moves would have to come out.
>
> Acclaim kept coming back and saying, "Look, we're going to make the Sega version, and it's going be right in line with the coin-op game. Having a toned-down version for Nintendo . . . Do you guys really want us to do that? Does that really make sense?"
>
> **—Howard Lincoln, former executive vice president, Nintendo of America**

---

[*] Acclaim also released Game Gear and Game Boy versions of *Mortal Kombat.* Amazingly, Acclaim sold 1 million copies of the Game Boy cartridge.

The home version of *Mortal Kombat* was released in September 1993, and the sales went through the roof. Over the life of the product, Acclaim sold approximately 6.5 million *Mortal Kombat* cartridges. The Genesis version, which included the original arcade fatality moves, outsold the edited-down Super NES version by nearly three-to-one, propelling Genesis hardware sales to new levels. Not only did the decision to remove the violence hurt sales, it also offended many Super NES owners. According to Howard Lincoln, Nintendo received thousands of angry letters, including a few letters from parents, warning Nintendo not to censor their children's games.

> Nintendo made a terrible blunder from a marketing standpoint in putting out a sanitized version of *Mortal Kombat*. Sega kicked their butt on that; probably sold 4 times as many units of *MKI* bloody than Nintendo did *MKI* sanitized.
>
> **—Tom Zito, founder, Digital Pictures**

Judgment Day

> I remember saying to Fischbach and to Rob Holmes [also of Acclaim], "I can guarantee you with *Night Trap* and now *Mortal Kombat,* we're all going to end up in front of Congress."
>
> **—Howard Lincoln**

> I think that all of this stuff that happened with the Senate was really orchestrated by Nintendo.
>
> **—Tom Zito**

A great deal of debate surrounds the events that led up to the 1993 joint hearings that investigated the marketing of video game violence to minors. People at Sega and Digital Pictures claimed that Nintendo encouraged the hearings to stop Sega's runaway sales. Some people claim that Nintendo director of communications Perrin Kaplan initiated the debates over game violence when she delivered a speech to National Organization of Women in the fall of 1993.

Others claim that Nintendo representatives went to Washington, D.C., and showed several people in Congress tapes of violent games, in the hope of stirring up trouble for Sega.

> I think Nintendo had taken such a trouncing that they decided to sort of go for broke and attack Sega. And they made these tapes up that showed *Night Trap* and showed *Mortal Kombat* on Genesis versus Nintendo. They hired a lobbying firm, and the lobbying firm basically started going around banging on doors to see if they could find a congressman who would be interested in taking this up as a cause. And I think that Nintendo was hoping that the public would be so outraged at what Sega was doing versus what Nintendo was doing that there would be pickets in front of every Toys "R" Us store, saying, "Don't buy Sega products."
>
> **—Tom Zito**

The official account of the events that led up to the hearings is that U.S. Senator Joseph Lieberman (Democrat of Connecticut) became concerned about video game violence when Bill Andresen, his chief of staff, told him about a hot new game named *Mortal Kombat*. Andresen's nine-year-old son wanted a copy of the game, but Andresen, having heard that it was "incredibly violent," did not want to purchase it for him. Out of curiosity, Lieberman suggested that they get a copy and see what it was about.

> I was startled. It was very violent and, as you know, rewarded violence. And at the end, if you really did well, you'd get to decide whether to decapitate . . . how to kill the other guy, how to pull his head off. And there was all sorts of blood flying around.
>
> Then we started to look into it, and I forget how I heard about *Night Trap*. And I looked at that game, too, and there was a classic. It ends with this attack scene on this woman in lingerie, in her bathroom. I know that the creator of the game said it was all meant to be a satire of Dracula; but nonetheless, I thought it sent out the wrong message.
>
> **—Joseph Lieberman, Democrat of Connecticut, United States Senate**

Once he saw *Mortal Kombat* and *Night Trap*, Senator Lieberman became concerned about the peddling of what he considered the equivalent of R-rated materials to children. He did some reading and found surveys that showed pre-Genesis demographics, with the average player being a seven- to twelve-year-old male. It should be noted that the 16-bit generation was only a few years old, and Sega was only beginning to gather data that showed the shift Genesis had brought to the market. It should also be noted that although only 10 percent of the games on the home market were violent, *Street Fighter II* and *Mortal Kombat* were huge sellers and fighting games seemed to dominate the market.

Having come to the conclusion that video game publishers were marketing violence to children, Senator Lieberman decided to see what his constituents thought. He asked parents in his home state of Connecticut about the games. Their answers gave him cause for further concern.

> I started to talk to people in Connecticut about it. Part of what I was hearing back from parents was that they didn't know what was in the game. Either there was a generational gap, which meant that they really didn't know how to use the machines, or they just didn't take the time. In a lot of these games, as you probably know, you have to spend a little time playing until you get to the so-called good parts.
>
> **—Senator Joseph Lieberman**

As to allegations that Howard Lincoln approached him, Senator Lieberman always insisted that Nintendo did not contact him to initiate the inquiry into the video gaming world. But he also remembers meeting with Howard Lincoln once the plans for the hearing were in place.

> He certainly didn't initiate the process; in other words, we went to him. We went to the industry. I had not heard about Howard Lincoln before we planned the whole thing. In fact, to be very honest about it, and there's nothing wrong with it, once the hearings were announced, I saw Slade Gorton [U.S. senator from Washington] on the floor of the Senate one day on a vote and he said, "I just got a call from the folks from Nintendo, which is real important in Seattle."
>
> I later learned that they had played this enormous and incredibly sort of civic role in helping Seattle to keep the baseball team there. So anyway,

> Slade was all tied in with them and he said, "There's a guy named Howard Lincoln who you've called to testify. Do you mind speaking to him or having your staff speak to him?"

—Senator Joseph Lieberman

As Senator Lieberman proceeded to arrange a hearing on the marketing of video games, Nintendo, Sega, and other companies found themselves in an untenable situation. They did not have their own lobbying organization. Many belonged to the Software Publishers Association, the same trade organization that represented Microsoft and WordPerfect. Their relationship with SPA, however, was shaky. Interactive entertainment companies, especially video game manufacturers such as Sega, Nintendo, and Electronic Arts, had long felt like the black sheep of the SPA community. The bulk of SPA's membership was made up of "serious" software companies that did not consider video game manufacturers legitimate members of the computer industry, and the top executives at the game companies did not expect to receive sufficient support during the hearings.

Senator Herb Kohl (Democrat of Wisconsin), chairman of the Subcommittee on Juvenile Justice, and Senator Lieberman, chairman of the Subcommittee on Regulation and Government Information, presided over the hearings that officially began on December 9, 1993. The proceedings started off on a strange note. One week before the hearings, Bob Keeshan, a.k.a. Captain Kangaroo, held a press conference in which he stated that "It would be hoped that software manufacturers would understand their role in a nurturing society and exercise that accompanying responsibility to commercial-free speech."[2] Keeshan did not participate in the hearings but submitted a prepared statement that was aimed at both the legislators on the panel and parents, reminding them of the responsibility to nurture their children.

Then, a few hours before the hearings began, representatives of several large game manufacturers sought to partially defuse the bad publicity by announcing that the industry had decided to endorse a rating system. The announcement was well timed, and several senators referred to it throughout the meetings.

Most of the hearing was taken up by the testimonies of expert witnesses from two panels: one consisting of experts on education and child psychology and the other made up of industry executives. The expert panel consisted of Parker Page, president of the Children's Television Resource; Dr. Eugene Provenzo, Jr., of the University of Miami; Robert Chase, vice president of the National Education Association; and Marilyn Droz, vice president of the National Coalition on Television Violence.

Page led the panel testimonies, citing the limited research that existed in the early 1990s into the effects of violent games on the children who played them. He finished with three recommendations for the industry: (1) that the federal government fund independent research projects into the effects of violent games and that the results of the research, along with a game-rating strategy, be made available to parents; (2) that future advertising should reinforce, not undermine, game ratings; and (3) that a voluntary industry-wide cap be placed on how much violence is allowed in games.[3]

From the start, an issue that came to the forefront of the hearings was concern about realistic-looking characters in games. *Street Fighter II* and even *Eternal Champions,* an especially violent fighting game for Genesis, were seldom if ever mentioned in the hearings. Neither were *Doom* or *Wolfenstein 3D.* The emphasis throughout the hearings was placed on games with digitized human images, that is, *Mortal Kombat, Night Trap,* and, toward the end of the hearings, *Lethal Enforcer.* Even the launch of an arcade game from Strata titled *Time Killers,* in which players hacked off each other's limbs with swords, saws, and axes, went unnoticed.

The next panel member, Dr. Eugene Provenzo, Jr., was well known to video makers, having published a book called *Video Kids: Making Sense of Nintendo,* which took a critical look at the impact that video games had on children. "Video games are overwhelmingly violent, sexist, and racist," he testified.[4]

> Now, if the video game industry is going to provide the foundation for the development of interactive television, then concerned citizens, parents, educators, and legislators have cause for considerable concern and alarm. During the past decade, the video game industry has developed games whose social content has been overwhelmingly violent, sexist, and racist—issues that I have addressed extensively in my research.
>
> For example, in *Video Kids,* I explored the 47 most popular video games in America. What I found out was that violence was the main theme. Of the 47 most popular games—this is based on *Nintendo Power* polls, industry polls—

> 40 had violence as their main theme. Of these 47 games, 13 included scenarios
> in which women were kidnapped and had to be rescued; i.e., the idea of women
> as victims. This represents a total of 30 percent of the games, a number which
> is even more revealing when we take into account that 11 of the 47 games were
> based on sports themes such as car racing and basketball.[5]*

> —**Eugene Provenzo, professor of social and cultural foundations**
> **of education, University of Miami**

The most telling testimony came from Robert Chase of the National Education Association. Chase warned about the instinct to censor materials and cautioned against it, while at the same time decrying the level of violence in some games. Throughout his speech, Chase stood firmly behind the idea of a rating system that would provide parents with "appropriate tools for making reasonable judgments." Then he made a statement that would later be echoed by much harsher and angrier critics.

> Electronic games, because they are active rather than passive, can do more
> than desensitize impressionable children to violence. They actually encour-
> age violence as the resolution of first resort by rewarding participants for
> killing one's opponents in the most grisly ways imaginable.[6]

> —**Robert Chase, vice president, National Education Association**

The last member of the panel was Marilyn Droz, whose testimony sounded more like an emotional plea than anything else. In the course of her testimony, Droz stated that "Girls are very offended by the lack of games for them to play" and that "playing video games has become a macho boy thing."

> The video industry has done the same thing that the movie industry has done.
> They have confused children's desire for action with violence. My 23 years of
> working with children directly has proven to me that children want action,

---

* It is interesting to note that if 11 of the 47 games were sports games and 40 of the 47 games had violent themes, then Dr. Provenzo considered a minimum of four sports games to have violent themes. In fairness, though, some psychologists have pointed out that although cartoonlike in nature, games such as *Super Mario Bros.* and even *Kirby's Dreamland* are violent.

> they want excitement. They do not need to see the insides of people splat-
> tered against the wall to understand. You know, they need action, but they
> do not need to find murder as a form of entertainment.[7]

—Marilyn Droz, vice president, National Coalition on Television Violence

Once Droz finished her testimony, Senator Kohl asked the members of the expert panel what they would say to the industry panel if they had the chance. Page said that he would ask about marketing techniques and encourage game makers to focus on action rather than violence. Provenzo said that "by manu-facturing games such as *Night Trap*," the game companies were "endorsing violence."[8] He went on to say that there was an obligation to make good games and to stop confusing violence for entertainment. As a closing remark, Provenzo called for guidelines for parents—the rating system that Senator Lieberman had advocated from the start.

Given his chance to speak, Robert Chase said that he would leave them with a message of responsibility. Finally, Droz called for a ratings panel that included people from outside the industry. "I feel to allow them to police themselves when they have already demonstrated that they are out of con-trol," she said, "is like leaving a classroom in charge of the troublemaker."[9]

Senator Lieberman asked Eugene Provenzo for examples of the video game racism he cited in his testimony and in his book.

> In interviews with children, what I found was that they talked about the ninjas
> as being bad. Then you asked them about who ninjas were, and they were
> sort of like the Japs and the Chinese. It turns out that they perceive Asians,
> any Asians, as being extremely violent, as being dangerous, as being evil. It
> is operating at a very basic level and at times simplistic.
>
> It carries over into other areas as well. There are depictions, I believe,
> although it is hard to prove, but my perception of homophobia operating in
> terms of how certain types of women are portrayed.[10]

—Eugene Provenzo

Throughout the question-and-answer period, the one game mentioned most was *Night Trap*. Senator Byron Dorgan of North Dakota started to comment that the committee had the testimony of Tom Zito, "who is not with us," when Zito interrupted him from the gallery, yelling, "I'm here, sir. I called, but there was no time to give a statement."[11]

Reading the transcripts of the 1993 hearings, it is hard to believe that anybody had ever actually played *Night Trap*. Few people bothered to acknowledge that the goal of *Night Trap* was not to kill women but to save them from vampires. Players did not even kill the vampires—they simply trapped them in Rube Goldberg–like booby traps. Nearly everyone who referred to *Night Trap* mentioned a scene in which a girl in a rather modest teddy is caught by the vampires and killed. The scene was meant to show players that they had lost and allowed too many vampires into the house. When this was pointed out to Marilyn Droz, she responded:

Oh, it makes me feel a lot better that if you are a loser, you are dead? No, it doesn't. We are dealing with self-esteem here. There are many magazines out there on the market like the several I brought in here today. These magazines are filled with game tips on how to play the game. In no time at all, children become winners and kill, and their kill ratio goes up. It tells them the secret codes and exactly what to do to become successful in murder.

My statement to people who feel that there is some value to these games is that if the Pentagon was to ever have suggested years ago that we put video games that teach children how to aim guns and train them at the age of eight to be soldiers, and ever invented a game to put in homes of young boys to train them to be in the military, I can't begin to tell you . . . you know what kind uproar there would be in this country if our government was to start training early killers.[12]

After interviewing the panel of experts, the senators turned their attention to a panel of industry representatives that included Howard Lincoln, executive vice president of Nintendo of America; Bill White, Jr., vice president of Sega of America; Ilene Rosenthal of the Software Publishers Association; Dawn Wiener, president of the Video Software Dealers Association; and Craig Johnson of the Amusement and Music Operators Association. The battle that was about to transpire was, if nothing else, bizarre.

Howard Lincoln led off by stating that Nintendo was "just as concerned about the issue of violence, whether in the movies, television, or video games, as anyone in the room."[13] Having made the decision to edit the violence out of the Super NES version of *Mortal Kombat,* Lincoln entered the proceedings with an air of innocence. Senator Lieberman even offered Lincoln an air of courtesy that was not extended to the people from Sega.

Lincoln went on to extol his company's virtuous endeavors. He said that thanks to the security chip, companies had to get Nintendo's permission to create games for the NES and Super NES. "Nintendo has video game guidelines which control game content, and we have applied these to every one of the more than 1,200 games released into the market by Nintendo and its licensees."[14]

> In the past year, some very violent and offensive games have reached the market and, of course, I am speaking about *Mortal Kombat* and *Night Trap.* Let me say for the record, I want to state that *Night Trap* will never appear on a Nintendo System. Obviously, it would not pass our guidelines. This game, which, as you have indicated, promotes violence against women, simply has no place in our society.[15]
>
> **—Howard Lincoln**

When Lincoln mentioned that Nintendo had been criticized by children and parents alike for "sanitizing" *Mortal Kombat,* Senator Lieberman interrupted him to ask about it. "We have received letters, we have received literally thousands of phone calls,"[16] Lincoln responded.

If Lincoln was the welcomed guest, Bill White of Sega was the man on the hot seat. Both of the games that had prompted the hearings were made for Genesis, and without ever mentioning Sega, Lincoln had pointed a scathing finger at the company during his testimony. White tried to improve his company's image by restating the vital information that Lincoln and the senators seemed to have ignored. He started by stating three points: Sega's customer base was older and broader than the previous experts had suggested; Sega already had a rating system; and Sega was trying to encourage the rest of the industry to adopt a rating system.

> In recent days, the glare of the media spotlight on this issue has resulted in the circulation of a number of distorted and inaccurate claims. The most

> damaging of these distortions, in my view, is the notion that Sega and the rest of the digital interactive industry are only in the business of selling games to children. This is not the case.
>
> Yes, many of Sega's interactive video titles are intended for and purchased by young children. Many other Sega titles, however, are intended for and purchased by adults for their personal entertainment and education. The average Sega CD user is almost 22 years old, and only 5 percent are under age 13. The average Sega Genesis user is almost 19 years old, and fewer than 30 percent are under age 13.[17]
>
> **—William "Bill" White, former vice president of marketing/communications, Sega of America**

White went on to explain Sega's "three-pronged approach" to informing parents. According to White, Sega not only placed ratings on all Genesis games but also included a toll-free hotline for consumers to get ratings, and informational brochures about the ratings were made available.

Listening to White, Howard Lincoln was apparently seething. Years later, Lincoln said, "I heard him saying these things that I knew he didn't believe, and I'm not sure what came over me." He sat quietly through Rosenthal's, Wiener's, and Johnson's testimonies, preparing a response to Bill White. Lincoln's anger may have been aroused by the way White tried to speak for the entire industry, and it may have been in response to the way he characterized Sega as being on the forefront of protecting children from adult material.* It may also have sprung from their past relationship. White had been Nintendo of America's director of advertising and PR and had joined Sega a few months after an ugly split from Nintendo. Whatever his reasons, Lincoln waited until the question-and-answer period after Johnson's testimony to speak.

Lieberman directed his first comment to White, stating that the clip he had seen of a woman being attacked in *Night Trap* was "gratuitous and offensive and ought not to be available to people in our society."[18] White responded by reiterating his message about the market maturing and the importance of

---

* In fairness, a 1991 suit between Sega of America and a game manufacturer called RazorSoft centered on a game called *Stormlord,* which Sega rejected because it contained statues of naked women.

ratings. Senator Lieberman continued to pick at White, pinning him down on whether or not *Night Trap* was a product for adults, then pointing out that if it was indeed being marketed only to adults, Sega should be obliged to enforce the ratings. He then proceeded to show the commercial for *Mortal Kombat* and commented that the boy in the commercial appeared to be under thirteen years of age—too young to buy the game, according to Sega's ratings.

Senator Lieberman then turned to Lincoln and threw him a softball question. After faintly praising Nintendo for its limited self-regulation, he asked if Nintendo would be willing to display ratings on advertisements and in brochures as well as on games. Lincoln said he would, then changed the subject.

> Let me make just a couple of other points. I can't sit here and allow you to be told that somehow the video game business has been transformed today from children to adults. It hasn't been, and Mr. White, who is a former Nintendo employee, knows the demographics as well as I do.
>
> Furthermore, I can't let you sit here and buy this nonsense that this Sega *Night Trap* game was somehow only meant for adults.
>
> The fact of the matter is this is a copy of the packaging. There was no rating on this game at all when the game was introduced. Small children bought this at Toys "R" Us, and he knows that as well as I do. When they started getting heat about this game, then they adopted the rating system and put ratings on it.[19]
>
> **—Howard Lincoln**

What could Lieberman say? He thanked Lincoln for his "forthrightness" and praised Nintendo for "having been a damn sight better than the competition."

> Well, the truth is that those statistics were very true and I think Howard knew those statistics were true. He would have to if they kept the same records that we kept. And having worked there [Nintendo], I imagine they did. Those were the primary player demographics that we measured, based on warranty card returns from our games, both software and hardware. And they represent the actual reported age of the people that play the games.
>
> **—William "Bill" White**

White shot back with a videotape showing violent games on Super NES. Nintendo's self-regulation did not go far enough, he argued. At least, Sega games had ratings. The tug of war continued, with Lincoln pointing out that without enforcement, ratings would not keep violent games out of the hands of children and White stressing the importance of ratings.

> One of the true highlights of the testimony, for me, was when after days of Nintendo claiming how pure they were in Lincoln's sanctimonious testimony, White pulls out the huge bazooka-like gun that Nintendo sold for use with the Super NES and asked Howard if this was what he meant by saying that Nintendo controlled the product it made and protected families and kids.
> Howard was shaken, ashen, and furious.
>
> **—Richard Brudvik-Lindner, former director of communications,**
> **Sega of America**

> I really had not planned on taking Sega on, but it became such a delightful opportunity. It was broadcast twice on C-SPAN, and the part when I really took White on was broadcast on CNN. It was everywhere. I don't remember what it was that he said, but it was so dumb. It just brought out the lawyer in me. I mean, it was a golden opportunity I couldn't pass up.
>
> **—Howard Lincoln**

> I was surprised when Howard Lincoln and Bill White went after each other like that. I thought that it looked awful. And I was surprised at the intensity of it. I guess it gave me this message that this was obviously big business.
>
> **—Senator Joseph Lieberman**

The meeting continued, with Senators Lieberman, Kohl, and Dorgan hammering Bill White, until it finally adjourned at 1:52 P.M. Before closing the meeting, Senator Lieberman called for a second meeting to be held in February to evaluate the industry's progress toward adopting a rating system.

> In a lot of ways, the hearings really changed the industry. It was a coming of age for the industry. It really marked the arrival of Sega as the industry leader.

> It created alliances and engendered animosities that exist to this day. It also created the opportunity for the PC entertainment industry and the video game industry to check each other out and see if they could be married. It forced these companies to develop a political savvy that they never really had.
>
> **—Richard Brudvik-Lindner**

Many changes occurred during the three months between the first Senate hearing in December and the much more serene second hearing on March 4, 1994. Howard Lincoln was promoted to chairman of Nintendo of America, making him co-equal with Nintendo of America president Minoru Arakawa. Work had begun on a rating system. Despite Sega's suggestion that the industry adopt its system, a new one was being created. Also, largely as a result of the publicity generated by the hearings, *Night Trap* had sold out all across the country. Sega CD had never been more than a niche product, with approximately 250,000 units sold in the United States. Had it not been for the hearings, *Night Trap* would have vanished as just another forgotten Sega CD game. Given new publicity from the hearings, it was later rereleased for both PCs and 32X.

> Sega wound up selling way more copies of *MKI,* probably as a result of the hearings. *Night Trap* came back to life. You know, I sold 50,000 units of *Night Trap* a week after those hearings.
>
> **—Tom Zito**

New Organizations

> Two things became obvious to people pretty quickly. One was that the industry ought to attempt to come up with a self-regulatory response to congressional concerns about content; and the second was that it ought to consider creating a trade association to represent its interests, not just in Washington and at the state level but in a variety of forms.
>
> **—Douglas Lowenstein, president, Interactive Digital Software Association**

Two organizations were formed as a result of the hearings. In 1994, game company executives decided that they had better create their own trade organization rather than depend on the Software Publishers Association.

Seven industry leaders met to discuss the formation of the organization: Nintendo, Sega, Acclaim, Electronic Arts, Phillips, Atari, and 3DO. The meetings, intense and private, took place over a six-week period, punctuated with hostile power struggles between Nintendo and Sega. The fighting eventually led to compromise and the creation of the Interactive Digital Software Association (IDSA), the interactive entertainment industry's own dedicated trade and lobbying organization, headed by a seasoned Washington, D.C., veteran named Douglas Lowenstein. In later years, the IDSA would prove to be very effective when the industry was under siege.

The creation of the rating system did not proceed without battles. In the beginning, Sega executives wanted the entire industry to adopt their rating system. When it became obvious that Nintendo and several other companies would not use the Sega rating system, Sega took a leading role in trying to establish a new system that would be mutually acceptable. Even this did not end the fighting. Several computer game publishers created their own rating system, which they used for more than a year before eventually accepting the video game ratings.

> Well, I think the real reason they didn't go with Sega's rating system was that it was Sega's rating system and . . . at the time the notion of Nintendo and Sony as fierce competitors, with Sega adopting a system identified with Sega's product, was . . . that was very unpalatable.
>
> **—Douglas Lowenstein**

> It's somewhat ironic that Sega was criticized the way it was, for having actually taken a lead in producing a rating system that would provide the very information that the senators wanted to see on every package across the industry. I think Sega should have been congratulated publicly for having taken a lead in establishing ratings for games, albeit amongst games that were proprietary or running on Sega platforms. And, of course, Sega was

> instrumental in the formation of IDSA and was very proactive in helping bring
> the industry into compliance with Senator Lieberman's requests.
>
> —**William "Bill" White**

Video game makers also created the Entertainment Software Rating Board (ESRB), an independent organization to rate games. Led by Dr. Arthur Pober, a highly respected educator, the ESRB won rave reviews when it presented its rating system to Senators Lieberman and Kohl. Though they resisted at first, computer game makers eventually adopted the IDSA's rating system, which reinforced the industry's new unity.

At Williams Manufacturing, Ed Boon and John Tobias made a modification to their basic game formula as they created *Mortal Kombat 2*. They kept the blood, brutality, and fatalities, but they also added a new kind of finishing move called "friendship." Friendships worked very much like fatalities—if a player defeated an opponent for two rounds, the opponent would stand dazed for a few seconds, during which time players had to tap in the right combination with their joystick and buttons. If the code was done correctly, instead of destroying the opponent in some gory way, the victor would give him a cake, a doll, or some other gift as the word *FRIENDSHIP* appeared across the top of the screen in rainbow colors.

> The "friendships" were a result of the hearings. They were put in specifically
> because we were getting so much publicity because of the violence in the
> game and stuff. We just thought we'd offset the fatalities with friendships.
>
> —**John Tobias**

With the ratings in place, Howard Lincoln and Minoru Arakawa decided that Nintendo no longer needed to sanitize games the way it had in the past. The Super NES version of *Mortal Kombat 2* contained as many fatalities and friendships as Sega's. This time, it sold better than the Genesis version.

CHAPTER 26

The "Next" Generation (Part 1)

Sega is sending a very confusing message to the customer, saying: "Buy Genesis," "now it's Game Gear," "no, actually it's Sega CD," "no, it's 32X," "forget all of that stuff, it's Saturn," "maybe it's Titan," "how about Pico."

—Trip Hawkins, founder, the 3DO Company

3DO a good value at $299? I'll sell you mine.

—Tim Stamper, cofounder, Rare, Ltd.

You Oughta Be in Pictures

Both Nintendo and Sega spun hit cartoon shows off their mascots. Nintendo went even further and worked on two movies: *The Wizard,* starring Fred Savage; and *Super Mario Bros.,* with Bob Hoskins playing the title role. Neither movie left much of a mark at the box office.

Sega's introduction into the film world is less well known and a bit more brutal. In 1994, Shenobu Toyoda, vice president of licensing at Sega of America, signed the company up as a sponsor of Robert Redford's Sundance Film Festival. Toyoda, who was said to be more interested in movies than games, saw convergence between the two media on the horizon, due largely to Sega CD. By sponsoring the film festival, he hoped to create some inroads into the industry.

> We were a significant sponsor of the Sundance Film Festival. These were heady times at Sega. This was a time period in which we really could see the merging of Hollywood and the filmmaking industry with the video game industry. We had the Sega CD, and we were the leading proponent of that marriage from the video game industry side.
>
> On top of all of that, it was really kind of a vision thing for Shenobu. A lot of people talk about his fascination or maybe his kind of . . . he was awestruck by Hollywood.
>
> **—Richard Brudvik-Lindner, former director of public relations, Sega of America**

Before the festival began, Sega rented an enormous estate outside of Park City, the Utah ski resort where the Sundance Film Festival is held. Although CEO Tom Kalinske did not attend and Toyoda only made a brief appearance, Sega sent a top-tier team that included Richard Brudvik-Lindner, director of communications; Michaelene Cristini Risley, group director of licensing and character development; and Joe Miller, head of research and development.

As one of the sponsors of the festival, Sega was invited to make a presentation one evening. Miller was to deliver a speech and show video clips of games under development, after which there would be a reception. Knowing of the "politically correct" attitude that prevailed in Hollywood, Lindner decided to have Miller put an emphasis on *Ecco the Dolphin,* in an effort to show that there was more to video games than simple shoot-'em-ups. After making his presentation, Miller opened the meeting for questions. He had expected a little animosity—what he got, however, verged on hostility. Members of the Screenwriters Guild and other trade organizations pounded him through the entire session with questions about how game makers would work with unions and whether game designers got adequate credit for their work.

The storm continued as the presentation ended and the reception began. Screenwriters and other movie people besieged the members of the Sega team.

> The questioning just continued, so much so, that I think most of the contingent of Sega people felt under attack. I noticed the Sega people getting more and more compacted together in this little group, and it was like they were surrounded. It got so bad that they wanted to leave before the reception was done.
>
> I remember stopping Joe Miller in the parking lot and saying, "You need to get back in there, these people don't understand the vision." I tried to get our guys to go back in there and be advocates and extol the vision. And I remember looking at Joe and Michaelene and some of the other folks who were there in the parking lot with me and seeing something that was almost like fear in their eyes. They kind of looked at me, they considered going back for a fraction of a second, then they said "no," and we all got in our Chevy Suburban and drove off.
>
> —Richard Brudvik-Lindner

New and Old Contenders

America's 3DO already has an advanced games machine on the market, though at a whopping $699. Atari will launch its Jaguar later this year; Sony has set up a new joint venture to market a 32-bit machine. Sega has teamed up with Hitachi to develop new machines.[1]

A number of historically insignificant consoles came out during the 16-bit era: a Japanese game manufacturer named SNK released a CD version of NeoGeo, Philips released an overpriced education/entertainment deck called

CD-i, and Sega released new reiterations of its CD product. Then, in October 1993, Matsushita (a.k.a. Panasonic) released a CD-based game console called the REAL 3DO Multiplayer. The introduction of 3DO marked the birth of the next generation of video game hardware.

The 3DO Multiplayer was the result of an interesting experiment in marketing economics, a partnership in which one company provided all of the technology while another provided the manufacturing—both without paying each other. The hardware itself was the creation of RJ Mical and Dave Needle, the same team of Amiga-veterans that developed the Lynx. Disappointed with the failure of Lynx, and furious at Atari for its poor handling of the product, Mical and Needle left Epyx and began working on their next invention the very next day. Meeting in a restaurant, they discussed possibilities for future plans. When they landed upon the idea of a truly breakthrough game console, they sketched out the needed components on a napkin right at their table.

Mapping out the hardware was easy enough—building it would be a different story. To do so, they would need capital and preferably an investor who would purchase the hardware rather than just help design it. They turned to Sega.

> Dave Morris, who replaced me briefly as president of Epyx, came to me with RJ and Dave Needle when I was president of Sega. They presented to me the concept of paying them $2 million and giving them two years to develop the next "ultimate revolutionary" video game system; and I was all for it, based on their credentials, because they had developed the Amiga computer and they had developed Lynx. I had just paid $1.7 million dollars to Joe Montana to get his picture on a game. I thought it was nothing to pay $2 million to get the next hardware system developed.
>
> So I recommended that they go to Japan, which they did two or three times, and present their concept to Nakayama. They were turned down.
>
> **—Michael Katz, former CEO, Sega of America**

One of the next people they met with was Trip Hawkins, the founder of Electronic Arts. Intelligent and ever fascinated by technology, Hawkins made a good audience for their presentation. As the CEO of a major computer and video game company, he understood the industry and had an army of contacts throughout Silicon Valley. And he would need them. Buying into Mical and Needle's project meant more than breaking into the console market; it meant taking on Nintendo and Sega. Anybody who signed on with Mical and Needle would need to be as much an evangelist as a venture capitalist. Trendy, witty, charismatic, and known throughout the high-tech world as the ultimate salesman, Hawkins was a perfect fit.

Taking 3DO from concept to reality was a lengthy and difficult process that required a large team. Looking back at everything that went into making the console, RJ Mical would later remark that "It took 17 people to design the Amiga. It took just Dave and me to design the Lynx, and we came in under budget. Turning the genesis of an idea into the reality of the 3DO took a small army. On the other hand . . . it was a small army."

Dave Needle, the hardware side of the Mical and Needle development team, had created a brilliant machine. Their console played games, music, and photographs on CD-ROM, hence the name "Multiplayer." It was built around a 32-bit ARM 60 RISC processing chip and featured 3 megabytes of memory. Unfortunately, time and the rapid evolution of technology had conspired against them. Shortly after Needle and Mical completed their work, a breakthrough in chip design made floating-point technology, an efficient way of making calculations for 3D graphics, more affordable for later consoles.

> Floating-point capability is something that we would have had to add at extra cost and might jeopardize the size of the chip. . . . Low-cost processors typically did not have floating-point capability until very recently. Then it finally became cheap enough and common enough to become available for use in video game machines.
>
> It would have speeded up the polygon calculations, but I don't really think that that makes a hell of a lot of difference, to be honest.
>
> **—Trip Hawkins**

From the start, Hawkins wanted to do things differently from other game companies. Nintendo and Sega manufactured their own hardware, while Hawkins wanted to create a hardware standard and license it out to electronics manufacturers. Nor did he want to publish games for his new console. In Hawkins's business model, he would simply develop the finest technology on the market, and his profits would come from licensing that technology to others. As the console went into development, Hawkins's strategy seemed to be working. Panasonic, Sanyo, AT&T, Creative Labs, and Gold Star all expressed interest in manufacturing hardware based on the new console's architecture. More than eighty companies, including Activision, LucasArts, and Microprose, signed on to make games for it. Since Hawkins was the head of Electronic Arts and some of the early development had been handled internally, there was never any question about whether Electronic Arts would support it.

> The creation of 3DO was shrouded in mystery to me. It felt pretty bitter. Trip Hawkins started the 3DO stuff internally and I think there were some real issues; but I'm not sure exactly what all went down.
>
> **—Don Traeger, former employee, Electronic Arts**

In the fall of 1993, Hawkins unveiled his 3DO game console to the press. Backed by Electronic Arts and headed by the electronics-entertainment world's best salesman, 3DO became the darling of Wall Street. Not everyone was impressed, however. Howard Lincoln, chairman of Nintendo, later said in an interview that he never worried about 3DO because of the way Hawkins set up the business model.

> They violated, in my opinion, the cardinal rule. And that is that you cannot rely on other people to make good games for your system. It's nice to think that they can, but these hardware systems need first-class software, and you have to do it yourself. The model just didn't work.
>
> **—Howard Lincoln, former chairman, Nintendo of America**

> I'd like to think that we would have had the smarts at Sega to market the 3DO in the conventional, successful way and not create this, if you'll forgive the expression, ridiculous new model that Trip came up with of how to market and sell 3DO. I mean, not manufacturing the hardware himself and licensing the technology to other people—it's ridiculous. Why would more than one company want to compete against someone else with exactly the same product? Why would a retailer want to buy the same product from more than one company? Everyone in the industry thought that was ludicrous.
>
> **—Michael Katz**

Behind the scenes, 3DO suffered from a bit of an identity crisis. Hawkins, whose background was in software, forgot some of the cardinal rules of video games. He decided to price the Multiplayer at $699, more than four times the price of Super NES or Genesis. A Commodore computer inspired this steep price. Remembering that Commodore had charged $700 for the complete Commodore 64 set up and feeling that his 3DO Multiplayer had many more capabilities than the Commodore 64, Hawkins thought consumers would pay the same price.

Sadly, the work and technology that went into 3DO technology were partially overshadowed by the console's poorly designed controllers. It came with flat, slender controllers that were reminiscent of the controllers on the Super NES. They had, however, one major flaw—the direction pad on the left side of the controller did not handle diagonal movement well. When consumers called in to complain about this problem, 3DO technicians suggested that they loosen the screws on the back of the controller. Although this fix helped diminish the problem, it did not completely solve it.

There was also some confusion about which game to pack in with the 3DO Multiplayer. Amazingly, the decision was made to bundle *Shelly Duvall's A Bird's Life* with the game player that Hawkins was trying to market as a toy for sophisticated adults. While *Shelly Duvall's A Bird's Life* was a respected piece of educational/entertainment software, it was a program meant to teach young children about birds. Fortunately, a company called Crystal Dynamics stepped in with an impressive new driving game called *Crash 'N Burn,* which was ultimately selected to be the bundled software. Even with *Crash 'N Burn* in the package, 3DO owners had little to play at launch. Few games were ready for the October launch of the 3DO Multiplayer, and only a space-flight game called *Total Eclipse* stood out as having much promise.

The public did not bite. According to one published prediction, only 125,000 units were sold in the United States in the entire first year.[2] Panasonic lowered the price of the 3DO REAL Multiplayer to $399.95 in 1994, but the initial excitement was already gone and sales remained low. In foreign markets, however, 3DO fared slightly better. Despite its "made in the U.S.A." image, the 3DO Company actively pursued worldwide sales and ultimately sold more consoles in Asia than in the United States.[*]

---

[*] 3DO handled digitized video better than other game consoles. Some of the more popular items available in the Asian market, which were not available in the United States, were pornographic CDs.

The first 3DO titles failed to demonstrate the superiority of its 32-bit technology. Over the next two years, Electronic Arts published games that highlighted 3DO's abilities and differentiated it from the competition. First a motorcycle combat racing game called *Road Rash* was ported to 3DO from Genesis. Then Electronic Arts followed up with a solid 3DO version of its titanic *Madden NFL* series. Tapping into the CD-ROM–based console's strengths, the new version of *Madden* featured digitized footage of the former Oakland Raiders coach and larger, more detailed, players. Next, Electronic Arts published a 3DO version of *FIFA International Soccer,* with multiple camera angles, a truly 3D field, streaming play-by-play audio commentary, and a repertoire of special kicks and realistic moves. This was the game that would demonstrate just how impressive "next generation" sports simulations could be. These games came out too late to save 3DO, however. By the time Electronic Arts finally teamed up with *Car and Driver* magazine to create a realistic auto-racing game called *Need for Speed,* consumers had moved on. None of these games were available in 1993 and by the time they began appearing more regularly, 3DO had lost its momentum.

Atari's Last Cat

In November 1993, Atari released one of the most controversial and ill-fated game consoles ever made. The system, called Jaguar, was a cartridge-based console with a Motorola CPU. Although Jaguar had only 16 megabits of RAM, it had two 64-bit RISC graphics processing chips. Atari marketed it as the first 64-bit game console ever to hit the market, but competitors argued that it was really a 16-bit game console.

> Their CPU is 16 bit. Ours is 32 bit, and our coprocessors are a lot more powerful doing the graphics and sound. Atari has trouble getting good sound during game play because of how they set up their bus structure. It's only because of an ambiguity in the law that they can even say 64 bit without having to explain what they mean.
>
> **—Trip Hawkins**

Atari president Sam Tramiel faced a tough battle from the moment he announced his new game console. His family's hardball style of business had alienated much of the industry. Many retailers refused to carry the new console, and while more than 200 developers signed up to make games for Jaguar, very few software publishers ever came through with any games. Only five games were available when Atari released Jaguar. Despite promises that more games would be out by Christmas, it took months before Atari released new games. Even worse, those first few games, which included *Cybermorph*, *Crescent Galaxy*, and *Evolution: Dino Dudes*, left consumers completely unimpressed.

Even taking into account the lack of games and the controversy surrounding the processing chip, Jaguar had some marketing advantages over 3DO. Retailing at $249.95, it was far less expensive. Atari created a catchy advertising campaign in which it instructed consumers to "do the math" when comparing Jaguar's 64 bits to 3DO's 32. Then there were the unique controllers that appealed to some players, yet infuriated others. Jaguar controllers were fat and wide, with curved edges and rounded rolls along their bottom to create an ergonomic feel. The controller featured a number pad in its center, giving a "retro" nod to the days of ColecoVision and Intellivision.

Although Atari never solved the dearth of games issue, two British game designers appeared on the scene to give the system a couple of outstanding titles. The first was by Jeff Minter, a former Vic 20 designer, who was known throughout the industry as "The Yak." *Tempest 2000*, Minter's first game, was a brilliant recreation of Dave Theurer's coin-op classic, updated with shaded polygonal characters and a techno-rock soundtrack. With its great sound and fast action, *Tempest 2000* proved that Jaguar could be a great game machine, given the right software.[2]*

Alien vs. Predator, Jaguar's second big game, came from a British developer named Andrew Whitaker. *Alien vs. Predator* was a first-person shooting game of the *Doom* variety that could be played from the perspective of the space parasites from the movie *Alien*, the intergalactic hunter from the movie *Predator*, or a space marine. Each character had its own goals, strengths, and weaknesses. It took Whitaker seventeen months to create *Alien vs. Predator*. The hardware was not completed when he began work on the project, and Atari engineers changed their design four times during the time that he worked on the game.

---

*Yes, for those of you who remember, I did give *Tempest 2000* a D+ score in *Electronic Games*. What can I say, I repent.

For every *Alien vs. Predator* or *Tempest 2000* that appeared on Jaguar, there were many more games such as *Kasumi Ninja:* a weak attempt at emulating *Mortal Kombat,* with characters such as a Scottish brawler who shot fireballs at opponents from beneath his kilt. Despite outselling the $699 3DO in 1993, Jaguar fell behind 3DO in 1994. In an effort to salvage his sales, Tramiel even tried running television infomercials.

The Consumer Electronics Battleground

CHICAGO: Sega kept a low-profile at the June 23–25 Summer Consumer Electronics Show here—in the basement, to be exact—while archrival Nintendo was roaring like a 200-pound *"Donkey Kong"* gorilla in a massive exhibit-hall booth that literally could not be missed.[3]

The 1994 Summer Consumer Electronics Show (CES), held in Chicago, was the scene of grand battles, with Atari and 3DO claiming technical superiority while Nintendo and Sega clashed on other fronts.

Nintendo entered the show on an unusual up-note. Having spent the last few years looking helplessly beaten by Sega in image marketing, Nintendo scored a hit with a game called *Super Metroid.* Designed by Gumpei Yokoi's Research and Development Team Number 1, it was built off an earlier game that they had created for the NES. *Super Metroid* was not enough to turn the tables on Sega, but it at least served notice that Nintendo was not to be ignored.

In 1994, Nintendo used CES to trickle out announcements about Ultra 64, the new 64-bit game console it was developing with Silicon Graphics. Company executives hired a bus and shuttled small groups of reporters to a hotel suite, where they were to be shown private screenings of Ultra 64 hardware. The groups were led into a small showroom with four televisions peering out of ceiling-high curtains. The reporters never actually saw the console, which they were told was nothing more than a prototype. Instead, they were shown a fighting game called *Killer Instinct* that they were told ran on Ultra 64 hardware. Nintendo did not announce a precise release date for Ultra 64 in those private screenings but indicated that the system would come out in the fall of 1995 for $250. That was the most Nintendo would release.

More salient to Nintendo's plans for 1994 was a curious little game adapter called Super Game Boy, which enabled consumers to run Game Boy cartridges on Super NES with some muted colors. At the time, Super Game Boy seemed like a ridiculous idea. Game Boy sales had slowed, and the Super Game Boy sold for $60, more than Game Boy itself.

Nintendo's other hope was a game that was designed using a new technology—*Donkey Kong Country*.

The Return of Rare

Though Rare, Ltd., had dropped out of active game development, the company did not remain silent for long. Chris Stamper began work on technology that would allow him to create games with 24-bit graphics on a Silicon Graphics workstation, then convert them into the kinds of two dimensional images that would run smoothly on the 16-bit Super NES. Once operational, Stamper's device would give Rare an edge over every other game company. While competitors would still be creating cartoon sprites, Rare would be able to pre-render art on high-end workstations. As Chris Stamper completed the device, his brother Tim began designing a boxing game that would serve as a demonstration of the new technology. Then they invited Nintendo of Japan out to their headquarters in the tiny English town of Twycross to see what they had created.

> We had a visit from Mr. Takeda [Genyo Takeda—one of Nintendo's top engineers]. We decided to show him a demonstration of a boxing game we had created, using rendered graphics on a Silicon Graphics workstation. He was very impressed and asked, "What would this look like on a Super NES?" So into the evening and the next day, we had two of our engineers work on taking the 24-bit true color imagery and converting it to Super NES.
>
> **—Chris Stamper, cofounder, Rare, Ltd.**

One of the strengths of Chris Stamper's design was that it showed objects on the Silicon Graphics workstation with the same amount of detail that they would have when displayed on the Super NES. Hence, when the Stampers showed

Takeda their boxing game on a Super NES the next day, it looked almost identical to the game they had shown him on the workstation the day before.

> When we took the guys from NCL [Nintendo Co., Ltd.] to the art department and showed them what we had, they kept looking under the table. I asked what they were doing. They said they were looking for the big computer because they didn't understand that everything was being done in the small box.
>
> **—Tim Stamper, cofounder, Rare, Ltd.**

Impressed with what he had seen, Takeda returned to Japan and reported the invention to Nintendo chairman Hiroshi Yamauchi. When Yamauchi responded by asking the Stampers what kind of game they wanted to make, Tim said that he wanted to make a game with the character Donkey Kong. With Yamauchi's and Donkey Kong creator Shigeru Miyamoto's blessing, Stamper and his design team began work on the game.

Knowing that they were working on an all-important holiday release, the people at Rare went to great lengths to ensure the quality of their game. Their in-house musician created several themes to accompany the game. The art was inspired by concept drawings that Miyamoto sent over, but Tim Stamper's team had license to take the concepts in their own direction. Stamper mapped out the levels for the game by drawing sequences of sketches on Post-it notes, then arranging them in a straight line.

The process for creating the objects and characters in *Donkey Kong Country* involved building 3D images using flat polygons. Once the shapes were complete, the artists would assign textures and colors to various polygons to add skins for their wire-frame creations. The artists used objects from Rare's converted farmhouse-headquarters to create images. When they needed textures for trees, they plucked leaves from a tree. When they needed a texture that resembled rusted metal for a wheelbarrow, they scanned an old shovel.

The end result was a side-scrolling game with characters that moved smoothly but looked as real and three-dimensional as the dynamations in a Ray Harryhausen movie. Rare had created new characters for the game, and the storyline was filled with British puns and humor.

When editors and buyers saw their first demonstrations of *Donkey Kong Country* at CES, they immediately knew what the big game of 1994 was going to be.

> The first time I saw *Donkey Kong Country*, I realized that Super NES could do everything that Nintendo said it could do.
>
> **—RJ Mical, former fellow, the 3DO Company**

Sega's Showstopper

> When you have an installed base as large as Sega has with the Genesis, and you come out with anything that costs less than $200, some people are going to buy it. That makes the release of the 32X a very nice financial event for Sega as a company.
>
> **—Trip Hawkins**

Sega's big CES product was 32X. Originally named "Mars," 32X was billed as the poor man's entry into "next generation" games. It was a mushroom-shaped peripheral that snapped into the cartridge slot of the Genesis console, giving it 32-bit processing power that Sega said would enable the system to work 40 times faster. In the heart of 32X sat two Hitachi 32-bit RISC chips, a 3D graphics processor capable of rendering 50,000 polygons per second, and some minor enhancements designed to work in tandem with Genesis audio and visual technology. Sega had already announced plans to release a superior 32-bit CD-based system called Saturn in Japan; but retailing at $159, 32X was supposed to be a much less expensive alternative for people who already owned a Genesis. The one question Sega was not answering, however, was whether a Genesis with Sega CD and 32X would be able to read Saturn software. Always happy to report his competitors' flaws, 3DO-founder Trip Hawkins charged that it would not.

> Everyone knows that 32X is a Band-Aid. It's not a "next generation system." It's fairly expensive. It's not particularly high-performance. It's hard to program for, and it's not compatible with the Saturn.
>
> **—Trip Hawkins**

Sega executives argued with Hawkins's rhetoric, furiously telling people that he did not know what he was talking about. Even as they did this, however, they refused to state once and for all whether the 32X and Saturn were compatible.

> Both systems have the same architecture. You read between the lines.
>
> Sega has never abandoned its customer base. When we released the Genesis, we created an adapter that allowed them to play Master System cartridges. The 32X lets you run titles from your Genesis library.
>
> **—Richard Brudvik-Lindner**

Hawkins, of course, had been correct. The 32X was not powerful enough to run Saturn software. It was, however, a huge improvement over the original design that was created by Sega of Japan. The project, which eventually turned into 32X, began as an entirely new console that was developed in Japan. When the unit was demonstrated to American executives, however, the reaction was less than favorable.

> We were told that there was going to be a thing called the Genesis 2. It was going to be another version of Genesis—an entire system. The only difference was that it was going to have double the colors and a lower cost.
>
> So Joe Miller said, "Oh, that's just a horrible idea. If all you're going to do is enhance the system, you should make it an add-on." He said, "If it's a new system with legitimate new software, great. But if the only thing it does is double the colors . . . "
>
> **—Michael Latham, former executive producer, Sega of America**

Joe Miller, head of Sega of America's research and development, fought against the idea of releasing an entire new game console that was little more than a Genesis with a larger color palette. At his suggestion, 32X was changed into a peripheral and made more powerful with a new set of processing chips. At Miller's suggestion, Sega of Japan made 32X a more significant product. What the company would not do is make it into a Saturn.

> Joe may have been "the father of the 32X," but in his defense, he had to choose between bad choice number one and bad choice number two. I think

> he picked the better choice and made a valiant effort to make the best of an impossible situation.

—**Michael Latham**

Once the design specifications were completed, Sega worked hard to evangelize the new platform in the third-party community, but the system was a tough sell. The top developers knew about Saturn and Ultra 64. They also knew about a new console that Sony planned to release in 1995. Anybody who had read the design specifications of any of the new consoles knew that 32X could never hope to compete, and no one felt any enthusiasm about its chances.

Sega got the same response from journalists. More seasoned journalists, such as *Electronic Games* editors Arnie Katz, Joyce Worley, and Bill Kunkle, questioned the logic of releasing inexpensive and full-priced game consoles that basically played the same games.

> Sega claims it is segmenting the market like General Motors. "The Saturn [the 32-bit machine] is the Cadillac, the Neptune [a never-released Genesis-32X all-in-one console] is the Oldsmobile, and the Genesis is the Chevrolet," says Rioux. Already analysts are worrying about this wide array of products. "There are too many planets; it is a confused strategy," says Edward Brogan of Jardine Fleming.[4]

In an effort to win journalists over, Sega held a huge party at a San Francisco dance club. The event turned out to be a fiasco. Sega flew journalists in from all around the country and put them up in the Sofitel, a hotel located beside Sega's Redwood City headquarters.* That evening Sega hired buses to drive the journalists to the dance club. The party began with Tom Kalinske giving a speech, then a local rapper performed a lengthy piece about the greatness of 32X. The music was too loud and the 32X games that Sega had placed around the dance club were so unimpressive that no one wanted to play them. Most attendees crowded into the lobby of the dance club to escape the loud

---

* Coincidentally, Sega headquarters was located on Marine Drive, a location that had once been used for a safari park and was the exact location Nolan Bushnell used for the coming out party that he threw for Sente Games.

music. Some journalists tried to leave, only to discover that the buses had departed and would not return until the party was over.

The retail community, on the other hand, greeted the news about 32X enthusiastically. Sega could not keep up with the demand among retailers, but when the unit actually went on sale, the public did not bite. One problem was that only six games were available at launch. While two of the launch titles were strong—*Virtua Racing* and *Doom*—other 32X games were inexplicably bad. One, a fighting game called *Cosmic Carnage,* looked and played so poorly that reporters made jokes about it.

> We were rushed. We had to get games out for the 32X and it was going to be such a close cycle. When *Cosmic Carnage* showed up, we didn't even want to ship it. It took a lot of convincing, you know, to ship that title.
>
> **—Michael Latham**

As some members of the press predicted, 32X did not sell well. Within a few months, Sega dropped its price to $99 and it was ultimately cleared out of stores at $19.95. And Sega's woes were just beginning.

The Return of Kong

The video game market fell into a three-year slump in 1993. In September 1993, Nintendo Co., Ltd., reported a 24-percent drop in profits. The following September, Nintendo reported a 32-percent drop in worldwide sales.[5]

After a decade of torrid growth, the market is slumping. Sega's earnings plunged 64 percent last year. Nintendo reported a 41-percent drop; its stock has declined drastically over the last year, and no respite is in sight. Nintendo has "another bad year coming," predicts Joseph Osha of Baring Securities in Tokyo.[6]

The late November release of *Donkey Kong Country* stood in stark contrast to the gloom and doom faced by the rest of the video game industry. After three holiday seasons of coming in second to Sega, Nintendo had the biggest game of the year. Sega still outperformed Nintendo in overall holiday sales, but the 500,000 copies of *Donkey Kong Country* that Nintendo sent out in its initial shipment were mostly sold in preorder, and the rest sold out in less than one week. Shortages were inevitable, and many retailers accused Nintendo of purposely undermanufacturing the game to drive up demand.

While analysts criticize Nintendo for trying to milk its existing technology, the 16-bit machine, even as others were leapfrogging that technology by moving to 32-bit machines with a CD-ROM drive, the bestselling item in the industry this Christmas was *Donkey Kong Country*, a game written for that supposedly outmoded 16-bit platform. In the last 45 days of 1994, Nintendo's new game sold 6.1 million units, making it the fastest-selling game in the 20-year history of the video game industry and clearly a hotter item than Sega's new *Sonic & Knuckles* title. Visually, the game is at least as impressive as those played on 32-bit machines.[7]

By the end of the 16-bit generation, Nintendo would go on to sell 9 million copies of *Donkey Kong Country*, making it the bestselling game since *Super Mario Bros. 3*. *Donkey Kong Country* made Rare, Ltd., Nintendo's most important second-party developer. It established the Super NES as the better 16-bit console and paved the way for Nintendo to win the waning years of the 16-bit generation. More important, *Donkey Kong Country* sounded the death knell for Jaguar and 3DO by convincing consumers that the first systems in the next generation of game consoles had little to offer that could not be found on Super NES. *Donkey Kong Country* may not have destroyed the competition, but it certainly cleared the way for the more impressive competitors that were about to arrive.

CHAPTER 27

The "Next" Generation
(Part 2)

For a company that is so new to the industry, I would have hoped that Sony would have made more mistakes by now.

—Trip Hawkins, founder, the 3DO Company

$299.

—The entire text of a speech at the first Electronic Entertainment Expo, Steve Race, former CEO, Sony Computer Entertainment of America

An Industry-Wide Low

By 1995, the video game industry appeared to be dying. According to the toy market-tracking NPD Group, the U.S. console market netted $4.55 billion in 1993. By 1995, that number was down to $3.07 billion. The NPD Group's TRST data showed a 17-percent drop in 1994, followed by a 19-percent drop in 1995.

> In 1992, the year Sega smashed Nintendo's dominance in the U.S., Sega's U.S. video game sales rose 50 percent, but it barely made a profit on them. In 1993, Sega's earnings dropped 64 percent to $112 million. In contrast, Nintendo profits fell 40 percent in 1993, but it still pulled in $500 million in net profits and over $1 billion in pretax profits. It also has no debt and $3.3 billion in cash, and controls 70 percent of the world video game market. Sega has $700 million in debt and about 25 percent of the world market.[1]

Having lost the temporary boost it received from *Street Fighter II* and *Mortal Kombat,* the arcade business was in even worse shape. Taito, the company that ushered in the golden age of arcades with *Space Invaders,* closed its U.S. offices in 1995, and Data East sold its pinball division to Sega of America. That year's Amusement and Music Operators of America show, held in Dallas, was even smaller than in previous years, and rumors of companies closing were rampant around the floor of the show. One Data East employee was so unsure of his company's future that he applied for jobs at the show in a unique fashion. Data East was demonstrating an arcade machine that took people's photographs and printed them on sheets of half-inch stickers. The employee made stickers of himself holding a little sign that said, "HIRE ME," attached them to his business cards, and handed them out to other companies.

The two companies hit hardest by the 1994 and 1995 drops in the market would ultimately be the 3DO Company and Atari. They had failed to build sufficiently solid customer bases to withstand the storm that was about to strike in Japan.

The Tsunami Hits Japan

On November 22, 1994, Sega released a 32-bit video game console called Saturn in Japan. Breaking with tradition, the launch took place on a Tuesday, causing added annoyance for Tokyo commuters because the response to Saturn was so phenomenal. The 200,000 consoles that Sega shipped sold for 44,800 yen, or approximately $469. Most stores had customers pre-reserve their consoles and sold out their entire inventories more than a month in advance. Days before the launch, lines formed in front of those stores that sold their Saturn inventory on a first-come, first-served basis. Their supplies came nowhere near to meeting the demand. But the star of the day was not the Saturn console but a Saturn game—*Virtua Fighter.*

It was developed by Sega's most famous internal development team—AM2, led by Yu Suzuki. Suzuki was Sega's answer to Nintendo's Shigeru Miyamoto. Having created such arcade classics as *Space Harrier, Hang-On, Out Run,* and *Virtua Racing,* Suzuki had reached minor celebrity status. But Suzuki's biggest console hit was the Saturn version of *Virtua Fighter,* a fighting game featuring 3D polygonal combatants using a variety of authentic fighting styles, ranging from Kung Fu to professional wrestling.

Suzuki's games reflected his wide-ranging tastes. Suzuki was a man of sophisticated discernment who collected fine wines and drove a Ferrari to work. His game designs often reflected his style, offering a nearly perfect mixture of realism and fantasy, wrapped in the most technologically advanced arcade cabinets on the market. Suzuki constantly pushed his managers to allow him to add features to his designs. His games generally had force-feedback controllers that rumbled or shook in response to action in the games and the largest and highest-resolution monitors of any games on the market. When his bosses balked at the cost of building his proposed *Space Harrier* cabinets, Suzuki promised to return his salary if the game bombed. It was a major success.

In the early 1990s, Suzuki was one of the first arcade designers to experiment with 3D polygonal graphics.* His first use of this technology was a game called *Virtua Racing,* which went on to become an international arcade smash. Suzuki followed up with *Virtua Fighter.*

The brawlers in *Virtua Fighter* were not as ornate as the 2D combatants in *Mortal Kombat* or *Street Fighter II.* Because of the early technology available at the

---

* Dave Theurer, the Atari designer who created *Missile Command* and *Tempest,* introduced 3D polygons into arcades in his 1984 game *I*Robot.* Suzuki openly admits that he got the idea of using his technology in a driving game after seeing a 3D racing game called *Hard Drivin',* which Atari released in 1989.

time, the artists who created the game had to create each character with less than 1,200 polygons. This resulted in fighters with square shoulders and boxy-looking arms. Although Suzuki's foray into 3D graphics did not compare well against the polished cartoon look of other fighting games, it paved the way for beautifully fluid body movements.

As an arcade game, *Virtua Fighter* was one of Sega's most successful games in Japan. The incarnation of *Virtua Fighter* that appeared on Saturn was almost indistinguishable from the arcade game. It did not come bundled with Saturn (no games were packed in with the console), but at a price of 7,800 yen (more than $80) the *Virtua Fighter CD* sold at nearly a one-to-one ratio with Saturn consoles.

On December 3, 1994, Sony launched a new console called PlayStation into the Japanese market. Unlike Sega, Sony was not an established game company, and only 100,000 consoles were shipped at a retail of 39,800 yen. The launch was not as highly anticipated, and many people who had not preordered consoles were able to purchase them at stores before the inventory ran out. Unlike Sega, Sony did not have famous in-house design teams. The most notable game for PlayStation was *Ridge Racer,* a solid translation of an arcade racing game. Namco published both the arcade and PlayStation versions of this game.

To show that consumers would choose Saturn over PlayStation, Sega waited until the day the Sony console launched to ship more Saturns. Once they did, and the systems were sold side-by-side, Saturn proved the more popular system.

A New Show

> So, for some period of time, there was a pitched battle between E3 expo and CES for exhibitors, with CES obviously arguing that they were the show of choice because Nintendo was going to be there and E3 Expo arguing they were show of choice because they had Sony, Sega, and most of the major third parties lining up.
>
> **—Douglas Lowenstein, president, Interactive Digital Software Association**

Back in the United States, Nintendo and Sega continued to wrangle for leadership of the video game industry. Sega lost the battle over the rating system, but a new struggle erupted over trade shows.

Since the early days of Atari, video game companies had unveiled their products at the Consumer Electronics Show (CES), a show run by a trade organization called the Electronic Industry Association. CES was about more than interactive games, however. It was the place where manufacturers unveiled new televisions, car sound systems, telephones, and refrigerators. Despite the bad years for video games, more and more computer software companies were publishing games, and floor space was becoming a limited commodity. In an effort to keep the game makers happy, the Electronic Industry Association proposed a show called CES-I.

With the creation of the Interactive Digital Software Association (IDSA), the video game industry had its own trade organization and was large enough and prosperous enough to run its own show. As the Electronic Industry Association made plans for CES-I, a large international publishing company called IDG Communications approached the IDSA with a proposal for an annual show called the Electronic Entertainment Expo (E3) that would supplant CES as the show for the interactive entertainment industry. Sega, Sony, Atari, and several leading software publishers immediately announced support for the show, while Nintendo and Microsoft threw their weight behind CES-I.

> When we decided to create a trade show, everyone, including Nintendo, supported a dedicated trade event for the industry. Two organizations were presenting and seeking our support at the time and we had to decide which one to endorse. EIA (Electronic Industry Association) had put together a version of its CES Spring show that was very broadly defined as Interactive television entertainment. At the same time, IDG had developed the concept for the Electronic Entertainment Expo. Both organizations were pitching for our support, and, ultimately, we voted to endorse E3, and Nintendo made a decision to sign up with the CES Philadelphia show.
>
> **—Douglas Lowenstein**

Nintendo became isolated. As more companies queued up in support of E3, Nintendo eventually had to fall in line.

> At the end of the day, after some period of time . . . Nintendo recognized that the industry had essentially voted with its feet, with an overwhelming

> number of companies signing up with the E3 event. They [Nintendo] then
> eventually joined the rest of the industry in signing up.
>
> **—Douglas Lowenstein**

The Electronic Entertainment Expo was about to become the next great battlefield.

Inside Sony

> The other thing that really helped us, and this is important, is that when you
> put those four letters on a product, S-O-N-Y, it gives you tremendous cred-
> ibility. It gives the customers great permission to buy, particularly when
> they've been burned by the 3DOs and the Jaguars of the world.
>
> **—Jim Whims, former executive vice president,**
> **Sony Computer Entertainment of America**

Ken Kutaragi, the engineer who created PlayStation, faced many obstacles while completing the game console that would eventually be known as the Sony PlayStation. His final unit bore almost no resemblance to the Play Station CD-ROM device that he was creating for the Super NES. He designed the final version around the 32-bit R3000A RISC chip, a processor that was supposed to be capable of rendering up to 500,000 texture-mapped polygons per second. PlayStation's performance, however, rendered approximately 350,000 polygons per second. While Saturn and PlayStation supposedly had fairly similar capabilities on the surface, there were several very important differences in both design and marketing.

PlayStation had a single processing chip with a 3D geometry engine in its CPU. This processor, along with the excellent development tools Sony made available, made PlayStation extremely easy to program. That ease of programming, along with Sony's liberal $10 per game licensing fee and its aggressive marketing plans, made PlayStation an attractive prospect for game designers. Nearly 100 game companies had signed licensing agreements with Sony by the time PlayStation launched in the United States, and more than 300 individual game projects were planned or underway.

Before Sony could become a serious contender in the game market, it would have to overcome its past. Along with being humiliated by Nintendo over the Super NES CD-ROM drive, Sony also had a dismal history as a entertainment software publisher. Sony Interactive, a small and unsuccessful software arm of the giant electronics company, had earned critical success with a game called *Mickey Mania* for Super NES, Genesis, and Sega CD, but most of its games were panned by the press and ignored by consumers. Sony published a series of ESPN Sports simulations that were generally acknowledged to be among the worst sports games on the market.

In what seemed like a poorly aimed attempt to buy its way into respectability, Sony bought Psygnosis, a Liverpool-based software company, for $48 million. At the time of the purchase, it seemed a strange move. Psygnosis's only hit, a game called *Lemmings,* had been created by outside developers; yet Sony paid top dollar for the company.

> We got into this business for one and only one reason, and that was to become leaders in the next generation marketplace. And eight months ago we were the new kids on the block, with a lot of hopes and dreams and aspirations and an absolutely o percent market share.
>
> **—Jim Whims**

When it came to marketing PlayStation in the United States, Sony left little to chance. Sony Computer Entertainment of America (SCEA), the American organization charged with the task, was built around a group of experienced game-industry veterans.

Steve Race, the president of SCEA, had been the vice president of Atari's European division during the heyday of the 2600. After the crash of 1982, Race and several friends founded Worlds of Wonder—the company that created Teddy Ruxpin and helped market the Nintendo Entertainment System. In 1990, as Tom Kalinske became the new CEO at Sega of America, he brought Race in as a marketing consultant.

Race's senior vice president of marketing was Jim Whims, who, like Race, was an ex–Worlds of Wonder executive who had a long history with video games that included stints with iMagic and Data East. Tall, comfortable around strangers, and athletically built, Whims had the look of a leader.

For his head of third-party relations, Race hired Bernard "Bernie" Stolar, whose roots in the industry reached all the way back to Marty Bromley and David Rosen. In earlier days, Stolar headed a small arcade company called Game Plan that made the 1981 game *Shark Attack.* Knowing that Sid Sheinberg, head of Universal Studios, might approach him about a possible infringement on the movie *Jaws,* Stolar met with and outsmarted the intimidating studio chief. Thinking he was giving Stolar a break, Sheinberg said that he would not demand a royalty on the first 1,000 machines. Stolar responded by cutting his manufacturing run after building the first 990.

As the person responsible for working with third-party companies, Stolar played a major role in luring outside developers to make games for PlayStation. Some of his decisions proved absolutely brilliant. Stolar actively courted Williams Manufacturing and arranged a six-month exclusive deal for the highly anticipated game *Mortal Kombat 3,* a move that virtually guaranteed PlayStation sales among members of the game's rather large cult following. On the negative side, Stolar felt that role-playing games, while very important in the Japanese market, were unnecessary in the United States.

Race hired an old friend named Peter Johnson away from Sega to handle marketing and communications. Though Sony was new as a company, its administrative team was composed largely of seasoned game executives.

> We had a lot of people with very, very good industry experience, and qualified guys who I could trust and women who I could trust who had either been in the industry or I had worked with before in some capacity. We got enormously lucky with the talent pool that we had, and we got dealt a great product, and then the rest we just put together.
>
> **—Steve Race**

In October 1994, tragedy struck Sony. Peter Johnson, the man Race had hired away from Sega to run marketing communications, was killed in a plane crash while traveling to the East Coast on business.

> I was a basket case for a long time. Peter and I had worked at three different companies together and he was a close personal friend. The night before the

> crash, I had gone to a Rolling Stones concert with him and his wife. I was
> devastated by it.
>
> **—Steve Race**

There was never any question about the quality of the PlayStation hardware or the personnel Race hired, but other issues plagued SCEA. Kutaragi and other executives at Sony did not always share Race's vision for how to run the company. They fought over everything from the length of the cords connecting the PlayStation's game pads to the launch price for the console itself.

> I'd been over to Japan a couple of times and we disagreed about pricing, po-
> sitioning, advertising, color, and ninety-nine other things that you would do
> for a product to Americanize it or to make it acceptable in the United States.
>
> It was funny. I would say, "Why are we doing this controller? It should
> look like this or it should be this size." Norio Ohga was the president of Sony
> at the time, and they'd sort of say, "Oh, no, no, no. Mr. Ohga wants it this
> way. Mr. Ohga designated this one."
>
> I kept thinking to myself, what is a guy running a $44 billion company
> doing going around with controllers for a game system?
>
> **—Steve Race**

Race's problems with Sony Computer Entertainment in Japan were well-known throughout the industry. Rumors about Race being fired were widespread. Opinionated and outspoken, Race sometimes seemed like a strange fit for the role of an American executive working in a Japanese company. The battles continued as Sony prepared for the official American unveiling of PlayStation at E3.

Inside Sega

> Clearly, Sega broke some promises about times and dates and all that. If you
> look at the recent legacy with Sega, between Sega CD and 32X and . . . well,
> I guess Nomad's still around, there were a lot of disappointing products that

> [Sega said] were next-generation systems that weren't fulfilled. They certainly weren't supported by the third-party community.
>
> **—Jim Whims**

As Trip Hawkins had predicted, Sega had stretched its resources by maintaining too many incompatible platforms. By the end of 1995, Sega of America found itself juggling seven separate and incompatible game platforms—Saturn, Genesis, Game Gear, Pico, Sega CD, 32X, and 32X CD. Amazingly, even Master System was rumored to still be active in some South American markets. There was no way one company could support every one of those systems. With an eye toward the future, Sega Enterprises CEO Hayao Nakayama made the logical choice to concentrate on Saturn.

From the Japanese perspective, Nakayama made the only possible decision. Mega-Drive, the Japanese name for Genesis, never caught on in Japan. Saturn, on the other hand, was outselling PlayStation and looked to be the dominant system. What made sense in Japan, however, was about to become a disastrous move in the United States.

> I would absolutely defend the American management on that. Tom knew that the 16-bit business was going to be there. Paul Rioux knew it, and so did Shenobu Toyoda; but Japan refused to believe. They were convinced, and they would not listen to Tom [Kalinske]. They would not listen to Paul [Rioux]. They would listen to no one and they absolutely bullied the U.S. into launching the system. It very much compromised their ability to keep the 16-bit business.
>
> **—Michael Latham, former head of Omega Team, Sega of America**

Back in the United States, the magazine *Next Generation* ran an article in which the internal components of PlayStation and Saturn were shown side by side. The editorial staff had developed a preference for PlayStation over Saturn, based on game performance, and that preference became far more pronounced as more games were published. *Next Generation*'s editors described PlayStation's design as "elegant" because all of the components fit neatly on one single circuit board. The Saturn design, by comparison, seemed jumbled, with its CD-ROM controller placed on a separate daughterboard.

> I think a lot of people are confused about that. I've heard a lot of people say, "Oh gee, look at all these chips they've got." Well, there's a reason for it and the reason is that our people feel that they need the multiprocessing to be able to bring to the home what we're doing next year in the arcades. That kind of power requires what we've got and we don't think the other machines can take advantage of.
>
> **—Tom Kalinske, former CEO, Sega of America**

In theory, Saturn, which featured two Hitachi SH2 32-bit central processing chips, was more powerful than PlayStation. The truth was that the SH2 chips were somewhat inferior to the chip Sony had selected. There was even a rumor that Nakayama had selected the chip as a favor to a golf buddy. All rumors aside, programming Saturn was difficult, and allotting different operations to both of the processing chips proved nearly impossible. In an interview with the press, Sega star arcade-game designer Yu Suzuki openly admitted having trouble with the dual-processor design while working on the Saturn version of his hit game *Daytona*.

As E3 approached in mid-May, Sega announced that the release of Saturn would take place on September 2—Sega Saturn Saturday. Behind the scenes, however, Sega was preparing an E3 surprise.

Inside Nintendo

> I realize that Nintendo keeps saying [that the Ultra 64 will be released in] 1995, but there is absolutely no evidence to support that. What they did in Chicago [at the 1994 Summer Consumer Electronics Show] was show people the coin-op hardware, which has absolutely no connection with the Ultra 64 from an internal standpoint. No way, Jose. It's a big promotional head fake.
>
> If he [Nintendo vice-president Peter Main] told you six months, mark your calendar and call him on that date. He'll tell you, "No, six months from now," and he'll still be blowing smoke at that point.
>
> **—Trip Hawkins**

On August 23, 1993, Nintendo announced plans to collaborate with Silicon Graphics on "Project Reality," a new technology that would be incorporated into a future game console. The pairing seemed perfect. Silicon Graphics was the leading company in high-end computer graphics. Hollywood special-effects studios used their workstations to create the effects in such movies as *Terminator 2* and *Jurassic Park*. The new system, which Nintendo claimed would be released in 1995, would include a modified version of the technology used in Silicon Graphics' expensive Indigo workstations and would sell for under $250. Nintendo would not give many specifics on what the system's architecture would look like, but it was stated that the final product would have a 64-bit processor.

He's [Howard Lincoln] convinced that the new Nintendo momentum will carry over into 1997. "One of the things I find most incredible," he says, "is how anyone could possibly conclude that Nintendo will not have a predominant share of the next-generation platform. We have the best technology—namely, Silicon Graphics' proprietary technology. Mr. Nakayama [Sega's president] wanted that technology as badly as Yamauchi [Hiroshi Yamauchi, president of Nintendo Co., Ltd.], but Yamauchi got it," he says. "Sega and Sony have world-class 32-bit systems. But unfortunately for them, we will be marketing a world-class 64-bit system at the same time."[2]

In 1994, Nintendo kept up a fairly regular rhythm of announcements. In March, Nintendo of America chairman Howard Lincoln announced that the British developer Rare, Ltd., would make games for Nintendo's new Project Reality console. This announcement was made two months before the unveiling of *Donkey Kong Country*, so few people knew anything about Rare. A quick scan of old Nintendo cartridges would have revealed that Rare was the company behind *Battle Toads*, but that was the only thing anyone outside of Nintendo knew.

On May 2, 1994, Nintendo announced that a Scottish firm called DMA Designs had signed up to do games for Project Reality. No better known than Rare, DMA had one significant claim to fame—it was the company that created *Lemmings*, Psygnosis's one big game. Three days later, Nintendo announced that Project Reality would use cartridge media instead of CD-ROM. This was a much more significant announcement.

At the time, Howard Lincoln claimed that the reason Nintendo decided to stick with cartridges instead of moving to CD-ROM was speed. With CD-ROMs, game consoles access information and load it into memory. These "access times" could take a few seconds with early CD-ROM drives such as the ones used in Sega CD and 3DO. Nintendo said that waiting for the games to load up diminished the experience. Because cartridges have ROM chips built into their circuits, access time is not a problem.

What makes Nintendo's platform so much cheaper than competing machines is the lack of a CD-ROM drive. Critics claim this is a great weakness. Everyone thinks the transition to CD-ROMs is inevitable because they can be manufactured much more quickly and inexpensively than cartridges. They also have much more memory, which allows developers to throw in movie and music clips. There is a problem, however. There is a difference in data-access speed of 1,000 times. To get around this, companies have had to build in lots of internal memory in the machines. But that is expensive. For software houses, it is cheaper to make CD games, but Nintendo says its cartridges will be priced the same as CDs and that for hot titles there will be plenty of margin for profit.[3]

Cartridges are a very expensive medium, however, and many game developers resented Nintendo's decision to continue using them. Sony's licensing structure was built around a $10-per-game arrangement that included manufacturing disks, manuals, and packaging. Compared to the cost of pressing CDs, manufacturing cartridges for Project Reality would be prohibitively expensive. At the time, it cost more than $20 to manufacture an 8-megabyte cartridge, compared to less than $2 to press a 640-megabyte CD. And the additional storage space on CDs could be used for video clips, animations, audio files, music, and larger games. Even as Lincoln told the media that Nintendo had forms of compression that would vastly increase the amount of information that could be crammed into an 8-megabyte cartridge, it was widely accepted that Project Reality games would simply be smaller than those on Saturn and PlayStation.

Speculation about why Yamauchi had chosen cartridges ranged from curiosity to antagonism. Tom Zito, founder of Digital Pictures, said that Nintendo went with the cartridge format because cartridges are harder and more expensive to copy—making it easier for Nintendo to avoid piracy. Other game company executives claimed Nintendo went with cartridges so that it would have complete control over the manufacturing of games for the console and maximize its profits.

> It was a combination of things. There was a technology element to it and there was that counterfeiting element to it, big time.
>
> The technology argument, I think, at the time was legitimate. . . . At the time, Takeda [Genyo Takeda, the Nintendo engineer working with Silicon Graphics to design Project Reality] and those guys felt very strongly that it was absolutely essential to have it on a cartridge in order to do the kind of things that we wanted to do with *Super Mario.*
>
> The counterfeiting thing, I think, turned out to be correct, with the huge counterfeiting problem that Sony has.
>
> I've seen speculation about how this was some plot to control third-party publishers. That's completely nonsense. There is just not a grain of truth in that thing. No discussion like that ever occurred; that was never an issue. It was strictly technology and counterfeiting.
>
> **—Howard Lincoln**

In the days leading up to the 1994 Summer Consumer Electronics Show, Nintendo made two more announcements. On June 5, Lincoln announced that Alias Research, one of the leading computer-graphics companies, would create custom software tools for Project Reality. On June 23, Lincoln announced that the final name of Nintendo's new console would be "Ultra 64" and that Acclaim Entertainment would create a game called *Turok: The Dinosaur Hunter* for it. Then came the closed-door meetings at CES, in which reporters and analysts were shown glimpses of *Killer Instinct* and told they were running on prototype Ultra 64 hardware.

On January 5, 1995, Nintendo announced that Silicon Graphics had completed the final chip set for Ultra 64 and gave the console's final specifications. Critics, such as Trip Hawkins, openly challenged Nintendo's assertion that Ultra 64 would be ready in 1995. But with the announcement that the chip set was complete, Nintendo's claim that a powerful system would be ready later that year seemed more believable.

According to the announcement, Ultra 64 would indeed have a 64-bit processor—easily the fastest processor in any of the next-generation consoles. Ultra 64 would also have a separate graphics processor that could generate 100,000 texture-mapped polygons per second, while handling several graphics-enhancing processes such as ray-tracing, anti-aliasing, and tri-linear mip-mapping interpolation—processes that were not available on PlayStation or Saturn.

After announcing that the chip set was complete, Nintendo began disclosing new partnerships with more "dream team" developers. Williams Manufacturing, the arcade company behind such Acclaim cartridge hits as *NBA Jam* and *Mortal Kombat,* joined on, as did noted PC flight simulation publishers Sierra and Spectrum HoloByte. Angel Studios, a computer-graphics company best known for making special effects for movies, and Paradigm Simulation, a company that designed high-end virtual reality software, joined the team. Then Ocean of America and GameTek—and the team started looking haphazard. Once, when asked why he selected Ocean as part of his "dream team," Lincoln was unable to stop himself from laughing. When he was able to respond, he smiled and said, "I'm surprised you did not ask, 'Why GameTek?'"

But Ultra 64 was not the only "next-generation" system Nintendo planned to release in 1995. Nintendo's research and development Team 1, led by Gumpei Yokoi, had created a portable game system called Virtual Boy.

Compared to the multimillion color-producing consoles being created by Sega, Sony, and Nintendo, Virtual Boy was an anomaly. Supposedly the heir to Game Boy, it had single-color graphics. The system was built around red LED arrays, so it only showed red objects against a black background. The catch, however, was that it had two mirror-scanning stereoscopic displays that enabled it to create the illusion of three-dimensional objects. Reflections Technology, a Massachusetts-based company that was not normally associated with games, had created Virtual Boy's stereoscopic LED technology years earlier. But marketing the idea to game companies had proved difficult.

> I turned down Reflections Technology twice. They came to me when I was with Mattel and showed me this thing called "Red World." Then they came to us before going to Nintendo and I looked at it and thought, "This looks very familiar."
>
> —**Tom Kalinske**

When Reflections Technology executives took their idea to Nintendo, they found a willing advocate in Gumpei Yokoi. Yokoi, who designed Game Boy, was looking for a new technology that might "encourage more creativity" in games.

> I saw that the market was so saturated with video games that it became nearly impossible to create anything new. There were a lot of creative ideas for games for the NES and for Game Boy. But there were not so many new ideas for games for the Super Nintendo. I think game companies ran out of new ideas. I wanted to create a new kind of game that was not a video game, so that designers could come up with new ideas.
>
> **—Gumpei Yokoi, former head of Research and Development Team 1,**
> **Nintendo Co., Ltd.**

Yokoi appears to have been less than excited about creating a system with a single-color display. He looked into making a color version of the technology but found that it would have to retail for over $500, far too expensive.

> In the beginning of the development, we experimented with a color LCD screen, but the users did not see depth, they just saw double. Color graphics give people the impression that a game is high tech. But just because a game has a beautiful display does not mean that the game is fun to play.
> I also wish to explain that LEDs come in red, yellow, blue, and green. Red uses less battery and red is easier to recognize. That is why red is used for traffic lights.
>
> **—Gumpei Yokoi**

As the project progressed, Yokoi made his new game console less like a virtual reality head-mounted display and more like a Viewmaster. Deciding that head-tracking caused motion sickness, he created his system without tracking technology. Then he decided that wearing a heavy helmet was uncomfortable, so he mounted the unit on a stand. Instead of a visor, he ended up with a console shaped like a diver's facemask with a rubberized seal for blocking outside light.

Nintendo first announced work on a virtual reality project in the summer of 1994. In November, the console was unveiled at Shoshinkai, a proprietary trade show Nintendo held in Tokyo every winter. The general reaction was less than favorable. One reporter dubbed the system "Virtual Dog."

> The November unveiling of Virtual Boy in Japan signifies an important change in direction for Nintendo. Either it has gone completely mad or it deems the future of videogaming to be crude, red, and likely to induce headaches.[4]

At the show, Nintendo announced that Virtual Boy would retail in Japan for 19,800 yen (approximately $207). Show attendees seemed unimpressed by the hardware and equally unimpressed by the games, which included a remake of the 1981 arcade classic *Mario Bros.*, a pinball simulation, and a boxing game called *Telero Boxer.* Of the three, only *Telero Boxer* tried to take advantage of Virtual Boy's 3D capabilities.

Even worse, several people who tried the system complained about having headaches after using it. Players needed to focus the mirrors inside Virtual Boy before every use to avoid getting headaches. And even if they did, staring at the red and black screen for prolonged periods of time could still produce headaches or dizziness. By the time Virtual Boy came to the United States, it bore a statement warning that extended use could cause headaches.

In January 1995, Nintendo of America unveiled Virtual Boy at Winter CES in Las Vegas but did not give specific launch information and only showed the partial games that were shown at Shoshinkai. For final launch information, reporters would have to wait for E3.

Nintendo Comes Clean

On May 4, 1995, a *Wall Street Journal* reporter named Jim Carlton interviewed Greg Fischbach about Acclaim's annual report. As he reviewed the report, he noted that while Acclaim had earnings projections for Saturn and PlayStation sales, there were no projections for Ultra 64 sales. When he asked Fischbach about this, Fischbach quickly said, "No comment."

Armed with this information, Carlton called Nintendo marketing and communications manager Perrin Kaplan and told her what he had found. She said she understood and asked for one hour to prepare a response. Kaplan went directly to Howard Lincoln, chairman of Nintendo of America, and Minoru Arakawa, president of Nintendo of America, and told them what had happened. With no other option, they admitted that Ultra 64 would not be released in 1995, and Carlton had a scoop for the next day's paper.

The next morning, Howard Lincoln came in early and called reporters around the country to warn them about the *Wall Street Journal* article and to let them know that Ultra 64 would not be out for another year.

The Really Big Show

The first Electronic Entertainment Expo took place in the Los Angeles Convention Center on May 11–13, 1995, and all the major players were ready to put on a show. On the first day, Tom Kalinske, president of Sega, and Olaf Olafsson, president of Sony Electronic Publishing, were scheduled to give keynote presentations from 8:30 A.M. to 9:45 A.M. Kalinske discussed Sega's heritage in arcades and as a game company. He announced that the retail price of the Saturn would be $399 and began describing what a powerful system it was. Then he gave the punchline—the console had already shipped. September 2, Sega Saturn Saturday, was still going to be the official launch date for Saturn, but 30,000 systems had already been shipped to four key retailers: Toys "R" Us, Babbages, Software Etc., and Electronics Boutique.

Next came Sony's turn to drop a bomb. Olafsson was supposed to discuss "what it's going to take to be successful storytellers in coming years." The topic obviously gave him room to discuss the technological strengths of PlayStation, and he was expected to announce the system's price and launch date. At the time, it was generally assumed that PlayStation would likely be as expensive, or possibly more expensive, than Saturn. Olafsson started his speech as expected, then interrupted himself.

> Olaf [Olafsson] was about two-thirds of the way through his speech when he said, "I'd like to call up Steve Race to tell you a little bit more about the Sony PlayStation." So I walked up. I had a whole bunch of sheets of paper in my hands, and I walked up, put them down on the podium, and I just said, "$299," and walked off stage to this thunderous applause.
>
> **—Steve Race**

Sony clearly won the first battle of E3. By sending Saturns to four retailers only, Sega offended several of its best outlets. Kay*bee Toys responded by dropping Sega from its lineup. More important, releasing in spring or summer, typically slow seasons for video game hardware sales, did not give Sega any advantage. Having a surprise launch meant that Sega had forfeited any chance of having a big send-off for Saturn and gave the appearance of being afraid of head-to-head competition with PlayStation.

> I think Japan was scared of PlayStation; at least more than we were in the U.S. Tom was not afraid. Tom was ready to go to battle because Tom was used to hardware that wasn't necessarily the best in the market anyway.
>
> **—Michael Latham**

Sony's surprise was more effective. Even though Saturn came bundled with a highly desirable game, *Virtua Fighter,* it was too expensive for the consumer electronics category. The $399 price point was known to be more of a high-end electronics ticket, something that people might pay for a stereo component but not for a video game console. Sega was making the same mistake Trip Hawkins had made with 3DO.

> I'm sure that price came from Japan. Tom was frequently dealt some very difficult cards to have to play, and he did a very good job of melding his deck and doing as much as he could with the cards that he was dealt. My hat is off to the guy.
>
> **—Steve Race**

While Nintendo, Sega, and Sony threw million-dollar parties at E3, Trip Hawkins held a quiet and elegant dinner at a fine restaurant. In his typical socially graceful fashion, he left one seat open at every table and shuttled from one table to the next through the meal so that he could speak with all of his guests. During the meal, a reporter asked him what he thought of Sony. Sighing and looking a bit tired, Hawkins replied, "For a company that is so new to the industry, I would have hoped that Sony would have made more mistakes by now."

Nintendo executives focused on Super NES, Game Boy, and Virtual Boy rather than Ultra 64. There were no Ultra 64 prototypes for guests at the Nintendo booth, and by this time everybody knew that Nintendo had no plan to release the console in 1995. Lincoln did announce, however, that Virtual Boy would come out in August for a suggested retail price of $179. Nintendo's other big announcements were three Super NES game—*Donkey Kong Country 2, Killer Instinct,* and *Yoshi's Island.**

The Launch Season Begins

One problem with launching Virtual Boy, along with the general lack of interest most consumers had in the product, was that the only way to see its 3D images was to place your face against it. This meant that shoppers would not see the 3D images as they walked past them in stores. Also, the system could not be effectively demonstrated on television.

Virtual Boy was released on August 14 to generally lackluster reviews. Although reviewers at *Entertainment Weekly* and *Popular Science* gave it glowing reviews,

---

* An interesting story lies behind *Yoshi's Island.* When Shigeru Miyamoto first demonstrated the game to Nintendo's marketing department, it was rejected because it had Mario-related graphics rather than the waxy, prerendered graphics of *Donkey Kong Country.* Rather than change to an artistic look he did not like, Miyamoto made the game even more cartoon-like, giving it a hand-drawn look. The second version was accepted.

Miyamoto, who is rightfully proud of his work, was offended that the first version was rejected. That same month, I interviewed Miyamoto and Tim Stamper, creator of *Donkey Kong Country,* together and noticed that Miyamoto was a bit hard on Stamper, making such statements as *"Donkey Kong Country* proves that players will put up with mediocre gameplay as long as the art is good."

In a later interview, Miyamoto admitted that *Yoshi's Island* had been a touchy subject at the time:

I think that it happened after *Donkey Kong Country* was introduced. In comparison with the graphics of the *Super Donkey Kong,* there was not enough punch to *Yoshi's Island.* That was what I was told by the marketing people.

I intensified my hand-drawn touch on *Yoshi's Island* from the initial part of the program. Everybody else was saying that they wanted better hardware and more beautiful graphics instead of this art.

Even while I was working on the *Super Mario World,* I was thinking that the next hero should be Yoshi. Other people have created games based upon Yoshi. . . . *Yoshi's World Hunters, Yoshi's Egg, Yoshi's Cookie,* and so forth—games that I don't really like. So I decided that I should make an authentic Yoshi game.

game magazines panned it. When the editors at *Next Generation* opened the box in which their Virtual Boy was packed, they began playing volleyball with the inflated bags Nintendo had used as packing material. "It was the most fun we were ever going to have with anything in that box," editor in chief Neil West explained when asked about it.

By mid-August, the industry had already lost interest in Virtual Boy, as Microsoft became the focus of worldwide attention. On August 24, 1995, Microsoft launched *Windows 95 (Win95)*, a major upgrade from previous *Windows* operating systems that included technology for running games smoothly. Though Microsoft published a few games to accompany the launch of *Win 95*, it would take months before people realized the deep impact the new operating system would eventually have on gaming. By the end of the year, people would even be able to play first-person shooters without leaving the *Windows* environment, making computer game installation suddenly easier.

Though it did not make computers as simple to use as consoles, *Win 95* went a long way toward closing the gap. Computer games did not catch up to console games in overall sales, and the top console games still sold at two to three times the rate of the top PC titles, but video game publishers began eyeing PCs as a viable new platform.

The next big event was the September release of PlayStation. One person who was not going to see this release, however, was Steve Race. On August 7, Race resigned as president of Sony Computer Entertainment of America and resurfaced quickly at Spectrum HoloByte. Few people were surprised by Race's departure; his ongoing battles with his employers in Japan were well-known.

> We had celebrated differences of opinion as to where the product should be and how it should be priced and positioned. I wouldn't say we had screaming matches, but we just had long pregnant pauses, and I questioned their heritage, from whence they came. . . . something about female dogs.
>
> **—Steve Race**

Sony shipped 100,000 PlayStation consoles for release on September 9, almost all of which had been prereserved. The entire shipment sold out. Two days after the release, Sony had already sold more PlayStations than Sega had sold Saturns in the five months since the surprise announcement at E3. By the end of the year, Sony boasted of having shipped 800,000 PlayStations into North America while Sega claimed to have sold 400,000 Saturns.

> We told people we would ship on September 9th. We shipped on September 9th. We told them we'd have 10 to 15 titles in the first 30 days, and we had 15 titles in the first 30 days. We said we'd have 50 new titles out by the end of the calendar year. We had 55 out by the end of the calendar year. We built credibility not only with the consumer, but with the trade.
>
> When you have two competitors as firmly entrenched as Sega and Nintendo, which are both great companies, make no mistake about it, you have to differentiate yourself. I think we did that.
>
> **—Jim Whims**

In the meantime, things unraveled for 3DO and Atari. As far as the public was concerned, Nintendo had blown a hole in 3DO's claims of technological superiority with *Donkey Kong Country*. In 1995, Crystal Dynamics released a game about a wise-cracking Hawaiian lizard called *Gex* that brought the same highly polished graphical look to 3DO and supplemented it with the voice files that would never have fit in a Super NES cartridge. Standup comedian Dana Gould performed the voice-over for Gex, the main character, giving the game a certain charismatic wit. Realizing that *Gex* was the most surefire game in the 3DO lineup, Panasonic bundled it with their company's version of the console.*

Gex and other highly improved games were not enough; 3DO had lost its position as the most desirable game console the moment Tom Kalinske announced that Saturn had already shipped. By the time Sony launched in September, the only tricks 3DO manufacturers Panasonic and GoldStar had left were to offer rebates and to bundle more software. As one GoldStar print ad stated, "The GoldStar 3DO system is jammed full of space-age technology and comes with lots of FREE stuff."

3DO's window of dominance had been shut, and, in his own evangelical way, Hawkins helped close it. Seeing that there was no way to compete with

---

* Once, while visiting a game store, Gould asked if a clerk had *Gex*. "It's pronounced Jex," the clerk replied. "it's about a dinosaur."

Sega and Sony, he began talking about the disappointment of the 32-bit generation and the real strengths that 64-bit processing had to offer. Hawkins changed his focus to M2, a 64-bit console that he promised would shame PlayStation and Saturn. M2 never materialized. 3DO sold the technology to Matsushita for $100 million, and though many game companies did receive M2 development kits, no M2 systems were ever released.

Things were even worse at Atari. Atari president Sam Tramiel struggled to find ways to bolster sales and cut costs. In 1995, he stopped manufacturing Jaguars and concentrated entirely on selling off the existing inventory. He slashed the price of the console to $149, released an attachable CD-ROM peripheral, and openly courted new game developers. He ran infomercials to try and sell additional consoles, but the infomercials did not reach the right audience. Toward the end of 1995, Atari finally convinced Wal-Mart to carry Jaguar in its superstores, but by that time people knew about Saturn and PlayStation and weren't interested. Nothing seemed to work. The company was hemorrhaging money. The end came when Sam Tramiel suffered a mild heart attack and his father, Jack, came in to run the show in his absence.

> Sam had just finished riding a bicycle. He got off the bike, felt somewhat faint, felt a pain in his chest, drove himself to the Stanford Medical Center, and there was informed that he had had a mild heart attack.
>
> Jack came back in [to Atari while Sam was recovering]. Jack knew how bad it was. It wasn't that Jack didn't know, Jack knew. Jack knew all the numbers, all the time.
>
> **—Bernie Stolar, president and COO, Sega of America**

Many theories arose about why Jack Tramiel purchased Atari. Some people said that he bought the company as a means for exacting revenge on Commodore, the company that he founded, then left under unpleasant circumstances. Another theory was that he purchased Atari to make one last fortune, enough money to ensure the future of his three sons, Sam, Leonard, and Gary. A third theory suggested that he bought Atari as a way of bringing his sons together. If any of these were his reasons, he succeeded. Atari outlasted Commodore, had a few enormously profitable years, and united his sons in a common goal.

On July 30, 1996, Atari Corp. merged with JTS Corporation, a company that manufactured 3.5-inch disk drives, in an $80 million stock swap. Jack Tramiel was active on the JTS board after the merger. Two years later, Hasbro Interactive purchased the Atari library from JTS.

> We were trying to license four products, including *Centipede, Missile Command, Tempest,* and *Pong.* During the licensing arrangement, we realized that JTS was in financial dire straits, so we decided to take it to a higher level. . . . we moved very quickly and very aggressively and turned this into an acquisition opportunity. We acquired all of the trademarks, patents, copyrights, and intellectual property for all of Atari. Jack Tramiel was involved in the discussions. He was a tough negotiator, as always, but they needed money. The acquisition cost us $5 million.
>
> **—Tom Dusenberry, president, Hasbro Interactive**

Time Warner put Atari Coin-Op on the sales block in 1996 as well. In an interesting twist, one of the first people to bid on it was Nolan Bushnell, the man who originally had founded the company. Time Warner turned down his offer, however, and sold Atari to a familiar competitor—Williams Manufacturing.

Nintendo Unveiled

In late November 1995, Nintendo finally unveiled its 64-bit, cartridge-based game console at its Shoshinkai trade show, held that year in a cavernous, warehouse-like convention center called the Makuhari Messe. As a proprietary show featuring only games for Nintendo systems, Shoshinkai was considerably smaller than E3 or the Tokyo Game Show. The entire show fit into one section of the Makuhari Messe and filled less than two-thirds of the floor.

Nintendo's next-generation console underwent three name changes by the time it was unveiled. First known as Project Reality, then Ultra 64, the final name of the console was "Nintendo 64 (N64)." Although Nintendo had released many details about the new console during the months leading up to the unveiling, no information was ever leaked about the system's controller. Created by Genyo Takeda and Nintendo Research and Development Team 3, N64 had a new and revolutionary three-handled controller that featured both a traditional digital directional pad and a new analog directional lever. The T-pad, which was especially good for fighting games, worked a lot like a light switch. It did not read how hard you pushed, it simply noted when you pushed down on it and from what direction you pushed, then moved you in that direction at a constant speed. The analog lever, on the other hand, responded to pressure. Push slightly to the right, and the character you were controlling would inch in that direction. Push the lever all the way over, and your character would run at full tilt.

> We tried a motion sensor wristwatch-style controller. We made a prototype and applied for a patent. Everything was good, but players didn't understand the internal mechanism and had trouble controlling it, so we abandoned it.
>
> **—Genyo Takeda, manager R&D Team 3, Nintendo Co., Ltd.**

Hiroshi Yamauchi was clearly proud of the new controller. In a lengthy speech given the first day of the show, he said, "If you think this is just another game pad, then you know nothing about video games."

Most of the floor space was dedicated to Super Famicom (the Japanese name for Super NES), with a fairly large section for Game Boy and a much smaller corner of the floor for N64. Obviously, most people at the show crammed in around the N64 area, taking turns playing the only two games on display— *Super Mario 61* and *Kirby's Air Ride*. Although the show ran smoothly, it was obvious that some decisions had not been made until the morning of the show. When an American reporter emerged from the N64 area, Howard Lincoln approached him and asked what he thought of the game. "The Mario game was great, but that other game wasn't amazing."

"We're only showing one game," replied Lincoln, who had not been told about a last-minute decision to show *Kirby's Air Ride.*

The Last Days of Yokoi

Across the floor of Makuhari Messe, in the corner farthest away from N64, Gumpei Yokoi manned the little booth where Virtual Boy was being displayed. As he always appeared when in public, Yokoi was impeccably dressed in a dark suit, crisp white shirt, and modest red tie. He was a thin man with narrow shoulders whose head always appeared slightly large for the tiny frame of his body. The touches of white along his temples added to his dignified air. Few people stopped by his booth, so Yokoi was able to personally demonstrate games to those who did.

This was his punishment, the Japanese corporate version of Dante's Inferno. Gumpei Yokoi, the engineer who had created Nintendo's first toys in his spare time, had been placed in the proverbial doghouse for creating the debacle that was Virtual Boy. Having received shipments of Virtual Boy less than one year earlier, Tokyo stores were now discounting it so heavily that customers could buy it for less than $100—under half the original cost.

When employees make high-profile mistakes in Japan, it is not unusual for their superiors to make an example out of them for a period of time, then return them to their former stature. Such seemed to be the case with Yokoi. Yamauchi would pretend to have forgotten that Game Boy, *Metroid,* and *Dr. Mario* had all come from Yokoi's team; would leave him to man a booth with a dying product; then eventually would bring him back into grace. So, armed with *Bound High,* a first-person perspective game in which players sat inside a bouncing ball and tried to steer it, and an adventure game called *Dragon Hopper,* Yokoi greeted buyers and the media and cheerfully tried to explain that there was still life in Virtual Boy. Not many people came by, but he seemed happy to have an audience when they did.

Yokoi left Nintendo the following August, after spending nearly thirty years with the company. He started his own handheld game company and named it *Koto,* a word meaning "small town." (It is also the name of a classical Japanese string instrument.) His company's first project was a monochrome handheld game system that was similar to Game Boy but slimmer and with a better speaker and a larger screen. Eventually named Wonder Swan, Yokoi's new game system had other nice touches, too. It had directional pads in two different corners so that it could be used to play games with either vertical or horizontal orientation. It also operated on a single AA battery. Yokoi licensed the new handheld to Bandai, Japan's largest toy manufacturer.

On October 4, 1997, Yokoi and a friend were involved in a small accident on the Horukiko Expressway in Kyoto when they rear-ended another car. Both men climbed out to inspect the damage and were struck by a passing car. While his friend suffered fractured ribs, Yokoi sustained much more serious injuries and died two hours later. As the father of Game Boy, his death attracted a lot of media attention. In the United States, Yokoi's obituary was read on National Public Radio and appeared in the *New York Times* and *People* magazine.

In 1999, Bandai released a new handheld video game system called "Wonder Swan." Though obsolete compared to Game Boy Color, Wonder Swan was launched with some fanfare. One of the first games for the new handheld was a curious strategy game in which players tried to complete circuits of lines by adding tiles with junctions. The game was called *Gunpei.**

---

* Several people who have written about Yokoi have used an "n" instead of an "m" when spelling his first name. Although his name appeared with an "m" on his business card, David Sheff chose to use the "n" in *Game Over*, which may be a more appropriate representation of his name.

The Mainstream and All Its Perils

Things are the same as usual here. Dudley's diet isn't going too well. My aunt found him smuggling doughnuts into his room yesterday. They told him they'd have to cut his pocket money if he keeps doing it, so he got really angry and chucked his PlayStation out of the window. That's a sort of computer thing you can play games on.[1]

—Harry Potter, Fledgling Wizard

Since 1957, in America, the per capita assault rate has gone up seven-fold. In Canada, since 1964, the per capita assault rate has gone up between four- and fivefold. In the last 15 years, in European nations, the per capita assault rate has gone up approximately fivefold, in Norway and Greece, fourfold in Australia and New Zealand. It has tripled in Sweden, and doubled in seven other European nations.

Now, the only common denominator in all of those nations is that we are feeding our children death and horror and destruction as entertainment. And the worst of these is the violent video games, the simulated training devices.[2]

—Congressional testimony, Lieutenant Colonel (retired) Dave Grossman,
professor, Arkansas State University, 1999 Senate Hearings

The Last Great Hope for Arcades

Steven Spielberg, a longtime fan of video games, made an annual pilgrimage to the Electronic Entertainment Expo (E3), often bringing his children with him. He was said to have several arcade machines in his home and was known to have visited Sega Enterprises in Japan on several occasions. In 1996, three elements came together at one time, creating the opportunity for Spielberg to enter the arcade business in a big way.

> I had been talking to Steven [Spielberg] about doing something in the arcade business for years. Then Steven formed DreamWorks, and Sega's home game business started getting into trouble, and Nakayama (Hayao Nakayama, CEO of Sega Enterprises) wanted to get more active in coin-op. I had introduced Steven to Nakayama the preceding year, and we were going to do this project, frankly, just with Sega and DreamWorks. Then Universal was sold and they had a friendly owner and joined us.
>
> But the core idea . . . a place where an adult wanted to go and could get good food, get Starbucks coffee, a good beer, have good music playing and meet other adults in a place that was attractive and appealing, that idea really had its core in Steven.
>
> **—Skip Paul, cofounder and CEO, Sega GameWorks**

Spielberg found the perfect partner for his arcade ambitions in Skip Paul, a man who had started with Atari as legal counsel and risen to president of the coin-op division. Like Spielberg, Paul was an avid fan of the arcade experience. He also had a great understanding of the video game business. Together, they formed an alliance between Spielberg's DreamWorks, Sega Enterprises, and Universal Studios, having all three companies throw their weight behind a chain of enormous and trendy entertainment complexes that would feature high-quality restaurants, bars, and enormous arcades. They called the venture "GameWorks."

The first GameWorks location, which had more than 35,000 square feet of floor space, opened in downtown Seattle in March of 1997. The opening was treated like a movie premier, with such stars as Will Smith, Gillian Anderson, and Weird Al Yankovic in attendance. MTV broadcast the event live, and Microsoft chairman Bill Gates walked the floor. The opening of GameWorks was a major press event as well. *USA Today, Time,* and many other national publications covered it.

The original GameWorks formula paid homage to the days of classic arcade games by featuring an alcove with two rows of 1980s coin-op machines.* As executives tweaked the GameWorks formula to find the best mix for the public, the classics corner was one of the first casualties.

After the Seattle debut, GameWorks opened several more locations in such cities as Columbus and Chicago. Although GameWorks was the most high-profile entry into the arcade business, other companies also experimented with location-based entertainment. There were still several Chuck E. Cheese franchises, the pizza parlor-arcades originally created by Nolan Bushnell around the United States. On a more upscale note, Disney opened virtual theme parks called DisneyQuests in Chicago and Orlando. More family-oriented than GameWorks, these high-tech wonderlands featured virtual rides and games with distinctly Disney themes. The most established arcade/eatery company, however, was Dave and Busters, a well-managed chain quietly spreading nationwide.

The Making of Mario

Shigeru Miyamoto, creator of *Donkey Kong, Mario, Zelda, Yoshi,* and *Star Fox,* entered the video game industry with a unique philosophy that was always reflected in his games. "When you draw a laughing face, your face should laugh," he once explained in an interview. "When you draw an angry face, your face should be angry. The character will capture your emotion. The emotions and fun in a game are not made while thinking about business."

By the time Nintendo launched Nintendo 64 (N64), Miyamoto had been creating games for nearly twenty years. He had witnessed and aided the evolution of the business, software, and technology of video gaming. His first

---

* Purists complained that the classic machines, which included *Donkey Kong, Moon Patrol, Gorf, Popeye,* and *Robotron 2084,* had been stripped out of their original cabinets and placed in matching oak cabinets.

game, *Donkey Kong,* was created by a five-man team and contained approximately 20K of code. Now, as he made the flagship game for N64, his team had swollen to more than fifty members. Instead of 20K, he and his team would write 8 megabytes of code—more than 400 times more code than in *Donkey Kong.* Instead of designing game levels that fit on a single screen, they created enormous 3D landscapes complete with trees, castles, and dinosaurs. Adapting to this new challenge, Miyamoto created a new philosophy. While most game designers were coming up with features, then building their games around them, Miyamoto worked on creating expressive landscapes, then created ways to use them.

> One thing that was different with *Super Mario 64* was [that] we wanted to make some snow mountain, a really big one. That came first, and afterward we asked [each other] for the ideas about how to make use of this mountain.
>
>   It was as if we were building up an amusement park. We first found our location. We purchased the mountain, and afterward, we thought of some interesting things we wanted to implement on the mountain.

> **—Shigeru Miyamoto, game designer, Nintendo Co., Ltd.**

Super Mario 64, Miyamoto's lead game for N64, did a better job of bringing a two-dimensional side-scrolling game into the world of 3D than any game before it. To accomplish this, Miyamoto's team used all of the old characters and objects made popular in earlier Mario games, then incorporated new devices that could only occur in the 3D environment. The big end battles, for instance, pitted Mario against a much larger foe on a huge 3D platform. The only way for Mario to win was to circle around the enemy.

Building from Miyamoto's amusement park analogy, *Super Mario 64* included huge slides and other kinds of activities that brought true variety to the game. Everybody at Nintendo recognized the game as a masterpiece; the only problem was that Miyamoto was taking too long to build it. According to Hiroshi Imanishi, Nintendo president Hiroshi Yamauchi's right-hand man, the release of N64 was delayed until Miyamoto was satisfied with *Super Mario 64.* The delay would have been even longer, but Yamauchi finally told Miyamoto that the game was good enough.

Another Battle at E3

> There may have been an agreement. I certainly wasn't a part of these conference calls that they had. Quite frankly, they have a CEO roundtable, and they weren't going to let lowly executive vice presidents on these panels.
>
> **—Jim Whims, former executive vice president,**
> **Sony Computer Entertainment America**

Concentrating on Saturn proved to be a tactical mistake that cost Sega millions, if not billions, of dollars at the end of 1995. According to TRST data released in 1997, 32-bit products made up less than 20 percent of 1995 video game sales, while 16-bit sales accounted for approximately 64 percent of the market. With only a few hundred thousand people owning Saturn, the market for Saturn software was tiny compared to the Super NES and Genesis markets. Nintendo concentrated on its 16-bit sales that Christmas and had the most lucrative holiday season of any game manufacturer. Cash-starved Sega did not have the inventory or new games to capitalize on Genesis.

Sega was also lagging in the 32-bit arena. In March, Sony sent out a press release announcing that it had shipped more than 1 million PlayStations into North America. By September, that figure would grow to 2.3 million units in North America and more than 8 million units worldwide.

Going into the 1996 Electronic Entertainment Expo, Nintendo looked strong, based on the glowing reviews N64 had received at Shoshinkai, an annual trade show Nintendo held in Japan. Sony also looked strong, having shipped more than 5 million PlayStations worldwide.

As they did during the days of the Consumer Electronics Show, Nintendo executives held a major press conference the day before E3 began. During this conference, held in the Biltmore Hotel, Nintendo chairman Howard Lincoln officially presented the N64 to the American press, and Nintendo spokespeople Ken Lobb and Isaac Marshall demonstrated *Super Mario 64* and *Pilotwings.* Lincoln announced that Nintendo 64 would be launched on September 30, at a retail price of $250.

Next, Peter Main, Nintendo of America vice president of marketing, described the future of the market as he saw it. Sony, he said, currently controlled

80 percent of the 32/64-bit market. Even calculating in the September release of N64, Main conceded that Sony would control 50 percent of the market in 1996, with Nintendo wresting 34 percent of the market away from Sega and Sony. By Main's figures, Sega was not much of a threat. He predicted that Sega would control only 16 percent of the market in 1996. And that 16 percent, he predicted, would drop to 8 percent in 1997, as Nintendo once again became the industry leader and claimed 53 percent of the market share, leaving Sony with only 39 percent. That night, Nintendo threw a lavish party in which Cirque Du Soleil performed. As far as Nintendo was concerned, the show had started perfectly. But Nintendo had no idea what Sony had planned.

As his predecessor had done the year before, Sony executive vice president Jim Whims decided to start the show "right" by making a momentous announcement during his keynote address. Though Sony could barely keep up with the demand for the PlayStation at $299, he announced that the company had decided to drop the price of the console to $199. The announcement caught Nintendo and Sega flatfooted. It was later revealed that there had been a gentleman's agreement barring price announcements at the show.

> Last year, Steve [Race] got up and said, "$299," and the place went crazy. So dropping to $199, this had been part of our plans for a long time. If we had to hire a streaker to run across the stage with a sign that said $199, we would have done it. This was part of our legacy now: don't miss the keynote address if Sony's up there.
>
> **—Jim Whims**

Whims's announcement sent shockwaves through the show. Sega had fought against dropping the price of Saturn to $299. Saturn hardware was more expensive to manufacture than PlayStation, and Sega did not have Sony's deep pockets to help absorb the costs of giving away hardware and profiting from software. Executives at Nintendo and Sega were not prepared to respond, but both companies eventually dropped their prices to match Sony's. Through Jim Whims's calculated game of chicken, Sony flexed its marketing muscle and proved itself to be the industry leader.

Sony's leadership came with a certain amount of arrogance. On the third day of the show, Sega spokeswoman Angela Edwards brought signs saying,

"Saturn, now only $299." As she stood outside the show, waiting for help carrying the signs, an employee of Sony approached her, looked at the signs, and said, "You're pathetic!"

Sega was in a bad position. Long known for its sports simulations, Sega did not have a football game ready for the 1996 fall season, and Electronic Arts did not release a 32-bit version of *Madden NFL '96*, meaning there was no football game on Saturn. Sony, on the other hand, produced an excellent game called *NFL GameDay* and took leadership of the sports category.

Sega had squandered its five-month lead to market, releasing only one new game all summer long. By 1996, Sony had a much larger library than Sega, and Sega's only hope at E3 would be new games. The company's hottest prospect was *NiGHTS,* a game created by Yuji Naka, who also designed *Sonic The Hedgehog.*

Naka may have established his reputation as a great designer with *Sonic,* but with *NiGHTS* he demonstrated his versatility. The game revolved around two young children who, in their dreams, gracefully flew through a surrealistic world and faced personal demons. Always the perfectionist, Naka, the main programmer on the *NiGHTS* project, fretted over every detail in the game.

> *NiGHTS* was a difficult game to make. . . . Very difficult. It wasn't just the 3D aspects, it was more the actual game itself, the worlds and the way the characters interacted. If the game was missing one important element, it was going to be a complete failure and everybody would look at it and say, "This is really a disappointment."
>
> **—Yuji Naka, leader of Sonic Team, Sega Enterprises**

NiGHTS showed the strengths and weaknesses of Saturn. The game's atmosphere and design were exceptional; but while the game had a free-flowing 3D feel, most of it actually took place in two dimensions. Although Nintendo and Sony had true 3D game machines, Sega had a 2D console that did a good job with 3D objects but wasn't optimized for 3D environments.

Interestingly, *NiGHTS* became part of a new kinder, gentler image that Sega tried to evoke in 1996. The Sega scream disappeared from the company's advertising and Sega held press events for educators and gave Internet-ready Saturns to schools. Things were closing in on Sega. The company that had once proved that the market was big enough for two competitors was now demonstrating that it wasn't big enough for three.

The Launch of Nintendo 64

In mid-June 1996, Nintendo shipped 300,000 N64 consoles for the June 23 Japanese launch date. Only three games were ready on the day that the console launched: *Super Mario 64, Pilot Wings 64,* and a Japanese chess game called *Shogi.* In what may have been the most orderly launch of a highly anticipated console ever, Nintendo sold all 300,000 consoles, plus 300,000 copies of *Super Mario 64* and nearly 200,000 copies of *Pilot Wings 64.*

Judging by the quiet Sunday morning launch, observers might have misjudged how excited people were over Nintendo 64. A Japanese fast food chain started serving "Mario milkshakes" and a new television game show based on Nintendo 64 appeared on television. Nintendo planned to ship more than 1 million more consoles by the end of the summer, but the euphoria did not last. Instead of shipping more consoles, Nintendo needed to ship more games.

In the meantime, Nintendo executives steadfastly tried to explain to the press why it was actually advantageous to launch after Sega and Sony.

> It has always been the contention of Nintendo that among the criteria for success, "first" is pretty far down the list. The three factors that most motivate our customers—and those of our competitors—remain constant, no matter how the technology advances. First, is the "content" or entertainment made possible by the technology. Second, does the new technology actually deliver performance which is immediately and palpably better than what they already own? And third, and perhaps most important, can they afford it?[3]

Milestones

By the spring of 1996, the industry was rife with rumors that Tom Kalinske was leaving Sega. People assumed he was going to work for Disney when he was seen having lunch with Disney CEO Michael Eisner. Indications hinted that Kalinske was ready to leave. Mike Ribero, a former hotel executive hired by Sega, was rumored to have told people that he was replacing Kalinske.

Moreover, there were stories about Kalinske falling asleep during company meetings and reports that he didn't seem as intense as he had been in earlier years.

> He [Tom] would fall asleep on occasion in meetings. That is true. These were nine-hour meetings. Sega had a thing for meetings. You'd get there at 8:00 A.M. and then you'd get out of the meeting at, like, 4:00 P.M., so he wasn't the only person.

> **—Michael Latham, former head of Omega Team, Sega of America**

Saturn continued to do well in Japan, and Sega's Japanese executives blamed their American affiliate for any problems in the U.S. market. Hayao Nakayama made frequent trips to Sega of America's Redwood City headquarters, and the Japanese team seized more and more control of how the company was run.

According to some people who worked with him, Kalinske seemed less interested in the work. People talked about walking into his office and seeing him staring out his window at nearby Oracle Headquarters. He didn't seem as ready to fight Japan on decisions he knew were incorrect, and when his marketing team sent out a poorly conceived advertisement, he replied with a surly memo that said simply, "Have we lost our collective minds?"

> It wasn't the failure of Saturn that made him lose interest; it was the inability to do something about it. He was not allowed to do anything. The U.S. side was basically no longer in control.

> **—Michael Latham**

On July 15, Sega announced that Kalinske had tendered his resignation. Within the week, Sega cofounder David Rosen resigned as chairman of Sega Enterprises and Hayao Nakayama resigned as CEO. Shortly after leaving Sega, Kalinske reemerged at Learning Technologies, a company founded by Oracle chief Larry Ellison and famed stock trader Michael Milken, both personal friends of Kalinske. Nakayama and Rosen remained with Sega, with Rosen acting as senior advisor.

One week after Kalinske left Sega, Sony Computer Entertainment of America announced that Jim Whims had resigned. For the next six months,

Sony executive Shigeo Maruyama would fill in as chairman, commuting from Japan on a weekly basis.

> Mr. Maruyama came in to become the chairman, and he did the infamous commute. He commuted between Tokyo and Foster City every week for six months. He would start the week on Monday, work in Japan Monday and half a day on Tuesday, then he'd get on a plane that would get him here Tuesday morning. He would work in Foster City Tuesday through Thursday, and then he'd catch a plane on Friday, which got him back to Tokyo on Saturday in the afternoon.
>
> **—Kazuo "Kaz" Hirai, president and COO,**
> **Sony Computer Entertainment America**

Maruyama eventually brought in Kazuo "Kaz" Hirai to run the American side of the PlayStation business. Hirai, who had been with Sony Music Corporation since 1984, was an excellent choice. Tall and elegant, Hirai spoke flawless English, though he was originally from Japan. He projected the very image Sony wished to convey—educated, sophisticated, and confident. Under Hirai's leadership, Sony Computer Entertainment America prepared for the launch of Nintendo 64.

These were busy months for Sony. On September 5, Sony released a game called *Crash Bandicoot.* The term *bandicoot* referred to a class of Southern Pacific marsupials that included Tasmanian devils. Hence, it surprised no one when the animal in Sony's new game turned out to be a dim-witted brute with a spin attack. Critics charged that as a game, *Crash Bandicoot* was too derivative. Like Mario and Sonic, Crash ran around jumping on enemies and collecting things—mostly apples. But Crash was a character with a strong personality, and the people behind the game had a great eye for gameplay. Hence the character seemed destined to become Sony's marsupial mascot. The character certainly took a step toward mascot status when an actor dressed in a Crash Bandicoot costume did a television commercial in which he visited Nintendo headquarters.

The commercial began with a quick glimpse of the sign outside Nintendo's Redmond, Washington, headquarters. (Except for that initial shot, none of the filming was done at Nintendo.) In the commercial, the actor playing Crash stood in Nintendo's parking lot, calling the "plumber boy" out for a showdown, until

Nintendo security escorted him away. While *Crash Bandicoot* was Sony's big game of 1996 and Crash became a popular character, Kaz Hirai and the rest of the Sony staff refused to acknowledge him as their mascot, though he would not have been Sony's first spokes-cartoon. Around the time of the first E3, Sony briefly flirted with the idea of using a character called "Polygonman" as its spokesperson. Polygonman looked like a stained-glass version of a *Simpsons* character. After E3, Sony quickly abandoned him and company spokespeople claimed to have never heard of the character.

> And if you take a look at Sony advertising, they never used any sort of celebrity or character endorsements. We never intended for Polygonman to be a character in a game. He was never going to be a Sonic or a Mario. He was always supposed to be something like the Master Game or something out there in the ether that was always challenging you. It was the challenge of video games that he was supposed to represent.
>
> And the Japanese took it much more literally and thought that this was something that we were trying to do that was going to supplant Sony. We introduced Polygonman at E3. The Japanese saw it and went postal on us.
>
> **—Steve Race, former CEO, Sony Computer Entertainment America**

Mario Returns

The American launch of Nintendo 64 was more phenomenal than the one in Japan. Nintendo made a press event of the shipping process by inviting a television crew to film pallets of consoles being loaded onto a plane. After more than a year of waiting for Nintendo to unveil the new game console, the media became a willing accomplice and the event made the national news. Nintendo originally announced that the release date would be Monday, September 30, then moved the launch up one day to the 29th. Having already presold their entire inventory, many stores started handing out their consoles on Friday the 27th, and all 500,000 units that Nintendo had shipped to the United States were gone by weekend's close. Though the stated plan had long been to release a very limited number of Nintendo 64s in the United States in 1996, Nintendo executives recognized what a vital market they were dealing with and scrambled to find more.

To accommodate the red-hot U.S. market, Nintendo rerouted consoles earmarked for the Japanese and European markets. Rerouting Japanese consoles was of little consequence; demand for the unit had slowed by mid-July. The fact that Nintendo had plundered the few consoles targeted for Europe, however, offended certain European retailers and game publications.

Back in the United States, demand for N64 held strong, but a problem that plagued the Japanese market was becoming apparent in the United States as well. The predictions of gloom and doom appeared to have been correct. Due to the cartridge format, there simply were not enough games for the new console, and many games that came out were expensive or small. *Super Mario 64* and *Pilot Wings 64,* the first games Nintendo released for N64, both came from Shigeru Miyamoto's design team and received rave reviews. The next titles, however, did not fare as well. *Cruis 'n USA,* a Williams arcade game published under the Nintendo label, had a slow frame rate, causing the game's motion to look jerky.

> Now, I'm going to be very direct with you. The very best games out there right now are N64 games. On the other hand, when it comes to *Cruis 'n USA,* I wouldn't be honest if I said that *Cruis 'n USA* was much of a game; but that product is selling. I think it would be fair to say that we know that some of the N64 software is not better than [the software you find] on other platforms. The challenge for us is to continue to try to keep that quality on the way up. Hopefully, we're going to succeed most of the time, but occasionally we're not. It's like saying to MGM, "You made *Gone with the Wind.* How come all the rest of your movies are not *Gone with the Wind?*" It just doesn't work that way.
>
> **—Howard Lincoln**

There were other disappointments, too. *Mortal Kombat Trilogy,* a game that many people thought would only come out on N64, was released on other systems. The PlayStation version was superior.

When played side-by-side, the PlayStation version makes the N64 version look like it's on a SNES [Super NES]. Then there's the sound: The digitized sound effects are utterly atrocious. In fact, it's so muffled that players may as well put their speakers on the other side of a cement wall before starting the game. The music is typical of a non-CD game—that is to say, worthless. It's tinny and very electronic sounding.

Mortal Kombat Trilogy proves that the Nintendo 64 is merely mortal. While it surpasses the PlayStation version in regard to load time, it still suffers a three or four second delay when loading a new character in multiplayer fighting. Ultimately, only *Mortal Kombat* addicts, who don't already own a PlayStation, will find this game worth picking up.[4]

When asked about these titles, Nintendo executives often defended them by pointing out that consumers had voted with their wallets—nearly every title released for Nintendo 64 was a million-seller. Nintendo's statistics were accurate: the company quoted TRST data with nearly religious reverence. The numbers, however, did not reflect the entire story. Millions of people purchased N64 hardware in the first year, then had only a few games to choose from. Every game for Nintendo 64 had reached bestseller status, but the sales were only being spread across a handful of games, whereas Saturn and PlayStation software sales were spread across five times as many games.

Nintendo did publish some brilliant games in the early days of Nintendo 64. During the first year after releasing the console, Nintendo released a few games that appealed to mainstream audiences, including *WaveRace 64, Mario Kart 64, GoldenEye 007,* and *Star Fox 64.* But the Nintendo 64 library was limited and expensive. By the end of 1997, PlayStation and Saturn had hundreds of games, most of which sold for under $50. By comparison, there were merely dozens of games for N64, some of which sold for nearly $80, and rumors were that future third-party cartridges might cost as much as $100. People outside Nintendo speculated that the console manufacturer had to sell its games at a loss and subsidize costs for other companies to keep prices down. Nintendo of America adamantly denied these stories, and the price of cartridges never reached $100. By 1998, the cost of cartridge manufacturing came down, and Nintendo 64 cartridges generally retailed for $10 more than PlayStation games.

Nintendo Loses Square

During this crucial time, Nintendo lost an important third-party partner called Square Soft. Square Soft specialized in publishing role-playing games (RPGs), adventure games in which players traversed elaborate worlds, gaining experience and learning fighting techniques while completing a quest. Although Square Soft published many highly respected games, its crown jewel was a series of games called *Final Fantasy*, created by Hironobu Sakaguchi, one of the world's most respected game designers.

Sakaguchi did not start out making RPGs. After joining Square Soft, he made three computer games, then switched platforms to Famicom and made *Highway Star* (released in the United States as *Rad Racer*), *King's Knight*, and *World Runner*. Sakaguchi was not excited by any of these games. His bosses assigned him to make 3D games because the programmer working with him, a notable Apple II game designer named Nasir Gebelli, was good at coming up with 3D code. Square sold approximately 500,000 copies of *Highway Star* and *World Runner*, pleasing Sakaguchi's employers. But Sakaguchi had become bored with game design.

In an effort to get more excited about his work, Sakaguchi decided to switch genres and work on a game that would be more interesting to write. He decided to create an RPG and brought the idea to his boss.

> The only person you had to go to at that time was the president [of the company], and he didn't really understand games that well. Selling him on the concept of an RPG wasn't that hard. I just went up and said, "I want to do an RPG."
>
> He said, "Is that good, is that interesting?" and I said, "Yeah, it's fun." So he said, "Okay."
>
> **—Hironobu Sakaguchi, president, Square USA**

Since he planned to quit making games after this first RPG, Sakaguchi named his game *Final Fantasy*.

> The basic concept was really a mythical concept of the whole earth, with fire and water representing everything on earth. I took that concept and represented those elements into a crystal, and that essentially became sort of the core theme for *Final Fantasy*.
>
> I took a preexisting idea—the four or five basic elements of the world; sort of an orthodox and mythical concept—then molded it into an original fantasy story.
>
> **—Hironobu Sakaguchi**

Creating *Final Fantasy* was a much larger and more involved task than making *World Runner.* Though he was able to create his earlier games with a three-person team, he needed a fifteen-person team for his RPG.

> I started with the story and the overall worldview of the game. I had the graphics designer do the drawings.
>
> Initially, the process was different from what we do now. Currently, we write the story completely and work from the storyline.
>
> When we first started *Final Fantasy I,* we were really limited, technologically. So what I had to do first was make a basic rough idea for the game [then we would test it]. We had to deal with the hardware first. By doing so, we would come up with the graphics on the screen and figure out, based on the limitations and the capabilities of the hardware, how big the world was going to be and how many locations I could have.
>
> After that, I would incorporate my rough ideas and build up a story based on what I had to work with. It was kind of working backwards.
>
> **—Hironobu Sakaguchi**

A huge bestseller, *Final Fantasy* was not the swan song Sakaguchi intended it to be. It resonated so well with Japanese audiences that Nintendo published it in the United States under its own label, and an unshakable relationship was forged between Square Soft and Nintendo.* In the early 1990s, as other companies flocked to Sega, Square Soft remained exclusive to Nintendo, publishing games like *Chrono Trigger* and *Secret of Mana* and always having its biggest sales with Sakaguchi's *Final Fantasy* games. Square Soft became one of Nintendo's most influential partners, a partnership that was covered by such publications as *Businessweek.*

The American audience was never as interested in RPGs as the Japanese. Though Square Soft's RPGs had a loyal U.S. following, sales were not as high as company officials hoped, and the company did not release *Final Fantasy V* in the United States. Then in 1994, as the market entered its major slump, Square released *Final Fantasy VI* for Super NES. (As there had been no American versions

---

* Square later released *Final Fantasy IV* in the United States as *Final Fantasy II* for the SNES.

of the previous three games, it published game six as *Final Fantasy III*.) *Final Fantasy III* was one of the top-selling games of 1994, but Square Soft employees were not satisfied.

> When you look at that game and the numbers in Japan . . . It sold 3 million copies in Japan. Judging by the [U.S.] population alone, we predicted millions. So, it didn't do that well.
>
> **—Hironobu Sakaguchi**

Square Soft's final title for Super NES was *Super Mario RPG,* a game that took Square Soft's signature in-depth stories and turn-based combat and applied them to the Mario universe. With the game's great graphics and a slowly growing base of RPG players, *Super Mario RPG* sales exceeded Nintendo's rather conservative expectations. Then, as Nintendo prepared to unveil Nintendo 64, Square Soft announced that it was switching allegiances. Like Namco before it, Square Soft was going to make console games exclusively for PlayStation. The split was bitter. So bitter, in fact, that even after Nintendo reestablished relations with Namco in 1999, Yamauchi still refused to work with Square Soft. When asked if Nintendo would allow Square Soft to publish games for a new console called "Dolphin" that would not be released until the year 2001, Minoru Arakawa quietly replied, "I do not think it is yet time for Square Soft."

Square Soft's decision to switch to Sony was largely due to aesthetic considerations. In a 1997 interview, Hironobu Sakaguchi explained that Sony's CD-ROM format allowed for more artistic freedom. His next game, released as *Final Fantasy VII* in both Japan and the United States, would be the biggest game of 1997 and one of the first RPGs to crack the U.S. market.

With PlayStation's 32-bit processing power and the seemingly unlimited storage of CD-ROM, Sakaguchi was able to increase the artistic qualities of his games. Sakaguchi had always had an eye for cinematics, art, and intricate storytelling, but working with CD-ROM gave him the opportunity to enhance these features exponentially. *Final Fantasy VII* had epic dramatic cut scenes with symphonic music. Sold under the Square Soft label in Japan, it was marketed by Sony with a huge budget in the United States. Nintendo had always published the bestselling game of the year in the United States, but with Sakaguchi's amazing animations and Sony's big-budget marketing, *Final Fantasy VII* became the biggest-selling game of 1997 worldwide. Once, when asked if the time and money spent on the game paid off, Sakaguchi happily replied, "Big time. It sold better in the United States than in Japan, and six million worldwide."

Violence Becomes the Issue

In August 1997, Nintendo released *GoldenEye 007*, a game that Rare, Ltd., developed, based on the James Bond movie *Goldeneye*. Few people paid close attention when Nintendo first announced plans to make a game based on James Bond, and interest waned even more when it was announced that the game would be a first-person shooter. When the game was released, it became a sleeper hit. PCs would remain the best platform for first-person shooters, but *GoldenEye 007* set the standard by which console versions of this genre would be judged.

The Rare team members who designed *GoldenEye 007* had been meticulous. They requested blueprints of set locations to be sure that their virtual locations matched those in the movie. They filled their game with Bond music and created a storyline that was reasonably true to the film.

As the game progressed, one designer asked Ken Lobb, the Nintendo of America executive in charge of second-party games, if he would like to appear in it. Tickled at the idea of becoming a virtual target, Lobb agreed. Curious to see what he would look like, Lobb looked for his image in each unfinished version of the game as Rare submitted them for review. When his likeness did not show up after several versions, he thought that Rare had decided against using it. Then, when a nearly completed version of *GoldenEye 007* came in for review, Lobb's team found a bug in the game and called him for help.

> They said they taped it and showed me the tape. It was me. They had made a tape of each of them shooting me, again and again.
>
> **—Ken Lobb, head of Tree House, Nintendo of America**

GoldenEye 007 was quietly released in August, a month not often associated with blockbuster game releases. But the game's popularity grew steadily. By the end of 1997, Nintendo had sold nearly 1.1 million copies. By 1999, that number would swell to more than 5 million copies worldwide.

This was a watershed game in the history of Nintendo. Rated "T" (or appropriate for players ages thirteen and up), *GoldenEye 007* was, like any other first-person shooter, about traveling through 3D environments and killing enemies. Nintendo, the last holdout of the video game industry, had shed its Disney image.

The Tragic Storm

On October 1, 1997, 16-year-old Luke Woodham of Pearl, Mississippi, used a baseball bat and a butcher knife to murder his mother. He then hid a rifle under his trench coat and took it to school. By the end of the day, he had killed three students and wounded several more before being stopped by Pearl High School assistant principal Joel Myrick, who grabbed a pistol from his car and brought Woodham down at gunpoint. "Mr. Myrick, the world has wronged me," Woodham told the stunned school official.

On the morning of December 1, exactly two months after the shooting in Pearl, 14-year-old Michael Carneal of Paducah, Kentucky, brought a 22-caliber pistol that he had stolen from his next-door neighbor to Heath High School and entered the lobby where 35 students had gathered together for a prayer meeting. Without warning, Carneal fired shots into the crowd, stopped to reload, and was wrestled down by Ben Strong, the boy leading the prayer. He wounded 8 students, 3 of whom died.

On March 24, 1998, 13-year-old Mitchell Johnson and 11-year-old Andrew Golden of Jonesboro, Arkansas, set off the fire alarm at Westside Middle School, then opened fire on students and teachers from nearby woods.

Two months later, on May 20, after being expelled from Thurston High School, 15-year-old Kip Kinkel of Springfield, Oregon, shot his parents and planted booby-traps around their bodies. He returned to school the next day with a 22-caliber semiautomatic rifle and shot 24 students, killing 2. When several boys tackled him to the ground, Kinkel shouted, "Shoot me!"

These events left the entire nation unhinged. Tragically, the violence did not stop there. On April 20, 1999, 18-year-old Eric Harris and 17-year-old Dylan Klebold of Littleton, Colorado, smuggled four high-powered guns and a stash of homemade explosives into Columbine High School and carried out a massacre that left 12 students and 1 teacher dead, and 23 students injured, before killing themselves. National outrage turned to horror and grief as the media showed the nation images of the wounded and the dead. As people tried to make sense of what happened, stories about school violence became a common theme in the media.

Video games were not immediately rooted out as a cause of the Pearl, Mississippi, shooting, and the Paducah shooting was said to have been inspired by the movie *Basketball Diaries.* Mitchell Johnson and Andrew Golden, on the other hand, were said to have spent a lot of time playing shooting games, including *GoldenEye 007,* before their 1998 Jonesboro assault. Most incriminating of all, however, was the shooting in Littleton. "The two became 'obsessed' with the violent videogame *Doom*—an interactive game in which the players try to rack up the most kills—and played it every afternoon," reported *Newsweek.*[5] Harris was said to have created a special version of *Doom* based on his high school.

Months later, the media reported that Klebold and Harris had made videotapes of themselves shortly before going on their killing spree. In the tapes, Klebold and Harris talked about their plans and related it to *Doom.*

Dylan Klebold sits in the tan La-Z-Boy, chewing on a toothpick. Eric Harris adjusts his video camera a few feet away, then settles into his chair with a bottle of Jack Daniels and a sawed-off shotgun in his lap. He calls it Arlene, after a favorite character in the gory *Doom* video games and books that he likes so much.[6]

"I hope we kill 250 of you," Klebold says. He thinks it will be the most "nerve racking 15 minutes of my life, after the bombs are set and we're waiting to charge through the school. Seconds will be like hours. I can't wait. I'll be shaking like a leaf."

"It's going to be like fucking *Doom,*" Harris says. "Tick, tick, tick, tick . . . Haa! That fucking shotgun is straight from *Doom.*"[7]

State legislators from Oregon, Arkansas, Florida, and other states proposed legislation to outlaw certain arcade games, and activist groups rose up, decrying violence in the media. In Washington, D.C., Senator Sam Brownback (Republican of Kansas) had long tried to hold hearings that investigated the marketing of violence to children. The events in Columbine gave his hearings a new urgency, and they began on May 4, 1999, just two weeks later.

> The hearings had been rescheduled at least twice. We had it previously sched-
> uled, and then an expert witness fell out or we had some objection, so this
> was like the third time it had been scheduled.

—Sam Brownback, Republican of Kansas, United States Senate

In light of recent events, it was only natural that this round of Senate hearings took on a more serious and heated tone than the earlier hearings. While
only a few senators appeared at Joseph Lieberman's 1993 hearings, fourteen made
an appearance at the latter ones. John McCain and Orrin Hatch, both of whom
would run in the 2000 presidential primaries, delivered statements at the hearings.* Reverend Charles J. Chaput, archbishop of Denver, Colorado, addressed
the hearing, as did Motion Picture Association of America president Jack Valenti
and Doug Lowenstein of the Interactive Digital Software Association.

The hearings, which focused as much if not more on movies than on video
and computer games, began with statements from each senator. Senator
Brownback started his statement discussing the connection between the Paducah
shooting and the movie *Basketball Diaries,* then turned his attention to video games.

> The violence in video games is, in some ways, even more disturbing. A game
> player does not merely witness violence, he takes an active part. Indeed, the
> point of such games as *Postal, Kingpin, Duke Nuke 'Em, Guilty Gear,* and
> others, is to kill as many characters as possible. The higher your body count,
> the higher your score.[8]**

—Senator Sam Brownback

Senator Kay Bailey Hutchinson (Republican of Texas) gave one of the most
accusatory opening statements.

> I think we need to find the connection between our violent art and our vio-
> lent culture. Modern video games are worse and more realistic than ever. An

---

* Ironically, Joseph Lieberman, who was also very much a part of these hearings, went
further than Hatch or McCain in the 2000 elections. Al Gore, who ultimately won the
Democratic nomination, selected Lieberman as his vice presidential nominee.

** This quote and many following quotes were taken directly from the Senate transcripts.

> eight-year-old can sneak off into cyberspace, assume a new virtual identity, and commit ghastly acts of violence and brutality. With the touch of a button, our children can torture victims, rip out their hearts or spinal cords, and then wave the bloody debris above their heads.
>
> The statistics on television violence are staggering. The average American child witnesses 100,000 acts of violence and 8,000 murders on television before leaving elementary school, but if a child is playing video games, that number is multiplied and the violence is at his own hands. He pulls the trigger, he likes it, he has fun, and his score goes up. What kind of message is that?
>
> One of our witnesses today says that video games deliberately use the psychological techniques of desensitization used to teach soldiers how to kill in battle. The difference, he says, is that video game violence is associated with reward and pleasure, and not tempered by a respect for authority or the revulsion of war.[9]

> **—Kay Bailey Hutchinson, Republican of Texas, United States Senate**

It was inevitable that the hearings would refer back to the tragedy at Columbine High School again and again, giving the impression that the senators held violent games and movies responsible for the killing. In interviews, however, the senators were more cautious about laying blame. "I don't know that you could quantify that. We do know, and we now have studies showing a correlation between playing the violent video games and violent behavior, and that correlation is actually higher than the correlation between smoking and lung cancer. So there is correlation, but I don't know that you can draw that directly on the Columbine case," Senator Brownback stated in an interview after the hearings.

Slade Gorton, the Washington State Republican who approached Nintendo for help in saving the Mariners, also participated in the hearings. Although he pronounced scathing condemnation of the executives from entertainment conglomerates who refused to appear at the hearings, he also spoke out in Nintendo's defense.

> Colonel Grossman yesterday on *Meet the Press* said that Nintendo marketed a game, or had a contract with the Army to market a game, for target purposes that is also used by children. Nintendo informs me that it does not now

> and never has had any contract with the Army or any Armed Service for any
> purpose whatsoever, and I think their response deserves to be on the record.[10]
>
> **—Slade Gorton, Republican of Washington, United States Senate**

After the senators finished their opening statements, the first of two panels came onto the floor. The members of this panel included Archbishop Chaput; Jack Valenti, of the MPAA; and Dr. William Bennett, former secretary of education and drug czar in the Bush administration.

"Exactly one week ago today, I buried the third of four Catholic teenagers shot to death at Columbine High School," the Archbishop began. "More than 1,000 people turned out for each of the funerals." Clearly unfamiliar with video games, the Archbishop mentioned the movie *The Matrix* in his brief talk. He finished by urging the senators to look at the causes, not symptoms, of our violent culture.

> The roots of violence in our culture are much more complicated than just bad
> rock lyrics or brutal screenplays. It is clear that the Columbine killings were
> planned well before *The Matrix* ever opened. But common sense tells us that
> the violence of our music, our video games, our films, and our television has
> to go somewhere. And it goes straight into the hearts of our children, to bear
> fruit in ways we cannot imagine until something like Littleton happens.[11]
>
> **—Reverend Charles J. Chaput, archbishop of Denver, Colorado**

Jack Valenti, the next speaker, brought a revivalist tone to the hearings.

> . . . there are three pillars, and only three, which support the rostrum from
> which springs a child's conduct: home and church and school. And mothers and fathers and priests and ministers and rabbis and teachers and
> principals have to insert in a young child's heart and mind early on an
> impenetrable moral shield against which all blandishments of peers and
> all the enticements of the mean streets and clannish cliques and visual and
> oral images crack and shatter.[12]
>
> **—Jack Valenti, president and CEO, Motion Picture Association of America**

> . . . absent all that, no abolition of constitutional rights and no presidential executive order, no amount of hand-wringing and fiery advocacy and no congressional law is going to salvage that child's conduct or locate what, in my judgment, is the missing moral core.
>
> Now I know that accusatory fingers point at movies. And I will accept that. Last year in America, we produced over 550 movies. And I will tell you something—when you make that many movies, some of them are going to be slovenly produced.[13]

> —Jack Valenti

The final speaker on the panel, Dr. William Bennett, who, as a former drug czar, former secretary of education, author of *The Book of Virtues,* and codirector of Empower America, came to the hearings with an air of authority. Bennett took the discussion in a philosophical direction, calling for social responsibility on the part of movie studios and entertainment companies. After his speech, the floor was opened for discussion, much of which focused on Valenti. Senator Brownback harkened back to Valenti's comment about "slovenly produced" movies and asked him to name examples. Valenti said that he would not do that. Brownback fired back that Valenti's voice would add "extraordinary force" to call responsibility. "Well, I plead with you, I just plead with you, to please—our country needs your voice to clean this up and to be specific on it. We are having a terrible problem, and we really need you."[14]

Impassioned as Senator Brownback's pleas may have been, Valenti, as the CEO of the Motion Picture Association of America, was in no position to single out movies of which he did not approve. As Senator Brownback continued to question him, Valenti pointed out that the crime rate among children ages 18 and younger had been steadily dropping since 1994. "Last year, 4/100ths of 1 percent of all young people, under the age of 18, were arrested—not convicted, arrested—for a violent crime. That means that 99.59 percent of all young people in this country are not into violent crime."[15]

After rather intense discussion, Senator Brownback called in the second panel, which included Lieutenant Colonel (retired) Dave Grossman, a former Army Ranger who had taught psychology at West Point and was currently teaching at the University of Arkansas, as well as consulting with law enforcement agencies and other organizations; Daphne White, executive director of a parent advocacy group called the Lion & Lamb Project; Interactive Digital Software Association president Douglas Lowenstein; and Dr. Henry Jenkins of the Media Lab at MIT.

Outspoken and direct, Col. Grossman had become somewhat of a lightning rod in the debate about the effects of video game violence. In his testimony, he discussed how the army had employed training simulators to teach soldiers to fire their weapons during combat.

> There is a broad leap, a vast chasm, between being a healthy American citizen and being able to snuff another human being's life out. There has to be a bridge, there has to be a gap. In World War II, we taught our soldiers to fire at bull's eye targets. They fought well. They fought bravely. But we realized there was a flaw in our training when they came on the battlefield and they saw no bull's eyes. And they were not able to transition from training to reality.
>
> Since World War II, we have introduced a wide variety of simulators. The first of those simulators were pop-up human targets. When those targets appeared in front of soldiers, they learned to fire, and fire instinctively. When real human beings popped up in front of them, they could transfer the data from that simulator.
>
> Today we use more advanced simulators. The law enforcement community uses a simulator that is a large-screen television with human beings on it, firing a gun that is identical to what you will see in any video arcade, except in the arcade the safety catch is turned off.[16]
>
> **—Lieutenant Colonel (retired) Dave Grossman**

In answer to the letter from Nintendo read by Senator Gorton, Colonel Grossman stated, "The Army has a device; I will bring pictures. The last time I trained on that puppy, it had a label on it that said "Nintendo."[17]*

> The industry has to ask how it can market one device to the military, whoever is marketing it, and then turn around and give the same device to your children, and claim that it is harmless.

---

* It later became clear that Nintendo never had a contract to create simulations for the Army.

> *Doom* is being marketed and has been licensed to the United States Marine Corps. The Marine Corps is using it as an excellent tactical training device. How can the same device be provided indiscriminately to children over the Internet, and yet the Marine Corps continues to use this device?[18]
>
> **—Lieutenant Colonel (retired) Dave Grossman**

Grossman next brought up the instructional value of flight simulators, then went on to call violent games "mass-murder simulators."[19]

> Now, what we have before us is a new national video game. The children are invested in racking up the new high score in a national video game. The high scorer on this game, instead of getting the three letter initials in the arcade, gets their picture on *Time* magazine and on every television in America. I have been predicting for close to a year now that the next major school shooting will see bombs. How could we have known that?
>
> Well, because if you want to get up to the upper levels in a video game and get that high body count, you have got to have instruments of mass destruction. And every video game incorporates that at the higher levels. We are scripting the children and they are carrying out the scripts.[20]
>
> **—Lieutenant Colonel (retired) Dave Grossman**

As he reached the end of his allotted time, Col. Grossman stated that "the willingness of children to commit" crimes was going up and up. Since 1957, he said, the assault rate in the United States had risen "seven-fold."[21] He then gave statistics for other nations.

Grossman said that video games should be classified as firearms trainers and, as such, should be judged under the second amendment instead of the first. "And as such," he said, "these things should be regulated, just like guns. Anybody who gives a child a gun is a criminal. Anybody who gives unrestricted access to these devices are criminals."[22]

> What we call for are three things, Senator: Education and legislation and litigation. We must educate America's parents, as a comprehensive national program, about what the AMA and the APA and the Surgeon General says about the link between violent media and violence in their children.

> Legislation: these devices that you see the ads for out there, these devices are law enforcement training devices that need to be legislated. And they are not even remotely a first amendment issue.
>
> And finally, litigation: Three ads here from the video game industry. One is for a joystick in a children's magazine. When you pull the trigger, it bucks in your hand like a gun. The ad says: Psychologists say it is important to feel something when you kill.[23]

> **—Lieutenant Colonel (retired) Dave Grossman**

> Keep your eyes on that Paducah case, Senator. It will be the Lexington and Concord of the culture wars. It will be the shot heard round the world, as we begin holding these individuals accountable for the toxic substance they are pouring into our children's lives.[24]*

> **—Lieutenant Colonel (retired) Dave Grossman**

After Col. Grossman's incendiary message, the rest of the proceedings seemed tame. Daphne White, head of the Lion & Lamb Project, echoed Senator Joseph Lieberman's concerns that games that the Entertainment Software Rating Board had given an "M" rating, meaning they were appropriate for players ages seventeen and up, were being marketed to children. One of her strongest themes was that it was ludicrous to give games with violent or sexual content an "M" rating and then make toys based on them.

> I have here a *Duke Nukem* [sic] action figure. The same game. One of these games is actually called *Time to Kill*. It says on it [the action figure]: Warning. Choking hazard. Small parts. Not for children under three.[25]

> **—Daphne White, executive director, the Lion & Lamb Project**

Though she caged it in dramatic tones by comparing regulating video games with the regulation of alcohol and tobacco, White was really asking for strict enforcement of the rating system.

---

* Col. Grossman may have been referring not only to the Carneal case itself but also to a suit that held video game manufacturers, movie makers, and other entertainment groups partially responsible for the shooting. That case was dismissed but is still up on appeal.

The next member of the panel was Douglas Lowenstein who, as the head of the Interactive Digital Software Association (IDSA), had the unlucky task of representing video and computer companies during the proceedings. This was a particularly unpleasant task, as Senator Brownback openly stated that one purpose of the hearings would be to humiliate entertainment company executives in the same fashion that cigarette manufacturers had been humiliated in other hearings. Brownback was disappointed, however, as all of the executives he invited chose to avoid the hearings.

Lowenstein started his testimony by reciting IDSA data showing that 70 percent of people playing PC games and 60 percent of people playing video games were over 18 years of age. He next cited Entertainment Software Rating Board statistics showing that most games were not violent. He then brought up, as a third myth, the lack of research specifically tracking the effects of video games. Having tried to attack these points, Lowenstein proceeded to present concrete plans for how the video game industry would work to prevent future violence.

First, we will be taking new steps to publicize and increase the visibility of the ESRB (Entertainment Software Rating Board) ratings, increase parental awareness, and encourage their use.

Second, we will explore ways to encourage retailers to enforce the ratings. While our industry has the ability to rate the product, we cannot impose policies on the retail community as to how they will manage those ratings. But our goal has been to work with retailers to put in place systems that directly or indirectly limit the ability of persons under seventeen to buy mature-rated games.

Third, we will review our advertising code of conduct to see what steps we can take to moderate the promotion of violent ads.[26]

—**Douglas Lowenstein, president, Interactive Digital Software Association**

The final member of the panel was Dr. Henry Jenkins, director of the Comparative Media Studies program at MIT. Jenkins, who has spent years studying popular culture, described theories he had formulated about the role of video games in modern "boy" culture. "Far from being victims of video games," Professor Jenkins told the senators, "Eric Harris and Dylan Klebold had a complex relationship to many forms of popular culture." Jenkins said that Klebold and Harris were "drawn to dark and brutal images, which they invested with their personal demons." He encouraged a "national conversation" about popular culture but suggested that such conversations should not take place until the current "climate of moral panic" had subsided.[27]

> We are afraid of our children. We are afraid of their relations to the digital media, and we suddenly cannot avoid either. These factors may shape the policies that emerge in this discussion, but they should not.
>
> Banning black trench coats* and abolishing video games does not get us anywhere. These are symbols of youth alienation and rage, not the causes. And we need to get back to the causes.[28]
>
> **—Dr. Henry Jenkins, director of comparative media studies,**
> **Massachusetts Institute of Technology**

Throughout the hearings, Senator Brownback used *Postal* as the example of irresponsible games. After Dr. Jenkins' testimony, Brownback questioned Lowenstein about the game and was surprised to hear that the game had not sold well and the company that published it was out of business. Even after learning this information, Senator Brownback continued to try to pin down Lowenstein on questions about the availability of M-rated games to children over the Internet and whether or not *Doom* had been licensed to the Marine Corps. While Lowenstein offered to work with the senator to locate this information, these were areas in which he was not prepared to speak. id Software, the company that created *Doom,* was not a member of the IDSA, and although Lowenstein said he had read articles discussing the Marine Corp's version of *Doom,* he claimed no personal knowledge. As to the marketing plans of individual companies, Lowenstein pledged to try and help Senator Brownback track down the information he wanted.

The final panel to address the hearing consisted of two college professors discussing the results of research tracking the effects of media violence. The first, Dr. L. Rowell Huesmann, a professor of psychology and communications

---

* Klebold and Harris hung around with a group of students at Columbine High School that referred to themselves as the "Trench Coat Mafia."

studies at the University of Michigan, discussed extensive research on media-viewing habits and applied some of the results to game playing. The second, Dr. Diane Levine, a professor of education at Boston-based Wheelock College, discussed cross-marketing efforts between TV studios and toy companies.

In truth, though they were far more dramatic, Senator Brownback's 1999 hearings did not have the deep impact on the video game industry that Senator Lieberman's 1993 hearings had. This probably reflected a certain sophistication that Douglas Lowenstein and the IDSA brought to the industry. Under Lowenstein's direction, the industry presented a unified voice and appeared to be much more anxious to cooperate.

> Not much came out of the hearings. It was a nice discussion, but I haven't seen much follow-up. We did push for the Federal Trade Commission to do a study on whether violence is being marketed to children by entertainment companies. I think the president put some pressure on the movie industry to be a little more diligent about seeing who's going to their R [rated] and violent movies, but that's about all I can come up with.
>
> **—Senator Sam Brownback**

CHAPTER 29

And the Cycle Continues

People say that I've been driven by vengeance in going after Sony, and I think they're probably right.

—**Bernard "Bernie" Stolar, former CEO, Sega of America**

The PlayStation 2 computer entertainment system is not the future of video game entertainment, it is the future of entertainment period.

—**Kazuo "Kaz" Hirai, president and COO, Sony Computer Entertainment America**

They [Sony Computer Entertainment America] also said they are not the future of video games, they are the future of entertainment; and God bless them. We're the future of video games.

—**Peter Moore, president and CEO, Sega of America**

The Eclipse of Saturn

> I felt Saturn was hurting the company more than helping it. That was a battle that we weren't going to win.
>
> —Bernie Stolar

As Nintendo executive vice president of sales and marketing Peter Main had predicted, much of the success of Nintendo 64 (N64) came at Sega's expense. With the launch of N64, Sega's already-low 32-bit sales were cut in half. By August 1997, Nintendo controlled 40 percent of the next-generation console market and Sony controlled 47 percent, leaving Sega with a mere 12 percent. Price cuts and big-name games did not help.

Bernie Stolar, formerly Sony's vice president of third-party, was president and CEO of Sega of America as Saturn entered its last days. Under his leadership, Sega stopped advertising Saturn on television. Then, on March 14, 1998, Sega announced plans to release three final games in the United States—*The House of the Dead, Shining Force III,* and *Burning Rangers.* After the release of these games, Sega of America discontinued the system.

> We tried to wind it down as cleanly as we could for the consumer. Again, we knew that the consumer was our judge, and we needed the consumer for the next round of what we were going to do as a company. So we did it slowly, maybe a little bit more slowly than I would have liked, but we did it that way. And I think we didn't hurt the consumer.
>
> —Bernie Stolar

The damage from Saturn's failure was extensive. At the time of the discontinuation, Sega had sold 2 million Saturns in the United States. By comparison, Sony had shipped 10.75 million PlayStations into North America.* Sega would have to absorb a $450 million loss (a 21 percent drop in sales) in 1998. The impact was devastating, but Sega did not bow out of the market for long. Sat-

---

* Sony always reported shipment statistics rather than sell-through, which was the kind of statistic that Nintendo and Sega generally used.

urn remained active in Europe and Japan longer than it did in the United States. In the meantime, Sega of America released several games for PCs. Word got out about Sega completing the design of a new system even before the final Saturn games reached store shelves. There were stories about the two systems being developed simultaneously, one in the United States and one in Japan. If these stories were accurate, Sega ended up manufacturing the system that was developed in Japan.

Largely stoked by Sega itself, the rumors continued. First known as "Dural," a metallic female fighter from the *Virtua Fighter* series, then as "Katana," a Japanese sword, Sega's new system was supposed to have a 128-bit processor, a 3D graphics chip from 3Dfx, and a Windows CE operating system. It was said to have a modem, and there were rumors that it would play games on DVDs (digital versatile disks) instead of CD-ROM.

On May 21, 1998, Sega put all the speculation to rest by announcing that "Dreamcast," the official name of the new 128-bit console, would be released in Japan on November 27. Most of the rumors proved fairly accurate. The final version of Dreamcast featured a Hitachi SH4 CPU and an NEC/VideoLogic PowerVR 3D graphics chip. The original specifications did call for a chip from 3Dfx, but Sega made a last minute change. Dreamcast's final design included a stereo chip from Yamaha and two operating systems—one from Sega, the other from Microsoft. Rather than a CD-ROM, it utilized a technology called GD-ROM—proprietary double-density CDs that held over a gigabyte of information. Most intriguing of all, however, was that the console included a 56K modem in a modular slot that would allow for updating should Sega choose to release broadband support. According to Sega officials, online gaming would be an essential element in their strategy for Dreamcast.

In Sega's Tokyo headquarters, a new CEO named Shoichiro Irimajiri hoped to use Dreamcast to reestablish Sega as a dynamic force in games. A former executive at Honda, Irimajiri was an energetic leader with ambitious plans, but before he could get the chance to launch his new system in Japan, Sony stole the spotlight. On March 2, 1999, Sony held a press conference in an enormous Tokyo opera house to announce the details of a "next generation PlayStation" that Sony promised would be released in the year 2000.

Putting on a fascinating show of internal politics, Sony's retiring chairman Norio Ohga began the meeting by reciting some of PlayStation's many successes.

Then Ohga made a statement that was meant to send a message to Nobuyuki Idei, who as Sony Electronics president and co-CEO was next in line to be chairman. "I remember when Ken Kutaragi proposed the PlayStation. I was the only one on the board who supported the idea."

PlayStation, which many Sony executives had viewed as little more than a side trip, had become Sony's biggest product of the 1990s. With more than 50 million units on the world market, PlayStation accounted for 40 percent of Sony Electronics revenues.

Trying to put a good face on the situation, Idei began his speech by saying, "I always believed in PlayStation." He then went on to say, "I believe this [the next-generation PlayStation] is something that will surpass a mere game machine."

Sony Computer Entertainment president Teruhisa Tokunaga came next to discuss the manufacturing partnership Sony had formed with Toshiba. Together, they were spending 20 billion yen (approximately $160 million against Japan's weakening yen) on the project. Tokunaga finished by describing the quickening pace of PlayStation sales. It had taken his company nearly two years to ship its first 10 million consoles. The next 10 million shipped in only nine months. Then Sony hit the next 10 million in six months, followed with another 10 million shipped six months later. According to Tokunaga, Sony went from 40 million to 50 million consoles shipped worldwide in just four months.

The final speaker of the day was Ken Kutaragi, the engineer turned Sony Computer Entertainment executive who designed the original PlayStation. As he explained the performance specifications of his new console, it became obvious that Sony had created a stripped-down version of a super computer. Sega's Dreamcast rendered 3 million polygons per second, nearly 10 times as many as the original PlayStation. This sounded impressive until Kutaragi revealed that his next-generation machine could render 60 million raw polygons per second. He conceded, however, that this performance was slowed as you added in effects such as fogging, shading, and curved surfaces. Even with these effects, however, the new console could render more than 16 million polygons per second.

Central to the new console's performance was an amazing new processor that Kutaragi called the "Emotion Engine." This processor was the result of brilliant out-of-the-box thinking. The computer industry had always followed a maxim called Moore's Law, named after Intel executive Gordon

Moore. According to Moore's Law, the typical high-tech manufacturer would double the speed of its fastest processor every eighteen months. This generally resulted in companies simply doubling the size of their processor. Realizing that doubling everything would make for a very expensive console, the engineers who designed the "next generation" PlayStation decided to isolate the operations that impact gaming and increase them exponentially. While the Emotion Engine was not going to be as fast as a Pentium II for some operations, its graphics processor had 1,000 times more bandwidth than current PC graphics processors at the time and its floating-point calculation performance was rated at 6.2 gigaflops (billion) per second, making it as fast as most super computers.*

Kutaragi's team had pulled out all the stops. The new console would run games on DVD, a medium that held 8 gigabytes on standard disks and 17 gigabytes on dual-layered disks. While he would not commit to whether the new console would play movies on DVD, the announcement led to widespread speculation that it would. What Kutaragi did confirm, however, was that the new console would be backward-compatible with the original PlayStation, meaning it could play the thousands of games that had been released for the Sony platform worldwide.

The event ended with representatives of Namco, Square Soft, and Polyphony, the outside development house that created Sony's bestselling *Gran Turismo,* running short demonstrations on a stack of computers set up to emulate the "next-generation" PlayStation.

Sega was caught flat-footed. Judging by the specifications Sony had released, Dreamcast was obsolete before it even launched. In an effort to respond, Bernie Stolar held a telephone press conference in which he addressed Sony's announcement.

> On paper, Sony's machine sounds impressive; but the fact is, it is still on paper. Dreamcast is here now. Frankly, Sony really has their work cut out for them creating a machine with the specs they unveiled on Tuesday and supporting it

---

* PlayStation 2 was so powerful, in fact, that *Star Wars* creator George Lucas later commented that it had more on-the-fly rendering power than all of the computers he used to make *Star Wars Episode One.*

> with a strong lineup of games. With a launch just one year away, [that] will
> be a challenge. And while Sony is working to create that hardware, Sega will
> already be in the marketplace with Dreamcast, building our installed base
> and developing an impressive library of games.
>
> **—Bernard "Bernie" Stolar**

Over the next few months, Sony parceled out small tidbits of information, revealing a master plan that would make its new console the center of entertainment in the home. It was later revealed that the console would indeed play movies. Sony announced plans to release an Ethernet connection, enabling it to handle high-speed connections to the Internet. The entire strategy, later tagged as Sony's "Trojan Horse," was to release a moderately priced console that would be the hub of a complete entertainment concept that merged television viewing, movie watching, video game playing, and Internet surfing into one device.

To help emphasize that new console's image as more than a game machine, Sony concept designer Teiyu Goto created a special case for the new console that suggested consumer electronics instead of simply video games. Goto, who also designed the look for the VAIO line of laptop computers, created a cabinet that looked like a stereo component. Instead of the sleek shape and smooth lines and top-loading design of a game console, the "next generation" PlayStation had a rectangular cabinet and a front-loading tray.

Nintendo Joins in the Race

With Sega launching a new system, and Sony well on its way, it was obvious that Nintendo would shortly join in the race. Nintendo made its announcement the day before the Electronic Entertainment Expo.

In typical Nintendo fashion, the announcement provided very little information, just enough specifics for reporters to create a rough idea of what the system might be able to do. To create the new system, which was code-named Dolphin, Nintendo had forged two new partnerships. The design of the processing chip would be handled by IBM. Dubbed "Gekko," the new chip would be based on IBM's PowerPC architecture and would feature 0.18 micron copper technology.

According to Nintendo chairman Howard Lincoln, the new console would have a DVD drive. However, like Kutaragi, he refused to specify whether it would play movies. He also refused to specify polygon-rendering rates. The most he would say was that Dolphin's graphics performance would meet or exceed anything on the market or going into production.

What he did say, however, was that Matsushita, known in the United States as Panasonic, had entered into a manufacturing agreement with Nintendo. Dolphin, Lincoln told the audience, would be released in 2000, just like the "next-generation" PlayStation.

A Shaky Dream Begins

On November 27, 1998, Sega launched Dreamcast in Japan. Although the system sold out, the response was quieter than expected. Sega shipped 150,000 consoles, which sold for 29,800 yen (approximately $260). Of the four games available at launch, only *Virtua Fighter 3tb* sold well. Based on the most successful arcade game Sega ever released in Japan, *Virtua Fighter 3tb* sold at a nearly one-to-one ratio with the console.* The other three games available at launch were *Godzilla Generations,* a ponderous game in which players controlled Godzilla as he pounded Japanese cities into rubble; *Pen Pen Tricelon,* a cute racing game for children, featuring a penguin and other cuddly animals; and *July,* a text-and-pictures adventure. In the weeks that followed, Sega shipped 300,000 more consoles, along with two new games—*Sonic Adventure* and *Sega Rally 2.*

Although the Dreamcast launch looked successful on the surface, it had in fact gone dreadfully wrong. With Sony's next-generation machine looming on the horizon, Sega wanted to shore up its installed-base as quickly as possible. Sega needed to ship more consoles and more games so that it could exploit the launch-day excitement. That, however, was prevented when NEC encountered manufacturing problems.

> We set up the whole program, and it seemed perfect except the supply of the graphics chips. . . . It was very sad to have the shortage of the graphics chips. We felt that 200,000 to 300,000 additional units could have been sold if we could have had enough supply.
>
> **—Shoichiro Irimajiri, former president and CEO, Sega Enterprises**

---

* *Virtua Fighter 3* did not do well in U.S. arcades.

Irimajiri had hoped to sell well over 1 million Dreamcasts in Japan by February 1999. Instead, he sold under 900,000. And the sales continued to be slow. Looking at the Japanese market from a historical perspective, Irimajiri calculated that he would need to sell more than 2 million consoles by the time Sony launched its new console. In the fiscal year that started on March 1, 1999, and ended on February 29, 2000, Sega sold less than 900,000 consoles. Sega's only hope was to beat Sony on the basis of price and games.

> We don't know what price point and what kind of performance the PlayStation 2 will have, but from the information we have already gotten, the PlayStation chip will be very, very nice, and we expect that it will be out of the range of the consumer console price.
>
> As you know, the $199 price point is kind of a magic price point for selling consoles and home electronics all over the world—$199 in the United States, 199 pounds in England, 19,900 yen in Japan. We have already reached that point. We are going to price down the Dreamcast in Japan from the 24th of this month (June) to 19,900 yen, and we are going to launch the Dreamcast in the U.S. at $199 and in the UK at 199 pounds. So we have already reached that price point, but PlayStation 2 will probably take a couple of years to reach that price point. Sony's starting point may even be almost double, placing it in a completely different category.
>
> **—Shoichiro Irimajiri**

Back in the United States, Bernie Stolar and other Sega of America officials scrambled to avoid the mistakes Sega Enterprises had made with the launch of Dreamcast. Stolar vehemently maintained that he did not want the four games available at Japanese launch to be used as launch titles in the United States. Working closely with Midway Games, Sega hoped to have a much better lineup, with fifteen games ready when Dreamcast went to market.

The American launch of Dreamcast was set for September 9, 1999.* As the launch approached, however, Bernie Stolar was ousted from Sega much as he had been from Sony. With Stolar out, the responsibility of directing the launch

---

* Sega marketing, always a sucker for alliteration, billed the launch as 9/9/99 for $199.

fell on the shoulders of Peter Moore, a former Reebok executive who had recently joined the company as senior vice president of marketing.

Sega of America had advantages never available to Sega of Japan. The success of Genesis gave Sega more clout in the United States than Sega Enterprises had in Japan. Sega had a sizable audience of loyal fans who liked the kinds of games Sega published. Also, in the ten months between the Japanese and American launches, several companies had managed to finish off truly polished games. Midway Games, for instance, had four games ready for the U.S. launch

> Fifteen. That's almost the minimum. At some point you have to draw a line in the sand and say, "enough." There are fifteen confirmed titles. We're still discussing some games with third-parties who, coming out of E3, are enthused about our launch plans.
>
> I think fifteen, quite frankly, is ample. In my brief career in this particular industry, it's pretty evident to me that no platform has ever launched with that breadth of titles.
>
> **—Peter Moore, former senior vice president of marketing,**
> **Sega of America**

Several of the games selected for the launch stood out as "breakthrough" products. Sega had a brilliant football simulation called *Sega Sports NFL2K* with fast gameplay, a wide array of play options, and excellent graphics. Midway created a comical boxing game called *Ready 2 Rumble* that had a nearly perfect mixture of humor, graphic panache, and fast action. Perhaps the best game at the Dreamcast launch was Namco's *Soul Calibur,* a superb home version of an arcade hit that actually looked better on Dreamcast than it did in the arcades.*

The U.S. launch of Dreamcast was hailed as a big event, with retailers selling out of the nearly 1 million units Sega shipped. But just as unforeseen circumstances slowed the Japanese launch, an unexpected hiccup earned Sega of America bad press. A slight manufacturing glitch in many of the Midway games caused the music to skip. The problem was easily corrected, but Sega's perfectly choreographed launch was marred.

---

* Of all the games released for Dreamcast in its first year, only *Soul Calibur* sold over 1 million units worldwide.

Appearing to have some momentum, Sega enjoyed great hardware sales, with over 1.2 million consoles sold by the end of the holidays. During January, Sega experienced an expected dip in sales. Unfortunately, that dip continued through spring, even as Sega and its third-party partners expanded the Dreamcast library with a wide variety of games.

Monster Pockets

> The initial shipment was just around 200,000 or so—fortunately, we were able to sell out. Then there were additional orders of 100,000 more and then another 100,000. By the end of 1996, we reached around 1 million. So we were very grateful. But we originally thought of it as a one-time product.
>
> **—Yasuhiro Minagawa, director of communications, Nintendo Co., Ltd.**

On February 27, 1996, Nintendo Co., Ltd., released a new cartridge for Game Boy called *Pokemon* (short for pocket monsters) into the Japanese market. What no one could possibly have suspected at Nintendo was that the company had done more than publish a game—it had started a small industry.

An outside company called Game Freak created the concept for *Pokemon* and proposed it to Nintendo at a time when Shigeru Miyamoto, the man who created *Mario,* just happened to be looking for a game that would allow Game Boy players to exchange items using Gamelink cables. Miyamoto oversaw the project from Nintendo's side as it evolved into a full-fledged RPG for children, a universe in which children captured and trained friendly monsters, then entered them to fight in competitions. To create a need for players to exchange monsters, Nintendo created two different versions of the cartridge, red and green, each of which had a few unique creatures. The only way to collect all 151 creatures would be to trade.

Believing that the game would have limited appeal, Nintendo shipped only 200,000 copies of *Pokemon* on its first release. But *Pokemon*'s popularity grew steadily, and several stores ordered more copies of the game. Seizing an opportunity, one of the teams behind *Pokemon* set up a partnership with an animation studio to create an *anime* cartoon for television. When the cartoon became the highest-rated kids' show in Japan, Nintendo started licensing

Pokemon to toy, trading card, clothing, and food manufacturers. *Pokemon* soon became a billion-dollar industry.

> *Pokemon* has become such a phenomenal success. . . . . At the very begin-
> ning just a few people knew this cartridge, and it was word-of-mouth that
> spread its popularity without the media noticing it. The cartoon came one
> year after the debut of the Game Boy game. We are continuing to sell a lot of
> the Game Boy games, but now we have movies. We have so much merchan-
> dise and the trading cards; but the growth was a gradual process.
>
> **—Hiroshi Imanishi, general affairs manager, Nintendo Co, Ltd.**

In 1998, Nintendo finally exported the *Pokemon* phenomenon to the United States as part of a massive movement designed to bring new life to the aging Game Boy. The U.S. release of *Pokemon* bore little resemblance to the Japanese one, as the cards, games, and television show all hit within a few weeks of each other; the success was immediate. The syndicated *Pokemon* cartoon show became the hottest kids' show on television, and *Pokemon Red* and *Pokemon Blue* became the bestselling games on the market. *Pokemon* trading cards became such a hot item that some elementary schools banned children from bringing them to class. Parents even initiated lawsuits, claiming that the way Nintendo and its partners marketed *Pokemon* trading cards was a form of gambling.

On November 23, 1998, Nintendo released Game Boy Color, a long antici-pated version of Game Boy with a color screen. In the spirit of Game Boy efficiency, Game Boy Color's 32,000-color screen did not use backlit technol-ogy. Like other Game Boys, it had to be played in a brightly lit area or players would not be able to see the images on the screen. On the other hand, it could run for 10 to 12 hours on two AA batteries.* With the launch of *Pokemon* and Game Boy Color, Game Boy sales shot into record territory.

---

* Energy efficiency was always the hallmark of Game Boy technology. Lynx, Game Gear, and TurboExpress all had better, clearer screens. Nomad, which played Genesis cartridges, had a library of larger, more visual, and generally better-made games. But Game Boy was the most portable system, in that it could go several times longer on two AA batteries than any of the previously named systems could go on six AAs.

NeoGeo Pocket Color (NGPC), a competitor that came out in 1999, on the other hand, had better technology and longer battery life. By the time it came out, though, Nintendo had already sold more than 80 million Game Boys worldwide. NGPC never stood a chance.

The boost could not have come at a better time. In 1999, nearly every video game company in Japan saw a significant drop in sales. Because of the relatively low cost of developing and manufacturing Game Boy cartridges and the brisk sales brought on by *Pokemon* and Game Boy Color, Nintendo had a profitable year.

In the United States, *Pokemon* sales gave the entire industry a boost. Video game sales generally drop in transition years in which new hardware systems are released, but U.S. game sales rose by $1 billion in 1999. The rise could be summed up in two words: Game Boy.

In 1997, the last year before the U.S. release of *Pokemon,* handheld game sales amounted to approximately $294 million. Nintendo released *Pokemon* in September 1998, and handheld sales surged to $466 million. From the moment they were released, *Pokemon Blue* and *Pokemon Red* became the hottest games on the market. In 1999, however, handheld game sales rose to $1.26 billion, representing 18 percent of the market. In short, the market had not grown; Game Boy did.

The Big Week

In February, Sony staged a trade show called PlayStation Festival 2000 to demonstrate the games that were under development for its new console, which was to be officially named PlayStation 2. By this time, the entire gaming world seemed consumed with excitement over the new console. But there were only nineteen games on display at the show, and PlayStation Festival 2000 left many attendees unimpressed.

Then rumors began circulating that for all of its power, PlayStation 2 was distinctly hard to program. Shinji Mikami, the Capcom designer credited with creating the popular *Resident Evil* and *Dino Crisis* games, complained that Sony had created insufficient tools to support PlayStation 2. Having created best-selling games for Dreamcast, Saturn, Nintendo 64, and PlayStation, Mikami said PlayStation 2 was the most difficult system he had ever worked with.

> Sony provided an extensive library with PlayStation. The library would do a lot of the work, but with PlayStation 2, there is no library. We need to create our own library, which poses its own set of problems in that there are so many choices to achieve the same effects.
>
> **—Shinji Mikami, game designer, Capcom**

> If you focus on making full use of all the specs, it will be very expensive and time-consuming to produce a game. Instead, if you can focus on one aspect of the game, then I believe you can produce a great game. For example, in an action game, accentuate the gameplay even to the point of compromising other aspects like graphics.
>
> **—Gozo Kitao, general manager, Konami**

Despite the bad showing at PlayStation Festival 2000 and the complaints of many developers, a few spectacular games were already underway for PlayStation 2. Keiji Inafune, the designer best known for his *Mega Man* games, was developing a samurai game titled *Onimusha: Warlords,* with spectacular graphics. While Inafune conceded that he did have some problems, he felt that many of those problems were partially caused by the huge amount of additional power PlayStation 2 offered, giving game designers too many options at once.

> Until now, because of the limitations of the hardware, when I asked a programmer if something could be done, [he] would say it couldn't be done. With PS2, [programmers] tell me, "Yes, maybe, but it will take a long time." How long, they don't know.
>
> So now, as a producer, my dilemma is what do I do? Do I let them go with the concept without knowing how long it will take to implement it? In a sense, there are no hardware limitations now and there is a large learning curve for programmers.
>
> **—Keiji Inafune, game designer, Capcom**

At Konami, Hideo Kojima quietly began working on *Metal Gear Solid 2,* a PlayStation 2 game in which players helped an ex–special forces soldier infiltrate a terrorist group and destroy a giant robot. Kojima, a self-described cinemaphile, claimed that PlayStation 2 was not as powerful as he had expected; but when he revealed video clips from his game at the 2000 Electronic Entertainment Expo, his videotape was the talk of the show.

> I was actually expecting something much better; and we were not getting what we expected. In the early days, I really dreaded going to work because

> I knew we were not going to get what we expected. The quality of the graph-
> ics that we have right now is the bottom line. They are going to get better.
>
> **—Hideo Kojima, game designer, Konami**

The Japanese launch of PlayStation 2 took place on Sunday, March 4, 2000. This was by far the most anticipated video game launch in history. *Newsweek* ran a cover story about the new console the week before the launch, and reporters and camera crews from all over the world descended on Akihabara, Tokyo's "Electric Town," to cover the story.

Sony promised to ship 1 million consoles for the launch. A few weeks before the launch, a high-level consultant working for Sony stated that the company would ship 2 million units, but Sony quickly released an official statement denying his claims.

The actual launch was a very orderly event. Most stores presold their entire inventory weeks before the deliveries were made. Long lines of customers who did not want to take a chance on shortages formed in front of these stores on March 3. The stores opened their doors and began handing the consoles out at midnight on March 4, and the distribution went smoothly.

A few electronics stores and several large department stores sold their PlayStation 2 allotments on a first-come, first-served basis. These stores generally opened at 11:00 A.M.. but to avoid causing traffic problems, they opened at 7:00 A.M. on the day of the launch. Thousands of people gathered in front of these stores. According to the manager of a Laox store, 4,000 people lined up at his door. When asked how many consoles he had to sell, he said he had about 200. Within three hours of opening, every store had sold out. In all, 600,000 consoles were sold, but it was obvious that Sony could have sold two or three times that number.

For the next few days, Japanese newspapers carried all kinds of stories about PlayStation 2. One big story concerned a boy who managed to purchase a PlayStation 2 and was riding his bicycle home from the store when two strangers drove by on a motorcycle and grabbed the bag out of his hands. Another story involved a teenager who tried to commit suicide by jumping out of an Akihabara building because he was unable to purchase a PlayStation 2. Strangest of all were reports that the Japanese government determined that

PlayStation 2 was a super computer capable of guiding missiles and imposed a limit on exporting the consoles.

The big sales of PlayStation 2 did not extend beyond the hardware, however. Of the thirteen games available on the day of the launch, only Namco's *Ridge Racer V* seemed to appeal to consumers. When asked, many consumers said they were looking forward to the April release of *Tekken Tag Tournament,* a fighting game that was also from Namco, but PlayStation 2 software sales remained low for the first few months. DVD players had not sold as well in Japan as they had in the United States. In the first few months after its release, the number-one use for PlayStation 2 was as a DVD movie player, and the leading software title for the console was the DVD version of the Keanu Reeves movie *The Matrix.*

Sega Enterprises chairman Shoichiro Irimajiri said he was elated with the results of the Sony launch.

> In Japan, PlayStation 2 is the first console that is selling only for hardware. In the past, the console was only a box without software; but people are buying the PlayStation 2 without any software. It's the image of this PlayStation that is interesting. So [people are really buying the] DVD player function and the big image of the PlayStation 2, which was created by Sony. I don't feel PlayStation 2 will have a big impact on the market this year.
>
> **—Shoichiro Irimajiri**

Sega's wounds ran deeper than the feisty Irimajiri confessed. In June, Irimajiri resigned as chairman of Sega Enterprises and took a lower post. He was replaced by Isao Okawa, chairman of Sega's parent company CSK. According to Okawa, Sega hoped to position Dreamcast as an Internet device both in the United States and Japan. Toward that end, Sega of America opened its own Internet service provider—Sega.com.

Three Horses and a Pony

When you consider the strength of the PlayStation 2 hype, the cost of marketing a new platform in the North American market . . . When you consider that Microsoft has announced a $500 million marketing program for the launch of Xbox and that Nintendo has a $5 billion war chest and the overall power behind Sony's PlayStation brand, Sega does not have the ability to compete against those companies.

**—Charles Bellfield, vice president of marketing and corporate communications,
Sega of America**

Well, it's good to see that not everybody squealed. It's amazing the stuff we've read about this product, you know, that . . . we [supposedly] had a developers' conference. None of us knew we had [one], but we had one in Redmond and everybody came from all over the world.

—Seamus Blackley, chief Xbox technical officer, Microsoft Corporation

Microsoft Joins

And we had some guys at Microsoft who came and said, we should do a console.[1]

—Bill Gates, Chairman, Microsoft Corporation

On March 10, 2000, less than one week after the launch of PlayStation 2 in Japan, Microsoft chairman Bill Gates stepped onto a stage in the San Jose Convention Center to give the most anticipated speech of the Game Developers Conference. Dressed in a leather jacket with a large green "X," he uttered the anticipated words that ignited the crowd:

It's very exciting to be here today and have the opportunity to announce a whole new platform, a platform that all of you are going to take in directions that we can't even imagine.

—Bill Gates

Gates's announcement was the culmination of a year of rumors and speculation.

The project began in 1999, around the time that Sega and Sony first started jockeying for position. Sega's modest plans for Dreamcast, which were virtually unchanged from the plans for Master System and Genesis except for the inclusion of a modem, might have gone unnoticed by Microsoft management; but Sony's "Trojan horse" strategy for taking over living rooms was another story. Sony's PlayStation 2 was attracting a lot of attention, and it would clearly do more than simply play games. Microsoft executives saw Sony creating a new market.

A couple of things happened [at] about the same time roughly a year ago. We hold an executive retreat [every year], in which the senior management of Microsoft goes away and ponders the company and the kinds of things they're doing. And one of the things they spent a lot of time talking about [last year] was rooms beyond the den, shall I say, where Microsoft . . . where important things are going on in the world of technology and Microsoft doesn't have a big presence. One of those rooms is the living room.

> Well, we're not a big player at this point [in living rooms], and if you look at the kind of entertainment that happens there, consoles are a huge part of it.
>
> **—Kevin Bachus, former director of third-party relations, Xbox Team, Microsoft Corporation**

Built by intelligent, technology-savvy people, Microsoft always attracted those who grew up playing video games. Some employees brought in arcade machines that they set on free-play and placed in buildings for employees to use. A skybridge between two buildings on the main Redmond campus had so many coin-operated games that it looked a bit like a video game arcade.

Microsoft also attracted many elite veterans of the video game industry. Joe Decuir, an Atari engineer who helped develop the 2600, moved to Microsoft.* Howard Phillips, Nintendo's "man who plays games for a living," joined Microsoft's entertainment division, as did David Thiel, who did the sound for *Q*Bert*.

With all of this talent and enthusiasm, it was only a matter of time before groups of employees got together and developed game systems on their own.

But Microsoft has never built a computer for sale, and in February 1999 it certainly had no official intention of making a game computer. Nonetheless, on the company's campus, in Building 27 and Building 5, a "garage-shop" game console was taking shape in the spare time of four engineers, Seamus Blackley, Kevin Bachus, Ted Hase, and Otto Berkes.[2]

Sony and Nintendo may have created unique machines with proprietary operating systems, but Microsoft's renegade gamers built their console around basic PC architecture. Their machine would have a customized operating system with a stripped down version of Windows, would use Microsoft's DirectX software, and would feature both a built-in hard drive and an EtherNet card for broadband communications. Although the final specifications for the console would not be ready for another year, the Microsoft board approved the project in March 1999.

---

*The processing chip in the 2600 was named "Stella" in honor of Decuir's bicycle.

Over the next ten months, the Xbox team remained a moving target for analysts and journalists alike. Microsoft neither confirmed nor denied work on the project, which most people recognized as a fairly reliable confirmation.*

Word about the Xbox often slipped out when Microsoft quietly discussed versions of its hardware with analysts and software makers. When Microsoft confirmed rumors that the console would include a graphics chip from a pioneering company called Nvidia Corporation, many analysts and game enthusiasts suddenly began praising the console.

As Bill Gates stood before the enthusiastic crowd at the Game Developers Conference, he unveiled a list of nearly final specifications that were guaranteed to dazzle a technically literate crowd. Analysts had already pronounced Xbox's Nvidia chip superior to the graphics processing unit in PlayStation 2. Coupled with an 8-gigabyte hard drive, twice as much memory as PlayStation 2, and an EtherNet card, Xbox appeared to be unstoppable.

That night, twenty-seven members of Microsoft's Xbox team ate a celebratory dinner together in a San Jose hotel. Other Microsoft employees saw them and sent bottles of champagne to their table in congratulations. Feeling like they had conquered the world, the team members joked and drank for hours. According to all reports, most team members were fairly drunk when they finally left the restaurant.

Rather than separate into groups when they reached the hotel elevator, the team decided to cram in together, far exceeding capacity. The last person in was Seamus Blackley. Well over six feet tall and quite sturdily built, Blackley saw that he could not cram through the elevator door; so he launched himself in horizontally, on top of the crowd. When the doors of the elevator slid shut, the elevator dropped three stories before coming to a safe stop.

Asked about this event later, Blackley, the college-trained physicist who once worked on the Fermilab Super Collider, commented, "Let's just say that when you cram twenty-seven celebrating people into an elevator with a seven-person limit, gravity happens quickly."

---

* Several newspapers, including *USA Today* and the *Wall Street Journal*, published articles with Xbox specifications that proved incorrect when the final specs were released. (I wrote the article for *USA Today*.)

Fall of the House of Sega

> Or better yet a terminator,
>
> Like Arnold Schwarzenegger,
>
> Try'n to play me out like as if my name was Sega.[3]
>
> **—Eric Shroddy, Larry Muggerud, Lou Donaldson, *Jump Around,***
> **House of Pain**

When Sega first announced Dreamcast, former Nintendo of America chairman Howard Lincoln sniped that considering Sega's faltering financial situation, the project was "completely irresponsible." According to Sega Enterprises cofounder David Rosen, both he and company chairman Isao Okawa had wanted to leave the hardware business after Genesis.*

The launch of PlayStation 2 broke huge holes in Sega's armor. While publicly remaining loyal to Dreamcast, several of Sega's top designers privately began admitting that they hoped to see their games on PlayStation 2. Yute Saito, the independent developer who created *Seaman*—the best-selling Dreamcast game in Japan, openly talked about releasing a PlayStation 2 version of his talking fish simulation.

Rather than keep its designer groups entirely in-house, Sega had spun them off into nine semi-autonomous organizations, naming its top designers as the heads of each independent studio. Within the industry, people quietly began speculating that this new corporate structure would open the door for supporting other platforms. When asked if his AM2 team—designers of such games as *Out Run* and *Space Harrier*—might investigate other platforms, Sega's Yu Suzuki commented, "I think so. Of course, we still have a relationship with Sega, so we cannot just move out right away. Maybe gradually."

> They have spun off from Sega and they are 100 percent owned by Sega. If they are successful, they will have an IPO. Theoretically, they can do any-

---

* Isao Okawa constantly pushed Sega to create Internet content and insisted that Dreamcast include a modem.

> thing [they want], but they are owned 100 percent by Sega—there is very,
> very little chance that they will make games for PlayStation 2.

—Shoichiro Irimajiri, former president and COO, Sega Enterprises

Under this new system, Suzuki's AM2 team, which had long had its own identity, remained largely unchanged but gained more independence, as did Yuji Naka's *(Sonic The Hedgehog, NiGHTS)* Sonic Team. Under this new structure, however, designers such as Hisao Oguchi *(Top Skater, Virtua Tennis, Crazy Taxi)* and Tetsuya Mizuguchi *(Sega Rally, Space Channel 5)* were able to expand their activities. Dreamcast needed an expanded library to survive, and between its independent studios and American publishing partners such as Visual Concepts *(NFL 2K, NBA 2K)*, Sega became the most prolific publisher in the business.

Long known for publishing innovative games, Sega also gave its design houses latitude to experiment. Temporarily abandoning his arcade roots, Yu Suzuki began work on a Dreamcast game called *Shenmue*—basically, an interactive sixteen-chapter novel. The first installment of *Shenmue*, which contained only one chapter, was rumored to have cost upward of $50 million to make. (Later chapters would cost less to make, since much of the money spent on the game went into developing new technologies.) With less than 3 million Dreamcasts sold worldwide, Sega could not possibly hope to make a profit on the game. In Japan, where role-playing games are especially popular and Yu Suzuki's notoriety as a game maker is second only to Nintendo's Shigeru Miyamoto, Sega sold 200,000 copies of *Shenmue*—a 20 percent penetration into the Dreamcast market.

> If we think of just the software business, very honestly speaking, we have not
> recouped yet. But when I think of the development advances we learned that
> can be applied to other games, that investment will someday be recouped.

—Hideki Sato, president, Sega Enterprises

With approximately one million Dreamcast consoles sold in Japan and well over two million sold in the United States, Sega focused more of its attention on the U.S. market. "The developers are starting to realize that they have to fish where the fish are biting," became a slogan that Sega of America president and COO Peter Moore repeated in many interviews during the eight months between PlayStation 2's Japanese launch and its U.S. debut.

Under Moore's leadership, Sega of America looked for ways to shore its base. One of its more dramatic moves was the formation of SegaNet, an Internet service provider created specifically for handling Dreamcast business. Slated for an official launch on September 7, 2000, the day of the MTV Video Music Awards, SegaNet was designed to reflect the aggressive new stance Sega was taking toward online games.

Up until the launch of SegaNet, Sega seemed to pay little attention to Dreamcast's 56K modem. (The only Dreamcast game with an online component available in the U.S. market was *Chu Chu Rocket,* a strategy game from Yuji Naka's Sonic Team.) Moore's stated purpose for initiating SegaNet was to beef up the American market. At $21.95 per month, Sega's new service was competitively priced, and subscribers who signed up for a two-year contract received a free Dreamcast and keyboard. If all things went according to plan, a plurality of future Dreamcast games would also feature online components.

E3 2000

As May approached, the industry looked toward the 2000 Electronic Entertainment Expo (E3) in Los Angeles for details about how Sony would launch PlayStation 2 in the United States and how Sega would respond. In the days before the show began, Sony, Sega, and Nintendo wrangled for position.

Sony announced that it would hold its pre-E3 press conference on Wednesday, May 10—during the noon time slot generally reserved for Nintendo's conference. Though members of Nintendo's PR team considered sticking to their original plans, they realized they could not compete. Sony would announce the price and launch date of PlayStation 2—the only big announcements Nintendo had would be new games. Nintendo gave up the slot.

Sony held its press conference in a Los Angeles sound stage not far from the convention center. Thousands of journalists and industry insiders crammed into the studio grounds and were fed a lunch of pasta and salad, as Sony executives prepared and made last-minute changes to presentations. When the doors opened, the excited crowd pushed in as if fighting its way into a rock concert. Sony's announcements proved worth the wait.

Sony Computer Entertainment America chairman Kazuo "Kaz" Hirai began the event by describing differences between the Japanese PlayStation 2 and the one Sony would introduce into the North American market. The American version would have its DVD drivers programmed into its circuits as firmware, avoiding some of the bugs that plagued the Japanese version. Also, the U.S. version had a built-in bay for a hard drive/Ethernet card peripheral that Sony had under development.

As for price and launch date, while Sony had to abandon its traditional September launch date, PlayStation 2 would be released in the United States on Thursday, October 26, making it to market in time for the 2000 Christmas season. Like the original PlayStation, this new and powerful machine that played movies on DVD as well as games would launch with a modest $299 price tag. But Sony was not just releasing a new game machine. PlayStation 2 would become the hub of the living room.

> The PlayStation 2 computer entertainment system is not the future of video game entertainment, it is the future of entertainment period.
>
> **—Kazuo "Kaz" Hirai, president and COO,**
> **Sony Computer Entertainment America**

Sony also addressed concerns about the lack of software during the Japanese launch. According to Hirai, PlayStation would launch with more than twenty games. To ensure this, Sony Computer Entertainment America paired up with Electronic Arts, a powerful ally that could provide the game content that was so obviously missing at the March launch. Electronic Arts showed clips of *Madden NFL 2001*, *NASCAR*, and *SSX* for PlayStation 2. While Sony demonstrated *Gran Turismo 2000*,* the third installment in a hugely successful series of realistic driving simulations, the only Sony-published game that would be ready for the launch of PlayStation 2 was *Fantavision*, a strategy game in which players grouped and exploded skyrockets streaming across gorgeously rendered night skies.

Due largely to the overall disappointing quality of the PlayStation 2 library, it took fifteen months for the first million copy–selling game to appear on

---

* Sony eventually "scrapped" *Gran Turismo 2000* and released a much-improved game called *Gran Turismo 3* in June 2001.

the system. That game, Capcom's *Onimusha: Warlords*, was followed closely by the Japanese release of *Gran Turismo 3*, which was an instant million-seller.

Like Nintendo, Sega was forced to compete against hardware by announcing new software. Sega held an all-but-ignored barbecue outside Sony's conference. Sega executives gave endless interviews about their plans for SegaNet, but as the preshow events finished up, most people were still talking about PlayStation 2.

And people continued to discuss PlayStation 2 throughout the show but in an increasingly poor light. As E3 2000 continued, it became abundantly clear that while more games would be available at the American launch, only a few of them lived up to expectation. Sega, on the other hand, left many attendees very impressed.

Visual Concepts, the Sega-owned U.S. game developer making most of Sega's sports games, completed *NFL 2K1* —a football game with a robust online component. Not having to compensate for such variables as processor speeds, modem speeds, and graphics cards as PC game publishers did, Visual Concepts was able to concentrate all of its efforts into optimizing the game for Dreamcast and its 56K modem. The end result was a game that ran nearly as smoothly online as it did offline.

Sega had other surprises, too. Sega showed *Seaman*—a game in which players used a microphone to communicate with an extremely ugly talking fish, *NBA 2K1*, *Shenmue*, and *Space Channel 5* (a game in which players helped a sexy news anchor with bright pink pigtails rescue a space station from aliens by dancing), and more. An air of desperation hung over the Sega booth and many attendees knew that the company was fighting for its life, but watching the go-go dancers and other trappings around the Sega booth, many people gained confidence that Dreamcast might survive. All Sega of America needed, according to COO Peter Moore, would be to somehow reach the 5 million consoles—sold mark—to double its install base—by the end of the year. Now that Sega was "giving" away Dreamcasts as a premium for joining SegaNet, and with a line of good games on the way, Moore believed he could reach his goal.

But the noose continued to close around Sega. On May 22, nine days after E3, Isao Okawa, the chairman of CSK, Sega's parent company, removed Shoichiro Irimajiri as president of Sega and took control of the company.

People who were unfamiliar with Okawa feared that he might close Sega. He openly advocated Sega's abandoning the hardware business, once publicly stated that there would be no follow-up console to Dreamcast, and felt that the futures of Sega and Internet games were inseparably connected. One thing no one could challenge, however, was Okawa's commitment to Sega. In the summer of 1999, he personally loaned the company nearly $500 million of his own money to help cover debts.

Rumblings in Japan

> The fact of the matter is that people are going to look for their entertainment to come from somewhere, and it does not necessarily have to come from games.
>
> **—Satoru Iwata, director and general manager of corporate planning, Nintendo Co., Ltd.**

The drop in the Japanese game market started so slowly that few people saw the shift take place. Just as the American arcade business started drying up in 1982, Japanese arcades showed signs of distress in 1998. Sega, Japan's largest and strongest arcade company, began closing locations in 1999. By the following year, the closures even included some of its flagship Joypolis virtual theme parks. In 2001, Namco and Taito, the other titans of the Japanese arcade industry, followed Sega's lead.

> We have closed many of our centers, which was hard business. We have almost finished for now, and we will begin looking into opening new amusement centers again. Of course, in the future, we will begin to build again. Fortunately, in the arcade business, Sega is dominant and is the main manufacturer of the machines. So, we will try to improve our position for the arcade business area.
>
> I think Sega is the only company making profits from the arcade business right now. Namco is losing money because they have not done the restructuring that Sega has done to this business center. Sega scrapped the bad amusement centers. Namco recently announced that they will close a couple of hundred amusement centers.
>
> **—Hideki Sato, president, Sega Enterprises**

But drops in the Japanese game industry did not stop with arcades. With Japanese consumers purchasing more games per console than other consumers, the Japanese market had long been the most lucrative of the three major video game markets—Japan, Europe, and North America. In 1997, Japanese consumers spent 750 billion yen (approximately $6.8 billion) on video game software and hardware. By 1999, overall game spending dropped to 600 billion yen, approximately $5 billion.[4]

Some of this was bound to happen. Having shipped approximately 18.5 million PlayStations into a country with an entire population of 127 million, Sony had saturated the market. By 2000, with the original PlayStation now six years old and PlayStation 2 only available in limited quantities, Sony's sales were bound to drop.

> The reason for the decline [in sales] is because the Japanese video game industry is experiencing a change in generations of hardware with Sony Computer Entertainment's launch of PlayStation 2, as well as Microsoft's announcement of Xbox and Nintendo's announcement of Game Cube.
>
> Throughout changes in hardware generations, consumers tend to refrain from purchasing old-generation products, and developers tend to lack the necessary skills to support the developments of quality products that fully benefit from the high-powered new generation hardware. These circumstances sometimes create a downward spiral. That is exactly what affected the sales of video games in Japan last year.
>
> **—Keiji Honda, president and COO, ENIX Corporation**

Some bright spots appeared in the overall picture. When ENIX Corporation released *Dragon Quest VII* (for the original PlayStation), thousands of young men camped outside of local game stores just as they had for PlayStation 2 game consoles. Predicting huge sales based on past popularity, ENIX was prepared. By the end of the year, the company had sold more than 3 million copies of *Dragon Quest VII.* Those sales eventually climbed over 4 million, making it the most popular PlayStation game ever sold in Japan.

The same week that *Dragon Quest VII* temporarily ignited the Japanese market, Nintendo unveiled its long-awaited next-generation game console at its annual Spaceworld trade show. Held in Makuhari Messe, the same convention center in which Nintendo 64 had been revealed in 1995, the show drew press from around the world.

First unveiled by Genyo Takeda, the man who succeeded Gumpei Yokoi as Nintendo's dean of engineering, the new system was called GameCube. Built around a 64-bit PowerPC processor, GameCube was the shape and size of a small Kleenex box—an approximately five-inch cube that would be manufactured in a number of bright colors and would use 2.9-inch mini DVD-ROMs. Unlike Xbox and PlayStation 2, GameCube would be a dedicated game machine with no ambitions of playing DVD movies.

The show closed with a lengthy presentation by star game designer Shigeru Miyamoto discussing the features he had requested in the new console and demonstrating the level of graphics it could achieve. The audience applauded wildly. Game enthusiast audiences always applauded wildly whenever Miyamoto spoke.

The Cataclysmic Christmas

> I shouldn't criticize; old habits die hard. But the real metric is how many Americans have got a PlayStation 2 in their home, plugged in, and are actively purchasing software. How many [PlayStation 2s] have left the factory is meaningless.
>
> **—Peter Moore**

Dreamcast started with a bang, then found itself adrift in the U.S. market. Sega crossed the one million units–sold mark after only a few weeks following its September 1999 launch, but sales ground to a halt by the first of 2000. Price drops and hot new games brought short spikes in hardware sales, and with an 8-to-1 software-to-hardware tie ratio, Dreamcast owners were clearly happy with their system and buying lots of software. But Sega needed to increase its install base; otherwise, the onslaught of PlayStation 2 would wipe Dreamcast out in the United States as it had in Japan. Yet nothing seemed to work. Sega dropped the price of Dreamcast to $149—half the price of PlayStation 2. Sales jumped briefly, then dropped. Even offering free Dreamcasts with SegaNet did not move the quantity of units Sega needed to sell.

> Sega failed to reach the targets we wanted to in terms of hardware sell-
> through. Therefore, our software, in the same time frame, didn't reach the
> levels that we had forecasted or expected. Although our tie ratio for the year
> 2000 was 8 to 1 . . . But 8 to 1 on a small install base didn't give us the revenue
> or the profit from that software that we needed for our business model to
> keep this platform viable in the medium to long term.
>
> **—Charles Bellfield, vice president marketing and**
> **corporate communications, Sega of America**

In mid-September, Sega received a stay of execution from the most unlikely of sources—Sony Computer Entertainment America. With the launch
of PlayStation 2 just one month away, stories began surfacing that Sony did
not have enough PlayStation 2 consoles to meet its promises. Rumor had it
that Sony had somewhere between 300,000 and 500,000 U.S. consoles ready for
shipment and that the company would either send half-shipments to retailers or postpone the entire launch. But if there was any truth to the rumor,
Sony refused to comment.

Then a reporter working for *USA Today* contacted executives at two top
electronic game specialty stores. Neither executive had heard about the shortages, but both took the rumors seriously and called Sony for an explanation.

(Reporter): What do you think of shortages of PlayStation 2?

(Unnamed executive): Well, you know, 1 million units is a lot less
than we would have wanted for such an important product; but we will
have to work with what we get.

(Reporter): What about 300,000 units? My sources say Sony only has
300,000 to 500,000 consoles to ship in.

(Unnamed Executive): Three hundred thousand? I haven't heard
that? Where did you hear that? How good is your information? I don't
have any comment.*

On September 20, Sony Computer Entertainment America president
Kazuo Hirai held a press conference, in which he announced cutbacks in
PlayStation 2 shipments due to parts shortages in Japan. Instead of shipping

---

* For the record, I was the reporter covering this story for *USA Today.*

1 million consoles, Sony could only ship 500,000 for the October 26 launch date, with an additional 100,000 consoles being shipped into the United States every week for the remainder of the year. In an industry rife with rumors and conspiracy theories, Sony's announcement led to wild speculation. People speculated that Sony was withholding shipments to build demand for the system, because there were no good games in the launch library, or because it did not want a major rollout until it had more first-party games available. Several publications sent reporters to visit electronics stores along Akihabara that October, where they discovered a small but steady supply of PlayStation 2 inventory. What few people knew was that the Graphics Synthesizer used in the U.S. version of PlayStation 2 was different than the one used in Japan. As Sony optimized its manufacturing, the company created a smaller version of its custom graphics chip for the United States, and glitches in manufacturing the smaller chip had caused the parts shortage.

Whatever had caused the shortage, the end result was that many retailers had allowed customers to reserve PlayStation 2 consoles based on twice the allocations they eventually received. When they learned that supplies were only half of what they expected, managers at stores such as Babbages, Software Etc., and Electronics Boutique were forced to inform customers that they would not receive the consoles they had reserved months in advance. Intended or not, Sony received a flood of positive publicity from stories of shoppers camping outside stores in the slim hope of finding a PlayStation 2.

The oddest story, however, dealt with Iraq. A persistent story surfaced that Iraqi leader Saddam Hussein was scouring the United States in the hope of purchasing a few thousand PlayStation 2s. News analysts immediately remembered the limitation that the Japanese government had placed on the exportation of PlayStation 2s and began speculating that Hussein might use them for launching guided missiles.* Of course, it would have been nearly impossible to find several thousand PlayStation 2s at regular retail prices. You could occasionally find them selling in toy stores in packages—finding the console, an additional controller, a memory card, and two games selling for

---

*I was interviewed by *NBC Nightly News* on this subject. My speculation was that if any truth lay behind this rumor, it meant that "Saddam's nephews were going to get a nice surprise under the old Ramadan tree."

$599 was not uncommon. You could also find PlayStation 2s selling through online auctions and in classified ads for anywhere from $600 to $800. According to news stories, Hussein ended up purchasing several hundred PSOnes—a new and smaller configuration of the original PlayStation.

In truth, Sony's hardware shortage was not as significant as many people said. Had Sony shipped two million PlayStation 2s in October, the supplies would still have been short.

Lack of adequate software was a more lasting problem carried over from Japan. A few PlayStation 2 games stood out as fairly strong. *Madden NFL 2001* and *SSX,* both from Electronic Arts, were the stars of the launch lineup. Rockstar Games, a tiny company that might normally have gone unnoticed, had two driving games—*Midnight Club* and *Smuggler's Run*—that did fairly well; and a company called THQ, best-known for its WWF wrestling games, received fair reviews for a role-playing game called *Summoner.*

This was Sega's golden opportunity. Sony did not have enough inventory, it did not have many good games, and its console cost twice as much as Dreamcast. Beyond that, with *NFL 2K1,* Sega scored a critical hit, and *NBA 2K1* and *Shenmue* followed closely.

> I think *Shenmue* did extremely well. *NBA 2K1* did very, very well. *Jet Grind Radio* was a little bit of a disappointment. We still believe it was a great game that somehow didn't catch the imagination of the gamer; but *Shenmue* hit its quota. *NBA 2K1* hit its quota. *NFL 2K1,* which was an earlier launch, clearly hit its quota.
>
> **—Peter Moore**

Retailers clamored to bump up their orders of Dreamcast on the theory that disappointed shoppers would purchase the Sega console rather than head home empty-handed. As Thanksgiving rolled past, Dreamcast sales surged and it looked as if Sega had been given a reprieve.

> We came out the day after Thanksgiving and had a huge day; but then the following week, U.S. retail went into the toilet. If you go back and check the news, you'll see that overall retail, and consumer electronics in particular,

> really fell flat. I think the PlayStation 2 effect that we were relying upon did
> not work for us. We had thought that we would get a spill-over effect.
>
> I think that we discounted what human nature really is [about], that people
> will hang on for as long as possible, working on the theory that they're going
> to get something in the second week of December. So they're hanging on to
> your video game dollars. What effectively happened is the PlayStation 2 lack
> of availability froze the marketplace within the video game sector. People were
> willing to wait to see what they could get their hands on or invest their dollars
> in different things—DVDs and other consumer electronics such as Poo-Chi.*

—Peter Moore

Sega stumbled into the new year, having fallen far short of Moore's stated goal of 5 million Dreamcasts. Even giving Dreamcasts away as a premium to SegaNet subscribers, Sega had not been able to lift its U.S. install base beyond 3 million units, and the worldwide install base was only at 6.5 million.

In January 2001, stories started circulating about executives from Microsoft and Nintendo visiting Sega to evaluate the prospect of purchasing the company. As early as December 27, the *New York Times* reported that Nintendo had entered into a discussion about purchasing Sega. Sega denied the story, but the rumors persisted. Then, in the last week of January, a small Japanese news service published a wire story claiming that Dreamcast had been discontinued. At this point, Sega admitted that while Dreamcast had not been discontinued, the manufacturing plant was no longer in operation because of inventory concerns. On January 24, Sega released a press release announcing the discontinuation of Dreamcast, and company executives Charles Bellfield and Peter Moore personally explained the situation to the press.

> Sega will adopt a multi-platform or platform-agnostic role or view of the
> video game hardware industry. We will develop content for multiple devices
> from cell phones right through and including video game systems—includ-
> ing those from our competitors.
>
> Secondly, Sega is confirming effective immediately a cease of the manu-
> facture of the Sega Dreamcast system. And effective as of April 1, 2001, we

---

* A toy robot dog created by Sega and marketed by Tiger Electronics.

> will have completed a management reorganization and a restructuring of Sega as a company to purely be focusing on a multiplatform strategy as a third-party publisher to multiple platforms.

> **—Charles Bellfield**

It took Sega 22 months to sell 6.5 million Dreamcasts worldwide. By comparison, Sony shipped 10 million PlayStation 2s in under 15 months, and its sales kept accelerating. With Sony squeezing Dreamcast out of the market and Nintendo and Microsoft preparing to launch new consoles of their own, Sega chairman Isao Okawa pulled his company out of the hardware business.

But Sega's dark times were only beginning. Okawa was losing a personal battle with cancer. Even as he struggled to find a new direction for his company, Okawa's body was failing him and he had to check into Tokyo University Medical Hospital. In his absence, Hideki Sato, the former head of Sega's software engineering, temporarily took the helm. Though Sato bravely maintained that Okawa was recovering,* that simply was not the case. In his last days, Okawa forgave Sega's debts to him and returned all of his shares of Sega and CSK stock as a gift—in Sega's case, a $695 million gift that would help the company survive the transition of becoming a multiplatform software manufacturer. On March 16, at 3:47 P.M., 74-year-old Isao Okawa died of congestive heart failure.

Upon learning of his friend's death, Sega cofounder David Rosen sent the following telegram:

To the Family of Mr. Isao Okawa:

I am very saddened to learn of the passing of my friend and business associate, Mr. Isao Okawa. He was a man of great vision, who dedicated his energy and his many abilities to whatever task he undertook. He always maintained a very strong sense of responsibility.

Mr. Okawa was always ready to listen and explore new ideas. He was an inspiration to the younger staff as well as management of Sega.

He was a man with charisma, who loved music and good conversation.

---

* I happened to meet with Sato the day that Mr. Okawa passed away, and Sato still claimed that Okawa was getting better and would soon return to the company.

My wife and I always found Okawa-san to be gracious and kind. We will miss him and retain fond memories of our past times together.

Sincerely,

David & Masako Rosen

When Sega and CSK held a special memorial service for Okawa a few months later, more than 6,000 people arrived to pay their respects to the man who had become a citizen of the world. Okawa, who started his career as an engineer before opening CSK and making the calculating investments that eventually made him a billionaire, was better known for his charitable foundations than for the companies he owned.

> As one would expect, if you've met him or sat across a conference table from him, he did everything, even his passing away, in a very organized and dignified manner. Over a number of months prior to his passing, it was one of the better getting your affairs in order before you leave type situations that I've ever seen in my life.
>
> I was privileged enough to go over two weeks ago to Japan to take part in the corporate funeral, which was attended by over 6,000 people, including Idei-san (chairman of Sony) and Kutaragi-san (president of Sony Computer Entertainment). . . . And I was the only gaijan [Caucasian] on the corporate receiving line that welcomed and said goodbye to the guests. It was an incredible affair that laid testimony to the effect that this man has had on the industry in Japan in general and in the computer services and digital entertainment world in particular.
>
> More than 6,000 were physically present, and it was Web cast to CSK offices in other cities.
>
> **—Peter Moore**

Video games, once thought to be a fad, have worked their way into the fabric of international culture. At present, Sony has shipped more than 80 million PlayStations worldwide and Nintendo has sold more than 110 million Game Boys. With every successive generation, the video game industry keeps growing.

And what of the people who built the industry? Odyssey designer Ralph Baer is retired; Nolan Bushnell, founder of Atari, is still a rogue entrepreneur looking for his next big Chuck E. Cheese; Howard Lincoln, who rose from corporate counsel to chairman of Nintendo, celebrated his sixtieth birthday by retiring from Nintendo to become the CEO of the Seattle Mariners; Vice President Al Gore selected Senator Joseph Lieberman as his running mate in his bid for the presidency; and Trip Hawkins, unwilling to give up after the demise of his hardware system, converted 3DO into a highly successful software publisher. On January 8, 2002, 55-year-old Minoru Arakawa shocked the industry by announcing his decision to retire effective immediately. At one time, Arakawa looked like the heir apparent to take over the company when Nintendo Co., Ltd. president Hiroshi Yamauchi retired. But Yoko Arakawa, Minoru's wife and Yamauchi's daughter, did not want to return to Japan.

That's the End?

In many ways, this book has become the project that never ends. I had hoped to finish the book in 1995, then 1996. In 2000, I finally published the damned thing myself. How could I have known that the next six months would become some of the most eventful months in the history of gaming—Midway Games finally abandoned the floundering coin-op video game business, Bill Gates introduced Xbox, Nintendo unveiled GameCube and launched Game Boy Advance, PlayStation 2 launched in the United States, Sega discontinued Dreamcast, and Isao Okawa passed away.

I am grateful that Prima Publishing has bought this book, but the deadline my editors set came up before the early November launches of GameCube and Xbox. And bigger battles are brewing. A recent study published in England predicts that the interactive entertainment market will double in size and could be as big as $49 billion worldwide.

To put it another way, the game never ends.

Source Notes

Chapter 2: Forgotten Fathers

1. Levy, Steven, *Hackers, Heroes of the Computer Revolution* (New York: Dell Publishing, 1984). The most comprehensive work that exists on this pivotal period in the history of computing. Though Steve Russell was helpful and offered much information, I found myself very dependent upon Steve Levy's book and direct any reader who wishes to know more about the beginnings of the computer revolution to Mr. Levy's book.

Chapter 6: The Jackals

1. Cohen, Scott, *Zap! The Rise and Fall of Atari* (New York: McGraw-Hill, 1984), p. 34.
2. Ibid., p. 42.

Chapter 7: "Could You Repeat That Two More Times?"

1. Cohen, Scott, *Zap! The Rise and Fall of Atari* (New York: McGraw-Hill, 1984), p. 50.

Chapter 8: Strange Bedfellows

1. Herman, Leonard, *Phoenix: The Fall and Rise of Videogames* (Springfield, NJ: Rolenta Press, 1994), pp. 18–21.
2. Cohen, Scott, *Zap! The Rise and Fall of Atari* (New York: McGraw-Hill, 1984), p. 52.
3. Herman, Leonard, *Phoenix: The Fall and Rise of Videogames* (Springfield, NJ: Rolenta Press, 1994), p. 20.
4. Robbins, Joe, "Arcades and Equipment Sales: Candid Thoughts," *RePlay Magazine* (March 1976): 58.
5. Cohen, Scott, *Zap! The Rise and Fall of Atari* (New York: McGraw-Hill, 1984), p. 57.

Chapter 9: The Return of Bushnell

1. Bloom, Steven, *Video Invaders* (New York: Arco Publishing, 1982), p. 21.

Chapter 10: The Golden Age (Part 1)

1. This history has been taken from: *http://zonn.com/Cinematronics/history.htm.*

Chapter 11: The Golden Age (Part 2)

1. Skow, John, "Games That People Play," *Time* (January 18, 1982): 50–58.
2. Ibid.
3. Ibid.
4. Ibid.

Chapter 13: A Case of Two Gorillas

1. "Boom Times in Bad," *Fortune* (February 7, 1983): 6.
2. Most of the information from this section was taken from *Universal City Studios, Inc. v. Nintendo Co. Ltd.,* 615 Federal Supplement (District Court of New York, 1985), pp. 838–865.
3. *Universal City Studios, Inc. v. Nintendo Co. Ltd.,* 615 Federal Supplement (District Court of New York, 1985), p. 845.
4. Ibid.

5. Ibid.
6. Ibid.
7. Ibid.
8. Ibid.
9. Ibid., p. 862.
10. Ibid., p. 842.
11. Ibid., p. 859.

Chapter 14: The Fall

1. Quote taken from Jeff Lee's *History of Q*Bert* site on the Internet *(http://users.aol.com/JPMLee/ qbert.htm)*.
2. Ibid.
3. Alexander, Charles P., "Video Games Go Crunch," *Time* (October 17, 1993): 65.
4. Marbach, William D., and Peter McAlevey, "A New Galaxy of Video Games," *Newsweek* (October 25, 1982): 123.
5. Wiswell, Phil, "Hard $ell, Atari's 5200 Will Take You for a Ride," *Video Games* (February 1983): 94.
6. Marbach, William D., and Peter McAlevey, "A New Galaxy of Video Games," *Newsweek* (October 25, 1982): 123.
7. Cohen, Scott, *Zap! The Rise and Fall of Atari* (New York: McGraw-Hill, 1984), p. 114.
8. Alexander, Charles P., "Video Games Go Crunch," *Time* (October 17, 1993): 64.

Chapter 15: The Aftermath

1. Much of this information is taken from Cohen, Scott, *Zap! The Rise and Fall of Atari* (New York: McGraw-Hill, 1984), pp. 149–150.
2. Cohen, Scott, *Zap! The Rise and Fall of Atari* (New York: McGraw-Hill, 1984), p. 150.
3. Ibid.
4. Taub, Scott, "A Noisy Decline: The Saga of Pizza Time Theater Runs into Difficulties as Sales Slide and Enthusiasm Wanes," *Financial World* (November 30, 1983): 40.
5. "The Zinger of Silicon Valley; Morgan Uses Drastic Measures in an Attempt to Save Atari," *Time* (February 6, 1984).
6. Ibid.
7. Ibid.
8. Tomczyk, Michael S., *The Home Computer Wars* (Greensboro, NC: Compute! Books, 1984), p. 33.
9. Ibid., p. 103.
10. Chakravarty, Subrata N., "Albatross," *Forbes* (January 17, 1983).
11. Ibid.
12. Tomczyk, Michael S., *The Home Computer Wars* (Greensboro, NC: Compute! Books, 1984), p. 185.
13. Ibid., p. 187.
14. Chakravarty, Subrata N., "Albatross," *Forbes* (January 17, 1983).
15. Ibid.
16. Rosenberg, Hilary, "Trouble in the Cabbage Patch," *Financial World* (July 25, 1984): 80.
17. Almost all of the information in this book about the close of Mattel Electronics has been taken from the second edition of *Phoenix: The Fall and Rise of Videogames*, by Leonard Herman. Herman has written the most comprehensive volume about the evolution of game hardware imaginable.
18. Alexander, Charles P., "Video Games Go Crunch," *Time* (October 17, 1983): 64.
19. "A Holiday Massacre in Video Games," *Fortune* (December 26, 1983): 100.

Chapter 16: Album Covers

1. Tomczyk, Michael S., *The Home Computer Wars* (Greensboro, NC: Compute! Books, 1984), p. 258.
2. Ibid., p. 257.
3. Chakravarty, Subrata N., "Albatross," *Forbes* (January 17, 1983).
4. "Okay, Jack," *Fortune* (February 20, 1984): 8.
5. Tomczyk, Michael S., *The Home Computer Wars* (Greensboro, NC: Compute! Books, 1984), p. 284.
6. "The Zinger of Silicon Valley," *Time* (February 6, 1984): 50.
7. Bagamery, Anne, "The Second Time Around," *Forbes* (October 8, 1984): 42.

Chapter 17: We Tried to Keep from Laughing

1. Sheff, David, *Game Over* (New York: Vintage Books, 1994), p. 152.
2. Ibid., pp. 154–155.
3. Ibid., p. 163.

Chapter 20: The New Empire

1. Pitta, Julie, "This Dog Is Having a Big Day," *Forbes* (January 22, 1990): 106.
2. "Please Daddy," *The Economist* (December 2, 1989): 35.

Chapter 21: The Legal Game

1. 17 U.S.C. #101 as quotes from *Atari Games Corp. v. Nintendo of America Inc.*, 30 USPQ 2d., p. 1405.
2. Ibid., p. 1404.
3. *Data East USA, Inc. v. Epyx, Inc.*, 862 Federal Supplement 2d., p. 209.
4. Ibid., p. 206.
5. Ibid., p. 206.
6. Ibid., p. 210.
7. *Atari Games Corp. v. Nintendo of America Inc., 30 USPQ 2d.*, p. 1403.
8. Ibid., p. 1403 (referring to 975 Federal Supplement 2d, p. 837).
9. Ibid., p. 1407.
10. Ibid., p. 1427.
11. *Sega Enterprises Ltd. v. Accolade, Inc.*, 977 Federal Supplement 2d., p. 1528.
12. Ibid., p. 1515.
13. Ibid., p. 1515.
14. Ibid., pp. 1515–1516.
15. Ibid., p. 1398.
16. Ibid., p. 1398.
17. Ibid., p. 1398.
18. Ibid., p. 1514.
19. Ibid., p. 1523.
20. Ibid., p. 1529.
21. *States of N.Y. and Maryland v. Nintendo of America, Inc.*, 775 Federal Supplement, p. 679.
22. Kichen, Steve, "Please, Br'er Fox! Don't Throw Me in the Briar Patch!" *Forbes* (December 23, 1991): 17.
23. *Lewis Galoob Toys, Inc. v. Nintendo of America, Inc.*, 780 Federal Supplement, p. 1295.
24. *Alpex Computer Corporation v. Nintendo Co., Ltd.*, 780 Federal Supplement, p. 162.
25. Riordan, Teresa, "After Nintendo's Victory, More Japanese Companies May Say They'd Rather Fight Than Pay," *New York Times*, November 25, 1996, section D, p. 2.
26. *Alpex Computer Corporation v. Nintendo Co., Ltd.*, SDNY 95-1191-1229.
27. Ibid.
28. *Alpex Computer Corporation v. Nintendo Co., Ltd.*, SDNY 212-791-1020.

Chapter 22: The Year of Hardware

1. "New Boy on the Block," *Time* (November 6, 1989): 73.

Chapter 23: Run for the Money

1. Sheff, David, "The Game Master," *Playboy* (June 1993): 216.
2. West, Neil and Chris Charla, "What the Hell Does Bill Gates Know About Games Anyway?" *Next Generation* (June, 1996): 60. This is Gates's response when asked about Spindler's statement.
3. Conour, Dale, "Sonic CEO," *Gentry* (August 1995): 88.
4. Ibid., 87.
5. Gray, Paul, "Boop, Beep, Blurp, Jingle, Jingle," *Time* (July 9, 1990): 15.
6. Dumaine, Brian, "When Delay Courts Disaster," *Fortune* (December 16, 1991): 104.
7. "NEC Lowers Price of TurboGrafx-16 to $99," *Playthings* (June 1991): 6.
8. Sheff, *Game Over*, p. 363.

9. Streisand, Betsy, and Richard J. Newman, "The Big Leagues' New Game Boy," *U.S. News & World Report* (February 17, 1992): 44.
10. Wulf, Steve, "An Outside Pitch," *Sports Illustrated* (February 10, 1992): 30.
11. Streisand and Newman, "The Big Leagues' New Game Boy," 44.

Chapter 24: The War

1. Tor, Matt, "Will Super Mario Halt Sega's Sonic Boom?" *Marketing* (a United Kingdom publication), April 30, 1992, p. 13.
2. Tetzeli, Rick, "Videogames: Serious Fun," *Fortune* (December 27, 1993): 110.

Chapter 25: Moral Kombat

1. Joint Hearings Before the Subcommittee on Juvenile Justice, One Hundred Third Congress, Serial No. J-103-37, December 9, 1993, March 4 and July 29, 1994, p. 22.
2. Ibid., p. 194.
3. Ibid., p. 12.
4. Ibid., p. 14.
5. Ibid., p. 15.
6. Ibid., p. 20.
7. Ibid., p. 22.
8. Ibid., p. 25.
9. Ibid., p. 25.
10. Ibid., p. 29.
11. Ibid., p. 30.
12. Ibid., p. 30.
13. Ibid., p. 35.
14. Ibid., p. 35.
15. Ibid., p. 36.
16. Ibid., p. 36.
17. Ibid., p. 41.
18. Ibid., p. 58.
19. Ibid., p. 62.

Chapter 26: The "Next" Generation (Part 1)

1. "Game Over?" *The Economist* (November 20, 1993): 74.
2. Bateman, Selby, "Movers and Shakers," *Next Generation* (March 1995): 29.
3. Miller, Cyndee, "Sega vs. Nintendo: This Fight's Almost As Rough As Their Video Games," *Marketing News* (August 29, 1994): 1.
4. Morris, Kathleen "Nightmare in the Fun House," *Financial World* (February 21, 1995): 32.
5. "Nintendo Expects," *Television Digest* (December 5, 1994): 13.
6. Meyer, Michael, "Fight to the Finish," *Newsweek* (December 12, 1994): 56.
7. Morris, Kathleen, "Nightmare in the Fun House," *Financial World* (February 21, 1995): 32.

Chapter 27: The "Next" Generation (Part 2)

1. Morris, Kathleen, "Nightmare in the Fun House," *Financial World* (February 21, 1995): 32.
2. Ibid.
3. Ibid.
4. "Nintendo Pins Hopes on Virtual Boy," *Next Generation* (March 1995): 20.

Chapter 28: The Mainstream and All Its Perils

1. Rowling, J. K., *Harry Potter and the Goblet of Fire* (New York: Scholastic Press, 2000), p. 25.
2. Hearing on "Marketing Violence to Children," U.S. Senate Commerce, Science and Transportation Committee, May 4, 1999, p. 117.
3. Harrison, George, "First to Market Is Good, but Not Always Best," *Brandweek* (December 4, 1995): 16. (Harrison was Nintendo of America's vice president of marketing and corporate communications.)

4. Gerstmann, Jeff, "Mortal Kombat Trilogy: Full Review," *GameSpot VG* [online], posted October 31, 1996, updated December 3, 1996.

5. Bai, Matt, "Anatomy of a Massacre," *Newsweek* (May 3, 1999): 26.

6. Gibbs, Nancy, and Timothy Roche, "The Columbine Tapes," *Time* [online], December 20, 1999.

7. Ibid.

8. Hearing on "Marketing Violence to Children," p. 5.

9. Ibid., pp. 13–14.

10. Ibid., p. 37.

11. Ibid., p. 67.

12. Ibid., p. 71.

13. Ibid., p. 72.

14. Ibid., p. 87.

15. Ibid., p. 91.

16. Ibid., pp. 113–114.

17. Ibid., p. 114.

18. Ibid., p. 114.

19. Ibid., p. 115.

20. Ibid., pp. 115–116.

21. Ibid., pp. 116–117.

22. Ibid., p. 120.

23. Ibid., pp. 121–122.

24. Ibid., p. 122.

25. Ibid., p. 126.

26. Ibid., p. 136.

27. Ibid., pp. 140–144.

28. Ibid., p. 143.

Chapter 30: Three Horses and a Pony

1. Taken from Game Developers Conference keynote address, delivered March 10, 2000.

2. Takahashi, Dean, "How Four Renegades Persuaded Microsoft to Make a Game Machine," *Wall Street Journal* (March 10, 2000).

3. Shroddy, Eric, Larry Muggerud, and Lou Donaldson, *Jump Around* (Tommy Boy Records, 1992).

4. *2000 Games White Paper,* Computer Entertainment Software Association, July 2000.

Index